AN IDENTIFICATION AND VALUE GUIDE

OLD FISHING
LURES
AND TACKLE

BY
CARL F. LUCKEY

THIRD EDITION

ISBN 0-89689-076-7

BOOKS AMERICANA
INC

ACKNOWLEDGEMENTS

I owe a great debt of special thanks to three men who went beyond the call with generous contributions of research and photography. Their kindness and generosity has made this a much better book.

JIM BOURDON, Croton-on-Hudson, New York
DENNIS "DOC" HYDER, Seymour, Missouri
CLARENCE ZAHN, Ann Arbor, Michigan

It is never possible to acknowledge all those individuals who contribute to a work of this sort. There are always so many helpful and cooperative people in on an endeavor such as this that it is not practical to thank them all in print. This is especially so when the work has gone through three editions over a period of ten years. The following is a list of those I have been able to keep up with over the years. I sincerely hope I have not omitted a deserving person, but at the same time realistically expect I have. To those folks I proffer my most heartfelt apologies. It is you and the rest of these folks that make this book possible. My continuing gratitude and good wishes to you all.

Frank Baron, Livonia, Michigan; Ray Barzee, Sumpter, Oregon; Ronald Bash, Lancaster, Ohio; Ed Blazek, Wadena, Minnesota; Stu Bonney, Falmouth, Maine; Charlie Brown, Sand Point, Idaho; Bruce Boyden, Providence, Rhode Island; Rex Butel, Apache Junction, Arizona; Jim Cantwell, Lake Forrest, Illinois; Harold Dickert, Muskegon, Michigan; Bruce Dyer, Labradore City, Newfoundland; Jim Frazier, Hollywood, Florida; Ron Fritz, Fife Lake, Michigan; Steve Fussell, Winter Park, Florida; Clarence Grimm, Columbia, Missouri; W.F. Hamilton, Port New Richey, Florida; Clyde and Polk Harbin, Memphis, Tennessee; Paul W. Haudrich, Bridgeton, Missouri; Emerson Heilman, Kunkleton, Pennsylvania; Harry Heinzerling, Garrett, Indiana; Ed Henckel, San Antonio, Texas; Harold G. Herr, Ephrata, Pennsylvania; Randy Hilst, Pekin, Illinois; Ray Homme, Bloomington, Minnesota; Clark Hunholz, Milwauki, Wisconsin; Noel Hutchens, Jacksonville, Florida; Ed Keiffer, Homosassa, Florida; Paul J. Lindner, Kentwood, Michigan; Dan Long, Rogersville, Alabama; Rick Loucks, Ashley, Indiana; Don C. Ludy, West Chicago, Illinois; Trygue C. Lund, Dowagiac, MIchigan; James F. Mallory of the American Fishing Tackle Manufacturers Association; Brian J. McGrath, Plano, Texas; Dave McCleski, Hoover, Alabama; Russ Mumford, West LaFayette, Indiana; Walter G. Murphy, Florence, Alabama; Leo J. Pachner, Momence, Illinois; Stephen K. Peterson, Denver, Colorado; Bill Potts, Cincinnati, Ohio; A. Barton Pride, Killen, Alabama; George Richey, Honor, Michigan; E. Nelson Robinson (dec.), Killen, Alabama; Ray Scott, Montgomery, Alabama; Doug Schelske, Minneapolis, Minnesota; Jeromw Schopp, Chenoa, Illinois; T. Layton Shepherd, Antigo, Wisconsin; John Schoffner, Fife Lake, Michigan; Richard E. Shook, Youngstown, Ohio; Tom Smith, Florence, Alabama; Tim Stallings, Orlando, Florida; Jim Stoker, Hastings, Minnesota; Oscar Strausborger, Edon, Ohio; John Thomas, Laramie, Wyoming; Rich Treml, Detroit, Michigan; Robert V. Vermillion, Huntington Woods, Michigan; Buck Vest, Claremore, Oklahoma; Tim Watts, Urbana, Illinois; Bill Wetzel, Hampton, South Carolina; Dave Whisman, Prestonsburg, Kentucky; Dick Wilson, Kent, Ohio.

AUTHOR'S NOTE TO THE READER

The information presented between these covers is the result of over ten years of study and research. That it is incomplete is a foregone conclusion. It is hoped however that it is more complete than any other work produced so far. I sincerely hope that any of you who wish to contribute any information toward helping to make subsequent editions more complete will not hesitate to contact me. This is especially true of photos, old catalogs, price lists, etc. As has been my habit in previous books, I invite anyone with constructive criticism or suggestions as to how the book might be improved, to contact me direct.

Do write me if you wish. **I cannot promise to acknowledge every single letter, but will attempt to do so** in time, as numbers allow. I hope you will remember to enclose a stamped, self addressed envelope. That goes a long way toward assuring a response from any author. **Please don't telephone me,** I regret that time and schedules do not permit me to accept any calls. I love to talk but I gotta work.

Good Fishing and Happy Collecting!
Carl F. Luckey
Rt. 4, Box 301
Killen, Alabama 35645

DEDICATION

PASS IT ON

What magic there is
    in togetherness alone.
    Unshared. Undivided.
Far away in your soft, green world
    of soltitude
    of things to fill the dreams
    of childhood;
The music of wind in the pines.
    Firelight. Night sounds.
Only for a little while
    will you stand
    the tallest tree in the forest.
Capture those fleeting moments!
While the child is catching fish
    fishing will catch the child.
And the child will need the green world
    someone else gave to you.
Pass it on.

CONTENTS

INTRODUCTION TO THE THIRD EDITION

Between these covers lies what is hoped to be a singularly valuable reference for the collector of old fishing tackle, particularly those whose interest is in the old fishing lure. The lure is a device made of some material, organic or inorganic, bearing a hook, a facility for tying it to a line and made in such a way as to deceive a fish into thinking it to be a delicacy worthy of pursuit. If successfully made and properly used, it will often net the user on the other end of the line a bit of fun and perhaps, turning the table on the fish's interest, a bit of good eating.

Since the first (1980) edition much has been learned and a tremendous additional amount of material has been turned up. Everybody who has had a serious interest has been generous with their information and material. Indeed, they have been anxious to share it with their fellow collectors. First edition publications have been revised and released and the National Fishing Lure Collectors Club (NFLCC) members have been at the fore in this effort. The excellent newsletter and members' research efforts (shared enthusiastically) have been excellent to say the least. Many of them have been of incredible help in providing new research materials for this third edition. Membership in this fine organization is inexpensive and an absolute must for any collector of old fishing tackle. It cannot be recommended highly enough.

There have always been collectors. You name it and someone, somewhere, collects it. The collectors of old fishing tackle number in the several thousands, if the number of sales of the first and second editions of this book is any indication. For every serious collector member of the NFLCC (genus and species, HOARDPLUGENS ENMASSUS), there are hundreds of casual collectors. Any one of these folks can become as engrossed in this fascinating hobby as the above-mentioned critter, Hoardplugens Enmassus.

The fascination with old lures is understandable and contagious. It is most likely that the first lures were conceived and fashioned when early thinking man first began to formulate ways of outwitting his prey in fishing. Whether early man's piscatorial pursuits were of a sporting nature or to supplement his diet is an academic point. What it does indicate is how long man has had to dream up new ways of tempting our fishy friends (foes?).

The province of this book is primarily that of manufactured artificial lures used since the earliest days of their production in the United States. There are few artificial flys in the listings, nor will you find many metal or metal spinner type lures. There have been numerous fine works about flys and fly tying already produced and there doesn't presently seem to be a large nucleus of metal spinner bait collectors. The latter group seems to be expanding, however.

The first edition contained a section on old rods. You will find that the listing of rods has been eliminated, but the history of rod development has been retained. The author and his publisher felt that the small listing was woefully inadequate to serve the needs of the rod collector. The enormous numbers of styles, types, materials, jobbers, manufacturers and habit of manufacturers supplying numbers of companies with their own trademarks make it all but impossible for it to be covered sufficiently here. A whole book for rods themselves would be required.

Reels have been retained and expanded a little, but it only covers a small number of earlier products.

Given the above you can see that the greatest majority of information presented is about fishing lures made beginning around 1890-1900 and ending in the early 1950's.

Think of it. Think how many thousands of fishermen have tried to think of a "better mousetrap" in those fifty or so years! Most producers of plugs in those years have experimented with a myriad of designs in the continuing battle to make the "secret weapon". The producers are represented by hundreds upon hundreds of operations, from the one-man shop to the large manufacturer, that have come and gone during this time. The types of lures that have come down the pike range from the sublime to the ridiculous, from the ineffective to the explosively successful fish-getter. Every single one of them, if you believe the advertisements, have been the proverbial secret weapon, the fabled supreme achievement. For example there is an old (1911) Ans B. Decker advertisement which boasts that he can catch more bass over 14 inches with his bait . . . "than you can!", and backs up his boast with a wager of "$1,000 against $500.00". Now that's a real challenge when you consider what a prodigious sum of money $1,000.00 was in those days! It would probably be prudent to suspect that Mr. Decker's skill was more likely the source of such confidence than was his bait design. Of course it is quite possible the bait was responsible, at least in part, for all fishermen are painfully aware of the apparent changing preferences of our fickle and apparently fashion-conscious, fishy foes.

For the collector of old tackle there follows here, a guide to the hobby. There is a history of artificial lures; a history of reel and rod development, a glossary of terms specific to the subject, illustrations of major developments and improvements, an illustrated guide to the identification and valuation, lists of clubs, related books, interesting periodicals, experts, appraisers and restorers. There is a section on care and practical, convenient display, and a very useful section on how to snag new items for your collection.

HISTORY AND SIGNIFICANT DEVELOPMENTS IN THE EVOLUTION OF AMERICAN FISHING TACKLE

This section is designed to give the collector some important general background information and some specifics in the development of fishing tackle in the United States. Knowledge of general history and significant events in the evolution of tackle will enable collectors to better understand and use this guide to properly identify, classify and possibly date the items in his collection. The first pages are devoted to a general chronology and that is followed by a separate and a bit more detailed history of the lure, rod and reel.

While there has never been any revolutionary event in the history of fishing to compare with what the invention of gun powder did for hunting, there have been technical advances in lure and tackle manufacture over the years. These can sometimes be identified as to an approximate date and are listed, following.

A GENERAL CHRONOLOGY OF DEVELOPMENT

PRE-COLONIAL TIMES

1. The Indians used their hands, traps, spears and lights for illumination at night. The latter, as we know and use them today, obviously attracted some fish. Light could be said to be one of the first artificial "lures."
2. Primitive American Indians as well as primitive peoples of other parts of the world used a "Gorge", the crude forerunner of today's modern barbed hook. The gorge, still used by some primitive peoples, is a straight bar made of bone, shell, stone or wood sometimes with a groove around it near the center for tying a line. It was utilized by inserting it lengthwise in the bait. When the fish swallows the bait, the line is tugged and the gorge becomes lodged lengthwise in the fish.
3. Eskimos and Indians used artificial lures made of ivory or bone. They were usually used as decoys in ice fish and/or spear fishing.
4. Eskimos and Indians used gill nets and seines.

EARLY COLONIAL TIMES

The first colonists had no interest in sport fishing as their immediate need was survival. History proves that there was much commercial fishing from the very earliest days of settlement in America.

EIGHTEENTH CENTURY

First appearance of fishing for sport in America.

1800-1810

1. First appearance of the Phantom Minnow in America.
2. George Snyder made the first "Kentucky Reels"

1835-1840

The first commercial manufacturer of the "Kentucky Reels" by the Meeks Brothers

1844-1925

The development of the "Henshall Rod",

*1848

Julio T. Buel began commercial manufacture of the Spoon lure. He is credited with its invention.

1852

Julio T. Buel - First U.S. patent on Spinner bait.

Various parts of Buel Spoons and Spinners. They may be found with either J.T. or H.W. Buel (Julio's half brother) and the patent date 1852 or 1854. The metal strips and spoons are the 1854 patent. The spinner body/blade is from the 1852 patent. Only that was provided. The angler had to attach his own hook and wire armature.

1859

First known patent for a lure that mentions wood as possible material for the lure body.

1874

First granted patent for an artificial lure **specifying** the use of wood for the lure body. Patented May 26, 1874 by David Huard and Charles M. Dunbar of Ashland, Wisconsin. (See page 73 for illustration).

1876

Early manufactured artificial lure incorporating wood as a component. Listed in U.S. patent records as patented by H. C. Brush,** August 22, 1876 (See page 69 for illustration).

1880

First known granted patent for an artificial lure specifying glass for the lure body. J. Irgens, Sept. 7, 1880. (See page 74 for illustration).

---

*Buel was actually fishing his invention as early as 1821 and made many for friends and neighbors over the years. The 1848 date is subject to speculation as there is a 1904 ad stating "Over 60 Years in Use."

**The 1876 H. C. Brush patent has heretofore been thought to be the first wooden plug. However study of patent records reveal the Huard and Dunbar patent precedes Brush by two years. It is not known if it was ever produced.

1883

Patent for "artificial bait" called The Flying Helgramite by Harry Comstock, Fulton, New York, January 30, 1883.

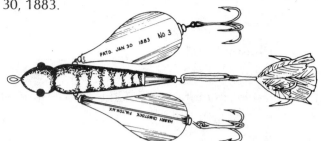

1883

Patent granted to Earnest F. Pflueger for artifical lures coated with luminous paint for fishing at night.

1885

The development of the "Chicago Rod"

1890

The beginning of widespread bait-casting in the United States. Although the bait casting reel was invented about 75 years previously, it wasn't until the 1890's that plugs were born.

1896-1998

James Heddon is generally credited with the first artificial lure we know as the "plug" today.

1900-1905

The beginnings of major plug manufacturers in the United States.

1907

The first appearance of jointed wooden plugs – the "K and K Animated Minnows".

1910-1920

The first widespread use of luminious paint on plugs began sometime this period. Pflueger was given the first patent on a luminous lure on Feb. 3, 1883.

c1912

The first water sonic plugs appeared. Probably the 1912 "Diamond Wiggler".

c1914

The first appearance of fluted plugs. Probably the Lockhart "Wobbler Wizard" later followed around 1917 by the Wilson "Fluted Wobbler".

c1914

The Detroit Glass Minnow Tube

1915

First appearance of a self illuminated plug to utilize a battery operated bulb. It was called "Dr. Wasweyler's Marvelous Electric Glow Casting Minnow".

c1917

Earliest known advertisement of a lure made of celluloid. The first advertisement found was in a May 1917 issue of **National Sportsman** magazine. It was for an Al Foss "Oriental Wiggler" - a pork rind minnow. Soon after his ads began to say pyralin instead of celluloid. These may be the first plastic lures.

c1922

The Vesco Bait Company of New York City advertised baits and spoons made of Dupont Pyralin. One of the first plastic plugs.

1932

Heddon introduced their "Fish Flesh" plastic lure. The first lures were produced in the 9100 and 9500 (Vamp) series. Soon thereafter came plastic "Spooks".

c1940

Appearance of the first American built spinning reels.

THE TACKLE COLLECTOR'S PRIMER

WHERE TO FIND IT

This business of collecting old fishing tackle can be one of the most interesting and natural extensions to the sport of fishing. It has been one of the most unexploited areas of collecting old Americana. Get cracking though, because the ranks are growing rapidly. Luckily there have been millions upon millions of pieces of tackle handcrafted and manufactured since the early days so there should still be plenty of nice examples to go around.

Try the oldest general stores, drugstores (used to carry bass plugs), bait shops and hardware stores in your area. There has been many a treasure turned up by feeling around a dusty top shelf or in a storage room. Anywhere tackle has been sold over a period of 30 years or more, there are bound to be some oldies. Some of these places may have sold tackle one time or another. Even if they don't now, they may have some old unsold stock stuck away somewhere. A friend of mine paid $1.29 for a Mill Site "Rattle Bug" in an old general store near the Alabama gulf coast. That plug possibly dates back to 1940 and had apparently been laying around unsold for all that time.

Remember trading boards? Well there are some shops that still use them. For an old or unwanted plug you pay a quarter or four bits, put your plug on the board and take another of your choice. There is one right near my home but alas, the owner is a plug collector. Many shops sell used rods and reels. You may find an old one or two this way.

Ask your family and friends if they know of an old timer who left his tackle box or other fishing gear in the cellar or attic. Look in your own box, there may be one in there under all that junk you haven't used or even seen for years.

The garage sales and flea markets of today are good places to try but so far they haven't been very good hunting grounds. So few of these folks think of old tackle as being very marketable. This source will grow in time. When attending these events ask, you may be surprised.

Another possible source for lures is the banks of old favorite fishing lakes and rivers. The latter are the best because of fluctuating water levels. I live on the banks of the Tennessee River and during low water periods, I have spent many enjoyable hours searching for lures among the driftwood, etc., deposited by the retreating water. The lake impoundments around here are not more than forty to fifty years old and most lures don't fare too well when exposed to the elements that long. However the search is pleasant and I have found dozens of salvageable modern plugs that are in my tackle box now. I feel it's an even trade because I know a few submerged stumps around here that must look like Christmas trees the way I have decorated them with lost lures.

Make up a want list with pictures or drawings (Copy 'em right out of this book. Be my guest.) and pass the list out among friends and relatives or post it on public bulletin boards such as provided by many grocery stores. Don't use names or numbers, just pictures. Names and numbers will just confuse them. When sending your want list to other collectors provide all the information you can; names, numbers, pictures, dimensions and complete descriptions.

In short, just use your imagination to come up with both likely and unlikely sources.

NOW YOU'VE FOUND IT – WHAT DO YOU PAY?

Now this is mighty sticky wicket, this business of pricing old tackle. It is an area probably as full of unseen hazards as there are standing hairs on a mad cat's back.

It would be safe to say that many tackle collectors, particularly plug collectors, would much prefer swapping and buying. For the most part collectors are "swappers and/or buyers", but generally not sellers. In fact there aren't a great bunch of lures that are valued at more than ten to fifteen bucks. In fact many of them are valued at less. The swap is by far the best way to expand your collection when your other sources dry up. The problem is there are precious few instances when one can pin down a value in swapping terms. You just can't say that a "Doctor Catchum's Surefire Killer Diller Spinner" is worth two "Magic Molly Gogglers" and half a "Big Bass Basher". Each swap is an individual negotiation between two collectors which ends in satisfying both. Most of the time, the only way to avoid the unsatisfactory alternative is to know your business. That takes study.

When hunting for old tackle, most of the time you find it already marked with a price in stores, garage sales, etc., and that's generally what you pay unless you're that enviable type, the "silver-tongued devil". In the above instances the price is usually more than a fair one, sometimes being a downright steal. The other sources discussed, Grampa's tackle box, etc. usually end up in no monetary outlay at all or if so an insignificant one. Witness my ten dollar purchase. It figures to less than fifty cents per plug. Beware of flea markets. You may find a bargain, but it has been my experience that most found there are grossly overpriced.

Generally speaking, the older the item the more it's worth, simply because the older it is the less thare are available in most cases. The simple law of supply and demand comes into important play in this case. Some old plugs, reels, and especially old split cane fly rods **can** and sometimes do soar into the hundreds of dollars. Older-worth-more is not set in concrete. Some lures of the 1920's and 1930's were made for a short period of time and are quite rare and valuable.

Another important consideration is how bad do you want it. It matters not a flit what someone or some book says it's worth if you're in a "I gotta have it" frame of mind. Let's say you have but one more necessary to complete a set and you're looking right at it **but** – it belongs to another collector who prizes it also. In this extreme case you probably will walk away empty-handed, but for the sake of argument, the conversation might go something like this: "Charlie, ole buddy, I just gotta have that Purple Plunker." "Aw, Bill, I can't part with it. Just look at it, it's mint." "Yeah I know Charlie, but you know that's the one I need to complete my set and it's the only one you got like that. It looks lonesome on your board." "Well, what'll you gimme?" "How about two Topless Torpedo Twisters and a six-pack of suds?" "No way, Charlie, I gotta have some long green. You know I've been savin' for one of those new super-charged boat trailers. Tell you what, a ten-spot and you can take it home." "Charlie, come off it, the book says it's only worth three, give me a break." "That's my price, Bill, take it or leave it." "Awright you old skinflint, here's your bounty."

Charlie paid over three times what the book said the plug was worth but he really didn't get ripped off. In the final analysis something is worth only what you're willing to pay for it. If Charlie already had his Purple Plunker, then Bill might not have gotten even the three dollars it was supposed to be worth. Or – if Bill had wanted the two Topless Torpedo Twisters more than the money, Charlie would have still gotten his Purple Plunker. In either case, the swap or the purchase, both were satisfied in the end.

All that for this: Take the value guide presented in this book as exactly that – a guide. It is after all, only one man's opinion. I couldn't say how many times I have heard: "This is worth about twenty dollars or so, but I wouldn't take three times that for it." **You** are the final authority. Don't forget it.

SOME HINTS FOR SUCCESSFUL BUYING, SELLING, TRADING

1. Arm yourself with knowledge. Get and study every piece of printed information you can get your paws on.
2. Mutual cooperation builds better collections and good friends and sources. Ask for help from knowledgeable collectors and give an edge to those who helped you in the beginning, after you get smart.
3. If you find you have a treasure, don't be greedy, be fair. If you don't deal fairly you may find many of your sources drying up.
4. If you find you have made a bad deal, don't worry over it - learn from it. Turn lemons into lemonade by knowing better next time.
5. Always make an offer. Nothing ventured, nothing gained. Remember one man's trash is another man's treasure.
6. Honest mistakes are made. If you have built up a good rapport with and a good reputation among your collector friends, most can be rectified. Keep in mind, however, that it is not possible to make all your deals mutually fair, only mutually acceptable. Don't squawk if you find later the deal wasn't so good. You can't win them all.

One last note about the way the values are presented in the individual listings. You will note that they are presented as "Collector Value Range". In many cases the range is quite wide. You may reasonably place the lower limits of the range as the approximate value of a newer item in less than perfect condition and the upper limit on those older or more rare pieces in an excellent condition. The final judgment is yours even to the extent that your opinion places the value outside the printed range. **All the value ranges in this book are for lures in good to mint condition. Any in less than real good condition will fall out the lower side range.** Valuation of these is strictly a matter of negotiation between individual buyers/sellers or traders.

NEVER MISS A CHANCE

How many times have you been out only to lose that special plug? I mean the only one that works; or worse, you and your fishing buddy are having a bad day and he starts hauling 'em in like he was bailing out a sinking boat. He found today's secret weapon and he's only got one copy and you're zeroed out in that type. Whatever the reason, we all have modified plugs in our tackle boxes in a sometimes vain attempt to land a lunker. Therein lies a problem the plug collector will invariably encounter. I have replaced spinners, hooks, lips, hook hardware, swivels, etc. and yes, even repainted favorite plugs. Think of the strange concoctions you might run across in an old timer's tackle box! Some may even defy the most expert collector but, most can be identified and eventually the proper hardware may be obtained and the plug restored to its original configuration: (More about this later). Moral: never discard old, beat up, mistreated plugs you find. Throw them in a box for cannibalization. The same applies to rods and reels.

SOME MISCELLANEOUS CONSIDERATIONS

Insurance - If you find yourself with a collection of old tackle that you cherish and/or is valuable then please consider some insurance. In the unfortunate event of a house fire those old wooden plugs and bamboo rods will be great kindling. Many reels have hard rubber parts and fires can reach temperatures high enough to melt some metals.

Check your homeowners insurance policy or personal effects rider. Most contain a clause that limits or excludes collectibles. I am not qualified to delve into the intracacies of insurance policies, but do emphasize the importance of proper coverage. It behooves you to discuss your particular collecting situation with a trusted agent.

Protection - There are numerous ways to protect and safeguard your collection which you can accomplish with ease if you will just take the time to do so. In the unfortunate circumstance of theft or destruction, the law enforcement authorities and/or insurance companies will be able to handle recovery, replacement or reimbursement much more efficiently if you have done your homework before the fact. This "homework" can be rewarding in itself by increasing your knowledge of the very things you collect.

Write It Down - Inventory your collection. Put it on your "Things To Do Today" list. Get yourself some index cards and file box, a looseleaf notebook, or whatever may be easiest for you to use to catalog your collection. Some of the important things to record in your inventory are when, where and how you obtained each piece. Record the price you paid or what you traded for it. Describe each with name, company name, catalog number, material, measurements, all signatures and other marks. It would be good even to assign each item a number in your collection and describe the location on the premises. The number may be your own or in the event there is universal number you may prefer to use it.

Photograph It - Photographs are evidence, should a piece be damaged, of its original condition. They are a positive means of identification by which it may be traced if stolen and assurance for insurance purpose. They can serve as an excellent tool in such process.

Many collectors find it convenient to use the back of each photo to record the description, etc., for their inventory. It is advisable to maintain duplicates of each, one set in a safe place at home so that you may use them when you wish, and the other set somewhere off the premises such as a safe deposit box.

Identification Marks - An additional safeguard is to mark each individually. If a piece is lost or stolen, the ability to point out a distinctive mark identifying it as your property is quite helpful.

If you are a purist, reluctant to permanently mark an object because it alters the original state, then there are other slightly more difficult ways.

You may want to use descriptions of unique properties of each item such as repairs, imperfections or areas of wear.

Should you choose to mark, do so in an unobtrusive location. However you mark, make sure it is permanent and very small.

Reproductions or Copies — The forgery is a copy or reproduction of an item specifically for the purpose of deceiving the purchaser. There are a lot of talented folks in this world of ours and some of them capable of doing an incredible job copying. That in itself is fine, but where that talent belongs to a dishonest individual, his product, the copy, becomes a forgery. The purpose of these few pages is not to help that nefarious forger, but to help the collector protect himself against the varmit and have a little fun to boot. There is no substitute for intimate familiarity with the nature and characteristics of what you collect, but the author has found another way to at least add a little to the understanding. **Try to make one yourself.** Reels are just about out of the question. Although not altogether impossible, it would not be economically feasible for anyone to try to forge an old reel. Do watch out for altered markings, however. The same applies to rods.

Old lures are a completely different proposition for obvious reasons. By attempting to reproduce an old plug yourself you will gain some insight into the problems a potential forger may encounter and that will help you to identify counterfeits.

A more enjoyable and satisfying experience however, is the making of lures that catch fish. Some of those old plugs actually were "performing fools." If fish do, as some insist, learn and remember lures which are constantly jerked by their noses then you will present them with a new, unfamiliar delicacy that they might just select for their breakfast. Many of those old successful plugs are not made anymore simply because the making of them costs the manufacturer too much to sell at a profit.

The best way to begin is in a book. There are two that I am familiar with, *Tackle Craft* by C. Boyd Pfieffer and *The Book of Old Lures* by Charles K. Fox (See bibliography page 13). The former is a highly detailed, excellent work dealing with fashioning your own tackle. The latter deals primarily with old lures, with some excellent hints on making plugs like the old ones. I found both in the smallish library in my home town. You might try the same or, that failing, your local book seller may be able to obtain one for you.

If you like the idea and are fairly handy with your hands, try it. There can't be any greater satisfaction than landing a lunker with a lure made by your own hands.

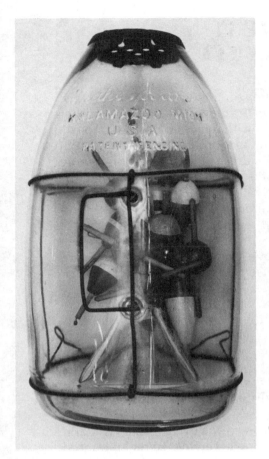

A small collection of old style hunting and fishing licenses ranging from 1935 to 1955. Could make a nice addition to a display of a collection of old lures and tackle.

A very early glass minnow bucket offered by Shakespeare. Note the old wooden floaters or bobbers inside. An interesting addition to any collection.

DEFINING YOUR COLLECTION

Sooner or later, you will have to decide what kind of collection you are building. The collector may approach his hobby in one of several different ways. You may want to specialize in wooden plugs only, lures or reels or rods made by just one manufacturer or even specialize in only one type. The choices are many. Mr. Clyde Harbin is a collector who began several years ago, trying to obtain one example of every single lure from one company. His collecting expanded to the same goal for products of several other companies. To date he possesses more than **ten thousand** lures!

An interesting and very attractive collection would be one made up of only those lures, rods, or reels in good to mint condition. This would be difficult but challenging. To add some variety to your collection and display, even the specialist collector should have a few pieces from other areas of collectible tackle. There are hundreds of accessories to be found illustrated in old catalogs, some quite curious, others interesting but unsuccessful attempts at making the fisherman more comfortable under adverse conditions. The old catalogs themselves are fascinating, incredibly entertaining to read and some are works of art in themselves.

An old Marshall Field and Company catalog (circa 1915) advertises a FISHING BELL ALARM at five cents, saying "It is called the sleepy fisherman's friend." A 1919 catalog shows that for $1.35 the unlucky fisherman may obtain a LINE RELEASER complete with leather case. The advertisement states, in part: "Ever have your fly in a tree? Got mad of course." It goes on to claim that the device will not save your temper but will save your line, leader, lure and possibly the tip of your rod. It is placed on the tip of the rod, cuts the twig and "...down comes twig and your belongings." I've seen many a day when I could have used one of those. Sometimes I think I should be casting for our feathered friends instead of the fishy variety.

NOW THAT YOU HAVE IT
HOW DO YOU DISPLAY IT?

There can be no end to methods of display if you use your imagination. To name but a few: the professionally made, glassed and sealed shadow box; open frames with burlap or other decorative, appropriate substances; custom made shadow box types with removeable glass or plexiglass; an arrangement on a wall; display shelves and cabinets; hung from ceilings or beams; in antique or modern display fixtures used by tackle shops or, in the case of some collectors, whole rooms or more, entirely devoted to display and enjoyment. The list is limited only by your imagination and individual requirements. All have advantages, but one will suit your needs.

For the serious or would-be serious collector, I would recommend a method that both protects and allows ease of access and removal. If you don't you'll regret it later.

One very effective method for lure display is the use of tray-like cases with foam rubber backing and a sliding or hinged plexiglass cover. It is quite easy to remove, add and rearrange plugs on the foam rubber, the plexiglass protects from dust and the box itself can be hung on the wall or transported if you wish. If you're handy with your hands you can build them yourself.

For reels, almost any cabinet with glass fronts and or sides would be very handy. Lights in the interior can add a very dramatic and decorative element to the room as the various metals and surfaces of the reels reflect it.

Rods could be shown to great advantage hung* on your walls (removeable of course) or perhaps a gun cabinet would be attractive. I have seen some beautiful old wooden rod racks that came out of tackle shops of bygone days. These are ideal for display and ease of removal.

You might add interest and contrast to your collection by displaying some of the very old with the very new, modern versions of the same thing.

If you are into rods, reels or lures alone, the inclusion of some example of the others will add enjoyment and interest to your display. An old rod looks a lot nicer with a vintage reel mounted on it.

Most of you are fishermen. Add trophy mounts to your collection. Old tackle boxes, patches and other gadgets and accessories add even more.

Old or reproductions of old catalogs serve two purposes. One is that they make fascinating reading and more importantly, they are the single most important source of information from which to learn about your hobby. Many of these old catalogs are rare and eminently collectible themselves. A word about using the catalogs as reference material: The manufacturers were not always entirely accurate when listing. This is especially true with regard to sizes. Frequently the size is rounded to the nearest half or quarter-inch. Use them as a guide only.

Whatever method or scope of collection and display you arrive at, you will always find it necessary to change, add or delete. That's part of the fun.

You Have It, It's Broken, Beat Up or Missing Parts.
What Do You Do?

Restoration and repair? Your first thought should be: "Wait a minute now." "How is this going to affect the value and does it really matter to me?" Each individual must make up his own mind as to what he prefers. It would be safe to say most plug collectors would rather have a plug with a beat-up or half missing original paint than a perfect looking repaint. Repaints are out except for the demonstration, or the fun of fishing an old lure and you would rather not risk those fine examples in your collection. Whatever the reason *all* repaints of old plugs, no exception, should be **permanently** marked as such somewhere on the body.

Save the old beat up plugs that are beyond help. Collectors have assigned a most appropriate name to these, "Beaters." Keep the beaters for hardware. They are a good source for replacing bent or broken hardware, eyes, etc., with authentic parts should you come up with a nice body and not-so-nice hardware. There's nothing wrong with that as long as you don't change the original configuration.

Rods in their original, "mint" condition are quite rare and highly sought by collectors. This is especially true of the old split cane rods. It is so unusual to find any old rod in new condition that repair and restoration is permissible under certain conditions. If the rod is rebuilt and refinished by a recognized rod smith in such a way that the original integrity of it is perserved then it does not devalue it.

Old reels are frequently found in near perfect working condition. There is usually a good bit of dirt or deposit of some sort, but this can be cleaned off without disturbing original condition.

Rods should always be displayed or stored vertically.   10

Just don't use any sort of abrasive cleaner or steel wool. It will damage the finish. If it is not working, take it to a competent professional for repair. Just make sure he knows you don't want any new parts unless they are authentic or taken from another older reel made by the same company. I know two good repair folks in my area and both have a lot of interest in old reels, each keeping a few busted down examples around for just such a case. If they are typical, I don't imagine you will have much trouble in this regard. Keep them oiled and free from dust. For heavens sake if you want to load the spool with line, use some old black line or braided line, never today's monofilaments. The latter can damage the reel.

Some Pitfalls You May Encounter

It may be that most collectors are interested in but one particular type of lure, or merely accumulating an interesting collection of plugs for nostalgia, or even just an attractive colorful display for the den or study. These and other casual collectors are not so concerned with authenticity as is the serious collector. However, he would be well advised to arm himself with at least a basic knowledge of the techniques of identification and authentication, for there are some worth hundreds of dollars and a few more worth up to forty or fifty bucks to a serious collector, although that serious collector would probably be more interested in swapping several attractive and interesting pieces out of his collection or trade box to obtain one.

There are some areas all must be aware of. We have already talked about modifying lures while fishing. This generally takes the form of bending a diving blade or taking a deep diving blade off one plug and placing it on another which happens to be our finny foe's favorite flavor of the day. The same sort of thing went on as much as fifty or sixty years ago. You may find a South Bend plug with Heddon or Barracuda brand-marked propeller spinners, or a Creek Chub with a Brooks style diving lip and, woe is me, you might even find all four or more on one body. In the case of hook hardware, there may have been some good and valid reasons for a fisherman to modify a newer plug with older hardware. He wasn't thinking of future collectors of tackle, but of his fishing luck that past Spring day on the lake. How about that old surefire fish getter that the paint has just plumb wore off? He might spend a winter afternoon doing an absolutely splendid job of repainting it, using another brand plug as his model. Illustrated here is a genuine old plug and another just as genuine in body and hardware, but repainted.

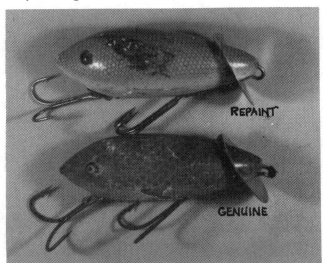

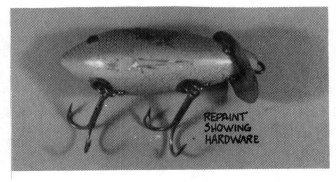

For the purpose of demonstration here, I took a badly beat up Heddon Crab Wiggler, removed the hardware and repainted it. I then "aged" the repaint job and replaced the hardware. At first glance it looks genuine. As a matter of fact, if there were no other Heddon plugs of the same vintage to compare it you might reasonably take it for the "real McCoy." However, if you are only casually familiar with the size of the scale pattern of that Heddon vintage it would jump out and holler "REPAINT!" at you. Repaints are interesting, but collectors do not value them as much as an original paint job in poor condition. If you were able to hold that lure in your hand right now, and know of the many layers of thick baked enamel and quality and size of the genuine scale finish, there would be no doubt in your mind as to its nature.*

*NOTE - The demonstration repaint shown in the photo was removed. The plug was again repainted, plainly marked Repaint and is now used in fishing demonstrations.

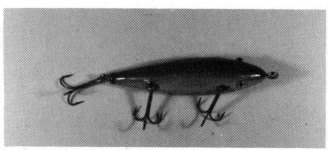

A wood-body, injured minnow type plug made from scratch by the author.

Upper plug in the photo is a mint condition late model Heddon lure. The lower plug is a genuine wood body, glass eye older Heddon with an extraordinarily good repaint in the original Heddon rainbow paint pattern.

There is wide availability of modern hardware on the market today. Fortunately it is easy to spot it, but the collector should be acutely aware that out of all the people in and around the tackle collecting hobby, there are bound to be one or two bad apples in the barrel. With the rapidly increasing interest in collecting plugs there naturally follows an increasing market for the genuine old item. There are some, unfortunately, who may attempt to take advantage of that. This is not peculiar to tackle collecting, but has followed virtually every area of collecting that has gained in popularity. Sounding somewhat negative there, I hasten to point out that all the dealers and collectors I have had any contact with are completely honest and trustworthy. I have never even heard one of them speak of a "bad apple." It is just that it is bound to happen and all need to be aware of the possibility.

American Fishing Lures and Fish Decoys

Cast your eye on some of today's newsiest collectibles.
By Seth Rosenbaum

There are two well-known stories about the origin of American fishing lures. The first has to do with the creation of the wooden minnow. According to this story, one day, about 1888, James Heddon, a rather famous Michigan sportsman, was sitting and whittling beside Dowagiac Creek. He idly tossed a chip of wood into the water and was startled to see a good-sized bass attack and try to devour it. Later, struck by the possibility of what might have happened if the wood had hooks and line attached to it, Heddon started turning out and selling hand-painted wooden minnows. The site where this event took place, a mill pond in Dowagiac, Mich., now boasts a commemorative plaque plus a hanging six-foot replica of an early Heddon plug.

Equally embedded in folklore is the story concerning J.T. Buel, the originator of the casting spoon. In the 1830s, Buel (like Heddon) had a fortunate fishing accident. He was fishing from a boat on Lake Bomoseen, Vt. With the approach of lunchtime, he unwrapped and ate his sandwich, and then reached for his favorite treat, a jar of preserved cherries. In doing so, he rocked the boat, lost his balance, and dropped his silver eating spoon overboard. As it sank, flashing, in the clear Vermont water, Buel saw a huge trout rush over and swallow the spoon. Shortly thereafter, Buel cut the handle off a household spoon and drilled a hole in both ends of the bowl of the spoon. He attached a hook through one hole and tied a line to the other. What his wife thought of this isn't recorded, but the fish liked the con-

traption and a new lure was born. In 1848, the J. T. Buel Spoon Co. was formed. Like the later-established James Heddon and Sons, it was a most successful lure company.

Lure and fish-decoy collecting is on the upswing. It started late—about 1950—and has grown very rapidly. Prior to this, the only sporting item considered collectible was a duck decoy made by a known carver. There was an abundance of wooden minnows and fish decoys around, but little interest.

Fish Decoys

Fish decoys are used in much the same way as duck decoys, which have been used for over 1,000 years, looking to a duck like another duck and bringing the real bird in for a visit. The duck could then be hit with an early spear or, later in history, shot with a shotgun. To use a fish decoy, you must have a frozen lake. You cut a hole in the ice, tie the decoy to a string, and dangle it in the water. The decoy is jigged up and down to attract a hungry or curious fish which, hopefully, is then speared by the fisher. Collectible fish decoys are usually made of wood, with the bottom hollowed out and a plug of lead inserted. This allows the decoy to sink into the water where the fish travel. The final

Continued on page 137

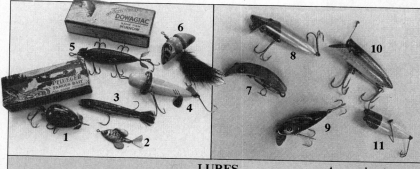

Name	Era	LURES Manufacturer	Approximate Value Today
1. Kent Frog	1923	Pflueger	$350 with box
2. Tin Liz Sunfish	1932	Arbogast	$200
3. Natural Minnow	1919	Louis Rhead	$350
4. Redfin	1908	Donaly	$600
5. Dowagiac Minnow	1925	Heddon	$150 with box
6. Wirl-Oreno	1939	South Bend Bait Co.	$200
7. Teas-Oreno	All from the 1940s	South Bend Bait Co.	All valued between $5 and $20 with box
8. Pike Flasher		Long Island Bait Co.	
9. Mustang Minnow		Pflueger	
10. Basser		Heddon	
11. Go-Getter		Abbey and Imbrie	

	FISH DECOYS			
Type of fish used to decoy or imitate	Carver	Era	State	Approximate Value Today
1. Abstract fish carving used to catch muskellunge and pike	unknown	1840	Wisconsin	$600
2. Imitation trout	Paul Henderson	1935	Michigan	$150
3. Imitation fish etched with a woodburning tool	Paul Henderson	1935	Michigan	$150
4. Imitation pike	unknown	1920	unknown	$75
5. Imitation frog used to catch bass	unknown	1920	unknown	$300

NTRY RE

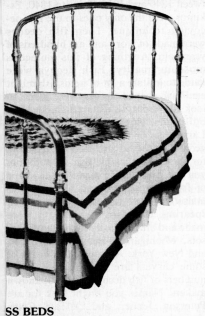

SS BEDS

ss heirlooms at affordable prices. All beds are
e with our 100% satisfaction guarantee. For a
Brass Company, Dept. CL75, 24 Park Lane Rd,

S LAMP
Hunting Horn (Order #2249)
" tall and has a
ck parchment
brass is hand-
protected with
r to last a life-
gift idea at
$4 shpg. each. Robelier, Dept. CLE7-5,
50th Street, Philadelphia, PA 19143.

2) Cecil Appreciation Days Craft Show (100 craftspeople). *When:* July 20–21. *Sponsor:* Crafts Guild and Art Assn. of St. Mary's County; (301) 994-1770. *Place:* Christmas Country Store & Old Mill, Great Mills. 3) Heritage/Ethnic Festival. *When:* July 21. *Sponsor and place:* Carroll County Farm Museum, 500 South Center St., Westminster 21157.

MASSACHUSETTS: 1) Kitchen Festival: Shaker-style meals. *When:* July 29–Aug. 3. *Sponsor and place:* Hancock Shaker Village, Inc., P.O. Box 898, Pittsfield 01202. 2) Art & Antiques Show. *When:* July 6–7. *Sponsor:* Antiques Dealers' Assn. of America, Inc., Mary Lou Sutter, Manager, RD Box 59, Frisbee St., East Chatham, N.Y. 12060; (518) 392-4690. *Place:* Springfield Civic Center Exhibition Hall, MA. 3) Ninth Mass. Arts & Crafts Summerfest (150 exhibitors). *When:* July 26–28. *Sponsor:* Todays Arts & Crafts Promotions, 152 Bliss Road, Longmeadow 01106; (413) 567-8542. *Place:* Topsfield Fairgrounds.

MICHIGAN: 1) Ann Arbor Antiques Market (300 dealers). *When:* July 21. *Sponsor:* Michigan Antiques Show & Sale, P.O. Box 1512, Ann Arbor 48106; (313) 662-9453. *Place:* Washtenaw Farm Council Grounds. 2) Heritage Days Art Show (50 exhibitors). *When:* July 4–6. *Sponsor and place:* West Branch Creative Arts Assoc., 124 N. Fourth St., West Branch 48661; (517) 473-2169. 3) Dearie Day Festival Arts & Crafts Show (130 exhibits). *When:* July 20–21. *Sponsor and place:* Old Village Assn., P.O. Box 483, Plymouth 48170; (313) 455-7011. 4) Seventh Annual Old French Town Days Festival.

When: July 20–21. *Sponsor:* Monroe County Historical Society, 126 S. Monroe St., Monroe 48161. *Place:* Hellenberg Park.

MINNESOTA: 1) Lace Making In The 19th Century. *When:* July 13. *Sponsor and place:* Murphy's Landing Historic Site, Shakopee 55379; (612) 445-6901. 2) Second Annual Pieces of Love Quilt Show. *When:* July 14–21. *Sponsor and place:* Kanabec County Historical Society and Museum, P.O. Box 113, W. Forest Ave., Mora 55051.

MISSOURI: Antiques Show & Sale (65 dealers). *When:* July 19–21. *Sponsor:* Wagner Promotions, Route 2, Box 152, Plattsburg 64477; (816) 539-3305. *Place:* Kansas City Trade Mart.

NEW HAMPSHIRE: 1) 10th Annual Antiques Show & Sale: *When:* July 20. *Sponsor:* Fitzwilliam Historical Society, K. Haeberle, P.O. Box 98, Fitzwilliam 03447. *Place:* Town Hall & Blake House Museum & Country Store. 2) 15th Antiques Show & Flea Market (25 dealers). *When:* July 13. *Sponsor and place:* New Castle Congregational Church Guild, Main St., New Castle 03854. 3) 10th Annual National Guild Rug School and Exhibit. *When:* July 16–18. *Sponsor:* National Guild of P.K. McGown Rug HooKrafters, Inc., C.L. Dugal, 10 Summer St., Dover 03820. *Place:* Rivier College, Nashua.

NEW JERSEY: 1) 27th Annual Antiques Show & Sale (13 dealers). *When:* July 6–7. *Sponsor:* Hope Historical Society, P.O. Box 52, Hope 07844. *Place:* Community Center. 2) Wilburs Country Craft Fair Days (100 craftspeople). *When:* July 6–7. *Sponsor:* Ray & Elizabeth Muriel, P.O. Box 443,

Continued on page 136

25

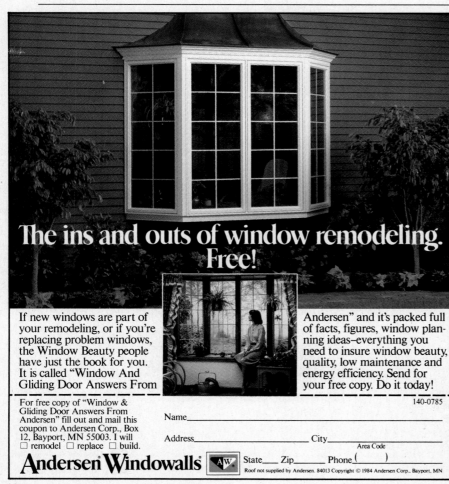

Refinishing Small Wooden and Paper-Mache Items

Practice and patience guarantee smooth results.
By Michael Varese

A nyone who has attempted to varnish a small wooden item has no doubt wondered how such a smooth finish was originally obtained—especially when the passage of the brush is hindered by molding, carving, or (in the case of trays) the gallery or rim running around the outside edge of the piece. It may seem that no sooner do you start the run of the brush than it is time to lift it away, and you cannot get into your stride. If the brush hits an uneven area, too much finish can be squeezed from the brush, making fat edges, runs, and conspicuous brush marks that will not even out when dry. In unpracticed hands, picture frames are notorious for collecting too much finish in the corner miters.

Smooth finishes used to be achieved

Spray finishes are easy to apply.

this way: After an item was cut out, fitted together, and adjusted where necessary, the various component parts were knocked apart, laid out, and secured along the workbench. Then they were finished—probably skillfully French-polished if they were Victorian boxes or caddies made of exotic woods. One can imagine how simple it was for a long length of picture-framing wood to be finished. All the parts were then reassembled, and fitted together. The result was a perfect finished surface.

Choosing a Finish

There are several practical finishes that the home handyperson can use on small wood pieces. The easiest are the rub-on varnishes that come in gel form, the increasingly popular tung-oil finishes, the spray cans of shellac, clear or satin varnishes, and polyurethanes. The tung oils and gel varnishes are so simple to apply they are considered foolproof, but the sprays take a little practice and patience.

The Professional's Finish

To obtain a flawless result, the spray process should never be hastened. The most common fault is holding the container too close and moving it too slowly along the work. Runs may appear, which too often are left, instead of being wiped away immediately.

Read and understand the instructions on the container, and soon you may find yourself addicted to this easy form of finish. A spray finish is more expensive than a liquid finish, but the unused portion of finish in the can will not deteriorate, form a skin, or harden as sometimes happens to a can of liquid finish when the lid is not pressed fully home. Be sure to clear the nozzle, as directed, each time you finish an application.

When you use masking tape to cover areas you don't want sprayed, apply it lightly so the old finish isn't lifted away when you remove the tape. Inexpensive masking tape works well because its adhesive is generally not too strong; it does the job and lifts away without causing damage.

In professional shops, the Preval Spray Unit is popular. This handy, inexpensive unit can be fitted with small replacement jars of any finish you choose. The unit is economical and can cope with all the usual finishing materials. Here again, instructions must be followed closely, particularly those that tell you how to thin various liquids before applying them. In addition to using this type of unit to spray small objects, it is ideal for "fixing" stain or for building up finish on small surface repairs. Pre-

HOOKED ON LURES

Fishermen call colorful wood or metal devices with attached hooks "lures" because they are made to attract and catch fish. Lures have caught collectors' eyes, too. This menagerie, ingeniously displayed in old shadow boxes, belongs to 12-year-old Jake Markezin, who discovered lures when his mother (a fish-decoy collector) took him along on antiquing expeditions. "Lures are neat-looking," says Jake. For more on lures and fish decoys, see Antiques and Collectibles.

Handcarved fish decoys.

Display boxes are valuable.

Bobber dips underwater when fish bites.

Hair hides the hook.

Some lures have more than one hook.

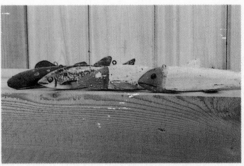
A school of decoys.

Propeller makes bubbles to lure fish.

Bug-like lure overlooks a tiger-striped lure.

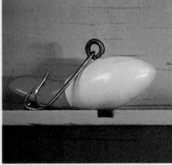
Color is a way to attract fish.

Some lures are designed to catch a particular fish.

A "Lazy Ike" lure under two line winders.

RECOMMENDED REFERENCES
and
SELECTED BIBLIOGRAPHY

There have been a few books written especially for the collector of old tackle. The first group listed here are the only ones I have found that are devoted exclusively to collecting old tackle. The remaining volumes listed are general history or contain some information useful to the collector. Some of these are out of print, but most can be found in a library of any size.

AMERICAN SPORTING COLLECTOR'S HANDBOOK; New Revised Edition by Allan J. Liu. Copyright 1982, Winchester Press, P.O. Box 1260, Tulsa, Oklahoma 74101.

This volume is available in soft or hardbound edition. It covers a wide range of sporting collectibles including rods, reels, lures and decoys. Useful to the collector and fascinating reading.

ANTIQUE FISHING REELS by Steven K. Vernon, copyright 1985. Stackpole Books, P. O. Box 1831, Harrisburg, Pennsylvania 17105.

The first comprehensive reference for fishing reel collectors.

THE BOOK OF BLACK BASS, James A. Henshall, M.D. Copyright 1881, revised 1904. The Robert Clarke Company, Cincinnati, Ohio. Out of print.

THE BOOK OF OLD LURES, Charles K. Fox. Copyright 1975 by Fox Publishers: Freshet Press, New York.

COLLECTING OLD FISHING TACKLE by Art and Scott Kimball, copyright 1980. Aardvark Publications, Inc., Boulder Junction, Wisconsin 54512.

Available in both hardbound and soft cover this is a new reference for collectors. Has some color plates. Recommended for any collector. May be out of print. They have a new book. See next listing.

COLLECTING OLD FISHING TACKLE by John Muma. Copyright 1987, National Child Publishing Company, P. O. Box 3452, Lubbock, Texas 79452.

A great little book crammed full of information. It would be useful to both the beginner and the veteran collector.

A COLLECTOR'S REFERENCE GUIDE TO HEDDON FISHING PLUGS by Bill Wetzel and Clyde A Harbin, Sr. Copyright 1984. 700 Ann Street, Hampton, South Carolina 29924 or CAH Enterprises, 1105 Marlin Road, Memphis Tennessee 38116.

Super handy little guide for the Heddon collector, but out of print and very difficult to obtain. None available from the authors.

THE COLLECTOR'S GUIDE TO ANTIQUE FISHING GEAR by Silvio A. Calabi. Copyright 1989 Wellfeet Press.

Recommended to any collector. Available from Book Sales, Inc., 110 Enterprise Ave., Secaucus, NJ 07094.

COMPLETE BOOK OF BASS FISHING, Grits Gresham. Copyright 1966, Outdoor Life, Harper and Row, N.Y.

EARLY FISHING LURES OF THE U.S.A. by Art and Scott Kimball, copyright 1985. Aardvark Publications, Inc., P.O. Box 252, Boulder Junction, Wisconsin 54512.

A very good soft bound book with a wealth of information about old lures.

ESQUIRE'S BOOK OF FISHING, Robert Scharff. Copyright 1933, Harper and Row, New York.

FIELD AND STREAM TREASURY, Greg and McCluskey. Copyright 1955, Henry Holt and Company, New York.

FISHING IN AMERICA, Charles F. Waterman. Copyright 1975, Holt, Rhinehart and Winston, New York.

FISHING AND COLLECTING OLD REEL AND TACKLE AND HISTORY by Albert J. Munger, 2235 Ritter Street, Philadelphia, Pennsylvania 19125.

Includes histories and photos of old reels such as Meek, Milam, Talbot, Leonard and more.

FISHING TACKLE, A COLLECTOR'S GUIDE by Graham Turner.

This is a large hard cover book that goes into great detail about the history of fishing and tackle. A exhaustively researched work. It is presently available from the author in England, but by the time this book is released it may be available in the states. The address is Hammerton's, 55 Hammerton Street, Burnley Lancashire, England BB 11 1LT.

FISHING TACKLE ANTIQUES by Karl T. White. Copyright 1987, Karl T. White, P. O. Box 169, Arcadia, Oklahoma 73007.

FRESHWATER FISHING, Arthur H. Carhart, Copyright 1949 by Carhart. Publishers: A. S. Barnes and Company, New York.

GREAT FISHING TACKLE CATALOGS OF THE GOLDEN AGE, Samuel Melner, Herman Kessler. Copyright 1972. Crown Publishers, Inc., New York.

THOSE OLD FISHING REELS by Albert J. Munger, 2235 Ritter Street, Philadelphia, Pennsylvania 19125.

GREAT TACKLE ADVERTISEMENTS BOOK I 1882-1930. Larry M. Smith, Editor. 3907 Wedgewood Drive, Portage, Michigan 49008.

A great collection of old tackle advertisment reprints in book form. Good research material.

GREAT TACKLE ADVERTISEMENTS BOOK II. 1874-1955. L. M. Smith, Editor. Copyright 1985. 3907 Wedgewood Drive, Portage, Michigan 49008.

A wonderful collection of old tackle advertisements reproduced in book form. A veritable treasure of information.

HISTORY OF THE SPORT OF CASTING, People, Events, Records, Tackle and Literature by Cliff Netherton. Copyright 1981. American Casting Education Foundation, Inc., P. O. Box 182, Herndon, Virginia 22070.

A HISTORY OF ANGLING, Charles Chevevix Trench. Copyright 1974. Follet, Chicago.

A HISTORY OF ANGLING AND ANGLING LITERATURE IN AMERICA by Charles M. Wetzel, Newark, Delaware.

JAMES HEDDON'S SONS CATALOGUES by The Bassman© Copyright 1977, Clyde A. Harbin, CAH Enterprises, 1105 Marlin Road, Memphis, Tennessee 38116.

This is a large book containing reprints of old Heddon catalogs beginning in 1903. In addition to the catalog reprints, the author has provided the collector of Heddon lures with a veritable treasure by meticulously describing and classifying each Heddon lure in organized charts throughout the book. A must for any collector of Heddon lures, but out of print and very difficult to obtain.

McLANE'S STANDARD FISHING ENCYCLOPEDIA, A. J. McLane. Copyright 1974. Holt, Rhinehart and Winston, New York.

THE NEW FISHERMAN'S ENCYCLOPEDIA, Ira N. Gabrielson and Francesca LaMonte. Copyright 1959. Stackpole, Harrisburg, Pa.

OLD FISHING TACKLE AND TALES by Albert J. Munger. Copyright 1987 Albert J. Munger, 2235 Ritter Street, Philadelphia, PA 19125.
book. A must for any collector of Heddon lures, but out of print and very difficult to obtain.

SALMON FISHING PLUGS, A History of Wood Salmon Fishing Plugs from Washington, Idaho and British Columbia by Jim Lone. Copyright 1983. 610 8th Avenue South, Edmonds, Washington 98020.

THE SPOONERS, Harvey W. Thompson. Copyright 1979, Eppinger Manufacturing Company, Dearborn, Michigan.

STREATER'S REFERENCE CATALOG OF OLD FISHING LURES by Richard L. Streater. Copyright 1978, Richard L. Streater, Mercer Island, Washington.

The author has provided the collector with a large, loose-leaf bound and index-tabbed book dealing with many different companies that produced lures over the years. Illustrated. Recommended for any new collector of old lures. Revised 1981.

TACKLE TINKERING, H. G. Tappley. Copyright 1946. A. S. Barnes and Company, N.Y. Out of print.

THOSE OLD FISHING REELS by Albert J. Munger, 2235 Ritter Street, Philadelphia, Pennsylvania 19125.

WHOLE FISHING CATALOG, Consumer Guide. Copyright 1978, Publications International, Ltd. Skokie, Illinois. Published by Simon and Schuster, New York.

There is a group of very informative scholarly studies privately published by the active members of the National Fishing Lure Collectors Club. While these were produced for other members of the club and may not be generally available, you might contact the authors or the club about the possibility. They are professionally prepared and are very detailed, valuable illustrated references for the particular companies chosen.

AL FOSS. A history of the company and their lures. By Jim Frazier. Copyright 1985. 312 North 46th Avenue, Hollywood, Florida 33021.

THE BOMBER BAIT COMPANY. A study of the company's lures, particularly the Bomber. Copyright 1983 by Jim Bourdon. Nordica Drive, Croton-on-Hudson, New York, 10520.

EARLY FISHING TACKLE OF NEW YORK STATE. Anyone with an interest in old tackle would be interested in this study chock full of old advertisements and a plethora of old patent application drawings. Copyright 1985, Jim Bourdon, Croton-on-Hudson, New York 10520.

HENDRYX. This is essentially a reproduction of catalog entries of Hendryx metal lures made prior to the 1919 acquisition of the company by Winchester. Copyright 1986 Harold D. Herr, D.D.S.

HENRY LOFTIE, FLY FISHERMAN, INVENTOR, TACKLE MAKER. Copyright 1987 by Richard R. Metcalf, 112 Sutton Drive, Syracuse, New York 13219.

A HISTORY OF THE ERWIN WELLER COMPANY by Harold G. Dickart. Copyright 1984. This very good study was written specifically for members of the National Fishing Lure Collectors Club and says so on the cover. Contact the club. May not be available to the general public.

JOHN H. MANN, THE MANN FROM SYRACUSE. A history of the man and his lures. Copyright 1986 by Richard R. Metcalf, 112 Sutton Drive, Syracuse, New York 13219.

MEMBERS OF THE CREEK CHUB PIKIE AND SURFSTER FAMILIES by Bruce Boyden. A good study that was produced specifically for members of the National Fishing Lure Collectors Club. Copyright 1984. Bruce Boyden, P.O. Box 752, Annex Station, Providence, Rhode Island 02901.

THE PONCA CITY BAIT CARVERS. Copyright 1986 by Jim Bourdon, Nordica Drive, Croton-on-Hudson, New York 10520.

SOUTH BEND Their Artificial Baits and Reels as reflected by the company's catalogs between 1912 and 1953. Copyright 1985 by Jim Bourdon, Nordica Drive, Croton-on-Hudson, New York 10520.

SOUTH BEND, Their Artificial Baits and Reels as reflected by the company's catalogs between 1912 and 1953 by Jim Bourdon. Copyright 1985. Nordica Drive, Croton-on-Hudson, New York 10520.

THE WATER SCOUT AND OTHER CLARK BAITS, A Preliminary Report by Ray Barzee and Jim Bourdon. Copyright 1984. Nordica Drive, Croton-on-Hudson, New York 10520.

VIDEOTAPES

Clyde Harbin has put together a series of four interesting video tapes that any collector would find useful. They are available in VHS from the following: Antique Lures - VHS Tapes, P.O. Box 154087, Irving, Texas 75015. Telephone: 1-800-634-8917. The tapes available are as follows:

Volume 1
   Antique and Collectibles: An Overview
Volume 2
   Antique Lures: Over 40 of the Rarest
Volume 3
   Antique Lures: The Heddon Collection
Volume 4
   Antique Lures: Heddon/Stokes Heritage
Volume 5
   Heddon Uncataloged Lures
Volume 6
   1903-1916 Heddon Catalogs
Volumes 7 & 8
   Heddon/Pradco Lure Collection I and II
      Ft. Smith, Arkansas

SOME USEFUL PERIODIC PUBLICATIONS

SPECIFIC TO OLD FISHING TACKLE

FISHING COLLECTIBLES. Brian J. McGrath, editor. 2005 Tree House Lane, Plano, Texas 75023.
This is a relatively new publication. It is devoted entirely to tackle and issued quarterly. Well worth subscribing to. A must for the collector.

SPORTING CLASSICS. John Culler, Editor. Editorial offices: P.O. Box 1017, Camden, South Carolina 29020. Subscriptions: Subscriber Service Center (Sporting Classics), P.O. Box 6669, Syracuse, New York 13217
An excellent bi-monthly magazine devoted to all sorts of sporting collectibles. Has frequent articles about old fishing tackle.

GENERAL TO COLLECTING

The following periodicals are aimed at collectors of all sorts of things. They can give you a wide scope of readership. A want ad or two in one of them might uncover a treasure in an individuals possession. I have seen occasional ads to buy or sell old tackle in most of them.

ANTIQUE TRADER WEEKLEY. P.O. Box 1050, Dubuque, Iowa 52349.
Weekly tabloid.

ANTIQUE WEEK. P. O. Box 90, Knightstown, Indiana 46148.
Weekly tabloid.

COLLECTORS JOURNAL. P.O. Box 601, Vinton, Iowa 52349.
Weekly tabloid.

SOURCES FOR OLD BOOKS AND MAGAZINES ABOUT FISHING AND TACKLE

Many of the old publications from catalogs and magazines to hard cover books are rich in information about tackle from the time they were printed. Many of the sources named here will be glad to supply you with lists of those they have available upon request. Be sure to specify type wanted and include a legal size stamped, self-addressed envelope (SASE). When writing to them, also don't forget to try your own public library. They can sometimes turn out to be very rich source of material.

Kenneth Anderson-Books
38 Silver Street
Auburn, Massachusetts 01501

The Anglers Art
P. O. Box 148
Plainfield, Pennsylvania 17081

Angler's and Shooter's Bookshelf
Goshen, Connecticut 06756

Avocet Books
827 South Horner
Sanford, North Carolina 27330

Back Number Wilkens
Box 247 A
Danvers, Massachusetts 01923

Bassman, CAH Enterprises
1105 Marlin Road
Memphis, Tennessee 38116

Judith Bowman Books
Pound Ridge Road
Bedford, New York 10506

James Cummings - Bookseller
859 Lexington Avenue
New York, New York 10021

Gary L. Esterbrook - Books
P.O. Box 61453
Vancover, Washington 98666

Gunnerman Books
Box 429a
Auburn Heights, Michigan 48057

Hampton Books
Rt. 1, Box 202
Newberry, South Carolina 29108

Henderson and Park
500 Main
Greenwood, Missouri 64030

Highwood Bookshop
Louis Razek
P. O. Box 1246
Traverse City, Michigan 49685

Melvin Marcher
6204 North Vermont
Oklahoma City, Oklahoma 73112

The Gamebag
P. O. Box 838
Twin Lakes, WI 53181

THE NATIONAL FISHING LURE COLLECTORS CLUB

There are hardly any national organizations of fishing tackle collectors that are known. The National Fishing Lure Collectors Club (NFLCC) is the only one presently known to the author. It was founded by three Missouri collectors several years ago and has grown into a national membership since. The club produces a periodic newsletter and the membership is very active in buy, sell and trade of old lures and tackle. For membership information contact:

NATIONAL FISHING LURE COLLECTORS CLUB
MEMBERSHIP CHAIRMAN
P.O. Box 1791
Dearborn, Michigan 48121

TACKLE MANUFACTURERS PAST AND PRESENT
Research and Reference List

The following list of American Fishing Tackle Manufacturers and/or distributors contains hundreds of names and addresses of firms that no longer exist and those presently in business. Over the years many of these firms went out of business, were bought by other companies, merged or changed their names. The primary reason for the inclusion of unknown or defunct companies is to allow those collectors who may live in or near the addresses given to embark on a little research of their own. Some detective work might ferret out the original owners, their children or relatives or maybe even some former employees. This kind of effort might net the collector a veritable treasure trove of unsold tackle, catalogs, records, etc., socked away in an attic, basement, or garage. In addition present day manufacturers (marked with and asterisk*) often print a little historical background in their current catalogs. These are usually available for the asking or for a nominal amount of money. So press on, those of you who want to 'tackle' it.

A

ABBEY and IMBRIE New York, N.Y.	MIXED	ALLSTAR BAIT CO. 1303 W. Jackson Blvd. Chicago, Ill.	LURES
ABC MFG., CO. 135 E. Jefferson Ave. Detroit, Michigan	LURES	FORREST ALLEN 1658 Summer St. Stamford, Conn.	LURES
ABERCROMBIE and FITCH CO. New York, N.Y.	MIXED	ALLIANCE MFG., CO. Alliance, Ohio	LURES
TONY ACCETTA 853 E. 144th St. Cleveland, Ohio	LURES	AMERICAN DISPLAY CO. Akron, Ohio	LURES
ACTION LURE CO. Hollywood, Calif.	LURES	AMERICAN ROD AND GUN Stamford, Conn.	LURES
ACTUAL LURES Cold Spring Harbor Long Island, N.Y.	LURES	J.E. ANDERSON 6224 May St. Chicago, ILL.	RODS
ADOLF ARNTZ 24 W. Western Ave. Muskegon, Michigan	LURES	ANGLER'S SUPPLY CO. Utica, N.Y.	MIXED
W. and J.M. AIKENHEAD 55 Front St. Rochester, N.Y.	REELS	*FRED ARBOGAST CO., INC. 313 W. North St. and 43 Water St. Akron, Ohio 44303	LURES
ALCOE LURE CO. Fern Park, Florida	LURES	ASSOCIATED SPECIALTIES Chicago, ILL.	LURES
FRANKLIN A. ALGER Grand Rapids, Mich.	LURES	T.F. AUCLAIR AND ASSOC., INC. 279 Highland Ave. Detroit, Mich.	LURES

B

BARR-ROYER CO. Waterloo, Iowa	LURES	THOMAS H. BATE and CO. 7 Warren St. New York, N.Y.	MIXED
BARRACUDA BRAND (Florida Fishing Tackle Co.) St. Petersburg, Fla.	MIXED	BEAR CREEK BAIT CO. Kaleva, Mich.	LURES
BASS-KING Brushton, N.Y.	LURES	BECKER SHEWARD MFG. CO. Council Bluffs, Iowa	LURES

BENSON-VAILE CO. Kokomo, Ind.	REELS	BRISTOL RODS HORTON MFG. CO. 23 Horton St. Bristol Conn.	RODS
BERRY-LEBECK MFG. CO. California, Mo.	LURES	BROADCASTER LURES 224 Phelps St. Youngstown, Ohio	LURES
BIEK MFG. CO. Dowagiac, Mich.	LURES	BRONSON REEL CO. 145 State St. Bronson, Mich.	REELS
BIFF BAIT CO. 4101 Meinecke Ave. Milwaukee, Wisc.	LURES	BROOK SHINER BAIT CO. Milwaukee, Wisc.	LURES
A.F. BINGENHEIMER 142 Second St. Milwaukee, Wisc.	LURES	BROWN'S FISHERETTO CO. Alexandria, Minn. Osakis, Minn.	LURES
BITE-EM BAIT CO. Warsaw, Ind. Ft. Wayne, Ind.	LURES	H. CORBIN BRUSH Brushton, N.Y.	LURES
BLEEDING BAIT MFG. CO. 3404-06 Main St. Dallas, Texas	LURES	JULIO T. BUEL Whitehall, N.Y.	SPINNERS
*BOMBER BAIT CO. 326 Lindsay St. Gainesville, Texas 76240	LURES	PAUL BUNYAN BAIT CO. 1307 Glenwood Minneapolis, Minn.	LURES
T.J. BOULTON 32 Lauderdale St. Detroit, Mich.	LURES	BURKE BAIT CO. 2314 West 12th St. Chicago, ILL	LURES
BRAINARD BAIT CO. St. Paul Minn.	LURES	AL BYLER Seattle, Wash.	LURES
BRIGHT-EYE LURE PRODUCTS 19646 Chalmers Ave. Detroit, Mich.	LURES		

C

CARTER'S BESTEVER BAIT CO. 25½ W. Washington St. Indianapolis, Ind.	LURES	HARRY COMSTOCK Fulton, N.Y.	SPINNERS
CASE BAIT CO. 208 E. Perry St. Detroit, Mich.	LURES	THOMAS J. CONROY 28 John Street New York, N.Y.	REELS
CHARMER MINNOW CO. Springfield, Mo.	LURES	MAX COOK 1608 Glenarm Denver, Co.	MIXED
CHICAGO TACKLE CO. 2752 W. Windsor Chicago, ILL.	MIXED	DAVE COOK SPORTING GOODS Denver, Co.	MIXED
THOMAS H. CHUBB Post Mills, Vt.	MIXED	CRALL BROTHERS Chicago Junction, Ohio	LURES
*CISCO KID TACKLE, INC. 2630 N.W. 1st. Ave. Boca Raton, Fla.	LURES	*CREEK CHUB BAIT CO. Garret, Ind. 46738	LURES
C.A. CLARK CO. Springfield, Mo.	LURES	D.J. CRITTENBERGER 3210 Ruckle St. Indianapolis, Ind.	RODS
COLDWATER BAIT CO. Coldwater, Mich.	LURES		

D

DAME, STODDARD and KENDALL   MIXED
374 Washington St.
Boston, Mass.

DAVID LURE CO.   LURES
Peoria, ILL

ANS B. DECKER   LURES
Nolan's Point
Lake Hopatcong, N.J.
and
DECKER BAIT CO.
6 Henry St.
45 E. Willoughby St.
Brooklyn, N.Y.

DETROIT BAIT CO.   LURES
12248 Woodrow Wilson
Detroit, Mich.

DETROIT GLASS MINNOW   LURES
TUBE CO.
55 W. Lafayette Blvd.
Detroit, Mich.

DETROIT WEEDLESS BAIT CO.   LURES
6906 W. Lafayette
Detroit, Mich.

DIAMOND MFG. CO.   MIXED
St. Louis, Mo.

DICKENS BAIT CO.   LURES
714 W. Superior St.
Fort Wayne, Ind.

LYLE DICKERSON   RODS
Detroit, Mich.

DILLON-BECK CO.   LURES
Address unknown

FRED D. DIVINE CO.   RODS
505 Robert St.
Utica, NY

JAMES L. DONALY   LURES
137 Court St.
Newark, N.J. and
Bloomfield, N.J.

HARRY F. DRAKE   LURES
900 S. 20th St.
Milwaukee, Wisc.

DRULY'S RESEARCH PRODUCTS   LURES
Prescott, Wisc.

*DUNK'S   LURES
4186 Vira Road
Stowe, Ohio 44224

E

*EAGLE CLAW   MIXED
(WRIGHT and MCGILL)
4245 E. 46th St.
Denver, Co. 80216

ECKFIELD BOAT CO.   LURES
Algonac, Mich.

EGER BAIT MFG. CO.   LURES
Bartow, Fla.

ELECTRIC LUMINOUS SUBMARINE   LURES
BAIT CO.
Milwaukee, Wis.

R.S. ELLIOT ARMS CO.   LURES
Kansas City, Mo.

ENTERPRISE MFG. CO.   LURES
Akron, Ohio

*LOU J. EPPINGER MFG. CO.   LURES
301 Gratiot St.
310-16 E. Congress St.
Detroit, Mich.

ESSENTIAL PRODUCTS CO.   LURES
201 Fifth Ave.
New York, N.Y.

ETCHEN TACKLE CO.   LURES
Detroit, Mich.

EUREKA BAIT CO.   LURES
Coldwater, Mich.

F

FENNER WEEDLESS BAIT CO.   LURES
Oxford, Wisc.

FISCHER-SCHUBERTH CO.   LURES
5820 S. Wentworth Ave.
Chicago, ILL

FISHATHON BAIT MFG.   LURES
CO., INC.
Okumlgee, Okla. and
Ypsilanti, Mich.

FLORIDA FISHING TACKLE CO.   MIXED
St. Petersburg, Fla.

H. and D. FOLSOM ARMS CO.   MIXED
314 Broadway
New York, N.Y.

AL FOSS   LURES
1716-1736 Columbus Road
Cleveland, Ohio

C.J. FROST   LURES
300 Ellis St. & 200 Normal Ave.
Stevens Point, Wisc.

H.J. FROST and CO.   MIXED
90 Chambers St.
New York, N.Y.

G

GARLAND BROTHERS Plant City, Fla.	LURES
GEORGE GAYLE and SON Frankfort, Ky.	LURES
GEN-SHAW Kankakee, ILL	LURES
GENERAL MERCHANDISE CO. 243 N. Water St. Milwaukee, Wisc.	MIXED
STAN GIBBS 35-39 Old Plymouth Road Sagamore, Mass.	LURES
*GLADDING CORP. (SOUTH BEND) 5985 Tarbell Road Syracuse, N.Y. 13217	MIXED
GO-ITE MFG. CO. Kokomo, Indiana	REELS
GOULD and GOULD Boston, Mass.	MIXED
GOODWIN GRANGER and COMPANY 1240 E. 9th Ave. Denver, Colorado	RODS
GRAND LAKE FISHING TACKLE Springfield, Ohio	MIXED
J.F. GREGORY St. Louis, Mo.	LURES

H

HAAS TACKLE CO. 8-10 N. Poplar St. Sapulpa, Okla.	MIXED
F.B. HAMILTON MFG. Pasadena, Calif.	LURES
JACOB HANSON 11 Ottawa St. 30 Manz Ave. 1700 Manz St. Muskegan, Mich.	LURES
WILLIAM B. HANSON CO. 939 Pollmey St. Pittsburgh, Pa.	LURES
C.R. HARRIS 449 River St. Manistee, Mich Niles, Mich. Mackinaw City, Mich.	LURES
HASTINGS SPORTING GOODS WORKS 418 Michigan Ave. Hastings, Mich.	LURES
HARDY SMAIL CO., INC. Fulton St. New York, N.Y.	MIXED
W.B. HAYNES 274 Park St. Akron, Ohio	LURES
JAMES HEDDON'S SONS 414 W. St. Dowagiac, Mich. 49047	MIXED
*HELIN TACKLE CO. 333 Elmwood Troy, Mich.	LURES
J.G. HENZEL 1313 S. Fairfield Ave. 2323 Greenshaw St.	LURES
BILL HERRINGTON BAIT CO. Green City, Mo.	LURES
HIBBARD, SPENCER, BARTLETT and CO. State Street Bridge Chicago, Ill.	MIXED
*JOHN J. HILDEBRANDT CO. 816½ High St. Logansport, Ind.	MIXED
JOE HINKLE 505 Augustus Ave. Louisville, Ky.	LURES
HOLLAND ROD CO. St. Joseph, Mich.	RODS
J.C. HOLZWARTH (Spring, Holzwarth and Co.) Alliance, Ohio	LURES
HOM-ART BAIT CO. 310 N. Howard St. Akron, Ohio	LURES
HOOKZEM BAIT CO. 3443 N. Harding Ave. Chicago, Ill.	LURES
HORROCKS-IBBOTSON CO. Rome and Utica, N.Y.	MIXED
HORTON MFG. CO. 245 Horton St. Bristol, Conn.	MIXED

I

IMMELL BAIT CO. 26 Main St. Blair, Wisc.	LURES
ISLE ROYALE BAIT CO. Jackson, Mich.	LURES

J

JACKS TACKLE MFG. CO. Oklahoma City, Okla.	LURES
W.J. JAMISON 736 S. California Ave. 2751 Polk St. Chicago, ILL.	MIXED
JENNINGS FISHING TACKLE CO. Olympia, Wash.	LURES

JENSON DISTRIBUTING CO. Waco, Texas	LURES
LOUIS JOHNSON CO. 40-B N. Wells St. Chicago, Ill, and Highland Park, Ill.	LURES
JOY BAIT CO. 221 W. Maple St. Lansing, Mich.	LURES

K

KALAMAZOO FISHING TACKLE MFG. 610 Douglas Ave. Kalamazoo, Mich.	LURES
KAUTZKY MFG. CO. Ft. Dodge, Iowa	LURES
FRED C. KEELING and CO. Rockford, Ill.	LURES
H.H. KIFFE CO. 521 Broadway New York, N.Y.	MIXED
KING BAIT CO. 4312 Chicago Ave. Minneapolis, Minn.	LURES

M.F. KIRWAN MFG. O'Neil, Nebr.	LURES
K & K MFG. CO. Toledo, Ohio	LURES
A. KLEINMAN 250 8th Ave. New York, N.Y.	REELS
S.E. KNOWLES 72 4th St. San Francisco, Calif.	LURES
JOHN KRIDER Second and Walnut Sts. Philadelphia, Pa.	MIXED
ARTHUR J. KUMM Dearborn, Mich.	LURES

L

LAUBY LURE CO. Marshfield, Wis.	LURES
LAZY DAZY BAIT CO. Preston, Minn.	LURES
*LAZY IKE CORP. (Kautzky) P.O. Box 4827 Des Moines, Iowa 50309	LURES
HIRAM L. LEONARD Bangor, Maine and Central Valley, N.Y.	RODS, REELS

LEX BAITS Louisville, Ky.	LURES
E.J. LOCKHART CO. Galesburg, Mich.	LURES
LOTZ BROTHERS 169 N. Main St. St. Louis, Mo.	LURES
W.T.J. LOWE Buffalo, N.Y.	SPINNER BAITS

M

MAKINEW TACKLE CO. Kaleva, Mich.	LURES
*MANTA-RAY CO., INC. 304 E. Wabash St. Montpelier, Ohio 43543	LURES
MARATHON BAIT CO. Wausau, Wisc.	LURES
MARINAC TACKLE CO. Kaleva, Mich.	LURES
*MARTIN REEL CO. (Martin Automatic Fishing Reel Co.) 30 East Main St. Mohawk, N.Y.	REELS

MCCLEAN SPORTING GOODS CO. 400 S. 7th St. St. Louis, Mo.	MIXED
MCCORMIC BAIT CO. Kalamazoo, Mich and Warsaw, Ind.	LURES
E.C. MEACHAM ARMS CO. St. Louis, Mo.	MIXED
B.F. MEEK and SONS, INC. Louisville, Ky.	REELS
A.F. MEISSELBACH and BRO. 10 Congress St. Newark, N.J.	REELS

*MEPPS (SHELDON'S INC.) Box 508 Antigo, Wisc. 54409	LURES	WILLIAM MILLS and SON New York, N.Y. and Central Valley, N.Y.	MIXED
MERMADE BAIT CO., INC. Platteville, Wisc.	LURES	MILLSITE FISHING TACKLE 1415 Michigan Ave. Howell, Mich.	LURES
H.H. MICHAELSON 912-914 Broadway Brooklyn, N.Y.	MIXED	MOONLIGHT BAIT CO. Paw Paw, Mich.	LURES
MICHIGAN TACKLE CO. 2550 Blaine Detroit, Mich.	MIXED	H.C. MOORE 432 N. Huron St. Ypsilanti, Mich.	LURES
B.C. MILAN Frankfort, Ky.	REELS	PHILIP MORRIS CO. Nashua, N.H.	MIXED
		MYERS and SPELLMAN Shelby, Mich.	LURES

N

NATIONAL SPORTSMAN STORE 75 Federal St. Boston, Mass.	MIXED	NEAL BAIT MFG. CO. 320 So. Cherry Street Columbus, Indiana	LURES
NATIONAL SUPPLY CO. Minneapolis, Minn.	MIXED	NEW YORK SPORTING GOODS CO. 15-17 Warren St. New York, N.Y.	MIXED
NATURALURE BAIT CO. 104 E. Colorado and 1218 Fair Oaks Ave. Pasadena, Calif.	LURES	FRANK T. NIXON 107 Mt. Vernon Ave. Grand Rapids, Mich.	LURES

O

ROBERT OGILVY CO. 78 Chambers St. New York, N.Y.	MIXED	W.E. OSTER MFG. 1620 N. Karlov Ave. Chicago, Ill.	LURES
ORCHARD INDUSTRIES Detroit, Mich.	LURES	OUTING MFG. CO. Elkhart, Ind.	LURES
ORCHARD INDUSTRIES, INC. 18404 Morang Rd. Detroit, Mich.	LURES	OZARK LURE CO. Tulsa, Okla.	LURES
*ORVIS CO. Manchester, Vt. 05254	MIXED		

P

F.A. PARDEE and CO. Kent, Ohio	LURES	PERRINE MFG. CO. 704 S. Fourth St. Minneapolis, Minn.	REELS
PAW PAW BAIT CO. Paw Paw, Mich.	LURES	JIM PFEFFER Orlando, Florida	LURES
PAYNE BAIT CO. 3142 Edgewood Ave. Chicago, Ill.	LURES	PFEIFFER LIVE BAIT HOLDER CO. 52 Clark Court Detroit, Mich.	LURES
E.F. PAYNE ROD CO. Highland Mills, N.Y.	RODS	*PFLUEGER SPORTING GOODS 1801 Main St. P.O. Box 185 Columbia, S.C. 29202	MIXED
JOE E. PEPER Rome, N.Y.	LURES		
PEQUEA WORKS, INC. Strasburg, PA.	LURES	PHILLIPS FLY and TACKLE CO. Alexandria, Pa.	LURES

*PICO LURES P.O. Box 5310 2617 N. Zaryamora San Antonio, Texas 78201	LURES	PONTIAC MFG. CO. Pontiac, Mich.	LURES
P and K 122 N. Dixie Hwy. Momence, Ill.	LURES	EDDIE POPE and CO. Montrose, Calif.	LURES
		P and S BALL BEARING BAIT CO. Whitehall, N.Y.	LURES

R

R.K. TACKLE CO. Grand Rapids, Mich.	LURES	C.L. RITZMANN 943 Broadway New York, N.Y.	LURES
RAWLINGS SPORTING GOODS, CO. 620 Locust St. St. Louis, Mo.	MIXED	C.C. ROBERTS Mosinee, Wis.	LURES
REDIFOR ROD and REEL CO. Warren, Ohio	REELS	ROD and CREEL TACKLE CO. 630 Helen Ave. Detroit, Mich.	LURES
LOUIS RHEAD NATURE LURES Brooklyn and Amityville, N.Y.	LURES	H.C. ROYER 335 Wilson Block Terminal Island Los Angeles, Calf.	LURES
FRED RHODES Kalamazoo, Mich.	LURES	J.K. RUSH 914 S. A. and K. Bldg. Syracuse, N.Y.	LURES
RICE ENG. CO. 912 Stephenson Bldg. Detroit, Mich.	LURES		
RIDER CASTING REEL CO. Ft. Wayne, Ind.	LURES	RUSSELURE MFG. CO., INC. 2514 S. Grand Ave. Los Angeles, Calif.	LURES

S

SCHMELZER'S Kansas City, Mo.	MIXED	G.M. SKINNER Clayton, N.Y.	LURES
SCHOENFELD GUTTER, INC. 63 Park Row New York, N.Y.	LURES	BOB SMITH SPORTING GOODS 75 Federal St. Boston, Mass.	MIXED
JOHN RAY SCHOONMAKER Kalamazoo, Mich.	LURES	JACK K. SMITHWICK Shreveport, La.	LURES
*SHAKESPEARE CO. 3801 Westmore Drive Columbia, SC 29204	MIXED	*SOUTH BEND TACKLE CO. (GLADDING) 1950 Stanley St. Northbrook, IL 60065	MIXED
SHANNON 816 Chestnut St. Philadelphia, Penn.	LURES	SPRINGFIELD NOVELTY MGF. CO. Springfield, Mo.	LURES
SHAPLEIGH HARDWARE CO. St. Louis, Mo.	MIXED	CHARLES STAPF Prescott, Wisc.	LURES
SHOFF FISHING TACKLE CO. 407 W. Gowe St. Kent, Wash.	MIXED	BUD STEWART TACKLE 1032 Ann Arbor St. Flint, Mich.	MIXED
SHURE-BITE INC. Bronson, Mich.	LURES	STOCKFORD REEL CO. 328 W. Kinzie St. Chicago, Ill.	REELS
SILVER CREEK NOVELTY WORKS Dowagiac, Mich.	LURES	SUNNYBROOK LURE CO. Tyler, Texas	LURES
SIMMONS HARDWARE CO. St. Louis, Mo.	MIXED	SURE-CATCH BAIT CO. Versailles, Ohio	LURES
T.S. SKILTON MFG. Winstead, Conn.	HOOKS. FLIES		

T

TALBOT REEL and MFG. CO. 314-316 E. Eighth St. Kansas City, Mo. Nevada, Missouri	REELS	**EDWARD K. TRYON, JR. and CO.** 10-12 N. 6th. St. and 220 N. 2nd St. Philadelphia, Pa.	MIXED
FRED E. THOMAS 117 Exchange St. Bangor, Maine	RODS	**TRUE TEMPER** (American Fork and Hoe) Geneva, Ohio	LURES
TOLEDO BAIT CO. 1944 Broadway Toledo, Ohio	LURES	**L. J. TOOLEY** 251 Hartford Ave. Detroit, Mich.	LURES
TRAPPERS SUPPLY CO. Oak Park, Ill.	LURES	**TULSA FISHING TACKLE CO.** 1402 East 6th St. Tulsa, Okla.	LURES
G. ED TREBING CO. Address Unknown	MIXED	**O.A. TURNER** Coldwater, Mich.	LURES
TRENTON FISHING TACKLE **and EQUIPMENT** 429 Greenup Covington, Ky.	LURES	**O.C. TUTTLE** 13 Tuttle Bldg. Old Forge, N.Y.	LURES

U

UNION SPRINGS SPECIALTY CO. Union Springs Cayuga Lake, N.Y.	LURES

V

VACUUM BAIT CO. 307 Walnut St. North Manchester, Ind.	LURES	**EDWARD VOM HOFE and CO.** 112 Fulton St. New York, N.Y.	MIXED
VAUGHN'S TACKLE CO. Cheboygan, Mich.	LURES	**VON LENGERKE and ANTOINE** 33 South Wabash Ave. Chicago, Ill.	MIXED
VESCO BAIT CO. 154 West 18th St. New York, N.Y.	LURES	**VON LENGERKE and DETMOLD** **INC.** 349 Madison Ave. New York, N.Y.	MIXED
VEX BAIT CO. 1917 N. Main St. Dayton, Ohio	LURES		
VOEDISCH BROTHERS 3429 N. Clark St. Chicago, Ill.	LURES		

W

WALTON SUPPLY CO. St. Louis, Mo.	LURES	***WEBER TACKLE CO.** (WEBER LIFELIKE FLY CO.) Stevens Point, Wisc. 54481	LURES
DR. C.S. WASWEYLER 461 Mitchell St. Milwaukee, Wisc.	LURES	***ERWIN WELLER CO.** 2105 Clark St. Sioux City, Iowa 51104	LURES
WATT TACKLE CO. 8500 Nottingham	LURES	**WEEZEL BAIT CO.** 6006 Wooster Pike Fairfax Cincinnati, Ohio	LURES
W.C. MFG. CO. 1142 Main St. Racine, Wisc.	REELS		

WIGGLE TAIL MINNOW CO. 162 Canfield Ave. Detroit, Mich.	LURES	CLINTON WILT MFG. CO. Springfield, Mo.	LURES
WILKINSON CO. 83 Randolph St. Chicago, Ill.	MIXED	WINCHESTER ARMS CO. New Haven, Conn.	MIXED
		ALBERT WINNIE Traverse City, Mich.	LURES
L.A. WILFORD and SON Jackson, Mich.	LURES	F.C. WOODS and CO. Alliance, Ohio	LURES
WILMARTH TACKLE CO. Roosevelt, N.Y.	MIXED	*WRIGHT and MCGILL (Eagle Claw) 4245 E. 46th St. Denver, Co. 80216	MIXED
THOMAS E. WILSON and CO. WILSON-WESTER W. SPORTING GOODS CO. New York, Chicago, and San Francisco	MIXED		

Y

YAKIMA BAIT CO. Granger, Wash.	LURES	YAWMAN and ERBE Rochester, N.Y.	REELS

Z

ZINK ARTIFICIAL BAIT CO. Dixon, Ill.	LURES	ZOLI, INC. 280 Hobart St. Perth Amboy, N.J.	LURES

THE HISTORY OF FISHING REELS

Reels, as we know them today, are direct descendants of the single action reels used by American anglers in the eighteenth century and early nineteenth century. There can be no doubt however that reels in some crude form were used several hundred of years ago. In fact, perhaps thousands of years ago, the ancient Egyptians had a reel of sorts. It was a spool-like affair, attached to the "rod" and apparently was merely for storing the line. In the Fifteenth Century an English angler Thomas Barker wrote a book entitled "The Art of Angling". In the first edition he spoke of a "wind" and his expanded second edition (1657) even illustrated this apparatus. He stated, describing the affair, in part: "Within two foot of the bottom of the rod there was a hole made for to put in a wind to turn with a barrell to gather up his line, and loose at his pleasure". It may be of interest to note here that in recent years manufacturers have begun to offer and represent as "the latest" or "newest", rods with reels built right into the handles or butts of the rig.

With the increase in popularity of these rods and reels in pursuing the black bass came the phenomenally rapid growth of the American fishing tackle manufacturing industry.

During the first decade of the 1900's, the manufacturers seemed to compete furiously, almost to the point of the ridiculous. Some companies actually advertised more than two hundred reel models and sizes as being available. By the 1920's this situation had generally settled down to more reasonable numbers.

During the Expansion age came widespread use of the level-wind mechanism, free spooling, and various experiments with anti-backlash devices. The old catalogs are full of various attempts to provide a preventative for this frustrating phenomenon which still plagues today's angler. Even with the highly efficient reels of modern manufacture, it takes practiced skill to avoid the lamentable "bird's nest."

The Spinning Reel

The fore-runner of todays modern spinning reels is the Peter Malloch reel. Made by Malloch in 1884 in Scotland and subsequently improved upon in England and France, the Malloch principle was incorporated in the first American built spinning reels. These reels began to become available in the 1940's but American manufacturers continued to import European models and often offered them under their own name rather than the European company name.

The three reels, various pieces of fishing gear and award medals were the property of Mr. Fred N. White of Chicago, Illinois. White at one time held the casting championship for all weights of plugs in the late 1920's. The reels are identified in the photograph value section beginning on page 50. All items came from White's tackle box.

The American spinning reel came into its own shortly after World War II and immediately became most poplular.

Spinning reels were used exclusively in salt water fishing until the late 1940's when anglers finally discovered its great potential in casting lighweight, artificial lures long distances.

The Four Ages of American Fishing Reels

In the fine book, **The American Sporting Collector's Handbook,** *Mr. Warren Shepard has set down "The Three Ages of Fine Reels". He has divided the history and development of reels very logically and in the interest and need of standardization we shall define these ages, add a fourth and use the same natural divisions in the discussion of reel history. The four ages are:

THE SMITH AGE-Reels & Rods that were handcrafted by American reelsmiths (usually signed) from about 1800 to roughly 1875. Reels from this period are represented by reelsmiths such as Clark, Conroy, Hardman**, Krider**, Meek**, Milam**, Noel**, Sage**, Shipley and Snyder**.

THE GOLDEN AGE-The beginning of the Golden Age is represented by the early machine-made reels. The period from 1875 to 1900 saw the development of high quality manufactured reels, usually made on a lathe, fitted and assembled by hand. Some of the best of this period are represented by makers such as Conroy, Vom Hofe, Leonard, Meek, Meisselbach, Milam, Orvis, Perey, and Talbot.

THE EXPANSION AGE-So called because of the surge in growth of American tackle manufacture. Mr. Shepard defines this period as being from 1900 to 1930. The most notable companies representing this period are Heddon, Hendryx, Horrocks Ibbotson, Pflueger, Shakespeare, and South Bend.

THE TECHNOLOGY AGE-The period of time from 1930 to the early 1950's saw the beginning of spin fishing and spinning tackle manufacture in the U.S. (about 1935-1940). It was during years that great technical advances in use of materials were made, modern plastics & alloys. Light weight highspeed reels were manufactured on highly mechanized assembly lines. The earliest reels of this

*Edited by Allan J. Liu, Copyright 1976 by Winchester Press.
**Kentucky reelsmiths fashioning the earliest brass and silver multiplying reels.

period are collectible but not quite so desirable as those from the earlier three ages. The exception of course would be the fine handmade products of Bogdan, FinNor, Vom Hofe, and Zwarg.

Undoubtedly the first mechanical reels in America were single action brought from Europe. The first known American were hand made and dated from about 1800. The handmade reels of George Snyder, dating about 1800-1810, are the most notable amoung the first.

Snyder was a Kentucky fisherman who was also a watchmaker and silversmith. He made spool reels in his shop and is credited with the development of the first multiplying reel. The reel has a four to one gear ratio. Snyder never went into a commercial enterprise but remained in his chosen profession. He fashioned the reels only for himself and friends. This was the birth of the Kentucky Reel.

The first Kentucky Reels were made commercially available through the efforts of another watchmaker, Mr. Jonathan F. Meek, who with his brother Benjamin F. Meek went into the business of commercial manufacture in 1835. An apprentice reelsmith, Benjamin C. Milam later became a partner also, leaving the company in 1851 to make reels on his own.

The Meeks developed the first mechanically actuated, adjustable clicks and drags, but both were rather crude at first and cumbersome to operate.

J.L. Sage, A.B. Shipley, and Thomas Conroy, all of Kentucky are other notable reelsmiths working during this period.

Until after the Civil War most reel bodies were made of brass and some were of silver. Thereafter the better reels were made of Nickle or "German Silver", an alloy of nickel, copper and zinc.

Before the advent of machine-made reels around 1875 most were unmarked, but many were signed by the reelsmith, ie: "J. CONROY, MAKER". Many of the truly fine old reels will also be found with a dated presentation inscription engraved in the beautiful script style of the day.

Reels from the Golden Age (1875-1900) are much more easily found than the early handmade ones. This era saw the advent of the "Henshall rod" and the "Chicago rod" (See pages 66-67). These were the first rods with which the multiplying reels could be used efficiently in bait casting. Used with these rods, the reels experienced an increased popularity and a more widespread acceptance and use. This development is responsible, in the main, for the rapid growth of the fishing tackle beginning around 1900, the birth of the Expansion Age of tackle manufacture.

Toward the end of the Golden age a new reel was patented (1887). It was called the "Henshall-Van Antwerp Black Bass Reel" and incorporated what is thought to be the forerunner of today's Star Drag.

IDENTIFICATION AND LISTING
OF OLD REELS

Many of the early craftsman and manufacturers identified their products by engraving or stamping their names and/or patent dates, etc., on them but later years saw the advent of decals, hot stamps, stencils, etc. The trouble is many others did not bother with this identification and those can defy the most knowledgeable to the point of frustration. Here we will discuss some specific and general methods of determining dates and origins of reels.

The scarcest and most valuable reels are those that were handcrafted from about 1800 to 1875. After that more modern mechanized production methods were prevalent in the industry. Those early reels were usually signed by the reelsmith. Often they also had beautiful presentation engravings: "Presented to so and so by so and so, dated".

George Snyder, the man usually credited with the beginning of the Kentucky reels made his earliest reels of brass and all were quadruple multipliers (4:1 ratio). They incorporated jewel pivots and square, steel gears. Watchmaker Snyder knew the jeweled movement to be the most advanced state of pivots at the time. These early models had the ends of the pillars riveted to one of the baseplates and the other ends secured by wire. Later this was improved by Milam and Hardman. They introduced screws to fasten them for easier dismantling for repairs and lubrication. The screws on Meek reels made after about 1840-45 were each numbered to match the number stamped beside each screw hole. After about 1865, the reels were also made larger and in a double multiplier model for the saltwater fisherman.

The reels of this period are exceedingly rare and valuable. The collector who obtains one should consider himself a lucky individual indeed, for few will ever possess even one example.

There are today six basic types of reels. They are the bait-casting reel, spinning reel, spincasting reel, fly casting, saltwater reel, and the special use reels. Of these, the bait-casting, the fly-casting and the early spinning reels are the most popularly collected types.

The following pages will aid the collector in identification of reels and where possible indicate an earliest possible date or manufacture. It is of necessity a sampling only. Because of the great variety of reels made prior to the 1800's, they are not listed individually. The early Kentucky reels of the 1840's are also quite scarce, but the collector may get lucky and happen upon one.

The reel listing is set up according to manufacturer. All reels could be found listed and priced, and reasonably attributed to that company as the actual manufacturer are listed as such. Because there were literally hundreds that had reels manufactured by others but bearing only the distributor's name, there is much room for error. It is hoped however that the lists will be of help in identifying reels in your collecting efforts.

ANATOMY OF A REEL

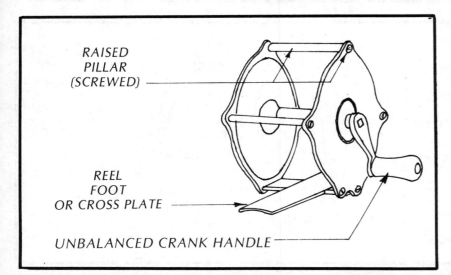

RAISED
PILLAR
(SCREWED)

REEL
FOOT
OR CROSS PLATE

UNBALANCED CRANK HANDLE

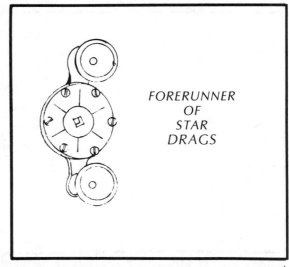

FORERUNNER
OF
STAR
DRAGS

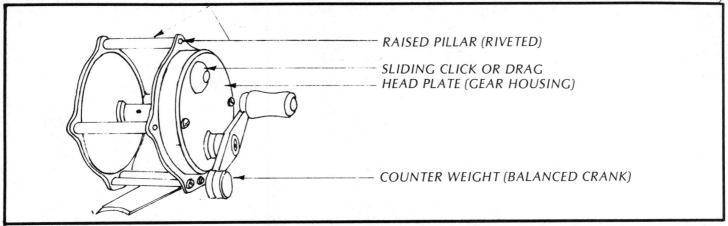

RAISED PILLAR (RIVETED)

SLIDING CLICK OR DRAG
HEAD PLATE (GEAR HOUSING)

COUNTER WEIGHT (BALANCED CRANK)

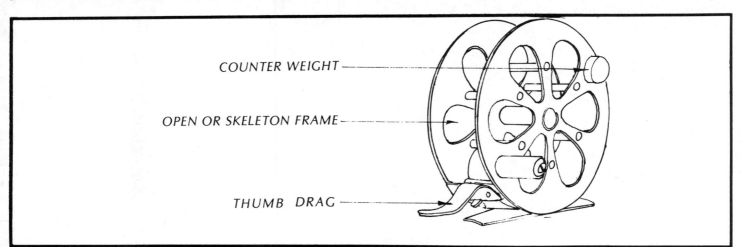

COUNTER WEIGHT

OPEN OR SKELETON FRAME

THUMB DRAG

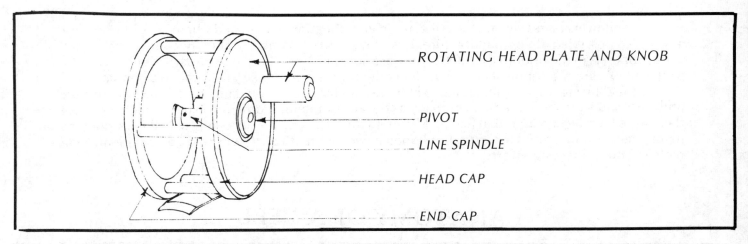

ROTATING HEAD PLATE AND KNOB

PIVOT

LINE SPINDLE

HEAD CAP

END CAP

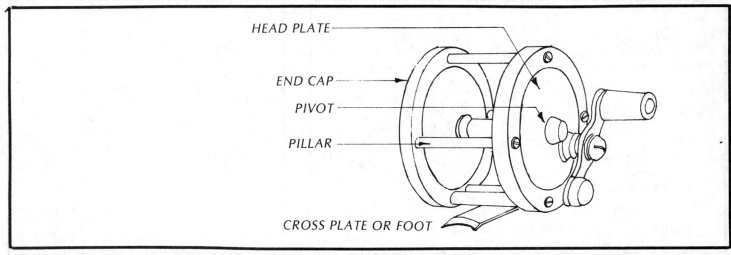

HEAD PLATE

END CAP

PIVOT

PILLAR

CROSS PLATE OR FOOT

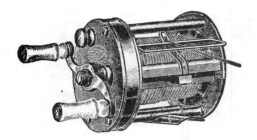

SOUTH BEND

LEVEL WINDING
ANTI-BACK-LASH REEL

Made of German silver with double ivoroid grip; jewel spool caps, one of which is adjustable; diameter of spool, 1½ inches; Quadruple multiplying.

Thumbing and spooling are entirely eliminated; Absolutely cannot back-lash or tangle; and upon reeling in it automatically spools itself, winding the line perfectly smooth and even. Adjustment screw on side of reel which allows drag on anti-back lash device to be taken off; thereby this reel level can be converted into a free winding type.

SOUTH BEND 550

No. 550 LEVEL WINDING
ANTI-BACK-LASH REEL

Frame is highly nickel and plated brass with double grip of black ivoroid riveted to crank. Quadruple multiplying gears of Hunting-tooth train type, that equalizes the wear on all teeth. Spool bearings run in bronze bushings; adjustable spool caps; spool diameter is 1½ inches; width, 1¾ inches.

SOUTH BEND

ANTI-BACK-LASH REEL

Made of German silver with double ivoroid grips and jewel spool caps, one of which is adjustable; diameter of spool, 1½ inches; Quadruple multiplying.

Anti-back lash enables beginner to cast with precision. The brake action applies itself only for a fraction of a second when the bait hits the water; there is no continuous drag to retard the cast; adjustment screw on side, which allows this reel to be converted into the free running type of reel.

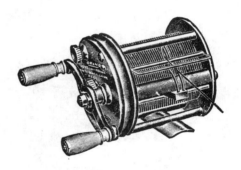

SOUTH BEND-ORENO

LEVEL WINDING
ANTI-BACK-LASH REEL

Highly nickel plated with ivoroid double grips, jewel spool caps, one of which is adjustable; diameter of spool, 1½ inches; quadruple multiplying.

Thumbing and spooling are entirely eliminated; absolutely cannot back-lash or tangle; and upon reeling in it automatically spools itself, winding the line perfectly smooth and even. Adjustable screw on side of reel which allows drag on anti-back lash device to be taken off; thereby this reel can be converted into a free running, level winding type.

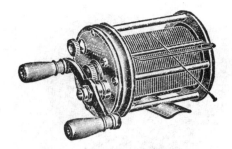

SOUTH BEND-ORENO

NO. 900 ANTI-BACK-LASH REEL

Nickel plated, brass with double ivoroid grips and jewel spool caps, one of which is adjustable; diameter of spool, 1 1/2 inches; Quadruple multiplying.

Anti-back lash enable beginner to cast with precision. The brake action applied itself only for a fraction of a second when the bait hits the water; there is no continuous drag to retard the cast. Adjustable screw on side, which allows this reel to be converted into the free running type of reel.

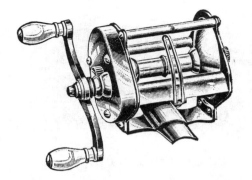

MEISSELBACH FLYER

Frame made of brass, heavily nickel plated; spool flanges; nickel silver; brass arbor; nickel steel pivots running in phosphor bronze bearings; adjustable end bearings; Pin which travels in groove of level wind shaft is made of long-wearing hardened steel. Copper-coated to prevent rust; back sliding click; double handle with white celluloid thumb pieces.

HEDDON CHIEF DO-WA-GIAC
THE REEL WITH THE
MECHANICAL THUMB

The mechanical thumb is an effective anti-back lash device, adjustable to any weight of bait and does away with constant thumbing of spool. Parts of level winding mechanism are chrominum plated, therefore non-rusting and non-corroding. Click made of hardened steel with phosphor bronze spring. Jeweled adjustable screw caps; reel has a highly nickeled finish; double handle with ivoroid grips.

MEISSELBACH NO.100
BULL'S EYE
LEVEL WINDING REEL

Heavy nickel plated brass frame; brass arbor and nickel silver spool flanges; nickel steel, rust resisting pivots run in phosphor bronze bearings; both adjustable and removeable; the end plates are made of "Permo", a tough, tenacious (not brittle) material; it is light and strong; highly polished and not affected by water or oil.

The one piece seat is a cross bar type; "Permo" end plates come in assorted colors of green, red, brown or black.

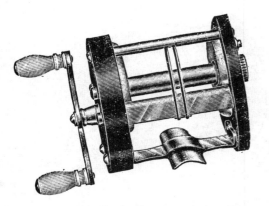

MEISSELBACH
LEVEL WINDING REEL

Frame constructed of heavy nickel plated brass; brass arbor and nickel silver spool flanges; nickel steel rust-resisting pivots; genuine bakelite end plates guaranteed against breakage; large double handle with tension adjusting end cap; full quadruple action; a substantial and well made reel.

MEISSELBACH
ALUMINUM LEVEL-WINDING
Take Down

Cast aluminum head cap and tail plate frosted finish, perfectly balanced double crank handle , special take down feature; bearings of nickel alloy, phosphor bronze; click level winding screw of phosphor bronze and tool steel pawl; click and drag combined in one unit; Quadruple multiplying.

MEISSELBACH
PEERLESS
LEVEL WINDING REEL
Take Down

Gears of tempered metal; line carriage of special alloy; bushings of best material; click and drag combined in one member. Head cap made of bakelite; balance nickel finished.

Transverse screw made phosphor bronze, pawl of tool steel. Slightly more than quadruple multiplying. Length of spool, 1 7/8 inches; diameter, 1 1/2 inches; weight each, 7 1/4 ozs.

MEISSELBACH
MODERN
LEVELWIND AND
ANTI-BACK LASH

Polished nickel finish scribed panels plated; perfectly balanced crank handle, celluloid grips; tempered and hardened gears; transverse screw and line carriage of special alloy; Bushings made of metal; drag lever made of nickel silver alloy; drag lever adjusting spring made of finest tempered bronze; Crank and drag combined in one member; length of spool, 1 7/8 inches; diameter, 1 1/2 inches.

MEISSELBACH
LION
ANTI-BACK LASH
LEVEL WINDING

Satin finish, equipped with adjustment screw for regulating anti-back lash device whereby, any tension desired may be put on back-lash drag. Also can be set to release anti-back last device entirely; equipped with double crank handle, tempered gears; transverse screw of phosphor bronze; line carrier of a special alloy; spool shaft of tempered steel running in metal alloy bushings. Quadruple multiplying click and drag combined in one unit.

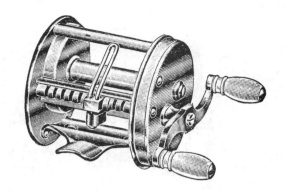

MEISSELBACH
LION LEVEL WINDING REEL

Satin finish throughout; equipped with perfectly balanced double crank handles; tempered gears; transverse screw of phosphor bronze; line carriage of a special alloy to give best possible service; spool shaft of tempered steel, running in metal alloy busings; quadruple multiplying; click and drag combined in one unit.

MEISSELBACH
MODERN
LEVEL WINDING

Plate frame supports; polished nickel head and tail plates; perfectly balanced crank handle with two celluloid grips; tempered and hardened gears; transverse screw and line carriage of a special alloy; brushing of both screw and spool made of special alloy metal; slightly more than quadruple multiplying; click and drag are combined in one member; length of spool, 1 7/8 inches; diameter, 1 1/4 inches.

DIAMOND KING
LEVEL WINDING REEL
Take Down

Plate frame construction with inserted heads; riveted gears; riveted steel plate; polished and buffed; head and tail plated; perfectly balanced letter "S" handles; Ivory grips; special head screw take down feature permits taking apart the reel without tools; tempered and hardened bronze transverse screw with special alloy steel pawls; full quadruple action.

DIAMOND KING
BASS CASTER LEVEL WINDING
Take Down

Plate frame construction; polished nickel head and plates; perfectly balanced crank handle celluloid grips; special head take down feature permits taking apart without tools. Riveted gears, tempered and hardened bronze transverse screw with special alloy steel pawl; click and drag are combined in one member quadruple action.

UNKNOWN

Frame constructed of heavy brass gun-metal finish, with nickel silver spool; double celluloid handle; tempered and hardened gears; has good substantial click; quadruple multiplying; diameter of spool, 1 3/8 inches; Length of spool, 1 7/8 inches.

DIAMOND KING
UNION

Polished nickle finish, with smooth head and end plate. Perfectly balanced crank handle with celluloid grips, tempered and hardened gears; hardened transverse screw; line carriage of special alloy hardened bushing of both screw and spool; good substantial click; stamped brass plate riveted and reinforced, set in with screws.

Diameter, 2 inches; length of spool 1 7/8 inches.

MEEK
B.F. MEEK and SONS
BLUE GRASS No. 3

German silver thoughout, satin and hand burnished finished; spiral gears; gear cut from finest bronze; steel cut spiral pinion; tempered tool steel pivots and stud; box pattern front head; absolutely dust and water proof; fine scroll counter balanced handle with genuine ivory thumb piece; accurately and smooth working adjustable steel click and drag on front head plate; screw-off oil caps; all parts handsomely milled, knurled and finished. Diameter of end plates, 2 inches; length of spool, 1 5/8 inches.

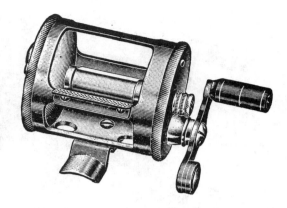

B.F. MEEK and SONS
BLUE GRASS SIMPLEX
IMPROVED TAKE DOWN STYLE
With New Style Thumb Rest

Brass nickel plated frame; one piece seamless drawn tubing; German silver plates and spool with polished brass shaft; spiral gear; gear cut from one piece hard drawn brass rod; pivots tempered, ground and polished; front plate rigidly fixed in frame; rear plate screwed into frame; sliding click drag on back plate; diameter of plates; 1 3/4 inches; length of spool, 1 3/8 inches; quadruple action; with plain German silver pivot bearings.

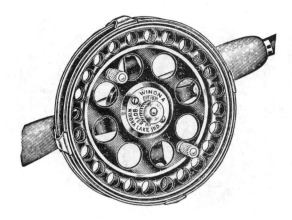

BOYER
WINONA

Spool made of one piece cast alumninum; finely machined to insure perfect balance and true running; entire reel highly nickel plated; bronze bearing; tool steel shaft; hard brass plate; very easily taken apart without tools; has only one place to oil; adjustable drag which can be set for heavy trolling; capacity, approximately 100 yards.

B.F. MEEK and SONS
BLUE GRASS

German silver take-apart improved design; German silver spool with hardened and polished brass shaft; hardened steel axles; Bronze gear and steel pinion; German silver sliding steel click with steel pinion, pawl and spring; No drag; German silver balance handle with celluloid thumb piece. Diameter of plates, 1-7/8; length of spool, 1-1/2 inches.

MEISSELBACH
TRI-PART No. 80

Tubular brass frame; brass end plates and ring frame cut from drawn brass tube; all nickel plated and polished; satin finish end plates; German silver spool; polished brass shaft and hardened steel axles; bronze gear and steel pinion; back sliding steel click; with steel pinion, pawl and spring; milled oil and friction adjusting cap on tail plate.

Quadruple action; diameter of plates, 2 inches; width of spool, 1-3/8 inches.

MEISSELBACH
TAKEAPART

Tubular brass frame; brass end plates and rings; frame cut from drawn brass tube; all nickel plated and polished; German silver spool, polished brass shaft and hardened steel axles; bronze gear and steel pinion; back sliding steel click with steel pinion, pawl and spring; milled oil and friction adjusting cap on end plate.

Quadruple action; diameter of plates 2 inches; width of spool, 1-5/8 inches.

DIAMOND BRAND
ST. LOUIS
CASTING

Highest quality German silver frame; spool and shaft steel axles running in hardened brass bearings; phosphor bronze gear; German silver double handles with celluloid thumb pieces; back sliding steel click accurately milled and nicely knurled.

DIAMOND BRAND
ULTRA
CASTING

Highest quality German silver frame; German silver spool with hardened and polished brass shaft; Steel axles running in phosphor bronze bearings; Phosphor bronze gear; double German silver balance handle, with celluloid thumb pieces; Back sliding steel click; accurately milled and handsomely knurled.

Diameeter of plates, 2 inches; length of spool, 1-7/8 inches; Quadruple action, with agate jeweled end bearing oil cups.

DIAMOND BRAND
MAYFAIR
CASTING

German silver finish; highest quality German silver frame and spool with hardened brass shaft; steel axis running in hardened brass bearings; phosphor bronze gear; German silver balance handle with white celluloid thumb pieces; back sliding steel click; knurled disc; oil caps and handle hub.

Diameter of plates, 2 inches; length of spool, 1-7/8 inches.

Quadruple action; with large ruby jeweled end bearings oil caps.

DIAMOND BRAND
SENECA

Brass, nickel plated and polished; brass spool and shaft; steel axles running in hardened brass bearings; machine cut gears; spring steel click and drag; knurled oil caps and handle hub.

Diameter of plates, 2 inches; length of steel spool, 1-7/8 inches.

Quadruple action; with agate jeweled oil caps.

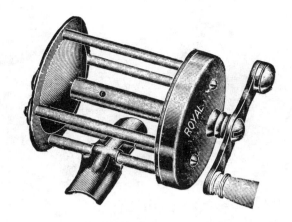

DIAMOND BRAND
ROYAL

Brass, nickel plated and polished; well balanced handle with white thumb piece; brass spool and shaft; back sliding steel click; all parts carefully milled, and the reel very nicely finished; will stand much use and hard service.

DIAMOND BRAND
BLUE HERON

Heavy brass frame; brass spool and shaft; steel axle running in hardened brass bearings; phosphor bronze gear; brass balance handle with white thumb piece; sliding steel click; knurled oil caps; nickel plated and polished.

Diameter of plates, 2 inches; length of spool, 1-7/8 inches.

Triple action; with agate jeweled end bearing oil caps.

UNKNOWN

Nickel plated brass frame; solid side plates with three cross bars; extension plate on right hand side for housing; solid one-piece base; extra axle reinforcement; white handle; brass gears and pinions; adjustable steel plate with agate jeweled end bearing oil cups.

UNKNOWN
DOUBLE ACTION

Made of brass, nickel plated and polished; solid side plates with three cross bars; complete with screws; extension plate on right hand side for housing; solid one piece base; extra axle reinforcement; complete with genuine bone handle; brass hubs; brass gears and pinions; adjustable steel click; knurled housing makes the reel more attractive.

BILTWELL
No. 2800
QUADRUPLE MULTIPLYING

Made of nickel plated brass; special "S" shaped crank insures a balanced double handle and eveness of action. Frame is very staunchly constructed; bearings are all tempered metal securely spun into the plates of the reel.

Diameter of spool, 1-1/2 inches; length of plates, 1-7/8 inches.

UNION

Double action; highly polished; raised pillars; back sliding steel click; well balanced handle with white wood thumb piece; 1-5/8 inch spool; substantially made.

UNKNOWN
SINGLE ACTION

Brass; nickel plated; riveted; raised pillars; black thumb piece; permanent click; end plate and bearings in one piece; size of plates, 2-1/4 inches; size of pillars, 1 inch.

UNKNOWN SINGLE ACTION
SINGLE ACTION

Diameter of plate, 2-1/2 inches; width of spool, 3/4 inch; line-carrying to attach to top or bottom or rod; made of cold rolled sheet steel; bright finish.

UNKNOWN
SINGLE ACTION

A remarkably staunch and rigid reel, entirely new, and something different in construction; rod clip has drilled holes for attaching reel to bamboo pole; Also designed to fit the reel seat of any bait casting rod; tail plate and head plate embossed; hub is provided with a line notch for fastening the line in the reel; diameter of spool 1-1/2 inch; length of pillars, 1 inch; assorted colors: Red, green, orange, blue and brown.

UNKNOWN
SINGLE ACTION

A combination trout and casting reel; rod clip has drilled holes which may be used for attaching reel to a bamboo rod; it will also fit the reel seat of any bait casting or fly rod; guide arms for winding accurately to the width of the spool and guide it properly when retrieving diameter of spool, 2 inches; width, 7/8 inch; height of reel, 2-1/4 inches; assorted colors: Red, green, orange, blue and brown.

UNKNOWN
SINGLE ACTION

A new and distinctively novel construction of reel; rod clip had drilled holes which may be used for attaching reel to a bamboo pole; also designed to fit the reel seat of any bait casting rod; diameter of spool, 2 inches; width 7/8 inch; assorted colors: Red, green, orange, blue and brown.

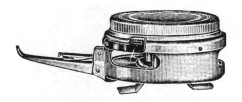

MARTIN AUTOMATIC
For Fly Fishing
FLY-WATE REEL

Made of duraluminum, a light, strong metal; milled brass gears that have large teeth insuring long life. The spindle is of hardened steel and the line spool is of light aluminum, fitted with a large, hardened steel, reversible line guide made the full size of the opening for the line which prevents piling and snarling of the line. The new spring tension throw-off is made practically flush with the side of the reel and operated by lifting the release with the thumb nail and allowing the drum to revolve slowly in the palm of the hand. Capacity 90 feet of "G" line; diameter of spool, 2-1/2 inches; width of spool, 3/8 inch; weight 6 ozs.

No. 1-Capacity, 75 feet; diameter of spool, 3 inches; width of spool, 1/2 inch; weight, 11 ozs.

No. 2-Capacity, 90 feet; diameter of spool, 3 inches; width of spool, 5/8 inch; weight, 12-1/2 ozs.

No. 3-Capacity, 150 feet; diameter of spool, 3 inches; width of spool, 3/4 inch; weight, 14 ozs.

MEISSELBACH
Automatic Reel

Beautiful in design, as light as a good automatic reel can be made; it embodies all the Meisselbach strength of construction and is built to give the everlasting service which made Meisselbach Reels famous; constructed of special metal light as aluminum; strong as steel and most important of all, it is rust proof; the strongly constructed winding mechanism is completely enclosed; paying out the line winds up the reel and a feather touch on the lever reels in the fish. Easy to disassemble for oiling and cleaning.

Diameter of spool, 3 inches; width of spool, 1/2 inch; actual weight each 12 ozs.

MEISSELBACH
RAINBOW
For Trout or Bass Fishing

Made of special alloy which combines lightness and strength; frame and reel seat strong and rigidly constructed; hardened and tempered steel click wheel and spring; phosphor bronze bearings; runs true and smooth under all conditions; every part is instantly accessible for oiling and cleaning; dull black finish; German silver trimmings.

Capacity, 35 yards; diameter, 2-7/8 inches; width, 3/4 inch.

MEISSELBACH WANITA FLY

Built of a special alloy metal combining both lightness and strength; Phosphor bronze bearings, click and gear of hardened steel; nickel silver reel seat; easily taken apart; dull black finish; wt. 3-7/8 ozs.

DIAMOND BRAND

Very practical high class single action casting reel; very light in weight; the holes in the spool and frame insure lightness and permit the line to dry quickly; had adjustable back sliding click; outside frame finished in dull black; inside is polished nickel finish.

DIAMOND BRAND

Brass; skeleton frame model; removeable spool; back sliding steel click; white thumb piece; very light in weight; weight, 4 ozs.

Nos. 90N and 90B capacity, 80 yards; balance, 60 yards.

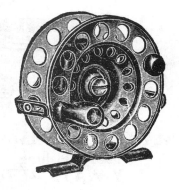

DIAMOND BRAND SINGLE ACTION

Made of brass; black Japanese finish; steel bearing; Wood handle; Metal ball balance; two line sleeve with loose ring line guides; Frame and base all one piece stamped metal.

Diameter of spool, 2-1/4 inches; Width of spool, 1 inch.

CATALINA FREE SPOOL
(Salt Water)

German silver, hard rubber side plates; metal bound; adjustable steel click; large well balanced handle with black rubber thumb piece; lever on side of top plate to adjust free spool action; all parts carefully milled and highly polished; leather thumb brake.

CATALINA FREE SPOOL
(Salt Water)

Steel pivot; adjustable click; fancy crank with specially shaped rubber handle; hard rubber plate reinforced with metal bands; fitted with leather thumb brake; lever on side of top plate to adjust free spool action; double multiplying metal disc on top plate with gear bridge and pivot bearing; all parts nickeled silver.

GULF SURF CASTING
(Salt Water)

German silver, hard rubber side plates; metal bound; steel pivots; adjustable steel click; black rubber thumb piece; all parts carefully milled and highly polished; leather thumb brake.

MIAMI FREE SPOOL
(Salt Water)

Best medium priced reel made for surf casting; extra heavy rubber side pieces; metal bound; lever free spool on handle side of reel; new style large handle, black rubber thumb piece; all parts carefully milled and highly nickel plated; leather thumb brake.

PACIFIC SURF CASTING
(Salt Water)

Double multiplying, hard rubber side plates; metal bound, thereby giving extra strength; steel pivot bearings; all parts carefully milled and highly nickel plated; large new style handle with black rubber thumb piece; adjustable steel click; leather thumb brake.

CALIFORNIA FREE SPOOL
(Salt Water)

Steel pivot; adjustable click; well balanced handle; black rubber thumb piece; lever on side of top plate to adjust free spool action; double multiplying; highly polished bronze finish; nickel plated spool; all parts carefully milled; leather thumb brake.

FAVORITE
(Salt Water)

Double multiplying; steel pivots; adjustable click and well balanced handle with black rubber thumb piece; Nicely nickel plated.

YANKEE
(Salt Water)

Double multiplying; steel pivots; adjustable click; well balanced handle with black rubber thumb piece; all parts nickel plated; built exceptionally strong.

REELS-REPRESENTATIVE VALUES

The following list is a sampling of several company's reels. The values were taken from actual advertised asking prices in various published and private collector's lists of those available for sale. Because many appeared in more than one list the values are placed in ranges rather than one specific figure. Where a reel falls in this range depends upon condition. It is impossible to assign a value to each and every one of the many thousands. This listing only includes around two hundred or so reels. There follows several pages of photos and illustrations of around one hundred reels from the value listing. Where possible, markings on the reel are described.

MAKER	NAME, DESCRIPTION and MARKINGS	COLLECTOR VALUE RANGE
*Abbey & Imbrie	"Lakeside", engraved	$5-12.00
*Abbey & Imbrie	"Top flight"	$5-10.00
Acme	"The Acme"	$3-10.00
Arrow	No. 60, raised pillar	$3-10.00
Atlas	Portage, sliding click, raised pillar, 100 yard	$5-10.00
Atlas	Portage, sliding click, raised pillar, 40 yd.	$5-10.00
Atlas	Portage raised pillar, sliding click, 60 yd.	$5-10.00
Atlas	Portage raised pillar, sliding click, 80 yd.	$5-10.00
Atlantic	"Surf Caster", 250 yd. Nickel plate and bakelite	$5-10.00
Atlantic	"Surf Caster", 300 yd. Nickel plate and bakelite c1925.	$5-10.00
Bass Caster	"Bass Caster", 80 yd.	$3-10.00
Billinghurst, William	Fly reel, Very early 19th Century	$150-250.00
Biltwell	"Biltwell" No. 2800 Metal bearings	$2-7.00
Bristol	"Bristol No. 65", 3½" x 1-1/8"	$5-10.00
Bronson	"Comet No. 2400R"	$2-8.00
Bronson	"Fleetwing No. 2475" jeweled, levelwind	$2-9.00
Bronson	"Biltwell No. 3300" jeweled "Bronson, Mich."	$4-11.00
Bronson	"Belmont" jeweled, engraved, levelwind	$4-12.00
Bronson	"Lion LW No. 1800, Bronson Reel Co."	$5-10.00
Bronson	"Mercury No. 2550" engraved jeweled	$2-10.00
Bronson	"Top Flight"	$2-8.00
Bronson	"Lashless No. 1700-A"	$3-9.00
Bronson	"Meadowbrook"	$2-9.00
Bronson	"Rouge No. 3000"	$3-9.00
Bronson	"Meteor", jeweled	$1-9.00
Bronson	"Jolly Roger"	$3-9.00
Bronson	"Spartan", jeweled	$3-10.00
Bronson	"Green Hornet"	$2-8.00
Bronson	"Torrent" fee spool, star drag	$4-10.00
Bronson	"X-Pert", jeweled	$3-8.00
Brookline	"Brookline No. 16"	$3-8.00

*ABBEY and IMBRIE
  Most Abbey and Imbrie reels are easily identified by the distinctive heart shaped, crossed hook trade mark.

Bunyan, Paul	Model No. 66	$1-7.00
Champion	"Champion, Model 805", pivoting base	$5-10.00
*Chicago Fishing Equip. Co.	"Gentleman Streamliner, No. 1372"	$10-20.00
Coxe, J.A.	No. 63, Star drag	$5-10.00
Coxe, J.A.	Coronet No. 25, c1940, aluminum	$20-40.00
Coxe, J.A.	Coronet No. 25N	$10-30.00
Davidson	No. 71, Wire line trolling reel	$5-15.00
Defiance	"Defiance", 60 yd.	$4-16.00
Defiance	"Defiance", 80 yd.	$4-16.00
Diktator	"Diktator No.D-1706", jeweled	$2-10.00
Empire City	"Empire City", Raised pillars, Sliding click and drag, 40 yd.	$4-14.00
Empire City	"Empire City", raised pillar 60 yd.	$5-16.00
Empire City	"Empire City", sliding click and drag, 80 yd.	$8-20.00
Expert	"The Expert, Casting Reel"	$5-10.00
Ferris-Lingren	Aluminum, "Ferris-Lingren Mohawk, New Rochelle, NY"	$3-14.00
Franklin	"Franklin" 100 yd. sliding click and drag	$3-14.00
Go-Ite Mfg. Co.	"Go-Ite Real Reels Patent Pending" aluminum	$10-20.00
Good-all Mfg. Co.	"Good-all El. Mfg., Co., R.A. Goodall, Pres., Good-For 30 years Ogalla, Nebr." Spinning reel, c1955	$2-6.00
Great Lakes	"Great Lakes"	$1-7.00
Heddon	"Heddon No. 3-15 Dowagiac, Mich." silver	$25-75.00
Heddon	"Winona No. 105SS", has line guide arm	$10-15.00
Heddon	"Winona No. 105FF", has line guide arm	$10-15.00
Heddon	"Winona No. 105H"	$10-15.00
Heddon	"Winona No. 105F"	$10-15.00
Heddon	"Pal No. P-41"	$3-10.00
Hendryx	Very early brass fly reel, c1890	$10-20.00
Hendryx	Very early nickel plate reel with click, c1900	$5-20.00
Hendryx	"No. 4906" raised pillar, 60 yd.	
Hendryx	"4-21-76/7-10-88", 2-multiplier, raised pillar	$10-20.00
Hendryx	Nickel plated, raised pillar, 25 yd.	$3-12.00
Hendryx	Nickel plated, raised pillar, 40 yd.	$5-20.00
Hiawatha	"Hiawatha No. 6515"	$3-9.00

*This is a rod built-in reel and wooden pistol-grip handle.

Higgins, J.C.	"300", Made by Bronson	$1-4.00
Higgins, J.C.	"537-31010", Made by Bronson	$2-5.00
Higgins, J.C.	"537-3105", Made by Bronson	$1-3.00
Higgins, J.C.	"537-3101", engraved	$2-7.00
Higgins, J.C.	"312-3101", No. 489	$2-7.00
Higgins, J.C.	"312-3111", engraved, jeweled	$2-8.00
Horrocks-Ibbotson	"The Captain" No. 1863 Model B, aluminum	$2-6.00
Horrocks-Ibbotson	Vernley Trout Reel, bakelite	$5-14.00
Horrocks-Ibbotson	Brass, raised pillar, 25 yd.	$5-10.00
Horrocks-Ibbotson	Commadore No. 1865	$1-5.00
Horrocks-Ibbotson	Minute Man No. 1810	$2-7.00
Horrocks-Ibbotson	Mohawk No. 1106, aluminum	$2-6.00
Humphrey	"Denver Model 3A"	$4-12.00
Indian	"Indian", 60 yd., raised pillar	$5-16.00
Kalamazoo Tackle Co.	"American Boy"	$5-15.00
Kalamazoo Tackle Co.	"Empress No. 1689"	$5-15.00
Kalamazoo Tackle Co.	"Miracle Silent Automatic, No. 1698 Model Co."	$2-8.00
Langley	"Streamlite Model 310KB"	$5-15.00
Langley	"Streamlite Model 310"	$5-15.00
Langley	"Streamlite Model 312"	$5-15.00
Langley	"Whitecap" No. 410, star drag, Free spool	$8-20.00
Langley	"Spinlite Model No.R-810"	$3-8.00
Langley	"Model No. 191-B"	$3-9.00
Langley	"Lurecast", Model No. 30-KC	$4-8.00
Lionel Corporation	"Airex Larchmont"	$2-8.00
Malloch	Brass Spinning reel, very early	$60-130.00
Martin	Martin Automatic No. 1, aluminum	$10-20.00
Martin	Martin Automatic No. 2, aluminum	$10-20.00
Martin	Martin Automatic No. 3, aluminum	$10-20.00
Martin	Martin Automatic No. 27/0, aluminum	$10-20.00
Martin	Martin Automatic No. 28/0, aluminum	$10-20.00
Martin	Martin Automatic No. 53, aluminum	$10-20.00
Meadowbrook	No. 3123460, engraved	$4-10.00
Meek, B.F. and Son	"No. 3"	$75-100.00
Meek and Sons	"Bluegrass No. 3"	$30-50.00
Meek and Milam	Hand made, brass, c1850	$200-300.00
Meisselbach	"Expert" fly reel, c1890	$10-20.00
Meisselbach	"Featherlight" fly reel, c1890	$10-20.00
Meisselbach	"Takapart". Nickel	$8-20.00
Meisselbach	"Takapart", Nickel, free spool	$8-20.00
Meisselbach	"Good Luck" wooden	$10-20.00
Meisselbach	"Rainbow" fly reel, aluminum	$10-25.00
Meisselbach	"Triton", Tripe multiplier	$8-20.00
Meisselbach	"Elyria" Ohio" No number, level/wind, bakelite end plates	$8-20.00
Meisselbach, A.F. and Bro.	"Newark, N.J." horizontal wire line trolling reel	$10-20.00
Meisselbach, A.F. and Bro.	Tripart style, no number, 80 yd.	$8-20.00
Meisselbach and Co.	"Tripart No. 580, 04, 04, 05, 07, 07	$8-20.00

Meisselbach and Co.	"Tripart No. 581, 04, 04, 05, 07, 07 free spool	$8-20.00
Meisselbach and Co.	Tripart style, no number, 80 yd.	$8-20.00
Meisselbach and Co.	"Simmons Special, Tripart", free spool	$10-20.00
Milam	"Milam, The Frankfort Kentucky No. 1"	$100-200.00
Milam, B.C.	"Frankfort, Kentucky"	$100-200.00
Milam, B.C. and Son	"No. 3, Frankfort, Ky."	$75-150.00
Ocean City	Very early star drag	$5-10.00
Ocean City	Early trolling reel made of German silver	$5-10.00
Ocean City	No. 35	$1-4.00
Ocean City	No. 305	$1-5.00
Ocean City	No. 306	$1-5.00
Ocean City	No. 1529	$2-8.00
Ocean City	"Interstate", jeweled, level wind	$8-15.00
Ocean City	"Nile"	$5-10.00
Ocean City	No. 970	$1-5.00
Ocean City	No. 1600	$3-8.00
Ocean City	No. 1810	$2-7.00
Orvis	1874 patent in script	Silver $150-200.00 Nickel $75-100.00
Pennel	"Peerless", 80 yd.	$5-10.00
Pennel	Serial No. 752, 50-60 yd.	$5-10.00
Portage	"Pastime No. 1743"	$8-15.00
Portage	"Topic No. 23" 2-multiplier, nickel plate	$3-9.00
Pflueger	"Atlas Portage", raised pillar	$10-15.00
Pflueger	"Akron No. 1893-L", jeweled level wind, nickel plated brass	$8-18.00
Pflueger	Trade reel, raised pillar	$12-20.00
Pflueger	"Capitol No. 1988", Stardrag, free spool, nickel plate, and bakelite	$10-20.00
Pflueger	"Captain", wire line trolling reel wood knobs	$5-25.00
Pflueger	"Gem No. 2094", c1940	$5-10.00
Pflueger	"Golden West", early fly reel	$20-40.00
Pflueger	"Knobby No. 1963"	$8-15.00
Pflueger	"Medalist No. 1495"	$4-10.00
Pflueger	"Oceanic No. 2859" patented 1907 and 1923	$18-35.00
Pflueger	"Pontiac"	$10-20.00
Pflueger	"Progress", open frame, raised pillar	$7-12.00
Pflueger	"Progress" anodized brass, raised pillar, wood knob	$16-30.00
Pflueger	"Rocket No. 1375, nickel plate	$7-15.00
Pflueger	"Sal-Trout No. 1554"	$4-10.00
Pflueger	"Sal-Trout NO. 1558"	$6-12.00
Pflueger	"Sea Star No. 1050"	$3-9.00
Pflueger	"Skilcast No. 1953"	$12-20.00
Pflueger	"Summit No. 1993"	$10-15.00
Pflueger	"Superex Automatic No. 775 pat. 1907"	$10-30.00

Pflueger	"Supreme" fly reel, Mod. No 578	$15-40.00
Pflueger	"Taxie No. 3138" wire line trolling reel	$5-20.00
Pflueger	"Trump No. 1943"	$3-10.00
Pflueger	"Worth No. 5039", jeweled nickel silver	$8-20.00
Shakespeare	"Acme No. 1904"	$3-9.00
Shakespeare	"Alamo"	$6-16.00
Shakespeare	"Automatic No. 1815"	$4-8.00
Shakespeare	"Criterion No. 1960 Mod. GE"	$6-16.00
Shakespeare	"Criterion No. 1922," level wind	$6-18.00
Shakespeare	"Criterion No. 1961, Mod. HO", engraved	$10-22.00
Shakespeare	"Dunce No. 1905, Mod. GA"	$5-15.00
Shakespeare	"Favorite No. 1733"	$3-12.00
Shakespeare	"Imperial"	$5-15.00
Shakespeare	"Intrinsic No. 1903"	$3-8.00
Shakespeare	"Intrinsic No. 1959 Mod. GK"	$3-8.00
Shakespeare	"Leader No. 1731"	$3-9.00
Shakespeare	"Leader No. 1909", level wind	$6-15.00
Shakespeare	"Marhoff No. 1964, Mod. GE", level wind	$5-15.00
Shakespeare	"Marhoff No. 1964, Mod. HE", jeweled	$5-15.00
Shakespeare	"Precision", 1914 model, jeweled	$10-15.00
Shakespeare	"President", c1940, bakelite	$5-10.00
Shakespeare	"President No. 1970, Mod. 31" engraved	$10-15.00
Shakespeare	"Russell No. 1895, Model GE", fly reel	$5-15.00
Shakespeare	"Russell No. 2062	$4-12.00
Shakespeare	"Service No. 1944, Model GK"	$7-12.00
Shakespeare	"Tournament No. 1922	$6-12.00
Shakespeare	"True Blue No. 1956	$5-10.00
Shakespeare	"Wondereel No. 1920, Mod. GA"	$6-15.00
Shakespeare	"Light Wondereel No. 1921	$6-18.00
South Bend	"No. 400 Level Winding Anti-Back-Lash Casting Reel"	$5-12.00
South Bend	"No. 666 Free Cast"	$5-14.00
South Bend	"No. 350-B Level Winding Anti-Back-Lash"	$5-15.00
South Bend	Oreno Saltwater Reel No. 850, Free spool, star drag	$6-12.00
South Bend	No. 30 levelwind Model D	$4-10.00
South Bend	No. 300 Anti backlash, level wind	$5-12.00
Talbot, Wm.	"No. 3, Nevada, Mo.," silver, late 1800's	$75-100.00
Talbot	"Kansas City, Mo.," silver, early 1900's	$65-90.00

Talbot	No. 4 Levison Special, 4 Jewel, c1907, 100 yds, 2-1/8" end plate diameter	$50-60.00
Talbot	No. 4 Talbot Special. 3 Jewel c1909, 100 yds, 2-1/8" end plate diameter	$50-60.00
Talbot	Meteor, 100 yds, 2" end plate diameter	$12-16.00
Talbot	Ben Hur fly reel, No. 100 and No. 101	$5-15.00
Talbot	Premier No. 2, No. 3, & No. 4	$20-40.00
Talbot	Club Special. 1-3/4" end plate diameter	$25-42.00
Union Hardware Co.	"Sunnybrook" fly reel	$10-20.00
Union Hardware Co.	"No. 71155" fly reel	$3-8.00
Union Hardware Co.	"Sunnybrook", brass, raised pillar	$5-10.00
Union Hardware Co.	"Sunnybrook", bright finish, raised pillar	$5-10.00
Union Hardware Co.	"No. 7169" aluminum, raised pillar	$3-10.00
Union Hardware Co.	Very small brass, raised pillar reel	$3-10.00
Union Hardware Co.	No. 7225S"	$4-10.00
Union Hardware Co.	"Samson" 60-80 yd.	$8-15.00
V.L. and A.	"Peerless", jeweled, 60 yd.	$7-15.00
Vom Hofe, E.	Small fly reel, nickel and rubber, "New York"	$10-20.00
Vom Hofe, E.	Small raised pillar fly reel	$10-20.00
Vom Hofe, E.	"4/0", 2-multiplier	$30-60.00
Vom Hofe, J.	"B Ocean" c1918	$30-60.00
Vom Hofe, J.	Small fly reel, nickel and rubber, "Brooklyn"	$10-20.00
Ward	"Ward's Sportking No. 60-6310, Mod. 5-C", engraved	$3-10.00
Winchester	No. 2726, wood knob	$15-35.00
Winchester	No. 4253, 80 yd.	$20-40.00
Winchester	No. 1630, aluminum fly rod, bone knob, c1920	$25-45.00
Winchester	No. 4350, 100 yd. Takapart	$10-15.00
Wright and McGill	"Stream and Lake", Mod. 14	$6-16.00
Wright and McGill	"Fre-Line, Mod. 10 BC", Side mount spinningreel	$5-14.00

Left: Arrow. No other markings, raised pillar. Right: Unmarked raised pillar reel. Collector Value Range: $3-10.00

Left reel is a Bronson Bitwell #3300. Jeweled. "Bronson, Mich." Collector Value Range: $4-11.00
Right: Bronson Comet#2400R. Collector Value Range: $2-8.00

Basscaster. No company name. Collector Value Range: $3-10.00

Two Bronson Coronets. Markings include "Bronson Reel Co., Bronson Mich. J.A. Coxe" on both reels. Left reel is the #25N and the right is the #25. Collector value range for the #25N: $20-40.00; for the #25: $10-30.00.

Bronson Fleetwing #2475. Collector value range: $5-10.00.

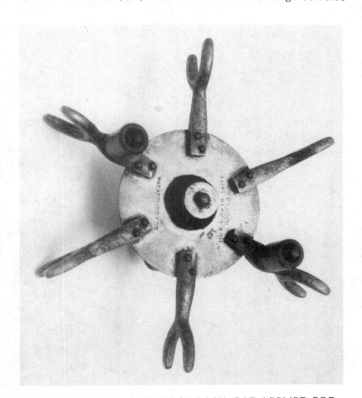

Markings: BENSON ANTI BACK LASH. PAT APPLIED FOR. Collector value range: $10-20.00.

Bronson Lion. Markings include "Bronson Reel Co. LION, LW, No. 1800". Collector value range: $5-10.00.

Markings: COZZONE. "200 YD" on foot. A saltwater reel with star drag. Collector value range: $15-25.00.

Chicago Fishing Equipment Company. "Gentleman Streamliner" #1372. Collector Value Range: $10-20.00

Both reels marked "Defiance". No company name. Collector Value Range: $4-16.00

"The Elite". 80 yard capacity with steel pivot bearings. Collector Value Range: $3-8.00

Markings: FREE Notangle SPOOL. Lou F. Eppinger DETROIT MODEL EE. Collector value range: $10-15.00.

Go-Ite with original box and pocket catalog. Collector Value Range: $10-20.00

Markings: GAYLE "SYMPLICITY" No. 2 FRANKFORT, KY USA. Collector value range: $5-10.00.

Heddon's Dowagiac. Non-level wind. Markings: HEDDON'S DOWAGIAC. A.F. MEISSELBACH & BRO. 80 yards. This reel was in the first Heddon catalog to feature a Heddon reel (1912). Collector value range: $20-40.00

Markings: THE "St. JOHN" FLY REEL. HARDY'S PAT. No. 9261 SIZE 3 7/8" MADE BY HARDY BROS LTD. ALNWICK, ENGLAND. It has a metal plate attached to it that says MADE FOR ABERCROMBIE & FITCH, NEW YORK. Collector value range: $30-60.00

Markings: Made by JAMES HEDDON'S SONS. DOWAGIAC, MICH. Heddon No. 45. Carters Patent. July 6, 1904 and Nov. 28, 1905. "#2" on bottom of the foot. Collector value range: $30-75.00

Heddon Pal #P-41 with original box. Collector Value Range: $3-10.00

Markings: Made by JAMES HEDDON'S SONS. DOWAGIAC, MICH. This reel has a wooden spool. Documented as once belonging to Fred N. White. Possibly made special for White Collector value range: $50-100.00

Markings: HEDDON LONE-EAGLE. JAMES HEDDON'S SONS, DOWAGIAC, MICH. "Made in USA Patented" on bottom of foot. A level wind reel that was offered in the 1932 catalog as a kit. May have been available earlier. Collector value range: $15-30.00.

Markings: WINONA JAMES HEDDON'S SONS DOWAGIAC, MICH. The one with the line guide (left) is marked No. 105-SS. The other is marked No. 105-FF. Collector value range: $10-15.00

Left: Hendryx, raised pillar, 25 yard capacity. Collector value range: $3-12.00
Middle: Hendryx #4906, raised pillar. Collector value range: $5-20.00
Right: Hendryx double multiplier. Marked "4-21-76 and 7-10-88." Collector value range: $10-20.00

Horrocks and Ibbotson Vernley Trout Reel, Plastic. Collector Value Range: $5-14.00

Left: Unmarked Horrocks and Ibbotson raised pillar brass reel. Collector Value Range: $5-10.00
Right: Empire City, brass, raised pillar. Collector Value Range: $5-15.00

Markings: No. 25 BLUE GRASS SIMPLEX. THE HORTON MFG CO. BRISTOL, CONN. The opposite side has an arrow with the word SCREWOFF under it. The letter E appears under the foot. Collector value range: $20-40.00.

Markings: No. 34 BLUE GRASS SIMPLEX FREE SPOOL. THE HORTON MFG CO. BRISTOL, CONN. The opposite side has an arrow with the word SCREWOFF under it. The letter J appears under the foot. Collector value range: $20-40.00.

Ideal. No other markings. Collector Value Range: $5-9.00

Marked "United States. INDIANA". No other markings. Collector Value Range: $6-10.00

Markings: Keystone Casting Reel. The number 60 appears beneath the foot. Collector value range: $10-15.00.

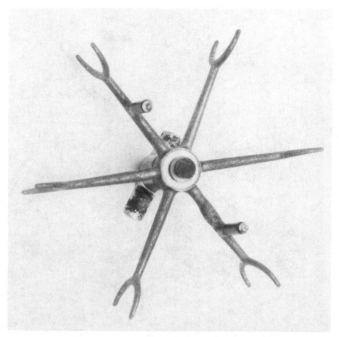

Markings: HENRY A. KIEST. MF'R KNOX, IND. PATENTED. Collector value range: $10-20.00.

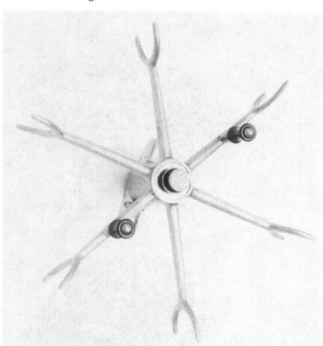

Markings: KIEST REEL CO MFRS KNOX IND PATENTED.

Langley Streamlite. Model #310-KB. Collector Value Range: $5-15.00

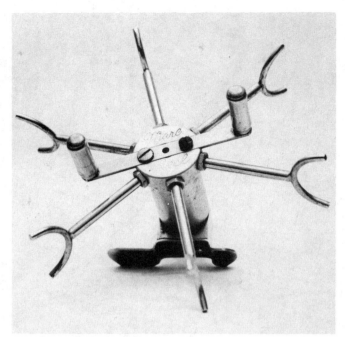

Markings: "Marc" or "Marl Reel" in script. PAT PEND. Collector value range: $10-20.00.

Markings: MARTIN AUT' FISH REEL CO. MOHAWK, N.Y. PAT APPLIED FOR FS No. 2. Collector value range: $10-20.00.

Markings: MARTIN AUT' SHORE CO. MOHAWK, N.Y. No. 3 PAT NO 2-175-756. Black in color. Collector value range: $10-20.00.

Markings: an arrow with the words SCREWOFF under it. "J.F. Hamilton, Chicago" in script. CARTERS PAT July 5.04 Nov 28.05. Markings on the other side: B. F. MEEK & SONS, LOUISIVILLE, KY. No. 33 BLUE GRASS. Collector value range: $30-50.00.

Markings: BLUE GRASS REEL. MADE BY B. F. MEEK & SONS, LOUISIVILLE, KY. No. 33. "H.B. Locker" in script. Markings on other side: CARTER'S PAT JUL 5.04 Nov 21.05. The number 7 appears on the bottom of the foot. Collector value range: $30-50.00.

Markings: B. F. MEEK & SONS, LOUISIVILLE, KY. No. 3. The numbers 3550 appear on the bottom of the foot. Collector value range: $75-100.

Markings: B.F. MEEK & SONS, LOUISVILLE, KY. No. 2. The numbers 4237 appear on the bottom of the foot. Collector value range: $75-100.00. This reel is documented as once having been owned by Fred N. White

Meisselbach and Co., Simmons Special Tripart Free Spool mounted on a 3½ Royal Steel Rod. (Simmons Hardware Co.) Collector value range: $10-20.00 (Reel)

Markings: No. 34 FREE SPOOL PAT NOV 26.01 NOV 28.05. Markings on opposite side: an arrow with SCREWOFF under it. B.F. MEEK & SONS, LOUISVILLE, KY. The letter C appears on the bottom of the foot. Collector value range: $30-50.00.

Left: Meisselbach and Bro., Tri part. Pat, dates marked "04, 04, 05, 07, Newark, N.J.". Middle: Meisselbach and Co., Tripart #580. Pat. dates marked "04, 04, 05, 07, 09". Right: Meisselbach and Co., Tripart #581, Free Spool. Pat, dates marked "04, 04, 05, 07, 09". Collector Value Range: $8-20.00

Markings: MEEK No. 3 FREE SPOOL. THE HORTON MFG CO. BRISTOL, CONN. The numbers 10570 appear on the bottom of the foot. This reel has been documented as having once been owned by Fred N. White. Collector value range: $20-40.00

Markings: MEISSELBACH - AUTOMATIC. A. F. MEISSELBACH & BRO NEWARK N.J. PAT PENDING. Collector value range: $10-20.00.

Markings: The Frankfort Kentucky Reel. No. 3 B. C. Milam & Son. Frankfort, Kentucky. Collector value range: $75-150.00

Unmarked English wooden reel with brass fittings. It has been identified as a c1880-1920 Nottingham with a Bicker Dyke line guard. Collector value range: $20-30.00.

Pelican. No company name. Collector Value Range: $6-15.00

Left: Pennell, serial number 752. Right: Pennel Peerless. Collector Value Range: $5-10.00

Pflueger Saltwater, 250 yards capacity. Has Pflueger's Bull Dog trademark. Marked: TEMCO Free Spool SURF CASTING.

Pflueger. Marked SKILKAST No. 1953. The round, screwed affair on the crank handle is marked PFLUEGER CUB No. 2542. Has plastic spool. Collector value range: $5-10.00.

Pflueger Akron. Left: is marked "4-3-1923 and others". Right: #1893. Market "Pat'd and pat pend". Collector Value Range: $8-18.00

Pflueger Knobby #1963. Collector Value Range: $8-15.00

Pflueger Skilcast #1953 with original box. Collector Value Range: $12-20.00

Pflueger Summit. Left reel has no number. Right reel is the #1993-L. Collector value range: $10-15.00.

Pflueger Summit #1993-L. Rubber guard on tailplate. Original box and chamois sack. Engraved. Collector Value Range: $15-30.00

Pflueger Supreme. Collector value range: $10-15.00.

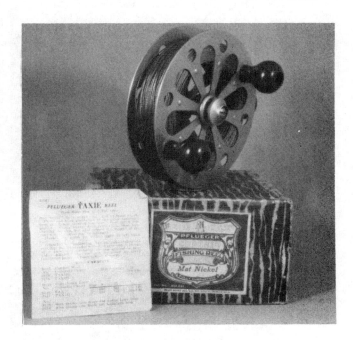

Pflueger Taxie #3138 loaded with braided copper line. Collector Value Range: $5-20.00

Pflueger Worth. 60 yard capacity. Marked "5039 Pat. 1-22-07, 4-10-08, 12-29-14". Collector Value Range: $8-20.00

Shakespeare Criterion Deluxe #1960. Model GE. Original box and cloth sack. Collector Value Range: $6-16.00

Russell Flyrod Reel #1895, Model NF. Collector Value Range: $5-15.00

Shakespeare Criterion #1961, Model HO. Engraved. Collector Value Range: $10-22.00

Russell Flyrod Reel #1889, Model GE. Green finish. Collector Value Range: $5-15.00

Shakespeare Duce #1905, Model GA 100 yard capacity. Original box. Collector Value Range: $5-$15.00

Shakespeare Triumph #1958, Model GE. Collector value range: $6-18.00.

Shakespeare Criterion Deluxe #1960. Model GE. Original box and cloth sack. Collector value range: $6-16.00.

Shakespeare Tournament #1922. Collector value range: $3-8.00.

Shakespeare Tournament #1922, 100 yard capacity. Collector Value Range: $6-12.00

Shakespeare Precision (23041) 1914 Model. Jeweled. 100 yard capacity. Collector value range: $10-15.00.

Shakespeare Wondereel #1920. Model GA. Collector Value Range: $6-15.00

Shakespeare Marhoff # 1964. Model HE. Jeweled. Collector value range: $5-15.00.

Markings: SHAKESPEARE STANDARD REEL No. 2 - 60 YDS - QUAD. PATENTED. Opposite side is marked Wm. SHAKESPEARE, JR. KALMAZOO, MICH. The numbers 1902/03 appear on the bottom of the foot. Collector value range: $20-30.00.

Shakespeare President #1970, Mode #31, 100 yard capacity. Original leather case. Collector value range: $10-15.00.

Markings: SHAKESPEARE "1918" MODEL MARHOFF PATENT LEVEL WINDING REEL 1964. Collector value range: $15-25.00.

Markings: SHAKESPEARE CLASSIC 23054. Beneath the foot is a fancy trade mark with these words within it: 1918 MODEL PATENTED 80 YDS KALAMAZOO, MICH. Collector value range: $10-15.00.

Markings: SHAKESPEARE UNIVERSAL 23038. Beneath the foot is a fancy trade mark with these words within it: 1918 MODEL PATENTED 80 YDS KALAMAZOO, MICH. Collector value range: $10-15.00.

Markings: SHAKESPEARE STANDARD PROFESSIONAL 13053. Under the foot appears a fancy trade mark with the words, 1912 MODEL PATENTED 80 YDS KALAMAZOO, MICH within the mark. Collector value range: $10-15.00.

South Bend #30, Model D. Collector Value Range: $4-10.00

South Bend #400, Model D, Anti Backlash with original box. Collector Value Range: $5-12.00

South Bend #666 Free Cast. Collector Value Range: $5-14.00

South Bend Perfectoreno #750. Collector Value Range: $8-20.00

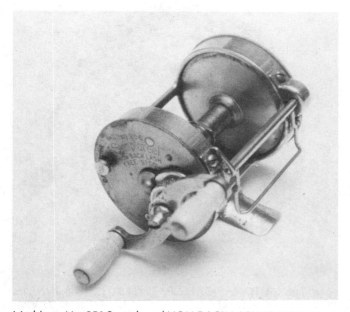

Markings: No. 256 Symploreel NON BACK LASH FREE SPOOL. Markings on opposite side: STANTON ST. NEWARK N.J. PAT. PENDING. Collector value range: $10-15.00.

Markings: NIANGUA. Wm. H. TALBOT CO., NEVADA, MO. U.S.A. Markings on opposite side: SMELZER ARMS CO., KANSAS CITY, MO. Collector value range: $75-100.00

Markings: FREE SPOOL "Tripart" 581. Has three patent dates on it: 04, 07, 09. Collector value range: $10-15.00.

Only markings on this reel are the letters U T K in a diamond. The diamond is surrounded with the words TRADE MARK Reg US PAT OFF with MADE IN USA beneath it. Collector value range: $5-10.00.

Left: Union Hardware Sunnybrook. Raised pillar, 60 yard capacity. Right: The identical reel but totally unmarked. This was apparently a trade model used by salesman. Collector value range: $5-10.00.

Winchester # 4450 Takapart mounted on a Winchester steel rod #5047. Collector value range: $10-15.00.

Union Hardware Samson. Collector Value Range: $8-15.00.

No company name. Marked "X-Pert, 311-75". Note round tension drag adjustor on handle. Engraved with a fisherman on the head plate. Collector Value Range: $10-20.00

Von Lengerke and Antoine. Marked "V.L. 8-A. Peerless". Collector Value Range: $7-15.00

Markings: AUTOMATIC REEL PAT'D FEBY 28, 1888. JUNE 16, 1891 YAWMAN & ERBE MFG. CO ROCHESTER, NY, USA PATENT AUG 1, 1899. There is another illegible patent date starting "JUNE 16..." Collector value range: $10-20.00.

Wayne. No other markings. Collector value range: $5-10.00.

Totally unmarked all brass reel. Very small. Raised pillar, clicker. Collector Value Range: $5-20.00

Unknown wooden reel with brass fittings. It measures 6" across. Collector value range: $10-15.00.

THE AMERICAN FISHING ROD
A Brief History

It has been said that the first fishing rod was the human arm. Soon after early man began to fish with primitive 'hooks' it probably occurred to him that if he attached his line to the end of a pole, he could increase his reach therefore increase his catch.

The first sport fishermen in America were few in the early colonial days. Generally most of them were visiting European aristocrats. Fishing as a pastime was looked upon with disdain by the hard-working early colonists for theirs was the strenuous business of surviving and building. They had little time in which to pursue such things.

The first fishing rods used in America were undoubtedly English-made. The first native American rod was more likely a long pole with a short line which allowed the presentation of an artificial bait. This long pole is the only American device that can have a possible claim to being an ancestor of the fly rod as we know it today. That we try to claim any of the original history of rods at all is vanity, for the English had already developed fly rods far superior to this crude pole and line. In actuality the first true claim we can make to any revolution in rod design, as the case with reels, is found in Kentucky history.

Until sometime in the late 1800's most American rods were of solid wood. They were cumbersome affairs of great length and casting or presentation of the bait with them required two hands. They were stiff and not well suited to fly casting or any type of casting for that matter.

About 1846-1848 a Pennsylvanian, Sam Philippi, improved on an English rod makers innovation of using flexible bamboo or cane for their rod tips. Philippi made an all bamboo fly rod by gluing four long strips of split bamboo together. Sometime in the 1860's Hiram Leonard improved the Philippi innovation by using six strips instead of four.

American rod makers can claim the history of today's fine baitcasting rods as theirs. In the 1880's, a Kentuckian, James Henshall (1836-1925), introduced a new rod that can be said to be the true fore-runner of the bait casting rod. It was made by the Orvis company. Although it was designed primarily for live bait presentation, when anglers used the new Kentucky reel with this shorter lighter rod, it became extremely popular. The Henshall rod was still long by today's standards. The original rod was eight feet three inches long and made of wood.

About 1885 James M. Clark introduced a rod for bait casting, called the "Chicago Rod", it was made of split bamboo and only six feet long. It took this rod a short five years to replace the longer Henshall rod almost completely. It was of course this very same time that we have noted that the artificial plug began its meteoric rise in popularity.

With the "Chicago Rod," the "Kentucky Reel" and the "Plug," there was no stopping the phenomenal growth in the popularity of bait casting. This was the beginning of the Expansion Age in the American fishing tackle industry.

IDENTIFICATION OF OLD RODS

Most old handmade rods were signed by their makers. The signature is usually found stamped on the butt cap, but some signed them on the shaft itself, just forward of the handle.

If there are no markings to be found at all, the collector should then check the metal fittings. If the fittings are of "German silver," the rod is probably an early hand crafted one. "German silver" typically tarnishes to a dull gray, sometimes tending toward green. There is occasionally found a greenish corrosion in crevices or joints. These early rods may also be found with nickel or brass fittings.

Early split cane rods had to be bound at short intervals for the entire length of the rod for glues & materials used prior to World War I were inferior. After WW I better glues and higher quality cane was used and the wrapped bindings were not as numerous. Frequently the bindings were necessary only at the ends of the rods.

Length of rods is a good clue to age. Most fly rods made prior to the early 1900's were ten to twelve or more feet long while those made afterward are found in six to ten foot lengths.

While in general, bait casting rods can be examined with the above length guide lines in mind, the collector should be aware that most are shorter and stiffer than fly rods.

Another method, but not dependable way, to date a rod is by examining the other hardware, the line guides, and handle styles.

Most of the earliest casting rods were made for a two handed grip. Then handles were wooden, mostly popularly ribbed for a better grip. Long about 1900 or so cork handles became popular but smooth or ribbed wooden handles continued in wide use. Trigger type additions to the grip were added occasionally to the one handed rods. This of course is still used today on some rods.

Early eye guides were sometimes made collapsible to protect them from breakage in transporting the rod. Snake guides and soldered eye or ring guides were developed early on with the snake guide probably coming first. For those of us who believe the ceramic eye guides are a recent development there is a surprise. Several early catalogs illustrate and offer agate eye guides. These are virtually the same only the inserts made of natural agate rather than ceramic. The reason for them was the same. Trumpet guides were also an early development not found on today's rods.

Earliest reel seats were simply a place to tie the reel to the handle with line. Quickly thereafter came the slide locking and screw type locking devices.

The collector should be aware that rebuilding rods, changing broken hardware, etc. is nothing new. Be wary of an old rod with brand new fittings unless the rod has been rebuilt by a competent rodsmith.

In the final analysis the business of identifying a casting rod by maker is almost impossible in the absence of an actual maker trademark or signature.

ANATOMY OF A ROD

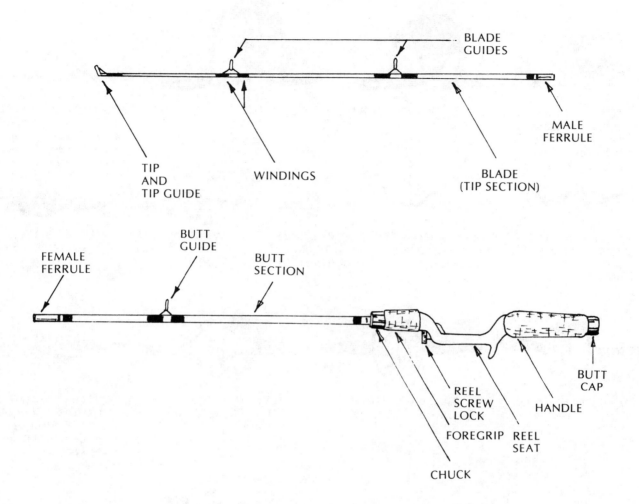

ROD MOUNTINGS

AGATINE GUIDE: Imitation agate; metal parts are 18% nickel silver, silver soldered.

GENUINE AGATE CASTING GUIDES

HARDENED STEEL BUTT GUIDE: Made of hardened steel; German silver arches; German silver soldered.

SNAKE GUIDE; GERMAN SILVER

SNAKE GUIDE; ENGLISH BRONZE STEEL

SPIRAL EYE GUIDE; BRIGHT WHITE METAL

TWO-RING EYE GUIDE, GERMAN SILVER

TUBE TYPE EYE GUIDE; BRASS

Spiral Casting Guide, German Silver.

Kalamazoo Casting Guide; German Silver.

Regular Casting Guide, German Silver.

BELL TRUMPET GUIDE; GERMAN SILVER. Made of one piece German silver; bell pattern.

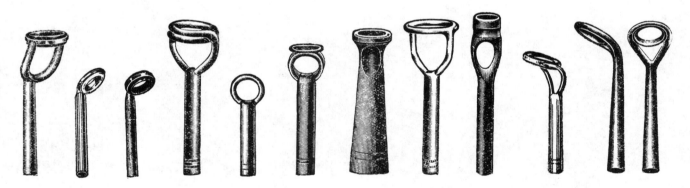

From left to right: AGATINE OFFSET TOPS: Imitation agate; metal parts are 18% nickel silver, silver soldered. Agatine Angle Fly Tip, German Silver, polished. ANGLE TIP: Genuine agate; metal parts are 18% nickel silver; silver soldered. SPIRAL CASTING TIP; GERMAN SILVER, POLISHED. SINGLE RING TIP; German Silver Polished. THREE RING TIP; German Silver Polished. TUBE TIP, BRASS: NICKEL PLATED. STIRRUP CASTING TIP: GERMAN SILVER POLISHED. PLAIN DOUBLE HOLE TIP; BRASS, NICKEL PLATED. GENUINE AGATE OFFSET CASTING TIP. CASTING TIP: Made of hardened steel; hard silver soldered; protected finish.

LURES
A History of Their Development in the United States

Legend has it that many years ago, after hours of fruitless hard work, a rather disgusted and altogether unhappy fisherman sat in his boat lamenting that all too familiar lament "Why the heck aren't they biting?!" After pondering his situation, punctuating his thoughts with muttered remarks about fish, luck and everything else connected with the sport of fishing, he made his final decision. He emphasized its frustrating impact by angrily flinging an empty cigarette box into the water. After the package landed, still causing a small disturbance in the water, something happened – something unseen jabbed hard at the box sending it several inches into the air. Not a little unsettled, the angler watched the box floating away and suddenly it happened again. This time however, the unseen force was seen. It was a big black bass that had smashed up through the surface hitting the box with such fury. An idea was born.

Perhaps this tale is a bit far-fetched, but on the other hand, who is to say? Whatever the case was there are some hard facts to follow the original idea and there is a story told and said to be true concerning a similar happening concerning the founder of Heddon (see page 219).

Plug development from that point, when initially conceived, was probably painfully slow at first. Proceeding from then it was a gradual process crossing many years from the first crudely painted, haphazardly hook-rigged carved, blocks of wood to the works of art we fish with today.

Probably the oldest manufactured ancestor of today's plugs was the "Phantom Minnow" sometimes called the false minnow. This artificial lure made in England originally appeared in America around the end of the first decade of the 1800's. The first of these were English-made and consisted of a metal head with metal fins on either side and soft body usually made of silk. The lure is illustrated in the photo below.

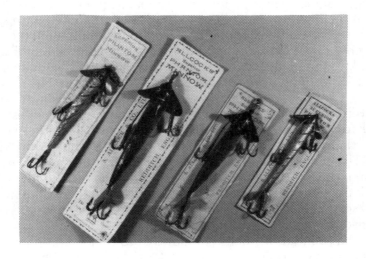

The Phantom Minnow remained essentially the same for the next 75-80 years. The lure was one of the first artificial baits to sport both the barbed and the treble hook together. The only significant changes in it for those years, was the addition and/or deletion of the number and type of hooks attached. An 1890's William Mills and Sons catalog illustrates a "Celebrated Phantom Minnow," available in twelve lengths, and that it is ". . . made of silk, coated with rubber, very light, very fine for black bass and pickerel." It can be found in several catalogs under various "Phantom" names until sometime in the 1940's. It appears that manufacturers settled upon three treble hooks, in the main, as the best design for the preponderance of them illustrated in these old catalogs, bear three treble hooks in various configurations.

The first American artificial bait listed in the United States patent records incorporating wood as a component and known to have actually been manufactured, is H. C. Brush's "Floating Spinner," Brushes Mills, New York. Patent, August 22, 1876. It is essentially a spinner bait, not a plug. It consists of a red painted or natural wooden (cork) float, center mounted on the shaft of a revolving spinner.

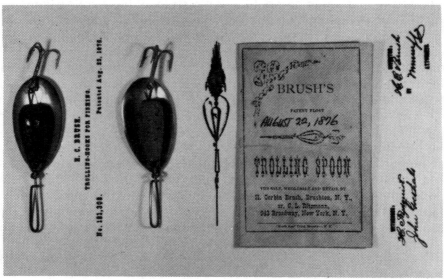

Here are two actual Brush Floating Spinners and a paper flyer that came with the lure. They are lying on a photo of part of the original patent.

There were no further major innovations in artificial lures until around 1890. About this time there began to appear the first artificial minnows made in the U.S. reflecting the look of a natural minnow. This bait, though sometimes found made of hollow aluminum (copies of the original in early years), was usually made of wood and the first manufactured bait known to be **purposely** made to actually look the same as a live minnow. This particular bait can be said to be the first "plug." Early on, artificial baits were fashioned to look like other critters and made of other materials. Frogs, mice, crawfish and minnows seem to have been the most popular ones imitated.

Although they were considerably eclectic in their offerings, American fishing tackle companies had but a small stock to offer the bait casting fisherman prior to 1890. These early catalogs catered primarily to the fly fisherman but did offer limited choices for those who wished to troll or cast spoons and spinners. The plug was rarely mentioned. It was just too new and not yet widely popular. Plugs began to appear more frequently in catalogs around 1892. Along with the "Phantom Minnow" began to appear such things as the Caledonian Minnow, the Protean Minnow, the Devon Minnow, and various hard and soft rubber minnows. The rubber minnows were usually offered in a luminous or non-luminous version.

James Heddon, the founder of James Heddon's Sons tackle company, was one of the early pioneers in the plug manufacturing industry that flourishes in the United States today. There is no concrete evidence to support the contention that he was the first to manufacture what we refer to as the plug today and certainly his company was not the first to produce artificial baits. His story however serves well to illustrate what was happening in that era.

In the years 1898 to 1901, Mr. Heddon whittled out a few wooden frogs and minnows for himself and some friends. These early plugs became the basis for the establishment of the Heddon company founded in 1901.

Naturally these baits were extremely limited in number and precious few exist today. A version of each was made commercially available by the infant Heddon company, but no early catalogs were found that illustrated them.

Along about the same time, or very shortly thereafter, the other bait companies were beginning to show a few plugs in their catalogs. One of the first was a revolutionary concept developed by the William Shakespeare company. This is the famous Shakespeare "Revolution" Bait and a variation, the Shakespeare-Worden "Bucktail Spinner." Both were made of wood.

Mr. Shakespeare writes in a 1902 catalog that the Revolution Bait "... takes its name from the fact that it has revolutionized fishing in the vicinity of Kalamazoo (Michigan), where it was developed. Whereas formally all anglers used live bait for bass, pickeral, pike and other game fish, now nothing is used but the Shakespeare baits. The reason is very apparent, as these baits catch good strings of fish where every other kind of bait fails."*

The variation, the Shakespeare-Worden Bucktail Spinner derives its name from Shakespeare's modification of the Revolution Bait by adding the bucktail originated from Mr. F. G. Worden of South Bend, Indiana, the founder of the South Bend Bait Company.

There were many other developments in the first decade of the 1900's. Mr. Ans B. Decker originated a top water plug which was and still is the old "Lake Hopatcong" plug. See page 171 for illustration.

There were several copies of this design not the least of which was the Mills Yellow Kid. Named after a popular comic strip character of the times, this lure was made of copper. Mills also brought out a similar plug made of wood called the Jersey Queen.

Also during this period were born the famed "Dowagiac Minnows" by Heddon, the "Coaxer" and the "Teaser."

The "Coaxers" and "Teasers" were developed by the W. J. Jamison Company. The original models were made of cork enameled white with wings of red felt and the tail was composed of a number of red feathers.

Variations of the original "Phantom Minnow" continued. 1906 saw the first Bing's "Weedless Nemahbin Minnow" by A. F. Bingenheimer of Milwaukee and in 1907 the K and K manufacturing company of Toledo, Ohio touted their "Animated Minnows" as an unprecedented development. They consisted of a divided wooden minnow, jointed at about the middle so that they wriggled along in the water .

A 1907 Abercrombie and Fitch catalog illustrated a soft rubber mouse ". . . covered with real skin. A splendid bait for black bass. Mounted with single hook of proper size and watch-spring swivel."

1910-1920

Between 1910 and 1920 appeared the "Famous Moonlight Floating Bait." This curious bait was called by its maker, the "Original and only successful night fishing bait." This apparently because it was painted with a luminous paint which allegedly glowed in the dark.

About the same time the Detroit Glass Minnow Tube Company introduced a lure in which one could place a live minnow. It was a glass test tube-like affair with a cap allowing circulation of water and four treble hooks.

According to their advertisement in the May 1915 issue of Field and Stream the bait had a "Magnifying glass tube" and the minnow would remain alive all day.

The earliest plugs which incorporated a design allowing water to flow through the body, thereby imparting movement and water disturbance characteristics was developed in this period. They are called "Water sonic" lures. It is thought this plug appeared around 1912.

There are several other interesting and curious plug developments during this decade. For instance there is "The Booster Bait." The advertisement in a pre 1915 Bob Smith Tackle and Camping Goods catalog states it was a prize winner at the Seattle Exposition. It was a plug ". . . filled with edible matter and containing a capsule which, when placed in water, dissolves, throwing off a strong taste and smell." One can only assume the taste and smell was irresistible to the fish.

Somewhere in this time period the Vacuum Bait Company was formed. It marketed an oddball affair ostensibly developed after years of research by a "Professor Howe."

The plug was a surface lure and the shape caused a spray, when retrieving, that attracted fish. It was later produced by South Bend.

A particularly clever weedless plug developed around 1914 was called "The Captor." It was invented by J. B. Fischer of Chicago and is illustrated on page 194.

Another ingenious invention, a "Spinner" plug was the "Chippewa" introduced in 1913 by the Immell Bait Company in Blair, Wisconsin. It was a wooden plug with the center portion cut out and a piece of twisted metal placed on an armature in such a way as to revolve when retrieved causing a flashing effect by reflecting light. It is illustrated in the Immell Bait Company section.

It was the years between 1900 and 1920 that Creek Chub, South Bend, Heddon, Pflueger, Jamison, Rush, Mills, etc., established themselves firmly in the plug business. Many of the designs developed then are still in use today! Perhaps modified but nevertheless the same basic concept is utilized.

*From Fine Points About Tackle - Being a Catalog of Fine Fishing Tackle, suited to the Needs of Anglers Who Follow the "Art of Bait-Casting." Copyright 1902 by William Shakespeare, Jr., Kalamazoo, Michigan.

1920-1950's

We have discussed most of the major developments in plugs in the early days. There were, of course many more produced in that era, but almost all were merely variations on a theme. Most will be discussed and illustrated in the expanded Collector's Identification and Value Guide beginning on page 100.

From 1920 on there were other developments in plugs but these were more of a technical nature such as improved swivel designs and better hook hardware. The experimentation with materials other than wood and metal such as the use of tenite and mother of pearl are good examples. Perhaps one of the most important influencing design and manufacture was the advent of plastics.

Other important influences were better and better paints and especially, increasing interest in researching the habits of fish. The latter had and still has an enormous influence on plug body design and surface decoration.

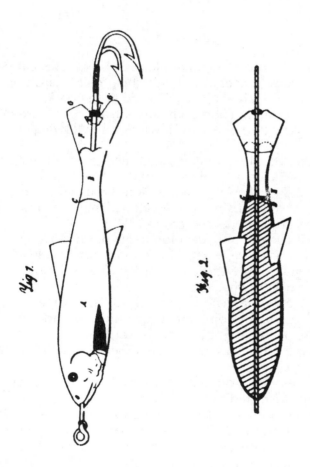

R. Haskell,

Fish Hook,

Nº 25,507,   Patented Sept. 20. 1859.

Drawing accompanying the patent application for the famous Haskell Minnow. It is the first known patent for a lure that mentions wood as a possible material for the body. A wooden version was apparently never made, but the metal version is well known. Originally silver-plated, this very rare lure has brought low five figure prices in the recent past, but may drop to a lower mid to high four figure amount. There are only about thirty known exist.

Witnesses:

Inventor:

RILEY HASKELL

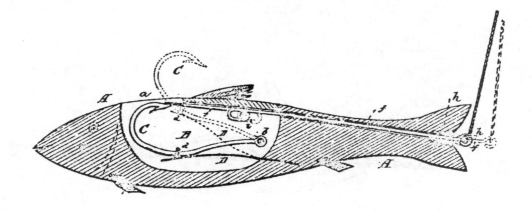

WITNESSES:

~INVENTORS~
David Huard
Charles M. Dunbar

per
C. H. Watson & Co.
ATTORNEYS.

Illustration accompanying the application for the first known granted patent for an artificial lure specifying "... wood or other suitable material" for the body.

J. IRGENS.
Fish Hook.

No. 231,912.

Patented Sept. 7, 1880.

Fig. 1.

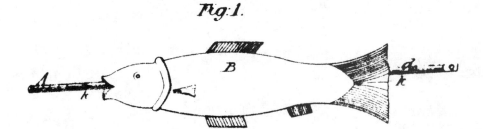

Fig. 2.

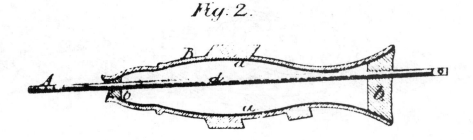

Fig. 3.

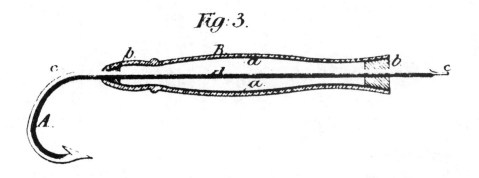

Witnesses:
Willy J. S. Schultz
John C. Tunbridge

Inventor:
Jorgen Irgens
By his attorney
W. Briesen

Illustration accompanying the U.S. patent application for the first known artificial lure specifying glass for the lure body. Granted Sept. 7, 1880 to Jorgen Irgens of Bergern, Norway.

E. F. PFLUEGER.
ARTIFICIAL FISH BAIT.

No. 272,317.   Patented Feb. 13, 1883.

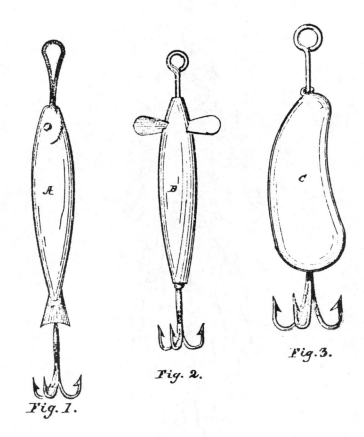

Fig. 1.   Fig. 2.   Fig. 3.

Witnesses: Inventor:

C. F. Wagoner   Ernest F. Pflueger,

Dayton A Doyle   by   C. P. Humphrey

                                Atty.

Lures on which Pflueger obtained the first patent for a lure coated with luminous paint. Granted Feb. 13, 1883.

C. J. W. GAIDE.
ARTIFICIAL FISHING BAIT.

No. 567,310.

Patented Sept. 8, 1896.

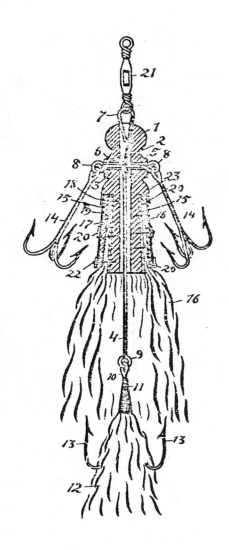

WITNESSES:

J. W. Wilson.

Emmett V. Harris

Carl J. W. Gaide INVENTOR

BY W. G. Burns

his ATTORNEY.

A very early wood body lure patented September 8, 1896 by Carl J. W. Gaide. Found advertised in a 1898 Smelzer and Son sporting goods catalog.

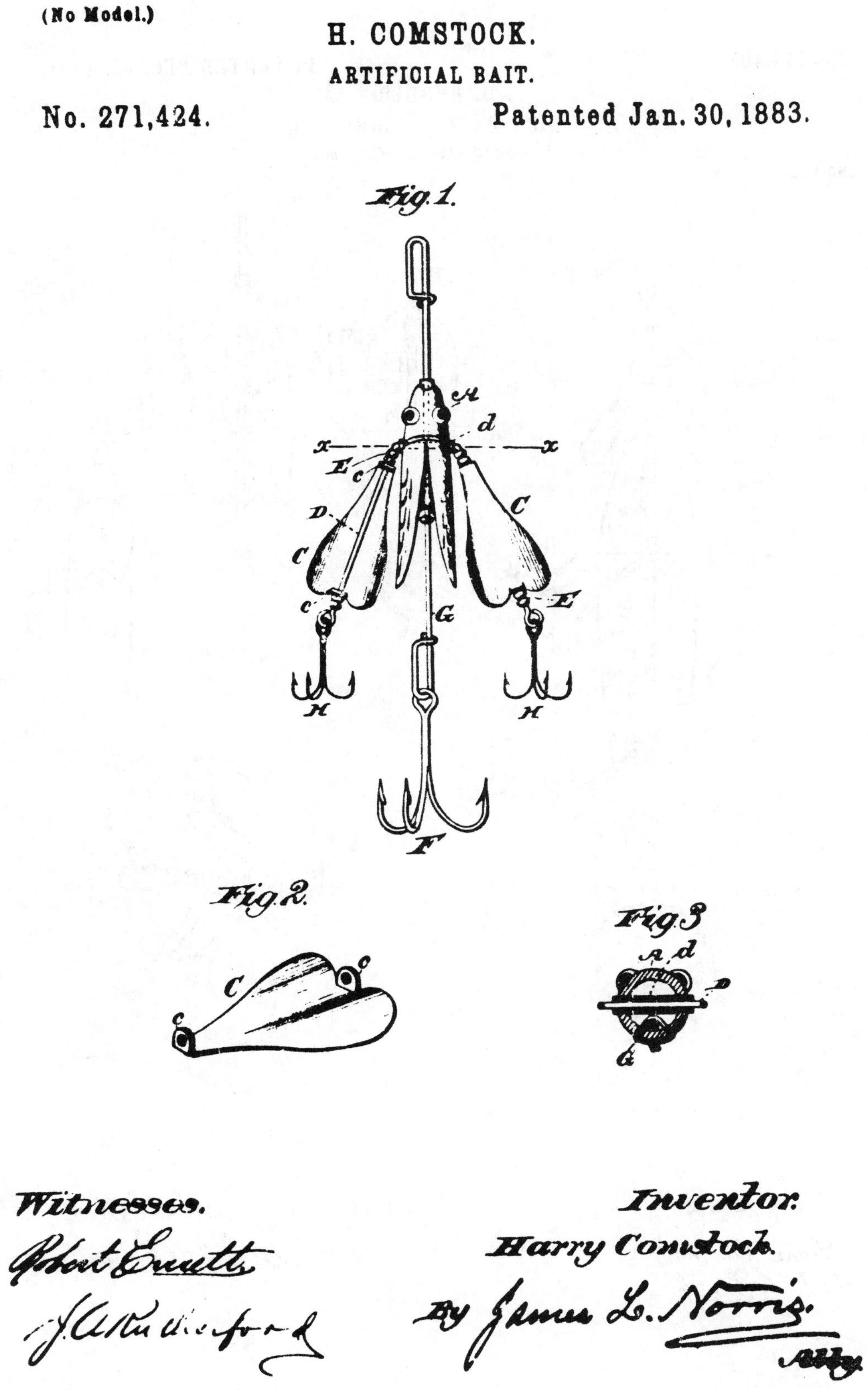

(No Model.)

H. COMSTOCK.
ARTIFICIAL BAIT.

No. 271,424.   Patented Jan. 30, 1883.

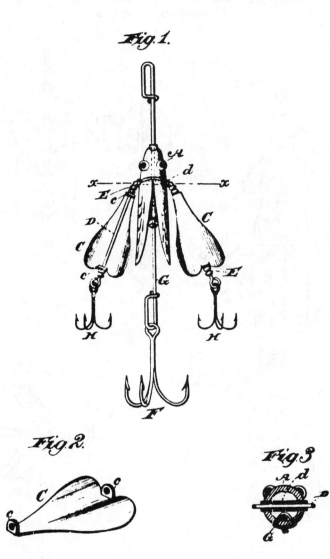

Fig. 1.

Fig. 2.   *Fig 3*

Witnesses.   Inventor.
Harry Comstock.

By James L. Norris.
Atty.

This is the original patent drawing accompanying the patent application for Harry Comstock's wood body Flying Helgramite. Granted January 30, 1883.

No. 777,488.

PATENTED DEC. 13, 1904.

F. D. RHODES.
FISH BAIT OR LURE.
APPLICATION FILED NOV. 2, 1903.

NO MODEL.

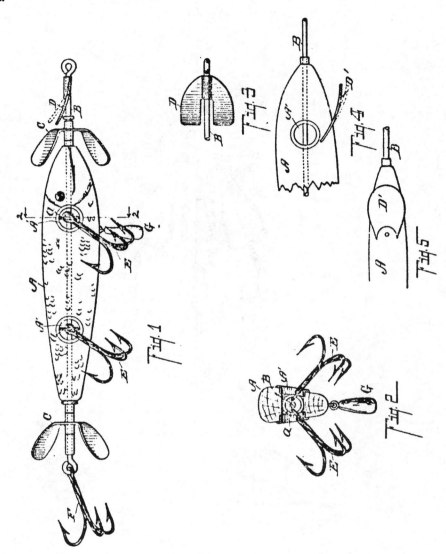

Witnesses:

A. Irene Adams

Otto O. Earl

Inventor,

Fred D Rhodes

This patent drawing illustrates the first time the see-through hook hanger shows up in patent applications and it is fully described in the text of the patent. The patent was granted to Fred D. Rhodes of Kalamazoo, Michigan on Dec. 13, 1904 and full rights were assigned to Frederick C. Austin of Chicago. The Shakespeare Company marketed the Rhodes Wooden Minnow.

954,691.

Patented Apr. 12, 1910.

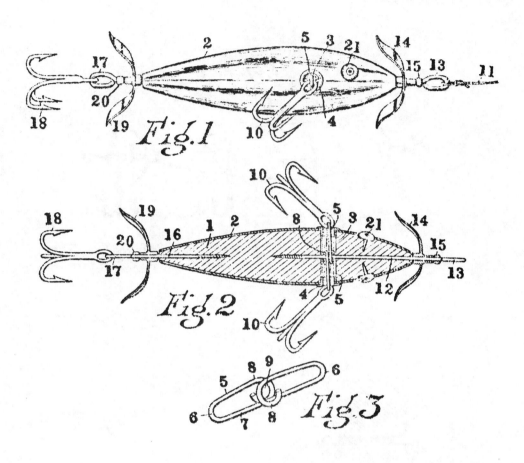

Fig.1

Fig.2

Fig.3

Witnesses:
Glenara Fox
Evelyn O'Linn

INVENTOR –
Joseph E. Pflueger,
By C. E. Humphrey,
ATTORNEY.

This patent drawing illustrates another see-through hook hanger claimed by Pflueger and granted on April 12, 1910. However there is a "disclaimer" attached to the end of the text. It is dated August 6, 1914, and withdraws the claim to the patent rights. This apparently because of the prior patent granted to Rhodes in 1904.

E. A. PFLUEGER.
ARTIFICIAL BAIT.
APPLICATION FILED MAY 12, 1911.

1,007,007.

Patented Oct. 24, 1911.

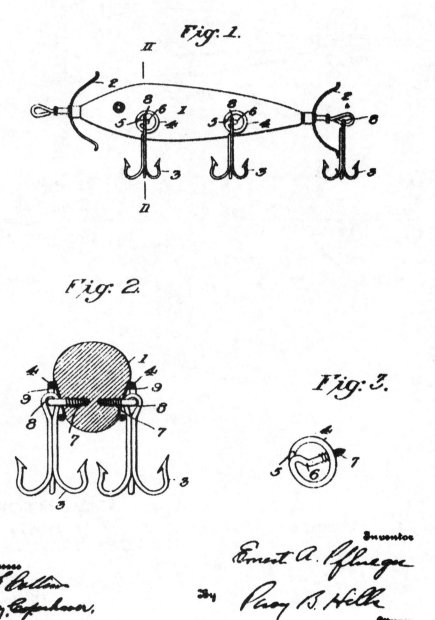

Illustration of the Pflueger patent of the "Neverfail" Hook hanger. Granted Oct. 24, 1911.

C. HEDDON.
FISH BAIT OR LURE.
APPLICATION FILED FEB. 27, 1914.

1,114,137.

Patented Oct. 20, 1914.

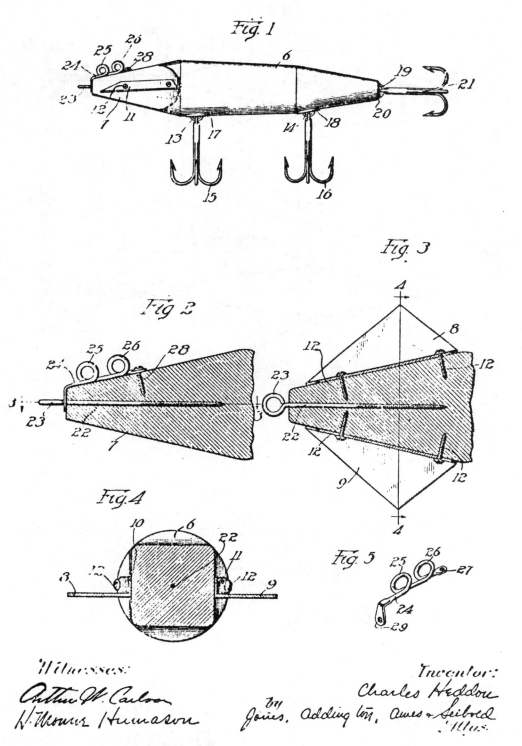

Patent illustration of Heddon's claim for the "pigtail" type Variable Line Tie. Granted Oct. 20, 1914.

1,133,724.   Patented Mar. 30, 1915.

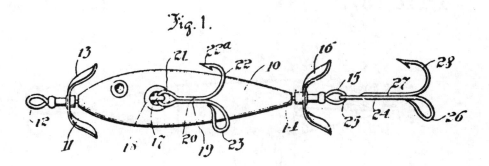

Fig. 1.

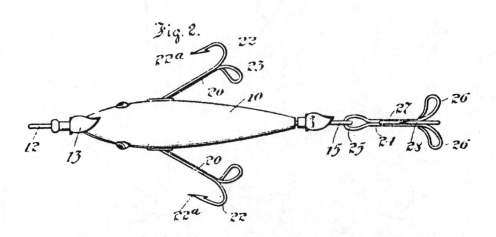

Fig. 2.

Fig. 3.

Witnesses
Charles G. Cope.
Mae Hanover

Inventor
Charles Heddon
by Jones, Addington, Ames & Seibold
Att'ys.

Patent illustration of Heddon's "Dummy Double" detachable double hook. Granted March 30, 1915.

W. SHAKESPEARE, Jr.
ARTIFICIAL BAIT OR LURE.
APPLICATION FILED JUNE 29, 1910.

1,150,635.

Patented Aug. 17, 1915.

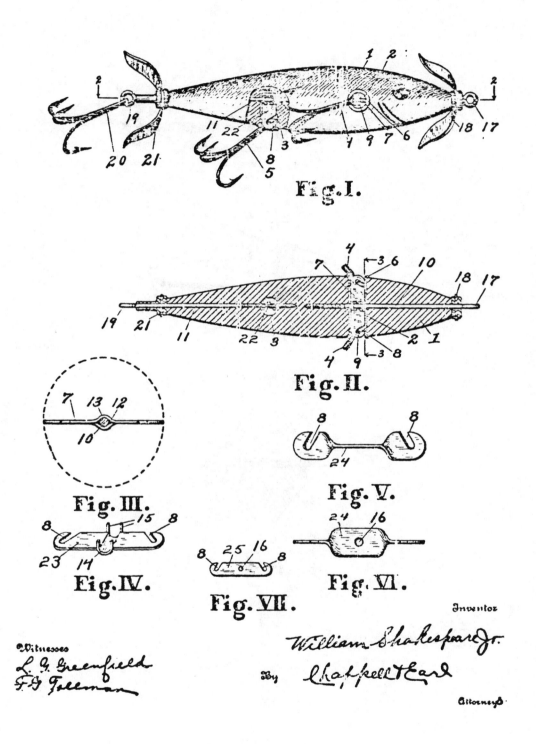

The Shakespeare patent for the one piece plate style hook hanger. Note there are four different types in the drawing. Granted August 17, 1915.

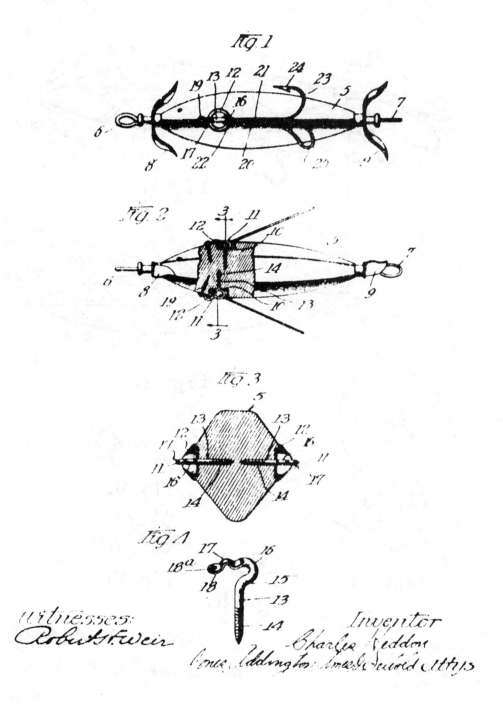

Illustration accompanying the patent application for Heddon's "L-rig" hook hanger. Granted to Charles Heddon August 20, 1918.

1,323,458.

Patented Dec. 2, 1919.

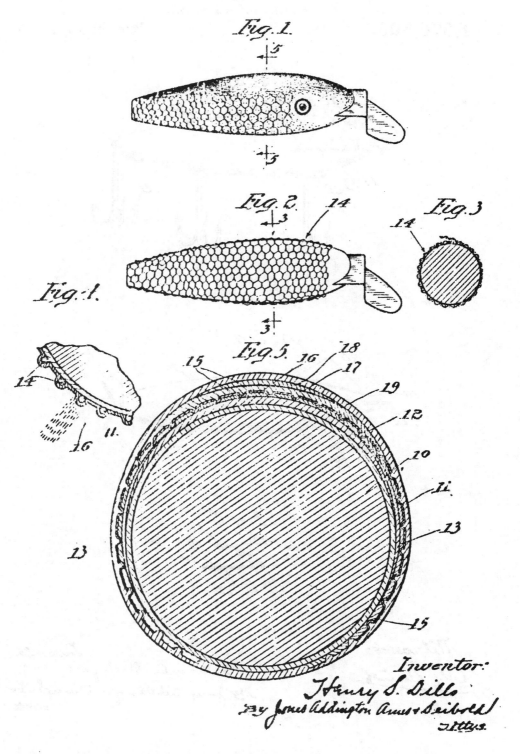

The original patent application illustration for a scale finish on an artificial lure. Granted December 2, 1919 to Henry S. Dills of the Creek Chub company and assigning one-half the rights to Heddon.

W. A. STOLLEY.
ARTIFICIAL BAIT.
APPLICATION FILED JAN. 22, 1917.

1,376,590.

Patented May 3, 1921.

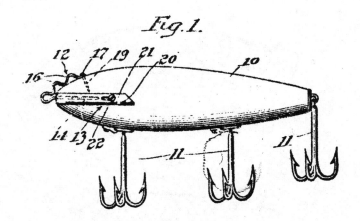

Fig. 1.

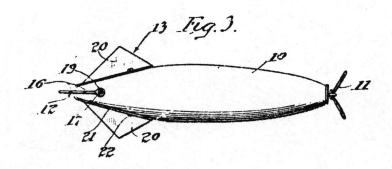

Fig. 3.

Fig. 2.

Witnesses:
W. T. Smith

Inventor
William A. Stolley.
By Jones, Addington, Ames Seibold
Attys.

The drawing accompanying Heddon's patent application for the "inch worm" type variable line tie. Granted May 3, 1921 to William A. Stolley, a Heddon employee, and assigned to Heddon.

1,418,326.

Patented June 6, 1922.

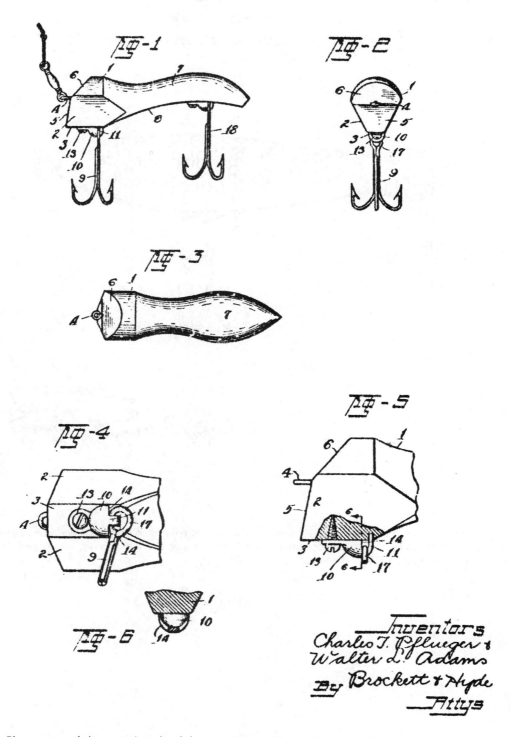

First patent of the one-piece hook hanger. Granted and assigned to Pflueger on June 6, 1922.

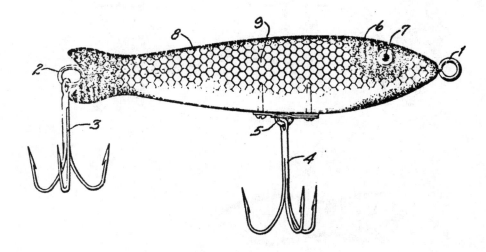

This Heddon patent drawing is the earliest found illustrating a lure with the first two-piece Hook Fastener. It is also the earliest application Heddon made for a plastic lure. The text stated that it may be made"...of celluloid or pyralin". Applied for in January 1929 and granted August 5, 1930.

E. L. BUCHANAN

1,801,951

ARTIFICIAL BAIT OR LURE

Filed March 3, 1930

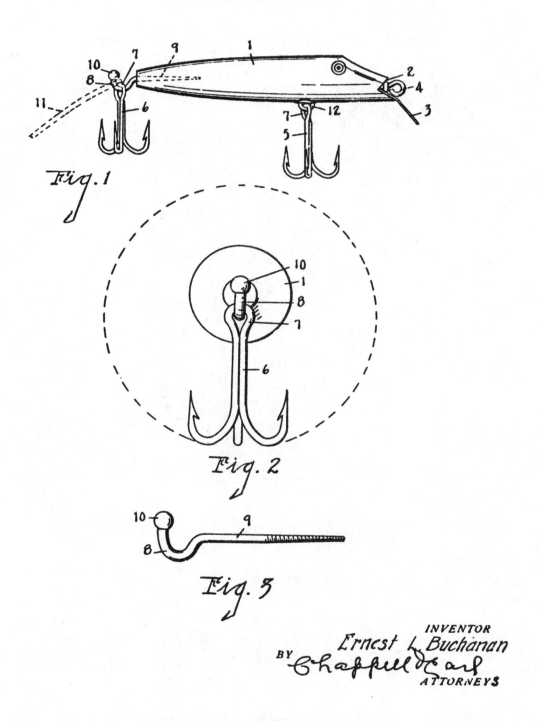

Shakespeare's "Ball Head Hook Retainer" patent. Granted April 21, 1931.

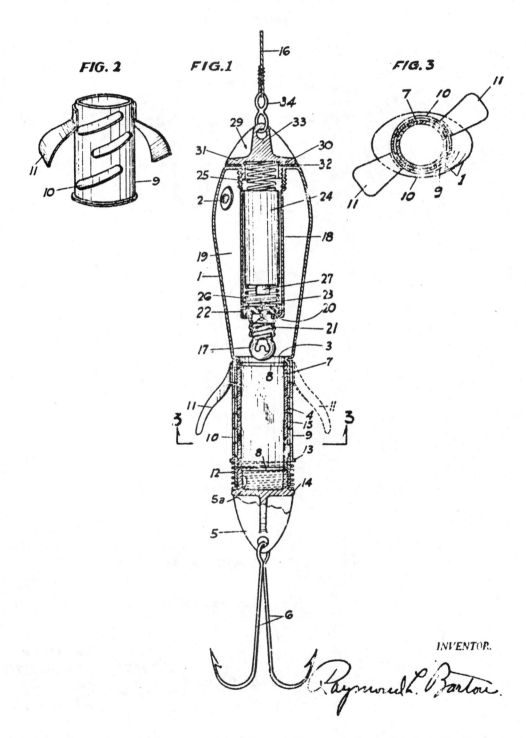

One of the many ingenious attempts at a self-illuminating lure using a battery and light bulb. This is the earliest one run across in patent records. Granted May 21, 1935 to Raymond L. Barton, San Diego, California.

HOOK FASTENING FOR FISH LURES

Filed Jan. 10, 1934

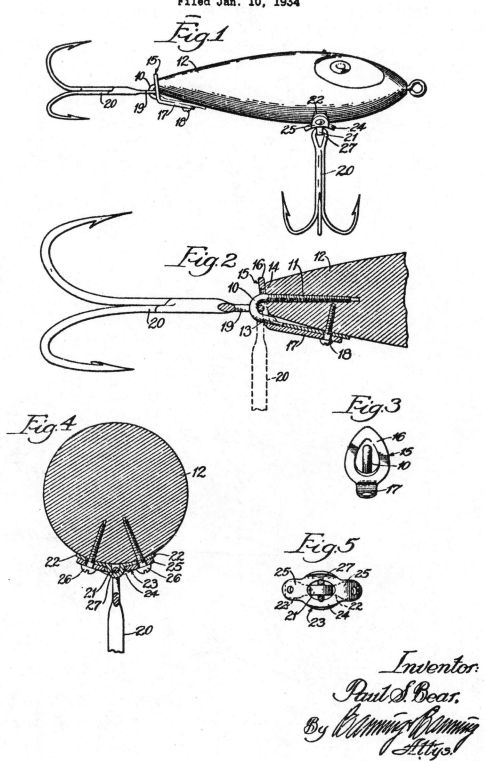

Fig. 1

Fig. 2

Fig. 3

Fig. 4

Fig. 5

Inventor:
Paul S. Bear,
By Canning & Canning
Attys.

*Granted to Heddon in 1935 the two piece tail hook fastener is familiar but the **cross-wise orientation** of the two-piece belly hook hanger has never been seen on a Heddon lure (See fig. 4 in drawing).*

May 14, 1935.   J. H. BIRD   2,001,652
                            HOOK GUARD
                         Filed Aug. 14, 1934

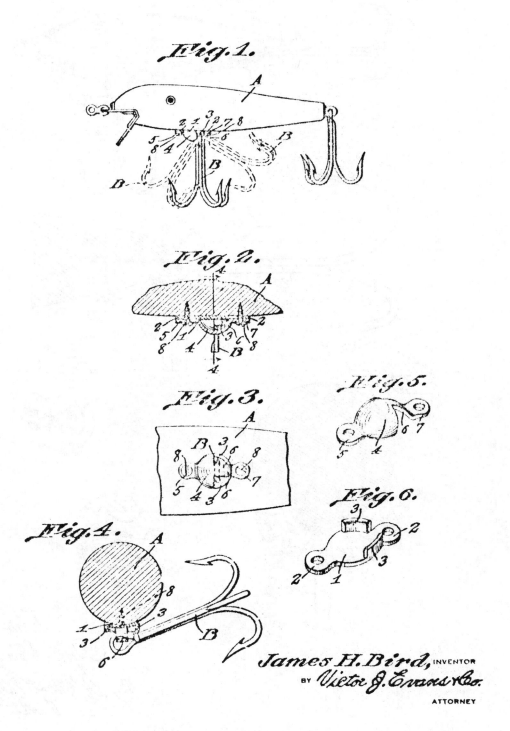

Fig.1.

Fig.2.

Fig.3.

Fig.5.

Fig.4.

Fig.6.

James H. Bird, INVENTOR

BY *Victor J. Evans & Co.*

ATTORNEY

This patent was granted to a James H. Bird of San Antonio on May 14, 1935. It is an interesting variation on the familiar one-piece hanger patented by Pflueger thirteen years before. As you can see it has the addition of a base plate.

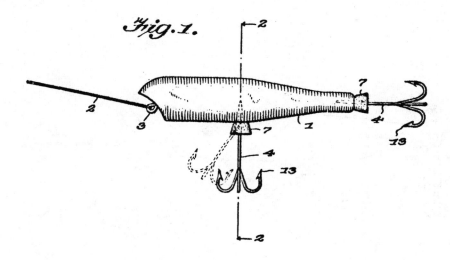

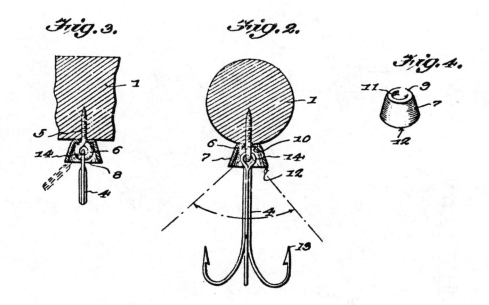

Inventor

OSCAR L. STRAUSBORGER

By

This illustration accompanied a patent filed in 1932 and granted to Oscar L. Strausborger of Edon, Ohio in 1934. It is a hook limiter made to prevent the hook from damaging the finish on the lure body. It is really an externally mounted cup. Many companies use this relatively inexpensive protective hook hanger even today, over 50 years later.

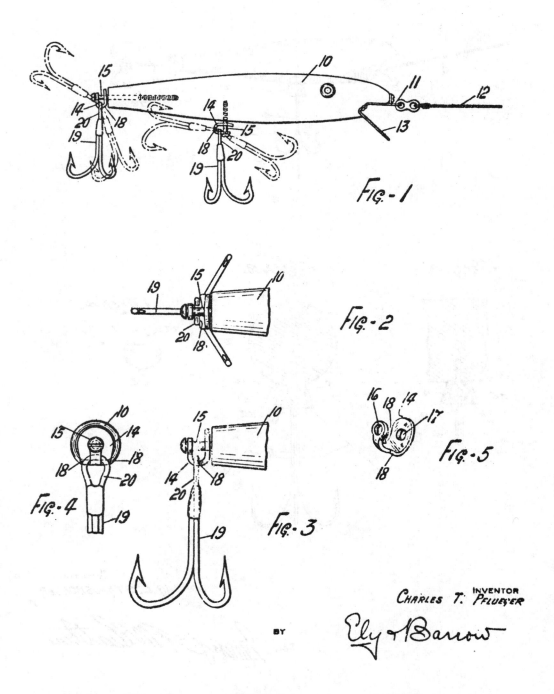

FIG-1

FIG-2

FIG-4

FIG-3

FIG-5

INVENTOR

CHARLES T. PFLUEGER

BY

Ely & Barrow

Patent of the Pflueger swiveled hook fastener. Granted August 13, 1935.

From the early 1890's on there were a number of rather amusing attempts at animation of artifical lures. Some of them would rival the fabled "Rube Goldberg Apparatus". a few of them were so complicated that the angler would have had to be an experienced mechanical engineer to repair and maybe even to operate the crazy things. Some of the patent drawings of these contraptions are illustrated on the following pages.

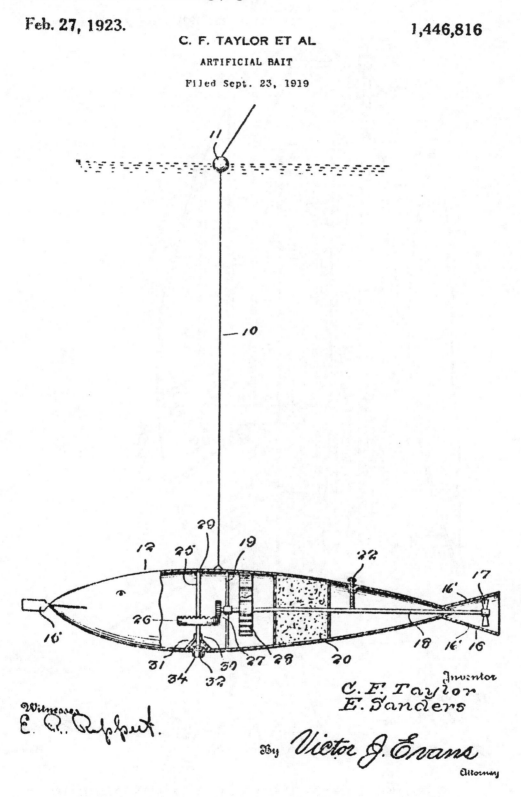

Feb. 27, 1923.

C. F. TAYLOR ET AL

ARTIFICIAL BAIT

Filed Sept. 23, 1919

1,446,816

SELF-PROPELLED!

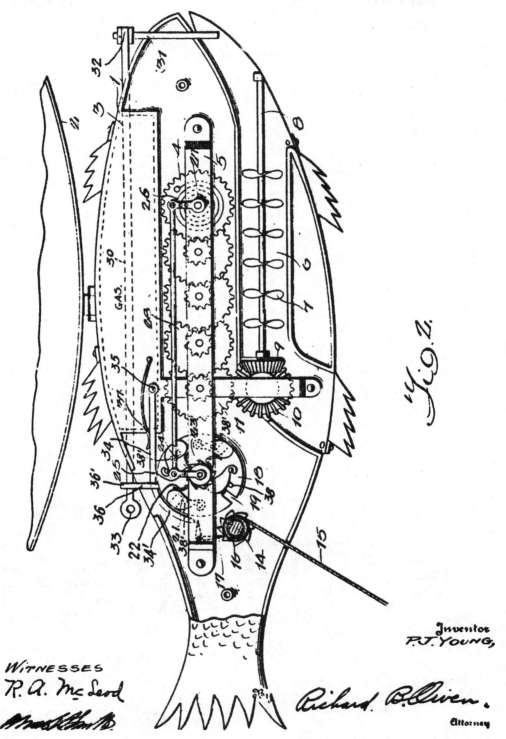

THIS FISH DECOY HAS TO BE A WATCH REPAIRMAN'S NIGHTMARE.

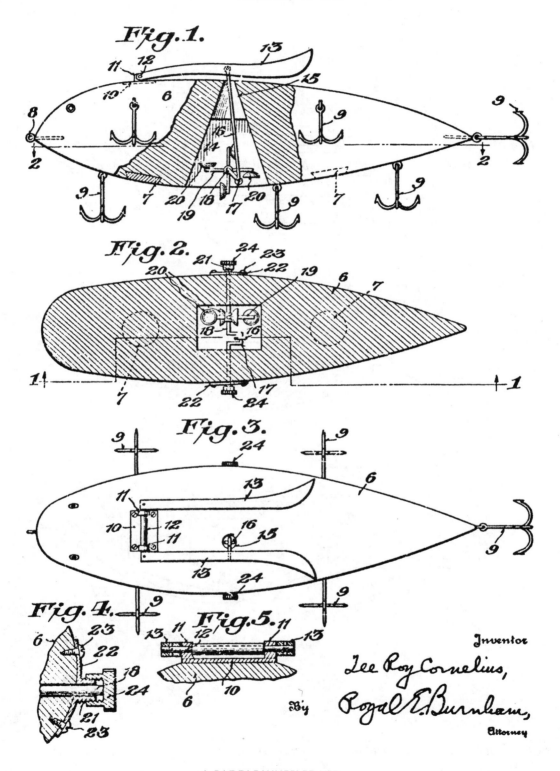

Fig.1.

Fig.2.

Fig.3.

Fig.4.   *Fig.5.*

Inventor

Lee Roy Cornelius,

By *Royal E. Burnham,*

Attorney

A PADDLE-WHEELER YET

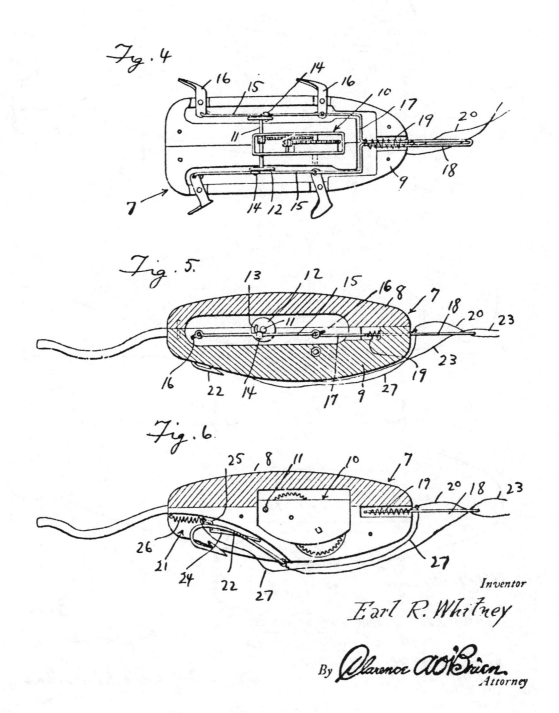

Inventor

Earl R. Whitney

By *Clarence A. O'Brien*
        Attorney

COULD THIS BE THE SAME E. WHITNEY OF COTTON GIN FAME? THE INTERIOR LOOKS LIKE IT COULD BALE COTTON.

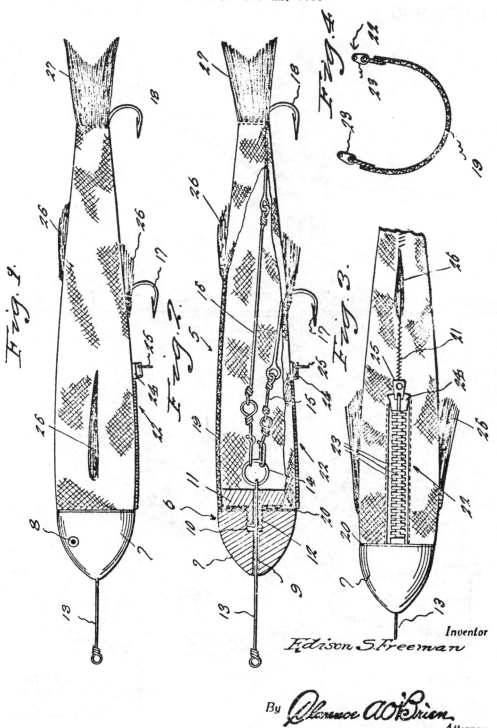

A ZIPPER! ONE CAN ONLY WONDER WHAT SALTWATER MIGHT DO TO IT. THE INVENTOR WAS FROM MIAMI.

1,068,908.

Patented July 29, 1913.

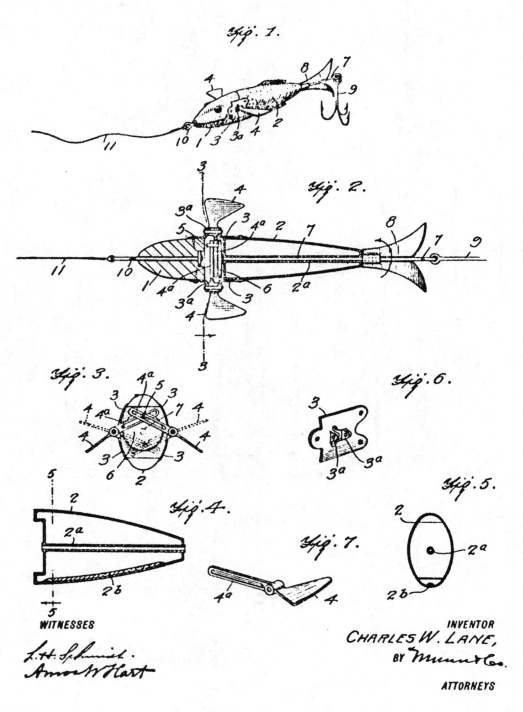

WITNESSES

INVENTOR
CHARLES W. LANE,
BY

ATTORNEYS

WITH THOSE FLAPPING WINGS IT MIGHT EVEN BE A FLYING FISH. THIS IS ACTUALLY A VERY DESIRABLE COLLECTIBLE LURE (See page 248).

THE PLUG
Some General Guidelines For Identifying and Dating

The first thing to do is study the overall appearance of the plug. Most of the older ones were made of wood and real marvels of craftsmanship. High quality enamels were used to paint them, most with several coats. Over the years this paint has a tendency to "check" or "craze". This is the appearance of hair line cracks in the paint. Be aware however that not all these plugs demonstrate the high quality production used by most in the early days.

The metals used in the first days of lure making were brass, steel, nickel, and sometimes even silver and gold plating.

The earliest hook fastener and line tie hardware was usually a through-body wire twisted into loops on the ends or a simple screw eye. There were many, many different methods, but those were the most common. The simple screw eye has been used throughout the years and is still in use by many manufacturers today.

Heddon, as far as can be determined, was the first to use a screw **hook** recessed in a hole or depression (c1902). Very soon after that, Heddon and others began using a flanged or rimmed metal cup to line the hole, reinforcing and protecting the body from the hook shank and points. This hole and cup served also to make a much better hook presentation. The Creek Chub Company has used this method almost exclusively all through the years. The Heddon Company patented the hook fastener known as the "L-rig" in 1917, but careful study of old patented records show that it is possible that even though he did not try to patent it, Edward J. Lockhart used a very close version of the Heddon "L-rig" in his application for a wooden plug patent in October of 1913. Heddon filed specifically for a patent on the "L-rig" in 1915 and it was granted in 1917. Heddon has a very specific progression of hardware changes. See following pages for detailed descriptions and illustrations.

Pflueger used a unique hook hanger called "Neverfail". It was patented Oct. 24, 1911 (See pg. 80).

Eye type and/or detail is another way to determine whether or not a plug is old. Most of the first lures had no eyes and there was a limited use of painted eyes. Probably simple round head tacks came next as eyes but it is not possible to determine presently if the glass eye preceded or coincided with their use. It is known that tacks were often used, painted or unpainted, by a few companies at the same time others were utilizing glass. the first glass eyes were slightly rounded having an opaque yellow iris and a small black pupil. The second was more rounded, has a clear outer section and yellow tinted iris and a larger black pupil. The yellow eyes varied in size generally the smaller size being the oldest. Then came the "Tack on Eye" which consisted of a cone shape plastic eye with a hole in the middle for the tack. Today almost all eyes are simply painted on.

The types of hooks found are really of no use as these may have been changed one or more times over the years as they were broken or bent out of shape, etc.

PLASTIC LURES

With few exceptions, the plugs we fish with today are plastic. The state of the art in lure manufacture is astounding with advances being made every day. Some of the plugs in our tackle boxes would look good enough to clean, cook, and eat if they were just a little bigger.

The earliest plastics were made up of compounds of animal and vegetable derived materials. Many consider these as "natural plastics" because of their make-up. The first of these plastics was Celluloid. An American named John Hyatt patented a mixture of cellulose and nitrate and camphor giving it the trade name "Celluloid." It was forty years later before Dr. Leo Baekeland developed a phenol-formaldehyde material he patented and called "Bakelit." The early years of the use of Bakelite were limited to darker colors, but by the mid 1930's the material had been refined and could be made in lighter shades of color. Some of the trade names of the early cellulose nitrate, phenolic plastics and their improved formulas are as follows:

Cellulose Nitrate	Phenolic Plastics
Celluloid	Bakelite
Pyralin	Durite
Nitron	Durex
	Catalin

The celluloid plugs were made in many colors and transparent as well. One of its properties is that it is highly flammable and subject to melting under heat or chemical reaction with other materials. It has tendency to yellow and become brittle with age.

Lure manufacturers experimented with many different plastics over the years and many of them were unstable. Illustrated here is an example of what can happen to some of those early plastics. Most of the earlier plastics are highly susceptible to damage from the compounds used in the plastic worms of today. Take care not to mix them.

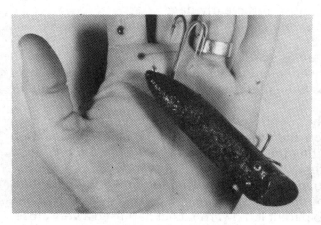

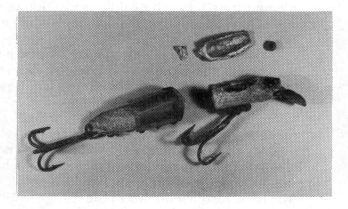

Some early plastics were not perfected. They were unstable and had a tendency to break down. Photo shows a messy example of this. An occurence as bad as this does not happen often fortunately.

This happened to a new plug while in its box. The proper mixture of ingredients for the plastic was apparently not carefully prepared resulting in the breakdown. It is thought that heat may accelerate the breakdown.

Lure Identification and Classification System

The following illustrated lure identification and classification system incorporates a code devised and set up by Clyde Harbin, The Bassman*, which was published in his book *James Heddon's Sons Catalogs.*** It is used with his permission. The system has been arranged in two forms, first according to category and second, alphabetically in order to facilitate its use in this collector's guide. The reader will find frequent references to the coding throughout the book. These codes can be readily used to classify and catalog your collection in short hand as it were. The collector will likely find it convenient to do so in corresponding with other collectors for trading or buy/sell negotiations.

*Registered trademark, Clyde A. Harbin.
**Copyright 1977, Clyde A. Harbin, published by CAH Enterprises, Memphis, Tennessee.

CATAGORY LISTING
Lure Identification
and Classification System

BODY SHAPES & COMPOSITION

FBL	Fat Body Lure
FSB	Flat Sided Body
HEX	Hexagonal (Six-sided body)
PEN	Pentagonal (Five-sided body)
TSB	Tapered Smaller Body
WFF	Webbed Foot Frog
PB	Plastic Body
PPB	Pyralin Plastic Body
WB	Wooden Body
RR	Reverse running lure
DEB	Double ended body (line tie on each end)
TenB	Tenite Body
BB	Bakelite Body

COLLARS

NC	Narrow Collar (oldest type)
NP	No Pen (friction fit)-oldest type
O	Type of Collar (completely encircles the lure body)
PNC	Penned or Nailed Collar (second oldest method of attachment)
S&FC	Screw and Flanged Collar
U	Type of Collar (similar to the 'O' collar above, but older and stops short of complete encirclement, thus: 'u' collar)

EYES

BE	Bead Eye
GE	Glass Eye
NE	No Eye
PE	Painted Eye
TOE	Tack, Peg, or Nail-on Eye
TBGE	Teddy Bear Glass Eye
TPE	Tack Painted Eye

HEAD TYPES

2 SH	Two Slanted (Sided) Head
4 SH	Four Slanted (Sided) Head

HOOK FASTENER HARDWARE TYPES

BHHF	Ball Head hook fastener (Shakespeare
CUP	Metal cup and Screw-eye hook fastener
HD "L"	Heavy duty Double Screw hook fastener
"L"	Double Screw hook fastener. Frequently called the "L" Rig
SH	Screw-hook fastener (used with CUP hardware)
SE	Screw-eye hook fastener

(Hook Fasteners cont'd.)

SEW	Screw-eye hook fastener with washer
WH	Wood hole (Screw-eye) hook fastener
BAR	One piece bar hook fastener
1 PC	One piece (surface) hook fastener
2 PC (1)	Two piece metal hook fastener. Frequently called the "Toilet Seat" fastener. (first Heddon style)
2 PC (2)	Second style of above (Heddon*)

HOOK TYPE AND POSITIONS

BH	Belly hook
DBL	Double hook
DHOT	Double hook on tail
NBH	No belly hook
SGL	Single hook
SHOT	Single hook on tail
STH	Side treble hooks
1-T	One treble hook
2-T	Two treble hooks
3-T	Three treble hooks
4-T	Four treble hooks
5-T	Five treble hooks
6-T	Six treble hooks

LINE TIE TYPES

LTHD	Line tie hump down
LTHU	Line tie hump up
SELT	Screw eye line tie
TL&SELT	Two loop and Screw eye line tie
VLF	Variable line fastener-known variously as the '3 loop', the 'Pigtail', or the 'Inch Worm'

LIP TYPES

APL	Adjustable position lip
BSL	Bell shape lip
HSL	Heart shape lip (appears somewhat like the profile shape of an inverted apple)
LLL	Long lower lip
PPL	Pyralin plastic lip

NAME PLACEMENT

NNBP	No name on big propeller
NNLP	No name on little propeller
NNOC	No name on collar
NNOL	No name on lip
NOBS	Name on both sides (collar or lip)
NOCF	Name on collar front
NOL	Name on lip
NOLP	Name on little propeller
NOB	Name on body

Pflueger used a slightly different style of 2 pc. hardware

Identification & Classification System (cont'd.)

NOSES

PN	Pencil nose
SN	Slant or slope nose

MISCELLANEOUS

PRA	Pork rind attachment
Pwts	Pennyweight (24 grains or .05 ounces)

TAIL TYPES

BT	Buck Tail
FS	Florida Special
FT	Feather Tail
NTC	No tail cap
TC	Tail cap
THI	Tail hook metal insert

ALPHABETICAL LISTING

Lure Identification
and Classification System

NUMBERS

1 PC	One Piece surface fastener
2 PC(1)	Two piece metal hook fastener. Frequently called the "Toilet Seat" fastener (first Heddon style)
2 PC(2)	*Second style of above (Heddon)
2 SH	Two Slanted (Sided) Head
4 SH	Four Slanted (Sided) Head
1-T	One treble hook
2-T	Two treble hooks
3-T	Three treble hooks
4-T	Four treble hooks
5-T	Five treble hooks
6-T	Six treble hooks

A

APL	Adjustable position lip

B

BAR	One piece bar hook fastener
BE	Bead Eye
BH	Belly hook
BHHF	Ball Head hook fastener (Shakespeare)
BSL	Bell shape lip
BT	Buck Tail

C

CUP	Metal cup and Screw eye hook fastener

D

DBL	Double hook (two points on one hook)
DEB	Double ended body (line tie one each end)
DHOT	Double hook on tail

F

FBL	Fat Body Lure
FS	Florida Special
FSB	Flat Sided Body
FT	Feather Tail

G

GE	Glass Eye

H

HD "L"	Heavyduty Double Screw Hook fastener
HEX	Hexagonal (Six-sided body)
HSL	Heart shape lip (appears somewhat like the profile shape of an inverted apple)

L

"L"	Double Screw Hook fastener. Frequently called the "L" Rig.
LLP	Long Lower lip
LTHD	Line tie hump down
LTHU	Line tie hump up

N

NBH	No belly hook
NC	Narrow Collar (oldest type)
NE	No Eye
NNBP	No name on big propeller
NNLP	No name on little propeller
NNOC	No name on collar
NNOL	No name on lip
NOB	Name on body
NOBP	Name on big propeller
NOBS	Name on both sides (collar or lip
NOCF	Name on collar front
NOL	Name on lip
NOLP	Name on little propeller
NTC	No tail cap

O

O	Type of Collar (Completely encircles the lure body)

P

PB	Plastic Body
PE	Painted Eye
PEN	Pentagonal (Five-sided body)
PN	Pencil nose
PNC	Penned or Nailed Collar (Second oldest method of attachment)
PPB	Pyralin plastic lip
Pwts	Pennyweight (24 grains or .05 ounces)

S

SE	Screw eye hook fastener
SELT	Screw eye line tie
SEW	Screw eye hook fastener with washer
S&FC	Screw and Flanged Collar
SGL	Single hook (one point)
SH	Screw hook fastener
SHOT	Single hook on tail
SN	Slant or slope nose
STH	Side treble hooks

T

TBGE	Teddy Bear Glass Eye
TC	Tail cap
TL&SELT	Two loop and Screw eye line tie
TOE	Tack, Peg, or Nail-on Eye (no paint)
TPE	Tack Painted Eye
TSB	Tapered Smaller Body
THI	Tail hook metal insert

U

U	Type of Collar (similar to the 'O' collar above, but older and stops short of complete encirclement, thus: 'u' collar)

V

VLF	Variable line fastener-known variously as the '3 loop', the 'Pigtail', or the 'Inch Worm'

W

WB	Wooden Body
WFF	Webbed Foot Frog
WH	Wood hole (Screw eye) hook fastener

TYPES OF HOOK HANGERS

SCREW HOOK
(recessed)

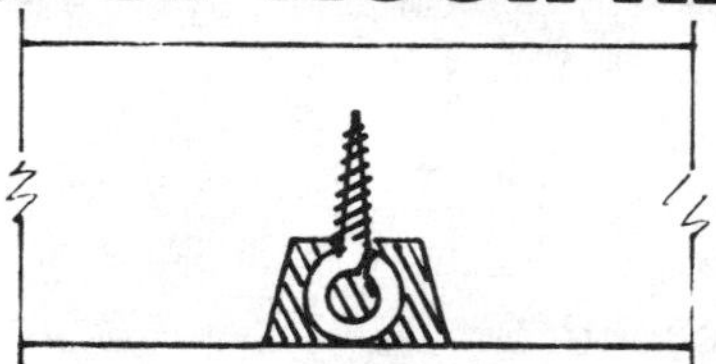

SCREW EYE
(recessed)

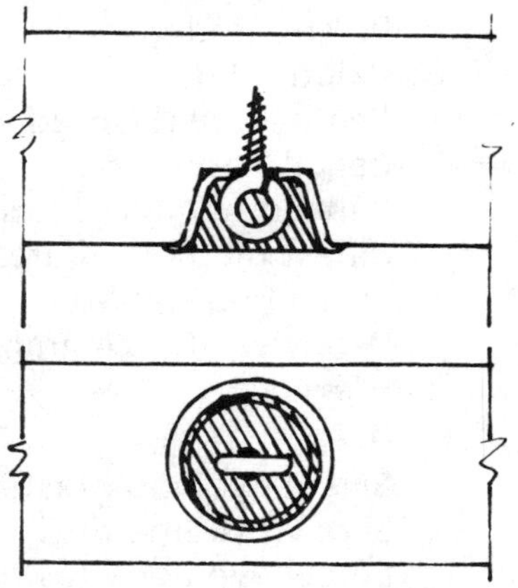

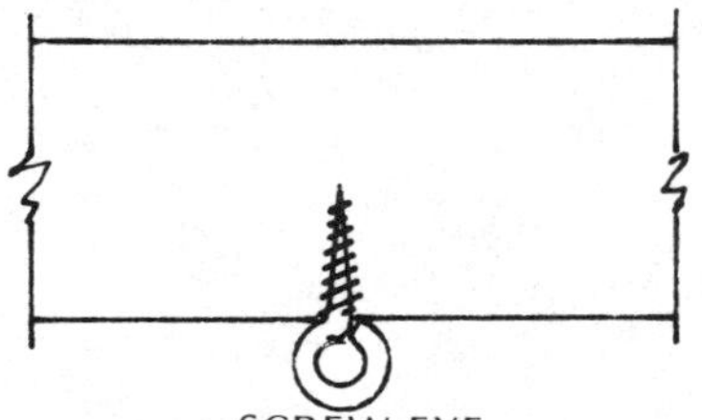

SCREW EYE
(Found with and without washer)

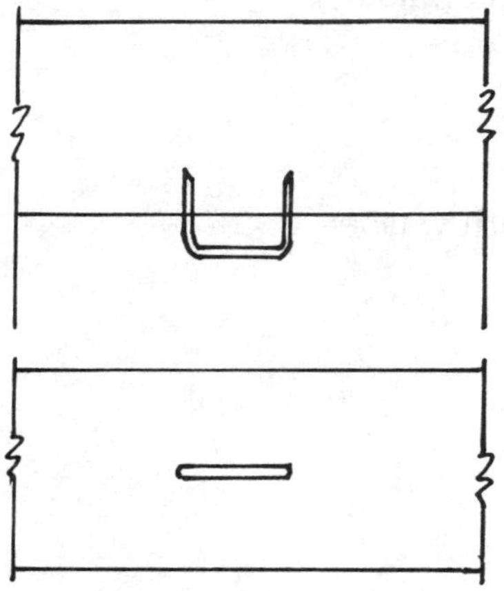

CUP
(Metal cup and screw eye)

L-RIG
(variation)

STAPLE type hook hanger.
Various shapes and sizes are found.

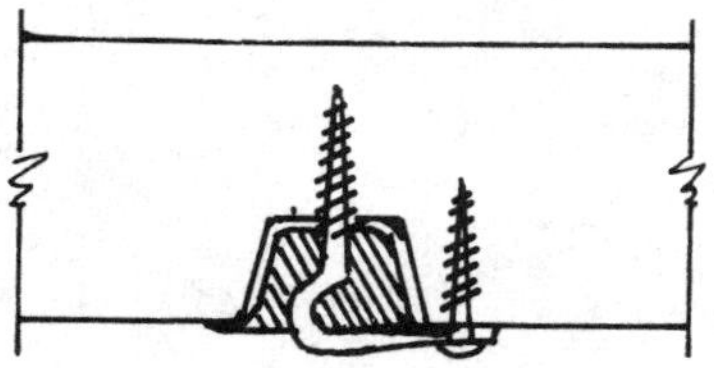

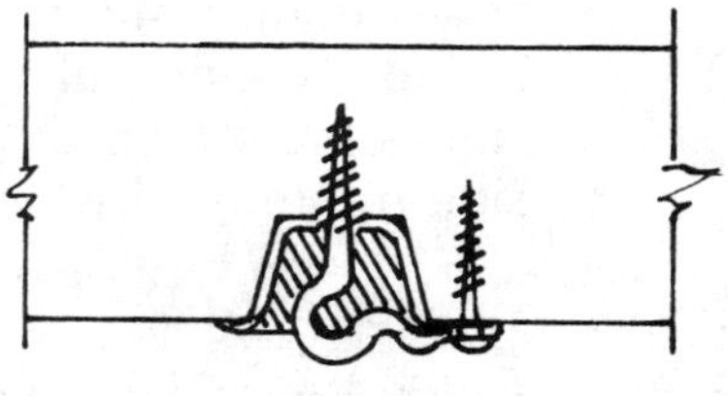

L-RIG
(Heddon style, most common)

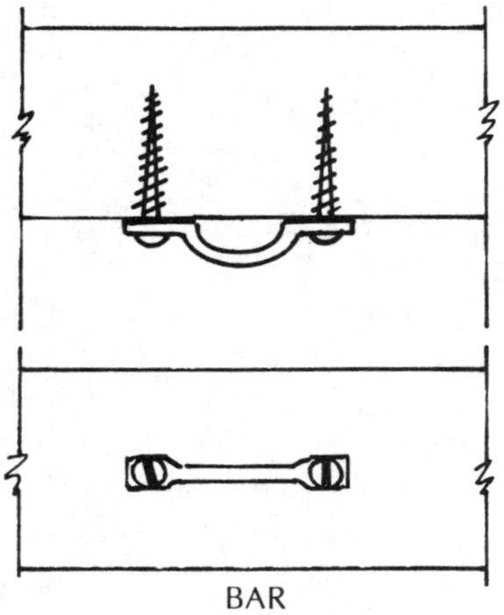

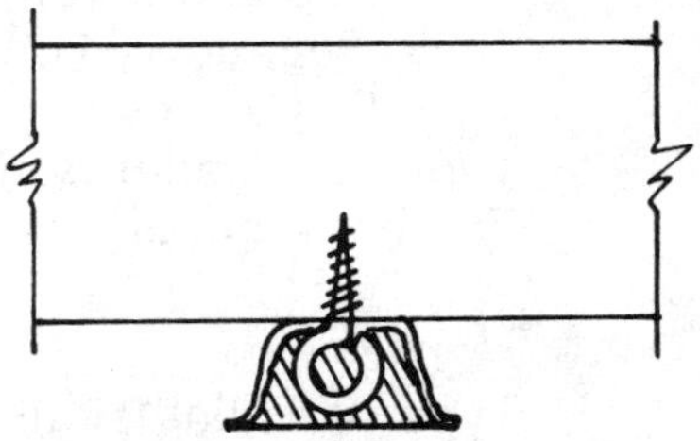

Surface mounted cup hardware

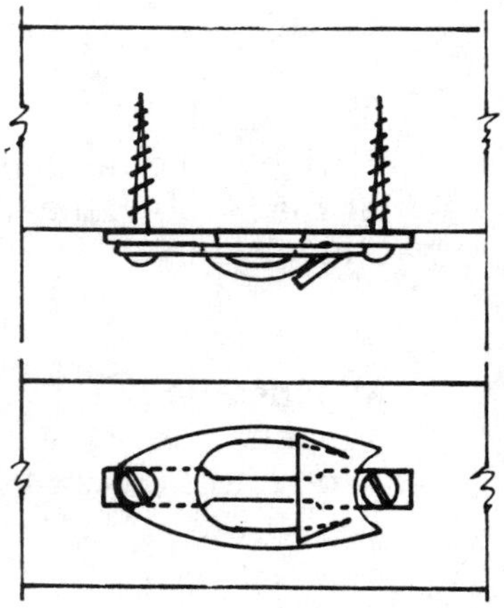

BAR
(one piece bar)

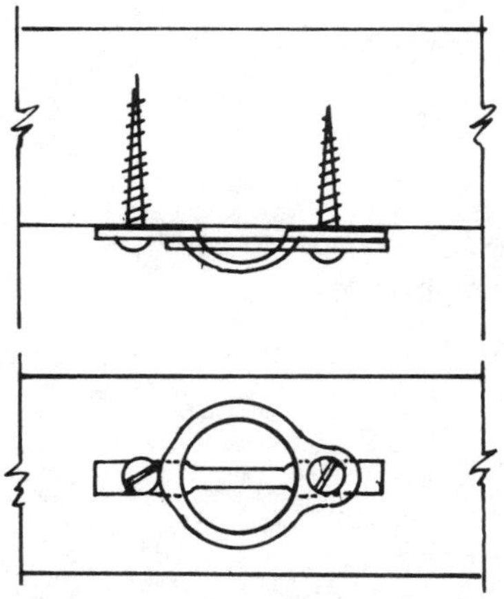

2-PC or TOILET SEAT
(first style of Heddon Two Piece)

2 PC (2)
(*Second style of Heddon 2-Pc)

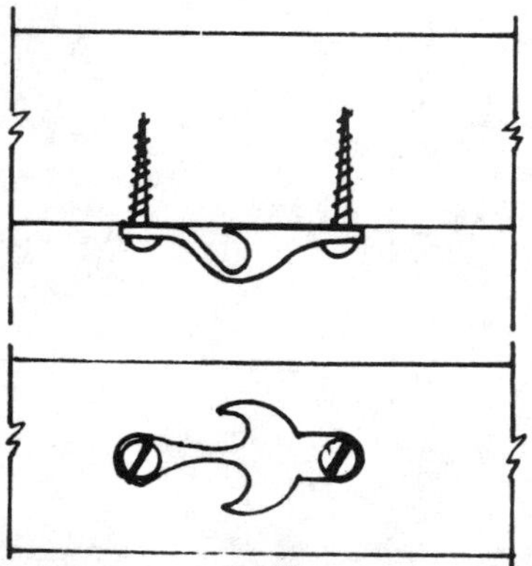

1-PC
(one piece surface)

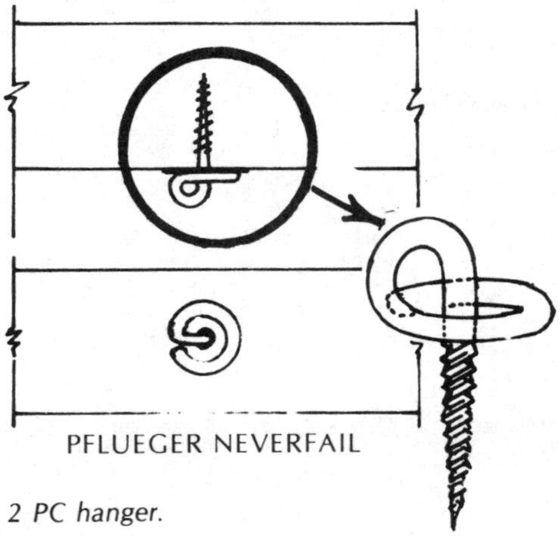

PFLUEGER NEVERFAIL

*Pflueger used a slightly different type of this 2 PC hanger.

ANATOMY OF A LURE

Various Types of Propellers

Al Foss style propeller spinner

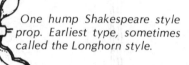
F. C. Woods style propeller spinner

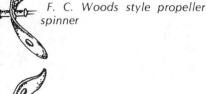
Clark and Keeling Expert style.

One hump Shakespeare style prop. Earliest type, sometimes called the Longhorn style.

Floppy prop style with no tube or bearing. Called Bow Tie Type when equipped with tube and/or bearings.

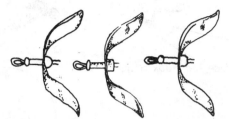
The Shakespeare smooth edge (no hump) prop. Latest style. Note the three types of bearings they are found with.

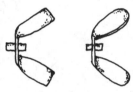
Two styles inexpensive tube type props found on various lures.

Creek Chub style propeller spinner. Found with several (at least two) washer type loose bearings to stabilize it.

Style used on early Holzwarth Experts and on later Rhodes and earliest Shakespeare wooden minnows.

Earth South Bend and Shakespeare (only a few used) two hump props.

Bow Tie type. Same as the Floppy Prop above but has tube and bearing. Location of the tube and bearing is found reversed also.

Winchester style tail propeller spinner.

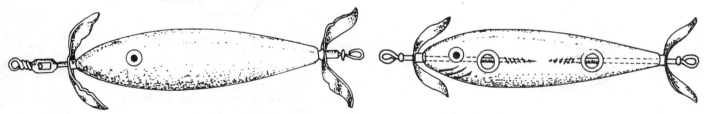
Various Styles of Propellers and Hook Hanger Hardware.

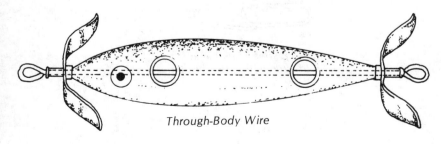
Through-Body Wire

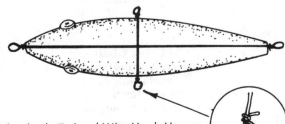
Thru-body Twisted Wire Hook Hanger. Thru-body Twisted Wire Line Tie and Trailing Hook Hanger.

107

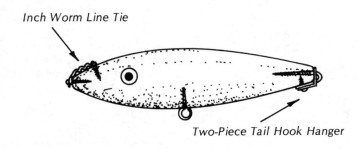

Inch Worm Line Tie

Two-Piece Tail Hook Hanger

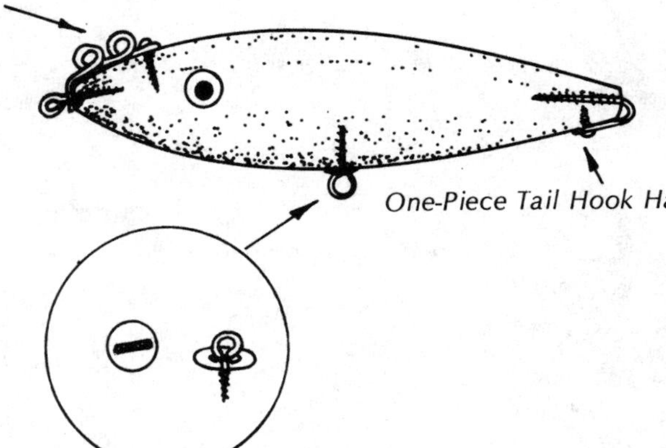

Pig Tail Line Tie

One-Piece Tail Hook Hanger

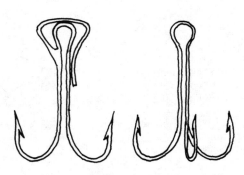

Detail of the Screw Eye and Washer style hook hanger

Heddon's patented Dummy Double detachable double hook

F. C. Woods patented detachable double and treble hooks

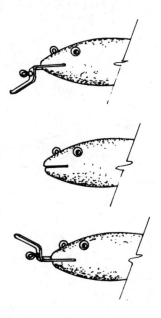

The Creek Chub convertible metal lip, three choices and two line tie options

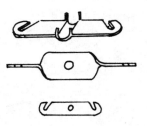

Three styles of plate hardware used in See-through Plate Hook Hangers.

Gem Clip style hook hanger. Usually utilized with a see-thru type.

ANATOMY OF A LURE
AND ITS COMPONENTS

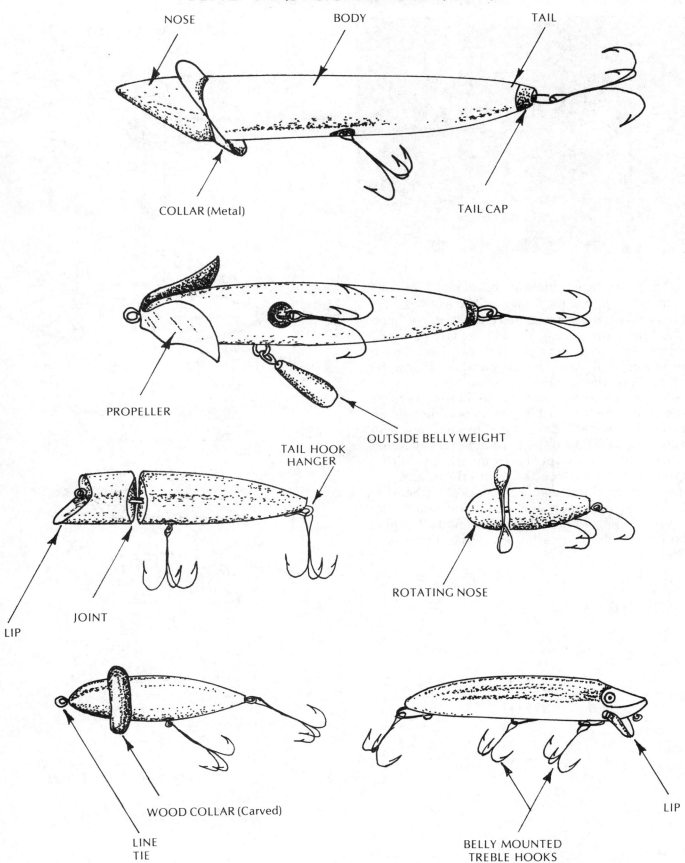

NOSE

BODY

TAIL

COLLAR (Metal)

TAIL CAP

PROPELLER

OUTSIDE BELLY WEIGHT

TAIL HOOK
HANGER

LIP

JOINT

ROTATING NOSE

WOOD COLLAR (Carved)

LINE
TIE

BELLY MOUNTED
TREBLE HOOKS

LIP

"A-B-C" MINNOW

George W. Bolton   **Detroit, Michigan**

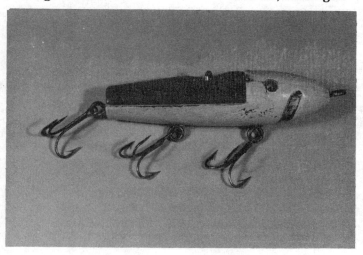

Dec. 18, 1923.   1,477,864

G. W. BOLTON

ARTIFICIAL BAIT

Filed Nov. 29, 1920

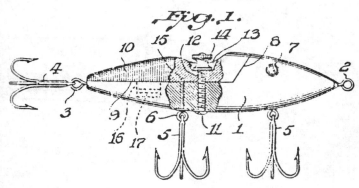

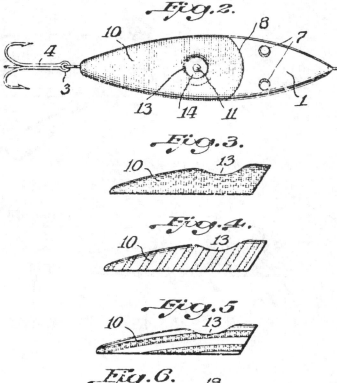

There are two models of this clever lure. Each has interchangeable back pieces. The available colors were black, white, red, green and silver. The photo of the single lure here is No. 100. As you can see it has a carved mouth and a pointed nose. Not very evident in the photo are glass eyes and cup/screw eye hook hangers. The accompanying illustration is of the patent granted to Bolton in December of 1923. As you can see, neither of the production models are exactly like the patent drawing. They are, however, close enough that the patent protected them. No patent models have as yet shown up. That would be a treasure indeed. Note the knurled nut and bolt fastener for the removeable backs used rather than the screw eye fastener on the production models. Collector value range: $40 to $80 with all parts. The glass eyed model will bring a bit more than the eyeless model.

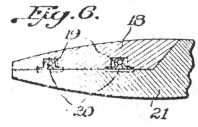

The A-B-C Minnow Patent Drawing

ABBEY AND IMBRIE FISHING TACKLE

This famous New York company was in active business long before they began to market fishing tackle to any great degree. If you examine ads and tackle catalogs with any knowledge of the old plugs from other companies you will find striking similarities. In fact it has been established that the company had many well known lure manufacturers to make their products with the Abbey & Imbrie imprint.

The photo of the lure with its original box here is a good example of this. It is no doubt a lure made by J. K. Rush (Rush Tango). The box is labeled "Go-Getter", but there is no identifying imprint anywhere on the plug itself. Collector value range: $2-4.00. I can't say with any sure evidence at this time that they ever actually manufactured lures themselves, but my inclination is to doubt it. The company was established in 1820 and earliest advertisements uncovered so far, that include lures, date in the mid to late 1880's.

ABBEY AND IMBRIE
MADE BY HEDDON

The lures in the following three photos are known to have been made by Heddon but marketed by A and I under their own names. What is not presently known is what those names were. Almost all the Heddon manufactured A and I lures will have "Abbey & Imbrie" stenciled on the belly. When fitted with metal plates, propeller spinners or diving lips they will have the same imprinted in place of the "Heddon Dowagiac" imprint.

The upper lure here is derived from a Heddon BASSER. It has no eyes and has the Heddon L-rig line tie. Collector value range: $10 to $30

This 3-7/8" glass-eyed A & I lure was made by Heddon utilizing their #140 FLIPPER body. The A & I version has the L-rigged hooks mounted on the side rather than the belly as Heddon did. Both the propeller spinners are marked with the Abbey & Imbrie imprint. Collector value range: $20 to $40

An A & I lure based on the Heddon TRIPLE TEASE. The metal minnow flippers are each imprinted with "Abbey & Imbrie." The center flipper is missing on this particular lure. Collector value range: $5 to $15

The "GLOWBODY" Minnow

This dandy was introduced in 1920. It has nickel plated hardware made so that the changing of hooks is made easy. The body is a glass tube with a smaller tube inside that is coated with a luminous material so that it could be fished at night. Length is about 3½ inches and the collector value range is $20 to $40.

HIAWATHA Wooden Minnow

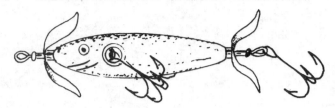

A 1914 Abbey and Imbrie catalog illustrates this plug as available in two sizes and hook configurations. Both sizes have nose and tail propeller. The smaller size had a side treble on each side of the body and a trailing treble (3T). The larger had two more side trebles (5T), these baits are remarkably similar to Heddons No. 100 and No. 150. They may have been made by Heddon for A & I. Collector value range: $4.00 to $8.00.

CATALOG SERIES #	BODY LENGTH	LURE WEIGHT	HOOKS
1100	2½"	3/4 oz.	3T
1150	3½"	1 oz.	5T

COLOR OR FINISH: *Fancy back; Rainbow; Solid White; Solid red; Blended green; Yellow perch.*

The OCTOPUS Wooden Minnows

These plugs were first observed in a 1911 catalog as available in two sizes: The No. 1 was 3½" long and had a pair of trebles on each side and a trailing treble (5T); the No. 2 was 2½" long and had only one treble on each side and a trailing treble (3T). Each sported nose and tail propeller spinner. Collector value range is from: $10 to $20.

CRIPPLED MINNOW

Some time in the 1920's this plug became available. It was wood and shaped somewhat like a minnow with a realistic tail fin shape. It had one left side mounted treble and left mounted trailing tail treble (2T). Collector value range: $6 to $14..

CATALOG SERIES #	BODY LENGTH	LURE WEIGHT
3400	4"	3/4 oz.

COLOR OR FINISH: *White with red head, Silver scale finish, Frog finish.*

MINNEHAHA Wood Minnow

In 1914 A & I marketed this plug in one size, three colors, and two hook configurations. They had one nose mounted propeller, one double or treble hook on each side and one trailing double or treble hook (3T or 3D). Collector value range: $8 to $16.

CATALOG SERIES #	BODY LENGTH	LURE WEIGHT
1100	2½"	

COLOR OR FINISH: *Red back, white belly; green back, white belly; Yellow back, white belly.*

MOUSE

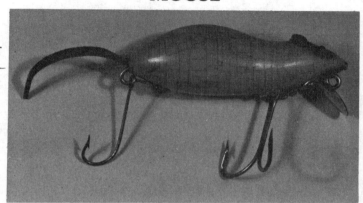

This is an A & I mouse lure made by Heddon from their MEADOW MOUSE design. The metal lip on this lure is imprinted "Abbey & Imbrie." It has black bead eyes, leather ears and tail and sports and L-rig belly hook hanger and the Heddon one-piece short loop (Stolley patent) tail hanger. It measures 2¾ without the tail. Collector value range: $4 to $10.

COLOR OR FINISH: *Gray mouse color, white body with red blush around eyes and chin.*

BASS-CATCHER

This is a 1920's vintage plug with a sloped nose and 1" wire leaded attached. It had one belly treble and a trailing treble hook (2T). Collector value range: $4 to $10.

CATALOG SERIES #	BODY LENGTH	LURE WEIGHT
2700	3½"	1 oz.

COLOR OR FINISH: *White with red head; Gold scale finish; Silver with red head.*

ASTRA WOOD MINNOW

This plug, circa 1925, came in only one color, white body with red head. It was 2½" long and weighed 1/4 ounce. It had one trailing double hook. Collector value range: $4 to $8.

CLEARWATER WOOD MINNOW

This plug was first marketed sometime around the 1920's It had a belly treble and trailing treble and was available in four color combinations. They are: White with red head; yellow with red head; red with black head; and white with blue head. Collector value range: $2 to $5.

WHIPPET

This lure first came along in 1929. It had a nose and tail mounted propeller, a belly treble and trailing treble hook (2T). Collector value range: $2 to $5.

CATALOG SERIES #	BODY LENGTH	LURE WEIGHT
2400	4"	5/8 oz.

COLOR OR FINISH: *White with red head; Gold, scale finish; Perch finish.*

FLASH-HEAD WOBBLER

This deep water plug was first put in the line about 1929. It had a nickel plated metal head, a wire leader, belly mounted and trailing treble hooks (2T). Collector value range is from: $4 to $10.

CATALOG SERIES #	BODY LENGTH	LURE WEIGHT
3700	3½"	1 oz.

COLOR OR FINISH: *Gold scale finish; Frog finish.*

WHIRLING CHUB

First found in late 1920's catalogs this is a minnow shaped plug with a nose propeller. It had one belly treble and a trailing treble hook (2T). Collector value range: $4 to $10.

CATALOG SERIES #	BODY LENGTH	LURE WEIGHT
3200	4½"	1 oz.

COLOR OR FINISH: *White with red head; Silver scale finish; Frog finish.*

EZY-KATCH WOOD MINNOW

This late 1920's plug was available in two distinctly different body designs even though both bore the same catalog number (No. 50). They were available to dealers in six plug counter display boxes (3 of each type). Colors were assorted. One style was more or less tear drop shaped with a nose propeller, belly treble and trailing treble (2T) and 3½" long. The other Ezy-Katch minnows were made by Heddon. The lure is actually a Heddon VAMP series plug. The two in the photo here have the Abbey & Imbrie imprint on the metal diving lips, glass eyes, L-rigs and the Heddon (Stolley patent) drop loop tail hook hangers. Collector value range: $2 to $5

"JIGOLET"
Tony Accetta, Cleveland Ohio

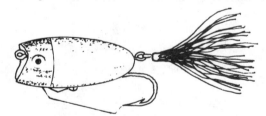

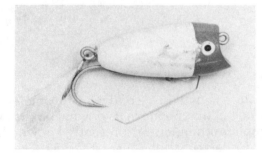

This was a circa 1941 2¾" Tenite plug with a single belly hook rigged snagless. The tail trailed a wiggling skirt and the head was concave vertically. Collector value range: $2 to $5.

ACTION LURE
Action Lure
Hollywood, California

Billed as the "WORLD'S FIRST SELF-PROPELLED LURE!", this crazy contraption was chemically propelled by the combination of a "blue pellet" and a "white pellet" in the "fuel tank", and apparently water. The plug was supposed to emit a buzzing sound while swimming ". . .various depths to 15 feet for up to one hour or more. . ." One can ony guess at its effectiveness. Collector value range: $2 to $4.

ALCOE MAGIC MINNOW No.401
Alcoe Lure Company
Fern Park, Florida

This lure is made of wood with flexible dorsal, ventral and tail fins. Found in its original box as in the photograph, nothing else is presently known about this lure. Collector value range: $3 to $8.

FRANKLIN A. ALGER
(1862-1940)
Grand Rapids, Michigan

Franklin A. Alger was a sportsman and an extraordinary craftsman/inventor. Besides making lures he also carved and painted bird decoys, made split bamboo rod and gun stocks. He fashioned his lure bodies on a lathe he made from a foot-operated treadle type sewing machine and his metal spinners were stamped out on a small home made hand-operated apparatus. He must have been an inveterate tinkerer for it is said that he designed and made over fifty styles of lures. I have seen photos of over forty of these myself. Few of these, however, were ever patented and marketed in any quantity as far as is presently known.

I am truly indebted to Clarence Zahn of Ann Arbor, Michigan for providing the aforementioned photographs many of which will appear following. Space constraints did not permit me to use all of them, but what is here is representative. Mr. Zahn was fortunate enough to have acquired Alger's personal tackle box after his death. It is those lures that appear in these photographs. These lures serve well to illustrate Alger's tremendous versatility and inventiveness in style and function. There really are no constants, no rules for identifying his products because of his versatility. There are a few things that appear from time to time and I will point these out as we go along. Just don't take them for gospel. He was apparently forever modifying his lures and their hardware.

Although it is thought that he made most of his lures for his own and friend's use, he must have had some commercial aspirations. He took the time and trouble to obtain patents on at least two of his lures. The only actual patent papers I was able to lay my hands on were filed in 1909 and the patent was granted to him on May 3, 1910.

This is the lure that is in the patent illustration. The name is unknown. It has yellow glass eyes, measures 3¼" long and has a small metal ventral fin. The hardware is brass. At present this is the only known example. Collector value range: $200 to $400.

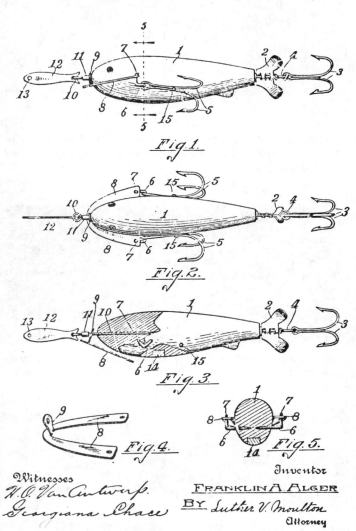

F. A. ALGER.
FISH BAIT.
APPLICATION FILED APR. 26, 1909.

956,872.

Patented May 3, 1910.

Fig.1.

Fig.2.

Fig.3.

Fig.4.   *Fig.5.*

Witnesses
N. O. VanAntwerp.
Georgiana Chase

Inventor
FRANKLIN A. ALGER
BY Luther V. Moulton
Attorney

Three GETSEMS from Alger's personal tackle box. Left to right: spatter finish, frog finish and then flowers. We can only speculate on the reason for the flowers. Perhaps it was to please a visitor to his workshop. Collector value range: $100 to $300.

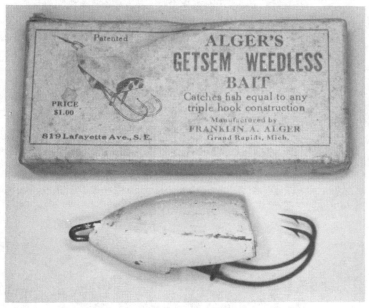

This lure with the printed box is evidence that Alger manufactured and marketed the GETSEM before Hastings Sporting Goods Works acquired the rights. $200 to $400.

These two lures are from Alger's personal tackle box. Note the unique reinforced propeller spinners on the bottom plug and the hook hanger/guard hardware. It is obvious from the wear that Alger used these two quite a bit. The years have taken their toll on the paint jobs.

(cont'd. next page)

ALGER'S GETSEM

This particular lure apparently gained in popularity and success because shortly after Alger began selling it, he and Hastings Sporting Goods Works came to some agreement giving them the rights to the patent. If you will turn to page 204 you will find more photographs and a detailed discussion of this unique Alger lure. Collector value range: $30 to $60

Another TANTALIZER, but this one is unusual with recessed, flattened glass eyes and propeller spinners reinforced with soldered twisted wire blade braces. Collector value range: $100 to $300.

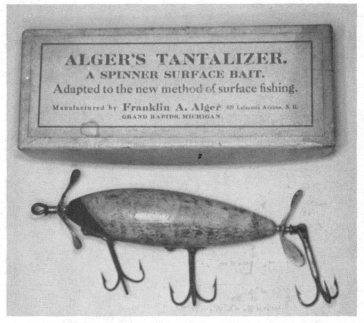

Another lure that was obviously manufactured and marketed by Alger as evidenced by the printed lure box. This 3½" plug has crude L-rig style hook hangers and no eyes. Collector value range: $100 to $300.

This spinner bait made by Alger plainly shows the spinner blade made and used by Alger on numerous of his lures. Collector value range: $40 to $80.

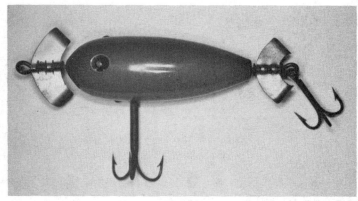

This is a small, 2-5/8", floating lure with recessed glass eyes. It clearly shows the often used Alger spinner. Collector value range: $100 to $300.

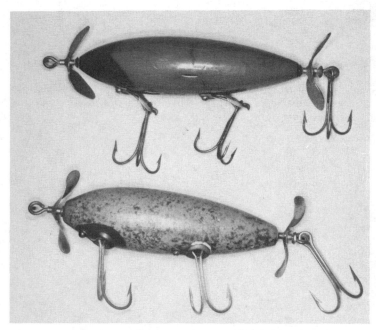

Two more TANTALIZERS. The upper lure has hold away hook hangers (designed to hold the hook away from the lure body). Lower lure illustrates the L-rig style used often by Alger. Collector value range: $100 to $300.

I strongly suspect this is a one-of-a-kind or prototype lure. It just doesn't have the polish of a production lure. It measures 3¼", has a metal lip and a grooved head to make it dive upon retrieve. It also has the GETSEM external belly weight and stand away hook hangers. Collector value range: $100 to $300.

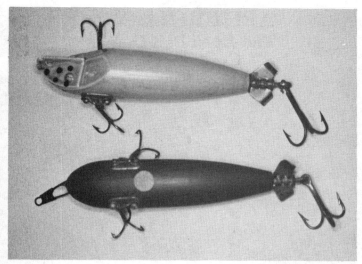

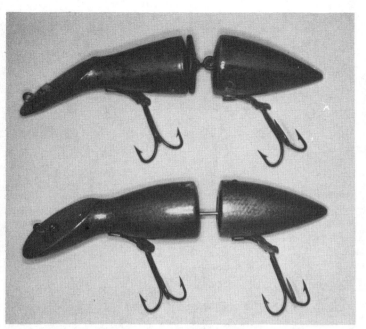

These 3½" no eyed lures (top and bottom view) have the Alger spinners at the tail and an unusual head plate incorporated the line tie. They have internal belly weights (see unpainted lure at bottom) and side hook hangers made by twisting wire and screwing it to the body with two screws through a metal backing plate. This is frequently found on Alger lures. Collector value range: $100 to $300.

Two jointed TANGO type lures with the stand away hook hanger. They each measure 5¼" in length. Collector value range: $100 to $300.

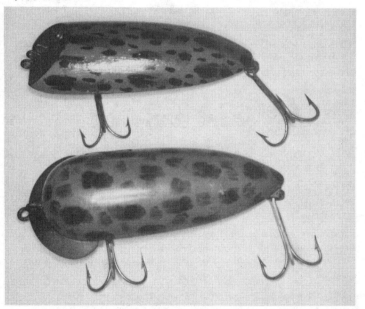

These two lures have chambers containing metal balls or shot attached to the belly. They could be the first of the rattle baits. They measure 3-5/8" and 2-5/8" respectively. Collector value range: $100 to $300.

Two flat belly Alger lures. The upper is 3½" long, has an Inch Worm style line tie and a slant head. The lower lure measures 3¾", has a metal diving lip and two line ties. Both have stand away belly hook hangers and very curious tail hook hangers. See next photo for details of this. Collector value range: $100 to $300.

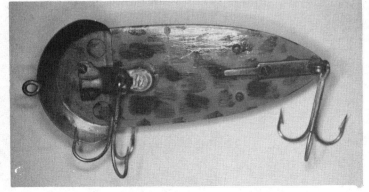

An Alger bug-type lure measuring 2¾". The legs are made of metal and there are two line ties. Collector value range: $100 to $300

A belly view of the lower lure in the last photograph. It shows the stand away belly hook hardware and the tail hook hanger. The metal strip is installed with the screw so that the whole strip can swing from side to side. Collector value range: $100 to $300.

A double ended by Alger. It is 3½" long and is designed to run underwater or topwater depending upon which end you tie your line to. Collector value range: $100 to $300

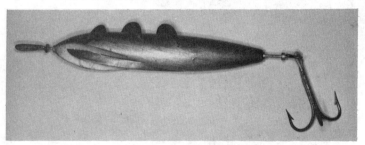

This lure has an unusual U-shaped heavy metal wire around its nose on which a line tie slides. Note the odd single round blade spinner at the tail. Collector value range: $100 to $300

A 4" lure with fins set into the body so as to make it spiral or revolve around the through-body wire armature on retrieve. Green, white and red in colors. Collector value range: $100 to $300.

This double jointed Alger lure is painted in a red and white candy cane style. It measures 3-1/8" long. Collector value range: $100 to $300

APEX BULL NOSE
The Apex Bait Company
Chicago, Illinois

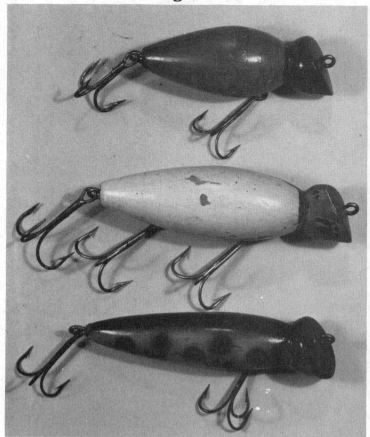

These Apex BULL NOSE lures measure 3", 4" and 3-7/8" from top to bottom. The upper two have washer and screw eye type hook hangers and the lower has the cup and screw eye hardware.

The earliest advertisement I was able to find for the BULL NOSE was in a March 1916 issue of *The Outers Book,* but it is reported to have been seen advertised as early as 1913. The 1916 ad pictured the large lure in the accompanying photo and noted the availability of a smaller one (APEX JR.). Both have screw eye and washer type hook hangers. The colors were white with red head, yellow with red head. The ad also mentioned an APEX UNDERWATER available in white or yellow with red head or a green back version with green or yellow spots.

There is another lure extremely similar to the BULL NOSE called the ALGONAC SNEAK BAC. It was illustrated in an ad placed in 1921 by the Eckfield Boat Company of Algonac, Michigan. The one in the ad seems to have a more narrow neck and slightly smaller head. I have never actually seen one so it may be easily distinguishable from the BULL NOSE. In any case be on the look out. Collector value range for the APEX BULL NOSE: $30 to $50.

DIVING DOODLE BUG
c1960
Aqua Sport Inc.
Noble Arkansas

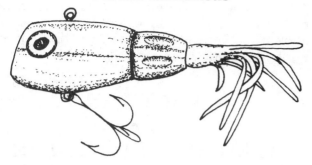

This crazy plug had provision for inserting a "Power Tab" to make it move erratically. Apparently it was caused by a chemical reaction between the tablet and water. It had one belly treble and a trailing rubber wiggler skirt, 2½" long. Collector value range: $2 to $4.

FRED ARBOGAST BAITS

Three plain Tin Liz lures.

Left to right: Tin Liz Twin, #3 Hawaiian Weedless Wiggler, Plain Tin Liz, #3 Hawaiian Weedless Wiggler with spinner, #1 Hawaiian Wiggler Single Spinner.

Earliest Sputter Fuss'es had hand made spinner blades and a three-corner wire armature as shown here. Bottom is earliest manufactured.

Until recently most collectors have thought that the Arbogast Company was founded in 1930. It is known he was in business as early as 1926. There is an advertisement for "FRED ARBOGAST'S Spin-tail Kicker" in the June, 1926 issue of *Hunting & Fishing* magazine, therefore one can deduct that he might have been active in business some time before that. Some place the date around 1924.

His most important contributions to the development of the artificial lure are the invention of the rubber "Hula Skirt" and the famous "Jitterbug." In fact the "Jitterbug" was selected by *Popular Mechanics* magazine a few years ago as one of the all-time classic fishing lures in America. We all know of the widespread use of the rubber skirt today of course, mostly made synthetic materials. He filed his patent for the skirt in mid 1938 and it was granted him August 8, 1939.

The earliest Arbogast lures were mostly metal, with wood coming along in the 1930's. The original wood lures were made of aromatic cedar.

Fred Arbogast died in 1947, but the Fred Arbogast Company, Inc. is still going strong in Akron, Ohio today. In 1980 they brought out "...a limited edition collector's replica of the original, classic, cedar Musky Jiggerbug."*

*From an Arbogast ad in the Sept./Oct. issue of Rod and Reel magazine.

TIN LIZ

In the first edition of this book I reported the Tin Liz was the first lure to be marketed by the company. This statement can no longer be made with authority. I have now found a catalog listing for the Tin Liz in a 1928 issue of a Shapliegh Hardware Company catalog. The entry illustrated the lure with a tear drop shaped spoon-type spinner attached to the hook with a swivel. It was then available in only two colors: natural chub finish and silver with a red head. I believe this to be the earlier version, for all subsequent ads and catalogs found so far show the more commonly found life-like fluted tail fins attached to the lure's hook.

In the first years of production the lure sported glass eyes with the subsequent ones having painted eyes. All were made of metal and had a single hook with the trailing fin tail attached. There were several versions made available after the initial plain Tin Liz. They are all listed following, with photo when available. Collector value range: $4 to $20.

NAME	LURE WEIGHT
Plain Tin Liz, c1924	½ oz., 5/8 oz., 1 oz.
COLOR OR FINISH: Chub finish; Perch finish; Red Head.	
Weedless Tin Liz	5/8 oz.
COLOR OR FINISH: Perch finish; Red Head.	
**Tin Liz Sunfish	½ oz., 5/8 oz.
COLOR OR FINISH: Sunfish finish.	
Tin Liz Snake	5/8 oz.
COLOR OR FINISH: Pike finish.	
Flyrod Tin Liz	1/64 oz., 1/32 oz., 1/16 oz.
Twin Liz Twins	5/8 oz.

WEEDLESS KICKER

Early Weedless Kicker, c1926

**Available in plain or weedless version.

First called the "Weedless Spin-tail Kicker" in ads, the earliest advertisement found so far was in a June, 1926 issue of *Hunting and Fishing* magazine. The ad stated they were available in two sizes, ½ oz. and 5/8 oz. They had glass eyes, a single hook, fancy feathers and a free, flipping tail fin attached to the hook. They were available in a Frog finish or Silver finish. Collector value range: $10 to $20.

WIGGLER or HAWAIIAN WIGGLER

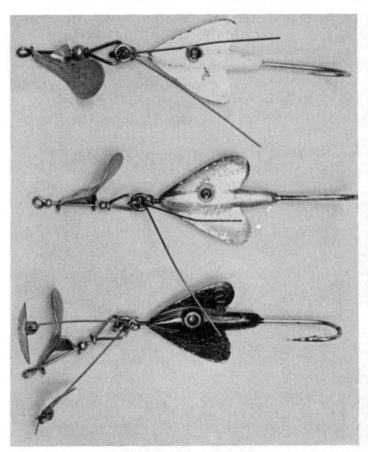

Various Hawaiian Wigglers.

New about 1930, this famous lure was preceded by the Al Foss Shimmy Wiggler (c1918) which had a bucktail attached to the hook. Along came Arbogast's wiggler, quite similar. He then patented the rubber skirt, hung it on the hook and thus was born the Hawaiian Wiggler. He used this skirt on various other of his lures and because of his patent, he had an exclusive on its use for many years. Collector value range: $2 to $5.

JITTERBUG

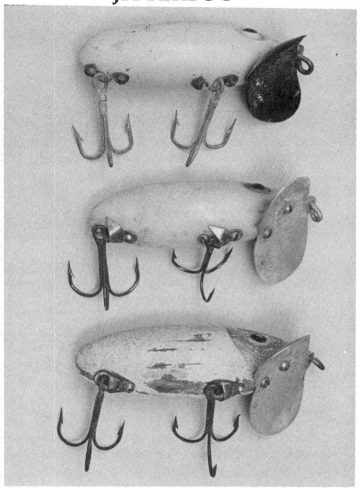

Perhaps one of the most famous of the Arbogast lures it was first introduced to the fisherman about 1937. It was first patented on July 9, 1940. The first Jitterbugs were made of cedar and initially had glass eyes. None in the photograph here have glass eyes. The bottom lure in the photo is made of wood. The name was derived from the dance craze of the time. The upper plug in the photo has a plastic nose blade. This was done because of the metal shortage during WW II. The plastic blades lacked the weight of the metal ones and the resulting plug did not perform as well as the other.

The story of the origin of the Jitterbug is interesting. It seems that Arbogast whittled a plug out of a piece of broomstick in the early 1920's, attached a spoon to the nose crosswise in an attempt to make a deep diving lure. It was a miserable failure gyrating wildly out of control on retrieve. As the story goes he chunked it in a drawer at home only to have it found during the visit of an old friend in 1934. Asked what it was, Arbogast said it was an underwater plug that didn't work. The two of them fooled around with it eventually coming up with the Jitterbug.

Today there are nine different models and sizes available including a jointed version.
Collector value range for metal lip, wooden Jitterbugs: $5 to $10.
Collector value range for plastic and metal lips, plastic Jitterbugs: $2 to $4.

HULA POPPER

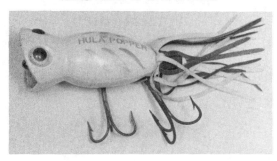

This lure was never manufactured in wood, only plastic, and it was introduced by Arbogast in 1948. However, it is known that Brooke Ortell, a consultant to Arbogast, whittled up to a possible one hundred models before he and Arbogast finally settled on the production design. These prototypes were carved from white poplar and it is reasonable to assume that toward the end of this prodigious effort, there were a few that came close to the final product. Whether or not any of these have made their way out of company hands isn't known. If any have landed in a collectors hands, he possesses a true gem.

The original plastic Hula Poppers were made in only one size, a casting weight for bass. They now come in four sizes from the smallest 3/16 ounce to the largest, 5/6 ounce. Collector value range for the earliest Hula Poppers: $2 to $3.

Right: Arbo-Gaster. Left: Hula Diver. Collector value range $2 to $3.

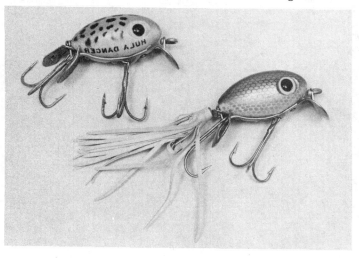

Hula Dancers. Collector value range $2 to $3.

121

UBANGI c 1955
Forrest Allen
Stamford, Connecticut

A small stubby plastic plug with a belly treble hook and a long deep diving lip blade. Collector value range: $2 to $4.

GEE-WIZ FROG LURE
c1931
All Star Bait Co., Chicago

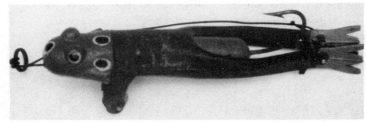

Another of the many attempts at animated frogs. It had one single hook mounted on the belly with the barb portion pointed up and between the legs. Probably pretty effective at being weedless. Collector value range: $4 to $8.

BASS BIRD c1946
J. J. Gill and Associates
Huntington Park, California

Found in its original box, little is known about this metal lure. The illustration on the box is of a two-hooker. The lure in the photo is missing the tail hook. Collector value range: $5 to $10.

This lure measures 2½". It is not known what the name is if any. It is placed here because the front half (spinning portion) is precisely the same as the BASS BIRD above. Collector value range: $5 to $10.

BASS CALLER
Detroit Bait Company
Detroit, Michigan

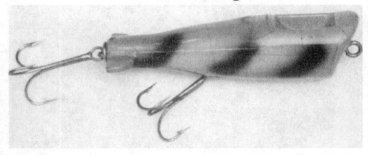

This topwater popper type lure has an interesting innovation. It has a scoop-out on top of its head that the company called a "vacuum cup" in a 1940 advertisement. It isn't too clear in the photograph here, but the tail end sports a pair of aircraft type tail planes that are part of the body, not attached or made of metal. Body length is 3½". Colors: red, green, cream, red head and luminous. Collector value range: $5 to $15.

BASS HOG
T. J. Boulton
Detroit, Michigan

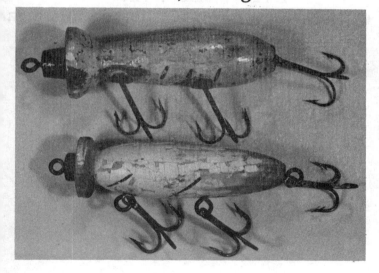

This lure was first found referenced in a 1911 publication. The upper lure is 4½" long and painted white with a red head and red stripes and dots on the belly. It has cup and screw eye hardware with a reinforcing metal tail insert. The lower lure is suspected to be a later model of the Bass Hog although this is not yet substantiated. It is 3-7/8" long, has screw eye only (no cup) hook hanger hardware and three gill marks as opposed to four found on the smaller, known Bass Hog. Collector value range: $15 to $35.

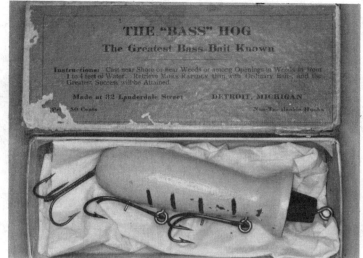

BASS HOG

BASS KING
National Bait Company
Stillwater Minnesota

These c1927 lures came in two sizes, 3" and 3½". They were white bodied with red heads and are usually found with cup and screw eye hardware. There are three flutes, one on either side and the third on the top.

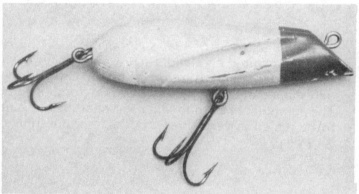

This is thought to be the earliest version of the BASS KING. Note that the flute on the body side is slanted down from the nose. It utilized the simple screw eye hardware. Collector value range: $15 to $25.

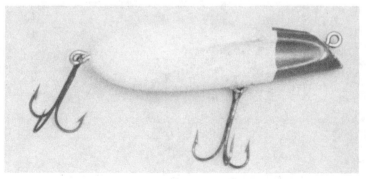

A later model BASS KING with cup and screw eye hardware and non-slanted flutes. Collector value range: $10 to $20.

123

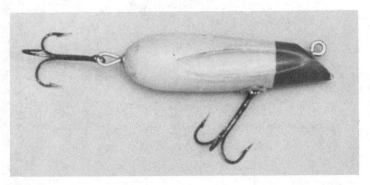

BASS KING JR. with cup and screw eye hardware. Collector value range: $10 to $20.

BASS KING
Red and Green Tackle Company
Detroit Michigan

Thought to be of 1940's vintage, this 2¾" lure has tack painted eyes and a screw eye/washer belly hook hanger. There is a protecting tail cap and the odd shaped diving lip has a cotter key for a line tie. The pamphlet in the box said it is a near surface bait to be reeled in very slowly. Collector value range: $5 to $10.

BERRY-LEBECK MFG. CO.,
California, Missouri

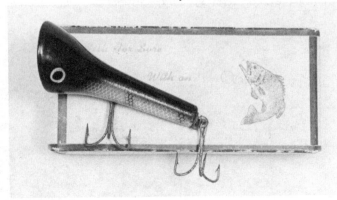

The two plugs pictured here are all the author was able to find from this company. There is no doubt there are others to be found. This Missouri Company sold their plugs under the brand name "OZARK LURES." These two are wooden and were in the original boxes. The upper plug is a TALKIE TOPPER (c1947) and the other is not identified as to name or number. The one advertisement found, said the Talkie Topper was available in 12 colors but did not list them. Collector value range: $2 to $3.

BIDWELL BAIT
Clifford W. Bidwell Kalamazoo, Michigan

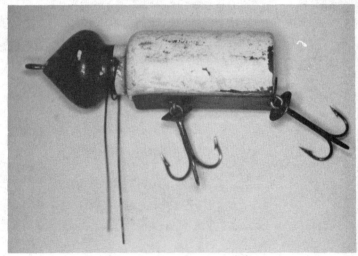

The name "Bidwell Bait" above is used by collectors to identify it. Not yet found in a box, advertising or any other identifying literature, we have no name for it. We do have a patent, however, so we do know that there was at least a serious intent at producing them in quantity. We also know that it's a rare one that's hard to find so it may have never gone into large scale production. The patent was granted to Bidwell in 1915 and the one in the photo accompanying is a match to the patent illustration. Take note of the brass plate on the bottom of and extending slightly up the tail. Also take note of the large brass washer-like hook preventers attached to the hooks. These appear in the patent, but several

124

lures have surfaced without these two features. It is speculated widely that they may have discontinued making them with the plate and preventers as a means of reducing manufacturing costs. It measures 3½″ in length. Collector value range: $60 to $150.

BIFF BAIT COMPANY
Albert R. Bayer   Milwaukee, WI

It is known that this company was doing business during the 1920's from catalog references. However the dates before and after are not presently known to the author.

THE MASTER BIFF PLUG c1926*

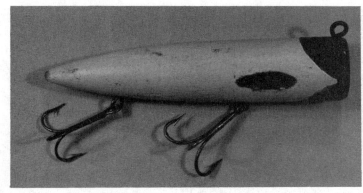

This 4½″ Biff plug was not found cataloged anywhere. It is placed here because of its similarity to the MASTER BIFF PLUG. It may turn out to have a separate identity.

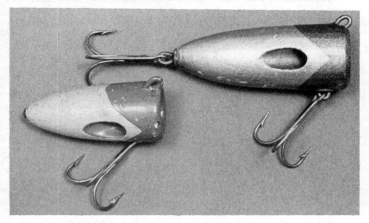

The upper right lure is a 2½″ MASTER BIFF PLUG. The lower lure is actually a 2″ WHOPPEE BIFF.

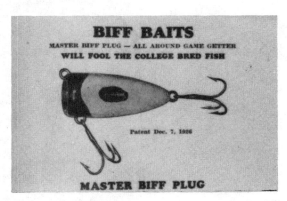

This lure was a "Water sonic" type, that is a plug with hole or holes to admit water at one point and expell it at the other end. It was cataloged as made in 2½″ and 2″ lengths but there is also a 4½″ known. It has a treble mounted under the head and a trailing treble hook on the 2½″ size. There are two color combinations to be found: red head with white body; copper color head with aluminum color body; Natural perch finish. Collector value range: $10 to $20.

SPIRAL SPINNER

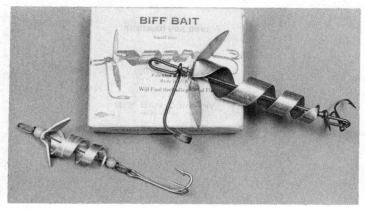

This lure was patented March 17, 1925 and marketed in two sizes, 2″ and 3″. The photo is of both sizes. Both were nickel plated brass and the interior of the spiral body was painted red. The larger size was also available in gold plate and brass. Collector value range: $10 to $20.

*Advertised in June issue of Hunting & Fishing magazine, page 20. Patent date on box is Dec. 7, 1926.

BASSEY BIFF SURFACE SINGLE WOBBLER

What a mouth full that is! The Bassey was patented December 22, 1925 but may have been available prior to that. Cork bodied mounted on aluminum plate, red beads at either end and a big counterweight at the nose, this plug was available in a swirling spattered type paint finish in green on white or red on white backgrounds. A double body version of the same lure was also available. Collector value range of each: $10 to $20.

Biff Single Wobbler. From a pocket catalog page, c1925.

Biff Double Wobbler. From a pocket catalog page, c1925.

GODEVIL BIFF

Patented December 22, 1925 this little devil was available in two colors, red and white swirled as in the photo and the same in green and white. It measures 1'' long. Collector value range: $10 to $20.

BING'S NEMAHBIN WEEDLESS MINNOW
A. F. Bingenheimer
Milwaukee, Wisconsin

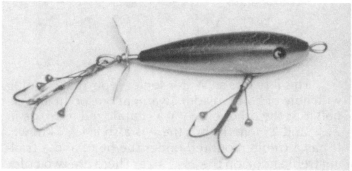

These particular plugs can be placed as early as 1905. An ad in a tackle dealers periodical of that year touts the lure as being "A NEW BAIT". The company can be found advertising tackle earlier, but not the Nemahbin lure. The lures pictured here are not the earliest. They are, however, 1906 vintage and the most commonly found though all are rare. Earlier versions (as pictured in the 1905 ad) show the weedless wires with loops at the end that attach to the hook points. Those hooks are single point and rigidly attached to the body. They have been found with nose or tail mounted propellers on both. Finishes available were Gold, Silver, Metallic, Crackle back and Green back with red or white belly. All I have observed so far have had glass eyes and lengths vary from 4" to 6". The weedless treble hooks, like those in the phtographs here, apparently were quite successful, as they are seen offered on lures in catalogs from other well known companies. In the Nemahbin Minnows the hooks are attached utilizing the gem clip type fasteners to the thru-body wire. Collector value range: $75 to $150.

BITE-EM-BATE COMPANY
Warsaw, Indiana (1917)
Ft. Wayne, Indiana (1920)

The dates with the two company locations above represent the dates of periodicals in which their advertisements with the addresses appeared. The name of the company had changed a bit in the 1920 advertisement. The name is found two ways prior to that: "BITE-EM-BATE" and "BITE-EM-BAIT." The 1920 ad read: "BITE-EM-BAIT SALES COMPANY" and the address was Ft. Wayne.

The earliest Bite-Em lure patent I have found so far was applied for in mid-1921 and granted mid-1922. The patent was granted to Claude M. Rodgers and Arthur W. Wenger. Some think Bite-Em became Wenger Manufacturing Company in the mid-1920's. The Wenger name on the patent and the change in address may have something to do with that. Only time and additional data will tell. The latest ads I have found for Bite-Em were in 1920 publications.

BITE-EM-BATE

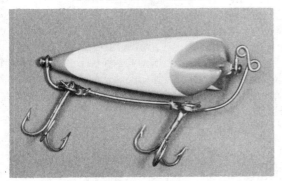

1920 Vintage Bite-Em-Bate, 2-7/8". Second style line tie.

This wooden plug was shaped so that it would rotate on retrieve. The body pivoted on an exterior wire half loop extending from the nose to the tail. The first (c1917) version had a treble hook attached to the wire loop and another attached directly to the tail end of the body. Later (c1920) the trailing treble was moved to the wire loop just beneath the tail. The method of hook attachment to the wire had also

changed by this point in time. It was available in seven different colors: White body, red head and red tail: Red body, white head; Gold body, red head and red tail; Aluminum body, red head and gold tail; Black body, white head and gold tail; Yellow body, red head and red tail; Choc. green, red head and red tail. Catalog entries state the size as 3½" overall length. Collector value range: $12 to $24.

LIPPED WIGGLER

It isn't obvious in the photo here, but the diving lip on this plug is adjustable enabling the fisherman to run it at the depth of his choice. Refer to the patent illustration reproduced here to find a clear illustration of this feature. The patent was granted in 1922. Hook hangers are a type of L-rig and the eyes are yellow glass. It was available with two or three treble hooks. Length of the one pictured is 3¾". Colors available are unknown. Collector value range: $15 to $30.

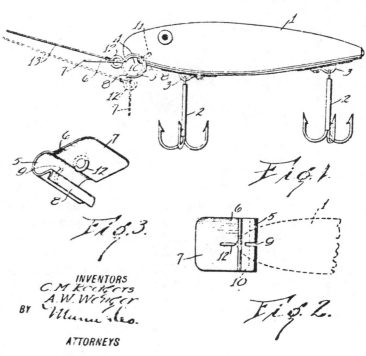

C. M. RODGERS AND A. W. WENGER.
CONTROLLER FOR FISH LURES.
APPLICATION FILED MAY 25, 1921.

1,423,025.   Patented July 18, 1922.

INVENTORS
C M Rodgers
A.W. Wenger
BY
ATTORNEYS

THE BITE-EM WATER-MOLE
c1920

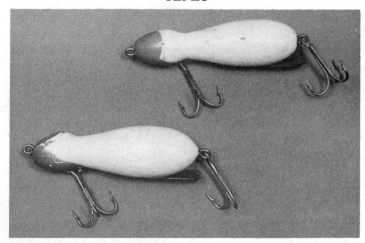

This 3" plug is shaped somewhat like a mole. As you can see in the photograph it is found with a round head or with a flattened head and slightly chubbier body (lower plug in photo). It is not presently known which version is the older. Though it has not so far been seen, a 1920 advertisement indicates the availability of this lure with a second line tie, ie. "...by tying the line in the upper line hitch...". It has a nickel-plated metal plate attached along the belly extending in a spoon shape slightly past the tail end. A treble hook is attached just aft of the head on the bottom and there is a trailing treble. Colors available were: White body, red head; White body, red head and red tail; Black body, white head and gold tail; Black body, red head and gold tail; Yellow body, red head and red tail; Yellow body, green head and green tail; Choc. green body, white and red head; Gold body, white and red head and red tail; Red body, white head; Aluminum body, red head and red tail. Collector value range: $15 to $30.

BITE-EM WIGGLER c1920

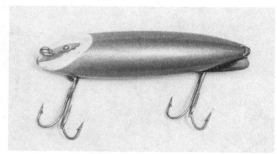

This is a 3-7/8" plug with a sloping head. It has a treble mounted beneath the nose and another under the tail. It has the same metal plate/spoon attachment as does the Bite-Em Water-Mole. The colors available were the same as for the Water Mole with the addition of Cream White. Collector value range: $15 to $30.

BITE-EM FLOATER MINNOW

This classic two propeller spinner floating lure was available in two sizes, 3" and 4" and has yellow glass eyes. Colors available are not known at present. Collector value range: $10 to $20.

BITE-EM BUG

Only one **illustrated** reference to this lure was found. The lure in the accompanying photograph is a genuine Bite-Em product, but differs from the one in the catalog illustration in some subtle and not-so-subtle ways. The catalog illustration shows a simple screw eye attachment of the trailing spoon, not as in the photo here. The body in the catalog is shaped slightly different and its paint design is simpler. It utilizes the same L-rig type hook hanger but is mounted in the opposite direction from the one in the photo. The available colors were: White body, red head; Black body, red and white head; Yellow body, red head; Choc. green body, white head; Roman gold body, red and white head; Red body, white head; Aluminum body, red head. Collector value range: $15 to $20.

BASS-ENTICER

This lure was reported as an unknown Bite-Em Bait product. We now know its name and the fact that it is actually a product of the Wenger Manufacturing Company of Warsaw also. We are still not sure which came first, Wenger or Bite-Em. Collector value range: $3 to 8.

BLEEDING BAIT MANUFACTURING COMPANY

This Dallas, Texas firm is known to have been doing business in the late 1930's, but the exact dates of existence are presently unknown to the author. All the plugs were designed with a receptacle hole and pivoting cover in which you placed a special tablet that stimulated the bleeding of a wounded bait fish when worked properly in the water. There were eight styles of lure and a hookless teaser. Some were available as a floater, diver or sinker making sixteen different plug types including the Teaser, for the collector to find. It would be a rare moment indeed to find a Bleedlure in the box with the vial of tablets for most are found without them. Each plug also came with detachable hook guards. The collector value range for all Bleedlures is from $10 to $20. They are listed in alphabetical order on the following pages.

THE B.P.S. 100

Made in floating, sinking and diving models, this plug is 4" long and weighs ¾ ounce. It has two side-by-side belly trebles and a trailing treble. This larger plug exhibits all the features of a Ranger though larger. A very poor photo copy of an old but undated ad shows a lure that appears to be the same as the one in this photo. We will tentatively ID this as the B.P.S. 100 until better evidence surfaces to confirm or discredit the assumption.

BROKEN BACK

This is a jointed lure weighing ¾ ounce and is 4" long. It has one belly treble mounted on the rear section and a trailing treble hook.

BUBBLER

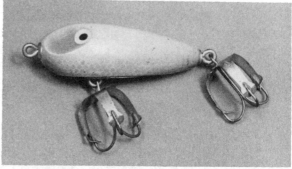

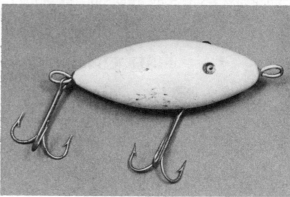

The lure on the top is a bubbler. The one on the bottom is interesting in that it has the bleeder feature, but was not found in catalogs or advertisements for the company. Could be a very early production lure or a prototype. Note that it has glass eyes, a feature not normally associated with the Bleeding Bait Company products. Painted eyes are the norm.

Available in floating (½ ounce) and sinking (5/8 ounce) models. Both plugs are 2-5/8" long. They each have one belly treble and a trailing treble hook.

CHUNKER

This plug has a notched mouth with the line tie in the roof of the mouth. It is 2¼" long and the weight is 5/8 ounce. It has one belly treble and a trailing treble hook. Note the unusual weedless features on the trailing treble hook. This is often found on Bleeding Baits.

(cont'd. next page)

DIDO

The Dido is a slow sinking plug weighing ½ ounce and 2-5/8" long. It was made with a belly treble and trailing treble hook only and a scooped out head where the line tie is located.

FISH KING

Made in diving, sinking or floating models, this lure is 2-7/8 ounces and 6¼" long. It sports three trebles, two belly mount and one trailing, and a metal lip blade.

MOUSE

This is a 2-5/8", ½ ounce mouse shaped plug complete with flexible tail. It had one belly treble and a trailing treble hook.

BONAFIDE ALUMINUM MINNOW

Bonafide Manufacturing Company
Plymouth, Michigan

Patented in 1907 by Hiram H. Passage with half the rights assigned to George E. Van de Car, this little gem was available in two sizes: a 3¾" 5-hooker and a 3¼" 3-hooker as in the accompanying photo. It is made in two halves of cast aluminum held together by a screw about mid-body. It is not solid but hollow allowing the fisherman to make it a floater or adjust bouyancy by adding water or other interior weight.

Note that there is a hole through the dorsal fin. This is to allow the lure to be used as an ice fishing decoy. The lures are rare and their Collector value range is as follows: The 3-hooker $100 to $300, the 5-hooker $200 to $600.

BRAINARD BAIT COMPANY
St. Paul, Minnesota

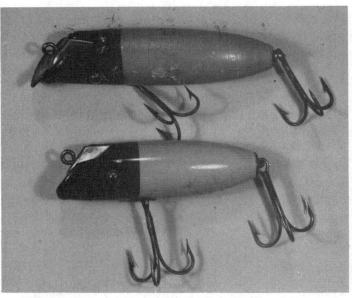

The lures in this photo are GOLD CUP DODGERS. The upper plug measures 3-3/8", has glass eyes and a screw eye only, belly hook hanger. The lower one is 2-7/8" long with yellow glass eyes and cup and screw eye hook hanger. It also has a different design metal head plate. Collector value range: $10 to $20.

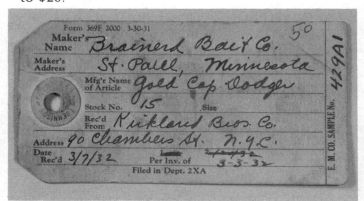

This photograph illustrates an interesting historical aside. It seems that everybody was watching everybody, with some even physically checking out the competition's products. The upper lure in the previous photo came from the Pflueger fctory with this tag attached. Not only did they obtain a competitor's lure for examination, but they actually tested it. The flip side of the tag indicated that the test took place five days after obtaining it. It bears the notation "Poor action. Bait turns over." It is initialed and dated by the tester and three witnesses. Collector value range: $10 to $20.

(cont'd next page)

W. H. GRUENHAGEN

PLUG BAIT WITH GROOVES

Filed Feb. 23, 1932

Oct. 31, 1933.   1,932,622

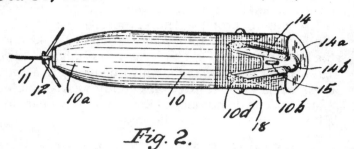

Fig. 2.

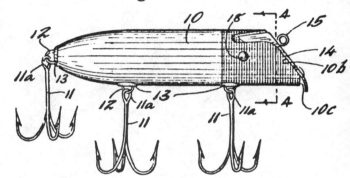

Fig 1.

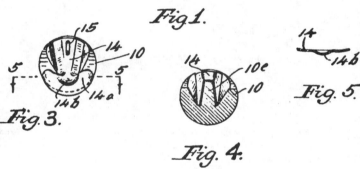

Fig. 3.

Fig. 4.

Fig. 5.

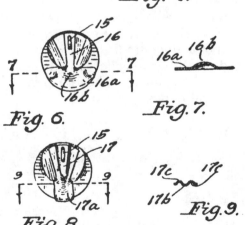

Fig. 6.

Fig. 7.

Fig. 8.

Fig. 9.

INVENTOR
WILLIAM H. GRUENHAGEN
BY *Reef & Braddock*
ATTORNEYS

This patent illustration shows two possible designs of the metal plane (see Fig. 6 and Fig. 8). That might explain the different planes on the preceding lures. The patent was granted to William H. Gruenhagen of St. Paul on October 31, 1933, but it was filed in February, 1932 so we can date it as early as that. It was likely in full production a good bit earlier than that.

BRIGHT-EYE-LURE
Bright-Eye-Lure Products
Detroit, Michigan

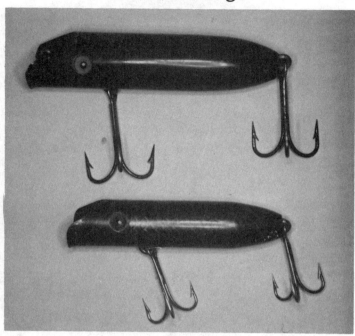

These lures are extremely unique and are also difficult to find. Their construction is what makes them so unusual. They are made of an aluminum shell around a wooden core. There are holes in the outer shell to accommodate the glass eyes so that they may be mounted in the wood portion of the body. The two in the photo measure 2¾" and 3¼" respectively. There is a third size, 4¼", also known to exist. They are thought to date around 1933, but little else is presently known. Collector value range: $10 to $30.

BROADCASTER LURES
Youngstown, Ohio

This plug, called the 4-IN-1 BROADCASTER, came along around 1933. A 1933 advertisement called it new in the text. The nose plane was adjustable so that the fisherman could change the lure into a deep diver, a wiggler, a darter or a surface teaser. Note that the metal plane is missing on the lower lure in the photo. The ones in the photograph measure 3½", but they also offered one in a 4½" length. Most are easily identifiable by the unusual nose plane and the peculiar belly hook hardware that makes hook exchange or replacement handy and the stamped or stenciled "4 IN 1 BROADCASTER" on the belly. The latter may or may not be readily discernible. The eyes are yellow glass. The color patterns offered are not known. Collector value range: $20 to $30.

BROOK'S BAITS
R-Jay Industries, Inc.
234 Portage Trail, Cuyahoga Falls, Ohio

A thorough search of the old catalogs and ads I have available turned up only four dated short references to Brook's. The earliest was a catalog thought to be dated somewhere around 1937-40, and the latest was found in *The Fisherman's Handbook For 1954*. The 1954 ad was the only one carrying an address (see above). It listed fifteen lures as available. As far as I can determine, all Brook's lures were molded of Tenite (plastic) or all metal.

BROOK'S No. 5 TOPWATER

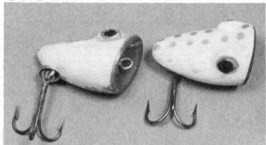

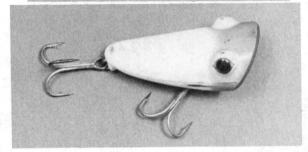

No references were found that corresponded with these two lures but their similarity to the #5 Topwater makes it likely that this is where they belong.

This is a ½ ounce popper type plug with concave mouth and bulging eyes. It is illustrated with a belly treble and a under-tail treble hook. It has been reported that it was available with single hooks as well. Colors available: Red head, Yellow, Frog, Scale. Collector value range: $2 to $4.

BROOK'S JOINTED TOPWATER

References turned up the following: Brook's Jointed Topwater, JTW Series; Baby Jointed Topwater also available. They came in six colors or finishes, but only four are known for sure. They are: Red head, Yellow, Frog and Scale finish. Collector value range: $2 to $4.

BROOK'S DOUBLE O and BROOK'S JOINTED DOUBLE O

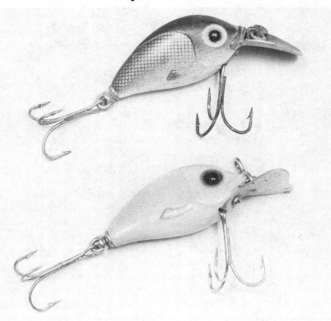

Note the two different styles lip on the Double O's in the photo.

These lures had a spoon type lip blade and a short wire leader attached to the nose mounted line tie. Each have a treble hook beneath the nose and another one trailing. Both weigh ½ ounce and the jointed model (see photo) has a tail-fin shaped second section. Collector value range: $2 to $4.

CATALOG SERIES #	BODY LENGTH	LURE WEIGHT
00	2½"	½ oz.
J-00	3⅓"	½ oz.

COLOR OR FINISH: *Red head, Black scale, Yellow Shad; Shiner; Perch; Pearl; Black dotted.*

BROOK'S NO. 6 REEFERS

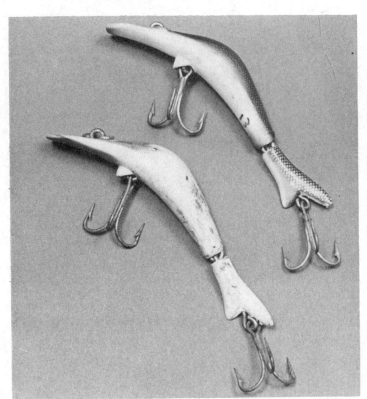

There are four types of Reefers to be found: The un-jointed Reefer and Baby Reefer, the Jointed Reefer and Baby Jointed Reefer. They were available in seven colors or finishes: Red head, Black scale, Yellow, Frog, Shiner, Perch and Pearl. Collector value range: $2 to $4.

BROOK'S JOINTED "DIGGER"

Identified in literature as Brook's Jointed "Digger", JO Series, ½ oz. Eight colors or finishes to be found: Red head, Black scale, Yellow, Shad, Shiner, Perch, Pearl and Black Dotted. Collector value range: $2 to $4.

BROOK'S NO. 4 WEEDLESS

This lure has a tail mounted single hook molded into the body during production. The hook is covered with a flexible rubber skirt and a wire weed guard extending back from the nose. There is a wire leaded that has a single blade spinner mounted on it. Collector value range: $2 to $4.

CATALOG SERIES #	BODY LENGTH	LURE WEIGHT
400	1¾"	5/8 oz.

COLOR OR FINISH: *Red head; Black scale; Yellow; Frog; Shiner; Perch.*

BROOK'S NO. 7 WEEDLESS

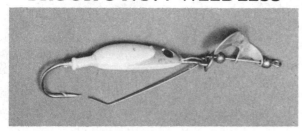

This is essentially the same lure as the Brook's No. 4 except smaller and lighter (½ ounce). It came in the same colors. Collector value range: $2 to $4.

UNIDENTIFIED BROOK'S LURE

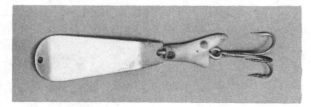

Of all the Brook's lures that were available to me for study and identification this is the only one that was left un-named. One of the ads I uncovered name some other as yet unfound Brook's lures and this one is likely to be one of them. They are listed following.

BROOK'S SPINNING NO. 5 TOPWATER
BROOK'S STUD SPINNER
BROOK'S JUMPER SPINNER
BROOK'S ¼ OZ. STRIPER JIG
BROOK'S PORK POD
BROOK'S NYLON LEADER (Bait)

This list is worded exactly as it was printed in the advertisement.

BROOK'S RANGER

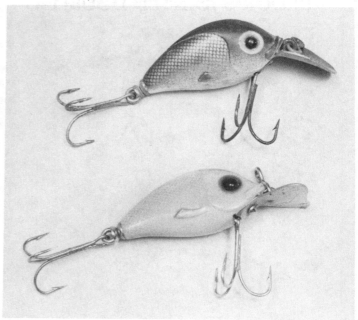

This lure was available in floating and diving models. Both weigh 5/8 ounce and are 2-5/8" long. There was also a BIG BOY RANGER that weighed ¾ ounce and was 4" long. Each had a belly treble, trailing treble hook and metal lip blade.

PAUL BUNYAN BAIT COMPANY
Minneapolis, Minnesota

This company made lures in the 1930's and 1940's. Little else is known presently concerning details of its existence. They manufactured and marketed several collectible plastic plugs, some wooden lures, and some metal spoon or spinner types.

FLOATING WEAVER

This plug had a series of grooves across the back of the body, a more or less flat belly and metal diving blade mounted under the nose. It sported one treble hook on the belly. The lure was 2¾" long and weighed 3/8 ounce. Colors available were white, pike scale, silver or yellow. The lure body was apparently slightly redesigned later without the flat belly. Collector value range: $2 to $4.

(cont'd next page)

TRANSPARENT DODGER (No. 900) and ARTFUL DODGER (No. 2100)

This plastic plug had rhinestone eyes. The three sizes available were #900, 4″, #2100, 1¼″ and #2100, 1¼″. Colors available were transparent clear, ruby, amber and green; solid black; and opaque white with red head. All have rhinestone eyes. Collector value range: $2 to $4.

DINKY

This was a tiny 1/20 ounce fly rod lure made of wood. It came in four colors not listed in the advertisement. Collector value range: $2 to $4.

ELECTRO LURE c1938

Here is another of those battery electric light lures. The hollow plastic body unscrewed for access to the battery and bulb. There was a clear plastic piece on top of its head through which the light shines. It had a cumbersome looking metal diving blade affair and came in white, green, yellow or silver, each with red head. Collector value range: $2 to $4.

SILVER SHINER or PAUL BUNYAN Minnow and GOLD FISH

All three of these lures were in the same body design. They were made of pyralin with a dorsal fin, ventral fins and tail fins. They were available with double and treble hook options and made in two sizes, 3-5/8″ and 1-7/8″. They also came with a diving lip or a single blade spoon type spinner at the nose in the 1-7/8″ size. Colors available were: silver shiner, gold fish, pike finish, or white with red head. Collector value range: $2 to $4.

MINNIE

A wooden minnow shaped lure with small spinning spoon mounted on a wire leader. It had a belly mounted double hook and trailing double. It came in three colors, white with red head, yellow with silver scale, or black with silver scale. Body length: 2¼″. Weight: 1/8 ounce. Collector value range: $2 to $4.

LADYBUG

This 2½″ tenite lure came in weedless or diving versions. The weedless lure had a belly double hook and was a reverse running surface plug. The diving version had a trailing treble and ran pointed end first. The body design for each was the same, having a dorsal fin running the entire body length and eyes on each end. Collector value range: $2 to $4.

PAUL'S POPPER

This surface lure came in two sizes, 2¾″ and 3½″. Each had a belly treble and trailing treble hook. Available colors were: white with red head, black with silver scale, yellow with silver scale, or green frog finish. Collector value range: $2 to $4.

TRANS-LURE

This interesting hollow plastic plug was made so that you could place a live minnow inside or one of twelve color combinations of body and head inserts. It came in two sizes, 4″ or 1¾″. Both had a belly treble and trailing treble hook. It is most unlikely the collector will find all the inserts unless lucky enough to find an un-fished lure in the original package. Collector value range: $2 to $4.

ALBYLER BASGETER SURFACE c1935
Al Byler, Seattle, Washington

Al Byler made and sold his lures under the name ALBYLER BASGETERS. He was a one-man operation in business somewhere around the 1930's. So far there have been only three different lures of his to turn up. All the colors that were available are not known but probably limited. Those plugs that have so far been found all have a paint job that includes the use of glitter. Various types of hardware is found on the lures. Apparently Byler used what he could find.

Albyler Basgeter Surface (cont'd.)

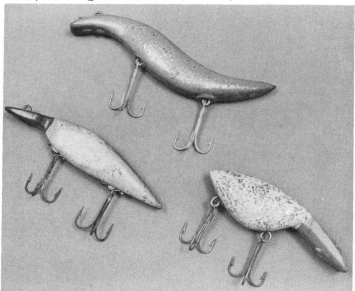

The three lures in the photograph are identified as follows: The lure on the left is the Basgeter Straighttail and is 4-5/8" in length. Top center plug is the Basgeter Surface, 5½" and the right plug is the Basgeter Underwater, 3½". Collector value range: $5 to $10.

CARTER'S
BESTEVER BAIT CO.
Indianapolis, Indiana
and
DUNK'S
American Display Company
Dayton, Ohio

In the beginning these two companies were entirely independent of each other. Patent application dates indicate Thomas J. Carter was in or at least preparing to go into business as early as the late 1910's. The earliest Carter patent found so far was for the Carter's Bestever. It was applied for on April 3, 1919 and granted February 12, 1924. The 5 year hiatus between application and patent grant remains unexplained. Mr. Milton S. Dunkelberger was apparently the owner of the American Display Company of Dayton, Ohio. They were in the tackle business in at least the early 1920's. They were either manufacturing and/or distributing lures under the name "STUBBY BRAND FISHING TACKLE" in advertising that also carried the American Display Co. name. A 1933 Dunk's catalog makes the statement that they had been producing lures for the "...last twenty years." That puts Carter back to around 1913.

Advertising date studies seem to indicate Dunkelberger either bought Carter's company or obtained his lure patents around 1930, for 1931 saw the first ads for "Dunk's-Carter's" and then just "Dunk's," both carrying the American Display Co. name and address.

Once the Carter lures were taken over by Dunk's there were improvements and additions to the line made. An important improvement was the addition of glass eyes to the Carter lures. As far as is presently known there were never any eyes at all on the Carter lures prior to the take-over. Dunk's is still in business today in Stow, Ohio. See accompanying photos for more hints on identification. The first two photos show the Carter's and Dunk's boxes.

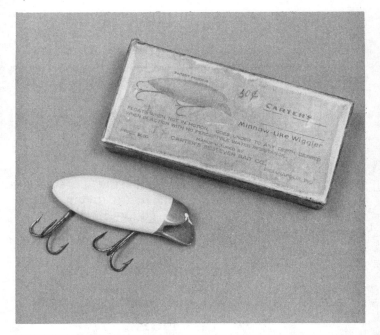

BESTEVER

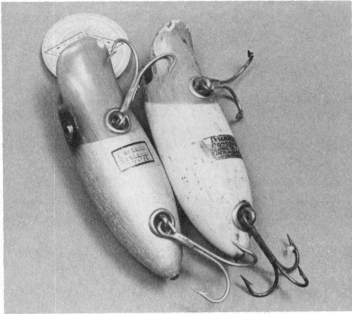

The label on the left plug is CARTER'S BESTEVER and the one on the right has the DUNK'S/CARTER'S label. As noted earlier the glass eyes was a Dunk's innovation, but here we have a Carter with glass eyes and a Dunk's without. These two must represent lures produced during the transition. The round tag is from the Shapleigh Hardware Co., distributors of tackle.

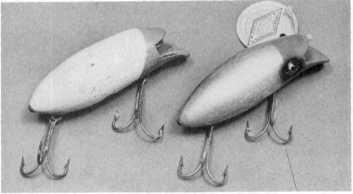

Same lures, side view.

Left is Dunk's tournament casting weight. For some reason it came in four different color schemes: white bodies with red head, green head, yellow bodies with red or green heads. The plug appears to be Bestever but measures 2". There were no 2" Bestevers cataloged in the available research materials.

There were several sizes and hook configurations available in this plug type. It has a very distinctive nose design that looks much like a bird's open beak. Most of the advertising copy and illustration indicate they were available mostly with treble or single hooks only. However one ad clearly states the three basic sizes were available in a double hook configuration too. Collector value range for all: $5 to $10.

NAME	BODY LENGTH	LURE WEIGHT	HOOKS
Pike	4½"	?	2T or 3T
Muskie	3-5/8"	1½ oz.	2T or 2D
Medium	3"	3/8 oz.	2T or 2D
Midget	2¾"	½ oz.	1T or 1D

COLOR OR FINISH: *White with red head; Aluminum with red head; Gold with red head; Yellow with red head; Solid red; *Solid black; **Half black, half white.*

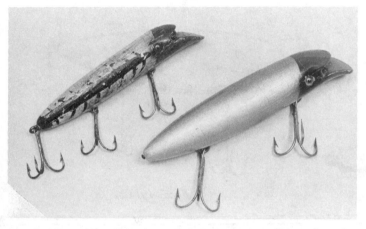

Pike and Muskie size Bestevers. Left is a repaint.

CARTER'S MOUSE

This is the same lure as the BESTEVER midget size but has a flexible tail. It has a single belly mounted treble hook. Collector value range: $5 to $10.

DUNK'S DUNKIT

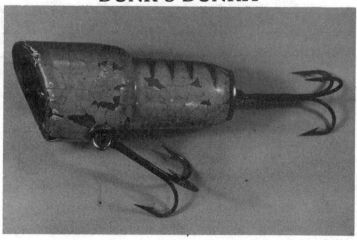

This is a 2" popper type plug with a concave (scooped) head, a belly treble and trailing trebles hook.

*Known as the "Old Black Joe."   **3-1/8" size only.

SINGLE HOOK WEEDLESS

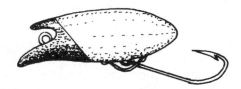

This is the same plug as the Midget Bestever except it has a single hook with a special guard to prevent the hook from turning to either side. Available in all the colors listed with the "Bestever" plugs. Collector value range: $5 to $10.

Feb. 12, 1924.   T. J. CARTER   1,483,842

ARTIFICIAL CASTING BAIT

Filed April 3, 1919

Fig.1.

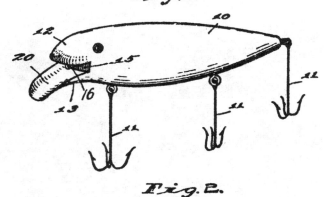

Fig.2.

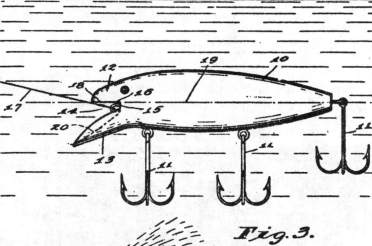

Fig.3.

Inventor
Thomas J. Carter,

Witness
Frank A. Fahle   By   Hood & Ohly
Attorneys

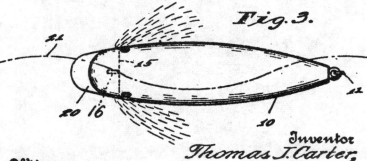

Illustration of the patent for Carter's "Bestever" lure. Granted Feb. 12, 1924.

CARTER'S SHORE MINNOW

Top is Bestever. Bottom is Shore Minnow.

This is essentially the same as the "Bestever" plugs except the rear treble hook is mounted directly on the tail end whereas the Bestever had it mounted beneath the tail. Collector value range: $10 to $20.00.

BODY LENGTH	LURE WEIGHT
3"	5/8 oz.
3½"	¾ oz.

COLOR OR FINISH: *Black head with silver sides and white belly; Solid black.*

BABY CARTER

This is a 1¼", 1/8 ounce Bestever design plug made for fly rod use. It was available in five colors and had one belly double hook. Collector value range: $10 to $20.

SURFACE TWIN

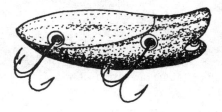

This lure is similar in design to the Bestever type. It is a 3" surface running plug with two same side mounted treble hooks. It was available only in a black and white color combination. Collector value range: $15 to $30.

DUNK'S DOUBLE HEADER

SWIM-A-LURE c1941

The plug in the photograph measures 2½" long. It has a flat head with a rotatable metal plate made so that it could be rendered a top water or an under-water lure at the will of the fisherman. You may have noted that this is not the case in the accompanying patent illustration. Its nose is a sloped wooden affair that could be rotated for the same reasons. Collector value range for the metal plate example: $10 to $20; for the patent model: Premium*

Heretofore collectors and writers, myself included, have considered this only one lure. This because of an old (c1941) Dunk's advertisement that carried only one illustration as reproduced in my drawing here. With the drawing was a list of what we thought were simply different paint jobs and finishes. While researching for this second edition I discovered that the advertisement actually read "Eleven models" not eleven finishes or colors. At that point I began to suspect there were eleven different lures to be found. While searching through my materials I came across a 1933 Dunk's catalog that confirmed my suspicions. There are indeed eleven different lures. I cannot draw or reproduce them for the photocopy available to me was of too poor quality to discern the details of each. What information I could pick out is in the list following on next page.

M. S. DUNKELBERGER
ARTIFICIAL FISH BAIT

Jan. 26, 1932.   Filed July 1, 1929   1,842,591

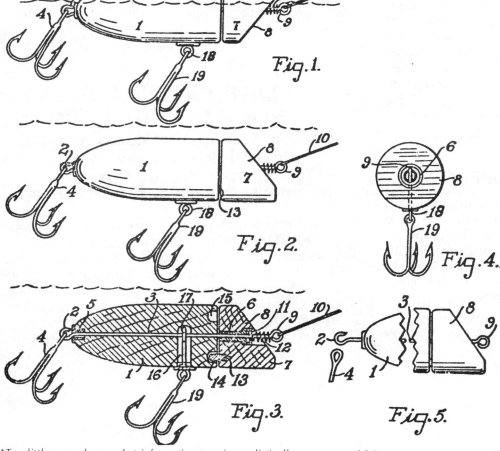

Fig.1.

Fig.2.

Fig.4.

Fig.3.

Fig.5.

INVENTOR
Milton S. Dunkelberger
BY *Noward S. Smith*
His ATTORNEY

1. **SUNFISH** ½ oz., 2″. Shaped somewhat like and similar to Heddon Punkinseeds.
2. **BLUEGILL**, 5/8 oz., 2½″. Shaped same as above, but elongated
3. **BIG CHUB**, ¾ oz., 3¼″. Body shaped like a Heddon Lucky 13 with a slope nose
4. **STRIPED MINNOW**, 5/8 oz., 3″. Minnow-like shape
5. **RED SHRIMP**, ½ oz., 2½″. Reverse running. Shaped a bit like a Carter's Bestever with a bird-like bill
6. **JOINTED PIKE**, 3/4 oz., 4″. Body shaped somewhat like a Creek Chub Jointed Pikie Minnow
7. **YELLOW JACKET**, size & wt. illegible. Shaped like a Heddon Moonlight Radiant
8. **FROG**, 3/4 oz., 2½″. Body similar to no. 5 above and reverse running
9. **BABY DUCK** model of the Dunk's Swim-A-Lure. This one measures 2-7/8″ long.
10. **PIKE**, 3/4 oz., 4¼″. Body same as no. 6 above but not jointed.
11. **CHIPMUNK**, 7/8 oz., 4½″. See drawing below

Some of the lengths and weights may not be exact as the copy in the ad was difficult to read. All of the Swim-A-Lures had adjustable lips the same as in my drawing of the Chipmunk, to make it a diving or surface lure. All were floaters if left still in the water. Looks like you better look in that bunch of unidentified plugs and see if one of these is there. Look for the distinctive adjustable lip as rendered in the drawing. Collector value range: $20 to $40.

STUBBY'S HYDROPLUG

This is a unique lure which was made so you could weight it for casting by filling with water. Dry weight is 5/8 ounce. It has a single blade spinner at the nose and a long shank trailing single hook with provision for attaching feathers, pork rind or live bait. The only color available was red and aluminum combination. Collector value range: $6 to $12.

DUNK'S CRAW

This is an all metal plug made to resemble a crawfish. It was 4″ long and weighed ¾ ounce. It was available in single or treble hook. There are two small trailing spoons, on either side. Collector value range: $10 to $20.

CARTER'S CRAW

This is a plug made in the same style as the "Bestever" design. It had eyes, two trailing spoons and two trebles, one belly mounted and one trailing. Collector value range: $10 to $20.

CAT'S PAW
Detroit, Michigan

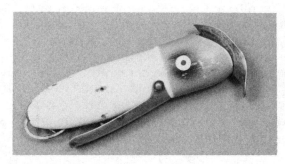

This lure appeared in the unknown section in the last edition. Two readers recognized the lure as the same as one in their collections. We still know very little. Stamped on the metal is "U.S. Patent 2200670." One had the box. All it said was "CAT'S PAW Guaranteed Weedless Casting Bait 2623 GD River Ave., Detroit, Mich." Collector value range: $5 to $10.

CEDAR PROPELLER and POCONO MINNOW
Malcolm A. Shipley (Cedar Propellor)
Philadelphia, Pennsylvania
J. L. Boorse (Pocono Minnow)
Allentown & Easton, Pennsylvania

Most of the information I was able to find regarding the CEDAR PROPELLOR was in an article by Sam S. Stinson in a 1921 issue of *The American Angler*. About the plugs he says in part, "Malcolm A. Shipley, a Philadelphia tackle manufacturer, made a surface plug in the late nineties . . ." It was illustrated in the article. I have copied the illustration and placed it here. As you can see, it is quite similar to the one in

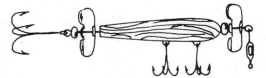

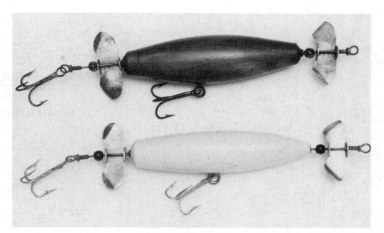

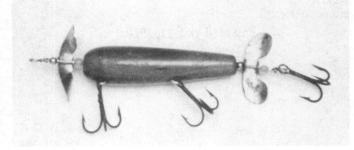

the photograph accompanying the illustration. The only big difference is the location of the second treble hook. The one in the photo may be a little later model. Stinson said he came across Shipley's retail outlet in Philadelphia about 1901-02 and bought half a dozen of them. He describes the lure as follows: "It was of plain uncolored cedar wood . . . equipped with two very light-weight metal propellers, one fore and one aft, connected by a copper wire that extended laterally through the conical body. It bore three treble hooks." We don't know for how long Shipley made his CEDAR PROPELLOR, but it is certain they were off the market by 1920. I can't pin the year down closer than that, but it was probably much, much earlier. Collector value range: $10 to $20.

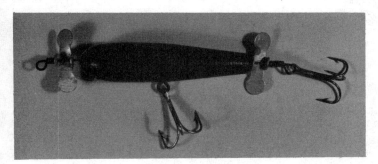

This 3½" 2-T lure is so similar to the 3-T model in the first photo that it was placed here in the third edition. It is only suspected to be a CEDAR PROPELLER. Collector value range: $20 to $40.

The two lures in the photo here are POCONO MINNOWS. They are 3⅛" long. The upper lure is natural varnished wood and the other is painted white. The only printed reference I could find attributed POCONO MINNOW to a J.L. Boorse and stated that they were manufactured in Easton and Allentown, Pennsylvania. Both cities are 30-40 miles north of Philadelphia where Shipley lived. Some collectors attribute the POCONOS to Shipley because of the similarity of the rigging and propeller spinners. I don't believe they were connected in any way other than one or the other copying the rigging. The body styles are significantly different and the strong, well-soldered eye construction at either end of the POCONOS suggest a more polished manufacturing operation than that of Shipley's apparently hand-made production method. Collector value range of the POCONO MINNOW: $20 to $40.

THE CHARMER MINNOW
Patent granted Oct. 11, 1910
The Charmer Minnow Company,
Springfield, Missouri

This early wooden plug had a nose mounted propeller and a tail propeller mounted to a rotating rear section of the lure body. The plug is usually found with eyes, has two opposite see-through mount side trebles and a trailing treble. The rear rotating body section was painted with corkscrew stripe. Must have looked a little dizzy to fish. Maybe that was its secret. A 1912 Charmer advertisement states "Body of red cedar, all mountings genuine German silver." The plug was available in eight different color finishes. They are listed below. Collector value range: $50 to $75.

COLOR OR FINISH: *Gold body, green stripes; Gold body, red stripes; White body, red stripes; White body, green stripes; Brass body, green stripes; Brass body, green stripes; Brass body, red stripes; Red Body, white stripes; Green body, white stripes.*

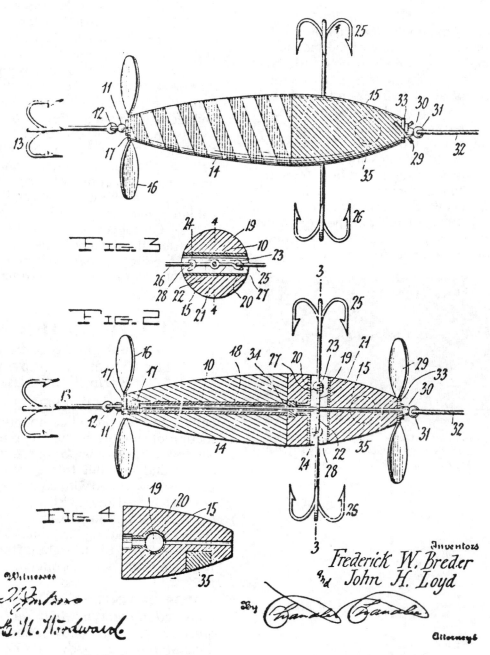

F. W. BREDER & J. H. LOYD.
ARTIFICIAL BAIT.
APPLICATION FILED APR. 19, 1909.

972,748.

Patented Oct. 11, 1910.

FIG. 1

FIG. 3

FIG. 2

FIG. 4

Witnesses

Inventors
Frederick W. Breder
and John H. Loyd

By

Attorneys

Original patent drawing accompanying the application for Charmer Minnow. Note no eyes and see-thru hook hangers. Granted October 11, 1910.

142

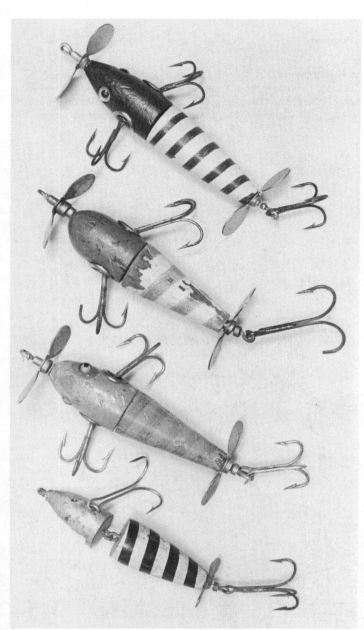

CHARMER MINNOWS. The plug on the bottom may or may not be a genuine Charmer. It could be an early prototype. The remaining three exhibit all the Charmer characteristics. The third from the left has no eyes as in the Patent application illustration reproduced on page 131.

CLARK
C. A. Clark
Manufacturing Company

There has been considerable research by others* on this company, part of which supports my first edition comments regarding the possibility of the Clark lures being manufactured as early as 1926. It is not conclusive however, and strongest evidence indicates that the 1930's is more accurate at this time. It is quite possible the "25 years" statement from the catalog is a boast including the years he was whittling out plugs prior to going into the formal manufacture of them. Whatever the case may be is yet subject to conjecture.

There was little information available to the author to establish the dates of either the company or its lures. However, there is a reference in what appears to be a 1950-51 catalog (undated) which states in part "... an example of where 25 years of doing one thing and doing it well, gives you a better bait for better fishing." I have examined a dated 1951 price list, therefore am reasonably assured that the company was doing business at least as early as 1926. The company was located in Springfield, Missouri, but there is no company by that name in Springfield presently.

Pictured on the following page is a patent page illustrating Water Scout on it. Note the drawing shows three small holes in a larger line tie. This was supposed to give three options for running depth. None have been found as yet. They may never have been manufactured this way.

Shown here from left to right are an original Water Scout, a handmade copy of the same lure, and on the far right is a modern version of the lure. This effective new plug is called the Spence Scout is is manufacturerd by the Strike King Lure Company.

*The Water Scout and Other Clark Baits, A Preliminary Report by Jim Bourdon and Ray Barzee. Copyright 1984.

(cont'd.)

Early wooden Water Scouts. Arranged left to right according to age. Left: no indent for eye; center: small indent with flat, painted eye; right large oval indent with raised painted eye. Indents were originally made by striking the lure with a ball-peen hammer.

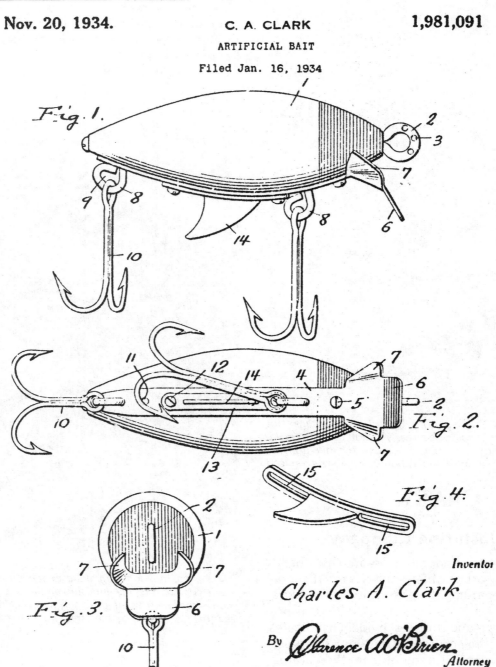

Nov. 20, 1934.   C. A. CLARK   1,981,091

ARTIFICIAL BAIT

Filed Jan. 16, 1934

Fig. 1.

Fig. 2.

Fig. 4.

Fig. 3.

Inventor

Charles A. Clark

By Clarence A. O'Brien
Attorney

Patent drawing for Clark's "Water Scout". Shows the typical Clark keel piece and the large screw-eye line tie with holes for changing line tie position on the screw eye. None have ever shown up with this particular line tie as yet. Patent granted November 20, 1934.

144

Clark (cont'd.)

300 SERIES WATER SCOUT

A small undated pocket catalog the "Water Scouts Bait Company," Springfield, Missouri, states this plug is "The original lure that gave the Water Scout family its world-wide reputation." It had two belly treble hooks, a metal band along the belly ending in a shaped metal diving lip plane. There was a small metal fin attached to the belly sort of like the keel on a sail boat. The lure weighed ½ ounce and floats when not being retrieved. It also exists in a sinking version (400 Series). The composition (wood or plastic) of this slow sinking water scout is not presently known to the author. Collector value range: $4 to $8. It was available in the following colors:

COLOR OR FINISH: *White with red head; Black with white head; Dace scale, black, red, yellow and silver; Deep green scale, blended with yellow; Rainbow; Shiner scale; Silver scale over white, red sheen on sides; Perch scale; Pike scale; Pearl; Black with white ribs; Yellow with white ribs; Green frog spot; White with silver ribs, red scale on sides.*

500 Series "DUCKLING"
(Water Scout Duckling)
600 Series "DUCK BILL"
(Water Scout Duck Bill)

Right: Water Scout Duck Bill; Left: Water Scout Duckling.

Both of these plugs are of the same design and configuration. The catalog listing of these plugs is the one in which the "25 years" reference quoted on page — was found. They are each the same basic design as the original Water Scout with the exception of the nose plane design. It is flat and longer than that found on the 300 Series Water Scout. The smaller one is 2" long and weighs 3/8 ounce, the larger is 2-3/8" and ½ ounce. Collector value range: $2 to $4. They were both available in the following colors:

COLOR OR FINISH: *White with red head; Black with white head; Deep green scale blended with yellow; Rainbow; Shiner scale; Perch scale; Pike scale; Pearl; Black with white ribs; Yellow with white ribs; Green frog spot; White with silver ribs, red scale on sides; Fluorescent red; Fluorescent yellow.*

700 Series
CLARK'S POPPER SCOUT

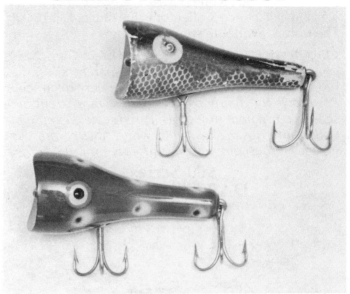

This ¼ ounce wooden plug was 2½" long and had a trailing treble and belly hook. Collector value range: $2 to $4. Available in the following six colors:

COLOR OR FINISH: *Pearl; Rich green scale etched with black; Perch scale; Green frog spot; Solid black; Solid yellow.*

800 Series
WATER SCOUT STREAMLINER

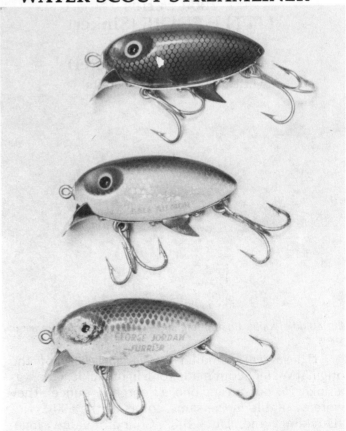

Water Scout Streamliner. Shown here are examples of special order lures that could be obtained in quantity with the angler's name or advertising on the body. Center plug says "Dale Allmon" and bottom lure, "George Jordan, Furrier".

Clark (cont'd.)

This was a sinking plastic water scout type lure weighing 5/8 ounce. Collector value range: $2 to $4.00. The colors available were as follows:

COLOR OR FINISH: *White with red head; Transparent, gold ribs, silver scale on sides; Transparent, silver ribs, red scale on sides; Transparent, silver ribs, green scale; Rainbow; Transparent shiner scale; Transparent pike scale; Transparent frog spots; Perch scale; Pearl; Black with white ribs; Yellow with white ribs; Fluorescent green; Fluroescent yellow, Fluorescent red.*

900 Series
DARTER SCOUT
(Top Scout)

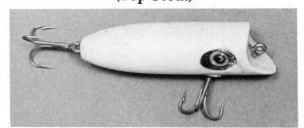

This wooden plug had a scoop nose shape, a belly and trailing treble hook. It weighted ½ ounce and was about 2¾" long. It was available in exactly the same colors as the "Popper Scout." Collector value range: $4 to $8.

1000 Series
LITTLE EDDIE (Sinker)
2000
LITTLE EDDIE (Floater)
(Little Eddie Water Scouts)

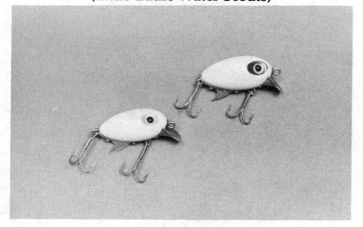

Little Eddie. Right: floater; left: sinker. Note slight difference in sizes.

These were smaller versions (1-5/8") of the original Water Scout made for a light tackle. One was a sinker (½ ounce) and one, a floater (¼ ounce). They were available in the same colors as the 500 Series "Duckling" and "Duck Bill". Collector value range: $2 to $4.00.

1500 Series
JOINTED SCOUT

This is a 3", ½ ounce jointed plastic plug with essentially the same design and configuration as the 600 Series "Duck Bill". Collector value range is from $2 to $4.00. The colors that were available follow:

COLOR OR FINISH: *White with red head; Transparent, silver ribs, red scale on sides; Rainbow; Transparent, green scale, silver ribs; Shiner scale; Brown scale; Perch scale; Peral scale; Black with white ribs; Yellow with white ribs; Transparent pike scale; Frog spot, green yellow and black spots; Fluorescent green; Fluorescent yellow; Fluorescent red.*

2600 Series
"GOOFY GUS"

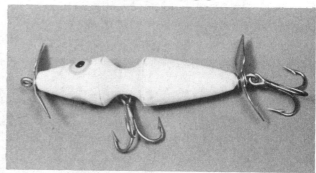

This ½ ounce plug has an odd shaped body. It is long and is thin in the middle something like an hour glass. It has nose and tail mounted propeller spinners and is a surface bait. Collector value range: $10 to $20. The colors available were:

COLOR OR FINISH: *Deep green scale, blended with yellow; Shiner scale; Perch scale; Pike scale; Pearl with red eyes; Pearl with blue eyes; Black with white ribs; Yellow with white ribs; Yellow with black ribs; White with black ribs.*

COLDWATER BAIT COMPANY

Willis E. Phinney   Coldwater, Michigan

EUREKA BAIT COMPANY

Samuel O. Larrabee   Coldwater, Michigan

It really is not yet known just what the nature of the relationship between these two men and their companies was, but research of wat material has been uncovered so far proves that they were connected in some way at some time in their early days. A look at patent dates and the grantees will demonstrate this.

LURE	APP. DATE	GRANT DATE	GRANTEE
Eureka Wiggler	June 2, 1913	June 9, 1914	Larrabee
Coldwater Weedless	July 18, 1916	Sept. 11, 1917	Phinney & Larrabee
Coldwater King	Sept. 7, 1916	Sept. 11, 1917	Phinney
Coldwater Hell Diver	May 17, 1917	May 14, 1918	Phinney

Note that the EUREKA WIGGLER is the earliest and granted only to Larrabee, but about two years later we find the COLDWATER WEEDLESS being patented with the rights being granted to both gentlemen. Furthermore, a Coldwater Bait Company (the Phinney Company) advertisement from 1931 offers the Eureka Wiggler (the Larrabee bait), but calls it the COLD-WATER WEEDLESS. From that it would appear that Phinney ended up in control by some means that only time will reveal to us.

Identifying which lure was made by which company is not always an easy task. A couple of general, though not always reliable, rules are one, that the Coldwater products will often have a washer-like tail protector device and two, most will have cup and screw eye belly hook hardware. The Eureka products are also found with simple screw eye hook hangers. Color patterns could help to separate them, but there are some known to be common to both. The colors found in lists and on the lures themselves so far as as follows:

COLDWATER COLORS	EUREKA COLORS
Fancy Spotted	Green Crackleback with White
Frog back with White belly	belly and red painted mouth
White with Red throat	Red Crackleback with White
White Luminous	belly and red painted mouth
White with Sprayed red head	Orange Crackleback with White
Red back with White belly	belly and red painted mouth

The Eureka crackleback finish is very unusual. Once you have seen an example you will recognize it from then on.

COLDWATER KING

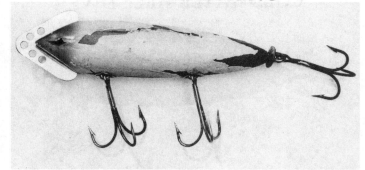

The patent for this plug was granted to Willis Phinney in 1917 and the example in the photo here conforms almost exactly to the patent drawing. Not evident in the photo is that the metal plate is installed at an angle so that the lure is erratic on retrieve. Note the typical Coldwater use of the slightly cupped washer at the tail hook attachment. Collector value range: $25 to $50.

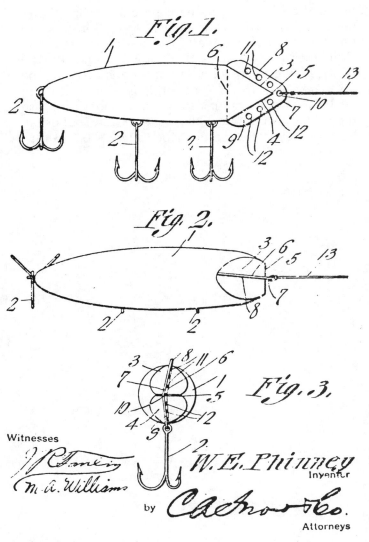

Original patent drawing for the Coldwater King. Note the seven holes (line ties) in the metal lip. The one in the photograph has only five.

COLDWATER HELL DIVER

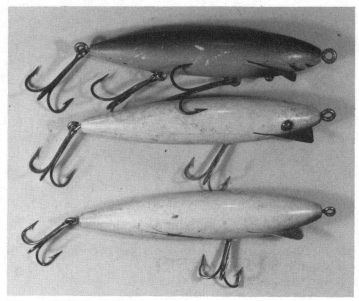

This lure, about 4¼" long, was patented in May of 1918 with rights being assigned to Willis E. Phinney. The lure in the photo here is essentially the same as the lure described and drawn in the original patent application. You may note the patent drawing shows vertical fins at the nose (see next page). This feature has not been found to date. The major feature of the Hell Diver is the adjustable diving lip. It is adjusted by loosening a screw under the nose and sliding the lip back and forth. This plug is similar to the Shakespeare Hydroplane so be careful not to confuse them. Has been found with glass eyes (rare) but usually has no eyes. Collector value range: $20 to $40.

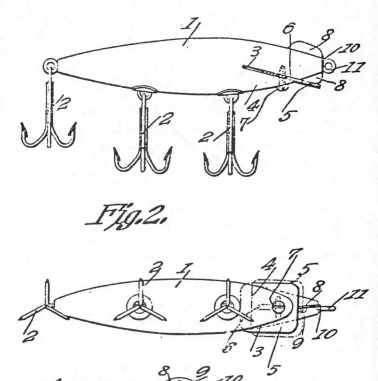

W. E. PHINNEY.
FISH BAIT.
APPLICATION FILED MAY 17, 1917.

1,266,311.

Patented May 14, 1918.

Original patent drawing of the Coldwater Hell Diver. Granted to Willis E. Phinney May 14, 1918.

148

COLDWATER WEEDLESS

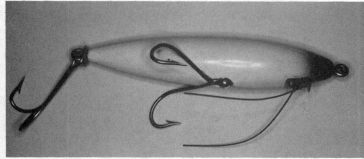

The COLDWATER WEEDLESS. White body with red head and no eyes 4¼" long. This is the rarest of the Coldwater lures.

This 4¼" weedless plug wasn't found in any of the catalogs and old periodicals available for study, but at least one actual lure (see photo) has been found. It is somewhat slimmer than the one in the patent drawing on the next page and has a trailing double hook. It is otherwise pretty much the same. The patent was granted to both Larrabee and Phinney in 1917. Collector value range: $40 to $80.

W. E. PHINNEY & S. O. LARRABEE.
ARTIFICIAL BAIT.
APPLICATION FILED JULY 18, 1916.

1,239,957.   Patented Sept. 11, 1917.

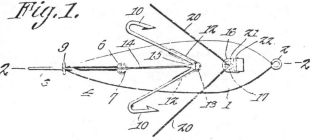

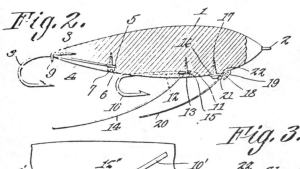

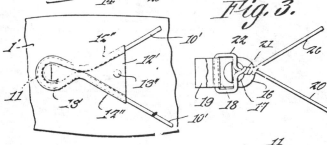

COLDWATER WIGGLER and EUREKA WIGGLER

The EUREKA WIGGLER was the original name for this lure. It was the first of the Coldwater/Eureka products being patented by Larrabee in 1914 as we

S. O. LARRABEE.
ARTIFICIAL BAIT.
APPLICATION FILED JUNE 2, 1913.

1,099,606.   Patented June 9, 1914.

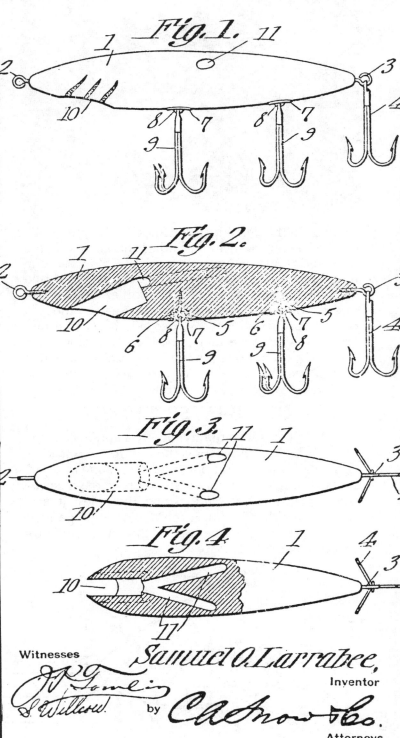

Original patent drawing for the Eureka Wiggler. Granted to Samuel O. Larrabee, June 9, 1914.

149

have seen. As you can see by studying the patent illustration here you can see that it is designed with a "Y" shaped water passageway so that when the lure is drawn through the water it passes through making the lure wiggle. Note that the mouth (usually painted red) is larger than the two exit holes on the sides. In the photo the lower lure measures 3-7/8" and is known

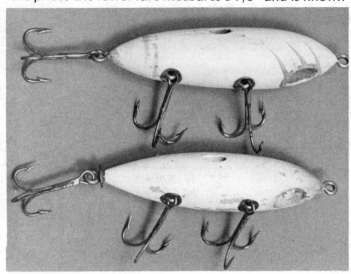

to be a Coldwater Wiggler. Although the upper (4") one has no tail washer all its other characteristics are typical Coldwater. Note the typical Coldwater cup and screw eye hardware. This lure is often confused with the Lochart Water Witch, another lure with an internal waterway. They are distinguished by the lack of cup hardware on the Water Witch and the fact that the Wiggler has an exit hole on each side while the other has but one (on the back). Collector value range: for the Eureka Wiggler: $40 to $60. the Coldwater Wiggler: $40 to $60.

COLDWATER GHOST

This lure is in actuality merely a curious version of the Wigglers above, or is thought to be. It is identical in all respects but one. It has the same large entry hole at the mouth but instead of the passageway splitting into a "Y" and exiting the sides, it gets smaller like the "Y" but it remains a single passage way and turns up to exit out at the back. Collector value range: $20 to $30.

COMSTOCK CHUNK

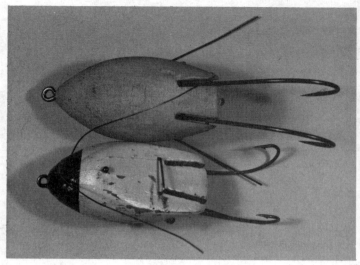

Aptly named, this lure is a "chunk" of wood with two trailing single hooks that can pivot downward through slots in the body. It has two wire weed guards originating at the nose. The lure in the photo measures 2½" body length. Available in white with red head or solid white. The Moonlight Bait Company obtained the rights to this lure around 1923. See Moonlight, page 302-313. Collector value range: $5 to $10.

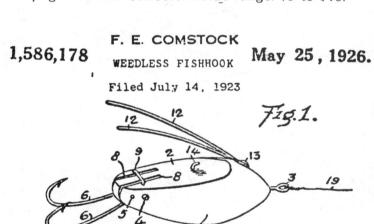

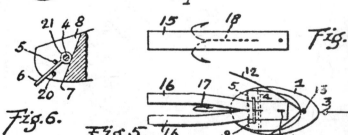

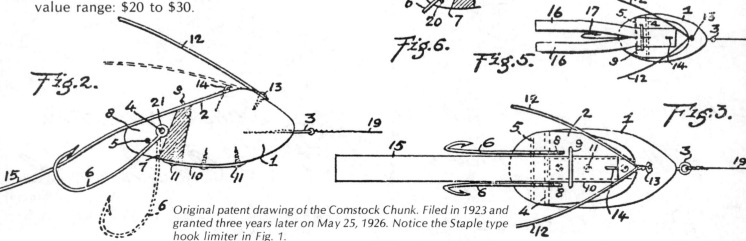

Original patent drawing of the Comstock Chunk. Filed in 1923 and granted three years later on May 25, 1926. Notice the Staple type hook limiter in Fig. 1.

COOL RIPPLE FROG c1947
Associated Specialties, Chicago, Illinois

This was a frog shaped weedless lure with a single hook. There were three brush type appendages, one protruding from the belly and two representing legs. The lure was made with Nylon skin and Rayon and weighted 5/8 ounce. Collector value range: $2 to $4.

CREEK CHUB BAIT COMPANY
Garrett, Indiana

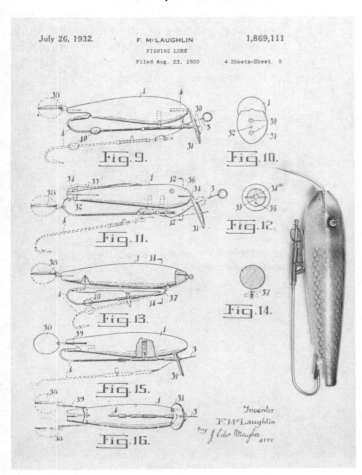

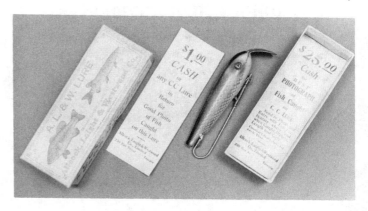

According to documented research so far the Creek Chub company began doing business around 1910 in Garrett, Indiana*, but there is strong evidence indicating the possibility of that date being as early as 1906. This latter date remains speculative as the 1910 date comes from the company records. The 1906 date comes from unpublished personal correspondence with the son of one of the original founders of Creek Chub. The original three founders were George Schultress, Carl Heinzerling, and Henry S. Dills. The first Creek Chub lure was the No. 100 Wiggler and they shipped the first one to the fisherman in 1911. A very significant contribution to the industry was their development of the natural scale finish for artifical lures. This finish was offered at least as early as 1917 and perhaps earlier. Like many other companies many of their earliest models lacked eyes, then glass eyes and so forth in the eye evolution of most companies' products. Creek Chub has however, stuck to the use of the cup and screw eye hardware since its initial development and uses it to this day. The first hook hardware was the simple screw eye with a flat washer. The earliest metal diving blades were plain with no name stamped on them. Next came the plain lip with their name (CCBCO) and usually a patent date of 9-7-20. The next change was the reinforced lip produced by stamping two paralled ridges in the lip for extra strength.

The company owned another plant in Canada. The name is Allcock, Laight and Westwood Company, Ltd. in Toronto. It is not known if that company still exists. The lure is boxed in the Canadian firm's packaging. The patent date is August 6, 1929 and was granted to F. M. McLaughlin, a Canadian. Recently I have found patents ranging from 1929 to 1932 for six additional variations of body and spring-loaded weedless hook methods. The one in the photo is probably the only one to be placed in production but be alert to these variations. They might turn up. Collector value range: $40 to $80.

*Creek Chub was sold to the Lazy Ike Corp., Des Moines, in 1979.

CREEK CHUB ICE DECOY

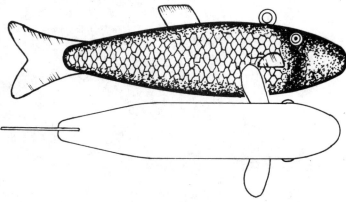

This is a very rare Creek Chub product. I have not found it in any catalog to date. It is 4¼" long including tail fin. It has glass eyes, metal tail fin and opposite mounted side fins in line with the line tie. There is a photo of the Ice Decoy in The Creek Chub color section. Sorry about the photo that was to be here. Some how it got lost in the shuffle. Collector value range: $300 to $450.

OBSERVATIONS REGARDING IDENTIFICATION AND DATING CREEK CHUB LURES

1. **Hardware**

   a. First lures had no metal reinforcing tail insert. This came along about 1920. Not all Creek Chub Bait Company lures utilized this.

   b. Earliest hook hardware was a screw eye and small washer. Next came the small cup (shallow) and screw eye. This was short-lived and the final was the larger cup and screw eye favored by many companies.

   c. The reversible metal lip plane was unmarked at first. Late teens to about 1920 saw the first of the lips with the company name stamped on them. At first the planes were fastened with a screw eye in the head. This was for ease of removal and reversal but provided a second line tie as well. Later this was replaced with a slotted screw. The double screw fastener came along in the early to mid-1930's. Most of the marked lips have a patent date stamped on them. Don't confuse this with dating the lure. The date reflects only when the blade was patented, not when it was made.

   d. Propeller spinners are unique. They were die cut and stamped out with a short raised rib on each blade extending from the pivot hole. You could call them "floppy" but the company used small discs on either side as bearings to help them stay straight and spin easily. See photograph of Spinnered Darters on page 157 for good examples.

2. **Colors and Finishes**

   a. Any time you find a lure with hand brushed gill marks you have a real early prize. A good example is shown on the top lure in the photograph of three Baby Pikie Minnows on page 143.

   b. Henry S. Dills patented the spray-through-netting method of attaining scale finish on lures in 1919, assigning one-half the rights to the Heddon company. The scale finish was used on Creek Chub Bait Company lures at least as early as 1917. See patent drawing on page 84.

   c. The company was very liberal with special order colors, so don't be surprised if you find some real strange combinations and patterns.

3. **Eyes**

   Eye type is not a very good method of identification or dating. We can be reasonably sure the very first Creek Chub Bait Company lures had no eyes, but collectors generally agree that the company was producing lures with no eyes and glass eyes at the same time early on. Painted eyes were commonly used on some of these lures very early also. The rarities would be glass eyes found on lures that were usually made with painted eyes. Tack eyes have also been found, but not often.

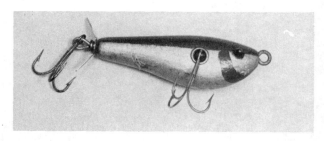

Handmade injured minnow from the Heddon archives. This is actually an original hand-carved CREEK CHUB INJURED MINNOW.

THE CREEK CHUB WIGGLER

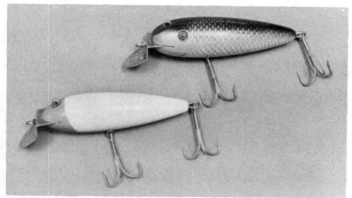

WIGGLERS. Lower is oldest with no eyes and no name on lip. Upper has glass eyes and name stamped on the lip. Neither one has the tail hook metal reinforcing insert.

WIGGLER, Yellow Glass eyes, red dace scale; Name on lip.

This lure came along in the 1910's. It was the lure illustrated in the 1920 patent for the Creek Chub Bait Company reversible lip. That patent was applied for in December of 1915. A 1917 catalog illustrates the lure with no eyes, but a 1918 catalog showed eyes. They have shown up both with and without eyes, with a marked lip and unmarked lip. They have always had the treble hooks (2T), one belly mounted and one trailing. The collector may be reasonably sure he has the earliest version if it has no eyes, no name stamped on the lip and no tail hook metal insert (THI). Collector value range: $5 to $10.

CATALOG SERIES#	BODY LENGTH	LURE WEIGHT
100	3½″	¾ oz.

COLOR OR FINISH: *Natural chub, Scale finish; *Perch with scale finish; *Dark gold color, scale finish; *Red side minnow, scale finish; *White with red head; *Solid red; Gold fish, scale finish; Natural mullet, scale finish; Green back, scale finish; Black with white head; Silver flash; Frog finish; Silver shiner.
*The pattern shown as available in the 1917 catalog.

THE BABY CHUB

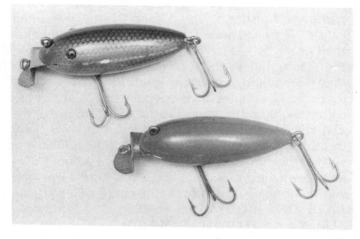

BABY CHUB. Lower has no eyes, upper has glass eyes. Neither have name stamped on lip.

Known in later catalogs as the Baby Chub Wiggler, the 1917 listing shows this plug to be essentially the same as the Creek Chub Wiggler but in a smaller, lighter version. It has the same hook configuration and the reversible metal lip blade is smaller. A 1953 catalog illustrates it as still being available. It is one of the first three lures available from the company. The collector value range is from $10 to $20.00.

CATALOG SERIES #	BODY LENGTH	LURE WEIGHT
200	2¾ #	½ oz.

COLOR OR FINISH: *Natural chub, scale finish; *Perch, scale finish, *Red side, scale finish; *Dark gold color, scale finish; *White with red head; *Green back, scale finish; *Solid red; Gold finish, scale finish; Black with red head; Solid red; Silver flash; Silver shiner, scale finish; Natural mullet, scale finish; Frog finish.
*The finish first available on the plug.

THE CREEK CRAB WIGGLERS
or
THE CRAWDAD
and
BABY CRAWDAD

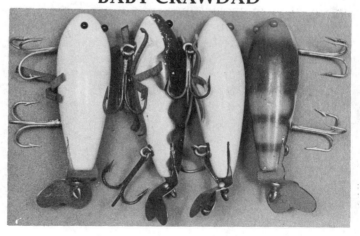

New in the mid to late 1910's, the Creek Crab Wiggler was renamed The Crawdad by 1920. At first

153

only one size (2¾") and one finish (natural crab) was available. In 1919 they added the Baby Crab at 2½" two more finishes, "Albino" and "Tan Color, Shell Finish." They had added the "River Peeler" (steel blue shell finish) by 1924. A 1917 catalog said this lure was the "Only Bait Without Nickel Plate." Presumably they were talking about the reversible diving plane, for earliest examples have a painted dive plane. It has eight flexible rubber legs protruding from the belly. The regular Crawdad is equipped with two belly trebles and the Baby size has two double hooks. The very earliest of these critters will have painted dive planes with no markings, red eyes, screw eye and washer hook rig. Collector value range: $8 to $16.00.

CATALOG SERIES #	BODY LENGTH	LURE WEIGHT
400	2½"	½ oz.
300	2¾"	¾ oz.

COLOR OR FINISH: *Natural crab, shell finish; Albino finish (white & red); Tan color, shell finish; River peeler, steel blue, shell finish; Perch scale; Silver flash.
*This was the only finish available until around 1918-1920.

OPEN MOUTH SHINER

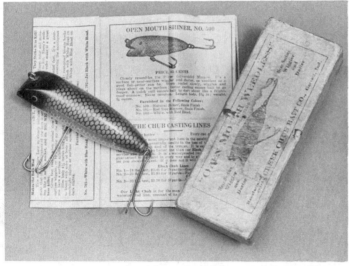

New in 1919, this plug closely resembles a shiner or silverside minnow. It has cut-out notch mouth, a belly mounted double hook and a tail mounted double with no THI. the 1931 catalog is the last one in the author's possession to illustrate this plug as available. Collector value range: $20 to $40.

CATALOG SERIES # NUMBER	BODY LENGTH	LURE WEIGHT
500	3¼"	¾ oz.

COLOR OR FINISH: Natural shiner, scale finish; Red side minnow, scale finish; White with red head; Silver flash.

HUSKY MUSKY

Newest on right (note 2 screws holding lip). Lip is reinforced (ribbed) and unmarked. This is the "Improved Husky Musky" introduced in 1936.

This is another very early Creek Chub lure. A large plug for musky fishing, it has the reversible metal lip blade, a belly mounted and a trailing treble hook. Prior to 1936 this hook hardware was the simple screweye. All after have the cup and anchored hook hardware. They must have made a few 3T models because several have turned up. They appeared in all catalogs into the 1950's. The collector value range is: $10 to $20.

CATALOG SERIES #	BODY LENGTH	LURE WEIGHT
600	5"	1½ oz.

COLOR OR FINISH: *Natural chub, scale finish; *Natural mullet, scale finish; Natural perch, scale finish; White with red head; Silver flash.

THE FAMOUS PIKIE MINNOW

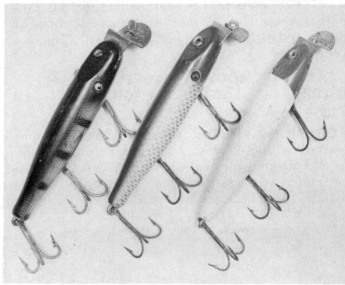

Right: Narrow lip, no name on lip, no eyes (oldest).
Middle: Narrow lip, no name on lip.
Left: Name on wide lip.

154

An undated pocket catalog of around 1919-1921 illustrates this plug with the reversible metal lip blade, slope nose, two belly mounted treble hooks and a trailing treble. The listing states "all hooks set in sockets". This plug appears to have been available throughout the years. Earliest models had no eyes and two line ties. Collector value range: $2 to $10. (See Deep Diving Pikie Minnow).

CATALOG SERIES #	BODY LENGTH	LURE WEIGHT
700	4½"	¾ oz.

COLOR OR FINISH: *Pikie minnow, scale finish; **White with blue head; **Black with white head; *White with red head; *Natural perch, scale finish; *Golden shiner; Silver shiner; Mullet; Rainbow; Silver flash; Orange and black spots; "New Black Scale"; Rainbow Fire"; "Fire plug".
*The original two finishes available
**The original finishes available (c1920).

DELUXE WAG TAIL CHUB

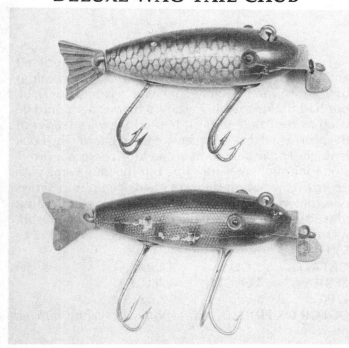

Top is newer, bottom is oldest Wag Tail Chub.

This lure appears in an early (c1918) pocket catalog as available with the reversible metal lip blade, two belly mounted double hooks (reversible to make the plug weedless), and a metal tail fin hinged to the lure so that it could flap on retrieve. It is illustrated in catalogs throughout the years as the "Deluxe Wag Tail" but the listing in the 1953 catalog is rubber stamped "DISCONTINUED". Collector value range: $10 to $20.00.

CATALOG SERIES #	BODY LENGTH	LURE WEIGHT
800	2¾"	½ oz.

COLOR OR FINISH: Natural creek chub, scale finish; Natural perch, scale finish; red side minnow, scale finish; Golden shiner, scale finish; White with red head; *Dace; **Silver flash.
*First available on this lure circa 1950.
**Became available between 1926-1932

THE BABY PIKIE MINNOW

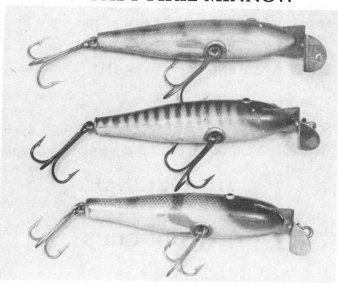

This is a smaller version of the famous Pikie Minnow No. 700. The other basic difference is the elimination of one of the belly mounted treble hooks. Note the slightly differing body shapes and the absence of the painted fins on the middle lure in the photo. The other comments regarding the No. 700 apply to this plug as well. Collector value range: $2 to $10.

CATALOG SERIES #	BODY	LURE
	3¼"	½ oz.
900	3¼"	½ oz.

COLOR OR FINISH: Natural pikie finish, scale; White with red head; Natural perch, scale; Golden shiner, scale; Silver shiner, scale; Silver; Rainbow; Silver flash; Orange and black spot; New Black scale; Rainbow fire; Fire plug.

THE BIG CREEK BUG WIGGLER
SERIES #1400, #1100 & #1000

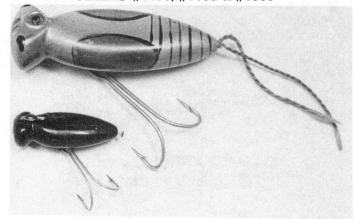

This plug originally appeared around 1918-1920 in three finishes and one weight and length. It was a bass plug but apparently wasn't offered in the bait casting size from about 1932 on. Around 1924 the same design appeared in two smaller, lighter sizes for fly fishing (Creek Bug Wiggler Series No. 1000 & No. 1100), but these too disappeared from the catalogs (around 1945).

155

They were all of wood, had a reversible, belly mounted double hook, and three tail mounted strings or red cord. All were available in the same three finishes. Collector value: $15 to $30.

CATALOG SERIES #	BODY LENGTH	LURE WEIGHT
1000	7/8"	
1100	1¼"	
1400	2½"	½ oz.

COLOR OR FINISH: *Bug finish; Black; White and red.

*Yellow gold body, painted brown wings and legs, dash of red on the head.

THE ORIGINAL
INJURED MINNOW
OR
FLAT SIDE CHUB

This plug is shown in a catalog as "... new for 1924", and was then called the "Flat Side Chub" and a smaller version, the "Baby Flat Side Chub". The larger one had three treble hooks, two *side-mounted, and one trailing. The smaller is equipped with one *side-mounted double hook and a trailing double, but the catalog states it could be ordered with treble hooks, therefore the collector may find it either way. The double hooks were reversible so as to make the plug weedless. Both sizes had nose and tail mounted propeller spinners. the design of the earliest models incorporated a flattened side so that the plugs swam on the side like an injured minnow. Much later models do not have this flat side.

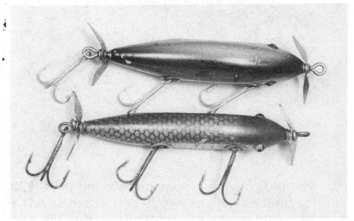

The photo of two lures shows a significant change in the width of the body. The lower plug, in the photo, is the oldest of the two. Still in catalogs of the 1950's and sometimes known as "The Crip",

*Technically these could be called belly mounted hooks because of the way the plug floats (side down).

these plugs have a collector value range of from $2 to $20. They are still made today in five sizes.

CATALOG SERIES#	BODY LENGTH	LURE WEIGHT
1500	3¾"	¾ oz.
1600 (Baby)	2¾"	½ oz.

COLOR OR FINISH: *Dark green, silver and red with scale finish; Natural perch, scale finish; Golden shiner, scale finish; Red side, scale finish; Silver flash; White and red; "Day-N-Nite" (Luminous); Rainbow fire; Fire plug; Dace; Yellow spotted; Frog finish; Red wing; White scale.*

THE POLLY WIGGLE

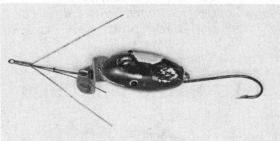

Introduced in 1923 this lure apparently didn't enjoy much success as it was gone from the catalogs by 1931. It was a weighted bait which would not float, but had the reversible metal lip blade so it could be used as a surface plug. It had a long wire leader at the nose which had a three wire weed guard. The hook is single and mounted near the tail. There is a provision for attaching a pork rind but the plug came with an artificial ribbon rind attached. The photo shows one that was left in a tackle box in contact with a plastic worm. The damage to the finish is the result, worm burn. The collector value range is from $15 to $30.

CATALOG SERIES #	BODY LENGTH	LURE WEIGHT
1700	1¾"	½ oz.

COLOR OR FINISH: *Natural pollywog; White with red head.*

156

THE UNDERWATER
SPINNER MINNOW #1800
and
THE CREEK and RIVER
FISHING LURE #1900

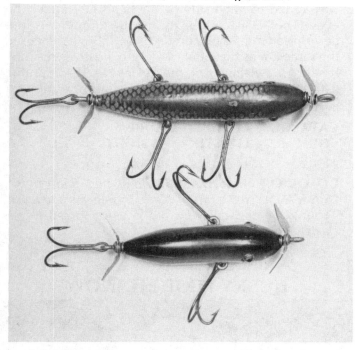

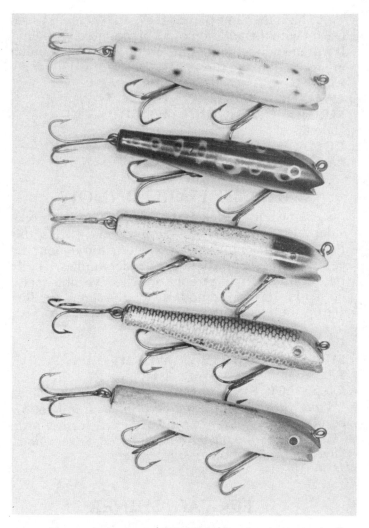

A 1924 catalog listing states this plug is weighted and both the large and smaller versions are available in the same three color designs. Both sizes have flattened sides, propeller spinners at nose and tail. Early catalogs show round-body lures in illustrations. The larger version has two double hooks mounted on each side and one trailing double hook. The smaller one has the trailing double, but only one double hook on each side. It had disappeared from the catalog by 1935. The collector value range is from: $40 to $80.00.

CATALOG SERIES #	BODY LENGTH	LURE WEIGHT
1900	2¾"	½ oz.
1800	3¾"	¾ oz.

COLOR OR FINISH: *Red side, scale finish; Green back, scale finish; Rainbow; Silver flash.*

CREEK DARTER
("The Two Thousand")

Appearing around 1922-24 this plug has two belly mounted treble hooks and one trailing treble. Just about all the Darters are found with painted eyes but a rare few have turned up with glass eyes. It continues in production throughout. Collector value range: $2 to $4. It is still made today in four sizes and a jointed model.

CATALOG SERIES #	BODY LENGTH	LURE WEIGHT
2000	3¾"	½ oz.

COLOR OR FINISH: *Frog coloration; *White with red head; *Yellow spotted; Silver flash; Pikie finish; Perch scale; "Rainbow Fire"; "Fire Plug".*

SPINNERED DARTER

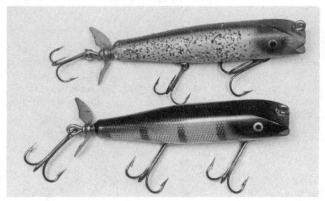

This is the same plug as the No. 2000 series Creek Darter with the addition of a tail mounted propeller. It was introduced sometime around 1946 continuing in production into the 1950's. Collector value range: $3 to $6.

CATALOG SERIES #	BODY LENGTH	LURE WEIGHT
2000 S	3¾"	½ oz.

COLOR OR FINISH: *Natural pikie; White with red head; Yellow spotted; Silver flash Frog finish.*

MIDGET PIKIE MINNOW

Same body shape as the other "Pikies" but considerable smaller. Appearing in the mid 1920's, this floating plug continues in production throughout the years. It has two line ties on the older models, a belly treble hook, a trailing treble, and the reversible metal lip blade. The newer models lack the screw eye line tie on the head. Collector value range: $2 to $10.

CATALOG SERIES #	BODY LENGTH	LURE WEIGHT
2200	2¾"	1/4-3/8 oz.

COLOR OR FINISH: *Natural pikie, scale finish; *White with red head, scale finish; *Natural yellow perch, scale finish; *Golden shiner, scale finish; *Rainbow; *Solid black; White and red; Silver shiner; Silver flash; Rainbow fire; Fire plug.

FIN TAIL SHINER

The lower lure has plain unstamped lip, two line ties and fiber dorsal and tail fins (oldest). The upper lure has a loose fluted metal, flopping tail fin, metal dorsal fin, unmarked lip and small metal flashers opposite mounted at sides of belly about one-third back from the nose.

New in 1924, this lure underwent a few significant changes before it was eliminated from the catalogs by 1944. First available as in the lower lure in the accompanying photograph; flexible fiber dorsal and tail fins. About 1930 another flexible fiber fin was added to each side of the head just under the eyes. The 1938 catalog is the first time the lure description mentioned metal fins although they used the same cut as the older models to illustrate the lure. It said "... swishing tail, metal fins." A 1945 catalog listed the lure but stated "Not Available". Collector value range: $10 to $20.

CATALOG SERIES #	BODY LENGTH	LURE WEIGHT
2100	4"	¾ oz.

COLOR OR FINISH: *Red side shiner, scale finish; *Silver shiner, scale finish; *Golden shiner, scale finish; *Yellow perch, scale finish; *White and red; Silver flash.

*These are the original finishes available.

HUSKY PIKIE MINNOW

This is an Improved Husky Pikie Minnow introduced in 1936. Note reinforced (ribbed) lip and two screws in head to hold the lip in.

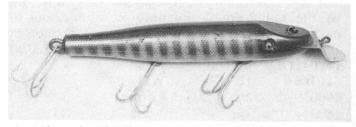

An early Husky Pikie Minnow. Has stamped lip and two line ties.

This plug came along early on (c1924) and appears in the line throughout the years. It is a large lure and has two belly mounted treble hooks and one trailing treble, the reversible metal lip blade and the sloped nose typical of all the Creek Chub Pikie Minnow plugs. Collector value range: $2 to $6.00

CATALOG SERIES #	BODY LENGTH	LURE WEIGHT
2300	6"	1½ oz.

COLOR OR FINISH: *Natural pikie, scale finish; *Natural perch, scale finish; *Golden shiner, scale finish; *White with red head; *Rainbow; Mullet; Silver flash; Orange and black spots; Black scale finish; Blue flash; Purple eel; Yellow flash; Rainbow fire; Fire plug.

*The original finishes available

WIGGLE FISH

The No. 2400 Wiggle Fish has been found with a plain tail. That variation is thought to be the oldest.

Appearing in the mid 1920's, this is a jointed plug with a fluted nickel tail, mounted so as to let it wag. It appears to remain in production all the way through. It has two line ties, two belly mounted treble hooks and the reversible metal lip blade. The collector value is from $5 to $10.

CATALOG SERIES #	BODY LENGTH	LURE WEIGHT
2400	3½"	¾ oz.

COLOR OR FINISH: *Natural perch, scale finish; *Silver shiner, scale finish; *Golden shiner, scale finish; *Red side, scale finish; *White and red; Natural pikie; Dace; Silver flash.

*The original finishes available.

BABY WIGGLE FISH

Baby Wiggle Fish. The one on the bottom has been erroneously called a Jointed Wiggler No. 100. It is either a Baby Wiggle Fish that has had its tail fin replaced by a treble hook or a new in 1936 Wiggle Wizard with its belly treble replaced with a double hook. Note the difference in the size of the slant sides on the forward body section.

This is essentially the same lure as the No. 2400 Wiggle Fish. It is a smaller version and has only one belly treble hook. *The same comments apply otherwise. The Baby Wiggle Fish was however, missing

from the catalogs from 1935 on. Collector value range: $5 to $10.

CATALOG SERIES #	BODY LENGTH	LURE WEIGHT
2500	2½"	½ oz.

COLOR OR FINISH: *Natural perch, scale finish; Silver shiner, scale finish; Golden shiner, scale finish; Red side, scale finish; White and red; Silver flash.*

*Could be ordered with a belly double hook.

THE JOINTED PIKIE MINNOW

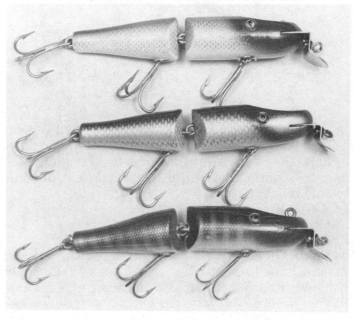

New around 1930 the Jointed Pikie Minnow stayed in production throughout. This is jointed version No. 700 series Pikie Minnow. Collector value range: $2 to $10.00

CATALOG SERIES #	BODY LENGTH	LURE WEIGHT
2600	4½"	¾ oz.

COLOR OR FINISH: *Natural pikie, scale finish; Natural perch, scale finish; Silver shiner, scale finish; Golden shiner, scale finish; white with red head; Silver flash; Rainbow; Mullet; Black scale; Orange and black spots; Rainbow Fire; Fire plug.*

159

THE BABY
JOINTED PIKIE MINNOW

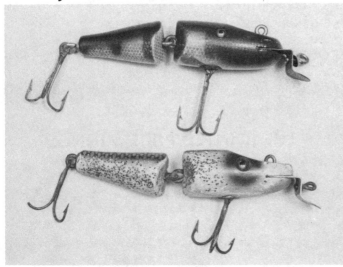

New around 1930, this plug is a jointed version of the Baby Pikie Minnow. The photo shows two older plugs. They have a line tie on the head that doubles as the securing device for the metal lip. Collector value range: $2 to $10.

CATALOG SERIES #	BODY LENGTH	LURE WEIGHT
2700	3½"	½ oz.

COLOR OR FINISH: *Natural pikie, scale finish; Natural perch, scale finish; Golden shiner, scale finish; Silver shiner, scale finish; White with red head; Rainbow; Silver flash; Silver flash, red tail; Silver flash, yellow tail; Orange and black spots; Black scale finish; Rainbow fire; Fire plug.*

THE CREEK CHUB WEED BUG

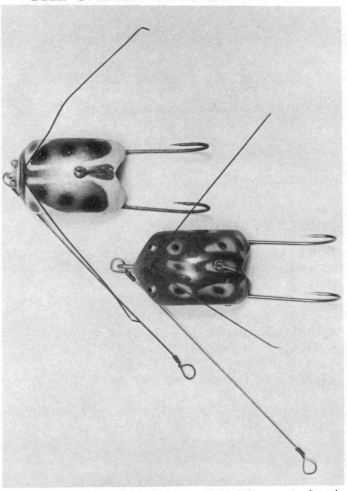

Upper left is the oldest. Note the location of the eyes (red) and pork rind attachment. The paint finish is old style.

This lure appeared in the late 1920's and the last catalog to list it is dated 1935. It is a weedless floater with two single point hooks trailing. Collector value range: $15 to $45.

CATALOG SERIES #	BODY LENGTH	LURE WEIGHT
2800	2"	¾ oz.

COLOR OR FINISH: *Yellow body, green wings; White body, red eyes; Meadow frog colors.*

THE GAR
UNDERWATER MINNOW

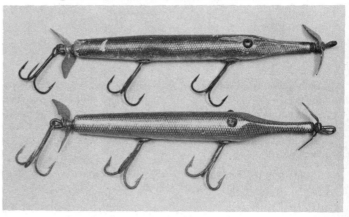

Upper lure is oldest version. Note the difference in head and snout dimensions and shape.

This plug was introduced about 1927-28 and was offered continuously until 1946. The 1947 catalog lists it but is overprinted "Not Available". It has a slender body almost pointed at each end (gar shape). It sports a propeller spinner at nose and tail, two belly mounted treble hooks and a trailing treble. Collector value range: $50 to $100.

CATALOG SERIES #	BODY LENGTH	LURE WEIGHT
2900	5¼"	¾ oz.

COLOR OR FINISH: *Natural gar, scale finish; Green gar, scale finish.*

JOINTED HUSKY PIKIE MINNOW
3000 Series

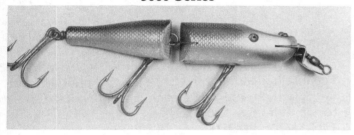

The 1936 vintage "Improved Jointed Husky Pikie Minnow introduced in the 1936 catalog.

The 1931 catalog states this as a "new" lure. It is a jointed version of the No 2300 series Husky Pikie Minnow and is available throughout the rest of the period covered by this book. The available colors & finishes are the same. The collector value range: $4 to $8.

THE CASTROLA

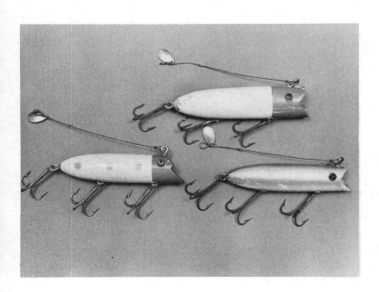

The left lure with the slant head is a variation of unknown origin. The upper lure is a larger (4") version of the Castrola thought to be a musky model. Not found in catalogs. The lower right is the standard 3-5/8" model.

Appeared on the market in the late 1920's-early 1930's and absent from catalogs from about 1942 on. The plug has two belly treble hooks and one trailing treble. There is a long wire leader extension attached at the top of the nose with a small spinner blade mounted toward the end of it. Collector value range: $10 to $20.

CATALOG SERIES#	BODY LENGTH	LURE WEIGHT
3100	3-5/8"	¾ oz.
(musky size)	4"	

COLOR OR FINISH: *Natural pikie, scale finish; Natural perch, scale finish; Golden shiner, scale finish; Silver flash; White with red head; Rainbow.*

THE PLUNKER

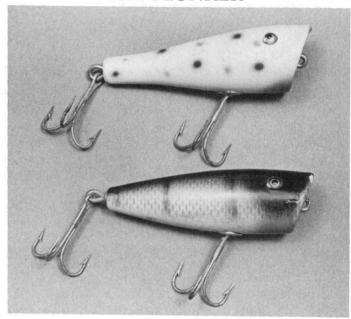

The top lure is a Creek Chub Plunker. The other is actually a Shur-Strike lure, but illustrates the oldest body shape for Plunkers.

Appearing around 1925 this plug continues in production for the entire period covered in this book. Sometime around the late 1930's it underwent a slight body design change. The original design had a fatter body whereas the later bodies were slimmed a bit toward the tail. All had a trailing treble and a belly mounted treble hook. Collector value range: $4 to $8. Made today in four sizes.

CATALOG SERIES #	BODY LENGTH	LURE WEIGHT	
3200	3"	¾ oz	or 5/8 oz.

COLOR OR FINISH: *Natural pikie, scale finish; Natural perch, scale finish; Golden shiner, scale finish; White with red head; Rainbow; Silver flash; Solid black; Frog finish; Yellow spotted; Red wing; White scale; Rainbow fire; Fire plug.*

THE "SARASOTA" MINNOW

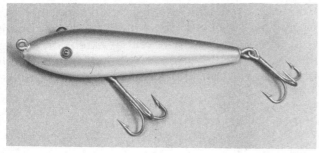

This lure was introduced into the line sometime between 1925 and 1930. It had disappeared from catalogs by 1935. It was rather slender, had a belly mounted treble hook and a trailing treble. Collector value range: $30 to $60.

CATALOG SERIES #	BODY LENGTH	LURE WEIGHT
3300	4½"	¾ oz.

COLOR OR FINISH: *Natural pikie, scale finish; Natural perch, scale finish; Golden shiner, scale finish; Rainbow; Silver flash; White with red head.*

THE SNOOK PIKIE

This lure shows up in catalogs around 1930 and continues in production throughout the years. Eventually it came to be known as the "Straight Pikie". It was made exactly like the No. 700 series Pikie Minnow except larger and much stronger. The belly hooks are swiveled and anchored entirely through the body. Collector value range: $2 to 4.

CATALOG SERIES #	BODY LENGTH	LURE WEIGHT
3400	4-7/8"	1-1/8 oz.

COLOR OR FINISH: *Natural pikie, scale finish; Natural perch, scale finish; Golden shiner, scale finish; White with red head; Rainbow; Silver flash.*

THE HUSKY INJURED MINNOW

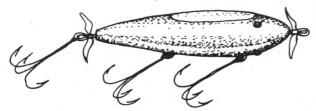

In production from around 1930 until sometime in the mid 1950's. This is the same lure as the No. 1500 series Injured Minnow except made larger and stronger. Collector value range: $4 to $8.

CATALOG SERIES #	BODY LENGTH	LURE WEIGHT
3500	5"	1½ oz.

COLOR OR FINISH: *Natural perch, scale finish; Golden shiner, scale finish; Red side, scale finish; White with red head; Silver flash; Pikie scale; Dace.*

LUCKY MOUSE

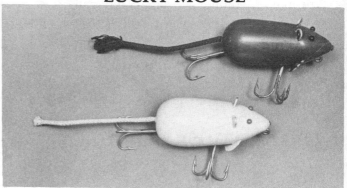

This lure first appears available around 1930 and is listed in catalogs up through 1947, however the 1947 listing has been over printed with "Not Available". The lure had aluminum ears, a flexible braided fabric tail, a belly treble, and a trailing treble hook. Collector value range: $20 to $30.

CATALOG SERIES #	BODY LENGTH	LURE WEIGHT
3600	*2"	¾ oz.

COLOR OR FINISH: *Natural gray mouse; Black mouse; White mouse with red eyes.*

RIVER RUSTLER

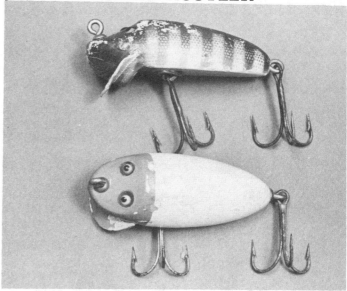

Called "New" in a 1931 catalog, it had disappeared by 1936. It has a slope nose, protruding eyes, a lip, one belly treble hook and a trailing treble. Collector value range: $10 to $20.

CATALOG SERIES #	BODY LENGTH	LURE WEIGHT
3700	2-5/8"	5/8 oz.

COLOR OR FINISH: *Natural pike, scale finish; Natural perch, scale finish; Golden shiner, scale finish; White with red head; Rainbow; Silver flash.*

The catalog listings all say 2" but some collectors list them at 2½".

THE BEETLE

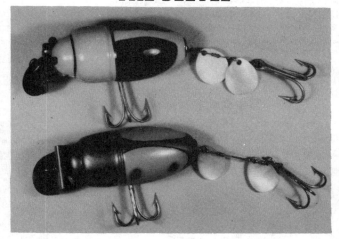

This plug appears in a 1931 catalog as "The New Creek Chub Beetle" and continued in production until some time in the 1950's. It is a deep running lure with a non-reversible metal lip blade. It has one belly treble and a trailing treble mounted on a wire extension which as two pearl finish blade spinners attached. Collector value range: $8 to $16.

CATALOG SERIES #	BODY LENGTH	LURE WEIGHT
3800	2½"	¾ oz.

COLOR OR FINISH: *Yellow beetle; Green beetle; White and red beetle; Orange beetle; Gold beetle; Black beetle; Pike scale.*

SUCKER

Called new for 1932 in that catalog, it was listed again in 1933 but not in any subsequent catalogs. It is 3½" long and available only as in the drawing above in two finishes: Natural yellow or natural blue sucker scale. Collector value range: $15 to $45.

TARPON PIKIE

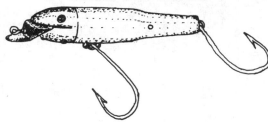

New around 1935 this lure is a large strongly built plug made for heavy salt water fish. The metal lip is heavily reinforced and the hook hangers are extremely heavy duty and anchored all the way through the body. It was available with either single or treble hooks and is listed in catalogs into the 1950's. Collector value range: $12 to $24.

CATALOG SERIES #	BODY LENGTH	LURE WEIGHT
4000	6½"	3 oz.

COLOR OR FINISH: *White with red head; *Natural mullet scale finish; Silver flash finish; Pikie scale; Perch scale.*

These finishes were the only ones offered until 1951. The 1951 catalog shows the addition of the last two listed above.

THE CREEK CHUB "JIGGER"

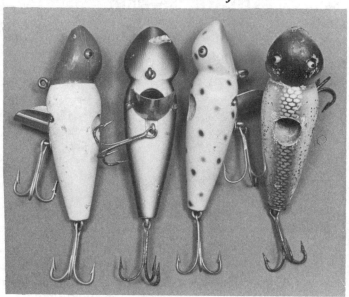

Introduced in 1933 this is Creek Chub's first and only "water sonic" plug. There was a hole with a metal scoop on the bottom to cause water to flow through the body on retrieve. It had a belly mounted treble hook and a trailing treble. It is illustrated as late as 1947 but the listing is stamped "Not Available". Collector value range: $10 to $20.

CATALOG SERIES #	BODY LENGTH	LURE WEIGHT

COLOR OR FINISH: *White with red head; Red side, scale finish; Yellow body, black and red spots; Silver flash; Frog finish; Black body with luminous head.*

THE RIVER SCAMP

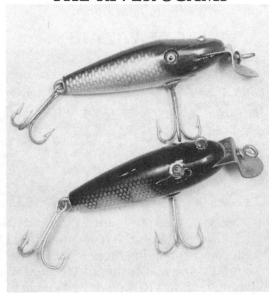

New in the early to mid 1930's the earliest River Scamps had two line ties. The Scamp continued to be listed in the catalogs as available until 1953 where it is stamped "Discontinued". The same catalog lists a "Deep Diving Scamp" as the same as the River Scamp except with a "Deep diving mouth piece." All had a metal lip, a belly treble and a trailing treble hook. Collector value range: $5 to $10.

CATALOG SERIES #	BODY LENGTH	LURE WEIGHT
4400	3¼"	5/8 oz.

COLOR OR FINISH: *White body with red head; Dace finish; Silver flash; Frog finish.*

FLIP FLAP

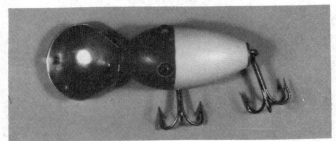

The first page of the 1935 catalog illustrates "Creek Chub's new FLIP FLAP! The Only Lure That Swims With an Up-and-Down Movement". This new "Startling Creation" must not have lived up to expectations for it was conspicuously absent from catalogs from 1942-43 on. It had a loose flapping spoon-like lip attached to the line tie at the nose. There was a belly treble hook and a trailing treble. The spoon was nickel but the plug could be ordered with a copper spoon if desired. Collector value range: $10 to $20.

CATALOG SERIES #	BODY LENGTH	LURE WEIGHT
4400	3¼"	5/8 oz.

COLOR OR FINISH: *White body with red head; Dace finish; Silver flash; Frog finish.*

WIGGLE WIZARD

Introduced in 1936 this jointed plug had two line ties on the earliest models the reversible metal lip, a belly treble, and a trailing treble hook. The 1938 catalog contains the last listing of the plug. Collector value range: $5 to $10. See Baby Wiggle Fish on page 147.

CATALOG SERIES #	BODY LENGTH	LURE WEIGHT
4500	2½"	½ oz.

COLOR OR FINISH: *Natural perch, scale finish; Silver shiner, scale finish; Golden shiner, scale finish; Red side, scale finish; Silver flash; White with red head.*

THE "SKIPPER"

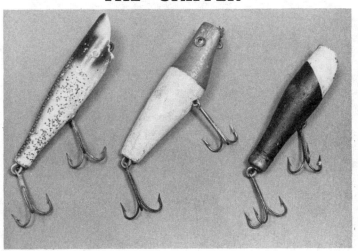

Skippers in three body styles. Newest to oldest, right to left

This lure is also listed as new in the 1936 catalog and as "Not Available" in the 1947 catalog. It had a weighted tail, a belly treble hook, and a trailing treble. Note the redesigned body on the later model (left plug in photo). Collector value range: $4 to $8.

CATALOG SERIES #	BODY LENGTH	LURE WEIGHT
4600	3"	5/8 oz.

COLOR OR FINISH: *Pikie finish; Perch finish; White with red head; Natural frog; Black with white head; Solid black; Silver flash.*

THE "WEE DEE"

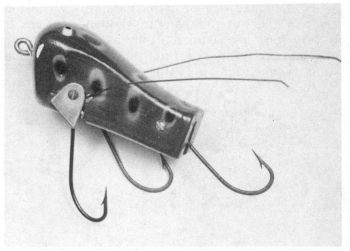

Introduced as new in the 1936 catalog, this lure had three single hooks rigged up with swinging pivots to be weedless. The 1947 catalog lists the Wee Dee but is marked as "Not Available". Collector value range: $20 to $40.

CATALOG SERIES #	BODY LENGTH	LURE WEIGHT
4800	2½''	5/8 oz.

COLOR OR FINISH: *Bug finish; Frog finish; White with red head.*

COLOR OR FINISH: *Natural pikie scale, brown legs; Natural perch scale, green legs; Golden shiner scale, Tyellow legs; White body, red head, red legs; Solid black; Silver flash body, red legs; Frog finish, green legs.*

THE CLOSE-PIN
5000 Series

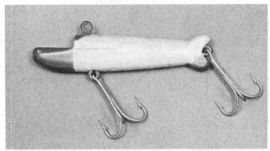

There are some very similar lures to the Close Pin. The Creek Chub lure has red paint on the bottom of the tail fin and yellow on the top part. The others do not have the yellow.

This lure is called new in the 1937 catalog and continues to be offered until 1947. It was made in only one finish, white body with a red head and yellow and red tail fins. The lure had gold plated treble hooks (2) and was made for saltwater fishing. Collector value range: $40 to $60.

THE SURFACE DING BAT
#5400 Series

This was new in 1938. The lure is quite similar to the other Dingbats but is designed without the metal lip. It has two double hooks, one at the belly and one trailing. The plug was available in exactly the same finish designs as the others but, around 1942-43 two more were added as available on the Surface Dingbat only, red wing and white scale, length 1¾'', weight 5/8 oz. Collector value range: $4 to $8.

THE DINGBAT MIDGET DINGBAT & HUSKY DINGBAT

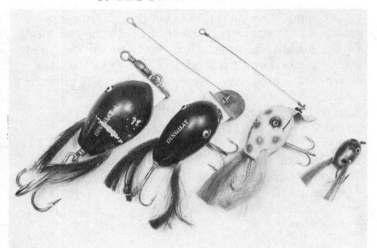

Left to right: The Husky Dingbat, new in 1943; The Dingbat; The midget Dingbat; The larger of the two fly rod sizes introduced in 1943.

New in 1937-38 these plugs had fluttering hair legs protruding from each side, a metal blade lip, one belly mounted treble and a trailing treble hook. They continue to be found in catalogs into the 1950's*. Collector value range: $4 to $16.

CATALOG SERIES #	BODY LENGTH	LURE WEIGHT
1300	-	-
1400	-	-
5100	2''	5/8 oz.
5200	1-5/8''	½ oz.
5300*	2½''	1-1/8 oz.

*The HUSKY DINGBAT was discontinued in 1946.

THE CREEK CHUB DINGER & THE MIDGET DINGER

Note the absence of the metal top head plate on the upperlure. The top two lures are Midget Dingers.

165

This plug was introduced in 1939 and continued to be available on into the 1950's. It has a metal lip, one or two ventrally located treble hooks, and a broom-like tail. A distinctive feature of this plug is a metal plate covering the top of the head although it is not always present. Note the design differences in the photo. Collector value range: $4 to $8.

CATALOG SERIES #	BODY LENGTH	LURE WEIGHT
5600	4''	½ oz.

COLOR OR FINISH: *Natural pikie, scale finish; Natural perch, scale finish; Natural dace, scale finish; Golden shiner, scale finish; White body, red head; Solid black; Silver flash; Natural frog finish.*

THE HUSKY DINGER

Appearing at the same time as the Creek Chub Dinger, 5600 series, this is merely a larger, stronger version. It was available only up to about 1947. Collector value range: $8 to $16.

CATALOG SERIES #	BODY LENGTH	LURE WEIGHT
6100 (Midget)	3½''	3/8 oz.
5700	5½''	1 oz.

COLOR OR FINISH: *Natural pikie, scale finish; Natural perch, scale finish; Natural dace, scale finish; Golden shiner, scale finish; White body with red head; Silver flash; Natural frog finish.*

THE HUSKY PLUNKER
& THE MIDGET PLUNKER

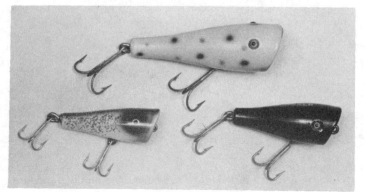

Both of these plugs appeared first around 1939. They are made in the same design as the original No. 3200 series Plunker but in different sizes. Collector value range: $2 to $4.

CATALOG SERIES #	BODY LENGTH	LURE WEIGHT
5800	4½''	1 oz.
5900	2¼''	3/8 oz.

COLOR OR FINISH: *Natural pikie, scale finish; Natural perch, scale finish; Golden shiner, scale finish; White with red head; Rainbow; Solid black; Silver flash; Natural frog.*

THE PLUNKING DINGER

Called "new" in the 1942 catalog this is the same design as the original Plunker but with the addition of the broom-like hair tail of the Dingers. The 1953 catalog lists it but it is stamped "DISCONTINUED". It was equipped with two treble hooks. Collector value range: $8 to $16.

CATALOG SERIES #	BODY LENGTH	LURE WEIGHT
6200	4''	5/8 oz.

COLOR OR FINISH: *Natural pikie, scale finish; Natural perch, scale finish; Golden shiner, scale finish; Natural dace, scale finish; White body with red head; Solid black; Silver flash; Natural frog finish; Red wing; White scale.*

THE POP 'N DUNK

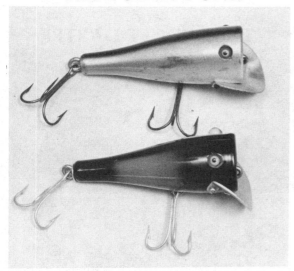

New around 1941-42 the Pop 'N Dunk was essentially the same as the Plunker with a metal lip added. It was stamped "DISCONTINUED" in the 1953 catalog. The upper plug in the photo is the older of the two (note the large glass eye). Collector value range: $4 to $8.

CATALOG SERIES #	BODY LENGTH	LURE WEIGHT
6300	2¾"	5/8 oz.

COLOR OR FINISH: *Natural pikie scale; Natural perch scale; Natural frog finish; Dace scale; White with red head; Silver flash; Red wing; White scale.*

TINY TIM

Introduced as new in the 1942 catalog this was a peculiarly shaped plug. It has a reversible metal lip, a belly mounted treble hook and a trailing treble. The plug illustrated in the photo is tagged as having been used to catch a record 8¼ pound small mouth bass on April 26, 1946. It was used by Tommy Thompson, a well known Memphis, Tennessee fisherman, on Willow Lake in Arkansas. It was given to Clyde Harbin in 1969 by Mr. Thompson and remains retired in his collection to this day. It continues available throughout the period covered by this book.

Collector value range: $2 to $4.

CATALOG SERIES #	BODY LENGTH	LURE WEIGHT
6400	1¾"	½ oz.

COLOR OR FINISH: *Natural pikie scale; Natural perch scale; White scale; White with red head; Silver flash; Red wing; White and red with wings; Spot; Gray.*

THE BABY BOMBER, THE BIG BOMBER and THE DIVE BOMBER

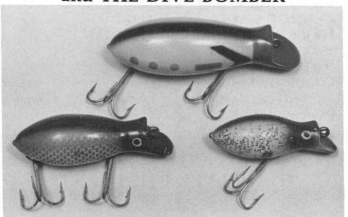

The Bomber was new in 1942 and by 1950 the name had been changed to the "KREEKER". At its introduction two of the color designs were called "Victory" finish. (illustrated in the photograph) The normal color codes used by the Creek Chub Company would indicate that these had either a white body with a red head or a yellow body with a red head. The illustration in the catalog shows the addition of three dots and one dash in black and a chevron in red, all oriented to form an arrow along the side of the body. Apparently this alluded to the spirit of the country during WW II. Indeed the Morse code for "V" (for Victory) is three dots and a dash, "dit, dit, dit, dah." The Victory finish wasn't found in catalogs subsequent to 1947. The lure had two belly mounted treble hooks and lip that is part of the plug, not attached with screws.

The Baby Bomber had only one belly treble hook. They appeared in the 1942 catalog and are marked "Not Available" in the 1947 catalog. They were available in the same finish designs as the Dive Bomber including the "Victory finish". Collector value range: $10 to $20.

CATALOG SERIES #	BODY LENGTH	LURE WEIGHT
6500	2¼"	3/8 oz.
6600	2-7/8"	5/8 oz.
6700	3-3/4"	7/8 oz.

COLOR OR FINISH: *Pikie scale; Perch scale; Golden shiner; Silver flash; *White with red head; *Yellow with red head.*

*These two were preceded by "Victory finish" in the 1942 catalog.

STRIPER PIKIE

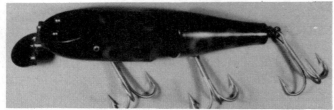

New in 1950 this is an extra strong, bigger and heavier version of the Pikie Minnow for saltwater or very heavy fish. The photo is of the jointed model. Collector value range: $2 to $4.

CATALOG SERIES #	BODY LENGTH	LURE WEIGHT
6900	6¼"	3¼ oz.
*6800	6¼"	3¾ oz.

COLOR OR FINISH: *Pikie scale; Perch scale; White with red head; Mullet; Rainbow; Silver flash; Fire plug; Rainbow fire.*

*This is jointed version of the same plug.

THE "SEVEN THOUSAND"

Introduced as "NEW" in the 1950 catalog, this plug is a very deep running lure. It was a reverse running plug with a metal diving lip. It had legs attached to the belly similar to the ones on the No. 300 series. Crawdad, and two belly mounted treble hooks. Although the catalogs don't mention any size difference, the two lures in the photo measure 2-3/8" and 2-7/8". Collector value range: $10 to $20.

CATALOG SERIES#	BODY LENGTH	LURE WEIGHT
7000	2¾"	¾ oz.

COLOR OR FINISH: *Pikie scale; Perch scale; White with red head; Solid black; Silver flash; Rainbow fire; Fire plug.*

THE JOINTED DARTER and THE MIDGET DARTER

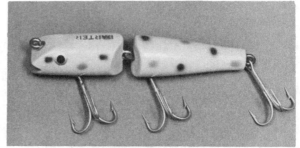

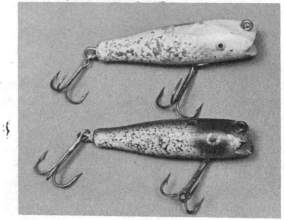

These two appeared on the market sometime between 1942 and 1945. The Jointed Darter is the same plug as the original Creek Darter but is jointed. The Midget Darter is a smaller version of the Creek Darter and has one less treble hook. Both continue in production throughout the period covered in this book. Collector value range: Midget $2 to $4. Jointed $2 to $4.

CATALOG SERIES #	BODY LENGTH	LURE WEIGHT
8000	3"	3/8 oz.
4900	3¾"	½ oz.

COLOR OR FINISH: *Natural pikie; White with red head; Yellow spotted; Silver flash; Frog finish.*

THE NUMBER 8000 C.B.

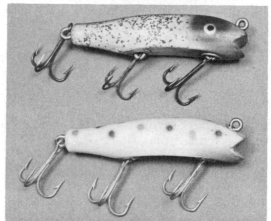

This lure appeared on the market around 1946 and continued in production into the 1950's. It was the same design as the No. 2000 Darter except the belly was made concave. Collector value range: $2 to $4.

The number 8000 C.B. (cont'd.)

CATALOG SERIES #	BODY LENGTH	LURE WEIGHT
8000 C.B.	3"	3/8 oz.

COLOR OR FINISH: *Natural pikie; White with red head; Yellow spotted; Silver flash; Frog finish.*

SPINNING PLUNKER

Showing up about 1950, this is the same lure as the PLUNKER but made smaller and lighter for spinning tackle. Collector value range: $1 to $2.

CATALOG SERIES #	BODY LENGTH	LURE WEIGHT
9200		1/4 oz.

COLOR OR FINISH: *Pike scale; Perch scale; White with red head; Silver flash; Frog finish.*

SPINNING DARTER

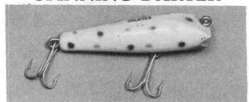

First produced around 1950, this is a very small and light version of the series 200 Darter made for spinning tackle. Collector value range: $1 to $2.

CATALOG SERIES #	BODY LENGTH	LURE WEIGHT
9000		1/4 oz.

COLOR OR FINISH: *Yellow spotted; Silver flash; Frog finish.*

SPINNING PIKIE

Introduced around 1950. This lure is the same as the Pikie Minnow but made smaller and light weight for spinning tackle. Collector value range: $2 to $4.

CATALOG SERIES #	BODY LENGTH	LURE WEIGHT
9300	2¼"	1¼ oz.

COLOR OR FINISH: *Pike scale; Perch scale; White with red head; Silver flash; Black scale.*

SPINNING JOINTED PIKIE

This is a very small, very light version of the Jointed Pikie made especially for lightweight casting and spinning. Collector value range: $1 to $2.

CATALOG SERIES #	BODY LENGTH	LURE WEIGHT
9400		1/4 oz.

COLOR OR FINISH: *Pike scale; Perch scale; White with red head; Silver flash; Black scale.*

SPINNING INJURED MINNOW

New about 1950 this lure is the same as the original Injured Minnow but made smaller and lighter for spinning tackle. Collector value range: $1 to $2.

CATALOG SERIES #	BODY LENGTH	LURE WEIGHT
9500		1/4 oz.

COLOR OR FINISH: *Pike scale; Perch scale; White with red head; Silver flash; Frog finish.*

FEATHER CASTING MINNOW

New in 1924 this lure disappears as a casting plug by 1931. It was then apparently redesigned for use with a fly rod. It has a propeller spinner at the nose and trails fancy feathers. The catalog listing states "Hook drops in slot behind body, making same more weedless and a better hooker." Collector value range: $15 to $30.

CATALOG SERIES #	BODY LENGTH	LURE WEIGHT
F10 or F11	1-5/8"	½ oz.

COLOR OR FINISH: *White and red; Creek chub, scale finish; Yellow perch, scale finish; Gold fish, scale finish.*

THE "WICKED WIGGLER"
#S1 Series

This wiggling spoon was new about 1926-27 and continued to be offered until the very early 1940's. The design never changed but initially the lure was offered in two hook styles, a feathered treble or a hook for pork rind. About 1933-35 a third option was offered, a single pointed rigid hook. Collector value range: $2 to $4.

"SINFUL SAL"

New in 1930-31, this is a wobbling spoon with twin blade spinners, and a single treble hook attached to the trailing edge of the spoon. The catalogs do not list this lure as available from about 1941-42. Collector value range: $2 to $4.

CATALOG SERIES #	BODY LENGTH	LURE WEIGHT
S-20	2¾"	¾ oz.

COLOR OR FINISH: *All nickel; Nickel inside, white & red outside; Copper inside, white & red outside; Nickel inside, white & black outside; Nickel inside, yellow spotted outside; Nickel inside, Frog finish outside.*

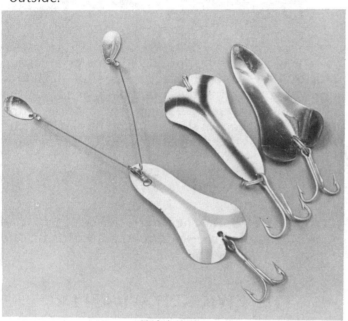

Sinful Sal

THE "CHAMP"

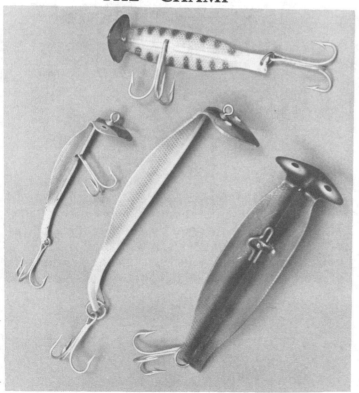

This lure is first illustrated as available in the 1937 catalog, but disappeared sometime in the mid 1940's. It was an all metal lure with a belly treble hook and a trailing treble. Collector value range: $2 to $4.

CATALOG SERIES #	BODY LENGTH	LURE WEIGHT

COLOR OR FINISH: *Pikie; Nickel; Copper; White with red head; Yellow scale; Green scale.*

THE "MUSKY" CHAMP
S-40 Series

This is exactly like the "CHAMP" above except the body is 5" long and weighs 1½ ounces. Continues in production all the way into the 1950's. Collector value range: $2 to $4.

THE SALT WATER "CHAMP"

The same lure as the two previous "Champs" but larger still. There was only one hook (trailing) but the buyer could choose either a tarpon hook or a treble hook. Continues in prodcution all the way into the 1950's. Collector value range: $2 to $4.

CATALOG SERIES #	BODY LENGTH	LURE WEIGHT
S-50	5"	3 oz.

COLOR OR FINISH: *Nickel; *Copper; White with red head; *Mullet.*

THE CROAKER
Croaker Bass Bait Company
C.A. Wilford and Son
Jackson, Michigan

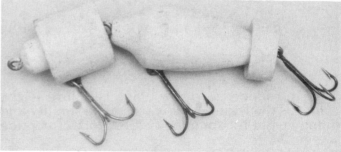

This jointed 4¼" plug was new in 1910. There are at least three slightly different body styles to be found. A flyer found in a Croaker box stated that they experimented for "weeks" in perfecting the lure. Apparently they continued to experiment with the design of the body parts even after they went into production. Colors were not listed, but the flyer did make an interesting comment about their finishes. "You will plainly see that our Wonderful Bait is not finished in the most handsome style and colors, as we have learned by experiment that this is done more for good sales and not at all to give the best possible results." It seems that that familiar controversy is an old one. Difficult to find, this lure has a collector value range: $80 to $160. (See Mushroom Bass Bait and next page).

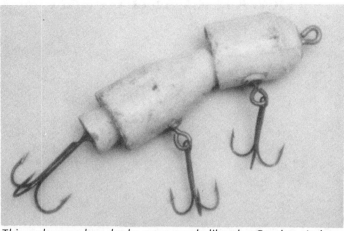

This unknown lure looks very much like the Croaker. It has Moonlight Bait Company style hardware. It measures 3¼".

ED CUMINGS, INC.
Flint, Michigan

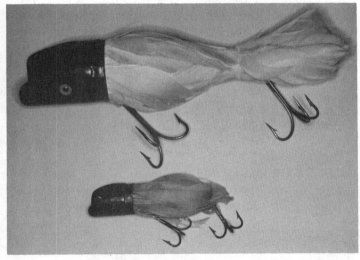

Very little is known about this company beyond its existence sometime around the late 1930's. The two lures in the photo are ED'S WAIKIKI, a glass eyed 9" musky lure and the smaller bass bait, ED'S HULA HULA, glass eyed at 4". Collector value range: $20 to $30.

LECTRO-LURE c1931
Davis Lure Company, Peoria, Illinois

Another of the battery lighted plugs. This one was of transparent plastic. It had nose and tail mounted propeller spinners, a belly treble and trail treble hook. Collector value range: $4 to $8.

DEAN'S LURE
Nashville, Tennessee

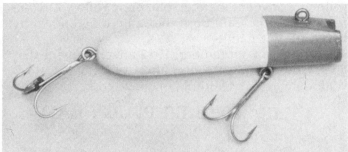

Little is known about this lure other than they were made by a man named Dean in Nashville, Tennessee. It is reported that only a couple of hundred were produced. Dean died sometime prior to 1939. Collector value range: $5 to $10.

DECKER LURES
ANS. B. DECKER
Lake Hopatcong, New Jersey

Mr. Decker was in business from the early 1900's to sometime prior to his death in 1925. One of his lures was in the celebrated fish-off with Jamison (see page 273). His plugs are found in advertising and catalogs as early as 1907 and perhaps before. Decker lures are fairly rare and there are many look-a-likes and copies. It is entirely possible that three body styles were produced by Decker for experimentation. To date, about the only sure way to identify a real Decker is to find his name stamped somewhere on the propeller blade. Even this is not foolproof owing to the unfortunate possiblity of the blades being switched around.

Since the first edition of the book I have come across an advertisement in a 1905 issue of *National Sportsman* that offers a very Decker-like lure available in two sizes (not given, only "medium" or "large") and three colors; red, white or yellow. The illustration shows single side hooks, one on either side and a trailing single. The manufacturer is Jacob Mick, 524 River Street, Paterson, New Jersey. Paterson is not too far from Lake Hopatcong and Mick likely fished the lake. There may be some connection between him and Decker or Decker may have swiped and patented the idea. All is subject to speculation at this time but it appears that Mick's plug predates Decker's plug for now.

To further confuse the issue regarding the "Which came first?" problem, an 1899 Wm. Mills and Son catalog lists the "Yellow Kid" as available. This is a very similar lure to the Decker lure and is made of copper. Also available in a 1906 catalog from the same company is a "Jersey Queen" made of cedar; very Decker-like and may be the Jacob Mick lure. Both of these were advertised well into the 1920's where they then disappeared from catalogs and

(cont'd next page)

magazines. Both are considered by some to be copies of Decker's plug. More yet: In a 1902 Schoverling, Daly and Gales (NYC) catalog there is a listing as follows: "Snyder Floating Spinner or Yellow Kid" inferring that they are both the same plug known by two different names.

There is a September, 1912 advertisement that gives the Decker Company address as 45-B Willoughby Street, Brooklyn, New York.

THE "DECKER PLUG" BAIT

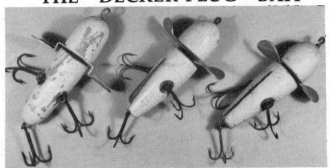

Left: Decker Plug Bait. Center & Right: Manhattans (Decker look-alikes).

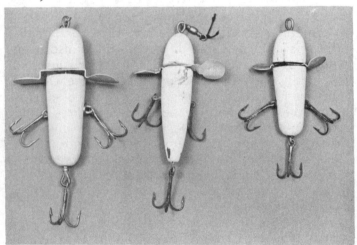

These three Deckers have his name stamped on the propeller blades.

The author first found this wooden lure illustrated in a 1907 Abercrombie and Fitch Co. catalog as available in two sizes either in white or yellow color. The propeller blades were of aluminum and the buyer had the option of three single or three treble hooks. It was illustrated with a box swivel attached. In a 1909 catalog from the same company there was an additional size option and a new color option, gray. Collector value range: $20 to $40.

CATALOG SERIES #	BODY LENGTH	LURE WEIGHT
No. 1	2¾"	unk.
No. 2	3½"	unk.
No. 3	3¾"	unk.

COLOR OR FINISH: *White; Gray; Yellow; *White with red head.*
**These two finishes had apparently been eliminated by 1950 for that catalog does not list them as available.*

TOPWATER CASTING BAIT

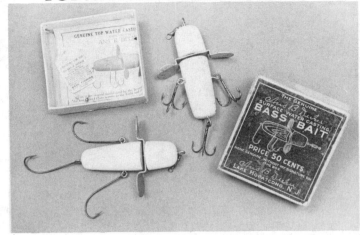

These are two Deckers and an original Decker box. Both have his name stamped on the propeller blades.

Found advertised in catalogs and sporting magazines from about 1908 on. This plug was shaped a bit different from the "Decker Plug Bait" at left. It was available with three single or three double hooks. As with all Decker plugs the hooks with screw eyes alone are oldest and those with "cups" around the screw eye mounts are newer. Collector value range; $20 to $40.

CATALOG SERIES #	BODY LENGTH	LURE WEIGHT
	2¾"	
	3½"	

COLOR OR FINISH: *White; Yellow; Mouse color; Red; Blue; Green; Yellow mottled; White with red head; White with red painted blades; Sienna gray.*

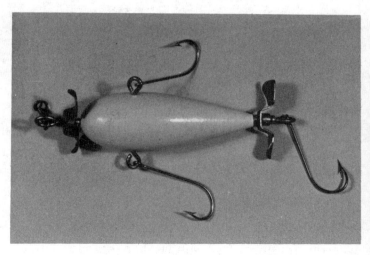

Another model of the DECKER TOPWATER measuring 2-5/8". It has screw eye hook hangers and each heavy gauge metal prop is marked "Decker". Collector value range: $100 to $200.

DECKER UNDERWATER

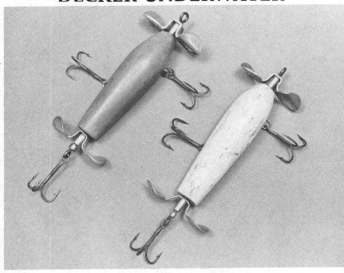

This Decker look alike is a 1926 vintage lure made by George Cummings of New Jersey. Conforms to the New Jersey hook limitation law of the time. Has screw eye and washer hardware. Collector value range: $10 to $20.

This is a little known Decker lure 3-1/8" in body length. It sported two propeller spinners made of heavy gauge metal, a trailing treble hook and two opposite side trebles that were offset. One was toward the nose and the other mounted about midway on the other side of the body. Available colors are presently unknown. Collector value range: $90 to $150.

DECKER LOOK ALIKES

There are so many variations on the theme they are almost impossible to sort out. Many are identified as to maker, but many are not. It seems every year more turn up. Perhaps one of you collectors could undertake a study and help straighten the rest of us out. In the meantime the following photos and information might be of some help.

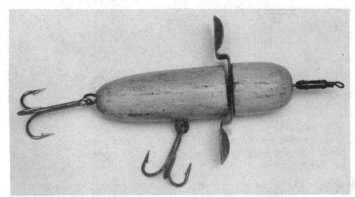

All white Decker type with a fixed box swivel at the nose. Collector value range: $10 to $20.

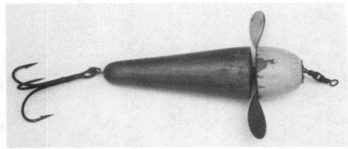

This single trailing treble plug has a round metal plate on the front of the nose. It is attached to the nose by four brads. This one conforms to the New Jersey three point (hook(s) limitation law. Collector value range: $10 to $20.

The Mills Yellow Kid. It is made of copper and painted yellow with gold spots. The earliest listing I found was in an 1899 William Mills catalog. Named after a popular comic strip character of the era, it continued to be offered in various catalogs up into the 1920's when it disappeared from listings. A 1902 Schoverling and Gales catalog offered the same lure as follows: "Snyder Floating Spinner, or Yellow Kid." Collector value range: $10 to $20.

(cont'd next page)

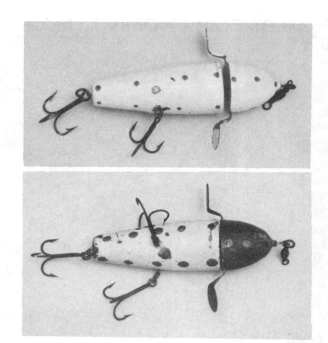

Two Success Spinners. One is white with gold spots and the other is white with gold spots and red head. Both are made of metal. Note one with 3-T and one with 2-T. They are also reported to have been available with single hooks. They are 1910-20's vintage and at least nine different colors schemes can be found. Collector value range: $10 to 20.

Three are two wooden Jersey Queens. These are the same as the Mills Yellow Kid except made of red cedar instead of copper. Hook hangers are staples with O-ring hook attachments. Collector value range: $10 to $20.

A partially disassembled JERSEY QUEEN showing the two screw attachment of the spinner blade and the unique screwed armature. This is a small (2-5/8") version of the lure.

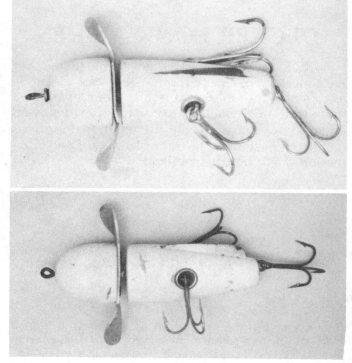

Decker look alikes that are known as "Manhattans." These are 3¼" and 3¾" with raised cup hardware. Note the metal keels ventrally. Collector value range: $10 to $20.

DELEVAN or NORTH CHANNEL MINNOW

Detroit Bait Co.   **Detroit, Michigan**

Very little is known about this lure. It is said to be made and/or distributed by the Detroit Bait Company arond 1903-1904. Whether the company is the same as the one operating later and producing the Bass Caller in the 1940's is not known. They are found in a three treble and a five treble version. The 3T model is usually around 3″ and 3½″ for the 5T. They have unusual large glass eyes with gold flecks in the glass. The line tie and hook hardware is thru-body twisted wire. Most are found with bow tie type tube propeller spinners although some will be found with the more crude prop as in the third photo here. The word DELEVAN or NORTH COAST is occasionally found stamped or stenciled on the side of the 5T model though not as yet on the smaller one. Collector value range: $40 to $80.

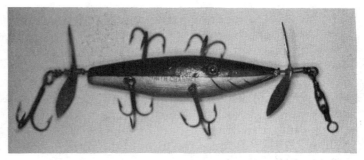

Here is an example of a 5-hooker labeled "NORTH CHANNEL". It measures 3½″ and has the gold fleck glass eyes. Collector value range: $50 to $100.

DETROIT GLASS MINNOW TUBE c1914

Detroit Glass Minnow Tube Co., Detroit

This 3½″ lure has all the characteristics discussed in the text. It also has DELEVAN inscribed on its side.

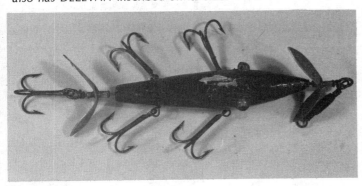

This lure measures 3¼″ and exhibits the same characteristics as above, but has no name inscribed.

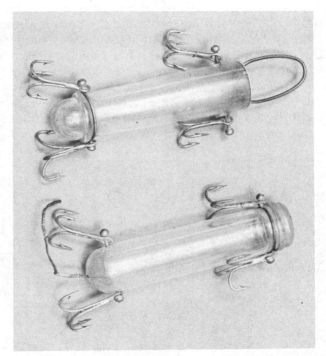

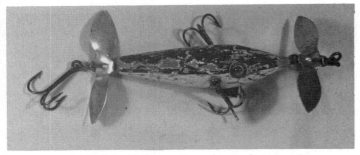

A 3T, 3″ model of the Delevan. Note the crude props. Some are reluctant to identify this lure with the Delevans because of the props, but the other characteristics do match.

The earliest advertisement I was able to find for this lure was in a March 1914 issue of The Outer's Book. It illustrated a glass lure like the upper lure in the accompanying photograph. Beneath the ad illustration is the inscription "Patent Pending" and with a magnifying glass, clearly visible are the words "DETROIT MINNOW" (with two more words unreadable) on the metal plug at the forward end of the lure. The company was the Detroit Glass Minnow Tube Company.

This was a hollow glass lure with four treble hooks side-mounted in opposite pairs. The angler was to place a live minnow in the tube and it was supposedly magnified to twice its actual size by the glass tube and water inside. There were holes in the front and rear so that the "Minnow will remain alive all day". It is the upper one in the photo and measures 3¼" body length.

Curiously what appears to be an identical lure was found illustrated in an ad in the August 1915 issue of The Outer's Book for PFEIFFER'S LIVE BAIT HOLDER, CO., also of Detroit. The ad states "None genuine unless Pfeiffer's name on stopper." It further states "It is the original bait of its kind. Patented March 3, 1914." Both of the lures in the photo above are products of The Detroit Minnow Tube Co.

In the same issue of the magazine is another advertisement, this time for another type of glass minnow tube, looking much like a test tube. This one has a screw-cap type rear end closure (see lower lure in the accompanying photograph). This ad was from the Detroit Glass Minnow Tube Company.

Yet again in the same issue is found another glass minnow tube advertised by Joseph M. Ness, Co., Minneapolis. Called the "Nifty Minnie" it is a glass tube with a metal cap and propeller spinner at the nose and tail. It sports two sets of opposite mounted side treble hooks, a trailing treble and the body is approximately 5½" long. The ad states it was patented December 9, 1913 and that it had been available for "...Two seasons."

Seems like there was a lot of interest in this oddity in lure development for a while. I sure wouldn't want to cast one of 'em toward any rocks. Collector value range: $60 to $90.

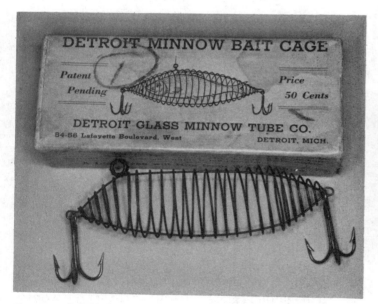

One wonders if this idea ever caught on. At least it wasn't as breakable as the glass tube. This scarce item has a collector value range of from $60 to $100.

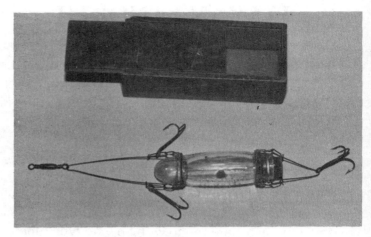

WELSH & GRAVES

This photo is of another glass minnow tube very similar, as you can see. It measures 3¾" in length and was found in the wooden box under circumstances that led the discovered to believe that it was the original box. Any identifying markings on the box that might substantiate this, however, are long since gone. Along the side of the lure are raised letters in the glass stating:

WELCH & GRAVES
PAT. JAN 3, '93
NATURAL BRIDGE, N.Y.

It has been reported that these have been found in three sizes and also with a screw cap closure as opposed to the cork closure on the one pictured. Collector value range: $80 to $160.

DIAMOND WIGGLER
Bignall and Schaaf   Grand Rapids, Mich.

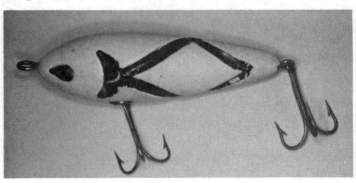

This is another "water sonic" type lure that seems to be a close cousin to the lures of the Eureka Bait Co. and the Coldwater Bait Co., both of Coldwater, Michigan (see pages 147-150). This one is 3⅝" long and has holes and flutes through which water may pass upon retrieve. It has cup and screw eye hook hardware. The lure dates about 1912-14. Collector value range: $40 to $80.

THE DICKENS BAIT CO.

John W. Dickens   **Fort Wayne, Indiana**

This company was started around the time of the granting of Dickens' first patent in January of 1916. It was for a lure with a head that could be turned up or down by means of a spring-loaded ap-

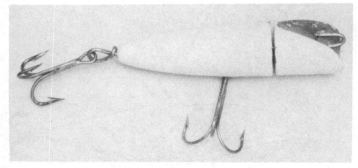

paratus making it a surface or diving lure at will. The lure in the photo here is almost exactly like that 1916 patent. It has not yet been named in any printed material found so far. Because the effect gained by turning the head is the same as that of the LIAR CONVERTIBLE MINNOW below, it may have been a forerunner to that lure. Collector value range for the patent model: $20 to $30.

THE LIAR CONVERTIBLE MINNOW

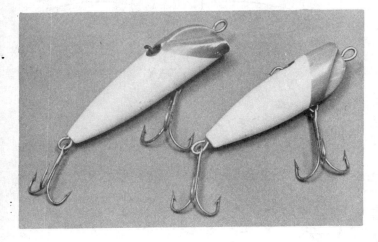

Patented in 1919 this plug had sloped nose, a trailing treble and another, removable treble, that could be attached to the back or belly thereby causing the slope to be down or up. This made it either a surface or underwater wobbler. Collector value range: $20 to $30.

THE WEEDLESS WONDER

I have measured various examples of this plug and the size varies from 1 ½" to 1-5/8". There is also a small ½ oz. fly rod size that is similar, but not exactly like it that is also called a Weedless Wonder. The ones in the photo here differ slightly in design and utilize different hardware. The upper lure is slightly larger, has a flat tail end and twisted or bend wire line tie and hook hanger. The lower example has a rounded tail end with a knob where the screw eye hook hanger is and a screw eye and washer line tie. Most came with the red feathered tail hook but were available with a leather tail. Colors are not known, but they were probably available in the same colors as the LIAR. Those in the photo are red and white and represent the most common finish they are found in. Collector value range: $10 to $20.

UNKNOWN DICKENS PLUG

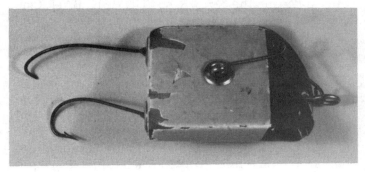

This Dickens plug remains un-named until we can find it listed in a catalog or advertisement. It measures 2-1/8" long and is obviously a deep diver. Note the unusual line tie treatment. Collector value range: $5 to $10.

KILLER-DILLER

Dillon-Beck Company
Irvington, New Jersey

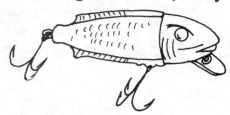

This c1940's company manufactured a line of about a dozen plastic lures. Some of them are duplicates of older Jamison lures such as the QUIVER-LURE, BEETLE PLOD and LUR-O-LITE. The drawing above represents one of their other lures, The KILLER-DILLER was made of transparent plastic and very fish-like in appearance. It has a belly treble, a trailing treble hook and the body length was 3¼". It was available in red and white, gold fish, pike, or rainbow finishes. Collector value range: $4 to $8.

JIM DONALY BAITS

James L. Donaly
Newark & Bloomfield, New Jersey

Donaly was active at least as early as 1908. He marked his lures under the REDFIN brand. Resources so far have turned up a patent application made in 1911 (the No. 27 REDFIN MINNOW). The earliest advertisement I was able to find was in a 1912 issue of *The Outer's Book*. It featured the No. 27 REDFIN MINNOW and the No. 57 CATCHUMBIG BAIT. One could deduce from these numbers that Donaly had been doing business for some time, if he numbered his lures sequentially. If so, the Donaly line could be more substantial than those found so far.

One of Donaly's lures the WOW, is the forerunner of Heddon's CRAZY CRAWLER (see page 250). The original patent was applied for in 1926 and granted to Donaly in 1928 (see accompanying patent illustration). It is known that Heddon acquired the rights sometime prior to 1940 when it first appeared in their catalogs. Donaly died in the mid-1930's, but his wife and daughter continued to paint and sell already assembled lures for a while after his death. They may have sold the rights to Heddon.

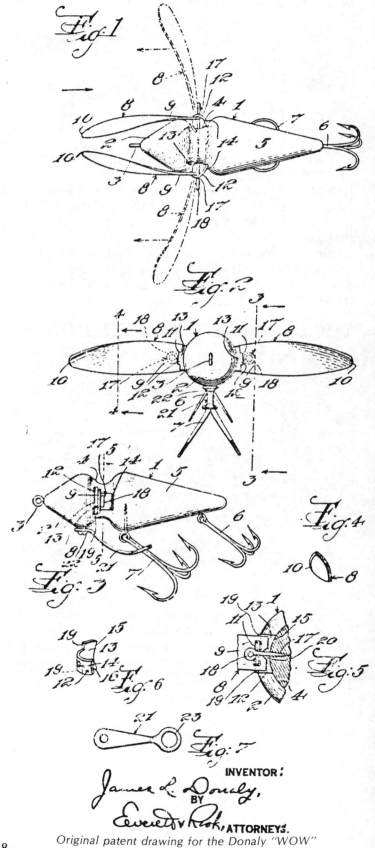

J. L. DONALY

July 17, 1928.   FISH BAIT   1,677,176

Filed May 28, 1926

Original patent drawing for the Donaly "WOW"

J. L. DONALY.
FISHING BAIT.
APPLICATION FILED DEC. 22, 1913.

1,243,391.

Patented Oct. 16, 1917.

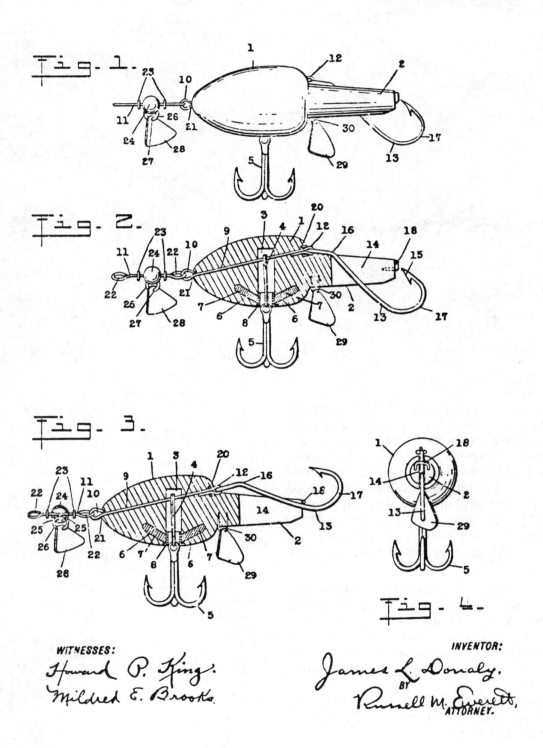

Original patent drawing for the Donaly "Weedless Redfin."

DONALY "WOW" and "JERSEY WOW"

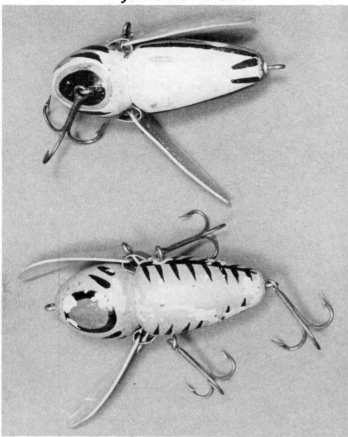

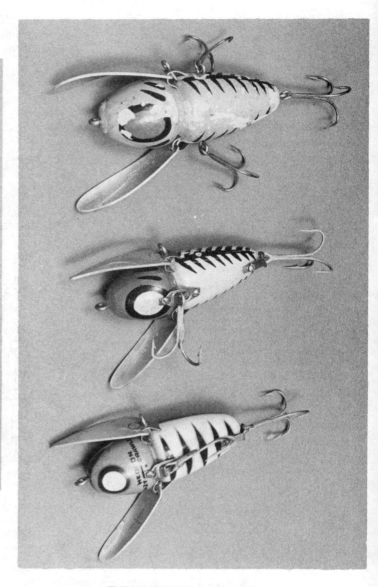

This lure was patented July 17, 1928. Both the WOW and the JERSEY WOW utilized the same body with the difference being in hook and line tie arrangement. Note these differences in the photo of the two WOWs here. The Jersey model has only one treble hook (New Jersey 3-point hook law) and was rigged for reverse running. The aluminum flapper blades are marked with Donaly's name and the Bloomfield, New Jersey, location. The regular WOW was made in two sizes, 2-¾" and 3". The Jersey WOW was made in 3" only.

The photo of the three lures following represents the transition from Donaly's WOW to Heddon's CRAZY CRAWLER. The top lure is a Donaly WOW. The center plug is the Donaly lure body, paint pattern and marked flapper blades, but the hook hardware is genuine Heddon. The lower lure is the pure Heddon product.

Colors available on the Donaly WOWs: red back, white belly; yellow body, white belly. Collector value range: $20 to $40.

REDFIN FLOATER

Advertised in a 1916 issue of *The Outer's Book* is the "New Redfin No. 77." The illustration in the ad shows a couple of features not often seen. The side

Donaly (cont'd.)

hooks are attached to the screw eyes with a safety pin or paper clip type affair and there is a small triangular flapper blade hung just beneath the tail of the lure.

The REDFIN FLOATER was made in two sizes, 2-1/4" and 2-7/8". It has two opposite mounted side treble or single hooks and a large nose mounted propeller spinner, usually marked with the Donaly name. It was available in red, yellow, gray, white or black. The white was luminous. Collector value range: $20 to $40. (see Spinning Barney).

THE WEEDLESS REDFIN BAIT NO. 67

I had no example to photograph but have included the original patent illustration (see page 164). I did find an illustrated advertisement in the April 1915 issue of *The Outer's Book* that shows a lure just about identical to the patent model. The patent was applied for in December of 1913, so we can be fairly sure they were around as early as 1914. Collector value range: $60 to $90.

CATCHUMBIG BAIT NO. 57

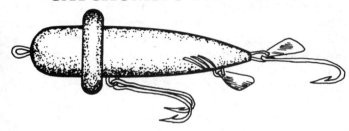

The earliest reference to this lure was in an advertisement in a 1912 issue of *The Outer's Book*. It was a floating lure painted white with a red collar. Size is 4". Available with double (Jersey rig) or treble hooks. Collector value range: $90 to $160.

REDFIN NO. 27

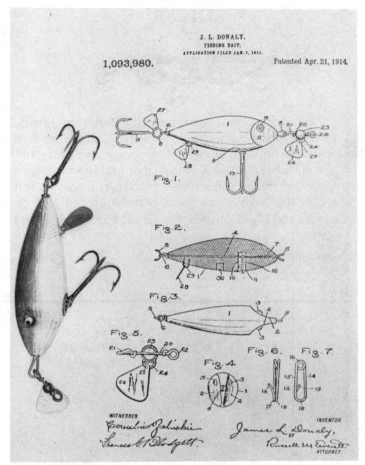

This lure was around at least as early as 1911 (patent applied for January 1911). It is a 3¼", ¾ ounce lure that was made with three flasher blades and available in single hook or treble hook models. Colors available were: White with a red band, green back with white belly, and white with red stripes. Lower plug in the photo of two No. 27's is probably a repaint. Collector value range: $60 to $90.

Donaly (cont'd.)

DIVER

This three inch wooden plug had a mid-body groove entirely encircling the body. There were two side trebles mounted off set opposite and undertail trailing treble. It had a metal diving plane mounted under the head, the colors available were: Green back, white belly and yellow with white belly. Both had red and black stripes. Collector value range: $60 to $90.

DOOFER
Uncle Hub's Enterprises
Ft. Lauderdale, Florida

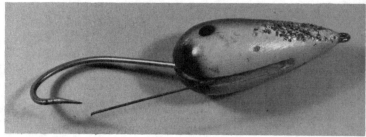

This lure is a floater and meant to be weedless. It is known to have been made in at least two sizes and color finishes. Sizes found so far are 2" and 2-3/8" and the finishes are frog back and as in the case of the one in the picture here, dark green back with glitter and pale green belly with a red flash at the broad end. Collector value range: $5 to $10.

SEA-BAT c1932
Harry F. Drake, Milwaukee

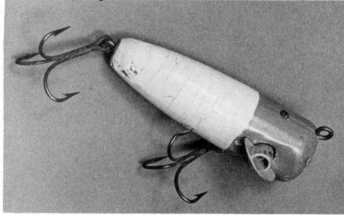

This 3-1/8" lure had two individually adjustable fins mounted opposite each other on the sides of the head and a BB rattler* inside. It had a treble hook mounted beneath the head portion and a trailing treble. It was apparently available only with a white body and red head. See patent illustration accompanying. Collector value range: $20 to $30.

*This is presently thought to be the first lure with a rattler.

H. F. DRAKE

ARTIFICIAL BAIT

Aug. 9, 1932.   Filed Feb. 27, 1931   1,870,559

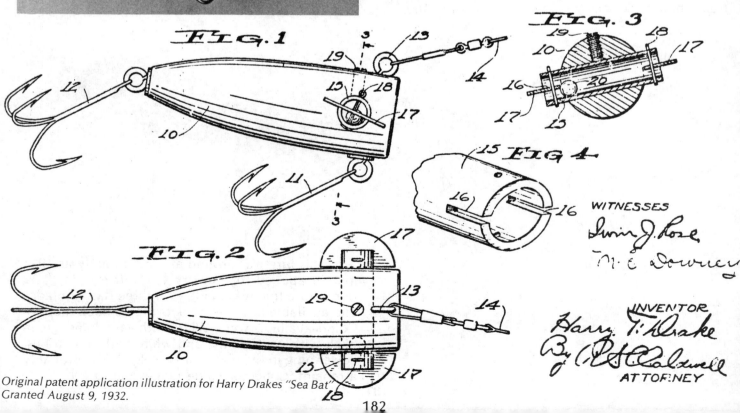

Original patent application illustration for Harry Drakes "Sea Bat" Granted August 9, 1932.

EDON BAIT COMPANY

Oscar L. Strausborger **Edon, Ohio**

Through the early development years of Strausborger lure making he experimented a good bit, carving many shapes and creating various finishes. Because of this diversity his early experiments would seem to be difficult to identify. Not so, because he consistently used a unique hook hanger apparatus that he invented. This external cup-like affair was fashioned from copper tubing. The result was a preventer/presenter that prevented the hook from contacting the lure body and damaging the finish but, perhaps more important, Strausborger thought it made for a more effective hook presentation to the fish. When he realized that his system was unique he applied for a patent in 1932 and it was granted to him in April of 1935.

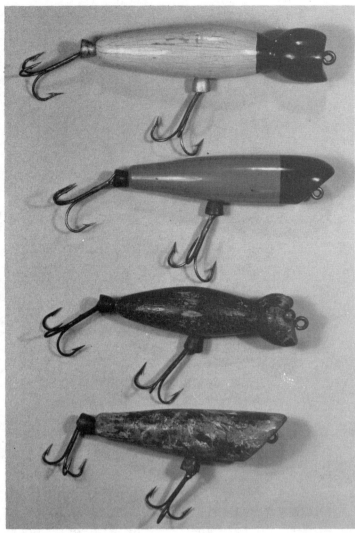

The lures in the following photograph represent typical models of Edon Bait Company products.

From top to bottom the lures are: Red head with white body, no eyes and measures 4" long; Red head and yellow body with no eyes measuring 3½"; Dark green scale finish, 3-1/8" long, this one has yellow glass eyes (glass eyes on any Edon lure is rare); Bottom lure is 3-¼" long and has a mottled red and green finish.

By the mid 1930's he had a number of people working for him. The lure bodies were then being turned on lathes for him by a wood-working company and they were hand finished. In 1938 he sold all rights and inventory to the South Bend Tackle Company thus ending the company's existance. Collector value range for Strausborger lures: $15 to $30.

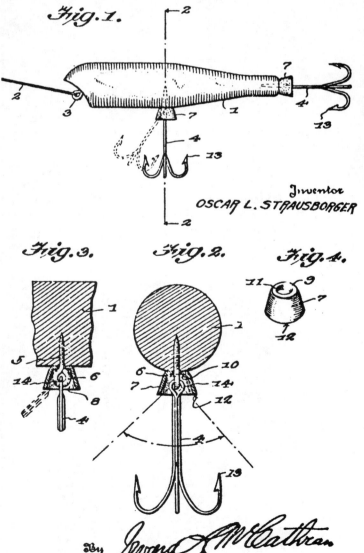

O. L. STRAUSBORGER

ARTIFICIAL FISHING BAIT OR LURE

April 9, 1935. Filed April 28, 1932   **1,996,776**

Fig. 1.

Inventor
OSCAR L. STRAUSBORGER

Fig. 3.   *Fig. 2.*   *Fig. 4.*

By Irving A. McCathran

Attorney

EGER BAIT MANUFACTURING CO.

Bartow, Florida, c1940's-1950's

300 Series MASTER DILLINGER

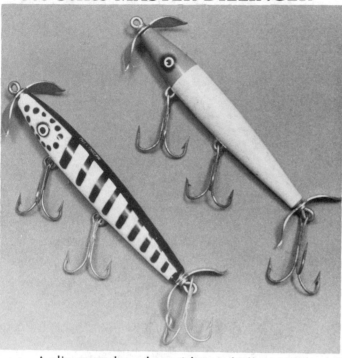

A slim wooden plug with two belly trebles and a trailing treble. It had nose and tail mounted propeller spinners. Collector value range: $2 to $4.

CATALOG SERIES #	BODY LENGTH	LURE WEIGHT
300	3-7/8''	3/4 oz.

COLOR OR FINISH: *White with black stripes; Red with red stripes; Canary yellow with red stripes; Chrome yellow with black stripes; Green with black stripes; Green scale; Silver flash; Gray scale; Gray mullet scale; Rainbow; Christmas tree; Yellow with polka dots.*

200 Series JUNIOR DILLINGER and O Series BABY DILLINGER

These are smaller versions of the "Master Dillinger" above and each has only one belly treble and trailing treble hook. Collector value range: $2 to $4.

CATALOG SERIES #	BODY LENGTH	LURE WEIGHT
200	3-3/8''	5/8 oz.
0	2-1/2''	1/2 oz.

COLOR OR FINISH: *White with black stripes; Canary yellow with red stripes; White with red stripes; Chrome yellow with black stripes; Opalescent pearl; Gren scale; Gray scale; Silver flash; Rainbow; Christmas Tree.*

100 Series WEEDLESS DILLINGER

Lower plug in photo has a red bead behind the spinner. The upper plug does not.

This was a 2-1/8'', 5/8 oz. plug with a single black spinner mounted on a wire leader. There was a hook protecting steel wire projected from the nose down over the point of the tail hook single point hook was rigid. The colors available were the same as the No. 200 series Master Dillinger. Collector value range: $2 to $4.

400 Series SEA DILLINGER

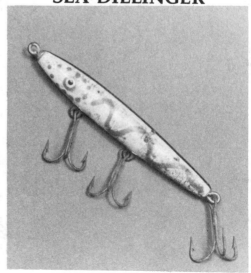

184

This is exactly the same plug as the "Master Dillinger" with the propeller spinners removed. Collector value range: $2 to $4.

CATALOG SERIES #	BODY LENGTH	LURE WEIGHT
400	3-7/8"	3/4 oz.

COLOR OR FINISH: *White with black stripes; Chrome yellow with black stripes; Canary yellow with red stripes; White with red stripes; Silver flash; Gray mullet scale; Rainbow; Christmas tree; White with red head; Yellow with polka dots.*

BULL NOSE FROG

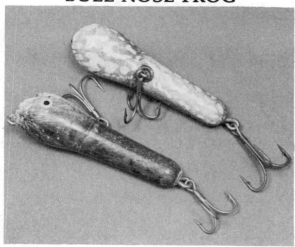

This was a plug with a bulbous nose and actually covered with real frogskin. Be careful not to confuse it with a very similar Shakespeare lure, the No. 6505 Frog Skin Bait*. It had a belly treble and trailing treble hook was 3" long and weighed 3/8 oz. Most are identified as Eger stamped on the belly in red ink. The belly up lure in the photo has faint red markings and the other has none. Collector value range: $6 to $12. (See page 372).

It is thought that Eger made Shakespeare's Frog Skin Baits.

FROG PAPPY

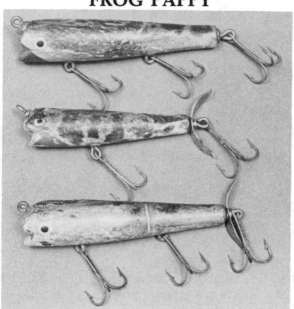

This is another plug covered with real frogskin. It was a top water lure with two belly trebles and a trailing treble hook; had a notched mouth and normally, a tail mounted propeller spinner. Weight: 5/8 oz.; body length: 3-7/8". Collector value range: $4 to $8.

FROGGIE JUNIOR

A small version of the Frog Pappy. It had only one belly treble (2T) and no propeller spinner. Body length was 3-1/8", weight 3/8 oz. Collector value range: $2 to $4.

1500 Series
EGER DARTER

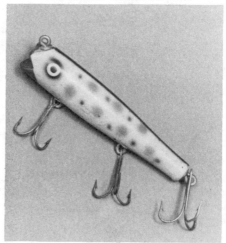

This lure appears to be the same body as the "Frog Pappy" above. Same weight, length and hook configuration. The tail propeller spinner was optional. Collector value range: $2 to $4.

CATALOG SERIES #	BODY LENGTH	LURE WEIGHT
1500	3-7/8"	5/8 oz.

COLOR OR FINISH: *Green scale; Perch scale; Gray mullet scale; Frogspot; Yellow with polka dots; Silver flash.*

1200 Series
EGER 1200

The "Eger 1200" is a larger plunker type lure. It had a belly treble and trailing treble hook (2T). Collector value range: $2 to $4.

CATALOG SERIES#	BODY LENGTH	LURE WEIGHT
1200	4½"	1 oz.

COLOR OR FINISH: *Silver flash; Gray mullet scale; Rainbow; Perch scale; Blue mullet scale; White with red head.*

Sept. 7, 1937. W. EGER 2,092,304

FISH LURE

Filed July 27, 1936

Fig. 1.

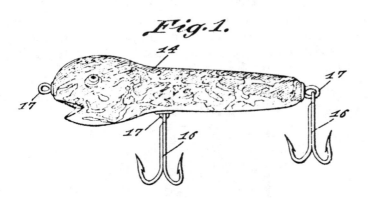

Fig. 2.

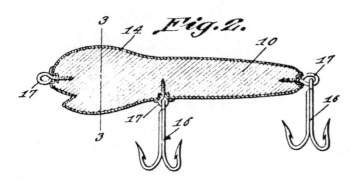

Fig. 3.

William Eger INVENTOR

BY Victor J. Evans & Co.

ATTORNEYS

William Eger's patent for using natural frog skin stretched over a lure body. Granted on September 7, 1937.

1400-½ Series
STUMP KNOCKER

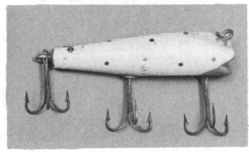

This plug had a concave belly, notched mouth, two belly trebles and a trailing treble hook. Collector value range: $2 to $4.

CATALOG SERIES #	BODY LENGTH	LURE WEIGHT
1400-1/2	3-1/8"	1/2 oz.

COLOR OR FINISH: *Green scale; Silver flash; Gray mullet scale; Frog spot; Yellow with polka dots.*

EGER No. 614
NAME UNKNOWN

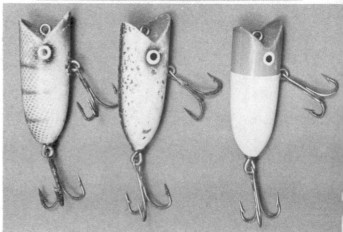

The plug in the photo is 2-3/8" long and clearly marked "EGER" on the belly. It has painted eyes and cup and screw eye hook hardware. Colors unknown. Collector value range: $2 to $4.

EGER No. 1019

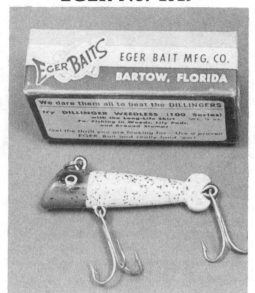

This is another plug for which no name has yet been found. It measures 2½" body length and is pictured here with the original box it was packaged in. It is likely a late 1940's to early 1950's vintage lure. Colors unknown. Collector value range: $2 to $4.

UNIDENTIFIED DILLINGER

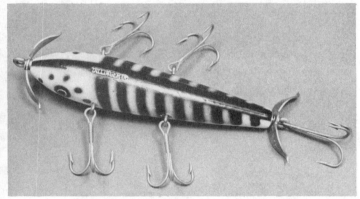

This 4¼" lure is clearly marked "Dillinger" on the back of the body but is not listed in any of those old catalogs in the author's possession. It is considerably wider or fatter than the other Dillinger plugs from Eger. The colors are unknown. Collector value range: $3 to $6.

UNIDENTIFIED EGER LURE

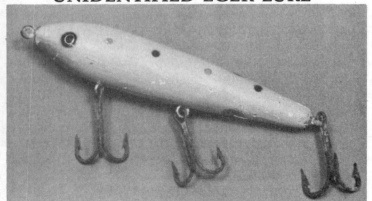

These plugs each measure 3-3/8" in body length. It was not found in any of the old catalogs in the collection, but the propeller spinners clearly identify them as Eger products. It might be reasonable to suspect that the propeller had been added or changed by someone if two had not been found in such good shape. Collector value range: $3 to $6.

1100 Series
WIGGLE TAIL

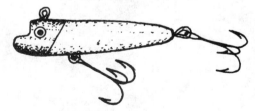

This was a strong plug made primarily for saltwater fishing. It had a notch in the top of the nose, line tie on top of head, a belly treble and trailing treble hook. Collector value range: $2 to $4.

CATALOG SERIES #	BODY LENGTH	LURE WEIGHT
1100	2½"	1 oz.

COLOR OR FINISH: *White with red head; White with red head and flecks; Yellow with red head and flecks; Yellow with red head.*

THE GLOW WORM c1915

The Electric Luminous Submarine Bait Co., Milwaukee

This has got to be one of the earliest of the many attempts at the battery operated lighted plug. The battery/light unit in this one was reversible. One way it throws the light forward and reversed it shines through little port holes on the tail. What a sight that must have been. It may even have worked! It had nose and tail propeller spinners, a belly treble and trailing treble hook. Collector value range: $8 to $16.

SIX IN ONE PLUG c1955

Essential Products Company, New York

This was a plastic plug that came packed with six different metal head plates. Each was supposed to impart a different action to the plug. It came in four color finishes: red head, perch, pike or frog. Collector value range: $4 to $8.

HELGA DEVIL c1946

Etchen Tackle Company, Detroit

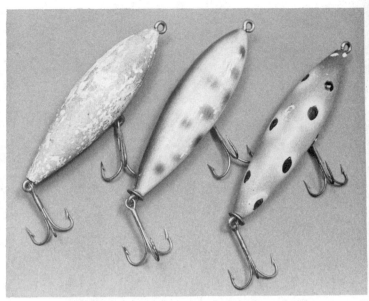

These are lures that could be either Eureka or Coldwater products. The body shape and cup hardware are the reasons they are placed here. No ads or catalog references were found for them under the Eureka Bait Company name. Lure on far right has glass eyes.

EVANS WEED QUEEN

E.S. Evans & Sons   Detroit, Michigan

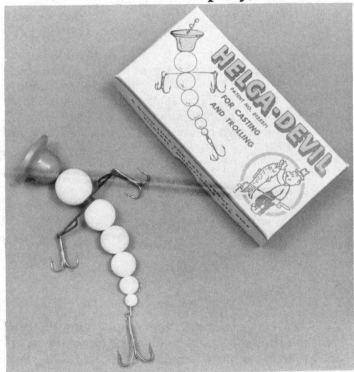

This lure consisted of six white plastic beads and a red head strung on a wire. It had two treble hooks mounted on a cross wire between the first and second beads, and a trailing treble. Collector value range: $2 to $4.

The patent for this very fine lure was applied for in 1934 and issued March 12, 1935. This lure is rendered weedless by placing the hooks beneath the metal plate at the rear. When a fish strikes the lure a lever on the belly is pushed in releasing the hooks to the position shown in the photo here. To find one of these with the original box is uncommon. They were most often marketed on twelve lure display cards. It has glass eyes and measures 2½″ in length. This particular one is in a red scale finish. Collector value range: $5 to $10.

THE "EXPERT" WOODEN MINNOWS

F. (Franklin) C. Woods and Company
Alliance, Ohio
Charles C. Shaffer, Alliance, Ohio
J. L. Clark Manufacturing Company
Rockford, Illinois
Fred C. Keeling, Rockford, Illinois

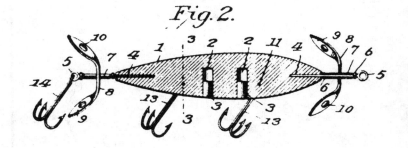

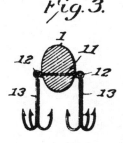

The four names above represent the transition of EXPERTS from 1901* to the 1930s (1928 was the date of the latest advertisement or catalog entry I could find). The 1901 date comes from the advertising of Experts in *Outers* that year. The patent was not even applied for until 1902. It was granted to Charles C. Shaffer March 17, 1903. Shaffer was working for the Post Office Department at the time and apparently felt that he should not use his own name in connection with the company. Herein lies the explanation for his name not being in the company name. Franklin C. Woods was a relative, it is thought, and they became partners. There is a variation of the EXPERT that has HOLZWARTH imprinted on the side. J. C. Holzwarth of Alliance apparently sold them, buying from Woods and marketing them under his own name. His ads show up in 1903 and 1904.

During the F. C. Woods era of the EXPERTS there were at least three patents granted, the basic EXPERT patent to Shaffer and two more to F. C. Woods. One was for a detachable treble hook in 1904 and the other, for a detachable double hook in 1906. It is interesting to note that the EXPERT used to illustrate the detachable double hook (1906) sports a newer, improved style of propeller spinner. All ads with illustrations beginning in 1906 and after, show this newer prop. The new prop came along sometime between 1904 and 1906.

The next step in the transition took place somewhere around 1907-08. J. L. Clark Manufacturing of Rockford, Illinois began making EXPERTS. The reason or exact date for this is not known presently, but the EXPERTS continued to be made. The Clark EXPERTS are generally thought to be of better quality than the F. C. Woods lures.

About 1914 Fred C. Keeling, also of Rockford, obtained the rights to the EXPERT continuing to make them and adding several other style lures. The Keeling company remained in operation until sometime in the 1930s when the company was sold the Horrocks-Ibbotson (see Keeling section). Collector value range for EXPERTS: $40 to $80.

One of F. C. Woods' advertisements in Sporting Goods Dealer of May, 1905 said they had been making them for ten years. That would place them as early as 1895. The same ad appeared in a 1906 edition, but the copy had been changed to read ". . . for many years." It looks as if someone may have called them on the claim.

Fig. 1.

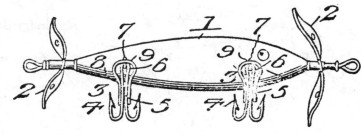

Fig. 2.

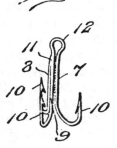

Fig. 1.

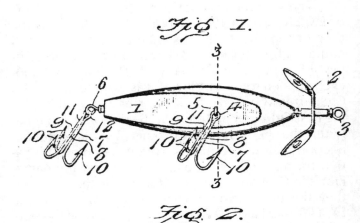

Fig. 2.

Fig. 3.

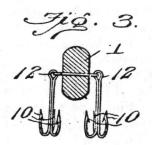

Witnesses

C. C. Hines.

By

Inventor
F. C. Woods,

Victor J. Evans.
Attorney

Witnesses

Chas. S. Hyer.

Inventor
Franklin C. Woods,

By Victor J. Evans
Attorney

Experts (cont'd.)

Some Tips For Identification of Experts

1. F. C. Woods/Shaffer EXPERTS will almost always have larger holes in the propeller spinner blades. The props themselves are tube-type with blunted or rounded blade points until about 1904-06. The line tie and trailing hook hanger are thru-body twisted wire.

2. It is my contention that the no-hole prop EXPERTS are either pre-production models or possibly not made by Woods/Shaffer at all. This latter observation is tempered by the fact that some of the Holzwarth models have shown up with no-hole props.

3. All classic EXPERTS I have observed and photographed so far have yellow glass eyes.

4. Most Experts have 'THE "EXPERT" ' imprinted on the body side. Many may have had the two words to wear off over the years.

5. 99% of all EXPERTS sport fore and aft propeller spinners.

6. J. L. Clark EXPERTS are found with four painted gill stripes as opposed to three being found on Woods and Keeling products. A few Keeling models have been found with four gill stripes, but this is most uncommon and likely to be a result of Clark's inventory left over at the time of the take-over.

7. EXPERTS of all three makers are found in both a round body and a shaped, slimmer body. Some of the latter are actually flat-sided.

8. Earliest classic EXPERTS will have thru-body twisted wire hook hangers and thru-body wire line tie and trailing hook hanger.

A 3-T model F.C. Woods EXPERT. It is 2½" long, has thru-body twisted wire hook hangers and line tie hardware and yellow glass eyes. Note the tube extension at the tail end.

Another lure suspected to be F.C. Woods EXPERT. 5-T, 2 belly weights, 3-5-8", yellow glass eyes, thru-body twisted wire hook hangers and soldered line tie.

A Woods EXPERT with typical pre 1904-06 tube-type bow tie propeller spinners.

Two 5-T model EXPERTS. It looks like the upper lure has its longitudinal thru-body wire and propeller spinner replaced by a fisherman.

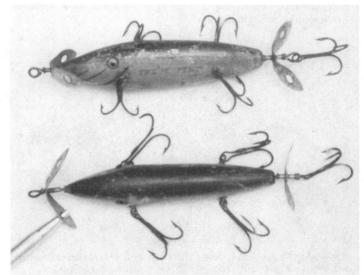

Two shaped body Woods EXPERTS. The Cross pen point is inserted to show the larger diameter hole. Later EXPERTS by others have smaller diameter holes. Pen point will barely fit the hole on the latter.

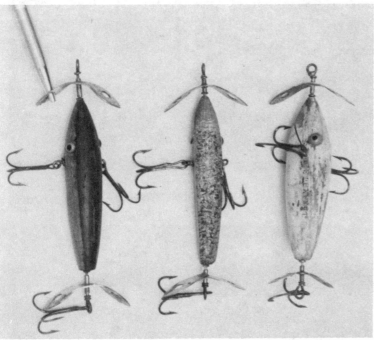

Three Woods EXPERTS. Note the flat sides on the center lure. Cross pen explained in the caption for previous photo.

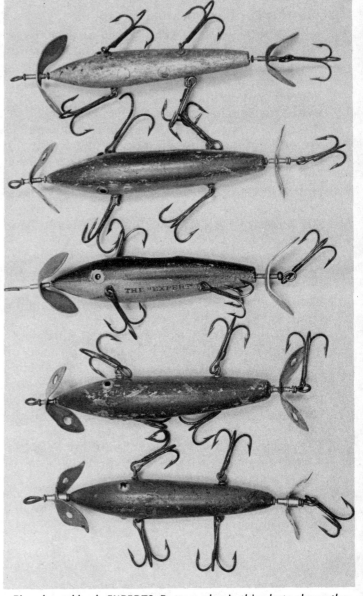

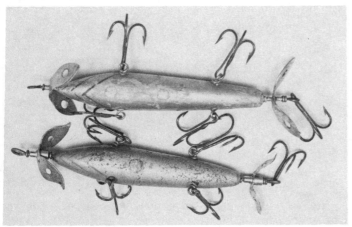

Belly view of two EXPERTS showing typical hardware, method of weighting and gill stripes.

Five shaped-body EXPERTS. Bottom plug in this photo shows the second style 1904-06 pointed blade propeller spinners.

A round-body Keeling EXPERT showing second style prop forward and no prop aft. This appears to be a production lure.

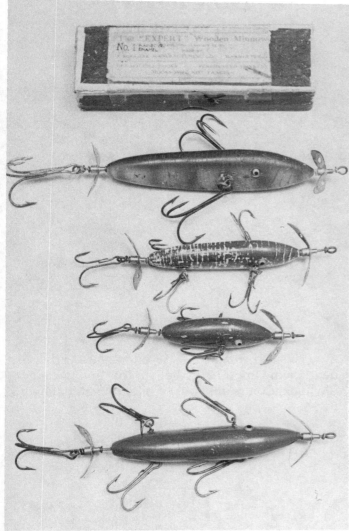

J. L. Clark box and EXPERTS. Shows detachable double and treble hooks. Some of the doubles are broken.

FALLS CITY BAIT COMPANY
Louisville, Kentucky

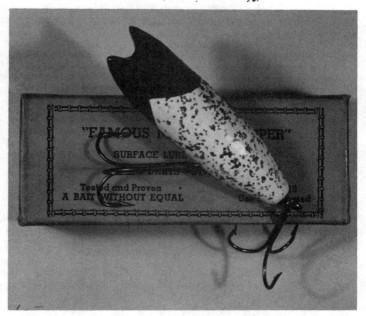

The lure pictured here is one of five that could be identified as being offered by this company. It is a MICHIGAN TIPPER. It measures 2-5/8", has a red head and white body with gold flitters. The hook hanger hardware is screw eye and brass cup. This particular example is mint in the box. A search through the available research turned up only a small, un-dated reference to the company. In it five lures are noted. They are as follows:

SNAFU - a 2-1/4" popper with two treble hooks
MICHIGAN TIPPER - pictured in the photograph above
DEEP SIX - a 2-1/4" underwater lure with a metal tip
S & W SPINNER - 2-7/8", typical 2-prop spinner minnow
HINKY - a 2-5/8" plug with slant dive plane cut in nose

All five of these plugs are wooden. Collector value range for any of the Falls City lures: $3 to $8.

WAB c1926
Fenner Weedless Bait Co.
Oxford, Wisconsin

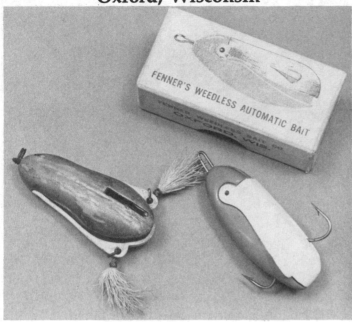

The name is taken from the first letters of "Weedless Automatic Bait." The lure was made of Pyralin, is 2¼" long, and the two single hooks were concealed in the body. Upon a strike they came out slots on the side. Collector value range: $5 to $10.

THE CAPTOR c1914
The Fischer-Schubert Co.
Chicago

This was an ingenious wooden plug made so that on casting and retrieve the two hard mounted single hooks on the tail protected each other making the lure weedless. If a fish strikes it the hinged plug closes at the tail and exposes the business portion of the hooks. It came in three sizes, 4", 5" and 5½". Colors are not known. Collector value range: $10 to $15.

DIZZY DIVER
Fishathon Bait Mfg. Co.,
Okmulgee, Oklahoma

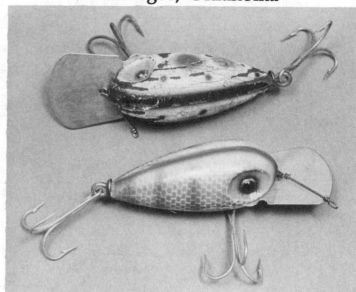

This is a small 1½", ½ ounce lure with a 5/8" deep diving lip. It had a belly treble and trailing treble hook. Colors unknown. Collector value range: $2 to $4.

DIZZY FLOATER

This 3¾", 5/8 ounce plug had a scooped out nose with a lower lip. It had two belly mounted treble hooks and one trailing treble. Collector value range: $2 to $4.

FISHERETTO

c. 1918-1945
Brown's Fisheretto Co.   Alexandria, MN
Osakis, MN

This company was formed sometime in the 1910's. In 1910, six brothers, Sam, John, Bill, Mike, Tom and Ed Brown opened a general store in Osakis, Minnesota. At some point between then and 1918 they began making and selling lures. Sam Brown applied for a lure patent in 1918 and it was granted to him February 24, 1920. That is evidence that they were serious about the lure business at least as early as 1918. They continued actively making and selling them until 1945.

They fashioned four basic styles of lures and two of ice fishing or spearing decoys. The following illustration and photographs represent these.

This illustration was taken from a Brown's letterhead. It is thought to be the original FISHERETTO. It is shaped somewhat like the patent drawing; at least more so than any of the others. It is most commonly found in a white body with red head finish, but has been found in other colors. I have not seen one of these personally so I can't say what type of hardware is common. I can say, however, that the one in the illustration not only appears to have cup and screw eye hook hardware, but also glass eyes. This is contrary to the norm for most of their lures. The usual hardware is a screw eye and washer and the eyes are painted. It may be that the illustration is of a prototype or early experimental model. Collector value range: $15 to $25 if found.

BROWN'S FISHERETTO — THE WORLD'S GREATEST FISH GO-GETTER

BROWN BROTHERS

MANUFACTURERS OF   BROWN'S FISHERETTO   PATENT ISSUED

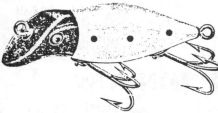

BROWN'S FISHERETTO
Red Head and White Body

"The BAIT THAT GETS 'EM"

It's a real fish getter that bass, pickerel, wall-eyed pike, muskies and even rainbow trout will strike at hard. Can also be used on the smaller salt water species with excellent success. Brown's Fisheretto has beauty and action—the kind that the fishing sportsmen demand.

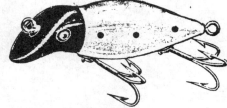

BROWN'S FISHERETTO
Red Head and White Body

OSAKIS, MINN., _____192 _

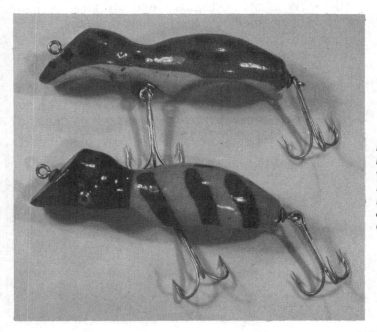

These two lures are examples of the most commonly found Fiserettos. Notice the distinctive concave belly. The upper lure has a frog finish and the lower has tiger stripes on a white body with a red head. These have the typical screw eye and washer line tie and hook hardware. The painted eye on the upper one is also typical, but the glued-on washer eye on the lower one isn't often found. They measure 3-3/4" and 3-5/8" long respectively. Collector value range: $5 to $10.

This is a minnow shape body with a floppy bow tie type propeller spinner at the tail. Note the use of cup and screw eye hook hardware. This is considered rare. This lure can be found in many different colors, some downright strange. For instance the upper lure in the above photo is white and pink! The other one is black and gold paint. They are 4-1/8" long. Collector value range: $10 to $20.

This 3-1/2" plug is considered the rarest of the Fisheretto lures. The one in the picture sports a Lady bug paint pattern with painted eyes and screw eye/washer hook hardware. Collector value range: $20 to $30.

They also made ice fishing or spearing decoys as you can see by these two photographs. The first photo is of the DARK HORSE SPEARING DECOY. It measures 5" long. The other is the FISHERETTO SPEARING DECOY. It is 5-1/2" long. Collector value range: $5 to $10.

For the most part these represent the line fairly well. Typical characteristics are screw eye and washer hook and line tie hardware and painted eyes. The lures were all hand-painted and no two were exactly alike. Most of the paint jobs would be considered crude by collectors, but they must have been successful fish getters for they were made for at least 26 years. It is possible for one of them to show up with the cup and screw eye hardware and glass eyes. They were made for a short while circa 1920.

FLOOD MINNOW

Frederick L.B. Flood   **Frostproof, FL**

The lure in the photo here is a particularly well made, carefully painted example of the FLOOD MINNOW or SHINNER, as Flood preferred to call them. The misspelling is his. It is said that Flood never went into commercial production with his plug though one wonders why he went to the trouble to obtain a patent on it. Perhaps he had intentions to go into production but some circumstance prevented that. In any case they all appear to be hand-made and painted, consequently they are each unique and all are fairly difficult to obtain. If you wanted to buy

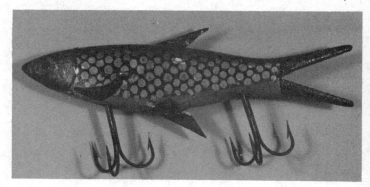

Flood Minnow (cont'd.)

one of his lures back when he was making them, you had to go to his house. There were no commercial sources.

Flood began making the lures shortly after building a house the back porch of which extended out over a lake. He began fashioning them about 1922 and had perfected his design by 1925. The earliest of his Shinners had leather tails, but sometime between 1925 and 1928 the leather was eliminated and the tails became wooden, carved integral with the body as in the example here. The dorsal and ventral fins are made of metal and are inletted into the body and the pectoral fins are painted on. Two odd characteristics that are unique to Flood's plugs are the rigid mount belly hooks and the side mounted line tie. The latter is barely perceptible in the photo here but if you look at the upper end of the painted pectoral fin you might be able to pick it out. About 1932 Flood made a deal with a man named Achter to product bodies for him. These were essentially the same as the ones Flood produced except that the Achter bodies had a sharply pointed nose whereas the Flood bodies had a more blunt, flat-topped nose as in the accompanying patent illustration. They remained pointed until Flood ceased production in 1935. The one in the photo here measures 5″. It is known that Flood produced at least two other sizes, one being larger at 6½″ in length. Collector value range: $100 to $200.

July 7, 1931.   F. L. B. FLOOD   1,813,843

FISH BAIT

Filed Sept. 22, 1928

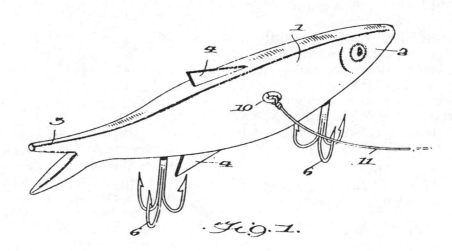

.Fig.1.

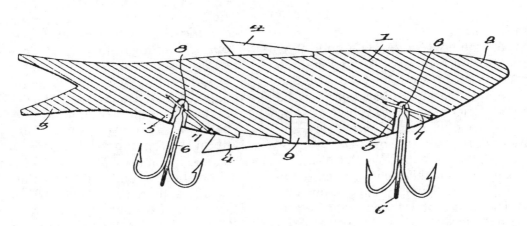

Fig.2.

By J. Destin Swecker
his attorney

F. L. B. Flood
Inventor

AL FOSS
Cleveland, Ohio
and
AMERICAN FORK
and HOE CO.
(True Temper)
Cleveland, Ohio
and Geneva, Ohio

Al Foss began making his famous pork rind lures first, then was later bought out by the American Fork and Hoe Company, now known as True Temper. (See Crippled Shad, page 349.) Al Foss was making (or at least experimenting with design) in 1915 or earlier. There is an ad in a 1916 issue of *The Outer's Book* offering the "Little Egypt Wiggler" and the "Skidder", both being all metal pork rind type lures. The 1915 or before date is derived from the fact that although his patent was not granted until 1918, Foss applied for the patent on his "Little Egypt Wiggler" on December 29, 1915. That is the earliest date patent research has turned up to date.

Dating Al Foss lures was made a little easier than many other company lure by Foss himself. He provided some valuable data for dating on an ad page in a 1929 issue of *The Sporting Goods Dealer* whereupon he provided an illustration with lure names and dates. "AL'S PORK RIND MINNOW TREE." "A staunch-sturdy oak-filled with good things for you." His listing follows:

LITTLE EGYPT - 1916
SKIDDER - 1916. Retired, exact date unknown but probably around 1918.
ORIENTAL - 1917
MUSKY ORIENTAL - 1918
SHIMMY - 1919
SHIMMYETTE - 1922
JAZZ - 1923
FROGS - 1926
DIXIE - 1928
NEW EGYPT - 1928

The patent for the now famous "Oriental Wiggler" was applied for on April 22, 1916 and granted to Foss two years later on April 30, 1918. The text of the original application infers that there may be some wood body "Orientals" to be found. It says, in part: "...preferably formed of **wood** (my emphasis), celluloid or other suitable material." No examples of a wood-body Oriental Wiggler have yet been found. It is not inconceivable but is highly unlikely that the collector will ever find a genuine one made of wood. The possibility of woodenprototype designs or a patent model* exists. Almost all Foss lures were designed to be used with pork rind or similar materials

*Until about 1920 all patent applications required the inventor to supply an actual working model with the paperwork.

Some time in the 1930's to '40's the American Fork and Hoe Company took over the Foss line and marketed them and a few additional lures of their own under the True Temper trademark.

The determination of the age of Foss lures is facilitated somewhat by the knowledge of spinner blade types used over the years. These types are: the Colorado spinner; the unmarked regular; the "AL FOSS" regular; the "AL FOSS" regular with 1918 patent dates; the Adam; and the Ponca 1928. They will be explained and identified in the following paragraphs.

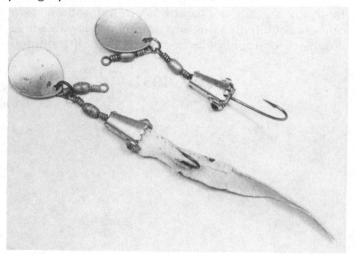

LITTLE EGYPT. Earliest style, with Colorado type spinner.

The earliest Foss lure found in patent research was the "Little Egypt Wiggler" mentioned above. The patent illustration shows a Colorado spinner at the nose of the lure. Advertisements for it in 1916 still illustrated this spinner as did all the "Skidders." After 1916 they began using the regular spinner (later called the "four" blade by the True Temper company). This blade is illustrated in the photograph of the five Al Foss wigglers accompanying the text here.

Early Foss spinner blades were unmarked and then he began stamping them "AL FOSS". Later, when True Temper took over, the patent dates from 1918 were added. This is true of all the Foss regular or "four" blades regardless of the type of lure on which they are used.

Oriental Wigglers are found with unmarked regular, the "AL FOSS", the "AL FOSS" with 1918 patent dates and the "Adam type blades. The "Adam" type blade can be seen on the far right lure in the bottom photograph on this page.

The "Shimmy Wiggler" came out about 1919 and has been found with four blade types: the unmarked regular; the "AL FOSS" regular; the "AL FOSS" with 1918 patent dates; the "Adam"; and the "Ponca 1928." The "Ponca" type spinner can be seen on the left three lures in the photograph at middle right.

Al Foss (cont'd.)

The ponca blades have a 1928 patent date on them.

The "Jersey Wiggler" was new around 1923 and so far has only been found with the "AL FOSS" with 1918 patent dates only.

"Frog Wigglers" became available in 1926 and as above have been found with the "AL FOSS" with 1918 patent blades only.

"Dixie Wigglers", new around 1928, can be found with the regular "AL FOSS," the "AL FOSS" with 1918 patent, the Ponca and a unique spinner that appears to be an unbalanced, two-bladed Ponca spinner.

The "New Egypt," also out in 1928, has so far been found with the "AL FOSS" 1918 and the Ponca blades.

"The Sheik" has shown up with the "AL FOSS" 1918 and another unique spinner, this one appeared somewhat like a modified Ponca blade but with single blade only. The "Hell Cat" has been found only with this latter spinner.

The chart below synopsizes much of the above spinner blade data. Collector value range for all: $3 to $12.

	Colorado Spinner	Unmarked Regular	"AL FOSS" Regular	Regular "AL FOSS" 1918	ADAM	PONCA 1928	UNIQUE
SKIDDER	X	X		X			
LITTLE EGYPT	X	X		X			
ORIENTAL WIGGLER		X	X	X	X	X	
SHIMMY WIGGLER		X	X	X	X	X	
JAZZ WIGGLER				X			
FROG WIGGLER				X			
DIXIE WIGGLER			X	X		X	*
THE MOUSE						X	
NEW EGYPT WIGGLER				X		X	
THE SHEIK				X			**
THE HELL CAT							

FROG WIGGLERS. Left is top view. Right two lures are belly view. All have the Regular ("Four") blade.

AL FOSS WIGGLERS. Left to right: Dixie Wiggler, The Mouse Wiggler, Shimmy Wiggler, Unidentified Wiggler. Each has the "Ponca" type blade except the far right. It appears to have a modified ponca type blade.

Various Al Foss lures. Left to right: The Shiek, Shimmy Spoon, Unidentified Foss, New Egypt Wiggler, Shimmy Wiggler with the "Adam" type blade.

*A unique spinner appearing to be an unbalanced two-bladed Ponca type.
**Unique spinner appearing to be somewhat like a modified version of the single blade Ponca type.

Al Foss (cont'd.)

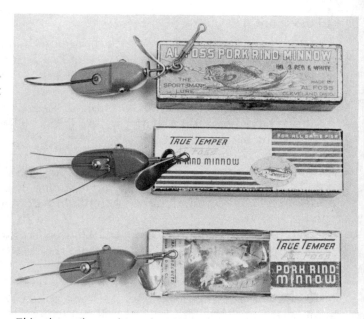

This photo shows the early "AL FOSS" spinner blade (top), the American Fork and Hoe Company blade (center) with patent dates and the last blade (bottom) with no identification on the blade at all. Each lure is shown with its original package.

The photo here shows the evolution of boxes from earliest tin to the later cardboard. Reading top to bottom, the first four are tin boxes and the bottom two are cardboard.

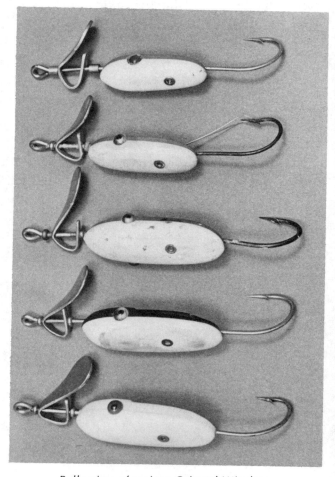

Belly view of various Oriental Wigglers.

W. A. FOSS.
ARTIFICIAL BAIT.
APPLICATION FILED APR. 22, 1916.

1,264,627.

Patented Apr. 30, 1918.

Fig. 1.

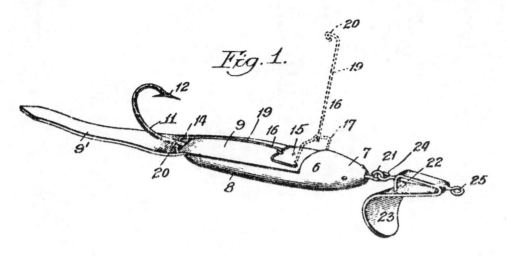

Fig. 2.

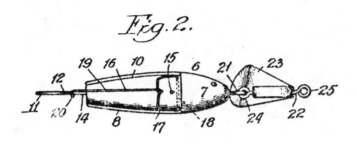

Fig. 3.

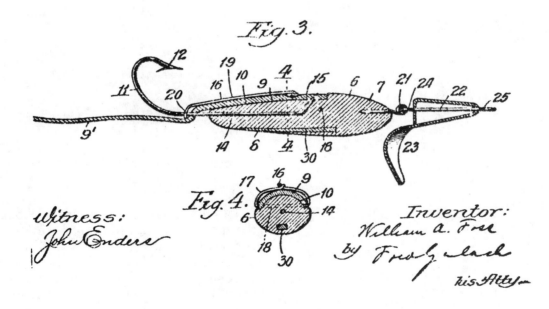

Fig. 4.

Witness:
John Enders

Inventor:
William A. Foss
by Fred Gerlach
his Atty

Al Foss (cont'd.)

Al Foss Shimmy No. 5 with original box and pocket catalog packed with it.

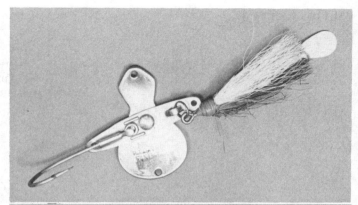

Fan Dancer . . . open and closed positions.

TWIN DANCER
Gardner Specialty Company
Gardner, Mass.

This lure was placed under the Arbogast listing in the first edition of this book because of its extreme similarity to Arbogast lures and it was otherwise unidentified. Little is yet known about the Gardner Specialty Company, but thanks to one of the many helpful collectors who have written me regarding the first edition we have the lure properly identified. The lure was likely made in the 1950's and is 3" long and the nose blade rotates to make it a surface or diving plug. Collector value range: $4 to $8.

CORK-HEAD MINNOW
Garland Brothers, Plant City, Florida

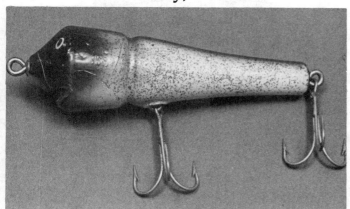

This plug has a wooden body and a head made of cork. The line tie has a very long shank that doubles as the device securing the head to the body by passing through the cork and screwing into the wood. The lure is 3-5/8" long and weights 5/8 oz. The lure dates from sometime in the mid to late 1930's. A lure box pamphlet listed the available colors as "Light Green Frog Finish, Dark Green Frog Finish, Green Silver Splash, and Red Silver Splash." Collector value range: $8 to $16.

GAYLE LURES
George W. Gayle and Son
Medical Lake, Washington

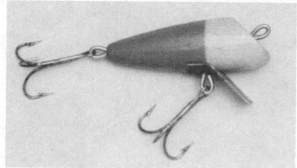

A thorough search of all the materials on hand for research turned up zero references to this maker. The only identifying characteristics I could find were the name Gayle on the propeller spinners of one lure and the name and city stamped on the metal diving lip of the other. Both lures appear to be old and fairly well made. George W. Gayle is known to have been a reel maker. Collector value range: $20 to $30.

GEN-SHAW
Kankakee, Illinois

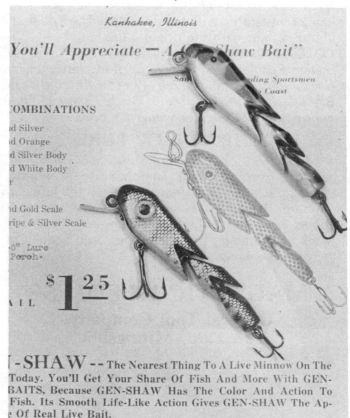

I reported in the last edition that the company apparently made only one lure. It is now certain that they produced at least two. The photo of the two lures on the 1950 catalog page are undoubtedly the same as the lure illustrated in the catalog photo but with a couple of small differences. Note the different line ties, eye size and diving lips. The lure in the photo for the WIGGLE-LURE below appears to be exactly the same as the one illustrated in the ad photo.

WIGGLE-LURE

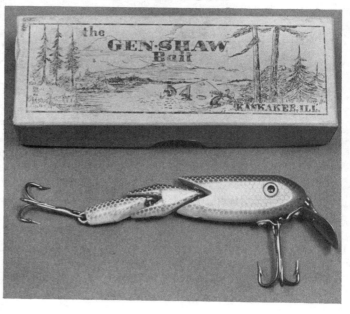

Gen-Shaw (cont'd.)

This is a triple jointed lure of plastic, 4½" long.* Note that it is the same as the lure illustrated in the ad above including the one-piece surface hook hanger integrated with the diving lip. The lure in the photo is mint with the original box.

COLOR OR FINISH: *Black and silver; Black and orange; Red head and silver body; Red head and white body; All silver color; Frog; White with gold scale; Black stripe and silver scale; Perch; "Spark-O" lure; Yellow perch. Collector value range: $5 to $10.*

THE "L & G" LURE

This 3-5/8" plastic lure showed up in a 1953 catalog from General Merchandise Company, Milwaukee, Wisconsin. It is a single jointed lure with the same hardware as on the Wiggle-Lure photo above. Available in the following colors: Red Head, Black and Orange, Green Sparkle, Gold Scale. Collector value range: $5 to $10.

MAGNETIC WEEDLESS
General Tool Company, St. Paul, Minnesota

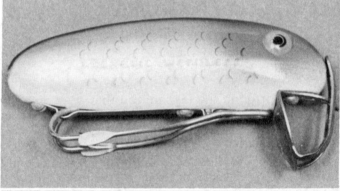

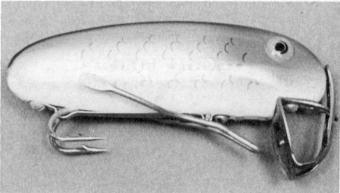

As you can see by the two plugs in the photos, they are well identified on the body. The lure is plastic and was made in the 1940's. It has a unique weed guard utilizing a magnet in the body that holds the guard out until a fish strikes it. The photos show the guard in the open and closed positions. It was available in four color combinations. Collector value range: $4 to $8.

The only reference to sizes found says the plug is 4½ inches long. The plug in the photo measures 3½ inches. Therefore there may be two sizes to be found.

GENTLEMAN JIM c1949
Associated Specialties

Made of plastic (Tenite) this lure had two belly mounted trebles and a twin tail molded in. They appear fragile, therefore the collector may encounter broken examples. Collector value range: $2 to $4.

GETS-EM

Keller   **Rochester, Indiana**

For years now, this particular plug has been grouped in with a group of lures all under the name Myers and Spellman. These lures were bunched together under that name because of their similarity in design, hardware and paint. They all resembled each other, but they never seemed quite close enough. It was a matter of convenience for there was really no other way to classify. At best it was thought they were related. Now some of this confusion has been sorted out (see Myers and Spellman and Jacob Hansen). We now know that the lures with KELLER stamped on the back were made by a Keller in Rochester, Indiana. We have a couple more we believe to be Keller products also. Little else is known presently, but there are folks digging around in the area. Perhaps we will know something more soon.

The photo above is of a Keller GETS-EM at the top and a Myers at bottom for comparison. Note the much larger knob at the nose of the Keller plug and its soldered, reinforced propeller spinners. It also has KELLER stamped along its back in all capital letters. Its side hooks are fastened by utilizing a thru-body twisted wire hanger. Collector value range: $30 to $60.

Both of these Keller Gets-Ems are 3-1/4", have metal nose caps (note different types) at the knobs, tail washers, thru-body twisted wire, painted eyes. Upper is blue/white, lower is orange.

Some collectors attribute these two lures to Keller, others to Myers and some to neither. They are here for want of someplace else to put them, so you see the confusion still goes on. They are essentially the same except for the hook arrangement and hanging method on the body. They have the same shape as the Keller GETS-EM and the similar Myers, but the propeller spinners are more like those used on the Keller lures. Both measure 3-1/8" and have the thru-body twisted wire arrangement. Collector value range: $50 to $100.

The two lures in this photo are attributed to Keller because they are the same shape, have the same hardwre and the fact that one just like the upper one in the picture has been found bearing a KELLER back stamp (the red paint at the tail wend was added by a fisherman). The smaller treble hook wired near the tail end of the lower lure appears to have been added by a fisherman also. Both are 3-1/2" and have metal nose and tail protectors usually found painted over, but could be loosened with use. Collector value range: $40 to $80.

GLOWURM
Oliver and Gruber
Medical Lake, Washington

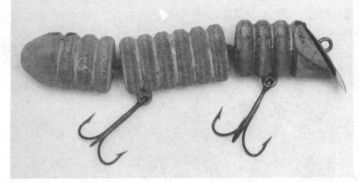

Advertisements for this 4¼" lure began to appear in the early 1920's. One ad contained a 1920 patent date. It was made in red and white stripes or yellow and green stripes. The one in the photo here has very little paint left on it. The lure is double jointed with three body sections. The head has a metal plate protruding slightly below forming a diving lip. The original box was very interesting. It was a long block of wood drilled out and cut in half longitudinally to accomodate the lure. It had slots in the bottom section to make room for the protruding third hook of the trebles. Collector value range: $5 to $15.

GOBLE BAIT

Bert G. Goble   **Tulsa, Oklahoma**

Very little is known about this particular lure or its maker. A search turned up patents for two lures by Bert Goble neither of which bears any resemblence to this one. The applications were filed in 1922 and 1924 and granted to Goble in 1924 and 1929. No examples of either have been uncovered as yet. The lure in the drawing here is handsome and well made. It is very sturdily built and measures 5-½" long. It has cup and screw eye hardware and clear glass eyes with yellow irises. The yellow scale finish is nicely done. The remaining paint has been carefully sprayed and the pectoral fins are brush painted. The metal diving lip is somewhat bell-shaped held in place by a screw and the screw eye line tie. The box says "patents granted and pending." There is no indication of model name or number. Collector value range: $20 to $40.

THE GO-GETTER

Hayes Bait Company   **Indianapolis, IN**
John J. Hildebrandt Co.   **Logansport, IN**

Sometimes known as the HILDEBRANT WOOD BAIT in the literature this lure was manufactured by The Hayes Bait Company and distributed by Hildebrandt, a company known widely for its metal spinners and other metal lures. Why they took on this one rather odd wooden lure is anybody's guess until more is learned. If you are lucky enough to find one in a box it may be in the original box as in the accompanying photo. Others have been found in the same box with Hildebrandt labels pasted on. The

lures date around 1927-30 as best as can be determined presently. There is a provision for easily removing and replacing hooks at will. It measures 2-5/8" and has painted eyes. All so far found have been painted white. Collector value range: $10 to $20.

THE GOPHER

Elmer J. Deuster   **Milwaukee, Wisconsin**
Gopher Baits   **Sheboygan, Wisconsin**

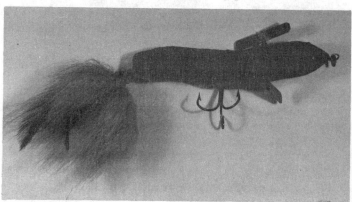

This big (5-3/4") funky looking lure was originally available in a brown, black, gray or yellow flocked finish. Sometime in the last ten years red was added to the choices. It is a musky or pike lure built quite strongly with an under belly wire comprising the line tie, the belly hook hanger and the bucktail hook at the tail. There are two metal paddle wheels, one at either side. An older box indicated that Mr. Deuster was the inventor, manufacturer and distributor. A later box has only the Gopher Baits name, but says "... All thanks go to E. J. Deuster, Milwaukee Inventor..." The address on that later box includes a Zip Code so one could presume that if they are not still in business they did last at least until the advent of the Zip Code. Collector value range: $10 to $20.

EARL PARKER GRESH
1896 - 1977
St. Petersburg, Florida

It isn't likely that you will come across many of Earl Gresh's lures very far away from St. Pete. All his lures were hand-made by him alone. He is a legendary figure around the St. Petersburg area. He was a true artist in wood. He built his home with his own hands during the Depression, making it a showplace in English cottage style. There he also established The Wood Parade where he also pursued his passion for woodworking.

Among his many talent were violinist, orchestra leader (many recordings with Columbia Records), boat builder and racer, avid conservationist with much recognition and fisherman. With a flair for fly tying, he made more than one for President Herbert

Gresh (cont'd.)

Hoover with whom he often fished. He also presented Hoover with a custom made wooden tackle box. Mamie Eisenhower saw this box and asked Gresh if he would make one for Ike, which he did. He was invited to dine at the White House as a result.

What we are interested in here are his lures. There is no accurate estimate as to how many he might have made, but the number must be limited due to the fact that they were all hand-made. Perhaps in the hundreds, perhaps more. The lures are highest quality, professional products. They were usually put up in sets in beautiful wooden boxes. He gave a few to friends and sold the rest. He must have made a number of sets of six (see photo) for he went to the trouble to have printed a set of instructions for the time and conditions under which to use the lures and provided one with each set. The lures are easily identified as made by him because he stamped each one with his name somewhere on the underside of the lure (see accompanying photos).

Presently it would probably not be fair to place a collector value on any of Gresh's plugs due to his relative anonymity among collectors outside the Tampa/St. Pete area, but I suspect this will change. I can, however, report that the large wooden box full of his lures in the photo accompanying sold for $450.00 at auction a few years ago. I doubt that figure would touch it now.

WATER COVERAGE

★ ★ ★

The lures in this mahogany bait box are designed to meet weather and water conditions. If the angler using these plugs will follow the numbers and directions he will obtain a maximum of results. Each of the lures has been carefully tested as to balance and usage conditions with coloration to meet outlined specifications.

No. 1 - Medium deep - - for dark days.

No. 2 - Deep sinking - - bright day fishing.

No. 3 - Slow sinking - for shoreline fishing around grass.

No. 4 - Top water - for dark days.

No. 5 - Bright day - top water, fish slowly.

No. 6 - Late evening lure - agitate by working rod tip.

Earl Gresh
The Wood Parade
St. Petersburg, Florida

This set of instructions was included in each of six lures like the box to the left.

This beautiful mahogany box of Earl Gresh lures was three trays of lures. It is the one mentioned in the text preceding.

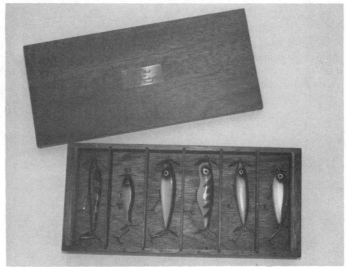

Box of six Gresh lures. The brass plate on top is inscribed "To _____ From the Old Woodworker, Earl Gresh." It was apparently a gift.

Gresh (cont'd.)

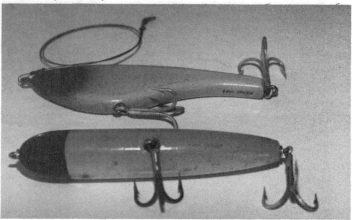

Both of these have recessed (no cup hardware) screw hook belly hook hangers. It appears the Gresh used this method most of the time. Note the swiveling tail hook on the lower plug.

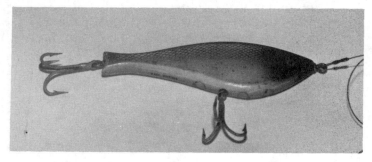

A good looking minnow with wire leader. Note the nose and tail cap protectors and the three internal belly weights.

The upper lure has a tail propeller spinner and a one-piece, sur-face belly hook hanger. Note the large plastic eye. This probably tags the lure as one of this later products. All others appear to have painted eyes.

HAAS TACKLE COMPANY
Sapulpa, Oklahoma
Haas' Liv-Minnow

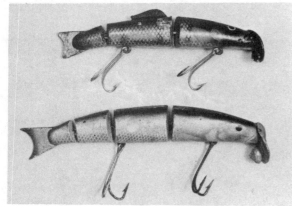

Pictured here are three lures from Haas and a reproduction of the original patent illustration. Patent applied for in 1933 and granted to Harry R. Haas on July 16, 1935. If you compare the photo with the patent you will note that the lure on the left in the photo is the one most like the patent. The other two have different types of lips, hook hardware and tail fin styles. They are however, so similar otherwise that they are most likely Haas lures as well. You may also notice that the patent shows a double jointed lure as do the two on the right in the photo. A 1930's advertisement illustrates a lure substantially similar to the one in my photo here except that the one in the ad is double-jointed. The protrusions at the lower edge of the lips are weights. The ad stated they were available in a 4" single-joint and a 5" double-jointed model. No colors were given. The left lure in the photo has glass eyes while the other two are painted eye types. We can reasonably place the glass eye version in the earliest category. Collector value range: $10 to $20.

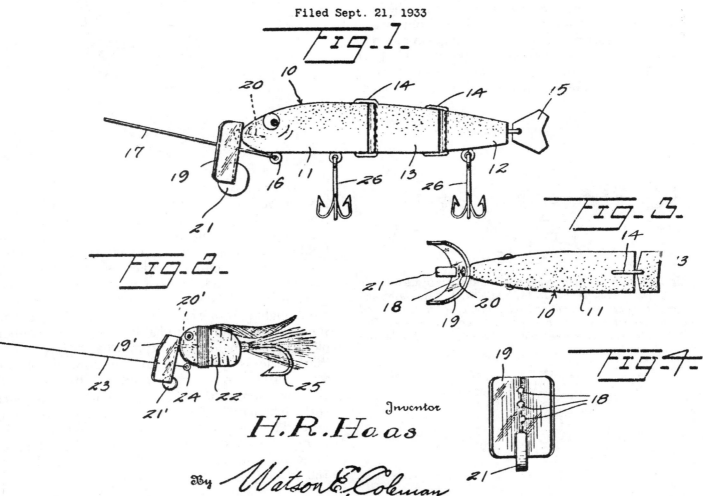

Patent on the Haas LIV-MINNOW. Granted to Harry R. Hass on July 16, 1935.

JACOB HANSEN
1866-1945
Muskegon, Michigan

For a long time there was very little concrete information to be had regarding this man. His name, along with Adolph Arntz, Edward Myers, Jack Spellman and a man named Keller were all associated with a sort of generic group of similar lures lumped under the name Myers and Spellman. When we found a lure that looked like any of those in the group, we just put it there for lack of anywhere else to put it. With the help of a few folks we can now sort this mess out for the most part. At the head of the list of these folks stands George Richey of Honor, Michigan. It was his research that uncovered much valuable information about Jacob Hansen thereby enabling us to cut through the fog.

Until now, the only thing we knew for certain was his association with Adolph Artnz with regard to the MICHIGAN LIFE-LIKE and the fact that Hansen was granted the patent on February 20, 1908. I reported in the last edition that Arntz was the manufacturer as a result of the advertisement I had found in a 1910 issue of *The Anglers Guide* that clearly stated "Manufactured by Adolph Arntz." We have known that Arntz was a sporting goods dealer in Muskegon and now know that Hansen made the lures and Arntz marketed them. Arntz bailed out after a couple of years because it was taking too much of his time. Hansen continued to make the LIFE-LIKE for a few years, but eventually abandoned it saying it was a good lure, but just too difficult to make.

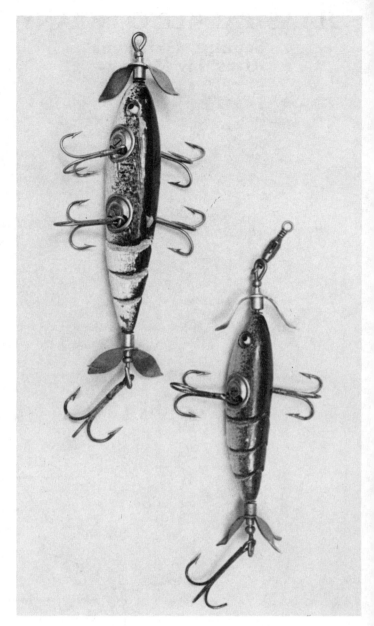

Illustrates one of the many types of forward single blade spinners used by Hansen on the SPOON JACK MINNOW. It was fashioned by punching out and bending back a portion of the metal and boring a hole through which the through body wire passed. This rendered the spinner more stable and held it away from the lure body.

The photo above shows the MICHIGAN LIFE-LIKE in both versions that were made. The smaller one was 2-3/4" long and had three treble hooks and the larger one came in a 3-3/4" length with Five trebles. Both sported glass eyes and three bladed tail spinners. The articulated bodies were extraordinarily well made. The side hook hangers shown on these two lures are of the style more commonly found and are thought to represent the oldest style. The second style protrudes further and although the same principle is in use, the design is somewhat different. The third style is illustrated in the drawing of the Muskegon Spoon Jack Minnow to the left. It looks somewhat like the common one-piece surface hanger that so many companies began using around the mid 1940's. It is, however, used as a hook *swing limiter* and covers the screw eye hook hanger. Collector value range for the MICHIGAN LIFE-LIKE: $80 to $160.

(cont'd next page)

COLOR OR FINISH: *Light green with speckled back and white belly, Dark green with speckled back and white belly, Aluminum color with dark back, Brook Trout, Dark back with yellow belly, Solid aluminum color, Perch, Green back with yellow sides and red belly, Natural wood finish.*

MUSKEGON SPOON JACK MINNOW

The drawing of the Spoon Jack Minnow shows what might be a typical one if indeed you can call any one of them typical. Hansen was known to be an inveterate tinkerer and it appears he couldn't keep from changing things about the lure. The majority are configured in the drawing with either three or five hooks. They have a round body tapered to a nose and tail, a two blade propeller spinner at the tail, a single blade spoon-type spinner at the nose, and a thru-body twisted wire line tie and tail hook hanger. The three hooker is found either in an opposite side mount or a two belly mount configuration. To add to the confusion there also exist, although fairly rare, two hook and four hook models. The two-hooker has one belly treble and the four-hooker has two side hooks on one side with a single mounted toward the tail on the opposite side. Both, of course, have tail hooks.

Sizes vary from 3-1/4" to 4-1/2" usually, but there is one known unusual 5" version that has flat sides.

With regard to eyes, they are found with no eyes, yellow and amber glass eyes and painted eyes.

The single blade spoon-type nose spinner is found made three ways. The first is illustrated in the drawing. Another type is made by simply drilling a hole in the tapered end of the spoon and the last is made by bending the small end back on itself and drilling through making two holes. Some collectors believe the simple single hole blade to be the earliest, but at the present time there is no way of being certain which of the types of blades or hook hangers came first.

Most Spoon Jack Minnows have a tail spinner also. For the most part these are the propeller spinner type, but from time to time you will find any of the three single blade spoon type spinners. With Hansen almost anything can happen. All of these variations will be illustrated in the photos to follow.

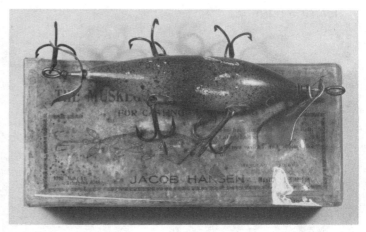

This Spoon Jack Minnow on its box measures 3-15/16" and is configured the same as the drawing above. It does not have the twisted wire thru-body fixture common to Hansen lures, however, it is characteristic of his lures in all other ways. Collector value range: $40 to $80.

This one measures 3-5/8" and has the single hole floppy style spoon-type single blade spinner at the nose. The rear propeller spinner is one made for use on the nose. Collector value range: $40 to $80.

Measuring 3-1/4" this one is easily identifiable as it is stenciled "Spoon Jack Minnow" on the belly. You don't find that very often. It has one internal belly weight. Collector value range: $40 to $80.

This 4" Spoon Jack Minnow is pretty typical. Probably more have this cup and screw eye hook rig than any other. Note the absence of a rear propeller spinner. Photo courtesy Clarence Zahn. Collector value range: $40 to $80.

This is a very atypical Spoon Jack Minnow. It is the only 5" one to be found so far. It has flat sides and odd ball wire extenders from the hook hangers to hold the hook away from the lure body. Note the presence of the single blade spoon-type spinner at both ends of the lure. From the George Richey collection. Photo courtesy Clarence Zahn. Collector value range: $40 to $80.

Hanson (cont'd.)

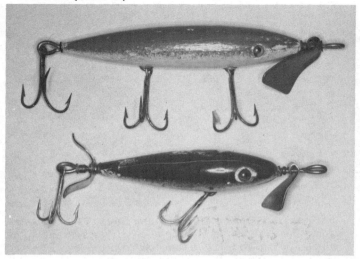

This may not be a Spoon Jack Minnow, but because of its hardware and configuration and lack of other classification it is placed here. It measures 4" and has a tail shaped a lot like the one in the previous photo. Note also the flutes at the head. This style Hansen is very scarce. Collector value range: $100 to $300.

The upper is 4-3/8" long. The front prop is brass. Note no rear spinner. The lower lure measures 3-1/4"-1/4". It has the typical spinners, but is the somewhat uncommon two hooker. Photo courtesy Clarence Zahn. Collector value range: $40 to $80.

This is an unusual Spoon Jack minnow in several ways. It sports two styles of single blade spinners, has long shank hooks and a spatter type paint job. Photo courtesy Clarence Zahn. Collector value range: $40 to $80.

PULL ME SLOW

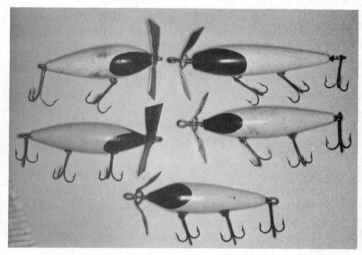

Hansen, true to his nature, made fat and fatter versions of this lure in sizes varying from 2-3/4" to more than 4-1/2". There are at least three versions of the large nose mounted spinners. They vary with the manner of mounting them on the armature, line tie. All the lures are cup and screw eye belly hook rigged. None have been found with other than a white body, red head paint job. They are found with three treble hooks, two treble hooks and a third version with only a trailing treble hook (rare). Collector value range for the Pull Me Slow: $20 to $50.

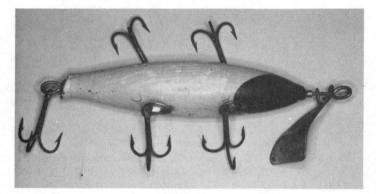

This 4-1/4" beauty exhibits a couple of unusual characteristics. This white body, red head pattern is not often found. Note the odd curved carving at the tail. It has no eyes, painted or otherwise. Photo courtesy Clarence Zahn. Collector value range: $40 to $80.

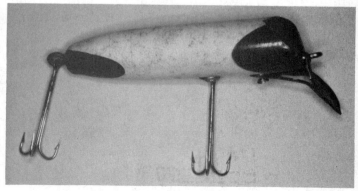

This is an unknown Hansen lure. Collector value range: $20 to $50.

HANSON'S IRRESISTABLE MINNOW

Wm. B. Hanson and Company
Pittsburg, Pennsylvania

This c1919 odd looking wooden lure was available as in the photograph and was also furnished with two double hooks. It has a raised cup and screw hook hardware. Colors available were: Brown mottled back with red painted mouth as in photo; Green; Red and Green. Collector value range: $80 to $160.

CHARLES R. HARRIS

1848 - 1922
Mackinaw City, Michigan
Niles Michigan
Manistee, Michigan

For years collectors have known Harris to be the inventor and maker of the Harris Floating Cork Frog. He was granted a patent for it on August 24, 1897. What was not widely known until recently is that he was also responsible for the Manistee Minnow, a lure of heretofore mysterious origin.

Harris was a railroad man and a hotel manager for some twenty years prior to his association with the fishing tackle business. Sometime during the 1880's or early 1890's, he was in the sporting goods business in Mackinaw City, Michigan. It was there that he first began making and marketing his lures. He later was located in Niles, and finally Manistee where he died at age 74 in 1922. Beside the two lures already mentioned he also offered a Phantom or Devon type lure he called the Featherbone Minnow. Collector value range for the Harris Cork Body Frog: $40 to $100; for the Manistee Minnow: $100 to $200.

The Manistee Minnow

This very rare lure has the words "The Manistee" on one side of the body. The photo here isn't too clear, but if you look closely you may be able to see the brass wire extending along the belly to the trailing treble hook and over the top of the tail where it is attached. There are metal hook restraining cups at the belly and tail. The spinner revolves on the armature connecting the head and body. This head does not rotate, only the spinner. Has zinc painted eyes.

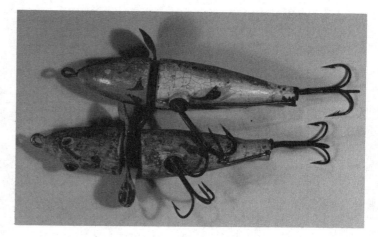

This photo shows belly views of two more Manistee Minnows. Both are 3-3/4" long. The lower lure has a slightly different method of hanging the tail and belly hooks. You may notice glass eyes on this lure. This is not the norm. These are obviously modern and have been added in recent times.

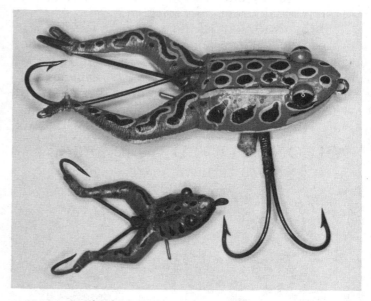

Harris Cork Floating Frogs. The upper lure measures 3-1/8" and the small fly rod size, 1-1/2". Each came with an external belly weight attached by a brass wire at the belly. The weight is missing from the small one in the photo.

WILSON WOBBLERS
Hastings Sporting Goods Company

The company has its origins in the early 1900's, probably around 1910-11. The first of their patents I could find was for the Wilson Fluted Wobbler. It was applied for in 1911 and granted to Richard T. Wilson and Aben E. Johnson on May 6, 1913 (see patent illustration on next page). It has been reported that an advertisement for this lure appeared in a 1911 publication the name of which is unknown to me. The earliest ad I could find for this lure was in a 1912 OUTER'S BOOK. What is interesting about this particular ad is that the company advertising was JOHNSON SPORTING GOODS WORKS, Hastings, Michigan. It specifically stated "Wilson's Fluted Wobbler" and illutrated same. The point here is that the next ad I found was in a 1913 OUTERS used the same illustration and some of the same text, but the company was then the familiar HASTINGS SPORTING GOODS WORKS. In addition to the above I came across a pocket catalog from "Good Luck Fishing Tackle" It featured a trademark that is a four-leaf clover with a Wilson's Fluted Wobbler superimposed. It said "Wobbler Brand." The catalog offered various Hastings Co. lures and said the company was located in Hastings Michigan. In any case all patents for "Wilson's" lures so far found have been granted to both Wilson and Johnson. Wilson was obviously the creative end of the company and Johnson the business end. It appears that all but one of the Hastings lures with Wilson's name as the prefix were invented by Wilson. Others will be discussed under the individual lure entries following.

Around 1927-28 Hastings company ads disappeared from catalogs and periodicals and about the same time the Wilson's Wobblers and Cupped Wobblers showed up in Moonlight (Paw Paw) catalogs and advertisements. It therefore follows that Hastings went out of business either merging with or selling their rights to Moonlight.

WILSON'S FLUTED WOBBLERS
(Good Luck Wobblers)

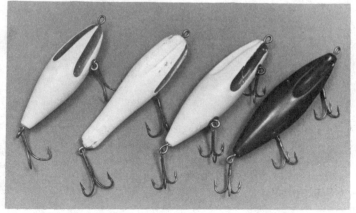

The illustration here shows four different bodies that were introduced. All had the distinctive four grooves or "flutes" in the forward portion of the body. They were available over the years mostly in two and three treble hook configurations and differing hook hanger hardware. It is possible that one or more copies or imitations because there were many individuals or companies jumping on the band wagon. There were floating and sinking models. Collector value range: $5 to $10.

NAME	BODY LENGTH	
Wilson's Wobbler	4"	3T
COLOR OR FINISH: *White, red flutes.*		
Luminous Wobbler	4"	3T
COLOR OR FINISH: *Luminous red flutes.*		
Sinking Wobbler	4"	3T
COLOR OR FINISH: *White, red flutes.*		
Red Wobbler	4"	3T
COLOR OR FINISH: *Solid red.*		
Yellow Wobbler	4"	3T
COLOR OR FINISH: *Yellow, red flutes.*		
Trout Wobbler	1¾"	2T
COLOR OR FINISH: *White, red flutes.*		
Super Wobbler	3½"	2D
COLOR OR FINISH: *White luminous, red flutes; Rainbow, Scale finish.*		
Musky Wobbler	4¾"	3T
COLOR OR FINISH: *Unknown.*		

There have been Wobblers found with gold and copper flutes but it is not known if they were produced that way or were repainted by others later.

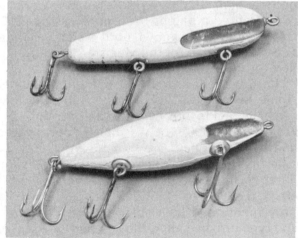

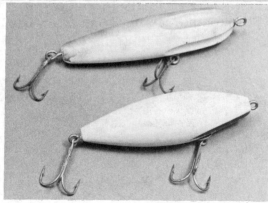

Fluted Wobblers. Photos show the various shapes to be found and are arranged according to the age of the hook hardware. All measure in the 4½" to 5" range.

R. T. WILSON.
ARTIFICIAL BAIT.
APPLICATION FILED NOV. 22, 1911.

1,060,873.

Patented May 6, 1913.

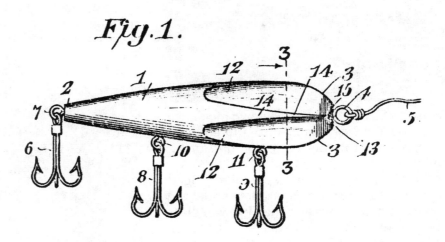

Fig.1.

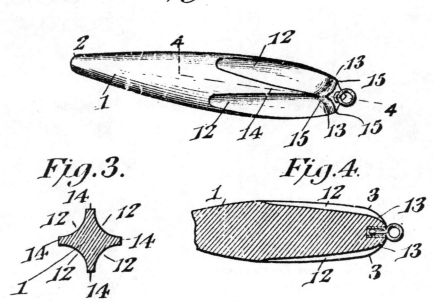

Fig.2.

Fig.3.

Fig.4.

Richard T. Wilson, Inventor

By

Witnesses
Jas F. McCathran

Atto'ney

The illustration filed with patent application for Wilson's Fluted Wobbler. Granted May 6, 1913 to Richard T. Wilson and assigning one-half the rights to Aben E. Johnson, both of Hastings, Michigan.

WILSON'S SIZZLER

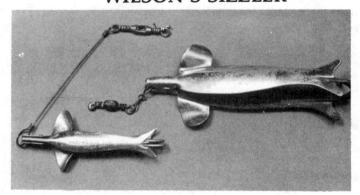

The Wilson's Sizzler is the only known incidence where Wilson's name was attached to a lure he did not invent. The inventor was John Hedlund of St. Cloud, Minnesota.

This is an all metal lure with a peculiar winged metal piece hinged at the nose and trailing under the body. It had two single hooks attached in a weedless manner. There were two sizes, 3¼" and 2½" and both are plainly stamped "PAT. AUG. 24-1904" on the back. Collector value range: $10 to $20.

WILSON'S GRASS WIDOW

This 2½" plug had an odd shaped belly (see illustration). It had one double hook. Colors available are listed below. Collector value range: $20 to $40.

COLOR OR FINISH: *Red body, mottled spots; Solid red; Solid white; Luminous; Solid green; Fancy green back, white belly; Rainbow; Brown scale.*

These colors are common to most Wilson's lures but may or may not apply to all plugs including the Grass Widow.

WILSON'S CUPPED WOBBLER

The three lures in the photos measure 4½", 3½" and 3-1/8" respectively. The center lure is identical to one illustrated in an ad in a 1921 issue of *Forest and Stream* magazine. The ad stated the lure was available in white luminous only. Note the top of the cupped head end is sliced off at the top. It is also found without the cut-off. These are found in various colors (see color listing under Grass Widow). They were new around 1915. Collector value range: $10 to $20.

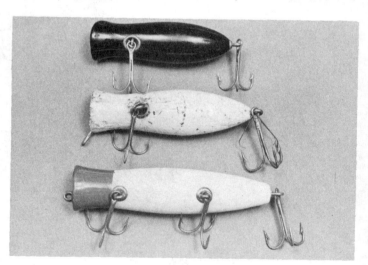

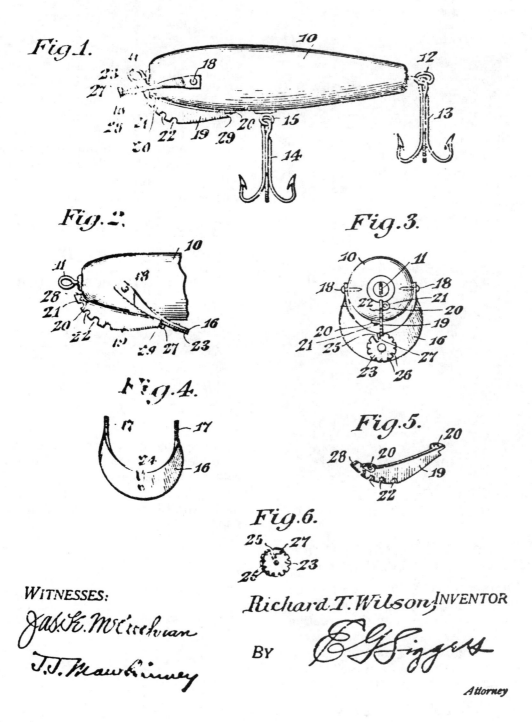

1,220,921,

Patented Mar. 27, 1917.

Fig.1.

Fig.2.

Fig.3.

Fig.4.

Fig.5.

Fig.6.

WITNESSES:

Richard T. Wilson, INVENTOR

BY

Attorney

Patent for the Wilson 6 in 1 granted March 27, 1917.

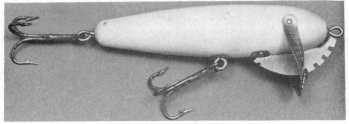

WILSON SIX-IN-ONE WOBBLER

See patent illustration on previous page. This lure was patented March 27, 1917 and has a unique six position adjustable diving lip at its head. It was first marketed in 1916, found advertised and written up in an article as new for 1916 (Outer's Book). It was available in white with red head, light green crackle back, or red stripes on a green back. Collector value range: $40 to $80.

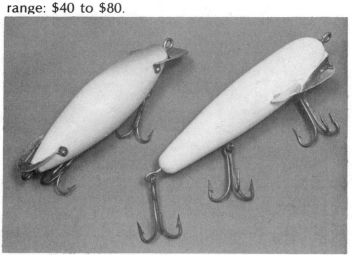

Photo shows BASSMERIZER on left and FLANGED WOBBLER on the right.

WILSON'S FLANGE WOBBLER or WILSON'S WINGED WOBBLER

This plug, patented Jan. 13, 1914, had a metal wing or flange piece fitted onto the bottom of the nose. The metal protruded from each side creating the "wings". It had two belly trebles and a trailing treble hook. The flanges were always painted red and the plug was made all the same colors as the "Fluted Wobblers". Collector value range: $10 to $20.

WILSON'S BASSMERIZER

This is a 3-5/8" double ended lure with a metal plane on each end. The angler may choose either end to render the plug action diving or surface. It had two belly mounted treble hooks. Collector value range: $40 to $80.

THE STAGGERBUG

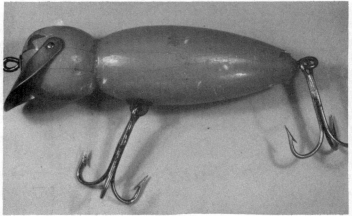

This lure has an adjustable metal plane on the head similar to the one on the "Six-in one" plug. The head is much smaller. It has one belly and one trailing hook and can be found in almost any of the colors listed with the Wilson's Grass Widow. The one in the photograph here has a cup and screw eye belly hook hanger. Collector value range: $100 to $300.

THE HAYNES MAGNET c1908
W.B. Haynes, Akron, Ohio

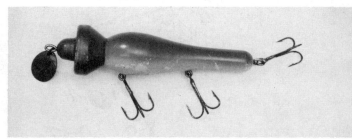

This is a plug very similar in basic design to the Woodpecker or Moonlight. The wood body is shaped with a collar carved behind the head. There is a small spoon attached to the line tie on the nose, a trailing treble and two belly trebles. Collector value range: $90 to $135.

THE HAYNES PEARL CASTING MINNOW

Although the text is not quite clear about it, in a 1907 ad it is inferred that the body of this lure is made of pearl (more likely Mother-of-Pearl). It is more probable that the lure is painted with an irridescent pearl finish. The odd looking protrusions at the head in the drawing above) are actually weights. They are affixed in such a way as to let them hold the lure in an upright position. The ad says they are made of "German silver." Don't let that fool you into believing it is real silver. That was a trade name of the day to describe an alloy that was shiny but anything but real silver. Length is about 3½". Collector value range: $20 to $30.

JAMES HEDDON AND SONS

Dowagiac, Michigan

James Heddon, 1845-1911
Will T. Heddon, 1870-1955
Charles Heddon, 1874-1941

These are six of twenty-four blank lures found in Mineola, Florida by Clyde Harbin. He carefully documented the find and authenticated them as having belonged to W.T. and Laura Heddon.

The Heddon company began humbly and became one of the giants of the tackle industry in its eighty plus years run. Founded by James Heddon and his son W.T. (Will) Heddon. The elder Heddon was quite an accomplished gentleman before he ever got in to the tackle business. He was an inventor recognized nationally as an expert on bee-keeping. He invented several devices and methods in this discipline and was widely published in the journals. He was into publishing (newspaper) and politics

*Article in a 1921 issue of American Angler.

(Mayor of Dowagiac) also. Son Will was something of an adventurer having done, among other things, hot air balloon ascents returning to the ground by parachute. The latter was particularly hazardous in those early days of its development. At the time he worked for his father in the newspaper business and became the manager of the Dowagiac electricity generating plant. At some point shortly thereafter he organized the Dowagiac Telephone company which he sold to the Bell Telephone Company in 1897. It was about this time that James Heddon started the company.

The story is old and has been told many times with little significant variation. It seems that Mr. Heddon was waiting for a fishing buddy one day by the side of the lake. To while away the time he whittled on a chunk of wood and upon satisfying the whittling urge casually tossed the result into the water. What happened next is the legend. To his amazement a big bass attacked the chunk so violently that it was knocked into the air. Some say the bass did this repeatedly. Whatever the exact event the idea of making artificial baits out of wood (hence the name "plug") was born in Heddon's mind in that moment. In Sam S. Stinson's *Whence The Plug? he says according to James Heddon's son, Charles, his father was using wooden plugs as early as 1890 and carved a few for family and friends. It was not until 1901 that Heddon Plugs were commercially available. The company has been under several ownerships in recent years.

The company continued to operate under the Heddon name until it was bought out by Ebsco Industries in 1983. Ebsco includes Rebel Lures.

A common story related in reference to the beginnings of the company is that early on in the production of lures there was a rush order for some lures whose paint was still wet and that to hurry up the drying process the lures were placed in Mrs. Heddon's oven. The result was a crackling of the paint on the back of the lures. Supposedly this was the birth of the so-called Fancy-back paint finishes. Whatever the case, the company was started in a small upstairs room at 303 Green Street in Dowagiac by James Heddon. He was soon joined by son Will who brought with him a $1000 investment. This is thought to be about 1902. The 1903 catalog read James Heddon and Son. Some time not too long after, younger son Charles joined the company. The 1909 catalog reads James Heddon and Sons. It seems that Charles turned out to be the one with the talent for business and Will the tinkerer. It was about 1903 that Will and his wife Laura went to Florida to experiment with various lure types and finishes. Apparently they and the company found that arrangement to their liking for it wasn't long after that they took up permanent residence in Mineola. They were both very talented fishermen and worked as a team in the experimentation and development of new lures. They also became important contributors to their newly adopted community. Each served in various community service and political capacities including terms as mayor. Will once and Laura three times. When James died in 1911, Will continued to serve in the research and development end and Charles continued to run the company. Upon the death of the father of the company became known as James Heddon's Sons. At some point in time Charles did become president. Upon his death in 1941 his son John took over as president. Will continued in his R&D capacity until 1945.

The following pages list the old Heddon lures by ascending catalog series number and dated where possible. Most of the plastic plugs are not listed.

Before getting into the listings, it is important to note three early lures, the Heddon hand carved frog, the model of the original Dowagiac bait, and the model of the first Heddon Wooden bait.

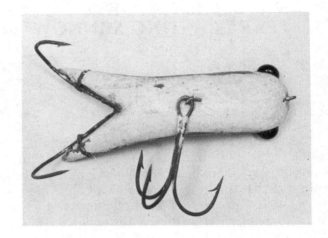

JAMES HEDDON'S WOODEN FROG c1898
Body Length: approximately 3''

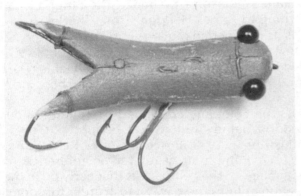

Pictured are three views of one of the first plugs used by James Heddon. He carved this plug for himself and a few others for friends, therefore it is

extremely rare and valuable. It would not be prudent to place a value on it. It is simply too unique to price. The collector who finds one should consider himself a lucky man indeed.

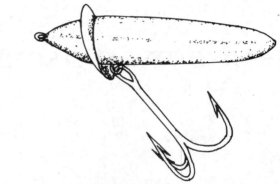

ORIGINAL DOWAGIAC BAIT. The first made by James Heddon.

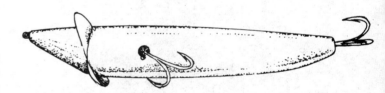

A model of the first wooden bait made by James Heddon.

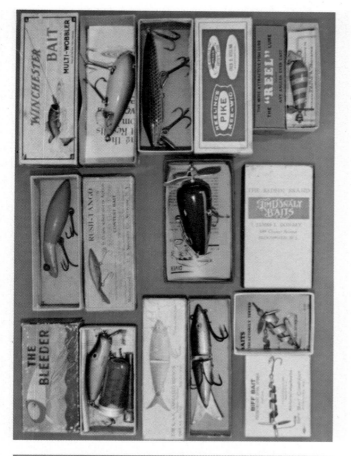

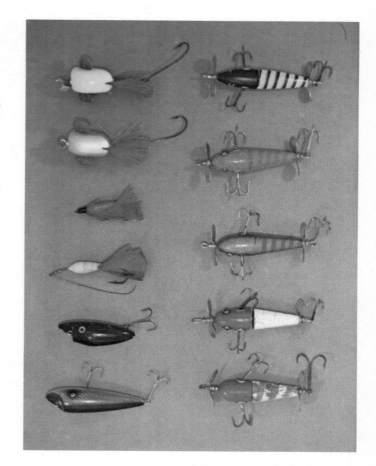

TOP LEFT: Assorted lures in original boxes.

TOP RIGHT: Bottom two lures in left row are **MOONLIGHT BAIT COMPANY** products. Remaining four are from **JAMISON**. Right Row: All are **CHARMER MINNOWS**.

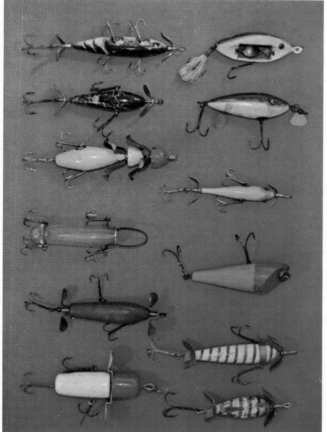

BOTTOM LEFT: Left row, top to bottom: **MICHIGAN LIFE-LIKE**; **WORDEN** lure; **MILLER'S REVERSIBLE MINNOW**; **DETROIT GLASS MINNOW TUBE**; **DECKER UNDERWATER**; and **DECKER** surface plug. Right row, top to bottom: **CHIPEWAH** from Immel Bait Co.; **REDFIN MINNOW** from Donaly; **NIXON UNDERWATER**; **ZIG ZAG** from Moonlight; and two **CLINTON WILT MFG. CO.** lures.

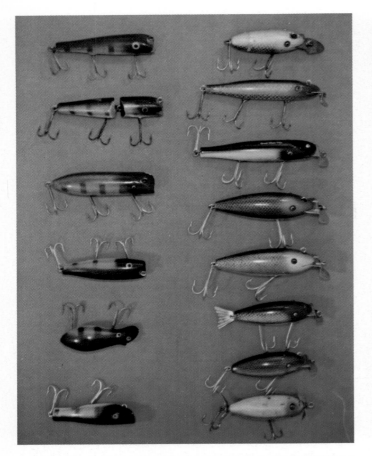

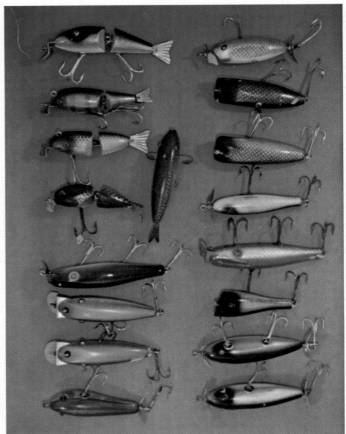

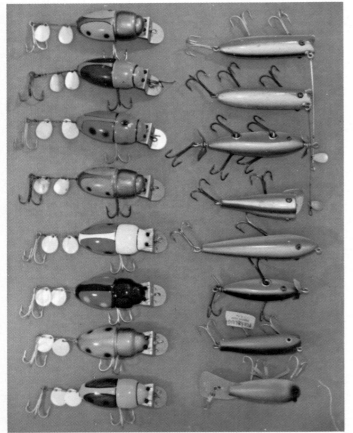

TOP LEFT: **CREEK CHUB PATTERNS.** *Illustrates various types of scale finishes found.*

TOP RIGHT: **CREEK CHUB PATTERNS.** *Bottom four lures in left row are four types of finishes found without scale pattern. The remainder are scale finish types to be found.*

BOTTOM LEFT: **CREEK CHUB PATTERN.** *Right row illustrates several rainbow type patterns to be found. Left row is of all patterns so far found on the "Beetle".*

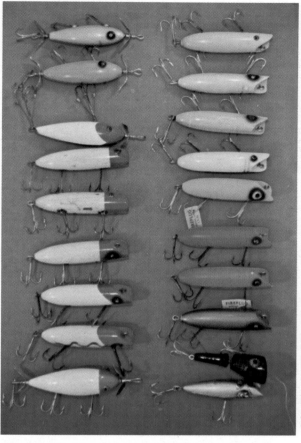

CREEK CHUB PATTERNS. Illustrates various two-color finishes, dot patterns, scale finishes and, frog types to be found. Note the "Victory Finish" demonstrated on the lower lure of the two lures appearing fourth from the left on the top row.

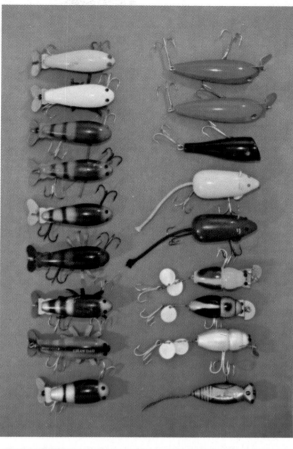

SOUTH BEND PATTERNS. Photo illustrates various solid colors found and the several two color combinations with the "arrowhead" and "straight line" head color paint.

CREEK CHUB PATTERNS. Bottom row illustrates various types of "glitter" or "sparkle" finishes to be found. Occurs in gold and silver glitter. Far left lure in bottom row is a fuzzy or flock finish. Top row is of the four patterns found so far on the "Wee Dee".

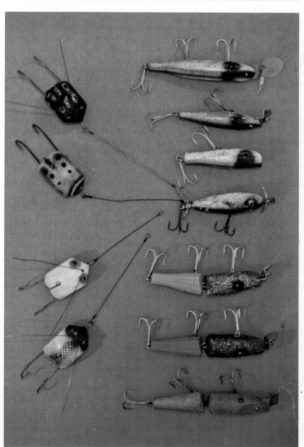

CREEK CHUB PATTERNS. Illustrates solid colors, pearl finish (bottom row, second from left), and all patterns found on the "Crawdad" so far.

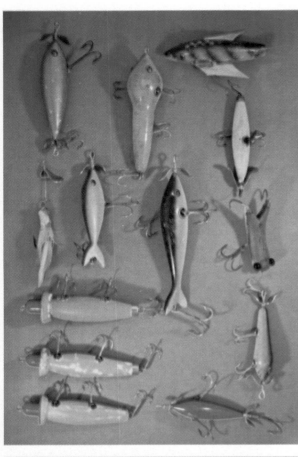

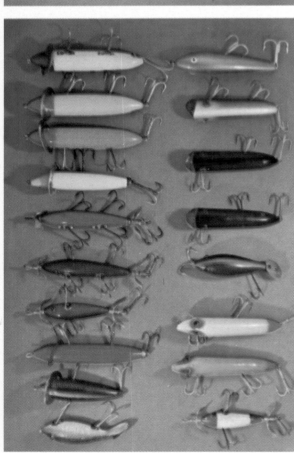

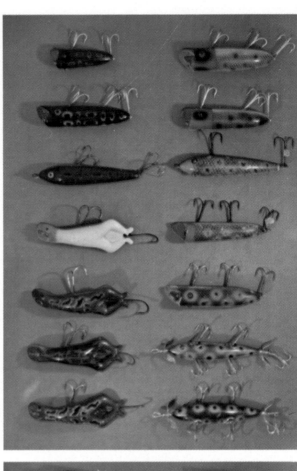

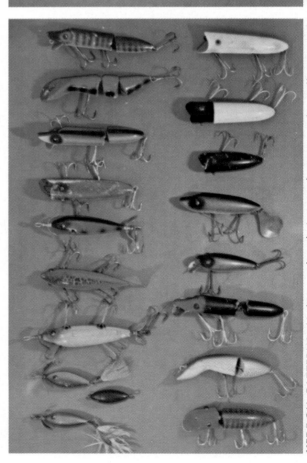

HEDDON PATTERNS. Photo shows a few of the very rare Heddon lures. Note the fish decoy at bottom right and the extremely rare frog, at bottom center, hand carved by James Heddon himself. See Heddon section text for identification of the others.

HEDDON PATTERNS. Various early color designs. Note subtle body shape changes demonstrated by two or three of the same lures placed side by side in the photo. They are placed in order from oldest on left to newer on the right.

HEDDON PATTERNS. Photo illustrates various frog and frog spot type finishes the collector may find. The top row, center lure is the very scarce red head, white body "Luny Frog." (Note webbed legs).

HEDDON PATTERNS. Various color designs and patterns the collector may encounter.

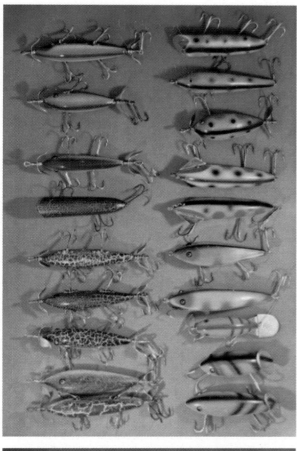

HEDDON PATTERNS. Illustrates various types of "Fancy Back" or crackle finish to be found. Remainder of the lures show several rainbow and spot multicolor patterns.

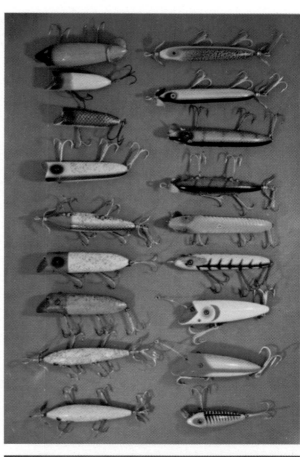

HEDDON PATTERNS. Illustrates several types of glitter type finish. The remaining lures show assorted paint and patterns to be found.

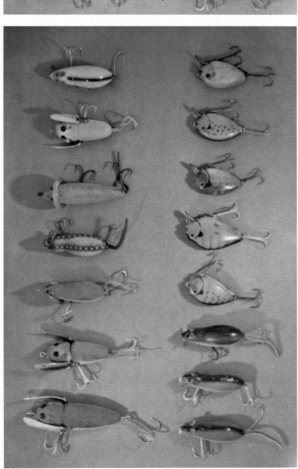

HEDDON PATTERNS. The first six lures in the top row are the various fuzzy or flocked type finishes to be found. Bottom row includes five patterns of the "Punkin Seed" lure.

PFLUEGER PATTERNS. Illustrates paint and pattern types encountered on Pflueger lures.

PFLUEGER PATTERNS. *Illustrates paint and pattern types encountered on Pflueger lures.*

PFLUEGER PATTERNS. *Illustrates paint and pattern types encountered on Pflueger lures.*

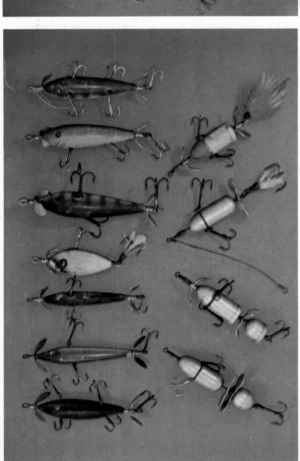

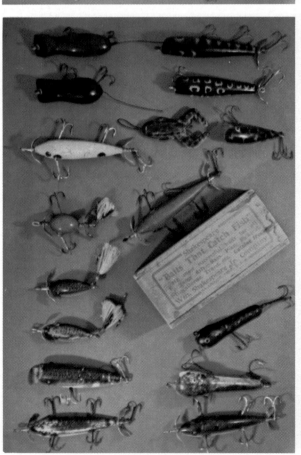

SHAKESPEARE PATTERNS. *Some very early lures. The bottom row shows the "Revolution" and "Bucktail Spinners".*

SHAKESPEARE PATTERNS. *Illustrates various "Crackle back" type finishes, solids, frog finishes and an early wooden box. Bottom row, second from left is a lure covered with actual frog skin.*

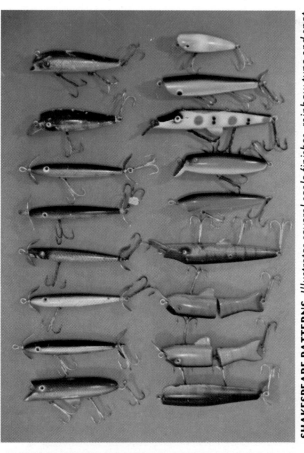

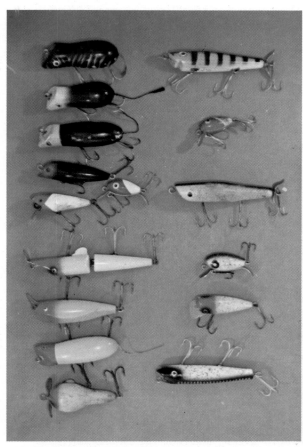

SHAKESPEARE PATTERNS. *Illustrates several scale finishes, rainbow type and spot color patterns.*

SHAKESPEARE PATTERNS. *Red and white, black and white, and other assorted styles including those found with glitter.*

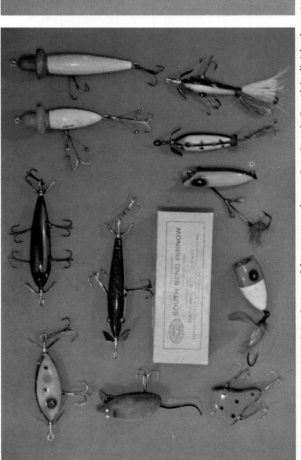

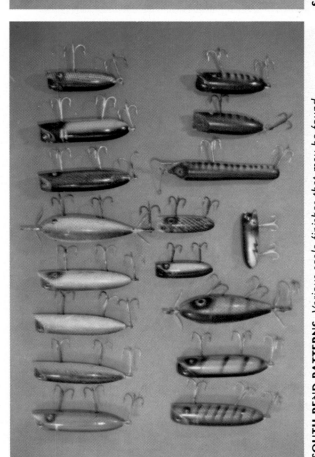

SOUTH BEND PATTERNS. *Some older, scarce lures. See South Bend individual plug listing text for identification.*

SOUTH BEND PATTERNS. *Various scale finishes that may be found.*

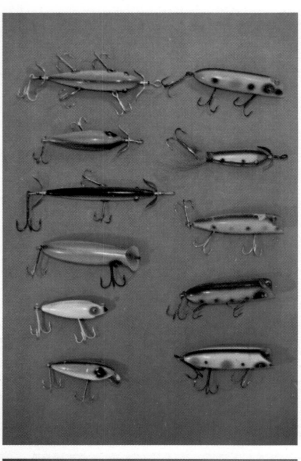

SOUTH BEND PATTERNS. *Assorted spot and rainbow type styles.*

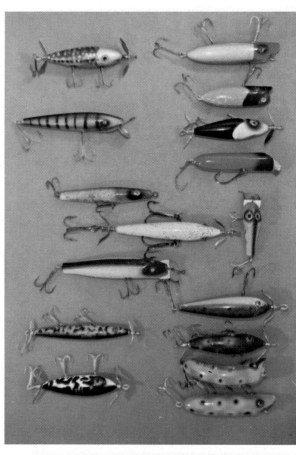

SOUTH BEND PATTERNS. *Types of head paint styles (straight, arrowhead, and blended), glitter styles, spots and frog spots, and miscellaneous.*

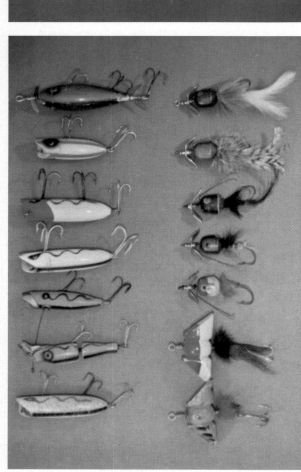

SOUTH BEND PATTERNS. *Assorted styles to be found.*

TOP ROW: **RUSH TANGO PATTERNS.** *Bottom Row: First five illustrate* **MEDLEY'S** *Wiggly Crawfish paint styles. Last three are typical* **KEELING** *paint patterns.*

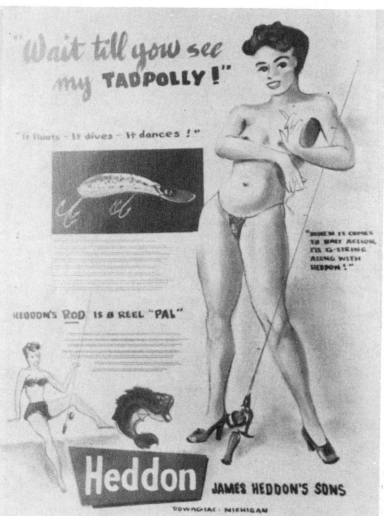

This rather risqué advertisement layout may have been a joke from their advertising agency or it may have been a genuine proposal. It is full of innuendos. There is a story that the boys' wives got wind of it and squelched the idea. Whatever the case it's fun and a humorous bit of Heddon history.

Some Specific Tips On Dating Heddon Lures

As discussed under the listing for the slope nose Experts, the first commercially produced Heddon lures had hook fasteners that were screw hooks recessed in a hole in the body (see patent drawing, page 224).

Shortly after this the recesses were fitted with metal flanged cups so as to protect the outside edges of the recess from the hook shanks. The first of these had a very thin flange or rim. Later the cup was made a bit larger and with broader rims or flanges. This "Cup" hardware is still in use by some companies today. A Heddon catalog of 1915 or 1916 illustrated and described "The new Heddon Double Screw Hook Fastening now used on all "Dowagiac Minnows...". It is headed "Heddon Patent Hook Fastening," but there is a patent number 1,276,062, applied for May 20, 1915 and not granted to Heddon until August 20, 1918. Although the statement said "all Dowagiac Minnows" it is reasonable to note the possibility of many old types still in warehouse inventory therefore one

can only date the first use of this double screw fastener (known to collectors as the "L-rig") approximately. The patent described and illustrated the L-rig as having two humps, but there have been one hump versions, and even a *no hump version found (probably pre-dates the patented rig).

There have been some plugs with the "one-piece bar" but generally collectors place the "two piece rig" as next in line. There were two versions. The first, referred to as the "toilet seat" for obvious reasons began around 1930 and the second style two piece rig came into use around 1935. The final style is the "one piece surface" replacing the "two piece rig" around the mid 1940s and is in general use today.

There are other more general rules, but they are not as reliable as noting the type of hardware. Even the hardware method is not entirely foolproof for it is possible to change some or all of it causing a lure to appear older than it really is. There are methods that enable the collector to reasonably determine whether this has happened but they are the highly technical, complicated procedures used by the very advanced serious collector. Perhaps as the hobby grows, we will cover these methods in depth in subsequent editions of this book. For now you may apply the hardware dating methods in combination with the general guidelines for identification of the 200 Series beginning on page 222.

This photograph of the early 100's shows difference in gill marks. Upper lure gill marks are curved. This is oldest manner. Bottom lure has more or less straight painted gill marks. Newer.

Only one is known to the author. There may be more. Possibly a modification by a fisherman.

THE DOWAGIAC UNDERWATER

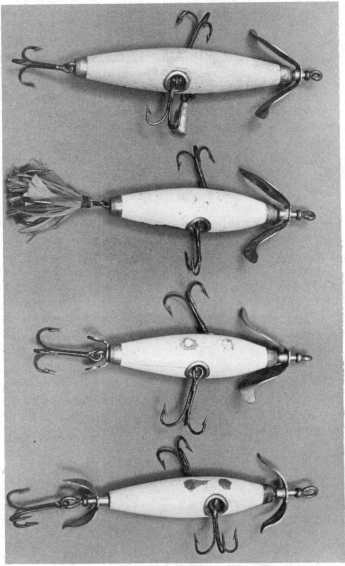

These four lures represent the evolution of the Dowagiac Underwater to what is thought to be its ultimate form, the No. 100 (see page 200). The first lure in the photo is earliest; note the external belly weight. The next is a smaller body. The third is the same body, but has addition of a small odd-ball prop at the tail. The last is the same body with No. 100 type propeller spinner and brass cup hardware. This is believed to be the transitional plug to the No. 100.

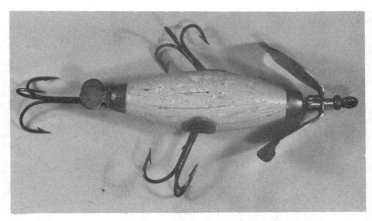

This is a shorter, fatter version of the third lure from the top in the previous photo. It has deep brass cups with screw hook hanger hardware, the earliest style sweeping front prop and the odd small one at the tail. Collector value range: $100 to $200.

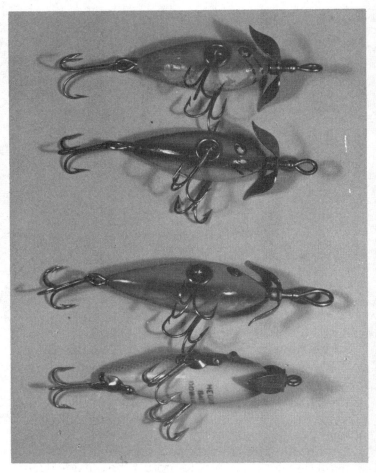

This 1904 Dowagiac Underwater is 3¾" long, had marine brass hardware, no eyes, and a nose mounted propeller with no name or trade markings. The earliest version has a lead weight swung from beneath the belly (see photo). Later versions have the weight inside the body. The hook hangers have cup hardware. Collector value range: $100 to $200.

DOWAGIAC "EXPERT" SURFACE LURE AND The 200 Series

Drawing copies the 1903 illustration in a Heddon catalog.

First called the " 'Dowagiac' Perfect Surface Casting Bait" the Expert had evolved into the 200 Series by 1912.

The Expert patent was applied for January 9, 1902 and granted to Heddon on April 1, 1902 (see next page).

This patent described four features as follows:
1. The metal angling collar (B on patent drawing).
2. The hook socket (A on patent drawing).
3. The screw hook or open-eye screw (B on patent drawing)
4. The sloped-up nose (A on patent drawing)

It was featured in the 1903 catalog as new and incorporated all specifications in the patent.

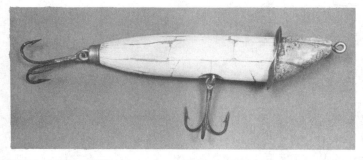

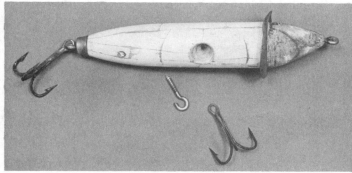

This is the 1903 vintage EXPERT in side and belly view. Note the addition of the metal reinforcing tail cap. The recess for the screw hook without any cup hardware is clearly visible. Collector value range for this particular Expert is: $50 to $200.

The Expert was first marketed in a second model the next year (1904). The original had one belly mounted treble and a trailing (2T) treble hook and the second ("Dowagiac No. 2") had two additional treble hooks, opposite side mounted (4T). Interestingly that 1904 catalog states, "We do not advocate the use of the 'No. 2', but offer this pattern to those who hold the false theory of 'more hooks, more fish'." The No.

2 did not appear in subsequent catalogs. All the catalog entries until 1912 stated it was available only in a white body, red painted collar and a blue nose*. The 1912 edition of the catalog said: "White body, blue snout and nickel plated collar; Frog colors, consisting of white belly, green spotted back." By then it was called the "No. 200 Special Series". The same catalog entry said it could be had with two, three or four treble hooks if preferred. By 1913 they had added a luminous finish. Most interesting to note in the 1913 catalog is that both the slope nose style and the round pencil nose style bodies are used in illustrations. The round pencil nose style was used to illustrate the Frog finish. All Experts and 200's catalog illustrations prior were of the slope nose type. This double body style illustrations prior were of the slope nose type. This double body style illustration remained this way at least through 1916. There is a gap in the catalog section here until 1921 where only the round nose model was available.

The following is a set of guidelines, observations and conclusions I have arrived at regarding the Experts and No. 200 Series lures:

1. It is **possible** that the earliest Experts were all white (c1902-03).
2. The first reference to other colors was in 1906 where it said "red painted collar and blue snout."
3. By 1912 the collar was described as nickel plated.
4. Regarding collars:
   a. First was friction mount (no pins)
   b. Next was a one pin mount under the nose
   c. About 1912 came the two pin collar mount simultaneous with the first one of the nickel plated cup hardware and tail cap
   d. About 1915-17 came the three pin collar attachment and the L-rig. Collar was marked Heddon Dowagiac. No collars prior to this were marked.
   e. Screws instead of pins to attach collars
5. At some point (c1912) they were made available with the belly trebles.
6. They lost the metal tail cap sometime during the L-rig period.
7. All were eyeless until about the first two-piece toilet seat hook hardware period when they acquired glass eyes.
8. Deviations from the above have been found but this is extremely rare. Consider yourself fortunate if you snag one.

No. 696,433.

Patented Apr. 1, 1902.

J. HEDDON.
FISH BAIT.
(Application filed Jan. 9, 1902.)

(No Model.)

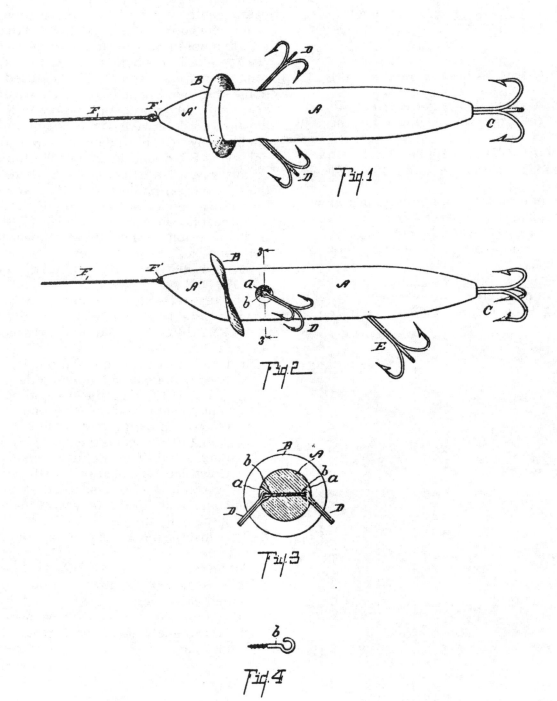

Fig. 1

Fig. 2

Fig. 3

Fig. 4

Witnesses:

A. E. Houghton

Otto A. Earl

Inventor,

James Heddon

By Fred L. Chappell

Att'y.

Original patent drawing for the Dowagiac Expert.

Evolution Of The Heddon Expert To Later Named Heddon 200 Surface

Please see photos on pages 226-228. Letter designations beside the descriptions are keys to the photos.

A. The original EXPERT from the 1903 catalog illustrating only this one lure. 4½" long, brass screw hook in the recess, friction mount collar (no screws or pins), brass tail cap, blue painted nose. Collector value range: $150 to $300.

B. Second model of the EXPERT. This one measures 4-3/8" and is the same as the one above with the addition of a brass thimble or rimless cup in the recess at the belly hook hanger. Slightly thinner body. Smaller line tie. Friction fit collar painted red. Collector value range: $100 to $200.

C. Same as B above except that the brass cup on this lure is rimmed. 4-3/8". Collector value range: $75 to $150.

D. Same as C above except that this one has one pin at the front bottom of the collar holding it secure to the lure body. The collar is painted red. This is the last EXPERT to use the small line tie. Collector value range: $60 to $120.

E. The earliest model to utilize the nickel plated deep cup and screw hook hardware. Two pins, at the top and bottom of the collar, secure it to the body (not through the body collar but adjacent). Large line tie and all nickel plated hardware. Collector value range: $50 to $100.

F. Solid red painted, cigar shaped (pencil nose, c.1915) body. Slightly small collar using 2 pins adjacent to the collar to secure it. Screw hook and very deep, almost coneshaped cup belly hook hanger, deep tail hook insert. All nickel plate hardware. 4-¾". Collector value range: $45 to $75.

G. Same as F above with but a slightly larger collar attached by a pin through the collar and a white body with blue nose. 4-5/8". Collector value range: $40 to $60.

H. Same as G above except the collar is not painted at all. 4-3/4". Collector value range: $40 to $60.

I. This is the first EXPERT to utilize a flanged collar (illustrated in lure M below). This is that there are two nibs or flanges on the collar through which the pins go to secure the collar to the body. Heretofore there was no flange; the pins simply went through the collar itself (illustrated lure H above). The tail cap on this lure is missing. 4-3/4". Collector value range: $40 to $80.

J. Same as above but is a 2T model. 4-5/8". Collector value range: $40 to $80.

K. This may be an experimental or prototype lure. It came from the Heddon factory archives. Oddities are the glass eyes, brass tail cap and friction fit collar. It is placed here because of body shape and hook hardware. The glass eyed models didn't show up with any regularity until around 1930-35. 4-3/4". Collector value range: $50 to $100.

L. First use of the three flange pinned collar. 4T. Deep cup and screw hook hangers, all nickel plated hardware and red painted collar. 4-3/4". Collector value range: $75 to $150.

M. First use of the L-rig hook hanger on this lure. Also this is the first appearance of the Heddon imprint on the collar. It appears on both sides. The other characteristics are the same as L above. Post 1915. 4-3/4". Collector value range: $35 to $45.

N. Same as M above except that it is a 2T model. 4-3/4". Collector value range: $35 to $45.

O. Same as N above except that it is a 5T model. 4-3/4". Collector value range: $50 to $100.

P. This is the first frog finish for Heddon and it helps to estimate the vintage of this lure at c. 1915. It is easy to distinguish the difference between the two frog finishes by noting the presence or absence of the mustache type marking at the nose. The mustache is the earliest. The Heddon imprint appears on both sides of the collar. L-rig hardware. 4-7/8". Collector value range: $35 to $45.

Q. Same as above except for finish and the fact that this is the first appearance of the flange collar held to the body with screws. 4-3/4". Collector value range: $30 to $40.

R. Second frog finish (no mustache). Tail caps disappear from the lures at this point in time. The Heddon imprint now apepars only on the front side of the collar. Other characteristics are the same as Q above. 4-3/4". Collector value range: $30 to $40.

S. Same as R above except for "HEDDON 200 SURFACE stenciled on the belly of the lure. 4-3/4". Collector value range: $30 to $40.

T. Glass eyes, three flange screwed unmarked collar, one-piece bar hook hanger, one-piece no hump tail hook hanger (P.S. Bear patent), "HEDDON 200 SURFACE" stenciled on belly. 4-3/4" Collector value range: $30 to $40.

U. Same as above except for the utilization of the two-piece toilet seat style belly hook hanger and the two-piece rectangular tail hook hanger. 4-3/4". Collector value range: $25 to $35.

V. Same as U above except for the screw eye tail hook hanger and lack of eyes. Collector value range: $20 to $30.

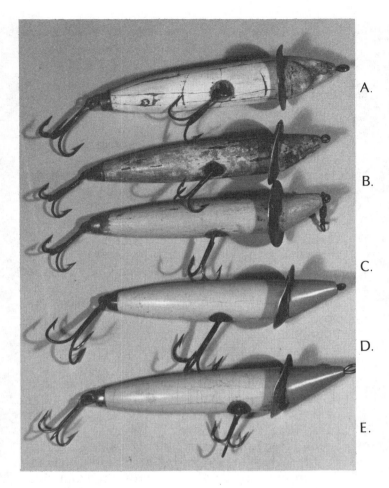

A.

B.

C.

D.

E.

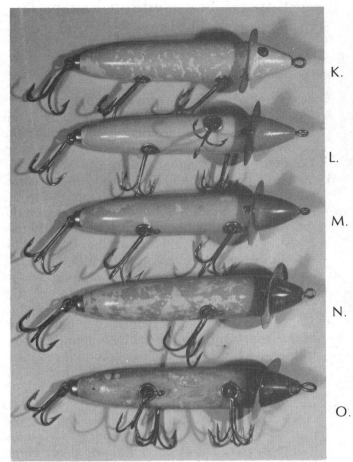

K.

L.

M.

N.

O.

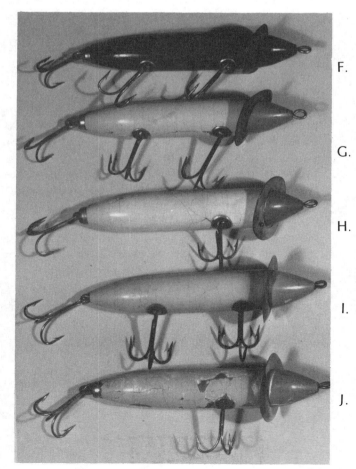

F.

G.

H.

I.

J.

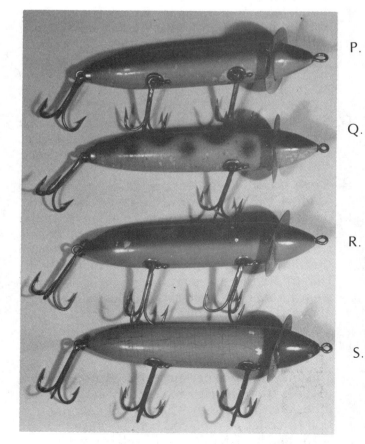

P.

Q.

R.

S.

Heddon (cont'd.)

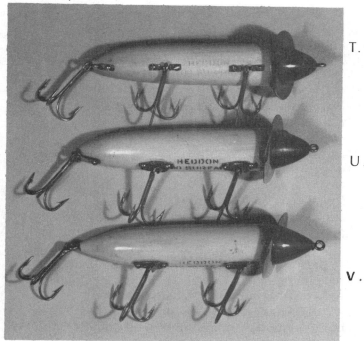

T.

U.

V.

MOONLIGHT RADIANT

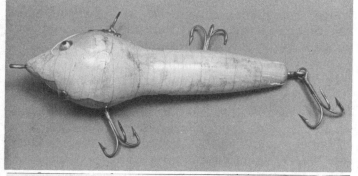

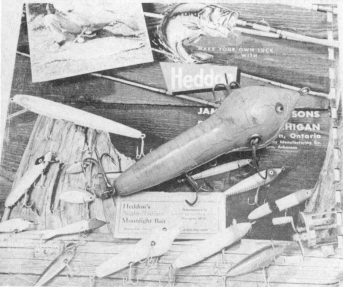

This interesting plug is *5" long and sports glass eyes. Two opposite side trebles on the bulbous head, a belly treble and trailing treble (4T). There has been only one reference to this lure in Heddon catalogs uncovered so far. This reference is only a photograph as part of the 1965 edition of a Heddon catalog. Collector value range: $100 to $200.

DOWAGIAC MINNOW
Series "O" and "OO"

A 1912 Heddon catalog says "Here's The New One." The accompanying photo shows the earliest at the top. They were first produced with the cup and screw hook hardware. The later versions had the "L-rig" as illustrated on the bottom two plugs. The "O" was about 3¾" long, had three trebles as in photo and two propellers. The larger "OO" was almost 4" long and has five trebles. It was otherwise the same. They were in catalogs until about 1927. The color offerings were: White body, red and green decorations; yellow body, red, green and black decorations; and red body with black decorations. Collector value range: $20 to $40.

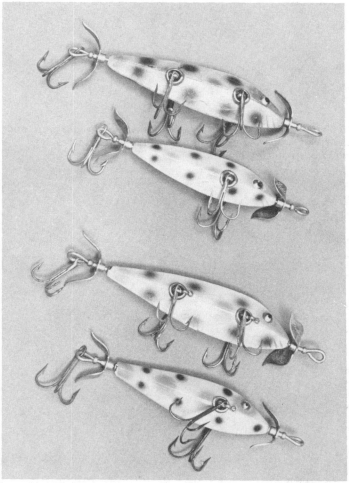

Top two Dowagiac Minnows show cup hardware. The two on the bottom have the L-rig hardware. Although the L-rig version is a later model, it is the rarest of the two. The later two-piece toilet seat style hanger is also difficult to find.

*It is also known to have been made in a 4" size. The name "Moonlight Radiant" may not be correct.

227

DOWAGIAC MINNOW
No. 100 Series and No. 150 Series

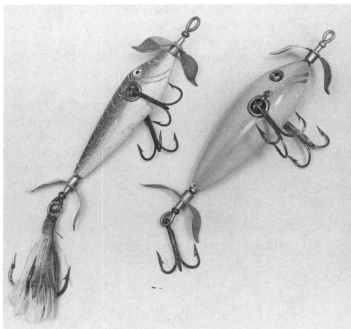

Left is an early No. 100 with high forehead, unmarked props and brass cup hook hanger hardware. Right lure is a later No. 100. Fatter body and L-rig hardware.

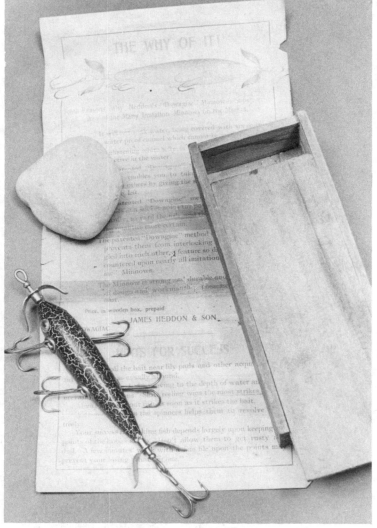

This is a cup and screw hook rigged Dowagiac No. 150 with original wooden box. Stone in the photograph is from Dowagiac Creek.

It is quite obvious that Heddon made **no** lures with propeller spinners in 1903 or prior for there is a paragraph in the 1903 and 1904 catalogs that says, "These devices, while churning water to a more or less extent, do not perform the very important function of throwing water into the air as does the "Dowagiac". It went on to denigrate the "spinners" and "paddle wheels" vociferously, all this, curiously, just before and in the same 1904 catalog that introduced the first Dowagiac Underwater with a forward mounted propeller spinner. That brings us to the No. 100 and the No. 150. Although the first catalog the No. 100 was found in was a 1905 edition, there is an advertisement for the No. 100 in the May, 1904 issue of *National Sportsman* magazine. That same 1905 catalog and all after make no reference to the Dowagiac Underwater, so presumably the 100's and 150's replaced it (Please see photograph of Dowagiac Underwater on page 222 for illustration of the transition theory).

The 100's and 150's are probably the first shaped body minnows Heddon produced commercially.

The very earliest of these have what is called a high forehead body configuration as in the photograph to the left and of the two early 100's on page 221 demonstrating gill stripe differences. Neither of them has marked propeller spinners and both have brass cup hardware.

The 100's were normally equipped with two opposite mount side trebles and a trailing treble (3T) and the 150's had five trebles (two on each side). There is a 1907 Abercrombie and Fitch catalog that offers it in a belly treble and trailing treble model (2T). The 2T is rarely found. The 100's lasted until about 1942-43 but the 150's continued in production for many years after still being made of wood, with glass eyes, as late as 1953. It was brought out in wood again in the late 1970's as part of Heddon's Wooden Classic Series. Collector value range: $10 to $20.

Dowagiac Minnow (cont'd.)

CATALOG SERIES#	BODY LENGTH	LURE WEIGHT
100	3-3/5"	7/10 oz.
	2¾"	⅔ oz.

COLOR OR FINISH: *Fancy green back, white belly; Rainbow; White body, red eyes; Aluminum; Red body; Yellow; Gold; Fancy sienna yellow.*

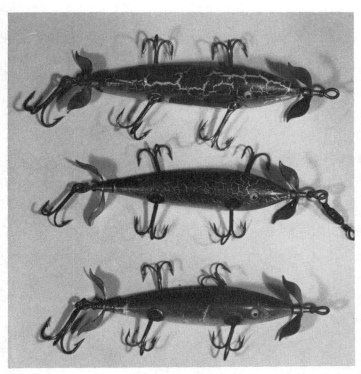

Heddon #150 Series. All three have opaque yellow iris glass eyes, unmarked big props and cup/screw hook hardware. The upper lure has two internal belly weights, nickel plate hardware and three long sweeping red painted gill marks, 4-1/4". The middle lure has two belly weights, brass hardware and a spray paint red throat, 3-5/8". The last has only brass cup and screw hook. The other hardware is a nickel plate. It has three belly weights. 3-9/16". Collector value range: $50 to $100.

Shows hardware progression for No. 150's. The top lure has see-through hardware. This is not typical of Heddon. It is not seen elsewhere and may have been an experimental prototype. The remaining lures show the classic hardware progression right up to the one-piece surface on the reissue No. 150 in the late 1970's Heddon Wooden Classic Series. Collector value range: from bottom to top: $25 to $50.

CATALOG SERIES#	BODY LENGTH	LURE WEIGHT
150	3-3/8"	9/10 oz.
	3¾"	¾ oz.

COLOR OR FINISH: *Aluminum color; solid red; Yellow; Gold color; Fancy sienna yellow; Red body, dark blended back; Yellow perch; Yellow perch, scale finish; Frog colors; Frog scale finish; Green scale finish; Red scale finish; Goldfish, scale finish.*

The nickel plated, large shallow cup hook hanger hardware and glass eyes should place this lure in the 1905 to 1915 era. The problem here is the presence of the unique Heddon Stanley propeller spinners. As far as can be presently determined, Heddon didn't acquire the Stanley company until the early 1920's. Perhaps the props are from Stanley prior to buying the company.

No. 175 Series

This lure, first found cataloged in 1909, is essentially the same as the No. 150 Series except that it is a 3T model having only two opposite mounted side trebles. It has the same specifications as the 150's and was available in fancy green back with white belly, rainbow, and blended white (grey back). Earliest models are 3-3/8" long and have rather larger than standard size cup hardware. Collector value range: $40 to $80.

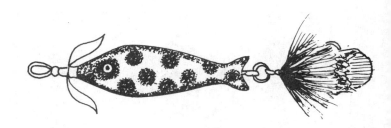

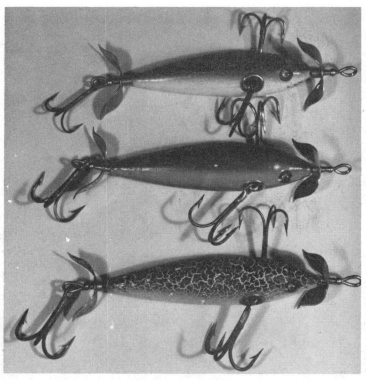

Top to bottom, oldest to newest 175's. Top lure has: large nickel plate cups with screw hooks, one internal belly weight, glass eyes and large unmarked props. 3-3/8". Be careful for it is easy to confuse this one with the #100 Series. The middle lure has the same hardware, but the body is slightly bigger all round. 3-3/4". The lower lure is the same except that the props are marked with the Heddon imprint and is 3-7/8" long.

HEDDON "DOWAGIAC" MINNOW No. 10 Series

The *upper lure measures 2-1/2" and the lower, 2-5/8". Each has glass eyes and marked propeller spinners.*

New in the 1912 catalog this little beauty was 2-3/8" long. My drawing here is a copy of the illustration in the 1912 catalog. One single feathered trailing hook and what they called "...the new Heddon Hexagon form..." This entry said it was available in a yellow body with red and brown spots, and white body with red and green spots. It was no longer available in the 1927 catalog. Collector value range: $40 to $80.

DOWAGIAC MINNOW No. 20 Series

This tiny (1¾", ½ oz.) plug first appeared in a 1909 Heddon catalog and promptly disappeared, not to turn up in catalogs again until 1922. It is the same size and weight as the Artistic Minnow and has a nose mounted propeller spinner. That is where this little critter's similarity ends though. The No. 20 has three treble hooks, one trailing and one on each side. That's a lot of artillery for such a small lure. Colors were: fancy back sienna, yellow finish, fancy green back, white, red, gold and silver white in 1909. In 1922 they were available in all the colors of the No. 150 Minnow. Collector value range for cup hardware: $20 to $40. for 1-pc. surface: $10 to $20.

LAGUNA RUNT No. 10 Series

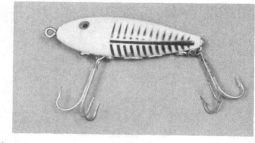

The 1939 catalog states that this is the "same body as the River Runt but without collar" (diving lip). It was made in two models, a sinker and a floater. The colors were exactly the same as the River Runt colors. Collector value range: $5 to $10.

230

WALTON FEATHER TAIL
#40 Series

This smaller plug was first found in a 1924 catalog and last found referenced in a 1926 catalog. It had a tail mounted single hook covered with feathers. There was a nose mounted propeller spinner, glass eyes, and came in four color designs. The colors were: red and white,; black body, orange tail; shiner scale, gray tail; and pike scale with green and yellow tail. Collector value range: $10 to $20.

A belly view of two Feather Tails showing the two styles of tail hook hangers to be found.

ARTISTIC MINNOW #50

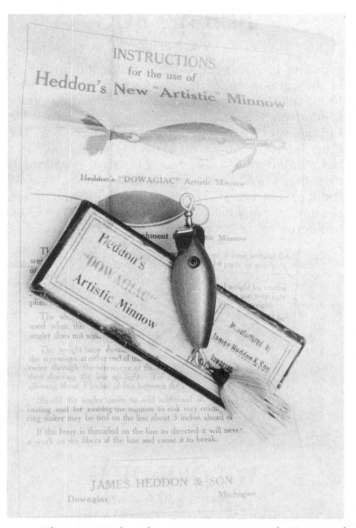

This 1¾" plug first appears around 1905 and seems to have been removed from the Heddon line by the 1910 issue of the catalog. The catalog states it was available in a fancy back sienna-yellow finish and a gold finish. The propeller was gold plated and the trailing treble was tied with fancy feathers or buck tail. It has glass eyes. It is thought the name was derived from the Artistic Wood Turning Works, Chicago, Illinois. This company turned out a lot of bodies for various companies in the early 1900's. Collectors of Heddon and Pflueger should be aware of the almost identical features of the Heddon Artistic and the Pflueger Simplex. Pflueger may have used the same company, for the bodies are identical. The best way to tell the difference is to compare the two and note the belly weights. Heddon Artistics invariably have only one belly weight whereas the Pflueger Simplex is often found with two. There are some belly weight (later model) Simplexes around, but the Pflueger weights are larger in diameter than those on the Heddon Artistic. The plug was sold with a weight to tie on in front if desired. To find the weight with the lure is rare. Collector value range: $50 to $80.

BUBBLE BUG
#90 Series

This lure was not found catalogued anywhere in the catalog collection studied. It was, however, found mint in a Heddon box. The exterior inscriptions printed on the box identified it as the Series 90, Bubble Bug. It was stamped "90 YB" on the box. The plug itself is yellow with black markings and has a red painted mouth. The feathers are also yellow. It measures 1-3/4" and is very light. It is probably a fly rod lure. The box style swivel, if it is original, places the lure at a very early era, perhaps the 1910's-1920-s. Collector value range: $30 to $40.

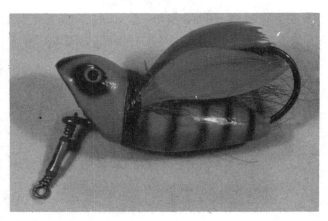

WILDER-DILG
Series #30 (cork)
Series #910 & 930 (plastic)

Introduced in the 1923 catalog this cork body, feathered lure was invented by a Louis B. Adams of New York City and named after B.F. Wilder, also of New York City and William H. Dilg of Chicago. The latter two gentlemen were credited with experimenting with and perfecting the lure in the 1924 catalog. In 1939 Heddon changed the body composition from cork to plastic and re-named it the Wilder-Dilg Spook. It was dropped from the line in 1953 after a thirty-year run. It was made in two sizes, a bass size at 3-1/4" overall and a trout size at 2" overall. Collector value range: $10 to $20.

HEDDON-STANLEY
WEEDLESS PORK-RIND LURE
Series #70

This lure was made of Bakelite and new about 1923 (changed to Pyralin in 1925). It had glass eyes and was available with or without the wire weedguard and surface attachment. Both are pictured belly-down in the photograph accompanying. Collector value range: $14 to $24.

CATALOG SERIES #	BODY LENGTH	LURE WEIGHT
70	1-1/8"	5/8 oz.

COLOR OR FINISH: *Solid white; White body, red top; Solid red; Green scale; Pike scale; Shiner scale.*

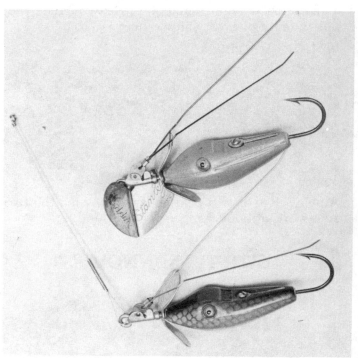

Two Weedless Pork-Rind lures. The upper lure has the scarce surface wiggler attachment.

TINY TEASE Series #80
and
WIDGET Series #300

The photo at top left of next page shows one 1929 vintage Tiny Tease and seven Widgets. They are all wooden and made for use with fly rods. The Widget came along around 1953 and the Tiny Tease about 1929. Collector value range Widget: $3 to $10; Tiny Tease: $20 to $40.

232

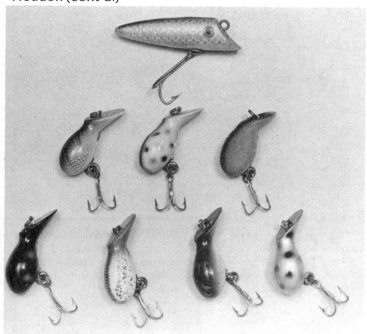

RIVER RUNT Series #110

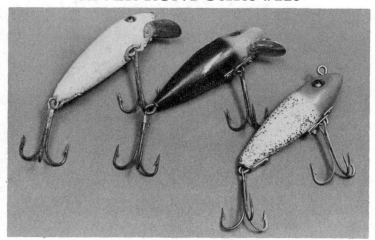

These four River Runts illustrate the hook hardware progression from L-rig to one-piece surface. Note the pork rind attachment on the trailing treble of the third lure.

These three lures illustrate hardware and style differences. Left lure is round nose with no eye depressions and 2-hump L-rig. Center lure has zinc eyes and toilet seat hardware. Right lure is a glass eyed Sea Runt, an early salt water No. 610.

New in 1929 the earliest models have the "L-rig" hook hardware. The photos here illustrate the subtle body style changes and the hook hardware progression over the years. It was made of wood all the way into the early 1950s. Collector value range: $3 to $10.

CATALOG SERIES #	BODY LENGTH	LURE WEIGHT
110	2-5/8"	½ oz.

COLOR OR FINISH: *Rainbow; White with red head; White with red head and silver specks; Solid red; Yellow perch scale; Red Dace scale; Silver scale; Natural scale; Shiner scale; Shiner scale with red head; Pearl; Silver with red head; Solid black; Silver Herring; Black with white head; Solid white; Allen stripey.*

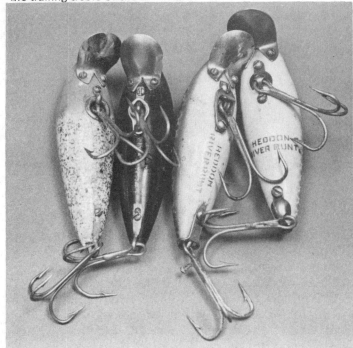

Belly view of the River Runts in the previous picture.

233

MIDGET DIGIT Series #B-110

The gang of plugs in the photo are all wooden with weighted bodies and painted eyes. This is a tiny version of the #110 River Runt. The Midget Digit was new in 1941. Collector value range: $2 to $3.

CATALOG SERIES #	BODY LENGTH	LURE WEIGHT
B-110	1½"	2/5 oz.

COLOR OR FINISH: *White body, spotted; White with red head; Black with white head; Yellow perch scale; Red dace scale; Shiner scale; Blue pearl; Red head, silver flitter; Silver scale; Black and white shore minnow; Yellow shore minnow.*

TORPEDO
Series #120 and #130

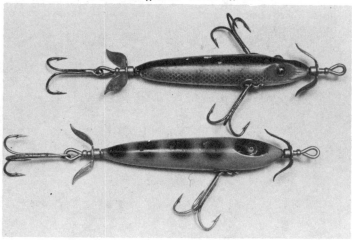

The first reference I could find for these two was in 1925. The entry, however, implied that it had been around long enough to become a "favorite." By 1930 the smaller size was no longer offered in the catalogs. The 2T model in the photograph is the normal No. 120, 3" Torpedo. The upper lure with two opposite mount side trebles is a rare bird. It was not found cataloged anywhere. The standard Torpedo No. 130 is larger (4½") and has two belly mounted treble hooks. All Torpedos so far found have L-rig, two-piece or surface

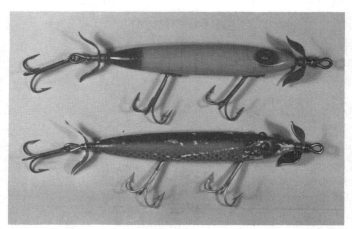

Of these two Torpedos, the upper one is the oldest. It sports tube type propeller spinners, has the L-rig hook hardware and "HEDDON TORPEDO: is stenciled on the belly. Note the later props on the lower lure. Both have glass eyes, the props are marked with the Heddon name and the bodies each measure 4-1/8".

These two represent the next two in line of age. The upper lure here has the 1-piece bar hanger. This was the first style after the cup and screw eye was abandoned. The lower lure is next in line with the 2-piece toilet seat style belly hook hardware. Both measure 4-1/8", have one internalized belly weight, glass eyes, marked propeller spinners and "HEDDON TORPEDO" stenciled on the belly.

This is a pair of saltwater Torpedos (#30s). The upper-glass eyed version is the oldest. Note it has a slightly fatter body and more blunt nose. The newer one measures 4-1/4" with the older being just a bit shorter.

234

Heddon Torpedo (cont'd.)

hardware. They are also found with the floppy round bladed floppy Heddon Stanley propeller spinners. They were offered in catalogs in wood until 1936 when they were replaced by the No. 3130 plastic Torpedo-Spook. Collector value range for wood Torpedos: $15 to $40 for the No. 120 and $10 to $20 for the No. 130.

CATALOG SERIES #	BODY LENGTH	LURE WEIGHT
120	3″	½ oz.
130	4½″	¾ oz.

COLOR OR FINISH: *White body, red eyes; Yellow perch scale finish; Green scale finish; Pike scale finish; Shiner scale finish; Rainbow scale finish; Natural scale finish; Blue scale finish; Rainbow scale, purple back; Orange black spots.*

THE S.O.S. WOUNDED MINNOW
Series 140, 160 and 170

The photos show the unique "banana" shape of all three sizes of this plug. If you look closely you will see from left to right, the one piece bar, the L-rig and the first style of the two-piece hook hangers. The No. 370 is the Musky size. It has the same length as the No. 170 (4¾″), but is much heavier. Hooks and hanger hardware are bigger and stronger. There is only one belly treble on it. S.O.S. means Swims On Side. All early plugs illustrated have glass eyes. They came on the market 1927-28 and lasted until the 50's. Collector value range: $8 to $20.

CATALOG SERIES #	BODY LENGTH	LURE WEIGHT
*140	3″	½ oz.
160	3½″	3/5 oz.
170	4¾″	4/5 oz.
370	4¾″	1-1/6 oz.

COLOR OR FINISH: *White with red head; Green scale; Perch scale; Shiner scale; Silver scale; Dace scale; Luminous.*

*The smallest (#140) size wasn't on the market until 1937 and by then a Pike Scale finish had been added.

This #370 SOS has cup and screw eye hook hardware, glass eyes and measures 4-3/4″ long. Note that it has "Heddon Stanley" marked floppy props. This is a rare occurence. Collector value range: $50 to $100.

YOWSER SPINNER BAIT #195

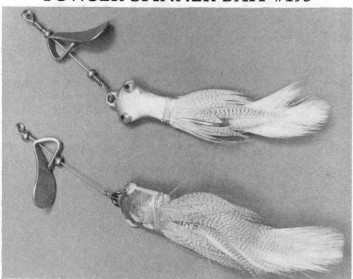

This lure came along about 1935 and only lasted until around 1939. The weight is 4/5 ounce and overall length is 4″ without measuring the fancy feather tail. It came in a single hook version only. Very rare. Collector value range: $20 to $40.

FLIPPER No. 140

These four Flippers are arranged oldest to newest, left to right. Each has glass eyes and the normal Heddon props of the era. The center two are 3-7/8″, the left one 3-3/4″ and right one is 3-1/2″. Far left has cup and screw eye hardware, center two have the two-hump L-rig hardware and the far right sports the one-piece surface hangers.

The Flipper came along about 1927. It is 3¾" long, ¾ ounce. The lure shows up again in the 1928 catalog, but is missing from listings from 1929 on. It must have been retired when stocks were exhausted. Whatever the case, the number 140 was given to the smallest S.O.S. Wounded Minnow added to the line about 1937. All those I have seen are glass eyed and have L-rig hook hardware. Collector value range: $20 to $60.

This 4-1/4" Flipper has a fatter body than usual, but what really makes it unusual is the presence of the "Heddon Stanley" marked floppy props. It also has glass eyes and the shallow big cup and screw eye hook hangers. Collector value range: $75 to $150.

DOWAGIAC MINNOW
No. 210 Series

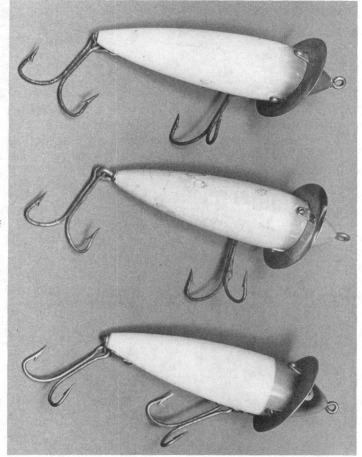

This is a short (3½") version of the 200 Series. It was first available somewhere around 1917-20. Earliest hook hardware I have observed is the L-rig. They are found with no eyes, glass eyes and painted eyes. As far as can be determined to date, they were always equipped with two double hooks in the

photograph. Colors in 1921 were: white body with blue head, white body with red head, frog and green scale. Collector value range: $4 to $20.

WEEDLESS WIDOW
Series No. 220

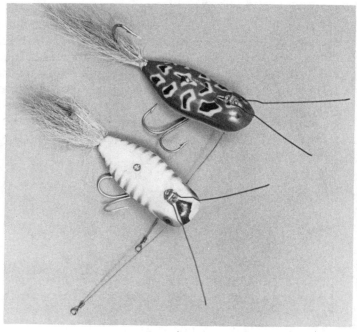

Top view

SURFACE MINNY #260 Series

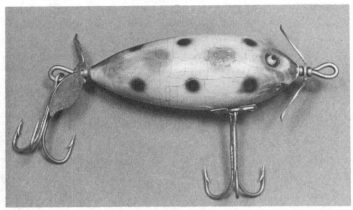

This scarce lure was in production only a short time. It appeared around 1934 and is absent from the 1936 and subsequent catalogs. Has been found only in the old 2-piece hardware only so far. Collector value range: $40 to $80.

CATALOG SERIES #	BODY LENGTH	LURE WEIGHT
260	3¼"	¾ oz.

COLOR OR FINISH: *White and red; Rainbow; Green scale; Perch scale.*

HEDDON SURFACE MINNOW No. 300 Series

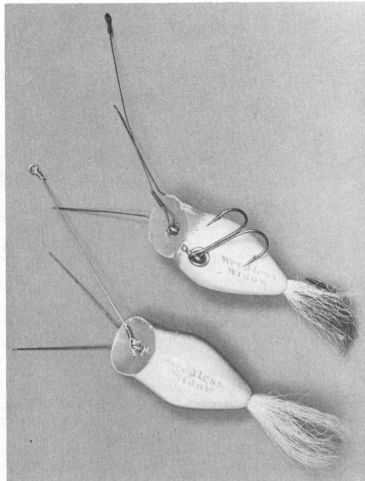

The first time this lure was offered was in a 1928 Heddon flyer as the WEEDLESS **WIZARD** (2½", ¾ oz., 6 colors). The text called it new. It had only a rigid feathered single hook on the tail. The 1928 catalog, however, named it the WEEDLESS **WIDOW**. The story is that Pflueger got a bit upset because of their own rather well known WIZARD lures, so Heddon changed the name. In 1930 they made them with a detachable belly double hook addition.

The photograph on page 206 of the white one with bead eyes is thought to be a proptotype. There is a hole bored in the back. Reason for this is unknown. Colors available were white with red head, bull frog, green scale, pike scale, shiner scale and silver scale. There was a JUNIOR offered in 1940 at 2¼" in the same colors and by 1949 this smaller size was the only one available. Collector value range: $6 to $20.

Called new in a 1905 catalog. The 1905 model is the upper lure in the photograph showing body style progression. The 1905 colors were: rainbow*, frog green back*, white*, aluminum, red, yellow or copper. The early 300's were 4" only and had one belly treble with cup hardware and a trailing treble. In 1911 the body had grown a bit fatter and shorter (3½") according to a catalog listing of that year. It also noted the availability of a 3T model on special order.

The only three finishes offered from 1906 through 1916.

Heddon No. 300 Series (cont'd.)

By 1922 the 300 is listed at 3¾" and they had added two finishes: white body with red and green spots; white body, red eyes. 3T model still available on special order. The 1925 catalog had renamed the 300 series, the Musky Minnow, and it had grown even fatter at 3¾". 1927 saw yet another name, the Musky Surf.

This #300 has one internal belly weight, glass eyes, brass cup screw hook hardware, unmarked props and measures 3-¾".

The No. 300 series was around for about 30 years and can be found with a classic progression of Heddon hook hardware from the brass cup to the one-piece surface. All had glass eyes. A 1937 catalog said it was "... regularly finished with three heavy trebles, also with six trebles or two trebles on special order." It had been renamed yet again. This time it is called the Musky Surfusser. It was gone after 1941. Collector value range: $10 to $30.

MUSKY SURFACE
No. 350 Series

Apparently this was a short-lived lure in the Heddon line. It is cataloged consistently from 1933 through 1936, but is conspicuously absent from then on. They may have been made long before 1933 The upper plug has unmarked big propellers, the same as found on early No. 700's. Colors were: spotted, white with red head, green scale and shiner scale. Collector value range: $50 to $100.

ICE DECOY

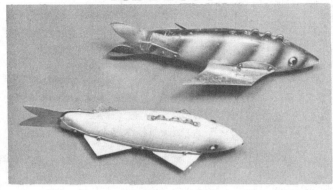

The earliest catalog entry I could find for a Heddon Ice Decoy was in a 1913 catalog. The illustration shows a body much like the top decoy in the photo of two here. It had a small screw eye line tie, much larger metal side fins than the one in the photo here and two additional metal fins (dorsal and ventral) and a natural (wooden) tail. It was listed as 5-1/8 inches long and available in fancy green back with white belly, or yellow perch finish. By 1916 the lure was listed as 4-3/8". The illustration was the same. One length may have been overall and the other the body only. A 1923 catalog shows fins like those on the lower decoy in the photo of two. This also is the first catalog illustration showing the inch worm line tie. By then they had added two more finishes: rainbow and green scale. They had disappeared from catalogs by 1928. All have glass eyes and fins are plainly marked Heddon. Final colors available had the addition of shiner scale finish and a white body with red eyes.

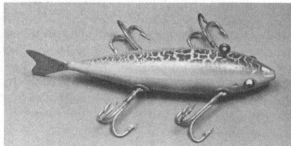

The photo here of the single lure is a real curiosity. It is generally the same body as the Heddon 150's and has the Heddon sienna fancy crackle-back finish. Decoy or lure? It is 4½" overall with a 3¾" body with a metal tail fin obviously production installed. There is a hole in the nose but no screw eye. The screw eye in the top is not typical of Heddon quality and may have been added later. The four treble hooks are installed utilizing cup and screw **hook** hardware. Eyes are glass. There are three weights beneath the nose. Collector value range for Heddon Ice Decoys: $60 to $120.

"KILLER No. 400"

The photo below includes part of a page from a 1905 catalog. The caption states "...in all essential respects the same as our No. 100 Minnow, excepting that it has but one propeller, is round instead of minnow shaped in body, and is without eyes or other decorations." The earliest have three small belly weights. Collector value range: $30 to $60.

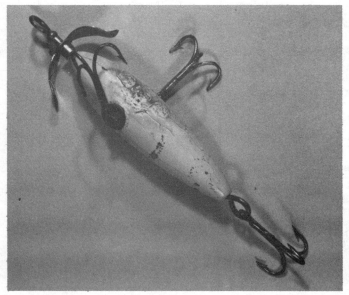

This KILLER #400 is 2-5/8" long, has unmarked prop, brass screw hook and cup hardware and three internal belly weights.

"KILLER No. 450"

This is a 1905 vintage lure that is exactly the same as the No. 400 except that it has an additional propeller at the tail. The lures in the photo are arranged to the bottom, oldest to newest. The key to age here is the number of internal belly weights.

The upper lure in the photo is so well painted that it is impossible to determine whether there are any belly weights much less the number of them. It is slightly larger than the other three, 3" long, round bodied, red in color, unmarked Heddon props and has double staple hook hangers. It could be a prototype for these 400's and 450's in this rather short-lived inexpensive line. The second lure measures 2-5/8", has unmarked props, brass cup and screw hook hardware and three belly weights. The third has the same characteristics except that it has only two belly weights. The last also has the same size and characteristics and only one belly weight. Colors available were: White, red, yellow, copper, aluminum, white body with red head and tail. Collector value range: $30 to $60.

MULTIPLE METAL MINNOW
No. 500 Series

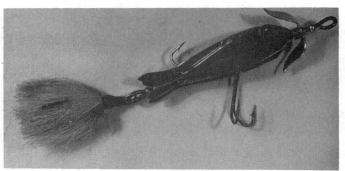

This lure is so similar to the accompanying patent illustsration that it is reasonable to presume it to be at least derived from the original patent. It first shows up as available in the early 1900's; some say as early as 1909 and that it didn't last long. If you look at the pictures or examples of the #500 and #600 Series Heddon Saltwater Specials you will note a striking similarity of body shape. In fact there is a listing in the 1934 catalog directly under the illustration and technical data listing for the Series 9600 Salt Spook that states "Metal-Minn NO. 510 Series (all-metal body). Similar to No. 9600 in shape and weight..." Now this may seem confusing until you realize that the Salt-Spook is merely the same-shape plastic version of the old Series #500 and #600 Saltwater Specials. In fact, just under the listing for the Metal-Minn is another listing for "Old Reliables... The same model as shown above except in wooden bodies." Listed there are the #500 and #600 Series and the colors available. All that for this: The similarity of Series number and the stated body shape could mean that the original metal remain in production, albeit limited, for twenty-five years or so. The example in the photo here is 2-1/2" long and nickle plated. They are known to have also been available in a gold finish and a larger, musky version at about 4-3/4". They may also be found with glass eyes. The one in the photo has rivet-like eyes. Collector value range: $40 to $80.

No. 861,116.

PATENTED JULY 23, 1907.

J. HEDDON.
FISH BAIT OR LURE.
APPLICATION FILED FEB. 4. 1907.

3 SHEETS—SHEET 1.

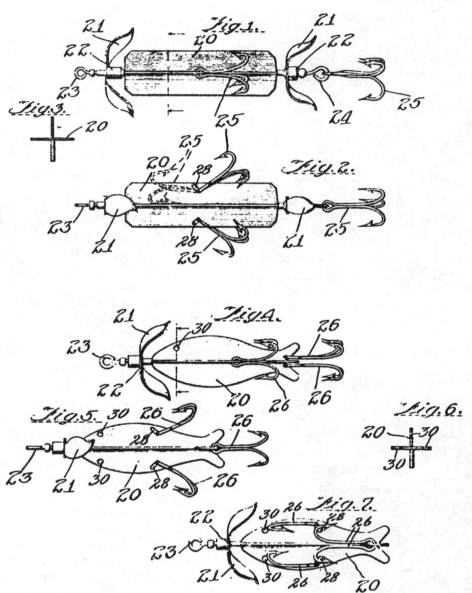

WITNESSES:

Ida Y. Avery

W. Perry Hahn

INVENTOR:

James Heddon

By Jones, Addington & Amos

Attorneys

SALTWATER SPECIALS
Series #500, #600, and #850

The catalog information regarding these wooden lures is confusing. They first appear around 1924 (#600 Series) in four sizes and five color designs. (Style is second from top in photo.) By 1925 another series number (#500) appears and the only sizes were as follows: #500 Series: ½ ounce, 2" #600 Series: ¾ ounce, 3½". In 1926 another style was added (third from top in photo), the #850 Series: 2", ½ ounce; and #800 Series: 3½", ¾ ounce. In 1932 a "plastic" plug identical to the #800 series was introduced as the #9600 "Salt Spook". All were gone from catalogs by 1949. The lure at the top in the photo is pictured only in a 1922 Heddon catalog as a #108 Florida Special. Collector value range for Saltwater Specials: $20 to $40.

CATALOG SERIES #	BODY LENGTH	LURE WEIGHT
500	2¾"	½ oz.
600	3-5/8"	¾ oz.
800	3-7/8"	¾ oz.
850	3"	½ oz.

COLOR OR FINISH: *White body with red head; White body, gold speckled, red head; White body, silver speckled, red head; *Yellow perch scale' **White body, red eyes; **White body, gold speckled; *White body, silver speckled; *Solid black; *Shiner scale; ***Aluminum color body, bronze back.*

WEE WILLIE
Series Number Unknown

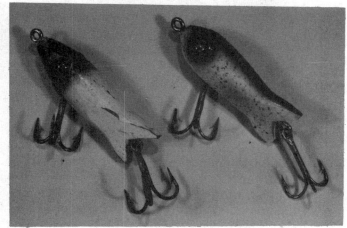

Called WEE WILLIE by some collectors, this lure is placed here because of its similarity to the SALTWATER SPECIALS above. The red head, white body plug in the photo is 3-1/2" long and has "HEDDON" stenciled on the belly. The other measures 2-1/8". Each has three internal belly weights and cup/screw hook hardware. Collector value range: $15 to $30.

SEA RUNT Series #610

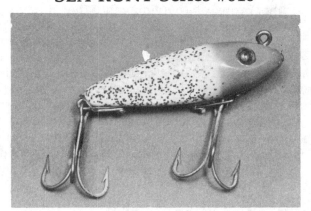

This lure was introduced as "new" in a 1937 catalog. It is somewhat similar to the #110 River Runt but has no diving lip and the line tie is located at the top of the nose. Collector value range: $10 to $20.

CATALOG SERIES #	BODY LENGTH	LURE WEIGHT
610	2-5/8"	2/3 oz.

COLOR OR FINISH: *Spotted; White with red head; White with silver flitter and red head; Silver scale; Yellow with red head.*

*#600 Series only.
**Pre-1930 only.
***#800 Series only.

COAST MINNOW #1, #2, #3, #4

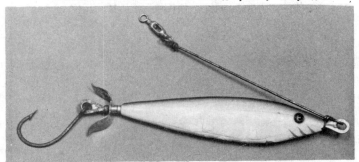

Appearing around 1913, the Coast Minnow was available in four sizes. The one in the photo above has Heddon paint and hardware, but this particular lure is not found illustrated in any Heddon catalogs. The Heddon catalogs illustrated a very similar lure beginning in 1913 and continuing consistently through 1922. Note the flat metal line tie and hook hanger and in particular the rear-mounted propeller spinner. The Heddon illustrations through 1922 show the same body but line tie/tail hook hangar on them all is twisted thru-body wire type and the prop is a very plain untwisted blade type completely unlike the one in the photo here. The next catalog (1923) listed the same lengths, weights and colors, but the illustration is more like the photo here. Same propeller spinner, but mounted at the nose instead of the tail and does have the flat metal line tie and tail hook hanger. The eyes on each end additionally are heavily reinforced with what appears to be wire wrapping. The text accompanying the illustration described this as "...a square phosphor bronze wire running thru the entire length of body." This same catalog listing and illustration continued until 1927 when it had disappeared.

Interestingly there was an almost identical lure called the South Coast Wooden Minnow available at least as early as 1910. It was offered by a Dr. H. C. Royer of Terminal Island, Los Angeles, California. Perhaps it wasn't patented and Heddon appropriated the design or acquired the rights. Pflueger's Catalina (later Bear Cat) is also remarkably like Royer's product. Collector value range for the Heddon Coast Minnow: $60 to $90.

CATALOG SERIES #	BODY LENGTH	LURE WEIGHT
1	4-4½"	1¾-2½ oz.
2	3-3½"	1 oz.
3	2½-2¾"	½ oz.
4	5"	2½ oz.

COLOR OR FINISH: *Fancy green back, white body, red and green spots; Rainbow; green scale; dark green back, gold speckles.*

DOWAGIAC MUSKOLLONGE* MINNOW #700 Series

The #700 Series was made in 3T and 5T versions. The 5T was the first to be offered (1909) and is the rarest. The 3T model was introduced about two years later in the 1911 catalog and continued to be available until 1928 when the catalog no longer listed them. They were cataloged at 4-3/4", but the lure at the top of the accompanying photo of three measures 5-1/2". It has four internal belly weights, glass eyes, cup and screw eye hardware and no name on props. The center lure has the same characteristics except it measures the standard 4-3/4" and has only three belly weights. The lower lure has the same characteristics as the center one except it has four belly weights and the props have the Heddon Dowagiac imprint on them. Colors listed as available are: Fancy back, white belly; fancy green back, white belly; Rainbow; fancy sienna back, yellow belly; red sides, **yellow perch, white body, red eyes. Collector value range: 3T $45 to $75; 5T $50 to $120.

*1909 catalog spelling.
**1922 on.

242

SPOONY-FISH
Series No. 490, 590, 790

This metal spoon-type lure in the shape of a fish is found listed in the Heddon trade catalogs of 1930 and 1931 only. It measures 2-3/4''. The catalog entry implies that it was available only in a heavy nickel plate finish, but as can be plainly seen in the photograph here it was made in at least one scale finish. The three Series numbers listed above denote the sizes it was made in. As listed in the catalog they are 2-5/8'', 4-1/4'' and 5-3/4''. Collector value range: $15 to $45.

PUNKINSEED
Series #730, #740, #380 and #980

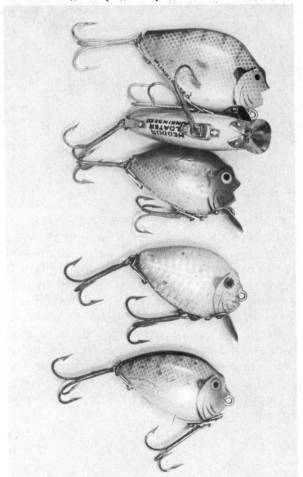

Lower lure in this photo is a renegade. As yet unknown as to why the lure was made with no lip.

A new lure in 1940 and made in floating and sinking models. It was a real departure from the traditional standard shapes for plugs. Made of wood it was a remarkably realistic looking "sunfish" type lure. The original versions had the line tie located under the notched mouth while a short time later it was moved into the mouth. There is a story that the famous Homer Circle, while working for Heddon suggested this change to Charles Heddon to impart better action to the lure, indeed later catalog photos show this change. A 1949 catalog states "The New Punkinseed." "Do not confuse this lure with any previous model." It goes on to say that the new model is strictly a sinking plug. Collector value range: $5 to $10.

CATALOG SERIES #	BODY LENGTH	LURE WEIGHT
730 (Sinking)	2¼''	⅔ oz.
740 (Floating)	2½''	3/5 oz.
**380 (Tiny)	1¾''	⅓ oz.
**980 (Fly Rod)	7/8''	1/20 oz.

COLOR OR FINISH: *Bluegill; Crappie; Shad; Rockbass; Sunfish; *Perch; Red and white shore minnow; *Black and white shore minow; *Yellow shore minnow.*

HEDDON SWIMMING MINNOW
or
DOWAGIAC SWIMMING MINNOW
Nos. 800 and 900

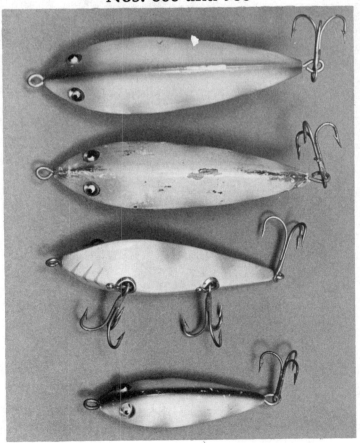

243   (cont'd next page).

Heddon Swimming Minnow (cont'd.)

The 800's are sinkers and the 900's are floating divers. First found cataloged in a 1910 edition (900 only, 800 appeared in 1911). The No. 800 was listed at 3¼" with a trailing treble only. The No. 900 was 4½" and had a trailing treble and a belly double with a locking pin. The 1912 and 1913 catalogs list only the large size (4½") and by 1914 it had disappeared altogether. I was unable to find any catalog reference at all regarding the 3T model in the photo here. It is 3-5/8" long and equipped with L-rig hook hangers as you can see in the photo. The L-rig patent wasn't applied for until 1915 so this may be simply a prototype never put into production or it could be a production model. It is known that Heddon didn't always catalog all their lures. The lures were available in two finishes: white body, green body and red spots; yellow body, green and red spots. Collector value range: $60 to $120.

*Sinking only.
**Plastic.

TRIPLE TEASER
Series #1000

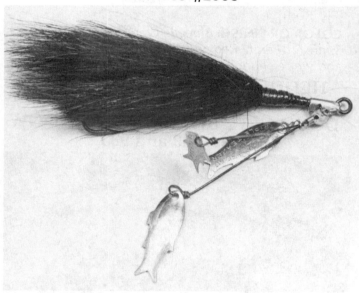

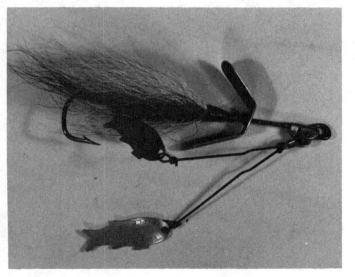

This unusual lure was first found listed in Heddon catalogs in the 1929 issue and last seen in the 1933 issue. It was made with either white, red, red and white, or natural bucktail and red or yellow feathered single hook. The example in the second photo here is atypical in two ways. The spinner on the shaft is not shown in any catalog illustrations nor is it present on most of the Triple Teasers found. It appears to have been placed there at the factory. If it was done by a fisherman he went to a great deal of trouble. The other difference is the absence of the third little metal minnow. It normally is found at the intersection of the two wires bearing the other two. It has been lost from this one. Each of the little minnow blades have "Heddon Triple Teaser" stamped on them. Collector value range: $5 to $10.

BLACK SUCKER MINNOW
#1300

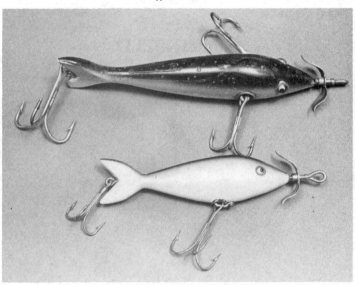

This lure was first listed in a 1913 catalog. It was described as being 5¾" long, weight 2½ ounces. Catalog entries consistently stated it was available in one color only. It has a very dark, almost black back blending down the sides into a light tint of red, ending in white down to the belly. Never was there any mention of the smaller size (3-7/8") shown in the photograph here or of any other colors or models. They are found in cup, two types of L-rig, belly treble, side trebles, rainbow finish and natural scale finish. All found so far have glass eyes. It is missing from Heddon catalogs from 1927 on. Collector value range: $80 to $160.

HEDDON DOWAGIAC MINNOW
No. 1400 Series

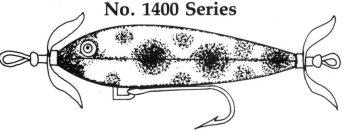

First found in a 1913 Heddon catalog it was never listed again although it may have continued in production for a time. The illustration (reproduced in my drawing above) is of the same hexagonal body as the Series 1500 Dummy Double but equipped only with a belly single hook with a unique attachment. The catalog entry said the hook was detachable. Colors available were white body with red, green and black spots and a yellow body with red, green and black spots. Body length 3". Collector value range: $200 to $300.

DUMMY DOUBLE
No. 1500 Series

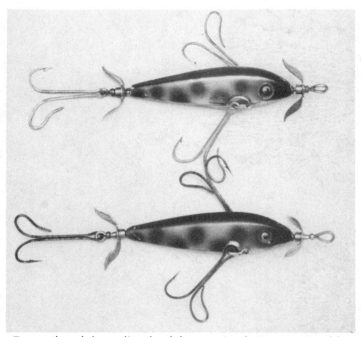

Two styles of the earliest hook hangers on the Dummy Double. An interesting note about the upper lure is that the hook hardware and the hooks were handmade by a fisherman just a few years ago. He found a good body and went from there.

Called new in a 1913 catalog entry, this rare plug cannot be found listed in catalogs any later than 1916. It, like the No. 1400 Series, utilizes the hexagonal body of the Series "0" Dowagiac Minnow. The lure was first made with the "football" style side hook hangers (see upper lure in photo), but the 1914 catalog illustrates the lure with an L-rig hanger. Text of the entry says this is a "new" type of screw hook. Note the very unique "Dummy Double" hooks. It came equipped with one on either side and one trailing. Body length is 3". Colors available were white body with red and green

spots, yellow body with red and green spots, blended white body with red eyes, blended red, rainbow, frog and fancy green back with white belly. Collector value range: $50 to $100.

STANLEY PERFECTION
WEEDLESS HOOKS

These are basically weedless hooks made in several variations and sizes according to application. The two in the photo here are a No. 2 with spinner and another No. 2 with bucktail. The others are rigged variously with or without weights on the hook shanks, pork rind attachments, spoons and even one that is meant to be fitted with a frog. The essential element on each of them is the unique hinged wire weedless hook guard. Details of this apparatus may be seen in the accompanying patent illustration. Note that the patent is dated 1931 having been applied for in 1929. If you will look at the Heddon Stanley Weedless Pork Rind Lure entry you will note the same apparatus is utilized on that lure. What is interesting is that the catalog entry for that lure in 1924 stated that the hinged weed guard was patented five years before the patent was applied for. Perhaps it was a bluff. We may never know. Another use for the weed guard was on the Triple Teazer. Collector value range for the Stanley Perfection Weedless Hooks: $4 to $8.

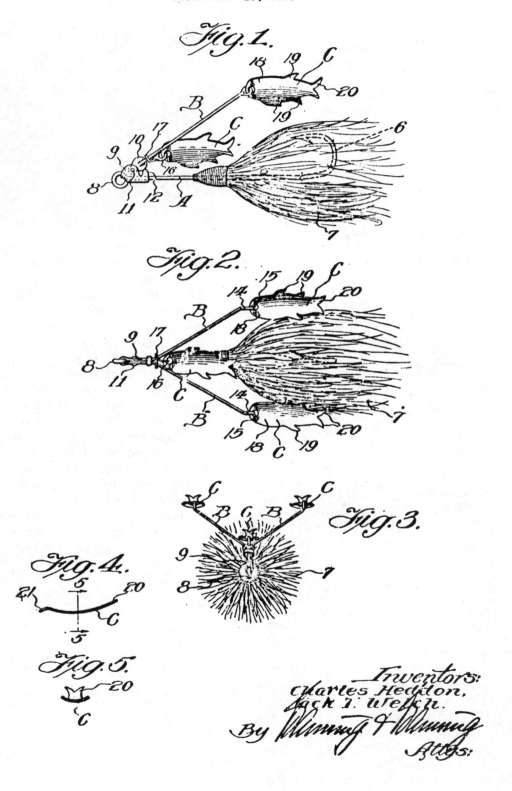

Fig.1.

Fig.2.

Fig.3.

Fig.4.

Fig.5.

Inventors:
Charles Heddon,
Jack T. Welch.

By   Attys:

DEEP DIVING WIGGLER
#1600 Series

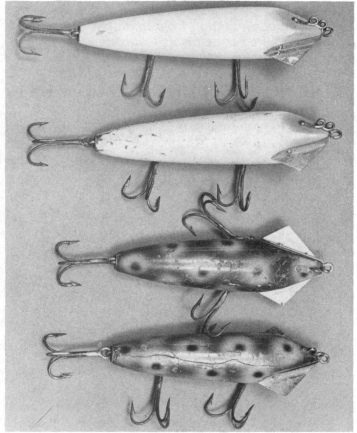

NEAR SURFACE WIGGLER
#1700 Series

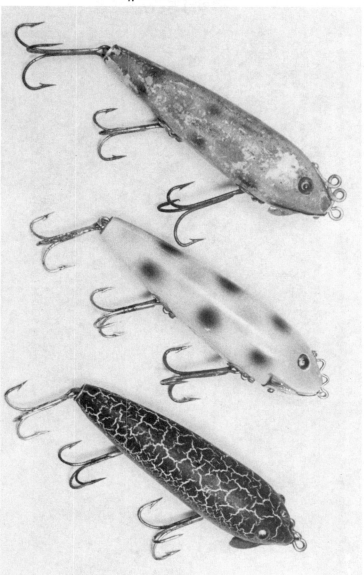

This lure and the following #1700 Series were the first Heddon production lures to utilize the L-rig hook hanger patented by Heddon in 1918 (applied for May 20, 1915. See page 83.) Both also sport the 1914 patent inch worm line tie. The DEEP DIVING WIGGLER was patented October 20, 1914. This patent included the aforementioned pigtail line tie (see page 80). It was manufactured in two different 3 treble configurations. There was one with two belly trebles and a trailing treble and other had two opposite side mounted trebles and a trailing treble. The plug body is found with subtle differences in the two or four slants cut into the nose portion. Each had two triangle shaped fins, one mounted horizontally on each side of the head. Each had triple line ties, but are found with slightly different designs. The very latest body design (c1926) had no slope cut into the top of the head but did retain the slopes on the head sides. This is illustrated on the bottom lure in the photo accompanying. The photo illustrates the evolution of the lure oldest to the latest, top to bottom. The first three have the combination pigtail/screw eye line tie and the other has the inch worm/screw eye line tie. These four all have the L-rig hook hangers, but there is a rare early one with the cup and screw hook hardware. None had eyes. Length 4½", weight ¾ ounce. Colors available were as follows: Fancy green back with white belly; white body with red and green spots; white body with red head; yellow body with red and green spots; yellow perch; frog finish; Rainbow; Shiner scale. Collector value range: $5 to $15.

This lure was first introduced in 1915 and lasted until about 1926. All found so far have had glass eyes. The multiple line tie changed several times over the years. The earliest (1916) catalog illustration I found showed a double pigtail type fastened at the nose with a screw eye (top lure in photo). The photo illustrates the transition from oldest to newest. Top plug as discussed above also has cup and L-rig hardware. Center plug has inch worm line tie and L-rig hardware. Bottom has a combination inch-worm/screw eye line tie. All of these have reinforcing tail cup hardware although it has been reported that the latest did not have this feature. All also have the metal under-nose plate with two side protruding fins. Earliest were mounted with two screws. Later ones have only one screw with the other fastener being integrated with the line tie fastener. Length 4½", weight 7/8 ounce. Colors available were the same as listed with the #1600 Series Deep Diving Wiggler. Collector value range: $5 to $15.

CRAB WIGGLER
#1800 Series

This reverse running plug was first introduced in 1915. The earliest models had the variable line tie and 'U' shaped collar as shown on the top plug in the photo. Then came the 'O' collars shown on the bottom. There was a slight modification of the 'U' collar before being changed to the 'O' type which completely surrounded the tail.* The line tie had been changed to a single tie type and was moved to the bottom of the tail* and utilized one of the same screws as the collar to secure it to the lure. Collector value range: $5 to $15.

CATALOG SERIES #	BODY LENGTH	LURF WEIGHT
1800	**4½''	9/10 oz.
1800	3½''	1 oz.
	3¾''	7/8 oz.
	4''	7/8 oz.

*Actually the front, as this is a reverse running plug.

**Earliest size.

***It is also quite similar to the #1600 with a two-slant head.

COLOR OR FINISH: *Fancy green back; White body, red and green spots; Rainbow; White body with red head; Yellow body, green back, red and green spots; Yellow perch; Imitation frog; Imitation crab; Green scale finish; Red scale finish; Goldfish, scale; Yellow perch scale finish.*

UNKNOWN HEDDON PLUG c 1915 CRAB WIGGLER?

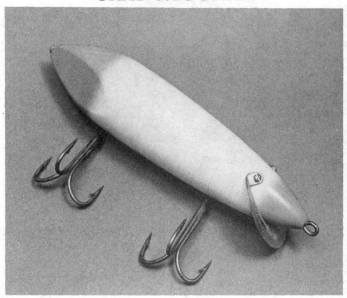

This 4-1/8'' lure is very like the #1800 Crab Wiggler***, but enough difference to consider it another type. It is possible that it was an experiment or prototype of the No. 1800. Note the flattened sides of the tail. There were no references to it in any catalogs and presently only five are known to be in collectors hands. This one has white body with red head and tail and no eyes. Collector value range: $40 to $80.

BABY CRAB WIGGLER (3'')
#1900 Series
MIDGET CRAB WIGGLER (2½'')
#1950 Series

These are smaller versions of the #1800 Crab Wiggler. They were introduced in 1915 and 1921 respectively. The earliest had 'U' collars and variable line ties as on left two lures in the photo. The last 'U' collar on this lure (before transition to the later 'O' collar) can be identified by noting that the script

248

Heddon (cont'd)

stamped on the collar is larger than on the earlier ones. Later plugs also utilize a single line tie secured to the body by using the same screw used to hold the center flange of the collar on. The colors are the same as the #1800 Crab Wiggler. The Midget model is in the photo for the Go-Deeper Crab. Collector value range: $5 to $15.

DEEP-O-DIVER
No. 700 Series

This is an unusual version of the Midget Crab Wiggler. It has the same body as the Midget. It has a unique line tie on **top** and a different style O-collar metal diving lip that is pointed. It sports only one double hook. New around 1919 it was first made with a pin type pork rind attachment on the body. By 1921 this was integrated into the double hook. This later version came with an imitation pork rind attachment. It is a ⅔ ounce sinker. The 1926 catalog was the last to offer the Deep-O-Diver. Collector value range: $10 to $15.

CATALOG SERIES #	BODY LENGTH	LURE WEIGHT
7000	2½"	⅔ oz.

COLOR OR FINISH: *White body, red head; White body, greenish black spots; Yellow body, black head; Green scale finish; Red, scale finish; Frog, scale finish; Goldfish, scale finish; Yellow perch, scale finish.*

GO-DEEPER CRAB
Series #D1900

The Go-Deeper Crab is the same as the #1900 Baby Crab, but has a deep diving lip instead of the collar and an optional spinner attached to the rear. These plugs came along in 1952. Collector value range: $3 to $10.

CATALOG SERIES #	BODY LENGTH	LURE WEIGHT
D-1900	3½"	½ oz.

COLOR OR FINISH: *Natural Crab; White with red head; Green crackle back; Black and white crab; Yellow shore minnow; Orange body, red and black spots.*

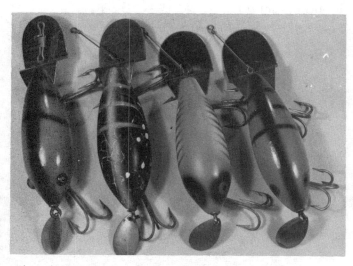

These four Go-Deeper Crabs are illustrative of the various names to be found stenciled on their bellys. Left to right they read: "HEDDON BABY CRABB", "HEDDON CRAB", "HEDDON DIGGER CRAB," and "HEDDON GO-DEEPER CRAB." The one on the left has yellow glass eyes and all four sport the 1-pc. surface hardware.

WIGGLE KING
Series No. 2000

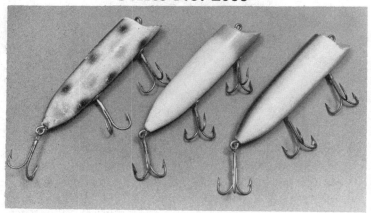

Not visible in the photo is an unusual decal sometimes found on the belly of WIGGLE KINGS. There is a gold colored oval shaped decal on the far left lure. Printed in the oval is "HEDDON WIGGLE KING."

The Wiggle King is extremely similar to both the Lucky-13 and the Basser. It probably represents the first stage in the development of both. It came alone somewhere around 1918-20. The Lucky 13 was new about 1920 and the Basser came out in 1922. The difference in the Wiggle King and the Lucky 13 is found in the shape of the face of the lures. The Wiggle King has no upper overhang at the top of the carved out head and Lucky 13 always do have a bit of an overhang. Please compare the photograph here to the ones accompanying the Lucky-13 on page 216. The Wiggle King is 3-7/8" long and came in five colors: White body with spots, White body with red head; Rainbow; Frog; Green Scale. They are found with cup and L-rig hook hardware. Collector value range: $10 to $20.

249

Heddon (cont'd.)

CRAZY CRAWLER
Series #2100

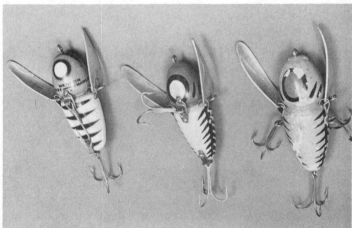

COLOR OR FINISH: **Bullfrog; **Gray mouse (fur finish with ears); **Red and white shore minnow; **Yellow with red head; Glow worm; **Silver shore minnow; **Black with white head; Luminous red and white; Luminous glow worm; Chipmunk (fur finish).

**Only colors available by 1949.

Note the huge eyes on this late model Crazy Crawler. It measures 2-3/4" and is black with a white head.

SAM-SPOON
Series No. 2160

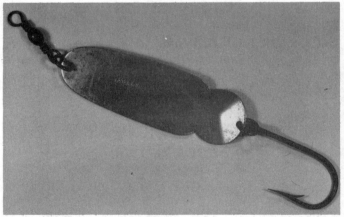

This surface lure appeared in the Heddon catalog first in 1940. It is interesting to note its startling similarity to the James Donaly "WOW" lure (see page 165). Indeed upon closer examination collectors have noted some interesting facts. In the second photo here (three plugs), the lure on the right is the Donaly "WOW." The center plug is the Donaly lure body, paint pattern and flapper blades but the hook hardware is genuine Heddon hardware. The far left plug is the Heddon product. This evidence served to convince most collectors that Heddon either bought the patent or the Donaly company at some point prior to 1940. It is now known that Heddon did indeed acquire the Donaly patent. It was first available in two sizes but quickly a third size was produced. Collector value range: $3 to $10.

CATALOG SERIES #	BODY LENGTH	LURE WEIGHT
320*	1¼"	⅓ oz.
2100	2¾"	¾ oz.
2120	2½"	3/5 oz.
2150	3½"	1 oz.

This lure was new about 1936 and was in the line regularly into the 1940's. It was available in either a single hook or a trailing hook model. Length is 6-1/2" and it was available in Allen Stripey or shiner scale, red and white or plain nickel plated. Collector value range: $15 to $30.

*New in 1957.

250

LUCKY-13
Series #2400 and #2500

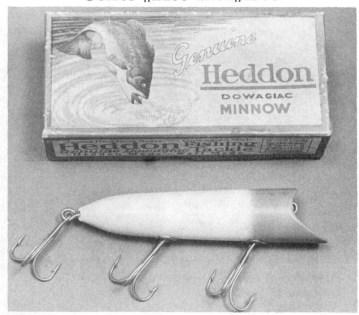

A mint condition early Lucky-13 with its original box. Note the long lower lip and no eyes.

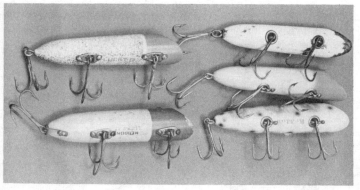

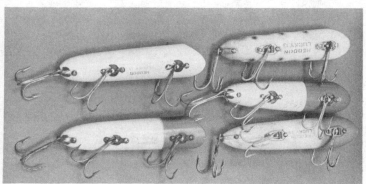

The Lucky-13 was preceded by the Wiggle King. The Lucky-13's appeared in the line about 1920 in two sizes, the regular at 3-7/8'' and the Junior at 3''. The regular size seems to have grown a bit by 1927 when listings begin to say they are 4'' long. The oldest sport cup hardware and follow the classic hardware changes over the years. The accompanying photographs illustrate the changes. The latest is the reissue of both in the Heddon Wooden Classic Series of the late 1960's. Collector value range: $4 to $40.

CATALOG SERIES #	BODY LENGTH	LURE WEIGHT
2400 (Jr.)	3''	
2400 (Jr. & Baby)	2¾''	3/8 oz.
2400 (reg.)	4''	5/8 oz.
2500 (reg.)	3-7/8''	5/8 oz.
*2400 (Classic Baby)	2-5/8''	5/8 oz.
*2500 (classic)	**3¾''	5/8 oz.

COLOR OR FINISH: ***White body, red head; ***Green scale finish; Red scale finish; Frog, scale finish; Goldfish, scale; ***Yellow perch, scale finish; ***White body, red and green spots; ***Pike scale; Shiner scale; Mullet scale; Orange, black spots; Blue scales; Rainbow; ***Frog scale, red head; ***Shiner scale, red head; ***Silver flitter, red head; Natural scale.

*The classics came out about 1965 in these colors only: Bullfrog, Perch, Frog scale, Red head, Silver flitter and Red head with Shiver scale.
**Actual measurement listed as 4'' in catalogs.
***These were the only finishes available by 1931.

SPIN-DIVER
#3000 Series

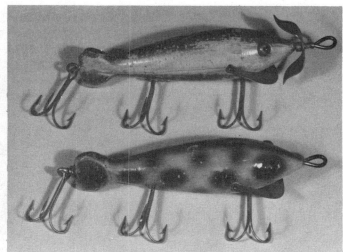

These are the propped and no-prop versions of the SPIN-DIVER. Both measure 4-1/2'' and have glass eyes. The no-prop model here has a plain unmarked metal lip and the other has a lip with the Heddon imprint.

New around 1918 this lure disappeared from catalogs after 1926. Found in L-rig only to date. Has been found with no prop and unmarked lip. A handsome 3T glass eyed, 4-3/8'', nose spinnered plug. It was available in many colors: green, red, frog, gold and yellow scale finishes; fancy green back; white body, red and green spots; rainbow; frog; yellow perch; white body with red spot on tail fin and enamel eyes. Collector value range: $25 to $50.

SPOON-Y FROG
#3200 Series

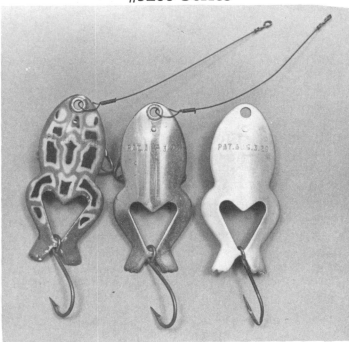

New in 1928 and gone from production two years later, this all metal lure was offered in four color designs. They were gold plated, silver plated, red and white striped, and green frog. They ran belly-up on retrieve. The photograph here shows the lures belly down. They are three inches in length and weigh 4/5 ounce. Collector value range: $10 to $20.

LITTLE LUNY FROG
#3400 Series

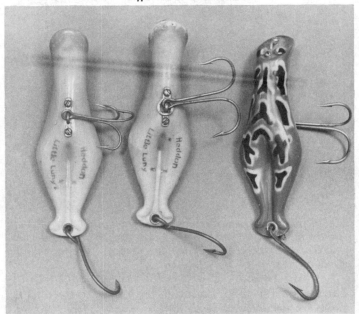

One year after Heddon introduced the #3500 Luny Frog they made this lighter, smaller version available (1928). It was also made of Pyralin and subject to the same brittleness for it too had disappeared from catalogs by 1932. It was available in the same colors as the larger one.* Collector value range: $10 to $20.

LUNY FROG
#3500 Series

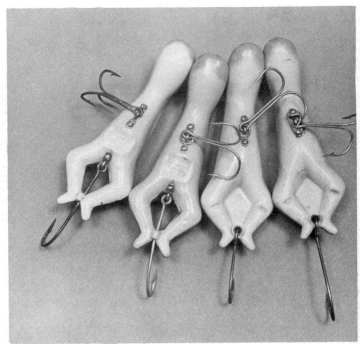

*No white body, red head Little Luny Frog is known to have been found yet.

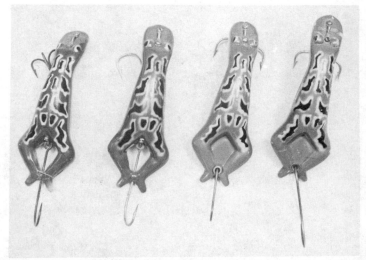

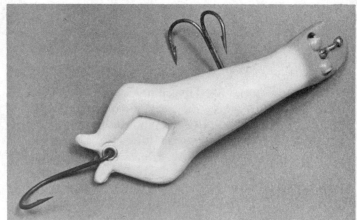

Although never listed as available in catalogs this is a rare red head, white body Luny Frog. $50 to $100.00

Heddon (cont'd.)

This interesting plug was introduced in the 1927 catalog and by 1932 it was no longer listed as available. The lure was made of pyralin and is known to be very brittle. It would shatter into several pieces if cast against rocks or other hard surfaces. The lure underwent a design change during its brief appearance in the Heddon line. The two photographs here illustrate the "web" that was added apparently attempting to strengthen the design. The plugs in the photo are arranged from left to right according to age. Note the hook hardware, identification style and location, and the webbed leg design. They were available with double or treble belly hooks. Collector value range: $10 to $15.

CATALOG SERIES #	BODY LENGTH	LURE WEIGHT
3500	4½"	7/8 oz.

COLOR OR FINISH: *Green frog; Meadow frog; White body with red head (rare).*

Arranged oldest to newest left to right according to hook hangers hardware. Note the last two have Vamp type lips. They have been found with this particular lip reversed, making it a surface plug.

MEADOW MOUSE
Series #4000

A 1929 catalog clearly states that this was a new plug for that year. The illustration also clearly shows the L-rig (post-1917) hook hardware. However, if you will examine the photo here you will note the use of

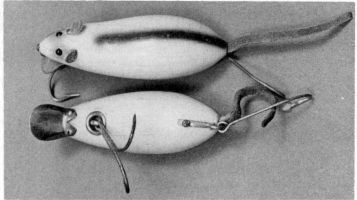

the pre-1917 cup hardware. The two lures are otherwise identical to the 1929 catalog illustration. Their metal diving lips say Heddon. They could be prototypes, but they are found so often it is doubtful. The lures are found with and without the name on the River Runt type diving lip. They are found with almost any combination of hook types but the first catalog illustration shows a belly double and a trailing single hook. A 1939 catalog shows the Meadow Mouse with a Vamp type diving lip, two treble hooks and two-piece hardware (see next to last lure in the photo of 6 lures). It also states that the lure is available with a double and single hook option.

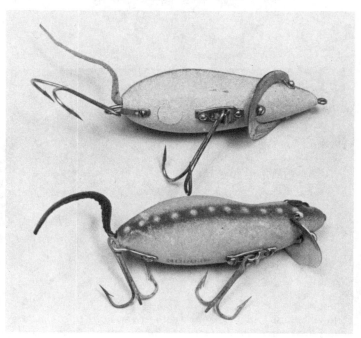

Upper is a Meadow Mouse with a Crab Wiggler type metal collar lip. Lower lure is the #4200 Munk-Mouse with a reversed Vamp type lip.

All the Meadow Mice had black bead eyes. Most any type of Heddon hardware can be found on the Meadow Mouse. Collector value range: $3 to $25.

CATALOG SERIES #	BODY LENGTH	LURE WEIGHT
4000	2¾"	⅔ oz.

COLOR OR FINISH: *Brown mouse; Gray mouse, white belly; White and red; *Black body with white head; **Fur finish brown mouse; **Fur finish gray mouse; **Fur finish white mouse.*

*New in 1930
**Fur finish new in 1934.*

TAD POLLY
Series #5000 and #6000

Shows earliest TAD POLLY and earliest Tad Polly box. This lure has a high hump line tie (earliest). It may not be readily visible on the lure, but the box illustration shows it clearly. This and the parallel arrangement of "Heddon" and "Dowagiac" on the heart or apple shaped metal head plate are characteristics of the earliest of the TAD POLLYS. Collector value range: $20 to $40.

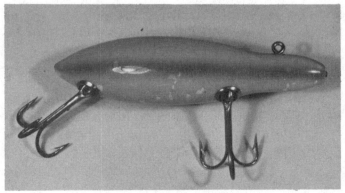

This unknown, un-cataloged lure is placed here because it bears a closer resemblence to the Tad Polly than any other Heddon Lure. It measures 4" long. Some collectors call them by the name "Bottle Nose." Collector value range: $15 to $45.

The smaller version (Series #5000) was the first to be introduced (1919) and the Series #6000 came along in 1920-21. The Series #6000 only lasted for seven or eight years disappearing after 1929. The Series #5000 was continuously in production until about 1941. There are at least two slighty differing body styles to be found one is a bit fatter than the other (see photo on previous page). A more significant difference in metal plate shape and the position of the identifying marks on the plate, oldest is the "Heart shape" or apple-like shape then the "bell-shape". The words "Heddon Dowagiac" are arranged in an inverted "V" shape on the bell plate and next, the words are in the upright "V" position then later rearranged in a curve following the rounded edge of the plate. The latter two arrangements are found only on the "bell shape" plate and are not illustrated in the photo of four here. They are found with double and treble hooks. Collector value range: $3 to $15 for the more commonly found versions. The left two in the photo of four will bring $20 to $40 because of the early high hump line tie.

CATALOG SERIES #	BODY LENGTH	LURE WEIGHT
5000	3-7/8"	5/8 oz.
5100 (Runt)	3"	½ oz.
6000	4-5/8"	¾ oz.

COLOR OR FINISH: Fancy green back; White body, red and green spots; Rainbow; White body, red head and tail; *Yellow perch; Frog coloration; Green, scale finish; *Red, scale finish; *Frog, scale finish; *Gold fish, scale finish; Yellow perch, scale finish; **Shiner scale.

  *Eliminated by c1930.

  **Added by c1930.

GAME FISHER
Series #5500
BABY GAME FISHER
Series #5400

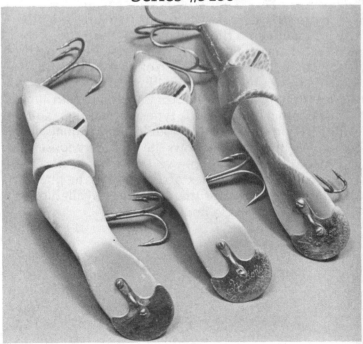

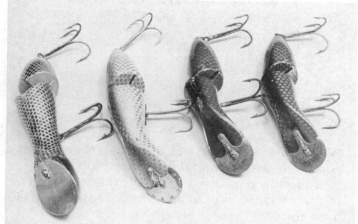

Dec. 18, 1923.   1,477,756

C. HEDDON ET AL

ARTIFICIAL FISH BAIT

Filed Aug. 16, 1922

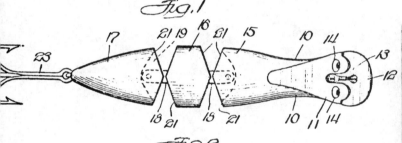

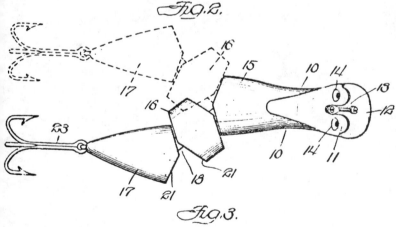

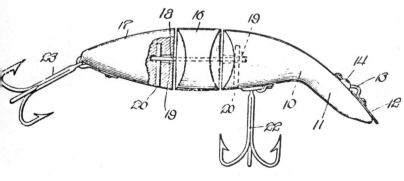

Inventors:
Charles Heddon
William A. Stolley

The #5500 came out in 1923. The smaller (#5400) came along about a year later. The Baby Game Fisher was only a two segment jointed plug. Both were missing from the 1934 and subsequent catalogs. The two photos on the previous page show both plugs and the three different metal lip plate styles. It is difficult to tell from the photos, but the major differences in the lips are as follows: left, no writing thought to be the very first model of the Game Fisher; third from left says "Vampir" (very rare); third from left and far left say "Heddon's Game Fisher." The lure was patented December 18, 1923 (see accompanying patent drawing). You will note the drawing (patent) indicates eyes. The patent text specifies glass eyes. There has been one glass eyed Gamefisher found so far. Considered very rare. All others found so far have no eyes at all. Left two are pre-patent models. They are valued at $25 to $50. Glass eyed model: $100 to $300. Others $3 to $10.

ZARAGOSSA MINNOW*
Series #6500

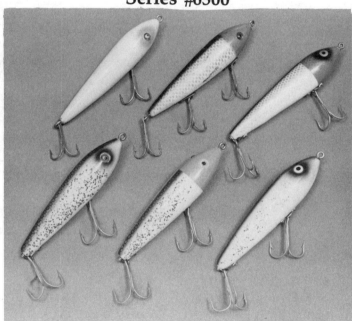

Originating around 1922 the earliest found so far had the L-rig hardware. The continue in production right into the fifties and on.

The top row in the photograph of six Zaragossas illustrates the lure progression from the earlies. From left the first has glass eyes and L-rig hardware, the center also has glass eyes but has the two-piece and the right plug has painted eyes and one-piece surface hardware. The bottom row shows three reissue Zaragossas. They are from the Heddon Wooden Classic Series of the late 1960's. Each of the Classics has stenciled on the belly "Original Heddon Wood Zaragossa." The photograph of the lure on the patent drawing is of the so-called "no-chin" model. It matches the original patent. Collector value range: $4 to $40.

*See Harden's Star, page 264.

255

Heddon (cont'd.)

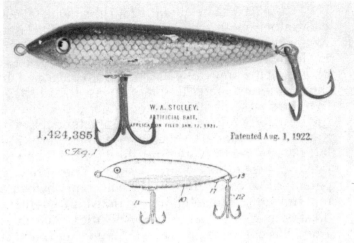

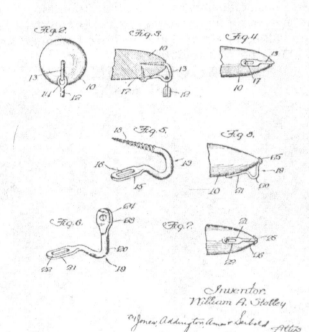

CATALOG SERIES #	BODY LENGTH	LURE WEIGHT
6500	4¼"	*½-¾ oz.

COLOR OR FINISH: *White body, red throat; Natural scale finish; Red scale finish; Frog scale with red eyes; Frog, scale finish; Goldfish, scale; Yellow perch, scale finish; Green cracked back; Rainbow; White with red eyes; Green scale; Pike scale; Shiner scale; Shiner scale with red head; White body, silver specks; White body, red and green spots.*

The catalogs list ½ ounce until 1926. From 1927 on the weight is listed as ¾ ounce. In 1935 the phrase "3 hooks now regular" would seem to indicate those made prior are usually found with two hooks.

MUSKY ZARAGOSSA

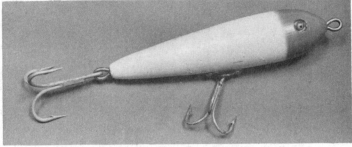

There was no catalog information found in regard to this plug. It is essentially the same lure as the other Zaragossas but made heavier and stronger. Collector value range: $60 to $90.

DARTING ZARA
Series #6550 and #6600

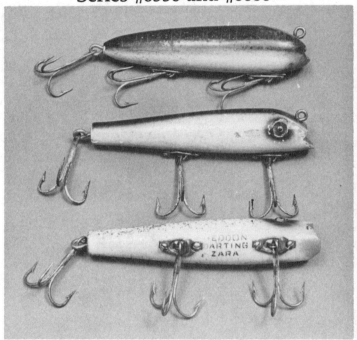

This lure dates back to at least 1928. A 1933 catalog says it was used to catch "two prize winning bass. . . in (the) 1928 Field and Stream Contest." They were made of wood up until the late 1930s when they became the Zara-Spook. The photograph of three Zaras are arranged by age from oldest at the top. All these have the second style two-piece hook hangers. The lure at the top inexplicably has a nail in the middle of the notch mouth. Collector value range: $20 to $60.

CATALOG SERIES #	BODY LENGTH	LURE WEIGHT
6550	3¾"	
6600	4½"	5/8 oz.

COLOR OR FINISH: *Orange with red spots; Bullfrog; Green scale; Silver scale.*

(cont'd next page)

Heddon (cont'd.)

This jointed version of the Darting Zara was not found referenced in any Heddon Catalogs. A case could be made that it is an altered unjointed Darting Zara except that the paint on the inside of the joint is an exact match to the remaining paint. Would you go to that much trouble if all you were doing was altering a lure in your possum-belly tackle box? This is a Heddon production model be it ever so rare. It measures 4-1/8", has glass eyes, one-piece bar hook hardware and "HEDDON" stenciled on the belly. Collector value range: $50 to $75.

FLAPTAIL Series #7000
FLAPTAIL JR. Series #7110

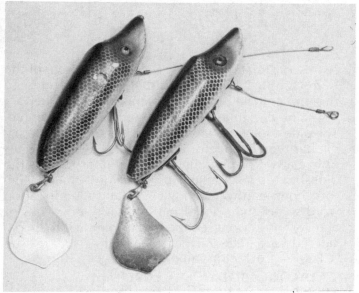

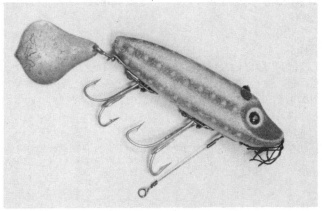

Chipmunk finish

These two were introduced about 1935. The Junior size is found with both one and two treble hooks. The regular Flaptails have two trebles. Collector value range: $4 to $15.

CATALOG SERIES #	BODY LENGTH	LURE WEIGHT
7000	4"	4/5 oz.
7110	3¼"	5/8 oz.

COLOR OR FINISH: *White with red head; Frog; Green cale; Perch scale; Pike scale; Dace scale; Silver scale; Grey mouse; *Brown mouse; **Chipmunk (fur finish).*

*Junior only.
**Added in 1942.

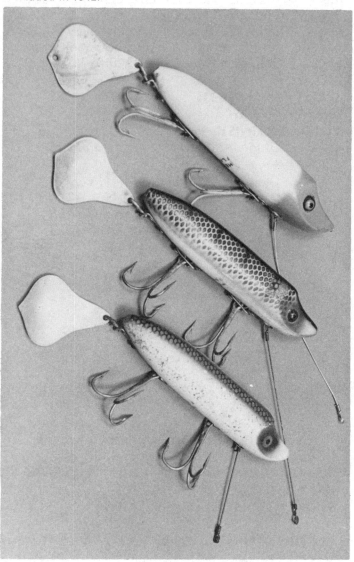

Heddon Flaptails

Heddon (cont'd.)

GIANT FLAPTAIL
Series #7050

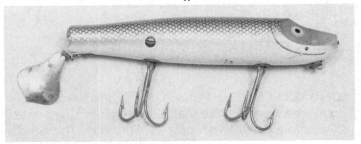

This is a relatively late model wooden plug coming out in the late 1940's. It is an exceptionally strong lure and is the same basic design as the earlier "Musky Flaptail" Series #7050 also, but much bigger. All have painted eyes. The example in the photo measures exactly 7". Collector value range: $10 to $16.

CATALOG SERIES #	BODY LENGTH	LURE WEIGHT
7050	6¾"	2¼ oz.

COLOR OR FINISH: *Shad; White red head; Blue herring scale; Shiner scale with red head and stripes.*

FLAPTAIL MUSKY
Series #7050

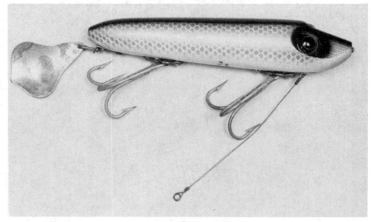

New in 1935 this lure is a heavier, sturdier version of the regular #7000 series Flaptail. Has "Teddy Bear Glass Eyes." Collector value range: $20 to $30.

CATALOG SERIES #	BODY LENGTH	LURE WEIGHT
7050	5¼"	1 oz.

COLOR OR FINISH: *White with red head; **Copper sheen; Natural scale; Shiner scale; Silver scale; Spottled; *Gray mouse; ***Chipmunk (fur finish).*

   *Added in 1936. Had ears and whiskers. Fur finish added in 1939.
  *Removed by 1939.
***Added in 1942.

JOINTED VAMP
Series #7300

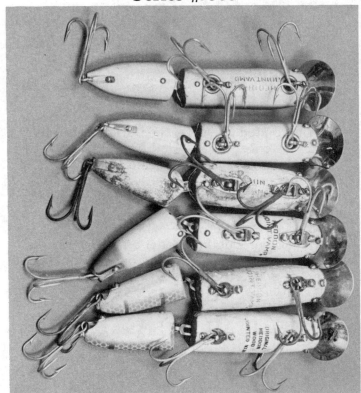

A 1927 catalog says ". . . newest member of the Vamp family". The 1928 catalog and after refers to this lure as "The Swimming Vamp Jointed." They are the same design as the #7500 Vamp except jointed. The oldest jointed Vamps can be identified by the signle bar type connector at the joint. The newer ones utilize a two piece connector. The photo shows the oldest to the newest, left to right. Note joint connectors, hook hardware body sizes, and identification word styles and orientation. All good indicators of age. A shorter front section of this jointed lure is considered rare. The farthest right lure is a reissue "Classic". Collector value range: $3 to $10.

CATALOG SERIES #	BODY LENGTH	LURE WEIGHT
7300	4½"	¾ oz.
**7300 (Classic)	5"	¾ oz.

COLOR OR FINISH: *Rainbow; White body, red head; Green scale; Perch scale; Pike scale; Shiner scale; Natural scale; Rainbow scale; *White body, silver specks, red head.*

  *Added in 1934.
**Classic is found only in Pike scale, Perch, White with red head, Shiner scale, Yellow shore minnow and White with red and green spots.

Heddon (cont'd.)

GIANT JOINTED VAMP
Series #7350

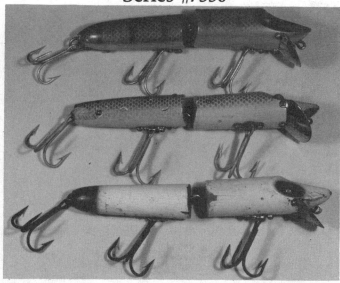

Upper lure is oldest. It measures 6-3/8", has glass eyes, Heddon name on metal lip and L-rig hook hangers. The center is 6-7/8", has "HEDDON JOINT VAMP" stenciled on the belly, glass eyes and toilet seat style hook hangers. The lower lure also measures 6-7/8", has "HEDDON GIANT JOINTED VAMP" stenciled on belly and glass eyes.

This is a jointed version of the #7550 Musky Vamp. Prior to 1935 it was called a Jointed Musky Vamp. From 1935 to the 1950's it is known as the Giant Jointed Vamp. They are all listed as 6" in length but the examples in the photo above actually measure longer. The upper lure in the photograph is the oldest of the three (1934-35). The middle lure was first illustrated in the 1937 catalog. It has a slightly slimmer body and a chopped off tail end. Colors are the same as the Musky Vamps. Collector value range: $7 to $20.

BABY VAMP Series #7400

New around 1925 this is essentially the same as the #7500 series Vamp but smaller. It is occasionally found with the metal lip in the 2 piece hook hardware vintage. Collector value range: $5 to $12.

CATALOG SERIES #	BODY LENGTH	LURE WEIGHT
7400	3½"	½ oz.

COLOR OR FINISH: *White body, red and green spots; Rainbow; White body, red eyes and tail; Green scale; Pike scale; Shiner scale; Mullet scale; Orange, black spot; Blue scale.*

VAMP Series #7500

Earliest Vampire. Has cup hook hanger hardware. Collector value range: $50 to $100 for this particular version.

The Vamp was born in 1921 as the "Vampire" minnow. First available in 4½" and five colors: white body, green and red spots; rainbow; white body, red eyes and tail; green scale; pike scale. The very earliest have cup hardware but the early Vampires are more often found with the L-rig. Refer to photograph of four lures on the next page. Another way to distinguish these early Vampires is by the manner of attaching the diving lip. In the photograph you can see that it is integrated with the L-rig hook hanger. The top three are Vampires. The bottom lure is a later Vamp. By 1922 they were called Vamps. The diving lips are marked as Heddon. Collector value range: $3 to $10.

CATALOG SERIES #	BODY LENGTH	LURE WEIGHT
7500	4½"	5/8 oz.

GREAT VAMP Series No. 7540
MUSKY VAMP Series No. 7550
VAMPIRE MUSKY Series No. 7600

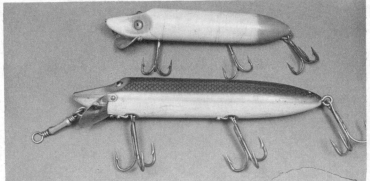

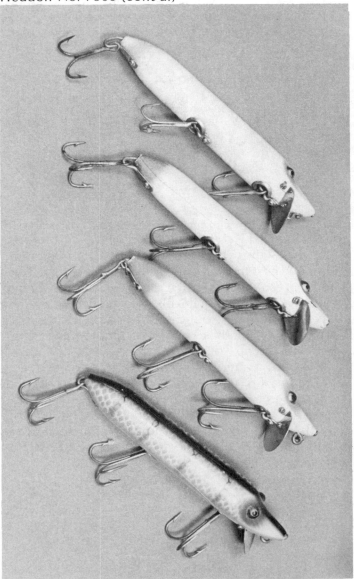

Upper lure is a 6" MUSKY VAMP. Lower lure is an 8" VAMPIRE MUSKY. The MUSKY VAMP became the GIANT VAMP by 1939.

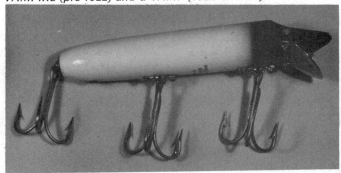

This is a VAMPIRE MUSKY #7600. It is 8" long and has glass eyes. Note the integrated forward hook hanger and metal lip hardware. This is an important clue in determining whether a lure is a VAMPIRE (pre-1922) and a VAMP (1922 or later).

COLOR OR FINISH: White body, red and green spots; Rainbow; White body, red eyes and tail; Green scale; Pike scale; *Mullet scale; **Red scale; **Frog scale; **Yellow perch scale; **Orange, black spots; **Blue scale; Silver scale; White, silver specks, red head; Luminous, red head and tail; Natural scale.

*Added in 1925.

**Added in 1926. The frog, blue scale and orange finishes were not listed after 1934.

A 5" long GREAT VAMP # 7540. It has glass eyes, no name on metal lip, but the name is found stenciled on the belly; heavy duty 2-piece toilet seat style hook hangers and a flat metal tail hook hanger held in by a screw from the bottom; metal tail hook insert.

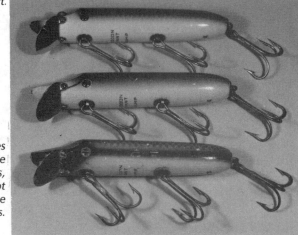

Three 5-3/4" GIANT VAMPS representing an evolution of the lures from glass eye to painted eye models. Oldest is at the top of the photo. It has glass eyes, heavy duty metal ribbon hook hangers, reinforcing tail hook insert. The middle has all the above except the eyes are painted. The lower lure is probably the newest due to the more economical use of screw hook and cup hook hangers.

Heddon (cont'd.)

The first of these to come along was the 8"
model in 1925 and the 6" version came along shortly
thereafter. The large one was gone around 1930 and
the smaller one had disappeared by 1932. The 5"
version was in the line from 1937 to 1939. They were
made quite large and strong to handle the big
muskies. Collector value range: $6 to $40.

CATALOG SERIES #	BODY LENGTH	LURE WEIGHT
7540	5"	1⅓ oz.
7550	6"	1-4/5 oz.
7660	8"	3¼ oz.

COLOR OR FINISH: *White body, red eyes and tail;
Green scale; Pike scale; Shiner scale; Natural scale;
White body, spotted.*

ZIG-WAG Series #8300
ZIG-WAG JUNIOR Series #8340
KING-ZIG WAG Series #8360

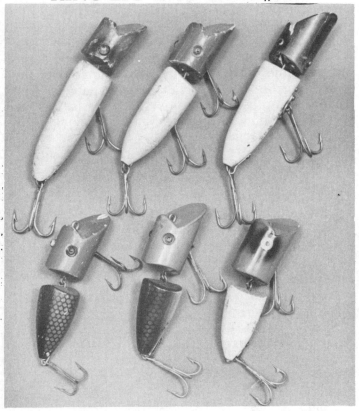

The #8300 was the first to come along (1928),
then the #8340 Junior in 1937. The #8360 King was the
last, becoming available about 1939, all three were
still being offered in the late 1940's and early 1950's.
When first encountered in catalogs (1928) the listing
stated "ZIG-WAG (Improved)." This seems to indicate
that the plug was already being produced. Even
though the author found absolutely no earlier
reference to the lure it is possible that it can be found
in an earlier and different design. Collector value
range: $10 to $20.

CATALOG SERIES #	BODY LENGTH	LURE WEIGHT
8300	4½"	¾ oz.
8340	3½"	½ oz.

COLOR OR FINISH: *White body, red head; *Green
frog; *Green scale; Green scale, red head; *Pike scale;
Pike scale, red head; *Shiner scale, red head; *Natural
scale; Natural scale, red head; Bull frog; White body,
silver specks, red head.*

*Eliminated by about 1934. Shiner scale finish was added again
in 1937.*

The King Zig-Wag sometimes came with a thumb tack
type attaching a fake (leather pork rind to its belly.
It was made in two different sizes and had string hook
arrangements. Both characteristics are evident in the
accompanying photos. Collector value range: $5 to
$10.

CATALOG SERIES #	BODY LENGTH	LURE WEIGHT
8360	5"	1-1/8 oz.
	6"	1½ oz.

COLOR OR FINISH: *White and red; White, red gills;
Shiner scale; Allen stripey; Blue herring; Yellow scale;
Pearl X-ray; Spotted, red head.*

HEDDON BASSER Series #8500

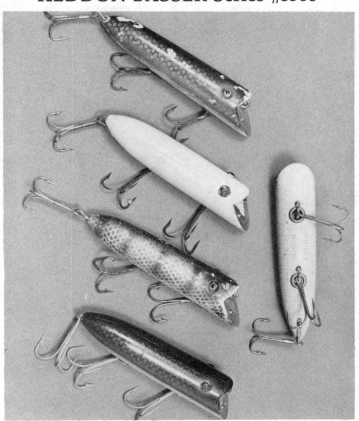

261

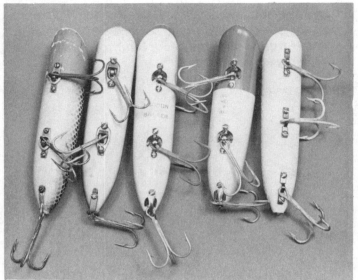

Above shows the evolution of hook hanger hardware on the BASSER. Not shown are the first two. Bassers are also found with the plain no-hump L-rig and the regular L-rig. Next (far left in the photo) is the 2-piece Toilet Seat style, then the second style 2-piece, 1-piece Surface and the 1-piece bar.

The original or first Basser came out in 1922 and was called the "Head-On-Basser" and these words were stamped on the metal head plate. In 1924 this had been changed to "Heddon Basser." The stamped identification has undergone some other style changes over the years, but the words have remained the same. Note the body style change over the years illustrated in the photos accompanying. The Basser is another of those reissued Classics around 1965 in wooden body and labeled "Original." Collector value range: $3 to $12.

*8540   4½"   1 oz.
*8540   4½"   1 oz.

CATALOG SERIES #	BODY LENGTH	LURE WEIGHT
*8400 (Plunking Basser)	3"	5/8 oz.
8500 (Regular)	4"	¾ oz.
*8510 (Salmon Basser)	4"	7/8 oz.
*8520 (Salmon or Deluxe)	4½"	7/8 oz.
*8540	4½"	1 oz.
8540 (King Basser)	4½"	1 oz.
*8550 (King Basser)	5"	1-1/10 oz.
*8560 (King Basser)	6"	2¼ oz.

COLOR OR FINISH: *Rainbow; White body, red head; Green scale; Red scale; Frog scale; Goldfish scale; Yellow perch scale; Pike scale; Shiner scale; White spotted; Mullet scale; Orange, black spots; Blue scale; White body, silver specks, red head; Luminous.*

*These were made no earlier than 1935 and all but the #8550 were out of production by the early 1950's.

KING BASSER
Series #8560

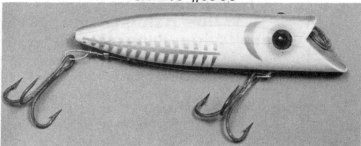

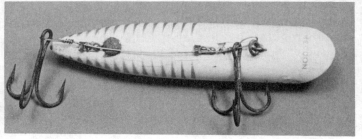

This lure is large and strong. It was obviously made for heavy fishing. Note the strong wire hook hardware set-up. Size: 6-1/8". Collector value range: $6 to $14.

SALMON RIVER RUNT
Series #8850

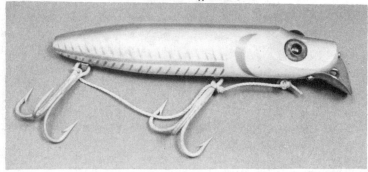

This strong 5½" wooden plug is obviously from the River Runt family but no catalog references could be found. In the photo, you will note the string arrangement in the hook hardware and a different type metal diving lip. The photo doesn't show it well but this particular example has "Teddy Bear Glass Eyes." It does state "Heddon Salmon River Runt" on the belly. Collector value range: $9 to $20.

SUPER DOWAGIAC
Series No. 9100

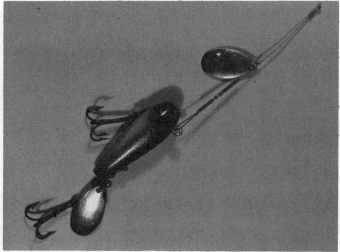

This particular lure is not found catalogued by Heddon in a wood body version. They were introduced in a plastic body model in a 1930 catalog so it would not be unreasonable to say the lures were produced prior to 1930 even though this cannot presently be proved. The name in that 1930 catalog was "New SUPER DOWAGIAC Spook." The body of the wooden model here measures 2". It has two-piece hook hanger hardware, painted eyes and is drilled from the nose and filled with lead so that it is quite heavy. Collector value range: $20 to $40.

CHUGGER
Series #9540

This CHUGGER is a red head, frog finish version with no eyes. It measures 4-3/8" and sports the second style Heddon 2-piece hook hanger. Collector value range: $25 to $50.

This is an interesting situation in that the first chuggers were the #9540 Series "Chugger Spooks." Spook means plastic in the Heddon line. The first Chugger Spook was released in 1938-39 and definitely was plastic. However there are several wooden Chuggers in collectors hands that were found purchased in the "Classic" boxes of 1964-65. They are definitely later models because of the eyes and hardware (see photo). The "Classic" lure was to be a reissue of four old time favorites in wood. The circular

HARDEN'S SPECIAL
HARDEN'S STAR
Walter Harden,
Connellsville, Pennsylvania

This lure is in actuality a Heddon product, at least in part. The story is that sometime in the late 1920's to early 1930's, Mr. Harden took a Heddon Zaragossa minnow and modified it for his particular brand of Florida bass fishing. It proved so successful that Heddon put the modified Zara on the market. The photographs show both of Harden's modified plugs along with a box with brown paper labels pasted over a regular Heddon label. Collector value range: Harden's Special - $20 to $30; Harden's Star - $200 to $300.

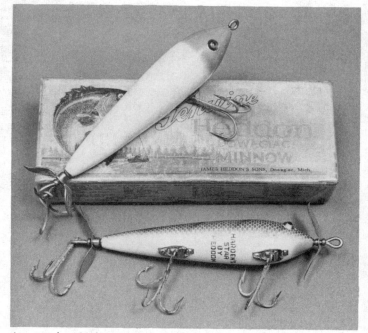

enclosed in the boxes state clearly that this style lure has been used "... for over fifty years and is one of the four great Heddon Wood Classics currently available." Perhaps the wooden chugger was a mistake or it may be representative of a prototype for several proven old timers to be reissued in wood regardless of age or original body material. They are not marked "Original" on the lure body as are the other four classics. In any case here they are. Collector value range: $40 to $80.

Lure on box is the Harden's Special (2T, 1 prop) and the other is the Harden's Star (3T, 2 props).

This lure is much like the #2000 WIGGLE KING except for the flat, straight slant head. The paint and hardware are obviously Heddon through the lure is not found in any catalogs thus far. It measures 4-1/8", has no eyes and has deep cup and screw hook hardware. Collector value range: $40 to $80.

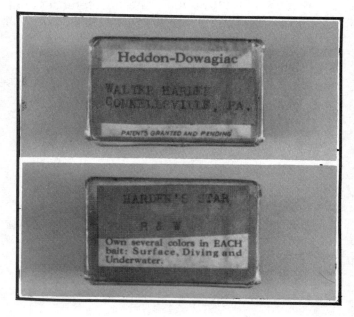

HARDEN'S WHIZ

There is just too little known about the Heddon/Harden relationship as yet. This is known to be a Heddon product. It is essentially a Heddon Baby Vamp body with flopy props, yellow glass eyes and two-piece toilet style hook hardware. It measures in at 3-1/2". There is another, larger one in existance measuring 4-1/2". It is not marked on the belly as is the 3-1/2" "HARDEN'S WHIZ BY HEDDON." The large one has only a tail propeller spinner. Collector value range: $100 to $200.

SOME UNUSUAL HEDDON LURES

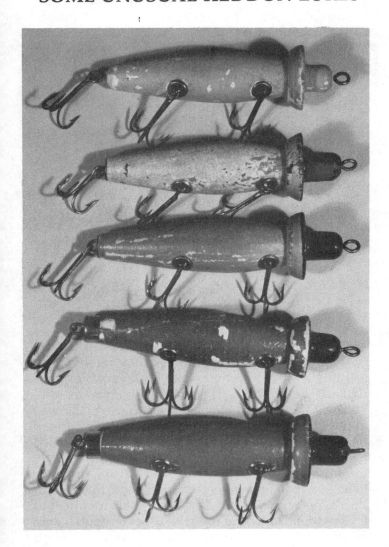

These woodpecker type lures are Heddon products. Information about them is elusive. They have never been found cataloged or advertised by Heddon. There is one obscure reference in a 1917 catalog that some collectors think may be this lure. It was a list of recommended lures for various fishing conditions. Under the list for night fishing there is an entry for the 1001RH. This number appears nowhere in catalogs for a lure that could have a red head. The number 1000 is used for the metal Triple Tease, but a red head is not practical for this type lure.

The accompanying photograph of five woodpecker type lures are positively identified as Heddon products. The oldest (at top of picture) measures 4-1/4", a screw eye tail hook hanger, cup and screw hook hardware and is painted all white (luminous). The next two down are 4-1/4" and 4-1/2" respectively. They have luminous white bodies with long, red painted heads. Each has cup and screw hook hardware and tail cup inserts imparting metal reinforcement. The fourth lure down measures 4-1/2" and has a metal tail cup clearly visible. It also sports cup and screw hook hardware and has a red head. The bottom lure is also equipped with the metal tail cap. It measures 4-5/8" and utilizes the 2-hump L-rig hook hardware. Note the slightly fatter body. The lures are arranged chronologically from the top. Collector value range: $50 to $100.

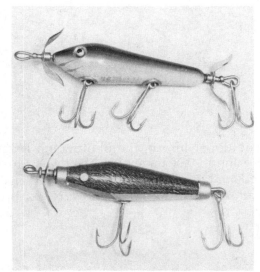

These two lures came from the Heddon factory archives. The lower lure is a dead ringer for a lure attributed to Leroy Yakely of Syracuse, New York. It is also almost identical to a lure in a series of drawings that were exhibits in one law suit in a series of law suits from 1913 to 1915 involving several men and companies. Yakely, J. K. Rush, Moonlight, Heddon and others were involved (see page 301). Heddon may simply have bought one of these for examination. It is included here because of where it came from and its possible influence on the design of the Heddon early 100 prototype on top.

Heddon (cont'd)

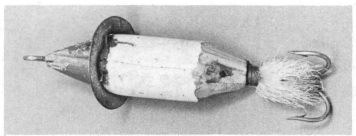

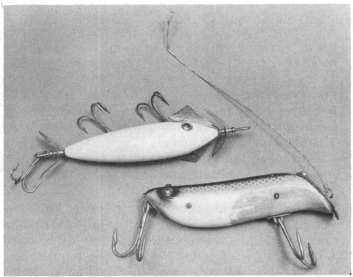

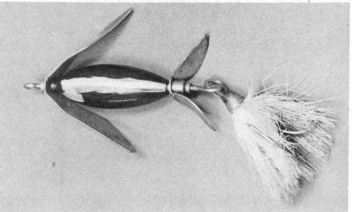

These two lures are also from the Heddon factory. Both are probably experimental or early prototypes. The upper lure has the No. 1600 Series Wiggler metal nose fins. The lower lure could be a prototype of the musky Tadpolly.

Two very early experimental Heddon lures from the factory archives. The top is obviously an old slope nose Expert that has been rather crudely whittled down short and fitted with a rigid mount buck tail double hook. Note the very crude propeller spinner on the bottom plug.

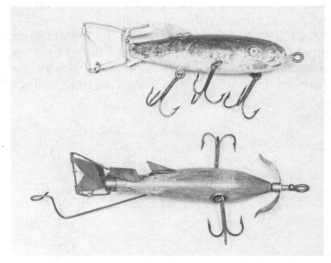

The upper lure in the photograph is the 1905 Smith Minnow (see page 416). The lower lure is from the Heddon factory archives. The latter is an obvious variation from the Smith Minnow. Never placed in production.

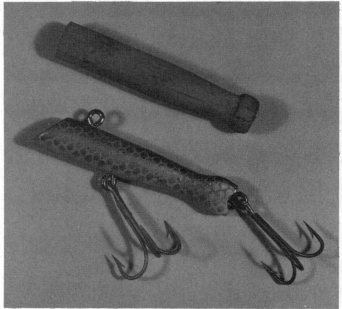

I have not been able to find any reference to this lure in all the Heddon catalogs available to me to date. This 2-5/8" lure is placed here for two reasons: The paint finish and the similarity to the blank also in the photo. Both lures have identical holes drilled from the nose. The finished lure has this hole filled with lead. The shape of the blank is almost exactly the same as the finished one after cutting the slant head and shaping the tail. This interesting thing about this is that this blank and several others identical to it were found in a cigar box with other Heddon blanks in what used to be W.T. and Laura Heddon's workshop in Osceola, Florida. Collector value range: $50 to $100.

266

Heddon (cont'd.)

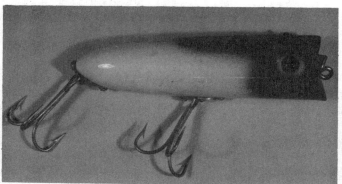

This interesting lure is a reworked Heddon LUCKY-13. It was apparently fashioned after the Heddon acquisition of the Makinen Tackle Company for it looks more Makinen than Heddon. It was obtained from a former Heddon employee. The body is the same shape as a Lucky-13 and shows evidence of being a body pre-drilled for Lucky-13 hardware with the holes filled. It measures 3-1/2", has Heddon tack/plastic eyes and one-piece surface hook hanger hardware. Collector value range: $20 to $40.

OUTING MANUFACTURING COMPANY
Elkhart Indiana
or
HEDDON OUTING
James Heddon's Sons
Dowagiac, Michigan

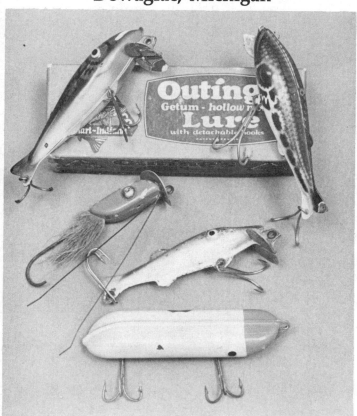

The Outing company manufactured at least six different hollow metal lures made of bronze and painted in various patterns. The company was bought by Heddon in 1927 and the lures were inventoried but not manufactured any more. Heddon closed them out at special prices. Collector value range: $5 to $10.

OUTING

CATALOG SERIES #	BODY LENGTH	LURE WEIGHT
700	3-1/8"	¾ oz.
750	2¾"	½ oz.

COLOR OR FINISH: *White and green; White and red; Solid black; Aluminum and red; No color and green.*

BASSY GETUM

Collector value range: $5 to $10.

OUTING

CATALOG SERIES #	BODY LENGTH	LURE WEIGHT
1200	3-7/8"	5/8 oz.

COLOR OR FINISH: *Black bass; Large mouth bass; Smallmouth bass; Rock bass; Calico bass; Silver bass.*

Top, on box: left is a BASSY GETUM and right is a PIKEY GETUM without the diving lip. Small lure is a BUCKY GETUM, then another PIKEY GETUM (with diving lip). Bottom is a FLOATEM GETUM.

Heddon (cont'd)

PIKEY GETUM

Collector value range: $10 to $20.

OUTING CATALOG SERIES #	BODY LENGTH	LURE WEIGHT
1000	3-5/8"	½ oz.

COLOR OR FINISH: *White and red; Rainbow; Red and green spots; Green scale; Pike scale; Perch scale; Silver shiner; Red throat and silver back; ? scale.*

FLOATEM GETUM

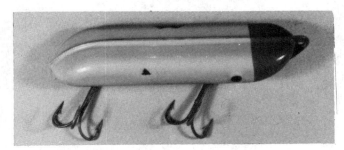

Collector value range: $15 to $30.

OUTING CATALOG SERIES #	BODY LENGTH	LURE WEIGHT
400	4-1/8"	¾ oz.

COLOR OR FINISH: *Four colors – unknown.*

BUCKY GETUM

See first photo in this section on page 230. Made in two sizes. Collector value range: $5 to $10.

PORKY GETUM and FEATHER GETUM

No illustrations available. Little catalog information concerning these two lures.

THE BOOSTER BAIT
c1907

J. G. Henzel, Chicago

The soft body of this lure is about 2½" long and is made without hooks. The fisherman was to place it on the hook of his choice. It was constructed so that it could be filled with a "stink bait." Colors: red, white, blue, pink, orange. Collector value range: $30 to $40.

BILL HERRINGTON BAIT COMPANY
Green City, Missouri
BAG-O-MAD

An ad stating that the lure was new for 1932 illustrates this lure as available in two sizes, the regular at 3¾". They had two holes in the notch at the nose, each of which went separately through the body exiting on each side of the lure. There were five color designs offered in the ad: Red head and white body, black head and yellow body, red head and yellow body, black head and white body, solid black. Collector value range: $2 to $4.

LIVINGSTON S. HINCKLEY
Newark, New Jersey

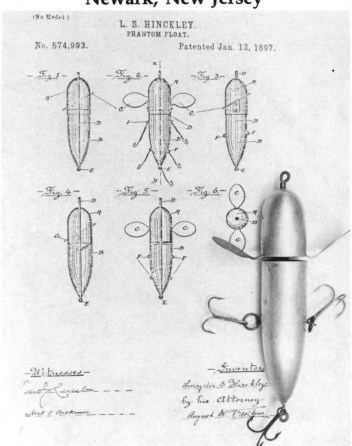

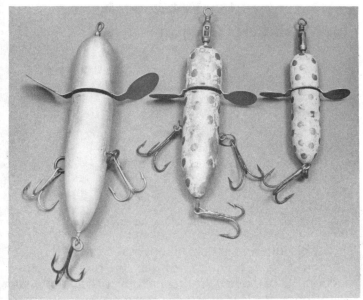

This is a three section jointed plastic lure made to look like a lizard. The line tie is at the throat. There are two opposite side mounted treble hooks and another treble mounted on the tail section but not trailing the end. It was about 6" long. Collector value range: $5 to $10.

HOLLOWHEAD
R-K Tackle Company
Grand Rapids, Michigan

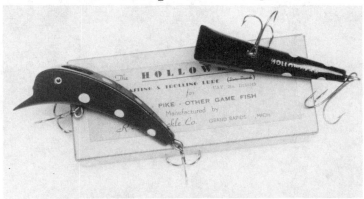

Little is known about this company and their other products if any. Note the hole in the top of the lure. It is made of wood but appears to be of fairly late vintage. Simple screw eye hook hangers. Collector value range: $3 to $5.

Since the release of the second edition a little bit more information has surfaced. The company operated only a short time (1948-1951). The name is derived from the first names of the owners, Ray and Kay Wiinika. The lures were made in only four colors. It is reported that several thousand were produced in the 3-4 years of operation.

Mr. Hinckley applied for a patent on a Phantom Float late 1896 and it was granted January 12, 1897 (see photo). The opening sentences of the patent application says in part"... have invented certain new and useful improvements in Phantom Floats." This seems to imply that this particular lure had been around a while. Whether the lure itself was invented by Hinckley or someone else and Hinckley merely improved it is not clear. A search of patent records does not however, reveal a previous patent of the Phantom Float. The photos accompanying illustrate the Phantom Float resting on the patent illustration and two sizes of "Yellow Birds" also attributed to Hinckley. Collector value range is from: $15 to $30.

THE HINKLE LIZARD
Joe Hinkle, Louisville, Kentucky

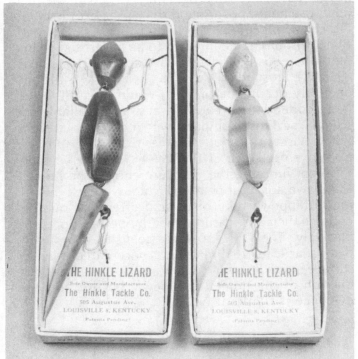

HOWE'S VACUUM BAITS
THE VACUUM BAIT COMPANY
North Manchester, Indiana

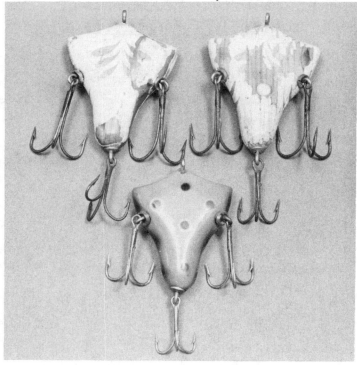

THE WEEDER
Ideel Fish Lures Company   Chicago, IL

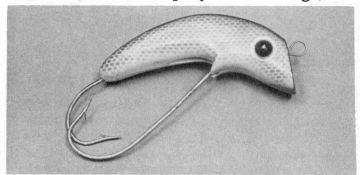

Small glass eyed weedless lure with scale finish.

This lure was in the Unknown section of the last edition. A reader recognized it as like one in his collection. He had one in its original box with a pamphlet identifying it. There was also a metal spoon type listed, but no other lures. The Weeder was made in nine finishes: Red head, Red and white stripe, Orange dot (don't have the foggiest what that means), Frog finish, Pike finish, Yellow scale, Perch scale, Aluminum scale and Black scale. Collector value range: $3 to $8.

THE CHIPPEWA C1913
Immell Bait Co., Blair, Wisconsin

It has been widely believed that the C. J. Frost company made the CHIPPEWA BAIT at one time and indeed the company did advertise it in a 1915 issue of THE OUTER'S BOOK. It seems possible, but I remain unconvinced for now. the lure was patented in 1910 (see patent illustration on next page), but was not introduced to fishermen until 1913 with the first advertisement appearing in the April, 1913 issue of OUTER'S, placed by the Immell Bait Company of Blair, Wisconsin. It continued to be advertised by Immell in various periodicals until about 1914-15. The 1915 C. J. Frost ad for the Chippewa Bait was the one and only occurence of this I could unearth in the large collection of catalogs and ads available for study. The Frost company was located in Stevens Point, Wisconsin, about 60 miles from Blair and they also advertised their CHIPPEWA SKIPPER, an entirely different lure (see the next lure entry). The Immell Chippewa ads disappeared, Frost advertised the Immell Chippewa only once, and after that one occurence their ads featured the Chippewa Skipper exclusively. The C. J. Frost ads seem to completely disappear after 1919. Perhaps more dated ads will surface, providing more data to support the Frost production of the Immell Chippewa, but for now the evidence is flimsy at best.

Of this wooden lure an old advertising folder says "The development of the bait has been the result of years of experience in bass fishing by Professor Howe, of who it has often been said, can catch bass any time...". Just exactly who Professor Howe was is not clear in the advertising, nevertheless the lure was consistently represented as "Howe's Vacuum Bait" by the company. As you can see by the illustrations, the lure had a curious shape. One can only wonder about the curious name as well. The shape of the lure is suspiciously the same shape of the old upright Hoover Vacuum Cleaner foot. It was a wooden surface plug with three swiveling treble hooks. These swivels were of great import to the designer and company as there was almost invariable use in all illustrations of a small hand pointing at them stating "See that Swivel!" They originally came in a tin box.

The lure was originally patented in 1909 and made available only in white with red stripes on the belly. As far as can be determined, the original was made in one size but there is strong suspicion that they may have marketed a second size and possibly added a red color option. In any case the South Bend company obtained the patent because about 1922 the plug shows up in their catalogs. (See page 336). The South Bend illustrations show some differences however. The slant on the face is different, the swivels are not always the same as on the original and some had glass eyes. Collector value range: $10 to $20.

(cont'd. next page)

Chippewa (cont'd.)

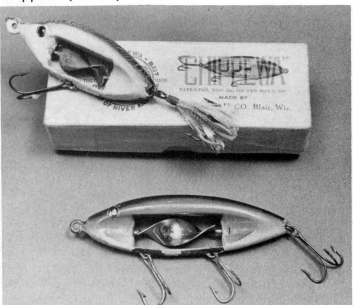

The Immell Bait Company CHIPPEWA Bait. Collector value range: $10 to $20.

The Immel Chippewa Bait was available in several sizes, floaters and sinkers. Sinkers are 3", 3½", 4" and 5". Floaters were available in 4½" and 5" sizes. It appears that all came with belly mounted detachable double hooks and a trailing treble. All found so far have glass eyes except the 5" size Floater. One of the ads breaks down the colors available as follows:

3½" Size
Yellow Perch
Solid White
Red and Yellow
Fancy Sienna
Green back, spotted sides
Rainbow
Fancy Green back
Green back, White belly
Fancy Green back, spotted sides

4" Size
Red and Yellow
Fancy Sienna
Rainbow
Fancy Green back
Green back, White belly
Fancy Green back, spotted sides

5" Size
Red and Yellow
Rainbow
Fancy Green back
Green back, White belly
Fancy Green back, spotted sides

Colors available in the other sizes remain unknown, but one ad listed Aluminum color and Red.

The Immell Chippewa Floater, 41-2". Collector value range: $20 to $60.

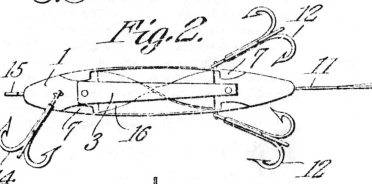

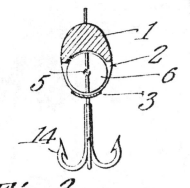

O. F. IMMELL.
MINNOW BAIT.
APPLICATION FILED OCT. 12, 1909.

974,493.

Patented Nov. 1, 1910.

Fig. 1.

Fig. 2.

Fig. 3.

Omer F. Immell.
By Cashow & Co.
Attorneys

Witnesses
E. W. Stewart
Nina B. Lawton.

Illustration accompanying original patent application for the Chippawa by Omer F. Immel. Granted Nov. 1, 1910.

CHIPPEWA SKIPPER
C. J. Frost,
Stevens Point, Wisconsin

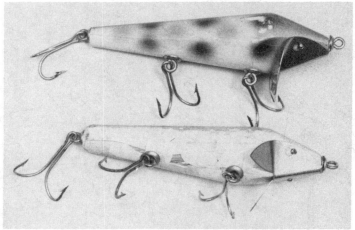

Although the plugs bear the same name, it is not probable that there was any official connection between the Immell and Frost companies. The Skipper had reversible double hooks, two belly mounted and one trailing (3D). It was sold with two interchangeable lips to impart different actions at the anglers option. It is very unlikely the collector will find both unless he finds the plug in the original package. The lure was 4½" long. Colors available were fancy spotted or green and white. Collector value range: $40 to $80.

ISLE ROYALE
Isle Royale Company
Jackson, Michigan

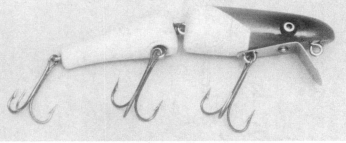

Isle Royale JOINTED PIKIE

Isle Royale JR. SOUTHERN BASSER #9999

Isle Royale POPPER #222

Isle Royale was in business from about 1940 to 1955. It is known that they made some lures for Shakespeare in the 1940's. Most of the Isle Royale lures I have seen have painted cup hardware. It appears that the cup was installed prior to painting, the paint was applied and finally the lure was rigged with the remaining hardware. Collector value range for all: $5 to $10.

JACK'S RIP-L-LURE
Jack's Tackle Co.   **Oklahoma City, OK**

This company is thought to have been in business as early as the 1930's. Most examples of the RIP-L-LURE found are made of plastic, however, this one is most assuredly made of wood. It has tack painted eyes, a tail cap and cup/screw eye hardware. The curious looking blade at the nose of this 3" topwater plug flips back and forth upon retrieve. There is a jointed version of this lure known to have been made and there is also another Jack's Tackle Company lure called the Wig-L-Lure. The latter is a feathered spoon wiggler. Collector value range: $5 to $10.

THE W. J. JAMISON COMPANY

Chicago, Illinois

Perhaps the most famous lure ever produced by Jamison was the Coaxer (patented January 3, 1905), but there were several others manufactured by the company. The company was established in 1904 and other than for the Coaxer it was heavy into metal spinner and spoon type baits not covered here. Jamison continued into the 1940's and manufactured some of the early plastic lures then.

It is interesting to note the following account of a famous fishing contest between the Coaxer and the Decker "Hopatcong" plug. It is taken from a W. J. Jamison Company, Chicago, Illinois catalog printed circa 1910.

WE PROVED IT
THE WORLD'S CHAMPIONSHIP
BASS FISHING CONTEST
WON BY THE "COAXER"

Desiring to prove in the most positive and satisfactory manner the "Coaxer" Surface Bait was superior to any other artifical bait on the market we issued a broad challenge in Field and Stream and National Sportsman to enter the "Coaxer" in contests with any other bait in the World. The contest to last three days and contestants to fish from same boat, taking hourly turns in choosing fishing grounds and positions in the boat. The challenge found only one taker. Mr. Ans. Decker, of N.J., a professional bass fisherman and manufacturer of the "Decker Bait." The contest was brought off under the auspices of Field and Stream and the Congress Lake Club of Canton, Ohio, on the latter's private lake near Canton. There were three judges, each contestant selecting one, the third being Field and Stream's representative, Mr. Macy, who was sent on from New York for that purpose. The date being set for June 16, 17 and 18, 1910, which was an unfortunate selection as the weather turned out very bad, there being two days of almost absolute calm and intense heat. It was agreed that eight hours fishing would be done each day. Owing to these bad conditions and also that the lake is well fished by the club's 100 members and their friends and had not been stocked for many years, the catch was not exceptionally large, though it was considerably larger than the average on this lake.

The "Coaxer" not only won the event easily but also scored the largest number of fish landed without a miss, landing five one day and seven another day without a miss. It also hooked the most strikes without a miss, hooking fourteen strikes in succession on the last day of the contest, but losing four of the fish in the heavy weeds.

As Mr. Decker used a bait fitted with three treble hooks most of the time against a "Coaxer" with but two single hooks it proves rather conclusively that good single hooks will hook and hold better than trebles. The "Coaxer" showed its superiority in open water fishing as well as in the weeds by raising all the fish that were raised in strictly open water. There were but three. Of these, but one was hooked, which was apparently of about 5 pounds weight. However, he dived into the weeds and got free. All agreed that this was the largest fish hooked in the contest. All had a good chance to see as he leaped fully a foot clear of the water. The No. 1 Convertible "Coaxer" was used but without the double hook most of the time. 26 out of the 28 bass were caught on the trailer hook.

As the bait used by Mr. Decker was of a style that is and has been recognized throughout the country for years as a most excellent lure and was in the hands of an angler of rare ability both as regards to his knowledge of the habits of the black bass and his skill as a sure and accurate caster, and also that the contest was of sufficient length to do away with any element of "luck." We believe that the "Coaxer's" superiority over all other baits has been most conclusively and thoroughly demonstrated. We challenged the world and accepted the first comer and beat him nearly two to one. We believe we have done all we claimed to be able to do and more.

NO. 1 CONVERTIBLE "COAXER"

Left: Luminous Bucktail Coaxer. Right: Feather tail.

This is the lure used in the contest described on the previous pages. Most of the Coaxers had red felt wings but some are found with leather. It is not known for certain if the leather was used in production or added by others later. The body was 1-7/8" long and made of cork. It had a single hook mounted in the tail and a second single hook attached to the first single hook. There was a removeable belly mounted double hook also. Available with a bucktail as well. Collector value range: $5 to $10.

NO. 1 WEEDLESS "COAXER"

This is the same as the No. 1 Convertible Coaxer above but does not have the detachable belly double hook. Collector value range: $5 to $10.

NO. 1 WEEDLESS BUCKTAIL "COAXER"

Same as above but with a bucktail. Collector value range: $10 to $10.

NO. 2 WEEDLESS "COAXER"

Essentially the same as the above Weedless Coaxers but smaller (1-1/8'') body with a slightly different shape. Collector value range: $5 to $10.

LUMINOUS BUCKTAIL "COAXER"

The same as the No. 1 Weedless Coaxer but with luminous paint. Collector value range: $10 to $20.

NO. 2 CONVERTIBLE COAXER

The same as the No. 2 Weedless Coaxer above with the addition of the detachable double hook on the belly. Collector value range: $5o to $10.

NO. 3 WEEDLESS "COAXER"

Made exactly the same as the No. 1 Weedless Coaxer only smaller. Collector value range: $5 to $10.

NO. 3 CONVERTIBLE "COAXER"

Exactly the same as above, but with the addition of a detachable belly mounted double hook. Collector value range: $5 to $10.

TEASER
or
TANDEM "COAXER"

Two 1'' body "Coaxers" mounted on a wire so as to make one run in front of the other. Collector value range: $10 to $20.

THE MUSKIE "COAXER"

Another of the Coaxer types this larger one is made for surface trolling. It has a 2-5/8'' body length a tail mounted single hook (optional trailing single) and a belly mounted double hook. Collector value range: $10 to $20.

THE "COAXER" UNDERWATER

This is similar to the other Coaxers, but the body is made of metal and has no wings. It has a tail mounted single hook. It was also available with luminous paint. Collector value range: $5 to $10.

WIGGLER

This plug came along about 1918 in three sizes and two hook type options. The sizes were 1¼'', 1¾'' and 2½''. They were available with double or single hooks and in eight colors: *Silver shiner; Golden shiner; Red side minnow; Red head, white body; Yellow perch; Solid white; Solid red; Solid yellow.* Collector value range: $5 to $10.

Jamison (cont'd.)

"MASCOT"

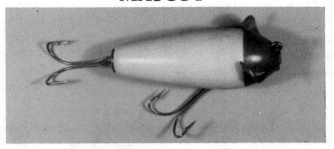

The #2 Winged Weedless Mascot.

In 1916-17 Jamison introduced several versions of a new lure called the Mascot. Collector value range of all: $10 to $20.

The No. 1 Weedless Mascot was 4" long, had two belly hooks and a trailing double. It had two line ties at the nose and was reversible. Colors available were: White with red head, solid red, white or yellow

The No. 1 Winged Weedless Mascot was slightly longer than the regular No. 1 Mascot and had metal wings attached to the head. Otherwise the plug is the same.

The No. 2 Winged Weedless Mascot is the same basic body design as the other Mascots. It was 2¾" long, had wings, and only one belly double hook and a trailing double. It was available in luminous paint or white body with red head.

The Weedless Muskellunge Mascot is almost exactly the same as the regular No. 1 Mascot but larger (5½") and with stronger hooks and hardware.

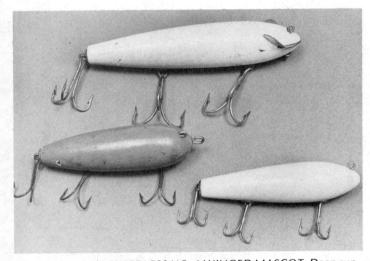

Upper lure is the WEEDLESS NO. 1 WINGED MASCOT. Deep running or surface lure choice (see line tie at top and under head. Left lure is a 1915 vintage WEEDLESS MASCOT. Near surface or surface running depending upon line tie choice (note nose protecting washer at line tye. Both upper and left lures were available in solid Red, White or Yellow or with White body, Red head. Lower lure is the CHICAGO WOBBLER.

FLOATING MINNO HOOK

This unusual lure has been attributed to Jamison, but has not been found catalogued as yet. It is thought to have been in the line in the late 1930's. Overall size is 4-3/4" and the wooden body measures 1-3/4". This one has a white body with red head and has a protruding belly weight. Note the smaller hook on the shank of the larger hook. It is attached in such a way as to allow the fisherman to squeeze the two shanks together enabling him to move it up and down the shank of the large hook at will. Collector value range: $5 to $10.

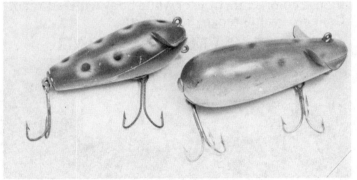

Left lure is a MASCOT. Right lure is the HUMDINGER.

CHICAGO WOBBLER

The lower lure in the photo of three plugs on the previous page is the Chicago Wobbler. Advertised as new in 1916 it is very similar in body style to the Mascot series plugs. Had only one line tie (top of nose). Available colors were solid Red, Yellow or White, or White body with Red head. Collector value range: $10 to $20.

HUMDINGER

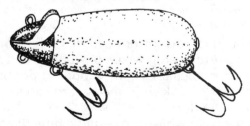

New in 1916 this plug was a tear drop shape with the fat portion to the rear. Photo of the Humdinger is the right lure in the photo of two lures above. It had two line ties, two metal up-swept wings on the head, a belly treble and trailing treble hook. Collector value range: $10 to $20.

275

STRUGGLING MOUSE

This plug was newly introduced around 1919. It had a reversible metal wing affair at the nose to render it underwater or surface running. It was available with either one or two belly trebles and a trailing treble hook or all double hooks. Colors were mouse color, crab, frog, or white body with red head. Collector value range: $20 to $30.

THE "NEMO" BASS BAIT

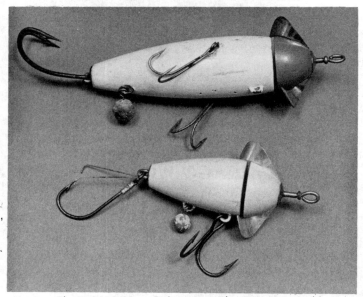

Lower: The "NEMO" Bass Bait. Upper: The "NEMO" Muskie Bait. Note the extra eye at bottom of the forward end. This feature allows the fisherman to move the external weight so as to make the lure run underwater.

This lure was introduced in 1910 as an underwater or surface plug. Made of wood, it had a revolving head, detachable belly mounted double hook, trailing single hook with weed guard and a moveable weight. The lure length was 2-3/8". The colors available were white, red, yellow, blue or green and they could be ordered in any combination. Therefore, the collector may find the plug in one of the five solid colors or a combination of twenty mixed for a total of twenty-five possibilities. Collector value range: $60 to $90.

THE "NEMO" MUSKIE BAIT

This is a larger version of the Nemo Bass Bait above. It has a trailing double hook, and a double hook mounted on each side of the body. The colors and combinations are the same. Collector value range: $80 to $120.

WIG-WAG

The photo for the WIG-WAG in the last edition was incorrect. It was a similar lure, but one that has now been relegated to unknown status. The new photo here is of the two sizes of WIG-WAGS, the bass size, 4-1/2", 3/8 oz. and the musky size at 6", 1-1/2 oz. There is a third size at 5-1/2". The lure was new in the 1930's and was made with glass eyes. Each was available in white body with a red head, silver body with a black head, and a yellow body and head with a brown back. Collector value range: $20 to $30.

PLASTIC OR TENITE JAMISON LURES

In the very late 1930's to early 1940's, Jamison began marketing molded plastic plugs. The following listing of seven plugs are examples of this use of plastic. Some were made in wood first for a short time.

WIG-L-TWIN

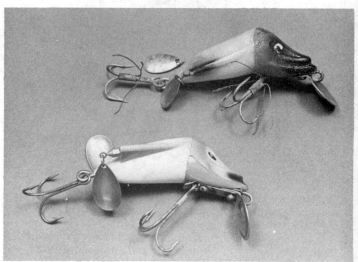

Thought to be new around 1939. The Wig-L-Twin was an odd shaped plug with a deep diving nose blade two laterally mounted horizontal fins each with a small flashing spoon attached to the trailing edge. It had a belly treble and a trailing treble (2T). Collector value range: $3 to $6.

Jamison (cont'd.)

CATALOG SERIES #	BODY LENGTH	LURE WEIGHT
1800		5/8 oz.

COLOR OR FINISH: *White body, red head, red fins; Black and white striped, white belly, black fins; Golden brown scale finish; Silver green scale finish.*

JAMISONS NO. 1500 c 1940

Made of plastic this plug had a pointed slope nose with line tie under it. There was a metal diving lip, a belly treble and trailing treble hook (2T). It was available in two sizes. Collector value range: $3 to $6.

CATALOG SERIES #	BODY LENGTH	LURE WEIGHT
1500	3¼"	5/8 oz.
S 1500	2½"	½ oz.

COLOR OR FINISH: *Red and white, Black and white; Target spot; Frog; Silver shiner; Perch scale.*

SURFACE WIGGLER

A 2¾" long tear drop shape plug with the fat portion of the body to the rear. It was originally equipped with either a barbless single hook or a double hook mounted on the belly. Collector value range: $10 to $20.

BEETLE-PLOP

Another plastic plug (c1940). It had two metal fins, one on either side of the body and a single trailing treble hook (1T). Collector value range: $5 to $10.

CATALOG SERIES #	BODY LENGTH	LURE WEIGHT
2000	2"	½ oz.

COLOR OR FINISH: *White body, red head; White body, black head; White body, yellow head.*

SHANNON TORPEDO
No. 1900

This is a very similar lure to the No. 1500. Same hook configuration and a metal diving lip. Made of Tenite and available in fourteen different colors. Collector value range: $5 to $10.

LUR-O-LITE
No. 1950

Occasionally a company has marketed a self illuminated plug and Jamison was no exception. The Lur-O-Lite was made of molded plastic and had a battery operated light internally. It was available only in a 4" size, 3 ounces in weight. The color was red head with white body. Collector value range: $5 to $10.

QUIVERLURE c1940

This plug was made of transparent plastic in the body and various head colors. The clear body allowed view of an internal shiny bar that quivered upon retrieve. The plug was made in three sizes. The collector value range is: $5 to $10.

CATALOG SERIES #	BODY LENGTH	LURE WEIGHT	HOOKS
1900	3¼"	5/8 oz.	2T
1910	2½"	½ oz.	2T
1920	4¾"	1 oz.	3T

COLOR OR FINISH: *Red head, chrome bar; Black head, chrome bar; Yellow head, chrome bar; Red head, red bar; Yellow head, green bar.*

JENNINGS
SURFACE MINNOW
Jennings Fishing Tackle Co., Olympia, Washington

This is a shaped plug with propeller spinners fore and aft. It has painted eyes, a side treble and trailing treble hook. Length 3¼". Collector value range: $2 to $4.

JENNINGS
BULLFROG PLUG c 1930

This 2¾" plug was designed for catching frogs, not fish. It had feathers concealing two single hooks and two wire antenna type appendages. Collector value range: $2 to $4.

JERSEY EXPERT

E.C. Adams   Morristown, NJ

IDEAL MINNOW

William E. Davis   Morristown, NJ

There is some amount of confusion surrounding these two very similar lures. Both of them were patented in 1907. Adams was first to get his patent with Davis getting his seven months later. The two were so close that there has to be some connection. The Davis patent was an improvement over the Adams patent in that there was a preventer device at the tail to keep the trailing hook from becoming entangled in the spinners and the hooks were readily removable. Because the two were so close in design, both men were from the same town, the second was an improvement over the first, and Davis is known to have offered both in advertising I think it reasonable to presume that the two struck some kind of deal. The drawing here was taken from an ad placed by Davis. It is the IDEAL MINNOW. If you

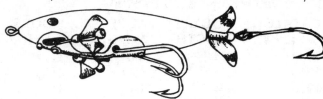

will compare it to the two photographs (side and belly views) accompanying you will note that they are essentially the same. Now compare the two patent illustrations reproduced here and draw your own conclusions as to whether they are related. Each has a Collector value range of $100 to $200.

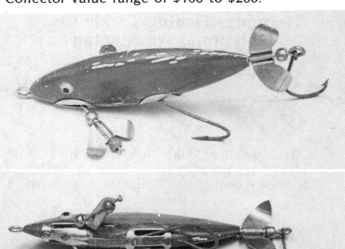

PATENTED NOV. 12, 1907.

No. 871,057.   W. E. DAVIS.
                               ARTIFICIAL BAIT.
                        APPLICATION FILED FEB. 2, 1907.

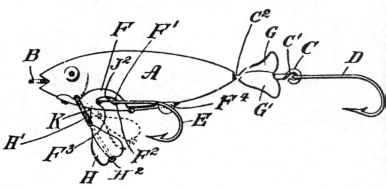

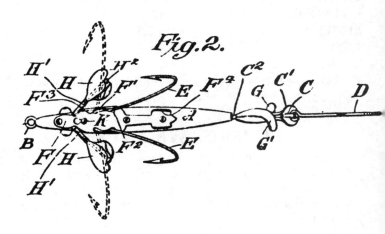

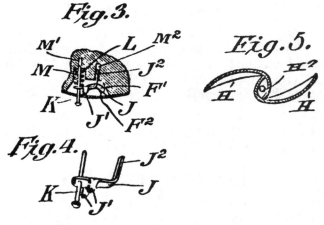

Attest:
Edgeworth Greene
Alan McDonnell

Inventor:
William E. Davis,
by S. S. Cox. Atty.

Patent illustration for the W.E. Davis IDEAL MINNOW

278

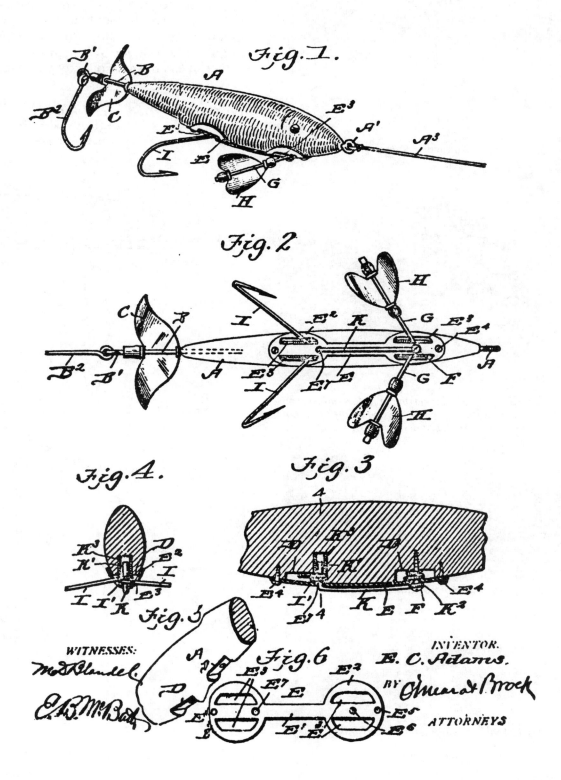

No. 849,522.   PATENTED APR. 9, 1907.

E. C. ADAMS.
ARTIFICIAL FISH BAIT.
APPLICATION FILED JUNE 7, 1906.

Fig. 1.

Fig. 2.

Fig. 4.   *Fig. 3.*

Fig. 5.

WITNESSES:

Fig. 6.

INVENTOR.
E. C. Adams.

BY

ATTORNEYS

Patent illustration for the E.C. Adams JERSEY EXPERT

JOHNSON AUTOMATIC STRIKER

Carl A. Johnson
Chicago, Illinois

Very little is known about Johnson, or production and distribution of the AUTOMATIC STRIKERS. Patented in 1935, they are quality-made and somewhat complicated (see patent illustration accompanying). On all but the smallest size, the design allowed for the hook to swing away from the body upon strike. Ostensibly this allowed more reliable fish holding capability. One small ad listed the following colors for the Junior size: Ivory body with red stripes, Ivory body with black stripes, Ivory body with green stripes and yellow tail, Ivory body with green head. Only a Silver Scale finish was listed for the larger size in the ad. Collector value range: $20 to $40.

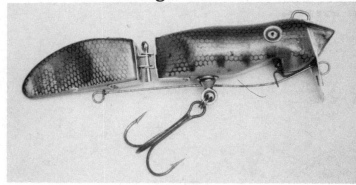

6½" Johnson Automatic Striker

3" Johnson Automatic Striker. The one on the right is missing some hardware and has a rounded diving lip. The one on the left is complete and the lower lip is fluted and squared off.

2" Johnson Automatic Striker.

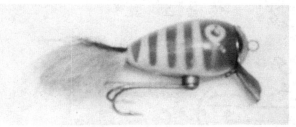

1-3/4" Johnson Automatic Striker Junior.

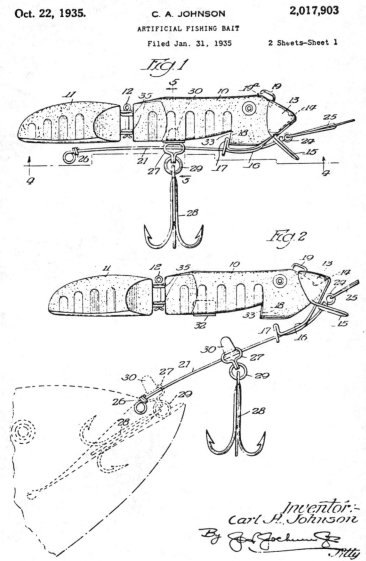

Oct. 22, 1935.   C. A. JOHNSON   2,017,903
                          ARTIFICIAL FISHING BAIT
                 Filed Jan. 31, 1935   2 Sheets—Sheet 1

Fig.1

Fig.2

Inventor:-
Carl A. Johnson
By

JOS. DOODLE BUG

Jos. Tackle Shop
Jasper, Indiana

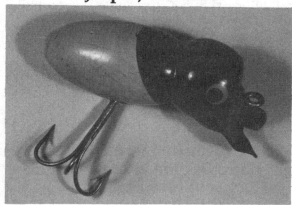

A 2-1/8" Jos. Doodle Bug. This one has a red head and white body with painted eyes. Cup and screw eye hook hardware.

A c1930 lure made with eight color choices: black, brown, gray, white with red or black head, orange with black head. Earliest models have glass eyes followed by painted eyes (see photo). They have been found with and without the pigtail style pork rind attachment on the tail. Collector value range: $10 to 20.

JOY'S WATER NEMESIS

Joy Bait Company
Lansing, Michigan

The two lures in the accompanying photo were illustrated in the unidentified section of the first edition of this book. As you can see they have now been identified as to maker but little else is known about the company. The upper lure in the photo (next page) is yellow with red head and measures 3-3/4". The other is white with red head and black stripes and measures 3-5/8". Collector value range: $5 to $10.

K & K MANUFACTURING COMPANY

No. 857,883.   PATENTED JUNE 26, 1907

J. D. KREISSER,
ARTIFICIAL MINNOW FISHING BAIT.
APPLICATION FILED JAN. 8, 1906.

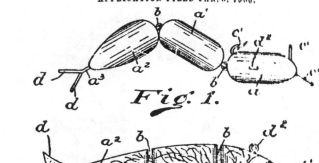

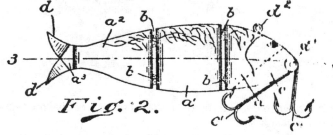

Witnesses
George H. Ricke
Geo. E. Heisel

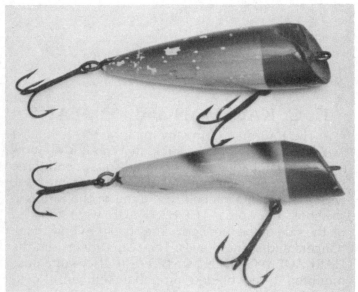

Joy's Water Nemesis

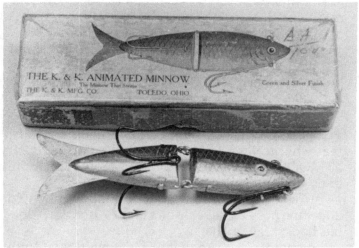

K & K Animated Minnow with original box.

281

K & K Animated Minnows. The bottom lure here has yellow background (iris) glass eyes.

Little is known about this Toledo, Ohio company but it is generally accepted that they marketed one of the first, if not the first jointed animated minnows. The following listing is from a 1907 K & K pocket catalog. Collector value range for all: $50 to $140.

THE K & K ANIMATED MINNOWS

#1A Golden Shiner, (female type), 4½", for black bass, 3 double hooks. Jointed body.

#2A Golden Shiner, (male type), 4½", for sea bass or muskellonge, 3 double hooks. Jointed body.

#1B for deep trolling, 4½", for bass, 3 double hooks. Jointed body.

#2C Deep trolling Silver Shiner, 4", for bass, large lake trout, land-locked salmon or striped sea bass, 3 double hooks. Jointed body.

"THE MINNOETTE"-3", silver shiner, for small bass, rock bass, trout, small pickerel, white bass, etc., 3 double hooks, red devil finish. Jointed body.

#3 King of Casting Bait (a surface bait). Swims about 3" under the surface. 3 double hooks, 4½". Jointed body, Red Devil finish (Bright red and gold on back and side, silver belly).

UNJOINTED K & K MINNOWS

#1 RAINBOW GHOST-One double hook on body, feathered trailing treble. Varigated colors.

#2 MOONLIGHT GHOST-Same as above with white body and red stripes.

#4-A THE WRIGGLER-One double hook mounted under the nose and a realistic tail fin. Also with 3 double hooks. Silver shiner.

More about K & K Animated Minnows (taken from a 1909 Abercrombie and Fitch Catalog).

The numbers 1, 2 and 5 each had three detachable double hooks and were sinking plugs.

#1	4½"	Gold, silver, black and silver
#2	3½"	Gold, silver, red, rainbow
#5	3	Gold, silver, red

The numbers 3, 6 and 7 each had three detachable double hooks and were surface plugs.

#3	4½"	Gold, silver, black & red, black & silver, white, rainbow
#6	3"	Gold, silver, red only
#7	3½"	Gold, silver, red only

HARKAUF MINNOWS
H. C. Kaufman and Company
Philadelphia, Pennsylvania
and
Pequea Works
Strasburg, Pennsylvania

Collectors have so far uncovered at least three, possibly four lures that are associated in some way with the name Harkauf or Pequea. Both are names of companies that were in Pennsylvania. I have positively identified three lures with the name Harkauf associated, but believe them to be products of two separate and unrelated companies, namely the two listed above. It appears that the Kaufman company preceded the Pequea Works by 5 or 6 years at least. Harkauf ads begin to appear in 1903 and the earliest Pequea ads show up around 1910. The two companies were located some 80 or 90 miles apart and there is no substantial similarity between their ads or their products.

H. C. KAUFMAN and COMPANY

The Kaufman Company manufactured at least two lures. **The Harkauf Bucktail Wooden Minnow** (new in 1904) had a nose mounted square end three bladed propeller spinner and one trailing treble hook with a bucktail attached to the tail of the lure, not the hook. The words "THE HARKAUF" were stenciled on the side of the lure body. They had thru-body hook hangers and painted eyes. They also advertised the HARKAUF WOODEN MINNOW. It also had a nose mounted three bladed propeller spinner. It was available in three unidentified finishes each with a "glistening silver belly" (1903 ad copy). Most have painted eyes. Collector value range: $50 to $100 for each.

PEQUEA WORKS

Pequea made the **Harkauf Trout Minnow.** The one in the photo here is in very poor condition, but is still obviously a much higher quality product than the Kaufman Company lures. The Trout Minnow sports glass eyes and well-made propeller spinners. There is a beautiful feather fly mounted forward of the nose (see photo). The body is 2½" long and finishes available are not known. Collector value range: $20 to $40.

NOTE: I have an undated "Catalog M" from J. E. Willmarth, Roosevelt, New York that contains both the HARKAUF TROUT MINNOW and the HARKAUF BUCKTAIL WOODEN MINNOW. The catalog also has a listing for the Heddon Triple Teaser which was new around 1929 so we can be reasonably sure the catalog is c1930. Interestingly, in this catalog, the Harkauf Bucktail Minnow is offered finished or in parts so that you may paint and assemble yourself. You may therefore find some crazy versions of that lure.

The listing for the Trout Minnow lists the 2½" size, but lists a smaller (1¼") size as well.

FRED C. KEELING and COMPANY KEELING BAIT and TACKLE

Fred C. Keeling
Rockford, Illinois

Keeling came on the scene about 1914 and was in business until the 1930's when the company was sold to Horrocks-Ibbottson. Keeling's early history is tied to the F. C. Woods Company, the first makers of wooden EXPERT minnows (please see THE EXPERT WOODEN MINNOWS on page 189).

Many Keeling lures had spinners or metal diving/wobbling planes that were made with holes in the blades. Although that is a very good way to identify a Keeling lure, it may not be foolproof. These holes are referred to in advertising copy rather vaguely as "Patented Spinners-The light shines through." Some almost identical ads do not contain this particular line and the accompanying illustration seems not to show the holes. There are a few lures without holes illustrated in these ads that are almost positively Keeling products.

The Keeling EXPERTS were just about identical to Woods or Clark (see page 189) Experts at first, but they began to change a little, soon after the take-over. Keeling made them in 2½", 3", 3½", 4½" and 5" sizes with hooks on the sides and in a few cases, on the belly. They were round, shaped, and flat-sided. All had holes in the propeller blades. In the 1930's they made what appears to be a cheaper version of the EXPERT with no-holes props, non-removable hooks and very simple paint jobs.

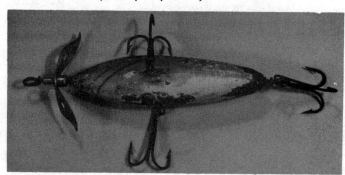

This 3" round body lure has no eyes, one belly weight and twisted wire line tie and tail hook hanger. At close examination it appears that the tail hook hanger may have been modified. There may also have been originally a tail mounted propeller spinner. Collector value range: $20 to $30.

A Keeling shaped-body underwater EXPERT. Says "The Expert" on the side. The long, 5" body is unusual. It has 5 belly weights, yellow glass eyes and a twisted thru-body side treble hook hanger. Collector value range: $30 to $60.

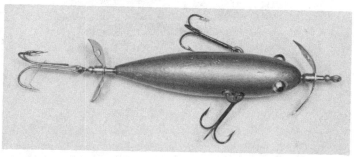

This 3-5/8" round body Expert type has Keeling characteristics including the odd-ball spring loaded side hook hangers. Collector value range: $30 to $60.

Keeling ST. JOHNS WIGGLE. This photo illustrates each of the three variations of the lure. Each is 3-3/4" long and has the typical Keeling spring loaded hook hanger. The top two have glass eyes and one internal belly weight forward of the belly hook. The center has five additional belly weights but it is obvious upon examination that they were added by a fisherman. Collector value range: $50 to $100.

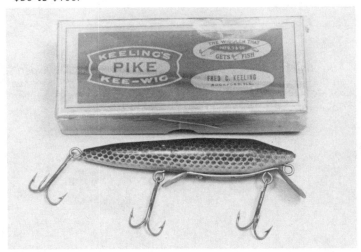

Keeling Pike Kee-Wig with box. Measures 4-5/8" body length. No holes in the spoon-like portions of the metal. Box states the patent date as July 6, 1920. Collector value range: $5 to $10.

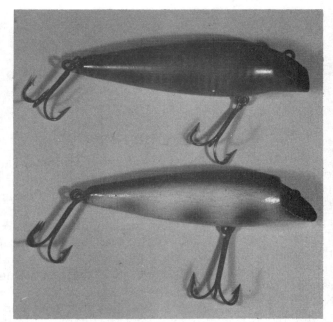

The upper lure in this photo is a BEARCAT. It is 3-7/8" and has plain screw eye hook hangers. The lower lure is the same size and shape and shares the same characteristics except for the slightly different lip design. Collector value range: $5 to $10.

This unidentified Keeling lure is in the style of the Heddon Artistic Minnow and the Pflueger Simplex. It is 1-13/16" long and has both the keeling prop with holes and spring loaded hook hangers. Collector value range: $50 to $100.

The upper lure is 2-5/8" long, has glass eyes and the Keeling belly fixture with holes. The apparent defect on the side almost appears as if it were done on purpose. The lower lure measures 2", is glass eyed and sports brass spoons soldered to the line tie and tail hook hanger. It must have been a nightmare to tune for running true. Collector value range: $20 to $40.

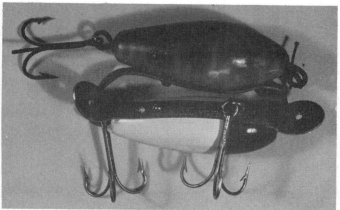

Two Keeling LITTLE TOMS measuring 2-1/2" and 2". Note the different body shapes. Both have the Keeling belly fixture with holes in the blades. Collector value range: $5 to $10.

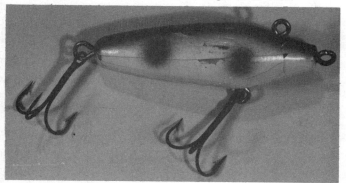

This lure is tentatively identified as a Keeling LITTLE FISH SPEAR. It is 2-3/4" long and has simple screw eye line tie and hook hangers. Collector value range: $5 to $10.

This lure is a probable Keeling. It is 2-3/4" long and has a typical Keeling paint finish. Note the unmarked double bend metal diving lip. Collector value range: $10 to $20.

Three Unknown lures attributed to Keeling because of their paint patterns. The one at top measures 4½" and is an early BEARCAT. The center and right lures measure 3½" and 3¼" respectively. Collector value range: $5 to $10.

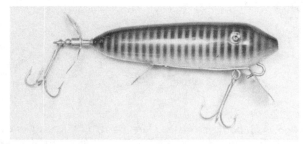

Typical Keeling paint pattern and blades. No holes in spoon-like portions of the metal, but propeller does have the holes 5-7/8" body length. Similar to BASS-KEE-WIG. Collector value range: $5 to $10.

A probable Keeling TOM THUMB WIGGLER, the 3¼" SURFACE TOM. Metal belly plate has "Keeling" stamped on it. Holes in lips. Actual measurement is 3½". Collector value range: $5 to $10.

285

Keeling (cont'd.)

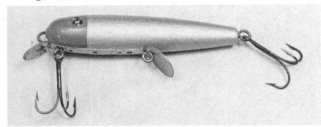

This lure measures 4" and has glass eyes and typical metal belly plate with lip at either end. The rear lip is stamped KEELING and the forward lip is stamped PAT'D 7-6-20. Probable PIKE-KEE-WIG. Collector value range: $5 to $10.

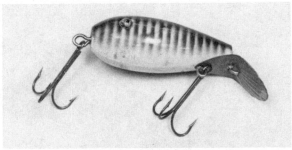

Unknown Glass-eyed plug with typical Keeling paint job. Note the unusual fluted metal lip. Collector value range: $50 to $10.

An early Keeling SURFACE TOM in "beater" condition. 3½" long, it has no holes in the lips but it is stamped KEELING. Collector value range: $5 to $10.

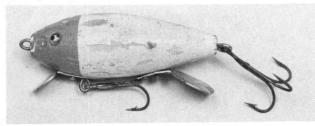

Unknown fat body, red headed lure. Has typical Keeling one piece metal belly plate with fore and aft lips. Collector value range: $5 to $10.

Keeling BABY TOM. Measures 2½" and has holes in blades. Collector value range: $5 to $10.

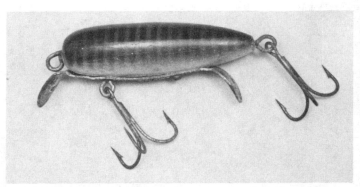

Probable Keeling LITTLE TOM. Measures 2½" and has holes in blades. Collector value range: $5 to $10.

TOM THUMB WIGGLERS

This plug had a metal plate on the belly the front and rear portions ending in metal spoon shapes. The spoons had holes in the center and the metal belly portion had "KEELING" on it. The lure came in five sizes, twelve colors and had one or two belly trebles and a trailing treble hook. Collector value range: $5 to $10.

NAME	BODY LENGTH
Baby Tom	2"
Little Tom	2½"
Pike Tom	2¾"
Big Tom	3"
Surface Tom	3¼"

COLOR OR FINISH: *Dark back, aluminum belly; Dark back, red belly; Green back, white belly; Green body, bronze speckled; Aluminum body, red head; Gold body, red head; White body, red head; Dark back, red sides, white belly; Rainbow striped; Yellow with red and green spots; Black with white head; Yellow with black head.*

SURF-KEE-WIG

This lure had two belly trebles and a trailing treble. It had only one spoon shaped metal plate and was located under the tail. Size and colors unknown. Collector value range: $5 to $10.

TIP-TOP

A tear drop shaped plug with one belly treble, a trailing treble and tail mounted propeller. Colors available were the same as the Tom Thumb Wigglers. Collector value range: $5 to $10.

RED-FIN

This was a lure with one trailing treble and tail and nose mounted propellers. It had glass eyes and came in an aluminum, copper, or white finish. Collector value range: $5 to $10.

BASS-KEE-WIG

The same lure as the TOM THUMB WIGGLER except the metal belly plate/double spoon rig is reversed so that the larger spoon is forward. Collector value range: $5 to $10.

286

Keeling (cont'd.)

PIKE-KEE-WIG

Much like the Bass-Kee-Wig but larger and shaped a bit different at the nose. It had a belly treble and trailing treble and came in three models: Baby, 3½"; standard, 4½"; and Musky, heavy duty 4½". Collector value range: $5 to $10.

NAME	BODY LENGTH
Baby	3½"

COLOR OR FINISH: *Dark back, aluminum belly.*

Standard	4½"

COLOR OR FINISH: *Green back, white belly.*

Musky (heavyduty)	4½"

COLOR OR FINISH: *Dark back, red sides, white belly; White body, red head; Aluminum body, red head.*

SCOUT

The Scout has two belly treble hooks, line tie on top of the head, and a metal diving lip mounted directly on the front of a flat nose. Colors available were: copper, aluminum, gold with red head, aluminum with red head, white with red head, and green speckled. Collector value range: $5 to $10.

KEEN KNIGHT

Keen Bait Manufacturing Co.   Detroit, MI

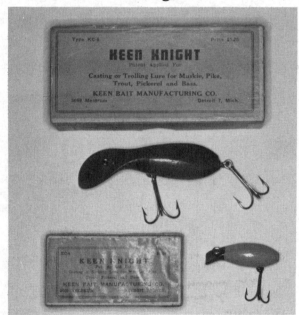

These two lures, found in their original boxes, are unknown other than the information that can be gleaned from the boxes. The upper lure is designated Type KC-6", is red with black spots and measures 3-1/4" long. The smaller one is designated "KC-4", measures 1-5/8" and has red head and white body. The body may have originally been white and has yellowed with age. It's hard to say. Collector value range: $20 to $30.

KENT FROG
and
KENT DOUBLE SPINNER ARTIFICIAL MINNOW

**F. A. Pardee and Company, Kent, Ohio
Samuel H. Friend, Kent, Ohio
Enterprise Manufacturing (Pflueger)
Akron, Ohio**

F. A. Pardee and Co. was doing business at least as early as 1900. There was an advertisement in RECREATION magazine that year, for the DOUBLE SPINNER ARTIFICIAL BAIT. This wooden plug is most likely the forerunner of Pflueger's TRORY UNDERWATER MINNOW or TRORY WOODEN MINNOW (see page 338). Similar ads for the same lure appear consistently until about 1904 and then seem to disappear from periodicals. By then Pardee was calling it the DOUBLE SPINNER ARTIFICIAL MINNOW. In 1906 a William Mills and Son catalog offered a "MANCO Wood Minnow" that is suspiciously similar to both the Pardee Double Spinner Minnow and the Trory Minnow by Pflueger which was offered in their early 1900's catalogs. The 1906 Pflueger catalog was the last to list it.

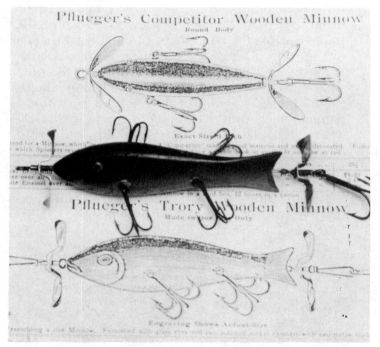

The photo of the lure on a catalog page here is of a lure that is probably a late Pardee or early Pflueger. It is either a TRORY or a DOUBLE SPINNER. The type of aluminum props on it were used by Pardee, but this prop was also one of the earliest types used by Pflueger. You will note the difference between the hook hardware on the lure and in the catalog illustration. The plugs are otherwise almost identical.

Kent (cont'd.)

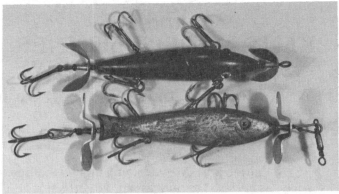

The upper lure measures 3-7/8", has yellow glass eyes, red glass beads for bearings, internal belly weights, thru-body twisted wire line tie/hook hangers and Friend patented split ring hook eyes. The lower lure measures 4" and exhibits the same characteristics as noted above. Poor paint is a result of improper cleaning of the plug. These two represent the transition from the KENT DOUBLE SPINNER (lower) to the PFLUEGER TRORY MINNOW (upper). See text for a more detailed discussion.

A 1906 advertisement announced that Samuel H. Friend had taken over the Pardee company. The ad copy indicated that Friend had long been the manager of the company and took over upon Mr. Pardee's retirement. The ad also illustrated the top lure in the photograph above. It was called "The KENT Double Spinner Bait." What is significant here is the elimination of the shaped tail fin visible in the lower lure and the use of newer type propeller spinners. Note the cone shape of the tube at the rear of the prop. Although the blades on the DOUBLE SPINNER are bow tie type now, most of the older style Pardee/Friend props had this same cone shaped tube. The red bearing beads are also common to Pardee/Friend products. All the hardware on this newer DOUBLE SPINNER is thru-body and strong. There are heavy duty soldered side hook hangers also. Except for the beads and the cone tube props, this lure is almost a dead ringer for the Pflueger WIZARD that came along about 1906. Collector value range for the Pardee//Friend KENT WOODEN DOUBLE SPINNER MINNOWS: $40 to $80.

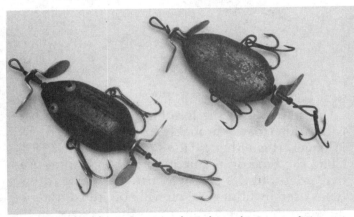

Pictured here are two hand made Samuel Friend KENT FROGS (as they are commonly known). They were listed in catalogs and ads variously as KENT CHAMPION FLOATER, KENT FROG FLOATER, KENT FLOATING BAIT, MANCO FLOATING FROG

and finally the "Pflueger KENT-FLOATER Bait." The one on the left in the photograph is said to be hand made by Samuel H. Friend. The earliest reference I found for the lure was as the "MANCO Floating Frog" in a 1906 William Mills and Son fishing tackle catalog. The one on the right (belly view) closely resembles the Manco frog. It has two words stenciled on the belly, but only the first word is legible, "THE." The only thing discernible about the second word is that it has four letters. Could be it once said "FROG." Both have glass eyes and twisted wire thru-body hook hangers. Collector value range for Samuel Friend KENT FROGS: $50 to $100.

Curiously, after the 1906 ad saying Friend had taken over operation of the Pardee company, I found no subsequent advertisments by Samuel Friend. The KENT FROG did, however, appear often in various tackle company catalogs. In addition it appears that the Pflueger company obtained the rights to the frog lure. There was a short reference with a drawing of the KENT FROG in the February, 1908 issue of FIELD and STREAM magazine that said in part "...Kent Champion Floater manufactured by Samuel Friend, Kent, Ohio." It said further that it was made or red cedar and the size was 2-1/8" x 1/8", 3/4 oz.

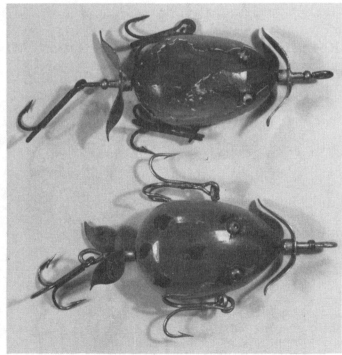

Here are two that must represent the transition from Friend to Pflueger. The one on the bottom has glass eyes, thru-body twisted wire side hook hangers and Pflueger style propeller spinners. The props are stamped with a "P" within a diamond, but they are also stamped with an "R" and "L" on the blades. The latter is typical of Pflueger props. The lure on the top is exactly the same, with the exception of the use of the screw eye hook hangers. Apparently toward the end of the Pardee/Friend company activity they were buying props from Pflueger. In any case the next development took place sometime prior to 1919. The Pflueger catalog collection I studied had a gap be-

Kent (cont'd.)
tween the 1897 and 1919 issues. The fully "Pfluergerized" KENT-FLOATER appears in the 1919 issue. Collector value range for the last PARDEE/ FRIEND FROGS: $20 to $40.

KINGFISHER WOOD MINNOW

Edward K. Tryon　　　　　**Philadelphia, PA**

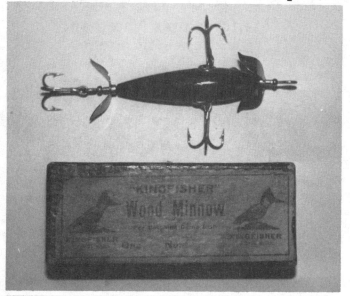

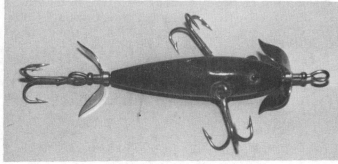

This lure is actually a Pflueger 2-3/4" NEVER-FAIL with unmarked propeller spinners. The Edward K. Tyron Company was a large fishing tackle dealer that did not manufacture any lures. They bought the products of other companies and sold them under their KINGFISHER house brand. Neverfail Collector value range: $15 to $30.

KING SPIRAL

**King Spiral Company
Detroit, Michigan**

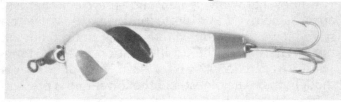

A strongly made 2½" plug. Note the tail and nose reinforcing metal cup inserts. The lure is made of white birch and a man named L. J. Rose is associated with the King Spiral Company. Little else is known about the company. Collector value range: $5 to $10.

KING WOBBLER c1918
King Bait Company, Minneapolis

This is a hollow tubular metal lure with a rounded end cap and a sloped nose painted red. One ad says it is 3" long and another states it is 3½" in length. The metal is nickel plated brass and there are two metal wings or blade-like protrusions on the sloped nose. Weight, 1 ounce, One belly mounted double and a trailing treble hook. Collector value range: $10 to $15.

KIRWAN'S BAD EGG c1923

M. F. Kirwan Manufacturer, O'Neill, Nebraska

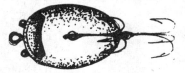

This plug was made in the shape of an egg. It had two small protruding eyes a belly treble and trailing treble hook. Made in white yellow or silver color. Collector value range: $30 to $45.

KUMM'S FISH SPOTTER
Arthur J. Kumm, Dearborn, Michigan

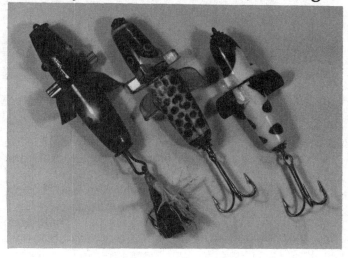

The far left lure in the photo is the original wooden model of the Fish Spotter. The rear section rotates on retrieve by means of two metal blades attached to the front of that section. The one trailing treble was originally offered feathered as shown. It has yellow glass eyes and measures 2-7/8" long. The other two, as you have not doubt noticed, are later versions made of plastic. Kumm applied for the patent in 1933 and it was granted in mid-1935. The earlier wooden examples are valued at $10 to $20 while the plastic ones are worth anywhere from $5 to $10. Both are difficult to locate.

FRANK L. KOEPKE
Ridgefield, Washington

Precious little is known about Koepke or his lures outside what the patent papers give us. Research has not turned up any other references to him or the lures. They are all hollow brass.

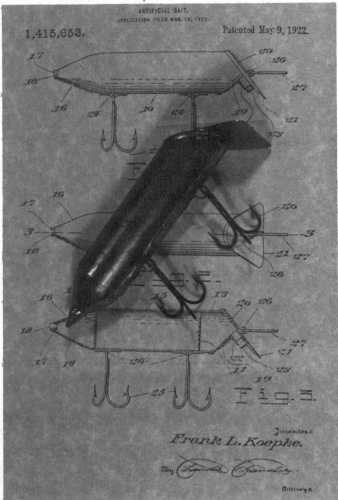

If you compare the lure to the drawing it is on you may note a subtle difference. Look at No. 17 and 23 on the top figure. Upon reading the patent I found that the lure was to be made with two hollow chambers, each with a filler hole and stopper enabling the user to choose the buoyancy he wished; nose up, nose down, floater, sinker. The combinations are endless. This particular lure measures 4-1/2" in length.

The three lures here are not addressed in the patent papers, but they are attributed to Koepke because the construction details are exactly the same as the patent model above. They measure 4", 3-3/4" and 3-1/2" respectively. Collector value range for the patent model Koepke: $15 to $30; the other Koepkes $10 to $20.

LAKE GEORGE FLOATER
Manufacturer Name and Address Unknown

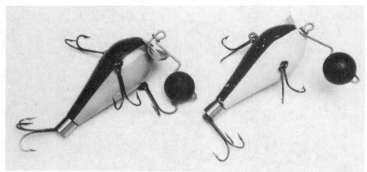

Very little is known about this little beauty.. It is believed that it is a Michigan lure from its name. There is a Lake George in Michigan. The lure has a metal blade at the nose causing the whole body to revolve on retrieve. It measures 2½" in length and 3" accross the front including the cork ball. Collector value range: $15 to $30.

LANE'S WAGTAIL WOBBLER
LANE'S AUTOMATIC MINNOW
Charles W. Lane, Madrid, New York

Pictured here are two Wagtail Wobblers. It is wood-bodied with a fluted metal swinging tail fin. The hook hardware is cup and screw eye. Earliest advertisment I was able to find was 1924. The ad stated it was available in three sizes, but did not list them. The one in the ad illustration is 2-7/8" long. These two are 2-3/4" and 2-7/8". The upper lure is thought to be the oldest, but the lower one is presently the most difficult to locate. It came in two finishes, Brown with gold sides and Green back with silver sides.

(cont'd. next page)

The accompanying patent drawing is the design for an earlier Lane product, LANE'S AUTOMATIC MINNOW. Patented in 1913, the only ad I could find was in 1914 issue of FIELD AND STREAM. The tail propeller spinner is mounted on a cam shaft so that when turning on retrieve it would make the pectoral fins move. The patent text says it was to be made of"...wood or any other suitable material." It has been found made of both. Collector value range: $40 to $80.

C. W. LANE.
ARTIFICIAL FISH BAIT.
APPLICATION FILED JAN. 14, 1913.

1,068,908.   Patented July 29, 1913.

Lane's Automatic Minnow patent.

LAUBY'S WONDER SPOON
Lauby Bait Company   **Marshfield, WI**

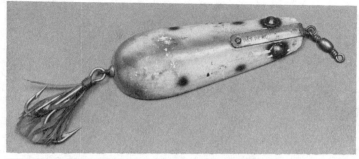

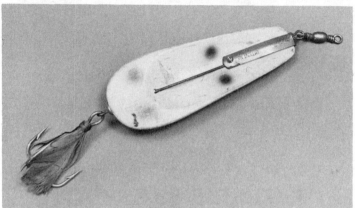

This lure measures 2-15/16". All that was found was the lure in its original box and a pamphlet. The pamphlet indicated that the company offered the above lure plus "...WEEDLESS WONDER SPOONS-SURFACE LURES-MINNOW FLIES-FLY RODS-CASTING RODS." There is a patent number on the metal head plate, if taken literally, that places this lure around 1910. It in no way has the appearance of having been made in that early era of lure making. If you add a "1" to the beginning of the number it comes out as being patented in the mid-1930's. That is more reasonable. The "1" must have either been left off or it was stamped so light, it just wasn't visible. Collector value range: $10 to $20.

LEAPING LENA
Ralph Miller, Miami, Florida

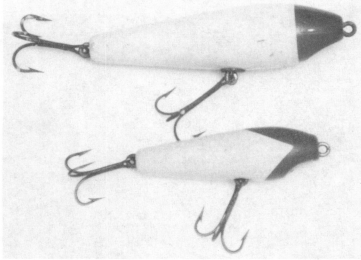

Very little is known about the campany or their well made lures. The two pictured here are white with red heads and are 3-5/8″ and 2″ long respectively. The company was doing business in the 1940's and perhaps earlier. Collector value range: $3 to $7.

LEEPER'S BASS BAIT
Henry Leeper, Fredonia, Kentucky

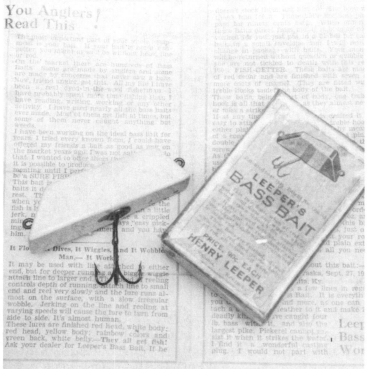

I have found a 1919 and a 1921 patent date listed in separate places, but failed to turn up an actual patent. The latest date I found the lure advertised was 1926. It was made in two sizes, 2¼″ and 2-¾″. They have line ties on both ends. Colors available were: Red head, white body; Red head, yellow body; white body with rainbow colors and green back, white belly; solid yellow, white or red. Collector value range: $15 to $30.

E. J. LOCKHART
OR WAGTAIL
MINNOW MFG. Co.
Battle Creek, Michigan*
Galesburg, Michigan

A careful search through old catalogs, periodicals and patent records turned up a lot of new data that helps to shed a little more light than reported in the last edition. Eleven ads and references, and three patents were found. The earliest reference found was for the WAGTAIL WITCH in an article about new lures in a 1911 issue of THE OUTER'S BOOK. It was illustrated and discussed briefly. The same article illustrated another Lockhart lure. It was captioned "The Lockhart Minnow", but no mention of it was made in the text. The lure pictured is actually the 4½″ Water Witch or Pollywog.

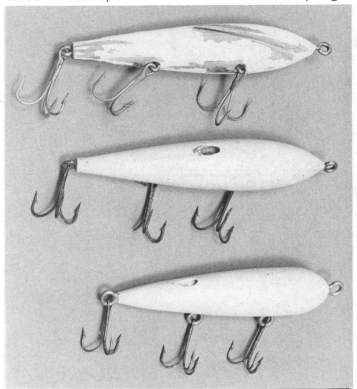

UPPER: Wagtail Witch. CENTER: 4½″ Water Witch or Pollywog. LOWER: Unidentified Lockhart lure. Could be a different model, a forerunner or prototype of the above Water Witch.

The Wagtail Witch in the photograph here has to be a very early one because it doesn't have the typical Lockhart hook hangers. The one illustrated in the OUTER'S article lacked them also. If you look over the patent illustration on page 250 you will see the hook hanger design. Look also at what appears to be a plate screwed on over the side body grooves or flutes. Although this has not yet been found, the lure in the OUTER'S article looks as if it has the plates on it. It also appears to have glass eyes. The patent was applied for in August of 1909 and granted November 11, 1911. This is actually Lockhart's second patent.

*Address given in the first Lockhart patent application.

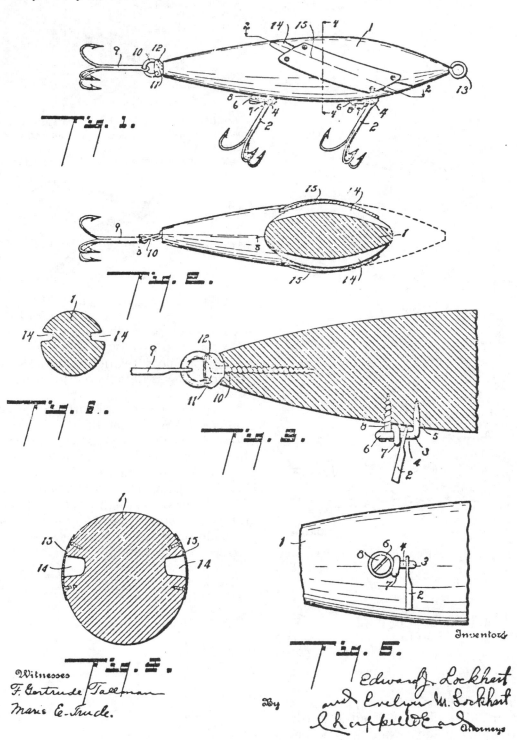

E. J. & E. M. LOCKHART.
FISH BAIT OR LURE.
APPLICATION FILED AUG. 27, 1909.

1,009,077.

Patented Nov. 21, 1911.

A 1911 Lockhart patent drawing containing details of their hook hanger hardware.

E. J. LOCKHART.

FISH BAIT OR LURE.

APPLICATION FILED SEPT. 19, 1908.

923,670.

Patented June 1, 1909.

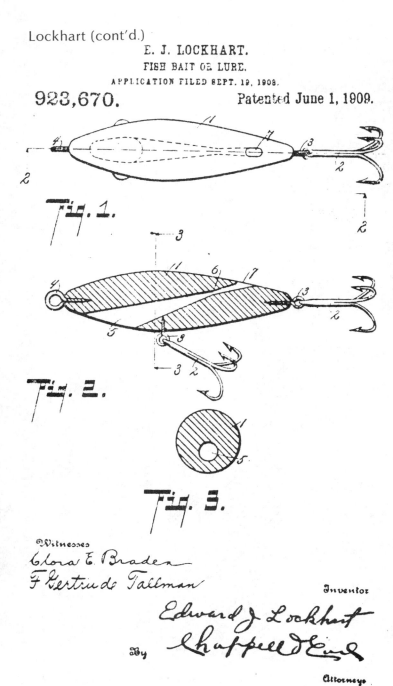

A 1909 Lockhart patent drawing of the Water Witch or Pollywog.

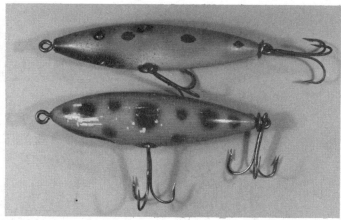

Two Lockhart WATER WITCHES. Note the shape variations. Both measure 4" long. They each have cup and screw eye belly hook hangers and tail protecting washer at the trailing treble hook. Upper lure sports glass eyes while the other has no eyes.

Illustrated above is the JERSEY SKEETER. No size or colors were found in any of the references. It came equipped with a single tail hook integral with the body and a belly double hook to comply with New Jersey hook restriction law. The ad stated that the double was detachable for replacement with a treble.

There are two Lockhart lures not pictured here; the WATER WASP and the WOBBLER WIZARD. The Water Wasp was advertised as being the same as the Jersey Skeeter "..but twice as long. Can be had with or without weed guard." The Wobbler Wizard or Wobbler Special has essentially the same body as the 4½" Pollywog or Wagtail Witch, but had very wide flutes or grooves that were oriented more horizontally as opposed to the upswept, narrow flute or groove on the Wagtail Witch.

The first patent (above) was applied for in September of 1908 and granted to Lockhart June 1, 1909. It was for the WATER WITCH or POLLYWOG (see photo at right). There are three sizes of the lure to be found.

It is interesting to note that the first patent was granted to Lockhart alone when he lived in Battle Creek, and the subsequent patents listed the grantees as Edward J. Lockhart and Evelyn M. Lockhart of Galesburg, Michigan a few miles down the road. Looks like Ed picked him up a wife and moved to the suburbs.

Lockhart (cont'd.)

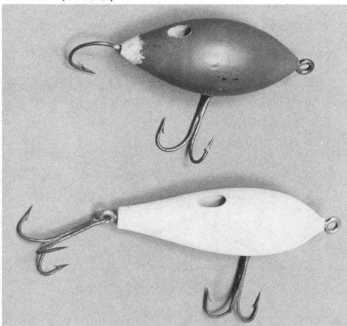

The 2½" and 3¼" Water Witches or Pollywogs. The smaller lure has apparently been modified by a fisherman as all ad photos show a trailing treble hook. Collector value range: $20 to $40.

It is important to note here, that there exists a lure made by another company that is very similar to the Water Witch. This lure is the EUREKA WIGGLER pictured and discussed on page 172.

In all there are seven different Lockhart lures known presently:

WAGTAIL WITCH
WATER WITCH or POLLYWOG (3 sizes)
JERSEY SKEETER
WATER WASP
WOBBLER WIZARD or WOBBLER SPECIAL

Colors mentioned in various advertisements are: White with Red head; solid White, Red or Yellow. Flutes or grooves are Red or Yellow. Collector value range for all: $20 to $40.

LUR-O-LITE
Sure Catch Lure Company
Irvington, New Jersey

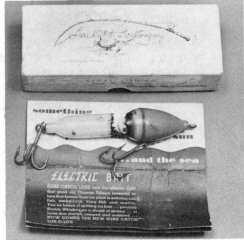

The lure above is the only one so far that I can

positively identify as from this company. It was a battery powered electric light plastic lure. Looks like the last time it was used it was put back in the box while still switched on. The heat from the bulb melted it in two. Collector value range: $5 to $10.

LONG ISLAND MANUFACTURING COMPANY c1935
Long Island City, New York

The lure illustrated here with the original box is mint. A 1936 William Mills & Son catalog listed two lures from this company. One of them appears to be the one in the photograph here, a JUNIOR PIKE FLASHER. The other is a JUNIOR BASS FLASHER and is listed as 2-7/8", 3/8 oz., Green back, Yellow belly. In five years that is the only additional info I have been able to find. Collector value range: $5 to $10.

THE McCORMIC MERMAID
McCormic Bait Company
Kalamazoo, Michigan

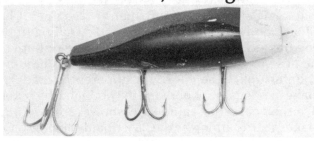

(cont'd. next page)

McCormic Mermaid (cont'd.)

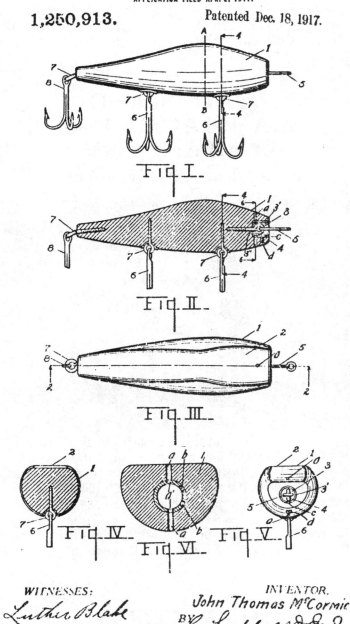

J. T. McCORMIC.
FISH BAIT OR LURE.
APPLICATION FILED APR. 2, 1917.

1,250,913.   Patented Dec. 18, 1917.

WITNESSES:
Luther Blake
Lynn Gilman

INVENTOR.
John Thomas McCormic
BY Chappell & Earl
ATTORNEYS.

Original McCormic Mermaid patent. Granted to John Thomas McCormic December 18, 1917.

This plug was found advertised in a May 1917 issue of The National Sportsmans Magazine. It had a 3-5/8" body, two belly trebles and a trailing treble. One unique feature was a small cupped-out area at the nose in which a short wire line tie was mounted (countersunk). The lure was apparently made for Shakespeare later or perhaps they bought the patent, In either case the same lure shows up in a 1920 Shakespeare catalog as the "Mermaid Minnow". Colors available from both companies are white, yellow, or red. It may also be found in white or black with a red head. The latter two colors were probably added by Shakespeare later. Collector value range: $20 to $40.

MARZ DOUBLE DUTY

Barnard Plating Company   Ann Arbor, MI

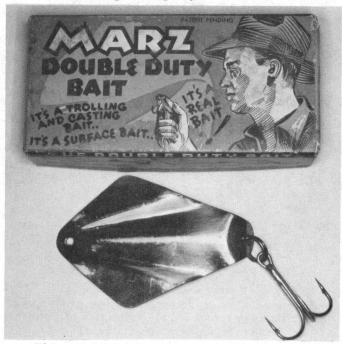

This metal lure measures 2-3/4" long and is apparently made so that you can pull it from either end depending whether you want a top water or underwater running lure. It dates from sometime around the late 1930's to the early 1940's. Collector value range: $5 to $10.

MEDLEY'S
WIGGLY CRAWFISH

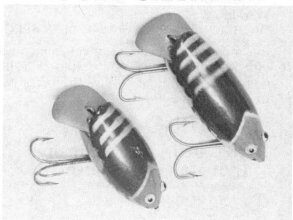

You will note in the photo that the patent date is May 25, 1920. There is another earlier patent dated August 5, 1919. Both show the same body, but the metal lip blade design is different. The earlier patent shows a metal lip much more like the actual product. The confusion lies in the fact that both patents were applied for on the same date, February 18, 1919. While both patents were filed for by Harry L. Medley of Los Angeles, California, the earlier one assigns one-third of the rights to Harry G. Hamilton of Youngstown, Ohio. The manufacturer of the lures was

(cont'd. next page)

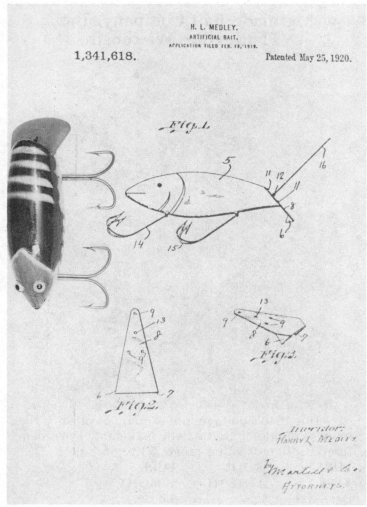

F. B. Hamilton Manufacturing of Pasadena, California and the patent date stamped on the metal lip was "8-5-19". Who was F. B. Hamilton? In any case there is an interesting story concerning the origin of the plug. It is said that Medley whittled the first plug out of a piece of pine and made the lip blade out of the tin from a Prince Albert Tobacco can. He made it initially for his own use but the patents serve to indicate that the plug was successful for he did go to the trouble to secure the patent. Apparently somewhere along the line Hamilton came along with the wherewithall to manufacture them.

The lure themselves were made in two sizes. The larger (3") had two belly double hooks and the smaller (2½") had only one double. There is reason to believe they may have been provided with trebles by the manufacturer as an option. This is evidenced by the 2" lure in the photo. Both lures in the photos were given to a man in Youngstown by Hamilton himself. All had glass eyes and were equipped with two flexible rubber antennae. They were reverse running plugs and came in twelve color combinations according to an ad in the June, 1922 issue of FOREST AND STREAM magazine. Collector value range: $20 to $30.

MEPPS
(Sheldon's Inc.)
Antigo, Wisconsin

By definition Mepps spinner baits are not particularly old nor is their history born in America. However any veteran fisherman should know what a French spinner is and of those who do, most recognize the Mepps name as representing the best French spinner to be had. The Mepps spinners came along in the fairly early days of spin fishing in America and therefore important to its development. Hence their inclusion in this book." ...This inauspicious lure has earned itself a lasting place in the hearts and folklore of many thousands of loyal Waltonians."*

The lures originated in France in the early 1930's and were made by Andre Muelnart and the firm name was Manufacturier D'Engins De Precision Pour Peche Sportive. The first letters of the letters in the company's Frence name form the acronym "MEPPS". Mr. Todd Sheldon brought them to the United States in the early 1950's. The majority of the components of Mepps spinners sold in the U.S. are made in France and assembled in the Wisconsin plant. The illustrations on the following pages will help you to identify the earliest Mepps spinners. These earlier lures will be of interest to those collectors who are attempting to assemble a collection representing the evolution of metal spinners and spoons in American fishing history.

IDENTIFICATION OF EARLY MEPPS SPINNERS

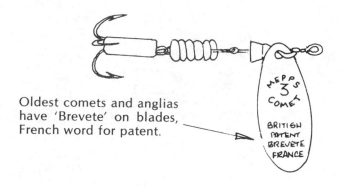

Oldest comets and anglias have 'Brevete' on blades, French word for patent.

*From **Millions and Millions of Mepps** by Roger Drayna. Autumn 1972 edition of Wisconsin Trails Magazine.

(cont'd next page)

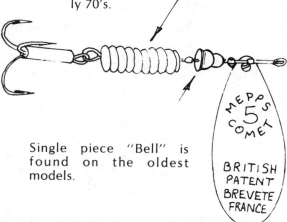

Twisted wire body was used on the first comets and continued in use until early 70's.

Single piece "Bell" is found on the oldest models.

MEPPS 5 COMET BRITISH PATENT BREVETE FRANCE

Older anglias in the #4 and #5 sizes had a red and yellow bead body.

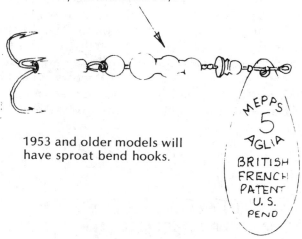

1953 and older models will have sproat bend hooks.

MEPPS 5 AGLIA BRITISH FRENCH PATENT U.S. PEND

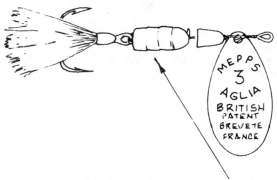

MEPPS 3 AGLIA BRITISH PATENT BREVETE FRANCE

Body style has changed substantially in the last ten years.

SCATBACK
Mermade Bait Company, Inc., Plattleville, Wisconsin

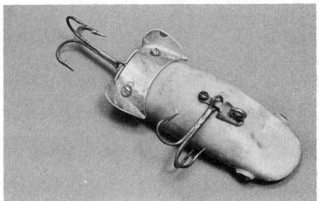

This 1940's vintage lure is made of plastic. The name is molded into the belly making it easily identified. Collector value range: $3 to $6.

LURE TYPE	BODY LENGTH	LURE WEIGHT
Bass size	2¾"	5/8 oz.
Musky size	unk.	1-1/8 oz.

COLOR OR FINISH: *Shiner; Perch; Red head; Frog; Yellow.*

MICHIGAN LIFE-LIKE
Adolph Arntz, Muskegon, Michigan

The origin and history of the Michigan Life-Like remains cloudy. The maker is in some way related to the Myers and Spellman confusion in the following listing on page 316. The patent for the Michigan Life-Like was granted to Jacob Hansen of Muskegon, Michigan on February 28, 1908. It has been assumed that he was the manufacturer and a friend, Adolph Arntz, distributed the lure. Arntz was a sporting goods dealer in Muskegon. This may or may not be true. The only advertisement I could find was in a 1910 issue of *The Angler's Guide.* It clearly stated: "Manufactured by Adolph Arntz." They are well made four section jointed lures. The forward section is the largest ending with three more smaller sections jointed so that there is a life-like motion to the plug. There are two sizes, 2¾" and 3¾". The smaller had three treble and the larger, five treble hooks. Both had glass eyes and propellers on the nose and tail. The tail propeller had three blades.

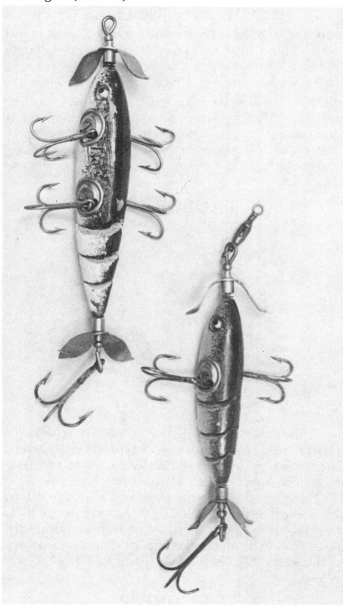

The side hook hangers shown on the lures in the photo are of the style more commonly found and probably represent the oldest style. It is a more or less flush mount. The second style protrudes further and although the same principle is utilized, the design is different. The third style is shown in the drawing of the Hansen Underwater Minnow on page 268. It looks somewhat like the common one-piece surface hanger. It is however, used as a hook limiter and covers the screw eye hook attachment. Collector value range: $80 to $160.

COLOR OR FINISH: *Light green, speckled back, white belly; Dark green, speckled back, white belly; Dark back, aluminum color; Brook trout; Dark back, yellow belly; Aluminum color; Natural wood finish; Perch; Green back, yellow sides, red belly.*

MILLER'S REVERSIBLE MINNOW
Union Springs Specialty Company
Cayuga Springs, New York

This extremely rare lure can be found in two variations. The earliest model (c1913) had simple screw eye or screw eye and washer hook hangers. It also had a slightly longer, much slimmer rear body section than the later version. The later one (c1916) utilizes the Pflueger type Neverfail hook hangers and a fatter rear body section. The 1916 lure seems much more refined in construction and finish.

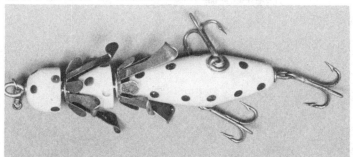

This lure is quite a wild looking contraption. Its propellers were colored gold and silver. The body was made of cedar, 4½" long. It came in three color schemes: No. 1, yellow with gold splots; No. 2, white belly, blended red and green spots; and No. 3, white body, red head with gold spots. The one in the picture has the Pflueger "Neverfail Hook Hardware". Collector value range: $100 to $200.

MILLSITE TACKLE COMPANY
Howell, Michigan

It is generally believed that this company has been around since at least 1920, but I have never run across any catalogs or ads earlier than the 1930's. Although the company is bound to have produced wooden plugs the greatest majority of those observed by the author and listed here are made of plastics. Just about all that have metal lips are stamped on the lip with the company name.

RATTLE BUG

It is thought this lure was first available around 1940. If so, it would be **among** the first to incorporate a loose metal ball internally so it would rattle on retrieve (see Sea Bat by Drake). It was made in the shape of a beetle, had a diving lip and one treble hook. Collector value range: $3 to $5.

CATALOG SERIES#	BODY LENGTH	LURE WEIGHT
900	1-7/8"	5/8 oz.

COLOR OR FINISH: *Black and red; Natural; Red and White; Goldfish; Frog; Pike scale.*

Millsite (cont'd.)

Rattle Bug

MILLSITE MINNOWS

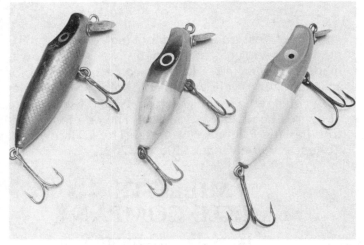

Over the years there were a number of different finishes, transparent or opaque, and lip types used on the plastic minnows. There were three basic body sizes, but all were shaped about the same as in the illustration. All had a belly treble and a trailing treble hook. The list of sizes and names follows here:

TRANSPARENT MINNOW (Floater)
      3"   3/5 oz.
OPAQUE MINNOW (Floater)
      3"   3/5 oz.
TRANSPARENT MINNOW (Baby Slow Sinker)
      2½"   ½ oz.
OPAQUE MINNOW (Baby Slow Sinker)
      2½"   ½ oz.

All were available variously with a deep diving lip, or in floating or sinking versions with smaller diving lip. Collector value range: $3 to $6.

MILLSITE COLORS

There were several colors used by Millsite but which colors available on which plugs is not clearly indicated in most cases. The list of those colors found follows here. The list is probably not complete.

COLOR OR FINISH: *Black and red; Natural; Red and white; Goldfish; Frog; Pike scale; Green scale, transparent; Gold scale, transparent; Silver scale, transparent; Yellow scale, transparent; Cardinal scale, transparent; Shiner scale, transparent; Orange and black spots.*

PADDLE BUG

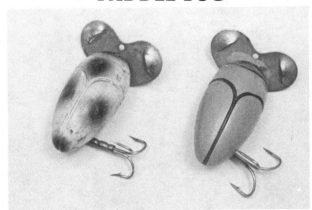

This is the same body design as the Rattle Bug. It had a large metal mouth piece much like the Arbogast "Jitterbug" but was slotted to allow water to pass through making bubbles. It had one treble hook, was 1¾" long, weighed ½ ounce and was available in the same colors as the "Rattle Bug." I have seen one that is the same design but there are no slots in the mouth piece. It may be an early model or it may have been modified by a fisherman. Collector value range: $3 to $6.

DEEP CREEP

The two plugs on the left in the photo are positively identified as Deep Creeps. The far right plug is thought to be the smallest of the three sizes that were produced but it is so unlike the other two (except for the diving lip) that we cannot as yet be sure.

Millsite (cont'd.)
There were no illustrations found in the catalogs. There were no sizes or weights listed either. As far as can be determined they could be purchased in all Millsite colors. Collector value range: $2 to $4.

DAILY DOUBLE

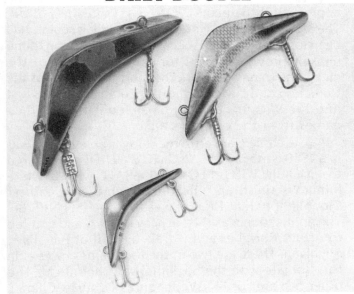

The photo shows the three sizes produced. They are double-ended so that the angler may choose shallow or deep running. Color list may be incomplete. Collector value range: $2 to $4.

CATALOG SERIES #	BODY LENGTH	LURE WEIGHT
700	4"	¾ oz.
800	2½"	5/8 oz.
unk.	2"	unk.

COLOR OR FINISH: *Red and white; Silver speckle; Perch spots.*

BASSOR BAIT

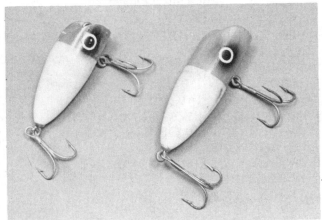

This plug was available in two sizes and one color clearly, but the head is molded with a scooped out nose. Collector value range: $2 to $4.

CATALOG SERIES #	BODY LENGTH	LURE WEIGHT
1201	2-3/4"	5/8 oz.
1301	2-1/4"	1/2 oz.

COLOR OR FINISH: *Red head, white body.*

WIG WAG

As you can see in the photo, this lure is identified as the Wig-Wag on the fish shaped tag attached. It weighs ½ oz. and is 2½" long. Colors produced are unknown. Collector value range: $2 to $4.

UNIDENTIFIED MILLSITE LURES

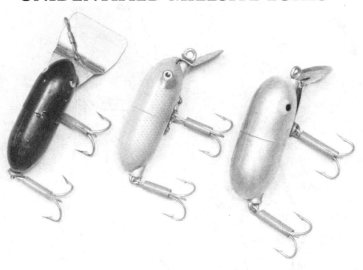

The plugs illustrated in the two photos here have not been identified for they were not found in any of the available old catalogs. The three plugs in the first photo are identified as Millsite products on their diving blades. The other is named on the belly as follows: "Millsite Spin-E-Bee ¼ oz." No other information other than this is presently known. Let's hope more old catalogs surface soon. Collector value range: $2 to $4.

THE MOONLIGHT BAIT COMPANY

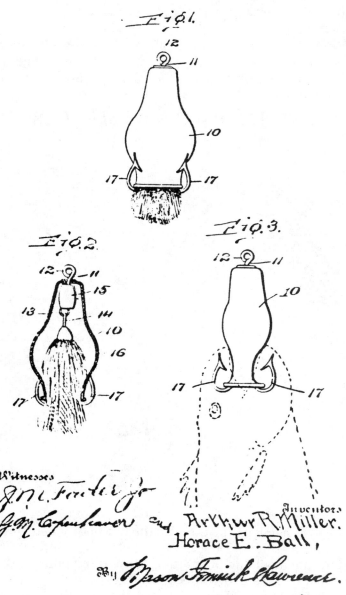

A. R. MILLER & H. E. BALL.
BAIT.
APPLICATION FILED MAY 28. 1910.

981,454.

Patented Jan. 10, 1911.

The Moonlight Fish Nipple patent granted to Miller and Ball, January 10, 1911.

The Moonlight Bait Company was formed by a legal agreement signed by Horace Emery Ball and Charles E. Varney on December 30, 1908 at Paw Paw, Michigan. A part of this document established Varney as the man who provided the start-up funds. The hand-written document is two legal pages long and after the signatures there is the beginning of a ledger starting in 1909. With this evidence we can now say with authority, that the Moonlight Bait Company began doing business in earnest in 1909.

The story behind this beginning is an interesting one. It seems there was a group of fishing friends who had little time for fishing in the daytime due to the constraints of employment so they began fishing at night. They soon discovered that nightime was the time to hook the big ones. In 1906 they formed the appropriately named MOONLIGHT FISHING CLUB. The aforementioned Horace Emery Ball, it seems, had been fashioning a very successful lure and soon found himself providing them for other members of the club. One thing led to another and the result was the formation of the Moonlight Bait Company and its first lure, the Moonlight Floating Bait, both deriving their names from the original club.

The earliest advertisement I was able to find was in a 1910 issue of THE ANGLER'S GUIDE. It featured the MOONLIGHT FLOATING BAIT with a white luminous finish and illustrated same. The earliest Moonlight patent I found was for the FISH NIPPLE. The application was filed in May of 1910 and granted to Arthur R. Miller and Horace E. Ball of Paw Paw, Michigan. These are two of the four names I was able to associate with the beginnings of Moonlight. The other two are Ford R. Wilber and, of course, Charles E. Varney. It has been reported elsewhere that the Moonlight Floating Bait was marketed as early as 1906. While we can accept its existence that early, we now know better. This report is apparently based upon the informal making and distribution by Ball to his fellow club members.

From 1909 to 1922-23 Moonlight enjoyed success and expanded their line a good bit. In the two years after the company was founded, they added a weedless version of the Moonlight Floating Bait, the Trout Bob and the Fish Nipple. By 1918 there were at least a dozen in the lineup. The following is a listing of those lures arranged, as best as I can determine, in the order of their appearance:

MOONLIGHT FLOATING BAIT (1908)
WEEDLESS MOONLIGHT FLOATING BAIT (1909-10)
TROUT BOB (1911)
FISH NIPPLE (1911)
DREADNOUGHT (1911-12)
THE "1913" SPECIAL (1912-13)
PAW PAW UNDERWATER MINNOW (1912-13)
PAW PAW PEARL WOBBLER (1912-13)
ZIG ZAG (1913)
PAW PAW FISH SPEAR (1914)
THE BUG (1915-16)
LADYBUG WIGGLER (1916-17)

Moonlight (cont'd.)

In 1923 Moonlight began a transition period by acquiring another lure company. This transition continued for the next five or size years with various acquisitions of the manufacturing rights to other lures until the company finally evolved into the famous Paw Paw Bait Company. The time between 1930 and 1935 is still a bit hazy as I have not been able to uncover any reliable information covering this period. The listing below approximates the transition through the years.

MOONLIGHT BAIT COMPANY   1909 to 1923
MOONLIGHT BAIT AND NOVELTY WORKS
1923 to 1930-35
PAW PAW BAIT COMPANY   1930-35 to 1960's

The 1923 acquisition of the Silver Creek Novelty Works of Dowagiac, Michigan resulted in the name change above and a considerable expansion of their line. That company had been making Pollywogs, the Silver Creek Wiggler and Pikeroons among other. Moonlight incorporated their line. You may also run across several lures from SEA GULL (Schoenfeld-Gutter, NYC) that look like Moonlight lures. They were made by the Silver Creek Novelty Works and/or Moonlight for that company. The Sea Gull company used the same catalog numbers as did Moonlight. About the time of the takeover of the Silver Creek Company, Moonlight apparently had to reorganize their numbering system for their burgeoning lure line. The 1923 Moonlight Bait and Novelty Works catalog lists them as follows:

FLOATING BAIT . . . . #1
WEEDLESS FLOATING BAIT . . . . #1
FISH NIPPLE . . . . #4
ZIG ZAG BAIT . . . . #6
PAW PAW PEARL WOBBLER . . . . #7
BASS-EAT-US . . . . 300 Series
BABE-EAT-US . . . . 400 Series
TROUT-EAT-US . . . . 500 Series
POLLY-WOG . . . . 700 Series
POLLY-WOG JUNIOR . . . . 800 Series
PIKAROON . . . . 900 Series
BABY PIKAROON . . . . 1000 Series
CASTING BAIT (3", 3T) . . . . 1100 Series
CASTING BAIT (3", 5T) . . . . 1200 Series
LIGHT FEATHER MINNOW (1-3/4" overall, 1/3 oz.) . . . . 1400 Series
WEEDLESS FEATHER MINNOW (3½" overall, 1/6 oz.) . . . . 1500 Series
FEATHER MINNOW (3½" overall, 1/8 oz.)
. . . . 1600 Series
WEEDLESS FEATHER MINNOW (3" overall, 1/10 oz.) . . . . 1800 Series

You will note that the TROUT BOB, DREADNOUGHT, BUG, FISH SPEAR, UNDERWATER MINNOW, THE 1913 SPECIAL and the LADYBUG WIGGLER are all missing from the catalog listing. As far as I can determine they never showed up in the line again.

The #600 Series is conspicuously missing from the list but it did show up in subsequent catalogs. About the same date as the above catalog, Moonlight obtained the rights to the lure patented by Frederick E, Comstock known as the COMSTOCK CHUNK (see page 150). The first listing of the #600 Series I found was in a 1926 Moonlight catalog. It was called the 99% WEEDLESS. The same catalog listed 'the WILSON WOBBLER. It is known that Moonlight also obtained the rights to the WILSON WOBBLER and the WILSON CUPPED WOBBLER around 1926 also (see Hastings Sporting Goods Works on page 214). The Wilson's Cupped Wobbler became the BASS SEEKER in Moonlight catalogs. There seems to be a four year gap in the Moonlight and Paw Paw catalog collection I studied (1927-30). Perhaps the collection was simply incomplete. In any case it is the period in which Moonlight became the Paw Paw Bait Company. Many of the same lures in the last Moonlight catalog are retained in the first (c1930) Paw Paw catalog available to me. The Paw Paw company remained in operation up into the 1960's. The Paw Paw Bait Company lures begin on page 321.

THE MOONLIGHT FLOATING BAIT
#1

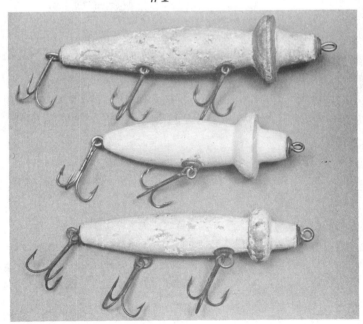

This plug was first mass-marketed by the company about 1909. The earliest versions were coated with a luminous paint and were 4" long with two belly trebles and a trailing treble hook. It was either solid luminous white or luminous white with a red head. It is not known for sure whether the weedless hook configuration was available then or came later. In any case soon after, a second, smaller size became

303

Moonlight (cont'd.)
available. The final available sizes and configurations available were as follows:

#1 Luminous white, 4", 3T or 2T
#1 Luminous white, red headd, 4", 3T or 3D
#2 Luminous white, red head, 3-5/8", 2T
#2 Luminous white, red head, 3-5/8", 2T (Weedless)
#3 Luminous white, red head,
Collector value range: $10 to $20.

THE TROUT BOB

This small 1-1/8" long plug first showed up in a 1911 advertisement in THE OUTER'S BOOK. The only known color is solid white. It sported a feathered trailing treble hook Sometimes known as the "Little Bob." Collector value range: $30 to $60.

THE FISH NIPPLE

Another of Moonlight's earliest lures, it first appeared in the same 1911 advertisement as the TROUT BOB above. It was patented January 10, 1911 by Arthur R. Miller and Horace E. Ball, two of the original founders of Moonlight. Collector value range: $10 to $20.

THE "1913" SPECIAL

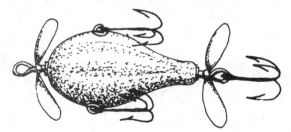

Apparently available in 1913 (or 1912) this plug was advertised as available in only one finish. It was painted and covered with a glitter-like material to make it sparkle. It has a treble hook one each side and a trailing treble. There was one nose mounted propeller and one tail mounted. Collector value range: $100 to $200.

THE PAW PAW FISH SPEAR

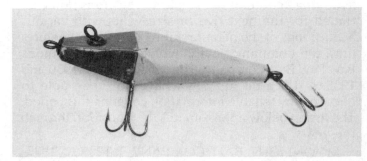

The FISH SPEAR was first found advertised in an August 1915 issue of THE OUTER'S BOOK. The size was not given, but colors were Red, White, Yellow or Fancy Spotted. Collector value range: $80 to $120.

LADYBUG WIGGLER

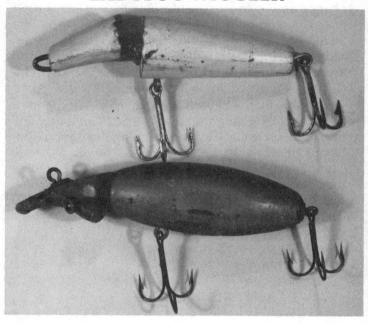

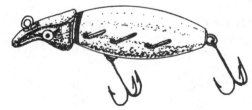

The patent for this lure was applied for in late 1916 and granted June 26, 1917. It was first found advertised in the May, 1917 issue of NATIONAL SPORTSMAN. The ad states "Newest and Most Attrractive Lure for Game Fish Ever Invented". It had an odd shaped diving plane head, a belly treble and trailing teble hook. It was available in three color finishes: White with red head and black legs; yellow with red head and black legs; and green back with red and yellow decorations, and black legs.

(cont'd.)

304

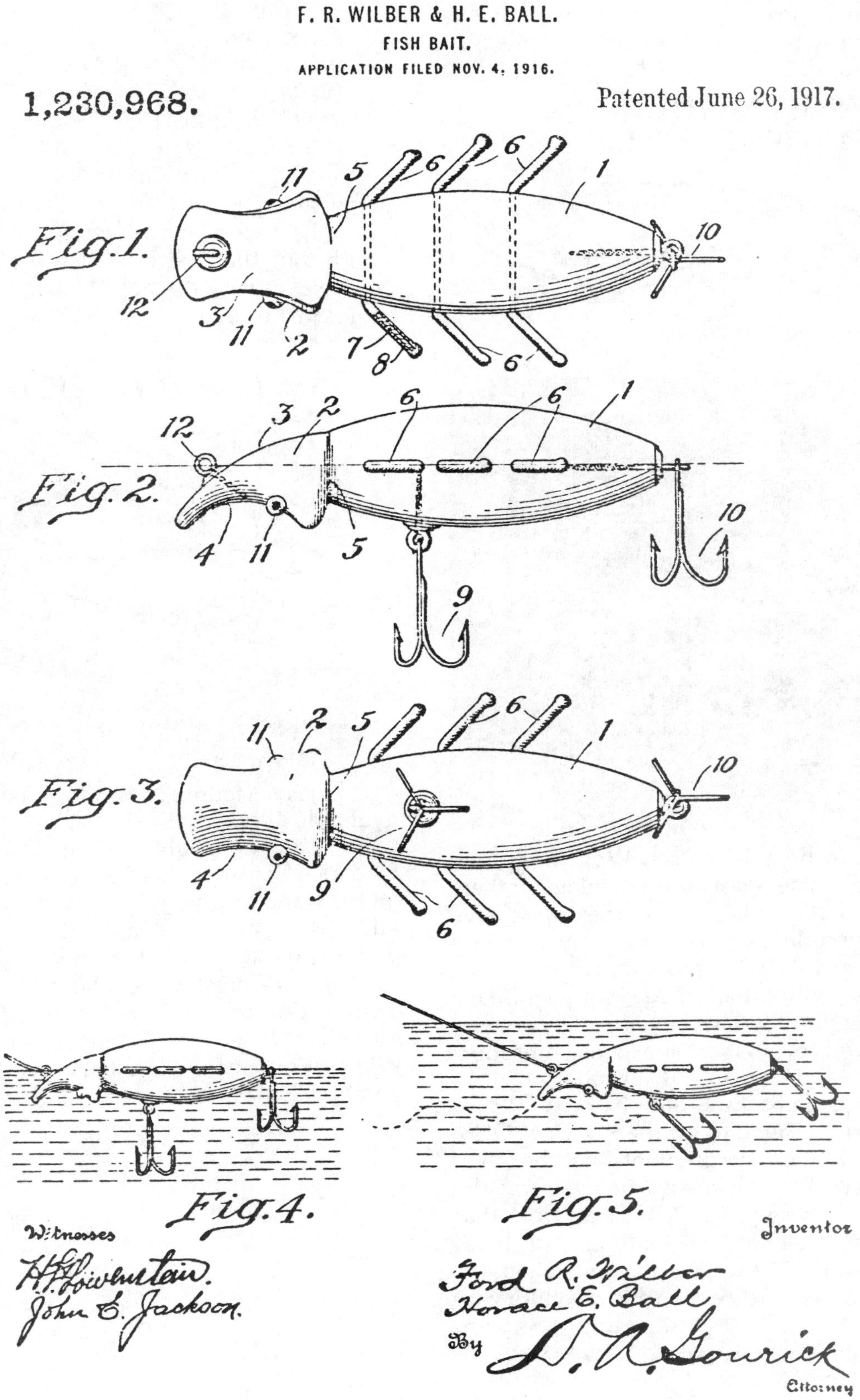

F. R. WILBER & H. E. BALL.
FISH BAIT.
APPLICATION FILED NOV. 4, 1916.

1,230,968.

Patented June 26, 1917.

Fig.1.

Fig.2.

Fig.3.

Fig.4.

Fig.5.

Witnesses

Inventor

Ford R. Wilber
Horace E. Ball

By

Attorney

Original patent drawing for the Ladybug Wiggler.

Moonlight Ladybug Wiggler (cont'd.)

The drawing and the lower lure in this photograph on page 304 are Ladybug Wigglers. The upper lure in the photo is thought to be an early experiment or prototype worth $20 to $40. Collector value range: $40 to $80.

POLLY-WOG
POLLY-WOG JUNIOR

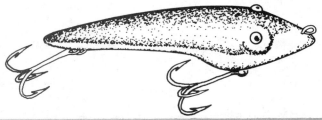

The top lure here is a Polly-Wog measuring 3-1/8". Though this size is not found catalogued there are so many of that size found that they must have been in regular production. This one may be a late Silver Creek or early Paw Paw product. The lower lure is a 4" Pikeroon. Both are painted simply and have painted eyes, suggesting that they are latter generation lures evolved to the most inexpensive production method.

A 1924 Moonlight Bait and Novelty Works catalog was the first found to list the POLLY-WOGS. It is known from other advertisements that the Silver Creek Novelty Works, Dowagiac, Michigan was the original maker of these plugs. A 1921 ad from that company stated: "Last year this bait made its debut in the angler's world." It was 4" long, weighed 4¾ oz. and colors listed were: Solid Yellow, White with Black Spots, White with Black Stripes and Moss back. A 1924 Moonlight catalog listed two sizes as available: 4", ¾ oz.; and the Junior size was 2½", ¾ oz. The illustration showed glass eyes (as did the Silver Creek ad) and the copy listed nine colors as available.

YELLOW
MOSS BACK
WHITE, RED STRIPES
YELLOW, BLACK SPOTS
RAINBOW
WHITE, BLACK STRIPES
WHITE
YELLOW PERCH
HORNED ACE

Sea Gull (Schoenfeld-Gutter, NYC) was also advertising the Polly-Wogs for sale at about the same time. The oldest and rarest version has a notched mouth, but the lure was then a product of Silver Creek Novelty Works, not Moonlight. Collector value range: $10 to $20.

THE 99% WEEDLESS

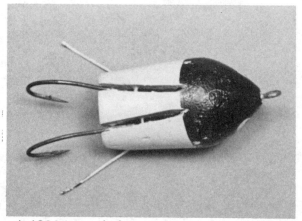

A 1926 Moonlight catalog first lists this lure as available. It is actually the COMSTOCK CHUNK (see page 150) or slightly modified version of it. Frederick Comstock applied for the patent on his lure in 1923 and it was granted to him in 1926. It was advertised as early as 1924 in catalogs and periodicals. It looks as if Moonlight obtained the rights from Comstock at about the time they were in transition to the Paw Paw Bait Company name. Moonlight listed it is six colors: White, Green back; White, Red head; Luminous; White, Black head; Perch; All Black. Collector value range: $5 to $10.

BASS SEEKER
and
BASS SEEKER JUNIOR

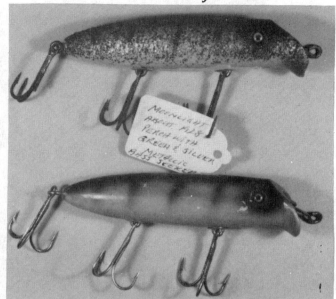

This is another acquisition of another company's lure during the Moonlight to Paw Paw transition period. The Bass Seekers were originally from the Hastings Sporting Goods company who called the WILSON'S CUPPED WOBBLERS (see page 214).

The lure has a scooped at nose, heavy wire link leader, a belly treble and trailing treble. It was available in six color finishes: Gold color body with red head; white body with red head; green scale finish; gold scale finish; blue scale finish; and perch finish. Collector value range: $10 to $20.

WILSON WOBBLER

As above, this lure was originally made by the Hastings Sporting Goods people and acquired from them at about the time of the Moonlight to Paw Paw transition. The lure was actually WILSON'S FLUTED WOBBLER (see page 214). Collector value range: $3 to $8.

LITTLE WONDER
THE #2100 Series c1925

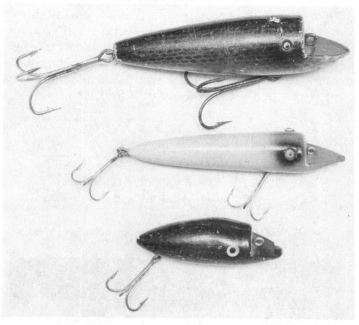

The lower plug in this photograph is the LITTLE WONDER. The other two are here because of the similarity of the body design. They have not been found catalogued as yet, but are tentatively identified as a bass size and a musky size version of the LITTLE WONDER.

The Little Wonder was found in a Moonlight advertisement that stated "BRAND NEW for 1925." No size or colors were listed in the ad but a 1926 catalog listing did contain the following six colors:

RED HEAD, GOLD BODY
GREEN SCALE
WHITE BODY, RED HEAD
GOLD SCALE
BLUE SCALE
YELLOW PERCH

Collector value range:

The Little Wonder - $10 to $20
Musky Size - $15 to $40
Bass Size - $40 to $80

PIKAROON
BABY PIKAROON
JOINTED PIKAROON

The following set of photographs should help you to identify the various PIKAROONS that were available. If you were to compare these to the Pikaroons in the Silver Creek Novelty Works section you may note a subtle difference in the style of the nose area. This is an unsubstantiated theory, but nevertheless one that is based on multiple observations; that the Moonlight versions have a little more refined looking, slightly turned up nose than those produced by Silver Creek before the 1923 Moonlight acquisition of the company. The Pikaroons were made in a Baby size, 1000 Series at 4-1/4" with two trebles, a regular size at 5-1/4" and found most commonly with two treble hooks, and the jointed version.

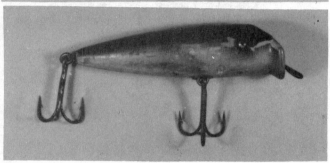

307

Moonlight (cont'd)

They are by no means limited to these sizes, but they are the most commonly found sizes and hook configurations. The color options they were available in are the same as the previously listed Little Wonder. There was also a Musky Special available. It is essentially the same lure as the Jointed Pikaroon, but made much larger and sturdier. It was made available only in Green Scale or White with a Red Head.

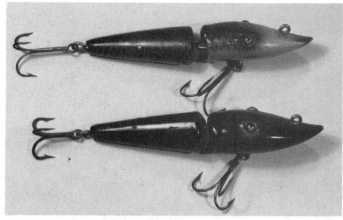

This is a full side view of the Jointed Pikaroons in the previous photo. They each measure 4-1/8", have yellow glass eyes and screw eye hook hangers. Note the turned up noses. Collector value range: $10.

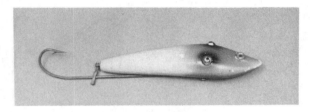

A 4-1/4" 2500 Series Pikaroon made for pikes and pickerels. Collector value range: $30 to $50.

This is a red head, white body 6" Musky Special. There are three types of connecting hardware to be found on jointed Pikaroons. The simple use of two connecting screw eyes on ths lure is thought to be the earliest. Collector value range for Musky Special Pikaroons: $10 to $20.

The following photo is a close-up of two Jointed Pikaroons showing the second and third styles connecting hardware. The one on the left has a large heavy wire loop from the trailing section wrapped around a heavy wire or brad placed laterally through the forward section. The one on the right has heavy cup and screw eye connectors. Collector value range: $10 to $20.

Note the Moonlight turned up nose on all three of the Pikaroons. They measure 4-1/16" at top and bottom with the middle plug at an even 4". Top and middle have glass eyes while the lower one sports tack painted eyes (TPE). Each has simple screw eye line tie and hook hangers. Collector value range for upper lure is $30 to $50. The other two are $10 to $40.

BASS-EAT-US c 1920
BABE-EAT-US c1920
TROUT-EAT-US c1920, 1926
BUG-EAT-US c1920

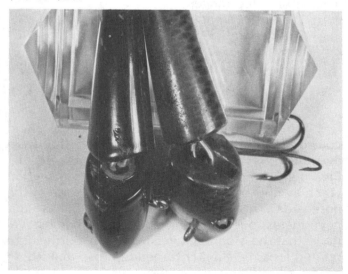

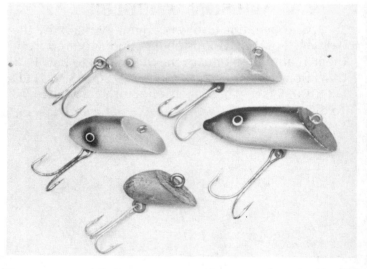

308

Moonlight (cont'd.)

Three were found listed and illustrated in a c1920 Moonlight catalog. The Trout-Eat-Us was listed as 1¾" in it and a later (1926) catalog illustrated a Trout-Eat-Us with an illustration but no size. The lure in the illustration is smaller than the 1920 version. It was described as a fly rod size in the 1926 catalog. The center two lures in the photo above match the two catalog illustrations. The upper lure in the photo is a Silver Creek 3" Bass-Eat-Us. The Babe-Eat-Us is smaller version of the Bass-Eat-Us at 2-1/2" with only two treble hooks. It is not pictured in the photo. The tiny lure at the bottom is the Bug-Eat-Us. All four of these lures were part of the Silver Creek Novelty Works at the time Moonlight acquired the company. Colors listed in the c1920 catalog were:

YELLOW
RAINBOW
MOSS BACK
WHITE, RED HEAD
YELLOW, RED HEAD

WHITE, GREEN HEAD
YELLOW, BLACK HEAD
WHITE, BLUE HEAD
YELLOW PERCH
HORNED ACE

Collector value range: $3 to $10.

MOONLIGHT MOUSE

This little fellow first showed up in a 1926 catalog. It has a very distinctive metal lip that is attached to the body by sliding into a slot cut horizontally into the nose. A center portion of the blade is cut and bent up to cover the tip of the nose and is held in place by the screw eye line tie. The small lure at the bottom of the photo of Ladybug Wigglers on page 260 has the same blade. The Mouse was available in White, Gold, Spotted or Mouse color. Collector value range: $10 to $20.

#1900 SERIES

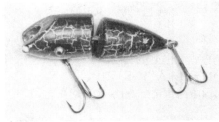

This un-named, jointed lure was listed and illustrated in a 1926 Moonlight catalog. It was available in the same six colors listed with the Little Wonder. No other references were found. Collector value range: $5 to $10.

#3300 SERIES

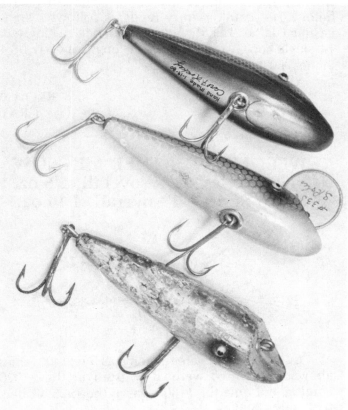

(cont'd next page)

309

Moonlight (cont'd.)

The #3300 is another un-named lure, shown on previous page. No catalog or advertising references were found that included this lure. It is included here and attributed to Moonlight because of the typical cup and screw eye hook hardware that was installed prior to painting resulting in paint being found on the cup rim or flange. The lower two lures in both photos are a Yellow or White with Green back and a Rainbow finish. The top lure in both photos is a close replica that I made in my workshop as an experiment. You can see on the belly-up photo that I identified it as such. My plug wouldn't fool most collectors, but could trip up a novice collector. That's why all of us who fashion replicas should identify them as such, prominently. Collector value range: $5 to $10.

LIGHT BAIT CASTING FEATHER MINNOW #1400 SERIES

A c1920 and a 1926 each list this lure and the small version of the WEEDLESS FEATHER MINNOW below. The catalog entry reads as follows: "Light casting Feather Tail Minnow for light bait casting. No. 1-0 single hook, weight 1/3 ounce, length of body 1-3/4 inches. Furnished in six colors:"

YELLOW	WHITE
ORANGE	BROWN
RED	GRAY

Collector value range: $10 to $25.

WEEDLESS FEATHER MINNOW
#1500 Series - 3½'' overall, 1/6 oz.
#1800 Series - 3'' overall, 1/10 oz.

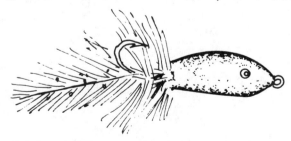

Colors available are the same as the #1400 Series above. These two were also listed in the c1920 catalog, but only the #1800 was in the 1926. Collector value range: $10 to $25.

FEATHER MINNOW #1600 Series

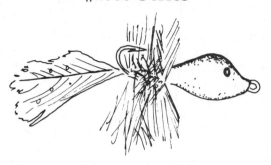

This lure was found in the c1920 catalog as were the above Feather Minnow types. It was listed as 3½'' overall length, weight, 1/8 ounce. Available in the same six colors as the others. Collector value range: $10 to $25.

CASTING BAITS #1100 Series #1200 Series

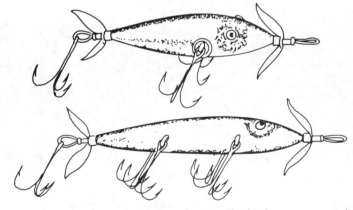

These two un-named Moonlight lures are truly beautiful examples of the classic, glass eye floating, propeller spinnered minnow style of Heddon, Shakespeare, South Bend and Pflueger. Found listed and illustrated in a c1924 Moonlight catalog only, they came in the two styles illustrated above. Both were listed as 3'' in length, but the catalog illustrations don't appear to support that entry. The drawings above are exact copies of the illustrations right down to the hardware detail. Colors available were:

YELLOW	YELLOW BODY, BLACK STRIPES
RAINBOW	WHITE
MOSS BACK	YELLOW PERCH
WHITE BODY, RED STRIPE	HORNED ACE
WHITE BODY, BLACK STRIPE	

Collector value range: $15 to $30.

WOBBLE BOY

This spoon type lure is likely to have evolved from the PEARL WOBBLER listed on page 313. It was found in a 1926 Moonlight catalog as available in six different "colorations." They came in two sizes, 2¾'' and 3½''. Ad copy reads in part: "...made of genuine

Moonlight (cont'd.)

South American irridescent pearl." This is probably
Mother-of-Pearl. Collector value range: $3 to $5.

#2900 SERIES
#3000 SERIES

These lures, found only in a 1926 catalog, were
illustrated with glass eyes and propeller spinners at
each end. No lengths were given but they appear to
be in the 3" to 4" range. They could possibly be the
forerunners of The Paw Paw Bait Co. Torpedo and
Slim Lindy. The #2900 was slim bodied with belly and
trailing trebles. The #3000's were fatter with same
hooks. Collector value range: $15 to $30.

This example from the 2900 Series is a 3½" long, has
glass eyes and sports cup and screw eye hook hardware. It has Heddon style thin metal propeller spinners. The lure is quite similar to the Heddon Torpedo.

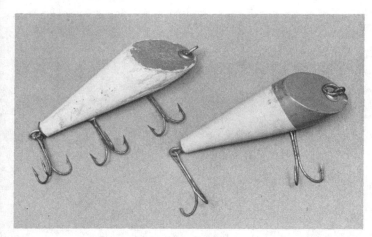

The Zig Zag was patented February 3, 1914 by
Ford R. Wilber and Horace E. Ball. The first advertisement for the ZIG ZAG was in a 1914 periodical.
According to advertisements it was only available
with two belly trebles and a trailing treble hook (3T),
but as you can see in the photograph there was obviously one made with only one belly hook and the
trailing hook (2T). The double hooks in the photo may
have been added by a fisherman. Ads stated colors
available as Red, White, Yellow, Luminous or Fancy
Spotted. You can see one in the photo that is white
with a red head. Perhaps the ad copy was a misprint
and should have read White or Yellow bodies with
Red Heads. There is also a 2½" two-hook MIDGET
ZIG ZAG, c1920. Collector value range: $5 to $10.

THE ZIG ZAG BAIT

F. R. WILBER & H. E. BALL.
ARTIFICIAL BAIT.
APPLICATION FILED SEPT. 8, 1913.

1,086,256.   Patented Feb. 3, 1914.

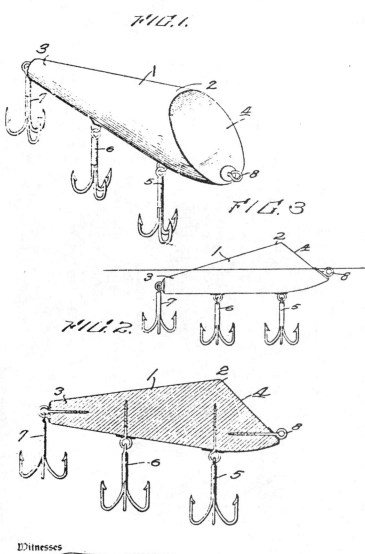

Original patent for the Zig Zag Bait

THE "BUG" #8

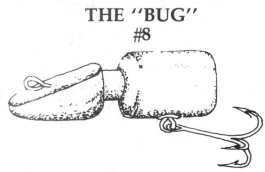

This very curiously shaped plug weighed ¾ ounce and came along around 1915-16. It had only one treble hook, mounted toward the tail but on the belly of the lure. Colors were: solid black; yellow and black with red head; yellow with red head; white with red head; white with red and black stripes; and yellow striped white body. Collector value range: $50 to $100.

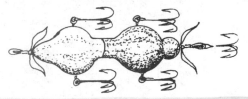

This little dude measures 2¾" long and has cup and screw eye hook hardware.

THE DREADNAUGHT

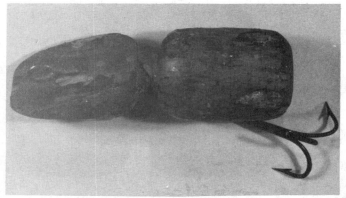

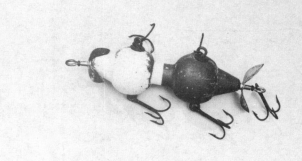

First found advertised in 1912 and called a "Fish Pirate" it goes on to say it was a "...new departure in bait design" and "makes a wake 'like a battleship'." I'll wager it didn't last long. More likely it scared all the fish out of the area. It had five treble hooks and two propeller spinners. The body was 4" long and was available in a red and white and a black and white finish. Collector value range: $80 to $120,

THE PAW PAW UNDERWATER MINNOW

This lure was first found advertised in the April, 1913 issue of THE OUTER'S BOOK. At the time it was available in White, Red or Yellow. It has a nose mounted propeller spinner and a trailing bucktail treble hook. Collector value range: $100 to $200.

THE PEARL WOBBLER

First made available in 1913 this was a spoon type lure with glass bead at the trailing end followed by a bucktail treble hook. The spoon was made of Mother-of-Pearl (see Wobble Boy on page 310). It is 2¾" in length and the collector value range is $5 to $10.

UNKNOWN MOONLIGHT

The lower lure has the cut-out dive plane described in the text. The upper represents another, less common style found. It has a larger portion of the lip cut out.

312

Moonlight (cont'd.)

These 2½" lures are attributed to Moonlight by many collectors because of the metal dive planes. The planes are exactly the same as the two shown on the mouse lures listed above. This is most likely a valid assumption unless the lip was obtained by Moonlight and some other company making this lure from an outsides source. I have found the exact same lure in a listing of lures made by Keeling in a mixed company catalog put out by the Shapleigh Hardware Company in 1928. It is called by the same name in the catalog, but the listing is printed with the name separated into two words: Lady Bug rather than Ladybug as Moonlight spells it. Collector value range: $40 to $80.

UNKNOWN MOONLIGHT

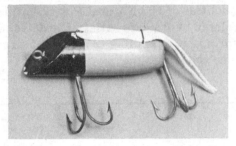

This lure is attributed to Moonlight because of its hardware, paint design and application. Not found in any catalogs or advertisement so far. No realistically derived value can be assigned at this time.

MOORE'S YELLOW PLUG
H. C. Moore, Ypsilanti, Michigan

COPYRIGHT—1926 BY H.C.MOORE

Moore's YELLOW PLUG

PAT. APP'D FOR
MADE ONLY BY
H. C. MOORE
YPSILANTI, MICH.
PRICE $1.00

H. C. Moore, the inventor of MOORE'S YELLOW PLUG, which came into use December 1st, 1924, after a careful study and experiments on Fish Lure. It proved to be a wonderful success, so in the first two weeks in November, 1925, and to my surprise, I sold 100 of these Plugs to fishermen from all parts of the United States.

The demand for my YELLOW PLUGS was so great that I found it necessary to make them by hand to supply my customers, so I made and sold, all told, 400 up to March, 1926. I have seen 75 fishermen casting at one time and every one was using MOORE'S YELLOW PLUG. Patent applied for.

MOORE'S YELLOW PLUG has a weighted head, the proper weight to make it an under-surface bait, and gets down where the big fish are, and can be drawn through the water at any depth you desire, and gets the big fish that will not come to the surface.

MOORE'S YELLOW PLUG has seven distinct improvements over all other wooden bait:

FIRST—The yellow body and black head is positively the most attractive color under all conditions. Fishermen, kindly notice these colors on delivery wagons and especially on road curve signs. Why? Because they can be seen a greater distance.

SECOND—MOORE'S YELLOW PLUG, having a weighted head, will actually cast easily 20 to 30 feet further than any other Plug.

THIRD—Its weight in casting takes up the slack line, reducing backlash 30 per cent.

FOURTH—When cast it travels tail foremost, thus causing less wind resistance.

FIFTH—It casts easily against the wind.

SIXTH—Travels horizontally, under the surface, any distance you desire, by reeling fast or slow.

SEVENTH—MOORE'S YELLOW PLUG is positively the strongest plug made, and excellent for night fishing.

The fishermen who have used this YELLOW PLUG gave it its name, and it is a yellow body with a black head, the colors being original with me, and is the most attractive color in the water for any game fish. Has the strongest Rust Proof Treble Hooks. ACE of all Plugs. Use MOORE'S YELLOW PLUG and you will use no other. Price $1.00.

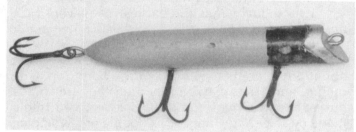

A strongly built, Metal-head plug with cup and screw eye hook hangers. Collector value range: $5 to $15.

MUD PUPPY

C.C. Roberts Bait Company   Monsinee, WI

This lure was first made in 1918. Consance Charles Roberts invented the lure and was granted a patent on it in 1928. At some point prior to his death in 1955 he took on a partner, Jim Rheinschmidt. He took over the operation at the time of Robert's death and was reportedly still making the lures in small quantities in 1987. This very unusual lure was designed so that the lure body would separate from the hook and line once the fish was hooked. This effectively removes the weight from the hook, thus making it more difficult for the fish to shake the hook out. After you boated your fish you were then supposed to retrieve the floating lure body.

The lure was made in two basic sizes, the Little Mud Puppy at 5½" and the regular size 7". Each could be had in what they called "Natural" or white body with a red head.

Now to confuse the issue. Although the sizes and colors listed above are true, they are not the only sizes and finishes to exist. Early in the manufacture the lures were all hand carved and smaller at about 6-7/8". The sizes and colors list as basic reflect the evolution of the lure at the 1946 point. By sometime in the early 1930's the lures had grown to 7¾". At that point they developed mechanized construction for lure bodies and they became a standard 7" for the regular size.

The earliest Mud Puppies have a pin style hook release. This proved faulty and he quickly developed a spring style that was much more effective.

It is thought that the earliest eyes were tack and/or painted. Then came glass and finally decals.

Hooks are usually trebles but during the WW II years trebles were in short supply so they used just about any type they could lay their hands on. One unique hook that may be found on the lures made during the war years was a hand assembled treble made by soldering a single to a double and wrapping the shanks with wire for reinforcing.

Although the majority of the lures will be found in the basic colors above, there were many more as a result of dealer requests. One rare finish is the sucker scale. Roberts developed this finish early on, but there was apparently a patent infringement and he discontinued it. Other colors to look for are black, black and yellow, blue, gold green, green perch, orange, purple, silver, tiger perch, yellow and yellow natural.

Over the 72 years they have obviously been extremely popular and successful. A lure pamphlet I read contained this testimonial, reading in part, "... catching two big muskies (24 and 28 lbs.) with your Mud Puppy." The testimonial was dated 1946, fully eighteen years after the patent date. Collector value range: $5 to $15.

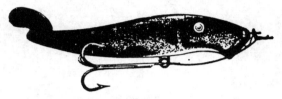

Natural Mud Puppy

The **NATURAL MUD PUPPY** resembles the actions of a live sucker and is used to good advantage by those muskie fishermen who ordinarily fish with live bait.

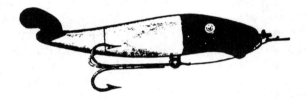

Red Head Mud Puppy

The **RED HEAD MUD PUPPY** has all the action and results producing qualities of the Natural Puppy, but is colored in order to satisfy the demand for a bait adaptable to different fishing conditions.

(cont'd next page)

How It Works

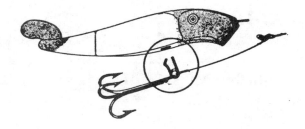

Put pin in nose of bait through ring in leader joint, pass hook end of leader across mouth and belly and press hook clasp into slot in bait and you are ready to fish.

CAUTION: Use leader, and keep hooks sharp.

———

Made in two sizes — LITTLE MUD PUPPY 5½ inches, 1¼ oz.; MUD PUPPY 7 inches, 2 oz.
Either size in Red Head or Natural finish.

MUSHROOM BASS BAIT

J.A. Holzapfel   Jackson, MI

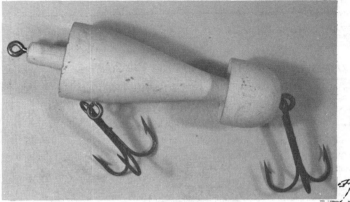

This unusual lure was made somewhere around the 1910's. It is known to have appeared in at least three different paint patterns, all red, all white and a froggy finish with some red. It has also been found in 3½" and 3-7/8" sizes. All the line ties and hook hardware are large brass screweyes. Collector value range: $25 to $50. (See THE CROAKER)

MYERS AND SPELLMAN

1914-15-16

Edward D. Myers
Jack Spellman   Shelby, MI

These two have had the honor of having a dozen or so lures attributed to them over the years when in fact it is now thought they produced only one. Until now all the lures of Jacob Hansen and a man named Keller were erroneously lumped into one group under their name. The following information regarding Myers and Spellman was unearthed by National Fishing Lure Collectors Club member Harold Dickert. They were not a full-time lure manufacturing company, but in fact they were partners in the local Ford automobile dealership. When Dickert visited Shelby in the course of his research, he talked to local historians who told him they believed that the lures were actually made in the dealership garage. The number of them made is not known, but they certainly had to have made a fair bunch, because they did advertise the lure.

The lure is quite similar to the Keller Gets-Em as you can see by the photograph reproduced here and comes only with a belly hook rig. The Myers and Spellman product is the lure pictured at the bottom. The name "Myers" is usually found stamped along the back of the plug. Be sure to note the other differences so you won't confuse them should you encounter one.

The accompanying patent illustration of a lure patented by Myers, but not yet found by collectors. It may not have ever gone into production. Collector value range for the Myers and Spellman lure: $25 to $50.

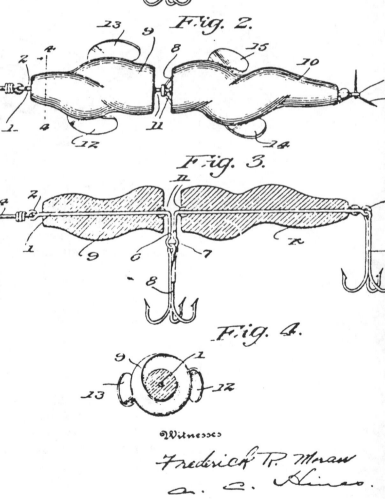

E. D. MYERS.
ARTIFICIAL BAIT.
APPLICATION FILED JULY 31, 1914.

Patented May 18, 1915.   1,140,279.

316

ARTIFICIAL MINNOW
R.F. O'Brien   Location unknown

There is very little known about this interesting lure. We have the example in the photograph and an incomplete patent application. We can't really even be absolutely certain the two match for there are differences. The lure and patent are so unusual and share so many characteristics, however, it is reasonable to match them up at this point in time. The body, painted red, white and black measures 3-5/8" and rotates around a thru-body wire armature. The words "PAT APPD FOR" are etched into the lower wire hook hanger and painted white. Collector value range: $40 to $80.

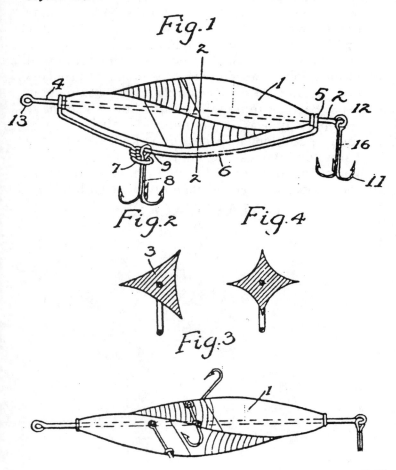

R. F. O'BRIEN.
ARTIFICIAL MINNOW.
APPLICATION FILED MAY 21, 1917.

1,256,155.   Patented Feb. 12, 1918.

Fig.1

Fig.2   Fig.4

Fig.3

NEAL SPINNERS
Columbus, Indiana

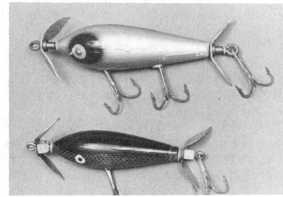

These two lures have only recently been discovered. Each has "Neal Spinner", Columbus, Indiana stenciled on the belly. No other information about the company or its products is known. The lures measure 3¼" for the larger and 2¾" for the smaller one. Note the unusual square piece on the propeller armatures on the lower plug in the photo. Collector value range: $5 to $10.

NIXON UNDERWATER
c1914
Frank T. Nixon, Grand Rapids, Michigan

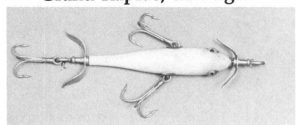

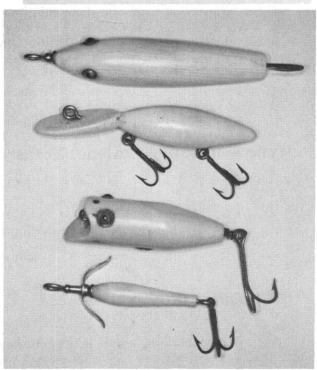

317

(cont'd next page)

Nixon (cont'd.)

The photo of the single lure accompanying is of the Nixon "THE ARISTOCRAT". It measures 3-1/4", has glass eyes and two propeller spinners. The lures in the photograph of four are all unidentified as to name, but are described as follows: The lure at top is glass eyed, has a flat belly and rigid mount single tail hook. The next lure has no eyes, measures 3-3/8" and is very similar to a Rush Tango. The third lure down has glass eyes, a belly hook (missing), tail hook and is 2-3/8" long. The bottom lure is a tiny 1 1/2" and has no eyes.

THE ARISTOCRAT is known to have been offered by Nixon as it was found in its original box. The box has a 1914 copyright date giving us a pretty good handle on the vintage. The box further stated that the lure was made of "PERSIAN IVORY" though this seems highly unlikely. It is more likely an early plastic and Nixon simply coined the name. They are handsome and look like ivory. The other four lures are included here as Nixon products because they are made of virtually the same material and utilize the same type hardware. Collector value range: $40 to $80.

NORTH COAST MINNOW
William Hoegee and Company
Location Unknown

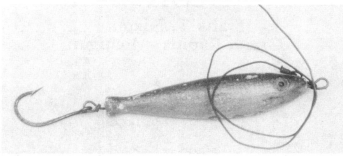

This 2 1/2" glass eyed lure is extremely similar to three other lures listed in this book. They are the H. C. Royer SOUTH COAST MINNOW, the Pflueger CATALINA, and the South Bend COAST MINNOW. It has a thru-body wire twisted on each end forming the line tie and the trailing hook hanger. There are three flush internal belly weights (visible in the photo). Collector value range: $20 to $40.

THE ACRO-JET
Ogene Company, Abilene, Texas

This is a 2 1/2" wooden plug. It is the only one found from this company so far. Perhaps some col-

lectors have other information to share. Probably dated around 1943-44. Collector value range: $3 to $6.

OSCAR THE FROG c1947
T. F. Auclair and Assoc. Inc., Detroit

This was an animated frog made of metal. It had a belly treble and a single hook mounted in each leg. Probably caught a lot of weeds. Collector value range: $4 to $8.

PACHNER and KOEHLER, INC.
Momence, Illinois

This company is better known as P and K. It had its beginnings in 1933 when Mr. Leo C. Pachner had a barber shop in Illinois. He began by selling a minnow saver hook put together and sold from the barber shop taking Koehler as a partner in 1934. In 1936 Pachner and his family went on the road pulling a house trailer and selling the hook to tackle retailers. As they began selling more and more items of tackle they founded the P & K corporation. They began manufacturing one of the first artificial lures made of rubber in 1939. World War II stopped their supply of hooks so they began manufacturing their own, eventually becoming the first U.S. manufacturers of treble hooks. The company blossomed into success but Pachner & Koehler liquidated the company in 1966. Pachner retired afterwards but like so many sedentary life was not for him. He is alive and well today, publishing a successful periodical called the **Farm Pond Harvest.** He still resides in Momence, Illinois. The following listing of P & K lures will cover the wooden and plastic plugs up to the early 1950's.

WALKIE TALKIE

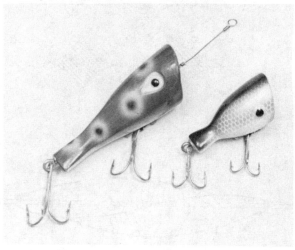

This was a plunker type lure made of Tenite. It had a belly treble and a trailing treble hook attached to a flared tail. It was available in two sizes (1-3/8" and 2-7/8"). By the 1950's the smaller size had been eliminated. Collector value range: $3 to $6.

CATALOG SERIES#	BODY LENGTH	LURE WEIGHT
43	1-3/8"	unk.
	2-7/8"	1/2 oz.

COLOR OR FINISH: *Red and white; Black and white; Frog; Yellow spot tail; Yellow perch; Pike; Green scale; Silver.*

AMAZIN' MAIZIE

This was a 5/8 oz., 2-1/4" lure made of Tenite. It had a diving lip, a belly treble, and a trailing treble hook. It is thought that the lure was named in honor of Pachner's wife. Collector value range: $3 to $6.

CATALOG SERIES–	BODY LENGTH	LURE WEIGHT
42	2½"	5/8 oz.

COLOR OR FINISH: *Red and white; Frog; Pike; Yellow perch; Black and white; Yellow spot tail; Green scale; Silver.*

BRIGHT EYES

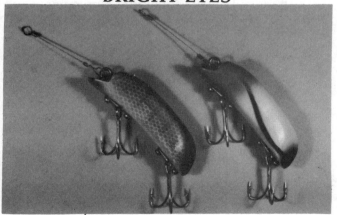

An odd shaped Tenite lure with two belly mounted trebles. It was a curved body and had a notch in the top of the head where the eyes and line tie are located. They were made a available with deep diving blade later. The weight is 1/2 ounce and body length, 2-3/4". Same colors as the "Walkie Talkie" Collector value range: $3 to $6.

DEEP RUNNING BRIGHT EYES

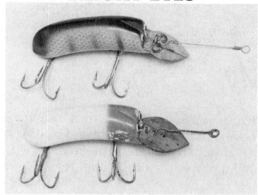

The same as the regular "Bright Eyes" but with the addition of a deep diving metal lip attached. Collector value range: $3 to $6.

SPINNING MINNIE

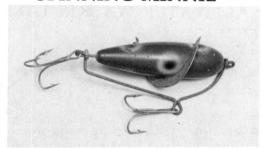

This is a Tenite plug with a small corkscrew ridge molded around the body to make it spin on retrieve. The hooks (2T) are mounted to a metal band attached to the nose and tail to allow the body to rotate freely maintaining the hooks in a down position. Available in two sizes (1½" and 3¼") the colors are not known. Collector value range: $3 to $6.

WHIRL-A-WAY c1942

This was a realistic looking plastic minnow with a double hook molded into the body. The minnow was attached to a wire leader with a weighted rudder on it. The lure was 3" and 5/8 oz. Apparently was available in only one color. Collector value range: $2 to $4.

LIPPY

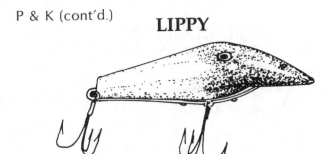

A strong saltwater plug with a sloped, sharp pointed nose. It had a belly treble and trailing treble hook, both attached to a metal piece running on the surface underside of the lure. Collector value range: $3 to $6.

CATALOG SERIES#	BODY LENGTH	LURE WEIGHT
63	7½"	3½ oz.

COLOR OR FINISH: *Red and white; Brown scale; Blue scale; Silver.*

SALTWATER WALKIE TALKIE

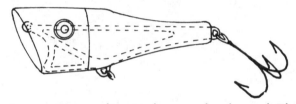

A very strong saltwater lure made of wood. There was a reinforced brass hook holding device, riveted and cemented into the body. It had a belly and trailing treble hook. Collector value range: $3 to $6.

CATALOG SERIES#	BODY LENGTH	LURE WEIGHT
62	5½"	3½ oz.

COLOR OR FINISH: *Red and white; Brown scale; Blue scale; Silver.*

CLIPPER TOP KICK

This lure was a plunker type. It had one belly treble and a trailing treble hook. It was available in only one size (3", ½ ounce) and the color options were: Red and white; yellow perch; pike; silver flitter; and frog. Collector value range: $3 to $6.

CLIPPER BASS WOBBLER

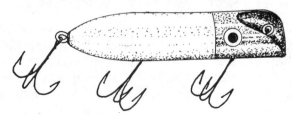

This lure had a scooped out nose, two belly trebles and a trailing treble hook. It came in two sizes: 2½", ½ ounce; 3¾", 5/8 ounce. The available colors were: red and white; yellow perch; pike; silver flitter. Collector value range: $3 to $6.

CLIPPER WIGGLER

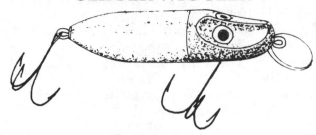

This plug was made in two sizes. It had two scooped out eye depressions rendering the nose slightly pointed. Both sizes had a round metal diving lip, a belly treble and trailing treble hook. Colors were exactly the same as the "Clipper Top Kick" above. Sizes: 2¾", ½ ounce; smaller size unknown. Collector value range: $3 to $6.

CLIPPER SURFACE SPINNER

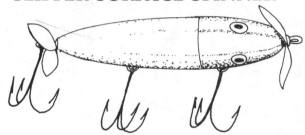

The Surface Spinner had a 3¾" body and weighed 5/8 ounce. It had two side trebles, a trailing treble hook, and fore and aft mounted propeller spinners. It was made in three finishes: red and white; frog; and pike. Collector value range: $3 to $6.

CLIPPER TINY MITE

This lure was a small 1¾", ½ ounce plug with round metal diving lip. It had one belly treble and one trailing treble hook. Colors were: red and white; frog; pike; yellow and black. Collector value range: $2 to $4.

(cont'd next page)

Clipper Tiny Mite (cont'd.)

Top row, left to right: SOFTY The Wonder Crab, two sizes of SPOTTY The Wonder Frog. Bottom left: a P and K fly rod popper. Bottom right: P and K Mouse.

CLIPPER ZIG ZAG

Made in two sizes (4", 5/8 ounce; 3", ½ ounce), both had two belly trebles and a trailing treble hook. Colors were: red and white; frog; pike; yellow and black. Collector value range: $3 to $6.

CLIPPER MINNOW

The minnow was made in two sizes: 4-1/8", 5/8 ounce; 3-3/8", 1/2 ounce. Each had a metal diving lip, two belly trebles and a trailing treble. Color options were: red and white; yellow perch; pike; and silver flitter. Collector value range: $3 to $6.

CLIPPER JOINTED PIKE

This was a jointed version of the "Clipper Minnow" above. The hooks and colors were the same. The joint was between the belly treble hooks. Collector value range: $3 to $6.

PAW PAW BAIT COMPANY
Paw Paw, Michigan

Catalog and all advertising studies have established that a transition of the Moonlight Bait Company to the Paw Paw Bait Company took place somewhere around 1927. Please see Moonlight Bait Company on page 302 for details leading up to the name change and early Paw Paw lures.

Paw Paw was in business continuously beginning around 1909 as the Moonlight Bait Company into the 1960's. In 1970 the Shakespeare Company bought out all Paw Paw rights and equipment, ending a long era of artificial bait production for the company.

It is known that Paw Paw produced many fine plugs with glass eyes but most found so far have tacks or brads for eyes. They were installed before painting the body and the greatest majority of those found have had the paint knocked off through use. The metal shows through in this case.

To help recognize a Paw Paw lure look for the one piece combination diving lip and forward hook hanger plainly visible in the photo of the Minnie Mouse at top left on page 324.

There are a number of lures listed and illustrated at the end of the section that have been attributed to Paw Paw because of the recognizable hardware or paint and pattern styles. They were not found cataloged.

(cont'd next page)

Paw Paw (cont'd.)

Here is an interesting piece of accessory fishing gear made by Paw Paw. They called it in the Scout. It was a collapsible shovel measuring 18¼ inches in the extended position and 11¾ inches collapsed. A 1930 catalog offered it to help get your vehicle unstuck or for use around a fishing camp. It was patented by Paw Paw.

LUCKY LURES BOX

It appears that Paw Paw began making a line or two of lures that were not as expensive to make as their regular lures. The second line was sold at lower prices or, as they say in some of their ad copy, "Designed to meet the popular demand for a good wood minnow at a moderate price." The unidentified plug on the "Lucky Lures" box is one of these.

I think the first of these to come along were the "Zipper" lures in the late '30's into the '40's.

PAW PAW FISH DECOY

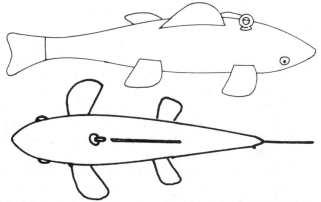

Found only in a 1929 catalog this critter was actually called "The Greatest Spearing Minnow." It had glass eyes, two painted metal fins on each side, a metal dorsal and tail fin. It has three internal belly weights. The only color listed was Perch, but there is at least one more called Red Horse. Collector value range: $20 to $30.

BULLHEAD SERIES

The lower plug in the photo here actually measures just a hair less than 4½" in body length although a 1931 catalogs states 4¼". This Bullhead is probably of earlier vintage than 1931 and most likely can be found with glass eyes. The examples above have tack or brad eyes (TPE). Collector value range: $10 to $20.

CATALOG SERIES#	BODY LENGTH	LURE WEIGHT
3500	4¼"	¾ oz.

COLOR OR FINISH: *Silver perch; White with red head; Pearl finish with red head; Frog finish; Dark brown; Black with red spots.*

THE CRAB

Not found in any of the available catalogs. This lure has a wooden body and two braided feelers trailing. The two examples shown here have glass eyes and measure 2¼" in body length. Dates and color finishes unknown. Collector value range: $10 to $15.

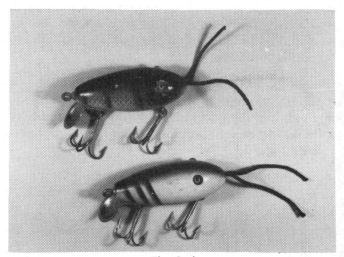

The Crab

322

Paw Paw (cont'd.)
CRAWDAD

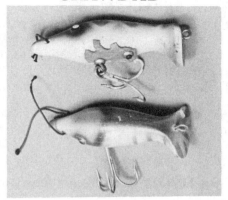

The two plugs in the accompanying photograph illustrate the typical condition they are found in. The lures both originally had two claws and six legs made of flexible rubber. Only a small piece of the rubber remains on the upper lure in the photo. Original models probably have glass eyes and occur only in a natural crawfish finish. Later models (c1931 and later) will have the tack painted eyes (TPE) and several other finishes as listed below.
Collector value range: $5 to $10.

CATALOG SERIES#	BODY LENGTH	LURE WEIGHT
500	2¾"	¾ oz.

COLOR OR FINISH: *Yellow with black stripes; Solid black; Green with black stripes; Solid red; Brown with black stripes; Black with yellow stripes.*

CRIPPLED MINNOW
PAW PAW INJURED MINNOW
3400 Series

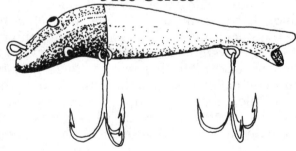

Sometimes called the Crippled Minnow in Paw Paw catalogs, this is an unusual lure that must have been difficult to make. It has glass eyes and two side mounted trebles. I have not actually seen one, but a very good catalog illustration shows what appears to be a through-body wire with line tie at the nose ending in the aft treble hook hanger just forward of the tail. First found listed in a 1928 Mixed Tackle catalog of the Shapleigh Hardware Company. Collector value range: $10 to $20.

CATALOG SERIES#	BODY LENGTH	LURE WEIGHT
3400	4"	5/8 oz.

COLORS OR FINISH: *Green scale; White with red head; Pearl with red head; Silver scale; Gold scale; Frog finish.*

LIPPY JOE LURES

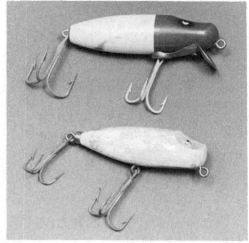

The two lures here are thought to be Lippy Joes. The catalogs in the author's possession list only two sizes the regular and the Baby Lippy Joe (sizes listed below). They measure 3-1/8" and 2-¾" respectively. Although only one matches the catalog size, the body styles seem to identify them. The smaller, light colored plug with the tail cup and no lip may be an early model. Collector value range: $3 to $6.

CATALOG SERIES#	BODY LENGTH	LURE WEIGHT
1200	2¼"	3/8 oz.

COLOR OR FINISH: *Yellow scale, silver ribs; White with red head and silver ribs; Black with silver flitter; Yellow perch; Frog finish.*

PAW PAW MOUSE BAIT

CATALOG SERIES #	BODY LENGTH	LURE WEIGHT
40	2½"	5/8 oz.

COLOR FINISH: *Solid brown; White body, red head; Black body, white head; Solid black; Solid white; Solid gray.*

CATALOG SERIES #	BODY LENGTH	LURE WEIGHT
*50	2½"	5/8 oz.

COLOR OR FINISH: *Mouse color (gray); Black body, white head; White body, red head.*
Also availble in brown, gray or white fur finish by 1949.

(cont'd next page)

Paw Paw Mouse (cont'd.)

Newer vintage Paw Paw Mouse (Series #40). Dates from about 1931 to the 1950's. Flexible leather tail. One-piece combination diving lip and hook hanger. Later called MINNIE MOUSE. Collector value range: $5 to $10.

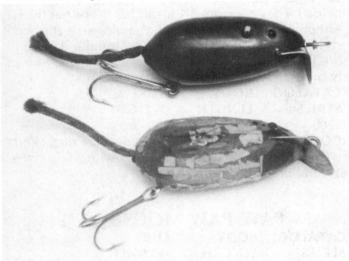

Oldest Paw Paw Mouse or early Moonlight Mouse (Series #50). Dates from around 1929 to 1930. Flexible braided tail, ears. Simple screw-eye hook mount. Collector value range: $10 to $20.

NATURAL HAIR MOUSE

Large and small Paw Paw Natural Hair Mouse lures.

The earliest reference found was in a mixed tackle catalog of 1928 from the Shapleigh Hardware Company. It listed and pictured the #60 Hair Mouse.

A 1929 catalog introduced the larger size as new. It was offered as the Musky Mouse and Sea Mouse, the latter being "...weighted for saltwater fishing." The photo above illustrates another model but no reference to it has been found to date. It had an arrow shaped metal diving lip that has the patent date "1-22-29" stamped on it. Collector value range: $10 to $20.

CATALOG SERIES#	BODY LENGTH	LURE WEIGHT
60	2½"	5/8 oz.
80	4¼"	

COLOR OR FINISH: *Gray; Yellow head; Red head; White.*

OLD FLATSIDE
OLD FLATSIDE JUNIOR
(also called Wounded Minnow)

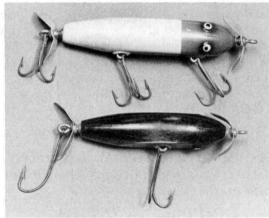

The earliest listing I found was in a 1939 catalog. This was for a flat side floater, 3½ inches long with only one side treble and a trailing treble (2T). A 1940 catalog listed a two side treble version (3T). In 1941 only the single side hook (2T) was offered and then in 1942 they were back to the 3T version. Why this swapping back and forth is anybody's guess. By 1949 both were finally offered in the catalog. All of these were cataloged at 3½ inches long but, as you can see in the photograph, the 2T version was shorter. It actually measured 2½ inches. The 3T actual measurement is 3 inches not as cataloged, 3½ inches. As you can see in the photograph, there are two distinctly different eye locations. Both types appear in catalog illustrations throughout the years. That probably represents the use of different cuts, regardless of design changes. Earliest Flatsides had glass eyes mounted at the sides of the head, then came tack painted eyes (TPE) on the sides, the TPE on top. In 1940 they introduced a version covered with real frog skin. Collector value range: $3 to $6.

CATALOG SERIES #	BODY LENGTH	LURE WEIGHT
1500	2½"	
2500	3"	3/4 oz.

COLOR OR FINISH: *Yellow perch; White with red head; Shad; Pike scale; Frog; Silver flitters; Dace; Black with silver flitters; Gold shiner scale; Green with gold dots; Rainbow; Perch scale.*

BASS SEEKER

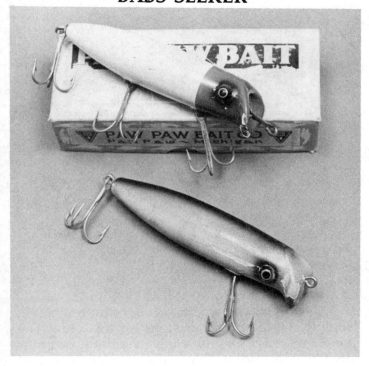

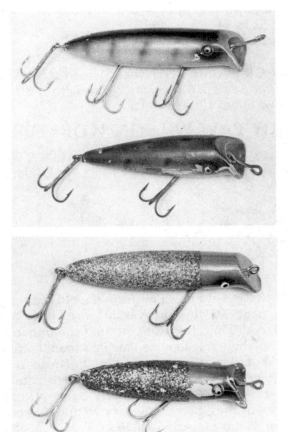

First found in a 1928 mixed tackle catalog, this is a lure retained from the old Moonlight Bait Company line (see page 258). It has a cupped head with a short heavy wire line tie attached to the screw eye and a projecting underjaw. They were first available with glass eyes than tack painted eyes (see photos). They came equipped with either two or three treble

hooks and were made in two sizes. The two examples in the photographs that do not have cupped heads were not found in any catalogs or advertisements, but they are obviously the Bass Seeker bodies. Collector value range: $5 to $10.

CATALOG SERIES –	BODY LENGTH	LURE WEIGHT
2600	4''	¾ oz.
4600	3¼''	¾ oz.

COLOR OR FINISH: *Green scale; White with Red head; Pearl finish with red head; Gold scale; Frog finish; Perch; Metallic Glitters; Red head, gold body; Red head, green body; Perch finish with green and silver metallic flitters; Red head, silver body.*

PIKE MINNOW LURE

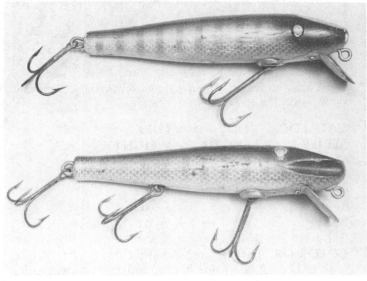

The photo here shows two body styles of this Paw Paw great. The upper plug in the photo is a dead ringer for the older model illustrated in a 1931 catalog. They were then available with only two treble hooks. Later models had three trebles and a groove on each side of the nose. All lures in the photos have the typical Paw Paw tack painted eyes and combination one piece diving plane and forward hook mount. Collector value range: $3 to $6.

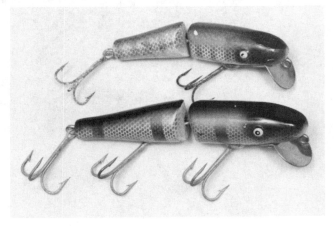

(cont'd next page)

Paw Paw (cont'd.)

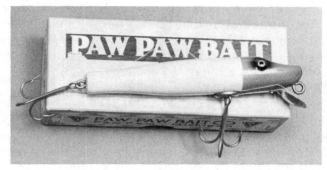

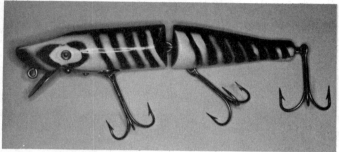

This is a rare glass eyed version in the musky size. 6¼". Collector value range: $10 to $20.

CATALOG SERIES #	BODY LENGTH	LURE WEIGHT
Musky	6¼"	2-3/8 oz.
Musky Jtd.	6¼"	2-3/8 oz.
Regular	4½"	3/4 oz
Regular Jtd.	4½"	3/4 oz.
Baby	3¼"	½ oz.
Baby Jtd.	3¼"	½ oz.

COLOR OR FINISH: *Green scale; Gold scale; *White with red head; Pearl finish; Frog finish; *Yellow perch; *Pike scale; *Silver flitters; **Shad; **Dace; **Black with silver flitters; **Gold shiner scale.*
*The only finish available by the late 1940's.
**Added in 1949.

PAW PAW RIVER TYPE

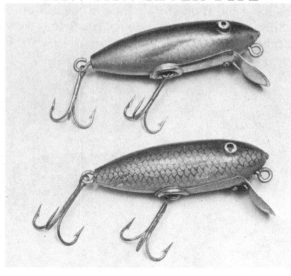

The photos below left and above represent two slightly different body designs for this plug. The more tapered body and relatively blunt nose plugs are likely the oldest. The body measurement of all four plugs in the photos is 2½". Collector value range: $2 to $4.

SERIES #	LENGTH	WEIGHT
900	2-5/8"	1/2 oz.

COLOR OR FINISH: *Perch scale; Green scale; Silver scale; Pike scale; Frog scale; White with red head; Rainbow; Silver flitters.*

PAW PAW WILSON WOBBLER

Carried over to Paw Paw from the old Moonlight line (see page 302) this lure was last listed in catalogs of the early 1930's. It is not certain if the one in the photograph here is a genuine Paw Paw manufactured Wilson Wobbler. It is pictured here because of the typical Paw Paw painted cup hardware. The catalogs listed it as 4 inches long, weight ¾ ounce. It came with three trebles, two trebles or two double hooks. Collector value range: $3 to $6.
COLORS AVAILABLE: *White with red flutes; Red; Yellow; Rainbow; Fox fire.*

BULL FROG

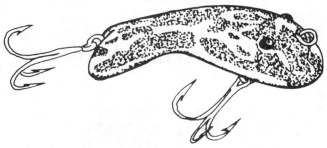

A 1929 catalog listed and pictured this unusual glass eyed lure. The drawing above is an exact copy of the catalog photograph. It was missing from catalogs by 1939. Size was not given but colors listed were: Bull Frog Finish and White with Red Head. Collector value range: $10 to $20.

FOX FIRE

This is the famous Moonlight Floating Bait (see page 259) retained by Paw Paw from the old Moonlight line. They simply changed the name and continued to offer it in their catalogs until 1939 when it disappeared from their line. They were 4 inches long with a belly treble and trailing treble hook (2T) and two color options: Fox Fire and White body with Red head. Collector value range: $2 to $4.

PAW PAW POPPER

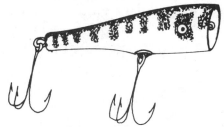

The Popper dates from about the early 1930's and was missing from catalogs by 1949. Earliest examples will have glass eyes. Collector value range: $2. to $4.

CATALOG SERIES #	BODY LENGTH	LURE WEIGHT
2200	3''	¾ oz.

COLORS AND FINISHES: *Yellow Perch; Rainbow; Green, Gold scale; Pike scale; Perch scale; White, Red head; Frog; Silver Flitters; Genuine Frog skin covering (1940).*

PLUNKER

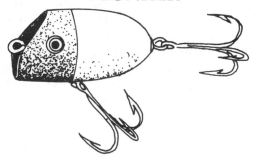

First found in a 1929 catalog this lure came in only one size: 2 inches, ¾ ounce. Catalog copy says "It is the result of a year's experimenting..."
COLORS: *Yellow; White with Red head; Black with White head; Silver; Frog; Perch.*
Collector value range: $2 to $4.

CASTING LURE

A 1930's propeller spinner bait that came only in White body, red head, and no eyes. It had only one treble (belly mounted) and was 2 inches long weighing ½ ounce. Collector value range: $2 to $4.

SHORE MINNOW

I could find only one illustrated catalog entry for this lure. It was in a new line of plastic lures for 1949. This one, however, is made of wood, in mint condition with original box. The box had no identification of the lure. Collector value range: $2 to $4.

PAW PAW PLENTY SPARKLE

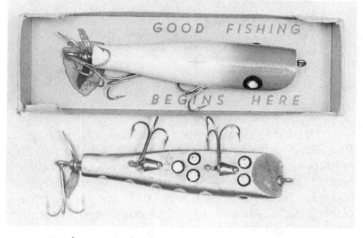

Aptly named, this wooden lure came in two sizes. The one in the photograph is the larger (4'') size and the other is the Plenty Sparkle Junior at 3¼''

Paw Paw Plenty Sparkle (cont'd.)

The larger size has five rhinestones on the belly as in the photograph and the smaller has only three. Both had rhinestone eyes. Box marking identified the series as No. 5500. Collector value range: $5 to $10. **Colors were:** *White with red head; Frog finish with white belly; Frog finish with yellow belly; Blue mullet; Silver Flash.*

CASTER BAITS

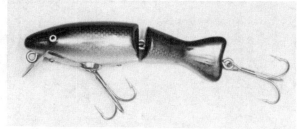

The three photographs here show five of this Paw Paw series introduced in 1941. All the series, sometimes called "Nature Baits", are wood-bodied and all but the large Saltwater and Muskie series Casters have the minnow tail shown in the photographs. All also have the combination round diving lip/forward hook hanger. There are nine different lures in the series, each in small and/or large size with different hook configurations and some

jointed versions making a total of 23 for the entire line. There are 18 different colors or finishes available, making the collection of all these quite a challenge if you're so inclined. Sizes range from 3¼" to 6½". Collector value range: $3 to $6.

PUMPKIN SEED

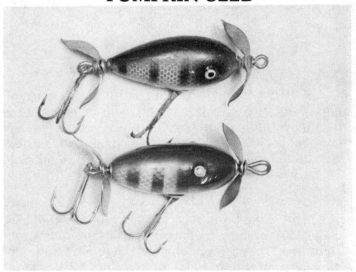

First available sometime in the 1930's, these small lures had two propeller spinners, trailing treble and belly mount treble utilizing cup and screw eye hardware. Made only in a 1-7/8 inches, ½ ounce size, the colors available were: Yellow Perch; Green, Gold dots; White, red head; Rainbow; Pike scale; Perch scale; Frog; Silver Flitters. Collector value range: $2 to $4.

SKIPPY MINNOW

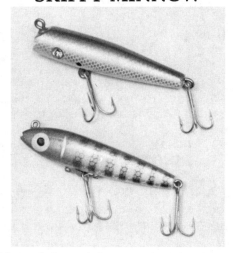

Neither of the two lures in the photograph above actually match the illustrations in the catalogs and are otherwise unidentified. They are placed here because of their similarity to the Skippy Minnow catalog entries. Collector value range: $2 to $4.

THE SHINER

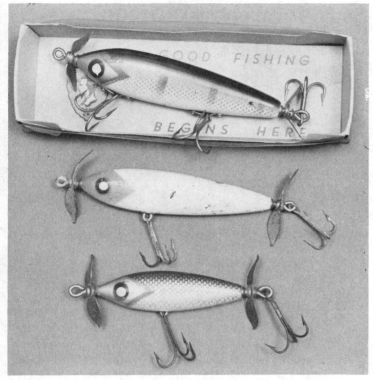

First available in a 1942 catalog. The boxed lure in the photo is the #8501 yellow perch finish. The lures were made in weighted and unweighted models and in a "Jr." size. Collector value range: $3 to $6.

CATALOG SERIES #	BODY LENGTH	LURE WEIGHT
8400 (Jr.)	2¾"	3/8 oz.
8500	3½"	½ oz.
8600	4"	¾ oz.

COLOR OR FINISH: *Yellow belly, brown and silver back; Yellow perch; Green scale; White with red head; Shad; Pike scale; Silver flitters.*

SLIM LINDY
or
TORPEDO

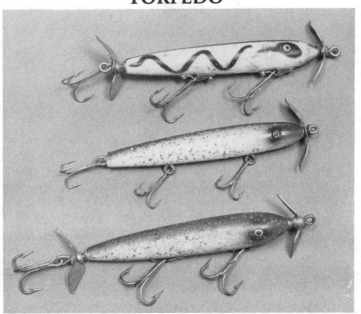

In a 1929 catalogs this lure was called Slim Lindy apparently in honor of Charles Lindbergh, who made his famous trans-atlantic solo flight in May of 1927. It was called the Torpedo by 1939 or so. The photo shows three hardware types to be found. The upper lure is the latest, having the one piece hook hanger. The center lure is probably the earliest of the three- because it has only the simple screw-eye hanger. The tail propeller has apparently been removed. The lure on the right has the cup hardware. Oldest of the Slim Lindys will likely have glass eyes. Collector value range: $3 to $6.

CATALOG SERIES #	BODY LENGTH	LURE WEIGHT
2400	4"	5/8 oz.

COLOR OR FINISH: *Green scale; *Gold scale; *White with red head; *Rainbow; *Frog finish; *Perch; Yellow perch; Pike scale; Silver flitters; White with black serpentine stripe; Whtie with green serpentine stripe; Green with black serpentine stripe; White with vertical black stripe.*

WEEDLESS WOW

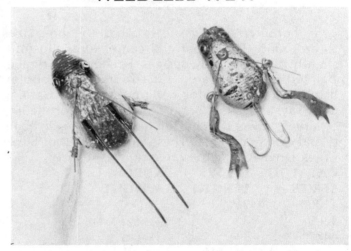

Called "New" in a 1941 catalog the photo here shows two sizes of Weedless Wows. The larger measures 2¼" and the smaller, 1¾" body lengths. Note the rubber legs and fixed double hook on the smaller size (not found in catalogs). Collector value range: $5 to $10.

CATALOG SERIES #	BODY LENGTH	LURE WEIGHT
600	1¾"	½ oz.
	2¼"	

COLOR OR FINISH: *Perch scale; Pike scale; Red head; Frog finish; Silver flitters; Flourescent.*

The original finishes available on the Slim Lindy. All but the white body red head pattern had been eliminated by 1950.

WOBBLER

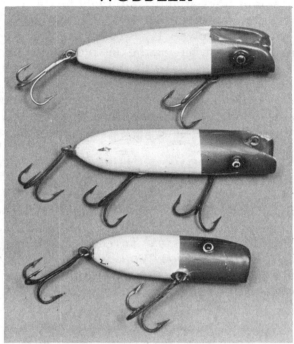

Photograph above shows two of the three sizes to be found. The upper and center lures illustrate slightly different body designs. Each has the typical painted cup hardware. I first found the Wobblers listed in a 1939 catalog calling them new. Catalog copy says they were part of an extension of the line of lures "...lower in price, but lacking nothing in quality and workmanship..." These were called the "Silver Creek Line." Collector value range: $2 to $4.

CATALOG SERIES #	BODY LENGTH	LURE WEIGHT
4100	2½"	
4200	3"	½ oz.
4400	3¾"	¾ oz.

COLOR OR FINISH: *White body, red head; Perch scale; Pike scale; Silver flitters; Yellow perch; Rainbow; Frog; White, red and green spots.*

CROAKER

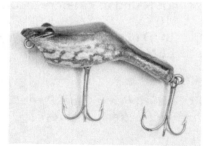

This frog plug was apparently new in 1940. It has a covering of genuine frog skin. It came in two sizes. The one in the photograph is the larger (3"). The smaller size (1¼") had a slightly different body design and only one integrated single hook. Collector value range: $5 to $10.

WOTTA-FROG
and
WOTTA-FROG, JR.

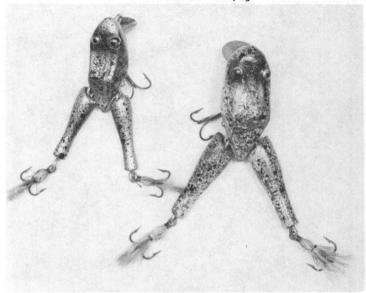

Catalog listing stated "New for 1941". As you can see in the photograph, they had hair or modified buck tail and tied to each of the three treble hooks. To find them with the hair/trebles intact is fairly unusual. Collector value range: $3 to $6.

CATALOG SERIES #	BODY LENGTH	LURE WEIGHT
#72	2½"	½ oz.
#73	3¼"	5/8 oz.
#74	4"	7/8 oz.

COLOR OR FINISH: *Found in green with paint spatter-finish only.*

#2400 Series
#200 Series

This boxed, mint condition plug states #2407 on the box. It looks very much like a #200 Series Shore Minnow except larger. The #2400 Series was not found in available catalogs and only a picture, name and number was found of the #200 Series. The #2400 in the photo above is white with a red head and measures 4-3/8" in body length. Collector value range: $5 to $10.

Paw Paw (cont'd.)

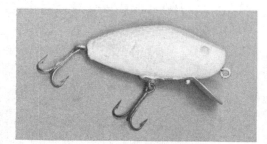

Unidentified Paw Paw lure.

Unidentified Paw Paw

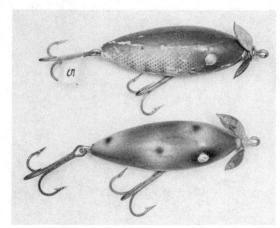

These two unknown Paw Paw lures bear a striking similarity to the Pumpkin Seeds but are much larger. Both have typical Paw Paw characteristics.

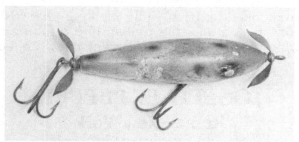

Unidentified Paw Paw lure.

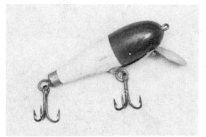

This little fellow has the characteristic Paw Paw combination diving lip and forward hook hanger hardware. Otherwise dissimilar to any Paw Paw lure found in catalogs and illustrations.

Unidentified Paw Paw lure.

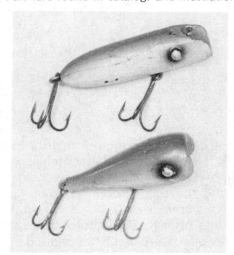

Two unidentified Paw Paw type lures.

331

PAYNE'S HUMANE WOGGLE BUG
Payne Bit Co.   **Chicago, IL**

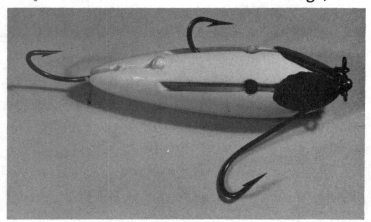

This 3¼" plug was available only in a white body, red head finish. It was first found advertised in an April, 1915 edition of THE OUTER'S BOOK, a popular outdoors magazine of the era, but seldom found advertised after. The same edition wrote the lure up along with five others as new for 1915. There were metal clips in the body slots to hold the hooks in until a strike whereupon the fish would pull the hook away from the lure body. The above mentioned article claimed that while fishing the lure a fisherman hooked a bass while fighting that fish a second bass struck the trailing lure resulting in a double catch. I have heard taller tales. Collector value range: $40 to $80.

JOSEPH E. PEPPER
Rome, New York

It is difficult to sort out all known and suspected Joe Pepper lures. Some are readily identifiable as Pepper by obvious characteristics and/or the Pepper name stamped on metal parts. Others attributed to him are as a result of his peculiar habit of painting gill stripes on the lure opposite to the direction of actual fish gills; the method used by just about every other lure maker. See examples of this characteristic in some of the photos following.

Not much about Pepper has yet been ferreted out. The first reference I was able to find was a 1902 advertisement for NEW CENTURY BALL SPINNERS. His use of "New Century" implies he was in business before or just at the turn of the century. Ads for Pepper lures seem to disappear about 1923. His products seem to run the gamut from crude to high gloss with quality hardware. This may have simply been the evolution from beginning to end in response to demand. They are found with no eyes, painted eyes and glass eyes and several quite dissimilar body styles. Often the glass eyes are placed in the head so that the lure appears to be looking forward, or for some strange reason, cock-eyed. This arrangement is, as far as I can determine, a uniquely Pepper characteristic. Many of the metal parts are stamped

with his name and/or patent dates though I was unable to uncover any actual patents. The metal fins he used are most often found painted bright red. Pepper seemed to have used whatever propeller spinners were readily available, for many different types are found on his lures.

ROMAN SPIDERS

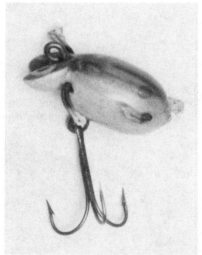

These came along sometime prior to 1915. The large (4-¾") Musky size had no notched or split head as do the two smaller sizes. The Bass or Pickerel sizes is 3¼" and the Baby Roman Spider, 1-3/4". Most found have a crackle back finish. All will have string or twine legs or at least the holes through the body where they once were. Each has painted eyes. All are very scarce and command a collector value range of $40 to $80.

Pepper (cont'd.)

REVOLVING MINNOW

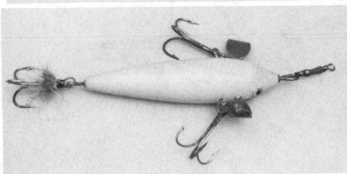

The REVOLVING MINNOW was introduced in 1911. They are extremely well made with high quality paint and hardware. A unique feature is the removable fins. If you didn't want the lure to revolve you simply unscrewed the fins. They were soldered to screw eyes to facilitate their removal without a screw driver. The sidehook hangers were twisted wire thru-body. Both in the photos here have yellow glass eyes. the large size is 3½" and the small, 2½". Collector value range for the REVOLVING MINNOW: $50 to $100 (small), $40 to 60 (large).

YANKEE AERO

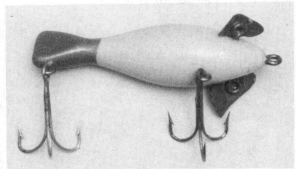

The photo is of the belly of the YANKEE AERO showing the method of providing adjustable or removable fins as discussed in the Revolving Minnow previously. Note the fins are soldered to screw eyes. The lure was said to be available in four colors in an ad, but the only one listed was White with Red tail. This very well made 4½" plug was also available in a jointed version. Painted eyes or no eyes. Collector value range: $100 to $150.

ROMAN REDTAIL MINNOW

The REDTAIL came along about 1912. Another well made quality lure by Pepper, it too had adjustable side fins. In addition it had another fin fixed at the bottom of the tail. It was made in two sizes, 2½" and 3¼", had glass eyes and thru-body wire line tie and tail hook hanger. The belly view photograph clearly shows the Pepper reverse gill marks. Collector value range for the ROMAN REDTAIL MINNOW: $50 to $100.

THE ROAMER BAIT

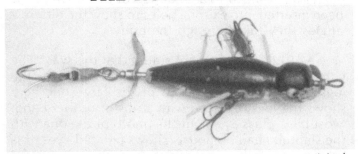

Pepper ROAMER BAIT. The rear propeller spinner is not original.

Pepper BABY ROAMER BAIT.

333

Pepper (cont'd.)

Pepper ROAMER BAIT body with a slant head (see text)

Two 3" ROAMER type lures. The wires sticking out each side of the lures are not part of them. They have been inserted into existing holes to show the different angles they take through the body.

A 1912 advertisement stated that this was "The Latest Bait on the Market." The ad text also said the legs were white. The photo of the large one here shows the legs replaced with strips of rubber band. Most have glass eyes, but the photo of the one with the slanted head obviously shows painted eyes. It is known this slant was production because it has the standard Pepper style painted eyes on the face. They were made in two sizes, 1-3/4" and 3". Colors were: Yellow body with green head and green back with yellow belly. Collector value range for the ROAMER: $20 to $100.

PEP'S DELTA BUG SPINNER. Collector value range: $5 to $15.

PEP'S STREAMLINE MINNOW. Lead body, red and white. Collector value range: $5 to $15.

PEPPER UNDERWATER MINNOW

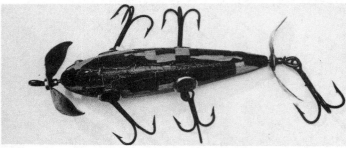

We can't be absolutely certain that the lures in the two photos here are Pepper products, but hardware and the reverse gill stripes make them likely candidates. Both have yellow glass eyes. The 5T model has cup and thru-body wire hook hangers. Collector value range: $50 to $100.

The upper lure in the above photo is a known Pepper UNDERWATER MINNOW. The lower lure is not, but was bought by a collector thinking it to be a Pepper because of the Pepper or Pepper-like hardware. Upon closer examination it was found to be a hand-whittled plug, with decidedly non-Pepper flat sides. It also sports unusual blue glass bead eyes. The latter would not necessarily be a surprise given Pepper's proclivity for using whatever materials were at hand, but the rest say it isn't a Pepper prodduct. This is placed here to illustrate how careful you need to be when identifying a possible purchase. If you bit on the lower lure you would have made a $40 to $60 mistake. Collector value range for Pepper Underwaters: $40 to $60.

MISCELLANEOUS PEPPER LURES

The following photographs are of mostly Pepper lures and a few other unidentified ones for comparison are offered as an aid to Pepper identification. Because of the wide variety of styles, quality and hardware encountered with the lures, identification can sometimes prove difficult.

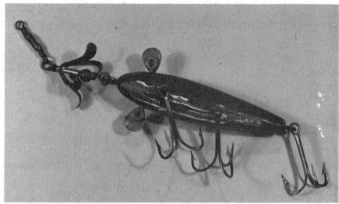

The two photos above are of the side and belly of a 3-3/8" lure with painted eyes and a black back and red belly. The fancy propeller spinner is exactly like one on the illustration of the 20TH CENTURY WONDER MINNOW in a 1904 Pepper advertisement. The propeller spinners are unmarked. It has simple screw eye hook hangers. Collector value range: $50 to $100.

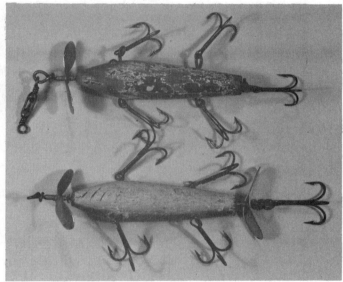

The 2-7/8" Pepper lures above share the same paint, same glass eyes and tube-type propeller spinners. The upper lure has thru-body bent wire hook hardware and the lower, thru-body twisted wire hardware. Both are found on Pepper lures. Note the typical Pepper reverse gill marks visible on the lower lure. Collector value range: $40 to $60.

The lure above measures 2½". It has the same propeller spinner as the previous lure. The inscription "JE PEPPER ROME NY" is stamped on one of the blades. It has yellow glass eyes and a single red glass bearing bead at the nose. There was apparently a second hook, in the belly, for the hole is there. Collector value range: in this condition: $50 to $100.

This plug has had the paint finish stripped off. It is a round body lure with big glass eyes. It has a pair of red glass bearing beads fore and aft and Pepper style thru-body hook hangers. The second set of hooks is missing from this originally five-hook plug. Collector value range: $30 to $50.

This little fellow measures 1¾" and is made very much in the style of the Heddon Artistic Minnow. The propeller spinner is typical Pepper as is the forward looking eye. Collector value range: $100 to $200.

Pepper (cont'd.)

Although they are not easily seen in this photo, the body is decorated with gold dots. This was often used by Pepper. The lure is 3¼" long and has forward looking yellow eyes. The two metal flippers are attached by a bent thru-body wire with washers. One of the flipper blades is stamped "JE PEPPER ROME, NY". Collector value range: $50 to $100.

This 3" plug is typical Pepper. It has forward looking yellow glass eyes, a single internalized belly weight and thru-body bent wire hook hangers and line tie. Collector value range: $50 to $100.

This jointed lure is 3" long. It is not found catalogued in any Pepper literature. It is attributed to Pepper because of the paint job and the fact that it was found in Rome, NY. It has a screw eye and washer belly hook hanger. Collector value range: $40 to $60.

This is another unknown lure that has been attributed to Pepper because of its typical Pepper paint finish. It measures 1-11/16" long. Collector value range: $20 to $40.

PFLUEGER

The earliest Pflueger research material available to the author is dated about 1921, but the company was actually established in 1864 by E. F. Pflueger as the American Fish Hook Company. Over the years it continued to exist in the Pflueger family hands variously as the Akron Fishing Tackle Works, The Enterprise Manufacturing Company, and finally, Pflueger Fishing Tackle. The company has almost always concentrated very heavily in reels and many types of metal spinner and spoon type artificial baits. These metal lures are numerous and not covered here. The following pages catalog the majority of the wooden plugs manufactured over the years to the early 1950's.

Pflueger patents include lumnious paint on the fishing lures (first used on his lures in the mid-1880's. The patent was granted to him on February 12 1883. It is reproduced on page 75. Another important Pflueger patent was for the Neverfail hook hanger granted on October 29, 1911.

The Pflueger Company continues in business today.

OBSERVATIONS REGARDING IDENTIFYING AND DATING PFLUEGER LURES:
1. Hook Hardware
   a. First was a through-body twisted wire type. Some were bare and some had a small washer against the body. Neither lasted long.
   b. There are a few very early Pflueger lures that used the see-through gem-clip type hangers. Pflueger even patented this in 1910, but it was quickly abandoned due to the prior Rhodes patent in 1904 for about the same thing (see pages 77 and 78).
   c. After the above problem, Pflueger developed their Neverfail hardware and it was patented in 1911.
   d. Patent date for their one-piece surface hook hanger was 1922, so the transition from Neverfail to one-piece surface should be in the 1920-22 time frame.
2. Propeller Spinners
   a. First use propellers were both bow tie floppy and bow tie tube types.
   b. By 1908 the propellers were more refined, smooth edge, pointed blade ends. It has been reported they used a few one-notch blades at this point, but this was very limited.
   c. They began marking their propellers sometime around 1910-12. The first ones were marked only with the word "PFLUEGER". The next mark was the Pflueger Bull Dog brand.

(cont'd next page)

336

Pflueger (cont'd.)

3. Eyes
   a. Eye types are not a very good guide to dating Pflueger lures as they used glass eyes, no eyes and painted eyes at the same time through many years, according to the four grades of lures they made.

Top: Whoopee Spinner - 1930, Middle; O'Boy Spinner - 1932, Bottom: Red Devil - 1926.

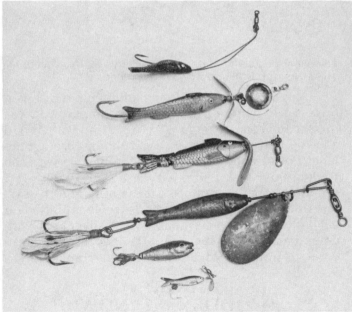

Top to bottom these rubber Pflueger lures are 1-Soft Rubber Casting Minnow c1897; 2-Razem Minnow; 3-Teelan c1930; 4-unidentified rubber minnow; 5-Biz Minnow #3400.

FLYING HELGRAMITE

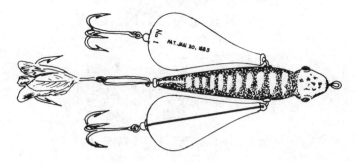

An 1885 catalog offers this very early, very rare wood body lure in four luminous models. It is obviously taken from the Comstock patent of January 30, 1883 (see page 74). I couldn't find it listed in any of the other Pflueger catalogs in the collection. The illustration with the entry clearly shows the Comstock patent date on the metal "wings." This is one of the earliest known wood body lures to be commercially produced. The only earlier one known is the 1876 Brush patent with a cork body. Collector value range: $400 to $600.

BREAKLESS DEVON

This all-metal lure was patented August 5, 1879 by Archer Wakeman of Cape Vincent, New York. It was routinely offered in the Pflueger catalog of 1897 (earliest in my possesion) in five sizes. By 1906 the Devon was available "Painted" in luminous and non-luminous or in "Bass, Nickel or Gilt." By 1919 the catalog entry was only "Polished Nickel Over All." In the 1920's it was Nickel and Copper only. It gained the single blade spinner in the photograph about this time as well. The lure was offered continuously in

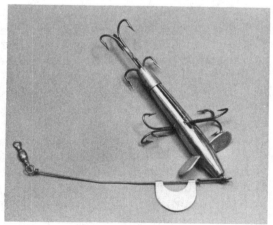

Breakless Devon

those two finishes and five sizes right on into the 1950's. Sizes were: 2", 2¼", 2½", 2-¾" and 3". Collector value range: $8 to $16.

WIZARD
(WOODEN MINNOW)

Wizard Wooden Minnow #315 with its original wooden box.

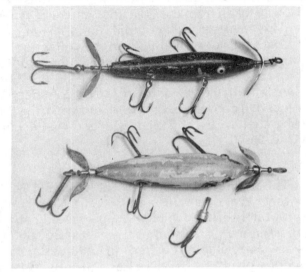

Upper lure is a Wizard #315 5T. Note the old propellers and especially the through-body twisted wire side hook hangers. Lower lure has machine threaded screw in hook hanger, is very strong and very unique. These are not found often and probably represent experimentation while they were looking for a new strong hook hanger. They finally settled on the Neverfail.

This glass eye plug is another of the earlier ones manufactured under the Enterprise name. The name was later used on an entirely different lure. (see page 296). It was made in four different sizes (2½", 3", The 2½" size had only one treble mounted on each hooks (two mounted on each side and one trailing). The 3½" size had only one treble mounted on each side and one trailing (3T). All four had nose and tail mounted propellers rotating on a common wire shaft running through the length of the wedge shaped body. It had glass eyes and finishes available are currently unknown to the author. This plug does not appear in the 1925 or subsequent catalogs. Collector value range: $40 to $80.

This is a three hook 2½" WIZARD. It has yellow glass eyes and 1 internal belly weight. You probably can't see them but the metal ball bearing beads at the aft end of each of the propeller spinners is faceted. Collector value range: $40 to $80.

COMPETITOR
(WOODEN MINNOW)

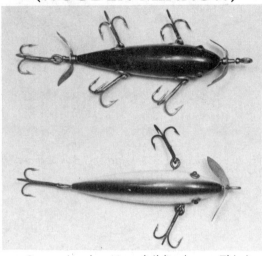

The upper Competitor has Neverfail hardware. This is unusual. The lower lure is typical of the Competitor.

This is another early lure manufactured by Enterprise (Early name of the Pflueger company). It was produced in four sizes (2½", 3" 3½" and 5"). It had a round body with a wire shaft running through the length of the body connecting the line tie with the trailing hook link and brass washer and tack eyes. It had a propeller mounted at the nose and the tail, one treble hook trailing, and one treble mounted on each side (3T). Colors available were: silver belly with green back; solid silver color. It does not appear in catalogs from 1925 on. Collector value range: $10 to $20.

TRORY
(WOODEN MINNOW)

This is probably among the earliest (c1900) wooden plugs in the Pflueger line (actually manufactured by Enterprise). It was shaped like a minnow with propellers fore and aft. It sported five treble hooks, one trailing and two mounted on each side. It had glass eyes and the body was about four inches long. These were only two finishes available, a luminous and non-luminous. It does not appear at all in catalogs from 1925 on. The collector value range is from: $150 to $300. Please read Kent section on page 287 for detailed discussion of this lures history. (photo on next page.).

Pflueger (cont'd.)

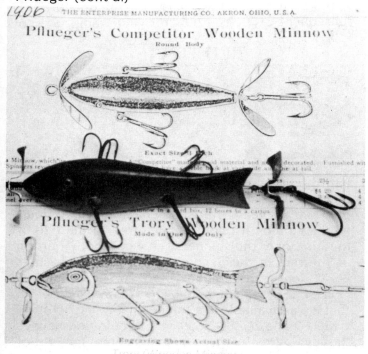

CONRAD FROG

Mr. Frog first shows up in this model in 1905. It was available in a weedless version in the same style as the regular one in the photograph here. Both were available in luminous and non-luminous finishes. The very first ones (pre-1905) were made of pressed ground cork but subsequent to that they were made of rubber. Collector value range: $5 to $10.

THE "MONARCH" MINNOWS
(pre 1925)(See Neverfail)

There were several types and sizes of plugs that were called "Monarch." They were made as floating, underwater, and strong underwater especially for Muskellonge fishing. It is known that the regular underwater and the floating versions came packed in wooden slide cover boxes. The collector will be fortunate indeed to find one in the very rare original packing box. None of these plugs are found in 1925 or later catalogs. Collector value range for the Monarchs is from $20 to $40.

The MONARCH Underwater (2100 series) was made in two different sizes (2¾" and 3-5/8"). The smaller had a side mounted treble hook on each side and one trailing (3T) and the larger size had two on each side and one on each side and one trailing (5T). Both sizes had nose and tail propellers. Each size was available in the following twelve finishes: *White belly, blended green back; White belly, blended slate back; Yellow belly, blended rainbow back; Yellow belly, blended brown back; Red belly, blended brown back; Silver belly, blended blue back, Silver belly, blended olive green back; Solid white; Solid red; Solid silver.*

The MONARCH Underwater Muskallonge (2200 series) was made in two sizes (3-5/8" and 5") for heavy game fish. Each size had the through-body shaft on which was mounted the nose and tail propellers. The plugs had one treble hook on each side (mounted to the shaft) and a trailing treble (3T). Both were available in one of only five finishes: *White belly, blended green back; White belly, blended slate back; White belly, blended rainbow back; Yellow belly, blended brown back; Red belly, blended brown back.*

The MONARCH Floater (2300) series) was also available in two sizes (2¾" and 4"), only the smaller being originally available with an optional buck tail trailing treble hook. The smaller had only a nose propeller but the larger one also had a tail propeller. Both had a trailing and belly mounted treble hook

Pflueger (cont'd.)

(2T). The available finishes were: *White belly, blended green back; White belly, blended slate back; White belly, blended rainbow back; Yellow belly, blended brown back; Red belly, blended brown back; Silver belly, blended dark blue back.*

This is a MONARCH floater. It has a Gem clip style hook hanger, glass eyes and measures 2¾" long. Collector value range: $40 to $80.

SIMPLEX MINNOW
(pre 1925)

This is a beautiful little wooden minnow made in only a 1-¾ inch size. They came in a small wooden box. These are sinkers, unless you use the buoy weight to hold it close to the surface on retrieve. Earliest catalog I was able to find it in was 1909. It was available in two qualities, the Favorite and Premium. The Premium came with gold plated hardware. The Favorite quality had Nickel plated hardware. They were made with one, two and three belly weights. The two weight models are the oldest. This lure is almost identical to the Heddon Artistic Minnow. See that listing in the Heddon section for a discussion of how

to tell them apart. They were not found in 1925 or subsequent catalogs. Collector value range: $15 to $30.

RED DEVIL

Pflueger brought this relatively hard to find lure into the line around 1920 and it disappeared from their catalogs in the 1940's. It was always available only in a red head, white body paint finish. Curiously, the catalog listing never referred to the size of the lure, only the spinner. The wood body portion of the one in the accompanying photo measures 2-5/8" long. The spinner blade on it is marked "PFLUEGER" on one blade and "2" on the other. In fact it was available in a spinner blade size 1 (1-9/16" x 15/32") and 2(1-7/8" x 39/64"). Would you believe those very precise measurements came right out of the catalog listing (1929)? They refer to the length and width of the blade. Collector value range: $10 to $20.

NEVERFAIL

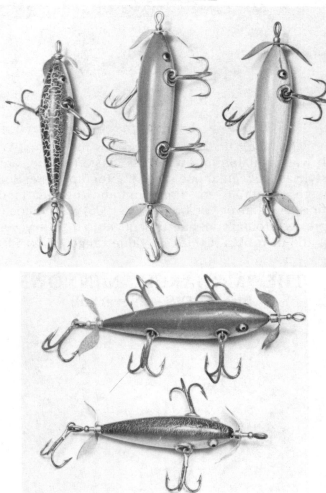

Neverfails. The crackle back lure has the single word "Pflueger" pressed into the propeller blade. This is rare. The solid color plug has the Pflueger Bulldog trademark on the front propeller blade and is an older Monarch with the see-thru wire hook hangers. Crackle back has Neverfail hook hanger.

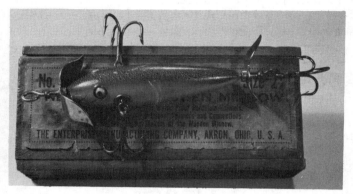

This is a very fine example of the NEVERFAIL. It measures 2-7/8" long, but the label on the box states it is "SIZE 2¾". The 2¾" size was not found in any catalog listing for the Neverfail. Note the label on the box says "THE ENTERPRISE MANUFACTURING COMPANY." Collector value range: $15 to $30.

This name first appears in catalogs around the late 1920's, but the plug is remarkably similar, if not identical to some of the older "Monarch" series plugs. The Neverfail was made right on into the 1950's (3" only in 1955) in two sizes both being underwater plugs. The smaller has two opposite side mounted trebles and a trailing treble 3T) and the larger had two additional side trebles (5T). Both had fore and aft mounted propellers. Collector value range: $15 to $30.

CATALOG SERIES –	BODY LENGTH	LURE WEIGHT
3100	*3"	¾ oz.
	3-5/8"	1 oz.

COLOR OR FINISH: *Luminous paint, gold spots; Natural frog, scale finish; *Natural perch, scale finish; Natural chub, scale finish; White body, frog back; White body, green and red spots; Yellow body, green and red back; *Rainbow; Solid red; *Green cracked back; *Yellow perch; *White body, red head; *White body, red, yellow and black spots.*

This size and these finishes were the only options available by 1955. The last finish on the list was new in the 1950's.

ELECTRIC WOODEN MINNOW

Small size 2-3/4" Electric Minnow with Neverfail hook hanger.

2-3/4" Electric Minnow with Neverfail hardware. Propeller spinner is marked "Electric Bulldog."

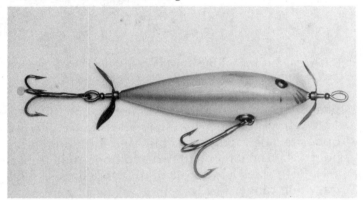

Electric Minnow with propeller marked "Metallized Bulldog." Catalogs say 3-5/8", but this one measures 4". Neverfail hardware.

This plug was first produced around 1920-21 in two sizes (2¾" and 3-5/8"). It had glass eyes, propellers mounted fore and aft, and a through-body wire shaft. The smaller version had two opposite side mounted trebles and a trailing treble (3T). The larger one had two additional opposite side trebles (5T). These lures did not appear in the 1925 or subsequent catalogs. Collector value range: $80 to $120. The available finishes are as follows: *White belly, blended rainbow back; Aluminum belly, blended olive green back; White belly, fancy (cracked) green back; White belly, blended rainbow back; White belly, blended olive green back; White belly, fancy (cracked) green back.*

Pflueger (cont'd.)

METALIZED MINNOW

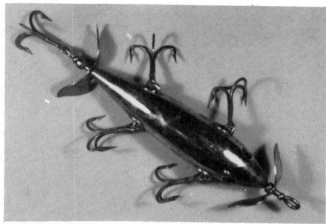

This Metalized Minnow has the Pflueger Bulldog trademark on the front propeller blade and the Neverfail hardware.

Patented around 1910-11 this plug doesn't appear in catalogs until sometime around the late 1920's. It was made in two sizes, the smaller with two opposite side mounted trebles and a trailing treble hook (3T). The larger had two additional side trebles (5T). Both sizes had fore and aft propellers. Collector value range: $15 to $30.

CATALOG SERIES #	BODY LENGTH	LURE WEIGHT
2887	3-5/8''	1 oz.

COLOR OR FINISH: *Metalized (polished nickel).*

KENT FROG

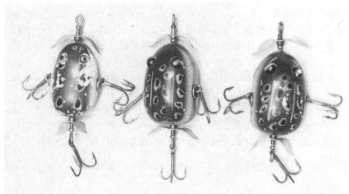

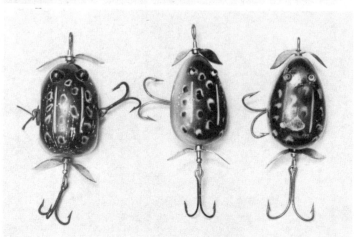

New for Pflueger around the late 1910's the form in the photographs illustrate changes in the Pflueger

Kent Frog over the years. Read them left to right, top to bottom. Note changes in eyes, hook types and arrangements, and body shapes. The last version has a non-tube floppy propeller. Available only in the finish pictured, Meadow Frog. Collector value range: $30 to $60.

Please turn to the Kent section on page 287 for detailed history of this lure.

MAGNET or MERIT 3600 Series

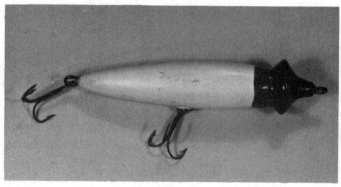

This is the first style of MAGNET or MERIT. Note the difference in the shape of the collar and the nose. This particular example is a repaint. Collector value range: $30 to $60.

Upper lure is a Pflueger Magnet. Lower is a Shakespeare Surface Wonder. See text for differences.

(cont'd next page)

Pflueger Magnet (cont'd.)

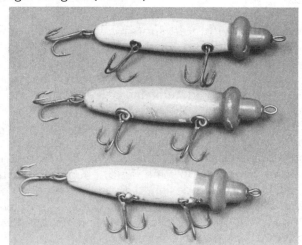

Three Magnets, oldest to newest. Top lure has through-body wire line tie and tail treble hook hangers with gem-clip type belly hook fasteners. Center lure has the Neverfail hook hanger and the lower plug has the one-piece surface hanger.

The oldest reference to the Magnet (first name) was a 1916 catalog entry with illustration. There are a couple of significant things about this entry. First, the illustration is identical to a Shakespeare Surface Wonder except for one small detail. The forward hook hanger is extremely close to the collar whereas on the Shakespeare model the screw eye is located farther back (see photograph for comparison). It looks as if Pflueger and Shakespeare were buying blank bodies from the same supplier at this time. The second observation came from the text of the entry. It stated as follows: "Joint on the screw eye at head is soldered to prevent line from slipping out." By the early 1920's the body style had changed to that of the lures in the photograph of three Magnets (Merits). The name remained "Magnet" until about 1935 when it was inexplicably changed to "Merit." The 1916 Magnet was offered in 3 color choices: White luminous, plain white, white with red head. By 1925 the all white non-luminous white body with red head was offered and that was it from then on. So, if you have an all white or white with gold spots, it's pre-1927, if it's not a repaint. It was gone by the end of the 1940's. It was listed as 4¼" long throughout the years. Collector value range: $10 to 20.

PEERLESS

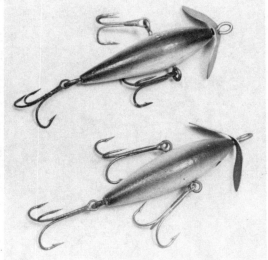

The Peerless minnow plugs were made as an inexpensive lure line with not quite the quality of the regular Pflueger line. All had opposite side trebles and a trailing treble hook (3T). They also had one nose mounted propeller. They came along in the late 1920's and apparently didn't stay in the line long after. Collector value range: $4 to $8.

CATALOG SERIES –	BODY LENGTH	LURE WEIGHT
4100	2½"	½ oz.
	2"	?
	3½"	?

COLOR OR FINISH: *White body, red head; White body, green back; White body, red back.*

PEERLESS
or
GEM MINNOW

This is a very inexpensively constructed critter that looks like another contender for competing with the Shakespeare Little Pirate. Collector value range: $4 to $8.

343

Pflueger (cont'd.)

GLOBE

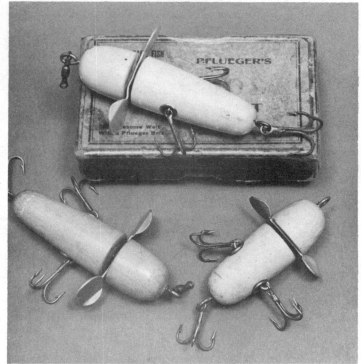

Three Globes and an original box. The one on the box is a "Portage" and has the wire see-through hook hanger (oldest). The remaining two lures have the Neverfail hardware.

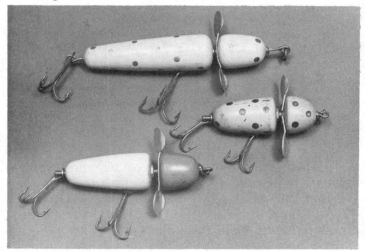

The three sizes of Globes each with the one-piece surface hook hanger (latest).

One reference found was a photocopy of a catalog entry that said at the bottom to insert this entry in "...our catalog No. F26". I have not seen this catalog but I have seen F25 dated 1909. So, this entry must be a 1910 or later. In any case the 3-1/8" Globe pictured there is much like a Decker (see page 158). The nose is a bit more pointed and rear body tapered more than a later Pflueger Globes. The next reference was in a 1916 Pflueger catalog. The 1916 illustration is the typical Globe shape, as in the photograph accompanying. It was called the Portage Reflex Bait in the entry. This one was available in two sizes, 2-3/4" and 3-5/8", and four finishes: Solid white, white with red head, yellow with gold spots, Mouse color. A 1919 catalog offers only luminous white body and the yellow with gold spots. By 1925 the red head was back, making three choices.

1926 Colors:
> Luminous with gold spots
> Yellow with gold spots
> White with red head
> Natural Perch scale finish with red head
> Natural Chub scale finish with red head

Pike scale finish with red head was added in 1928 and in 1929 they added a larger size, 5¼". Black body with red head was added sometime in the 1940's. These color changes may be of some help in dating your Globes. However, changes pretty much reflect the typical evolution. One major change took place about 1930. They redesigned it so that the head could be pulled forward away from the body for easy weed removal. They were available right on into the 1950's. Collector value range: $3 to $6.

CATALOG SERIES –	BODY LENGTH	LURE WEIGHT
3700	2¾"	5/8 oz.
	3-5/8"	3/4 oz.
	5¼"	1-1/3 oz.

ALL-IN-ONE
(pre 1925)

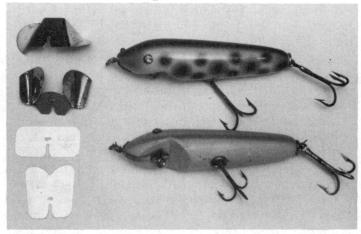

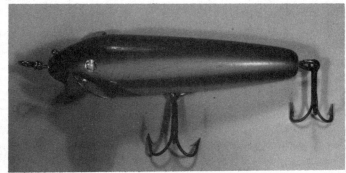

This 4" ALL-IN-ONE has the Pflueger patent Neverfail hook hanger for the belly hook and a simple screw eye for the tail hook. Note that the rhinestone eye has no metal retaining clips. They are glued in. The retaining clip is a later innovation.

This interesting plug will probably be a very difficult item for the collector to find intact. It was furnished with four different interchangeable metal nose pieces. Each was different so that depending upon which you chose to use, the plug would rotate, dive shallow, deep dive or plane along the surface when

344

Pflueger (cont'd.)

retrieved. Because these metal planes were removable, it is not likely that you will find any but the one attached to the body. The plug had a belly mount treble and a trailing treble hook. It was not found in catalogs of 1925 or after. Collector value range: $120 to $160 with all four planes. Value range without extra planes: $49 to $80. The colors available were as follows: *Luminous paint; Solid white: White belly, blended green cracked back; White belly, blended rainbow cracked back; White belly, blended frog back; White belly, green and red spots.*

BEARCAT
(pre 1925)

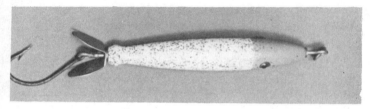

The Bearcat is almost identical to the Catalina (5500 series) except that it has a belly mounted treble and a trailing treble hook. Patented in 1922, it appears in a 1925 catalog as available in natural mullet with scale finish, white with red throat, and white with a yellow and green back. It was missing from catalogs by 1930. Collector value range: $15 to $30.

SURPRISE

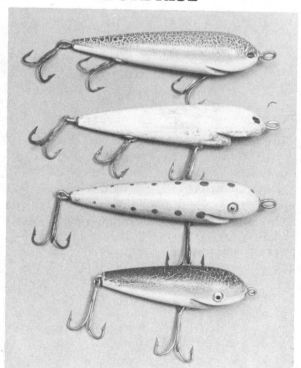

This beautiful mint condition 4" SURPRISE has no eyes of any sort. It is one of only two known to exist in private collections. Collector value range: $50 to $100.

The patent for the Surprise was applied for in 1913 and granted in 1915 so it must have been introduced around then. When first entered into the line there was only a 4" size and it had two belly treble hooks and one trailing treble. By 1919 a 3" size two hooker had been added and the 4" size had become a two hook model also.

The earliest models of the Surprise had empty eye sockets for eyes, just empty holes. This is a puzzling characteristic until you read the patent papers. It seems that someone thought they had a really bright idea. Ostensibly the sockets had a tendency to retain air when pulled under water in a diving motion. Further, it was thought that when you brought the lure to a horizontal position or stopped it, the air would be released in the form of tiny bubbles giving the appearance of the lure exhaling in a lifelike manner. By the early 1920's they were sporting the normal glass eyes of the time. I guess someone finally figured out that fish don't breathe air. The lure was absent from the Pflueger catalogs by the mid 1930's. Collector value range: $15 to $30.

CATALOG SERIES –	BODY LENGTH	LURE WEIGHT
3900	3"	½ oz.
	4"	5/8 oz.

COLOR OR FINISH: *Luminous paint, gold spots; Golden shiner, scale finish; Natural mullet, scale finish; Natural frog, scale finish; Natural perch, scale finish; Natural chub, scale finish; Black body, white head; *White body, red head; Rainbow; *Green cracked back.*

**These were the only finishes available in 1931 and the 3" size had been eliminated.*

(cont'd next page)

PAL-O-MINE

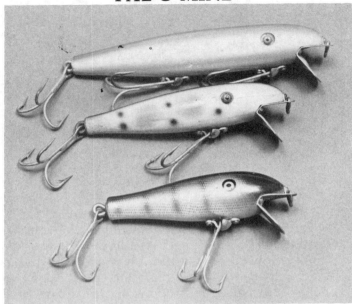

First introduced about 1925 the Pal-O-Mine continued to be offered throughout the years right into the 1950's. It was first available in only two sizes (3½" and 4¼"). In 1932 a smaller (2¾") size was added. The basic design of these plugs didn't change but various color finishes were eliminated or added at particular year intervals. This will enable the collector to establish the approximate age of some of them (see listing below).

The larger (4½") had always been offered with two belly trebles and one trailing (3T). The 3½" and 2¾" sizes have always sported only one belly treble hook and the trailing treble (2T). All had a metal lip fitted into a cutout notch at the nose. The collector value range is from $4 to 8. (See Jointed Pal-O-Mine).

CATALOG SERIES –	BODY LENGTH	LURE WEIGHT
5000	2¾"	1/3 oz.
	3¼"	½ oz.
	4¼"	¾ oz.

COLOR OR FINISH: *Golden shiner, scale finish; Red side, scale finish; Natural mullet, scale finish; Natural pike, scale finish; Natural frog, scale finish; Natural perch, scale finish; *Solid black, white head; Rainbow; †Solid red; Green cracked back; Solid white, red head; **Solid white, red head, silver specks; **Red, green and yellow scramble finish; **Solid white, red splash, gold specks; **Solid white, red and green spots; ††Red head, pearl specks.*

All finishes other than those listed above date the plug 1941 or later.

Eliminated in 1931.
**Added in 1931, eliminated in 1938.*
†Eliminated in 1932.*
††Added in 1932.*

JOINTED PAL-O-MINE

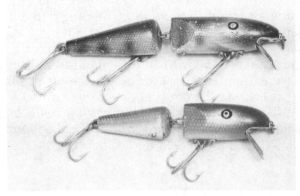

By 1936 the original Pal-O-Mine had become available in a jointed version. It was available in two sizes and the body design was the same as the unjointed version (see above). Collector value range: $3 to $6.

CATALOG SERIES#	BODY LENGTH	LURE WEIGHT
9000	3¼"	½ oz.
	4¼"	¾ oz.

COLOR OR FINISH: *Red side, scale finish; Green mullet, scale finish; Natural pike, scale finish; Natural perch, scale finish; White with red head, silver sparks; Rainbow blend.*

O'BOY

The O'Boy came along around the mid 1920's and by 1931 it was no longer to be found in catalogs as a plug (the name was reused on a spinner bait). It was made in two sizes and three weights. The heavier stronger version was for big fish. All had a metal lip, a belly treble and trailing treble hook. Collector value range: $10 to $20.

CATALOG SERIES #	BODY LENGTH	LURE WEIGHT
5400	2¾"	½ oz.
	3½"	¾, ⅞ oz.

(cont'd. next page)

Pflueger (cont'd.)

COLOR OR FINISH: *Golden shine, scale finish; Red side, scale finish; Natural mullet, scale finish; Natural frog, scale finish; Natural chug, scale finish; Black body, white head; White body, green and red spots; Rainbow; Green cracked back; White body, red head; Red side, scale finish; Natural chub, scale finish; Silver color body, red head; Rainbow.*

WIZARD WIGGLER

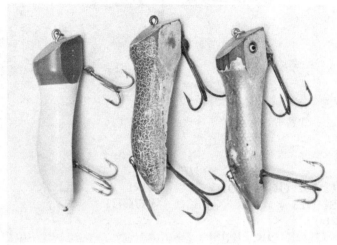

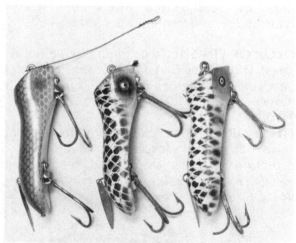

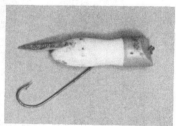

This lure was first found in a 1927 catalog. It was patented June 6, 1922. It had disappeared form catalogs by 1936. Although the patent drawing did not include it, they have a top tail mounted metal flasher attached loosely so it would wiggle on retrieve. The left lure in the first photograph is not like the regular production models. It is more like the patent drawing. Note the pork rind attachment on the tail (not in patent). Interestingly, the Pflueger style one-piece surface hook hanger is part of this 1922 patent (see page 86). Collector value range: $10 to $20.

CATALOG SERIES #	BODY LENGTH	LURE WEIGHT
4700	*1½"	1/20 oz.
	1¾"	1/10 oz.
	2¼"	¼ oz.
	*3"	½ oz.
	3½"	5/8 oz.

COLOR OR FINISH: *Luminous paint, gold spots; *Natural frog, scale finish; Natural perch, scale finish; *Natural chub, scale finish; White body, green and red spots; *Rainbow; Green cracked back; *White body, red head.*

NOTE: The Wizard reappeared in a 1938 catalog in only the 3" size and in six finishes: Natural perch, scale finish; Black with silver lightning flash; Luminous with red lightning flash; Green cracked back; White body, red head; Gray mouse.

The only sizes and finishes available by 1929 and the 1½" size was not available in Luminous paint or frog finish at this time. The frog finish was eliminated as an option in 1931.

WIZARD MOUSE

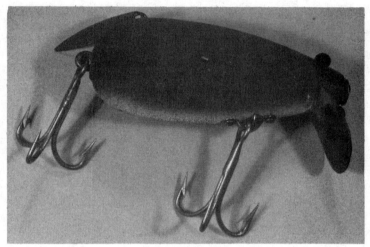

A thorough search through the Pflueger catalog collection available turned up no mention of this lure. I have named it Wizard Mouse and placed it here because of the presence of a metal flasher on its back just like the one on the Wizard Wiggler. The blade does have "PFLUEGER WIGGLER" stamped on it. The body measures 1-5/8" in length and the finish is fuzzy brown with a white belly. The eyes are large black beads. Belly hook hardware is one piece surface and the tail has a protective metal insert. Collector value range: $40 to $80.

(cont'd. next page)

Pflueger (cont'd.)

CATALINA
(pre 1925)

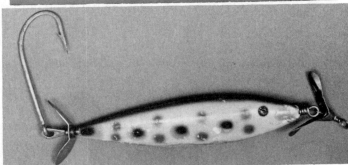

This plug was patented in 1910, but it is not presently known exactly when it entered the Pflueger line. It was in catalogs from 1925 to 1936 then disappeared. The bait is a long slim wooden type with a bronze wire shaft running through the length of the body. The shaft begins as a line tie as the nose and a hook link for the trailing single hook. There is a propeller mounted on the shaft at the tail. The spotted one in the photo has a non-standard prop on the nose added by a fisherman. Collector value range: $20 to $40.

CATALOG SERIES #	BODY LENGTH	LURE WEIGHT
5500	4¼''	?

COLOR OR FINISH: *Natural mullet, scale finish; White with red throat; White with yellow and green back; Solid red; Metalized (polished nickel-plate all over).*

LIVE WIRE

Sometime around 1931 the Live Wire appears in only four color designs and two sizes. It was made of celluloid and very slim. It had a nose and tail propeller spinner, two belly trebles and a trailing treble hook (3T) on the larger size and only one belly treble on the smaller (2T). There was a dorsal fin very realistic in shape and appearance. By 1932 a saltwater version was in the line. It was a 4½'' body, with only the tail propeller and one trailing single hook (1T). by the 1937 catalog the plugs were still available in the saltwater version, but only one size of the regular lure was still being offered (3½''). The 1941 catalog saltwater version was still offered in the original body design. Both had disappeared by 1955. Collector value range: $5 to $10; new $6 to $12.

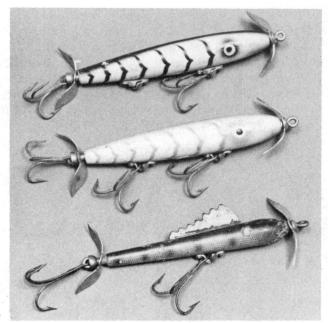

Live Wire.

CATALOG SERIES #	BODY LENGTH	LURE WEIGHT	HOOKS
7600	5½''	1 oz.	2T

COLOR OR FINISH: *Natural perch, scale finish; *Green gar, scale finish; *Silver sides, scale finish; *White body, red head, gold sparks.*

7900	5½''	

COLOR OR FINISH: *Green mullet, scale finish, silver sparks; White body, red head, gold sparks; Whtie body, yellow and green back; Solid red; Pearl sparks all over.*

*9400	3¾''	¾ oz.

COLOR OR FINISH: *Yellow body, red decorations; Yellow body, black decorations; White body, black decorations; White body, red and green decorations.*

*The four finishes available in the 1931 catalog.
**The latest version.

FRISKY

Some time in the mid 1930's this bait appeared in catalogs. It had a very unusual nose shape, one belly and one trailing treble hook (2T). By 1952 the Frisky as it was, was gone. The name was retained but it applies to an entirely different lure. Collector value range for the original Frisky: $3 to $6 and for the new: $5 to $10.

CATALOG SERIES –	BODY LENGTH	LURE WEIGHT	HOOKS
8400	3''	½ oz.	2T

COLOR OR FINISH: *White body, green back, red splash; White body, red head; Mouse finish.*

This is the new FRISKY appearing first in a 1952 catalog. It has unpainted eyes, one-piece surface hook hardware and measures 2-5/8".

PAKRON

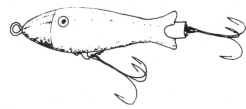

Appearing around 1931 this lure had a metal head with belly treble and a trailing treble. This trailing treble was hooked to a fastener that extended through the body to the metal head (2T). The lure was absent from catalogs by 1936. Collector value range: $30 to $60.

CATALOG SERIES #	BODY LENGTH	LURE WEIGHT
7000	2¾"	1 oz.

COLOR OF FINISH: Green mullet, scale finish; White body, red head, gold sparks; White body, red head.

MUSTANG

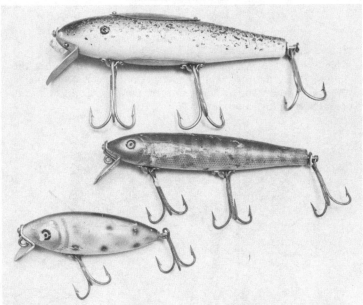

This plug begins to appear in the catalogs about 1937. It can be found in four different sizes. The smaller three sizes are fitted with a metal diving lip, a belly treble and a trailing treble the larger two have an additional belly treble. The body design of the smaller two is a bit chunkier than the larger one. The largest is a strong saltwater version and has a metal flasher plate on the back and belly. Photo is of the smaller sizes. Collector value range: $3 to $6.

CATALOG SERIES #	BODY LENGTH	LURE WEIGHT	HOOKS
8600*	2½"	½ oz.	2T
8900	2¾"	½ oz.	2T
8900(c1939)	4½"	5/8 oz.	3T

COLOR OR FINISH: Red side, finish; Green back, silver finish; Natural pike, scale finish; Natural perch, scale finish; White body, red head, silver sparks; Black with silver lightning flash; White body, green and red spots, **Sunfish, scale finish, **White body, red, yellow and black spots.

9500	5"	1½ oz.	3T

COLOR OR FINISH: White body, red head only.

*The only size listed in 1937 and 1938.
**New about 1941.

POPRITE

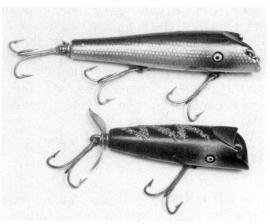

The Poprite first appears around 1935-36 and stays in catalogs into the 1950's. It was first available in one size only (4"), but around 1940 a smaller size (3") was added. The larger sported two belly trebles and a trailing treble (3T) and the smaller had only one belly treble (2T). The 1955 catalog shows only the 3" size and there has been a tail propeller added. Collector value range for older plugs is from $3 to $6.

CATALOG SERIES #	BODY LENGTH	LURE WEIGHT
8500	3"	½ oz.
	4"	5/8 oz.

COLOR OR FINISH: *Red side, scale finish; *Natural pike, scale finish; Natural perch, scale finish; Meadow frog; *White with silver sparks and red gills; *White with green and red spots; **Green back, silver sparks; **White with red head, silver sparks; **Yellow with red stripes; **Black with silver lightning flash.
*Eliminated by 1940-41.
**Added in 1940-41.

Pflueger (cont'd.)

SCOOP

This is an unusual plug in that it has a **three-bladed** propellers, fore and aft. Both sides of the body are slightly flattened and the body trebles are side mounted. New around 1937 it was first available in only one size (3-5/8''). By 1941 a second, smaller size (3'') was available. The large size had two side trebles and a trailing treble (3T) and the smaller, only one side treble (2T). Both were removed from the line sometime in the late 1940's or early 1950's. They are very similar in body design to the Creek Chub Injured Minnow except for the three blade propellers. Collector value range: $5 to $10.

CATALOG SERIES #	BODY LENGTH	LURE WEIGHT
9300	*3''	½ oz.
	3-5/8''	¾ oz.

COLOR OR FINISH: *Red side, scale finish; Silver sparks, green back, Meadow frog; *Natural perch, scale finish; *White with black stripes.*

*Added around 1940-41.

TNT

This all metal body plug was patented in 1929 and first observed in a 1931 catalog. It had a deep diving metal lip, a belly treble and a trailing treble. It had disappeared from catalogs by 1937. Collector value range: $15 to $30.

CATALOG SERIES #	BODY LENGTH	LURE WEIGHT
6900	3¼''	1-1/10 oz.

COLOR OR FINISH: *Natural pike, scale blend; Natural perch, scale blend; White with gold sparks, red head; Spotlite finish with gold color lip; Rainbow blend; Polished nickel.*

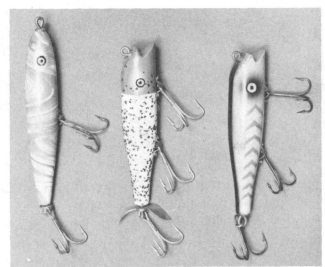

Three late 1940's Pflueger lures. Left is the Ballerina #5400 Series. Middle is the Tantrum #8400 Series and right is a painted eye Darter of unknown vintage.

PICO LURES
Padre Island Company
San Antonio, Texas

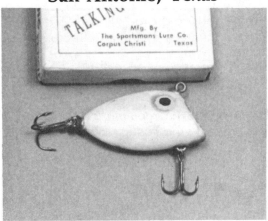

This little fellow, found in its original box, is so much like the tailless Pico's that it is included here. Could be a forerunner of Pico or a copy. Made by The Sportmans Lure Co., Corpus Christie, Texas. Collector value range: $5 to $10.

(cont'd.)

350

Pico (cont'd.)

a tendency to break off so they may be difficult to locate unbroken. The next one and the top lure on this page represent the last of the wooden Picos. The simplified design proved more durable and easier to carve. They were produced until about 1946-47. The second lure above is the first plastic Pico and the last represents the present day Pico Perch. Collector value range of the wooden plugs: $5 to $10.

THE PONTIAC RADIANT
THE PONTIAC MINNOW
Pontiac Manufacturing Company
Pontiac, Michigan

The smaller Pontiac Minnow here measures 2-7/8" and the larger one, 3¾". Both have yellow glass eyes, bow tie type propeller spinners and a single internal belly weight. Top lure: $40 to $80. Bottom lure: $100 to $200.

An article in a 1958 periodical takes an historical glance back 50 years to one of their 1908 issues and reprints an article headlined "1908-Luminous Lures Big News in Latest Lineup of Tackle Items." The article describes "The Radiant Minnow developed by the Pontiac Mfg. Company." Pontiac produced these lures in two sizes plus the same lures in other non-luminous colors. Each of them has a unique hook hanger making them easily identifiable. The side trebles were mounted utilizing a screw placed through the eye of the hook and a raised or convex cup on the body. The screw is not tightened down against the hook and the shank of the hook is bent outwardly near the eye. This system allows the hooks to rotate through 360 degrees without touching the body or each other (It has been reported that there may be a cheaper version by Pontiac utilizing the same cup, but with an L-rig type attachment). Each of those I have seen have had glass eyes and rounded blade propeller spinners fore and aft. There are two sizes, a three hooker and a five hooker. The smaller is about 3" in body length and 4½" overall. The non-luminous colors available were Red, White, Yellow or Green. Collector value range: $40 to $80.

Photos courtesy Ed Henckel, President, Pico Lures.

This present day company dates from 1933. The center right on the previous page is one of the original vibrating lure designs, hand carved from cedar by Fred Nichols in 1928. It had glass eyes. Reading from top to bottom the next two are also of wood, improved designs of the original and were sold along with it until about 1936. The tail fins had

RHODES

Bert O. Rhodes
Kalamazoo Fishing Tackle Co. Kalamazoo, MI

Fred D. Rhodes   **Kalamazoo, MI**

Jay B. Rhodes
Kalamazoo Fishing Tackle Manufacturing Co.
Kalamazoo, MI

There is some confusion when you try to sort out the relationship between Fred D. Rhodes, his uncle Jay B. Rhodes, Bert O. Rhodes, Frederick C. Austin and the Shakespeare Company. As you will see they are all tied to each other by way of a family or a business relationship of one sort or another. These particular relationships are a bit hazy in some instances. In any case, the following is what we do know.

1. Fred D. Rhodes was the inventor of THE PERFECT CASTING MINNOW and was granted the patent for it in 1904 (see patent illustration on page 78). The rights for the patent were assigned to Fred C. Austin of the Fred C. Austin Company of Chicago.

2. Jay Rhodes, Fred Rhodes' uncle, was the inventor of the KALAMAZOO MINNOW and his mechanical frog lure, the KALAMAZOO FROG.

Nowhere in the text of the patent application is any mention of just what material the frog lure was to be made from. It was probably made of rubber, but the drawings seem to suggest wood. Perhaps the patent model was made of wood and the production version was rubber.

3. It is known that Jay Rhodes worked for Fred C. Austin at the time of the 1904 St. Louis World's Fair. He apparently also worked at making and selling his own lures before, during and after his employment with Austin. In exactly what capacity he was employed is not known.

4. Bert O. Rhodes was probably a relative of the other two Rhodes. He was also granted a patent for a mechanical rubber frog (see patent illustration

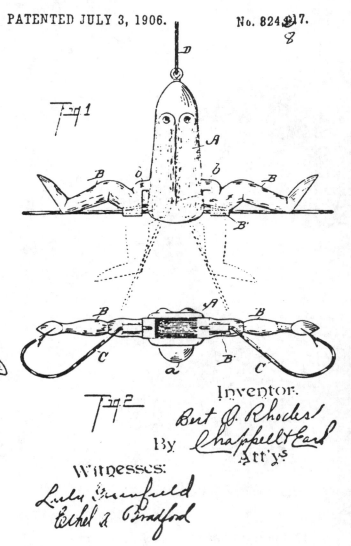

reproduced in part above and the drawing in the Shakepeare section). The patent was granted to him on July 3, 1906. What is interesting here is that at the time of granting the patent also says that all rights were assigned to William Shakespeare, Jr. More about this later.

352

Rhodes (cont'd.)

5. Art and Scott Kimball reported in their book, *Early Fishing Plugs of the U.S.A.* (copyright 1985, Aardvark Publications, Inc.), that Jay Rhodes sold the rights to his KALAMAZOO FROG. Fred Rhodes' PERFECT CASTING MINNOW and Bert Rhodes' mechanical rubber frog to Shakespeare in 1905. Since Bert Rhodes' frog was patented in 1906 (after the transfer of rights), it may be that Shakespeare asked him patent a heretofore unpatented lure, assigning the rights to them for protection.

6. It is obvious by the above, that somehow Jay Rhodes had obtained the rights to Fred's lure from Frederick C. Austin and the rights to Bert's rubber frog at some point prior to 1905, but after the 1904 patent date of Fred's lure.

In conclusion, it would seem that most, if not all, the Rhodes lures ended up in the Shakespeare line early on in that company's development years. It is not certain whether all were eventually offered as a regular part of the line, but it is known that at least three were. These will be discussed in the Shakespeare section.

The following photos are of Fred D. Rhodes' PERFECT CASTING MINNOWS. Each of the three have five treble hooks (5T), but he made a shorter 3T model also. The 3T model seems to be in short supply as they are seldom found. Collector value range: $60 to $100.

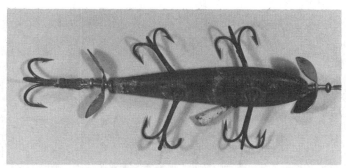

Measuring 4-1/8" this PERFECT CASTING MINNOW'S principal difference from the previous two is that it is sporting early Shakespeare tube type bow tie propeller spinners.

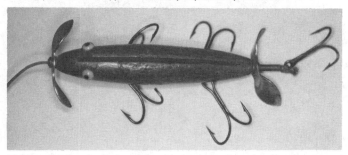

This 3¼" 5-hooker has glass eyes. Note the long brass tube placed at the tail eand. This was to prevent the tail hook from contacting the tail propeller spinner. What makes this lure unique is the manner of hook attachment. It utilized string through the body. The slot along the back of the body enabled access to the string. Collector value range: $200 to $400.

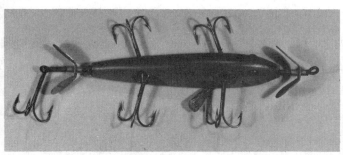

This lure is fairly typical of the early model PERFECT CASTING MINNOWS. The propeller spinners have stamped on the blade "PAT'S. PNDG." It has an external belly weight with a staple hanger, brass tack eyes, and the side hooks are rigged two to a split ring around a thru-body wire armature. Note the tube extender aft of the rear prop. The lure measures 4" long exclusive of hardware.

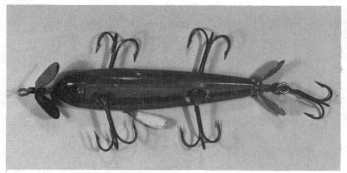

This 4" lure has the same hook hardware, marked props and staple hung external belly weight as the previous lure. The only significant difference is that this one has painted tack eyes.

ROLLER FLASHER

B & J Tackle Company   **Detroit, MI**
Roller Flasher Company   **Detroit, MI**

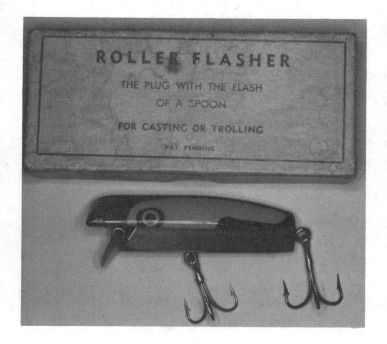

Roller Flasher (cont'd.)

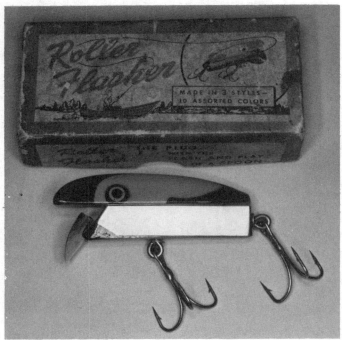

The B & J Tackle Company is the name found on the plain, undecorated box in the photo. The lure that came in that box is made of wood, is 3″ long, has painted eyes and a metal band extending all round the lower portion of the plug body. The lure with the decorated box has the same characteristics except that it is only 2½″ long and is made of plastic. Except for this the lures are almost identical so obviously from the same design. The name change could signify the company changed hands and went to plastic construction at that time. The wood lure probably dates from the 1930's and the plastic one from the 1940's. Collector value range: $10 to $20.

ROTARY MARVEL
Case Bait Company
Detroit, Michigan

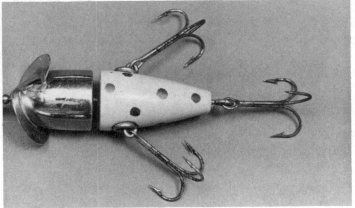

This strong well-made 3″ lure has a nickel-plated rotating head. The one in the photo here has the Pflueger Neverfail hook hangers. I have never seen the earlier version personally, but from all illustrations they appear to have hard staple-type side hook hangers. Earliest reference I found was a 1914 ad in Field and Stream. This ad said they were available in either red, yellow or white bodies. As you can see in the photo they must have included at least the polka-dot finish at some point. My research turned up no more exactly like this one. I did, however, find another very similar lure called The Rotary Marvel. It was offered in a 1919 sporting goods catalog. I have drawn the lure as it appeared in the catalog.

The ad text indicated it was made all of brass and was hollow. I don't know if there is any connection between the two. There does seem to be some sort of connection between the wooden Rotary Marvel and the Miller's Reversible Minnow on page 256. When you examine them together it's easy to come to the conclusion that they were each made by the same people. The hardware and especially the paint job are remarkably alike. Collector value range: $60 to $90.

RUSH'S TANGO MINNOWS
J. K. Rush
Syracuse, New York

Early development of the Rush Tango Minnow is mired in confusion. I reported in the last edition, one, that Le Roy Yakely was credited with the invention of the Rush Tango Minnow and, two, that I would not (at that time) attempt to sort out the confusion surrounding its early development. The first statement was wrong, but, happily, the second can now be resolved to a greater degree.

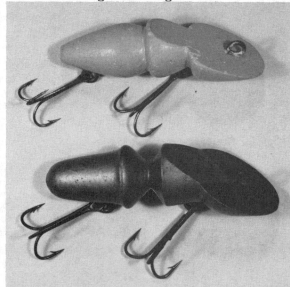

The lower lure measures 4″ long, has simple screw eye hook hanger, is colored gold with a red head and is stamped "WELLES PATENT." The upper 3½″ lure has the same characteristics as the other, but lacks the Welles patent stamp. It is white bodied and is placed here because of its similarity to the genuine article. Collector value range: $20 to $40.

Rush's Tango (cont'd.)

It seems, as in many cases during early lure development that there were several simultaneous individual revelations to occur regarding the invention of an at rest floating plug with a sloped nose (flat planed) making it dive upon retrieve. This naturally gave rise to a dispute.

The design for the patent for the Rush Tango Minnow was filed on September 4, 1914, granted to Le Roy Yakely of Syracuse, New York and assigned to Joseph K. Rush on December 22, 1914. From this it would seem that Yakely was the inventor, but wait – the plot takes a twist here. The above patent apparently came swiftly to the attention of one Fillmore M. Smith. Smith held rights to two patents filed in 1912 and granted to a Henry S. Welles in 1913 and 1914 that described "...floating artificial baits ... which shall dive beneath the surface when drawn through the water..." Believing the Rush Tango infringed upon his patents Smith filed a law suit in 1915, seven months after the granting of the Yakely/Rush patent. The Welles patent lure was declared the first and from that point on Rush Tango boxes incorporated the words "Fully recovered patents include Welles basic patents." Interestingly, I have seen an advertisement with the Welles misspelled "Wells." One can only speculate whether that was accidental or on purpose. It could be that the licensing arrangement between Rush and Smith was less than friendly and that was one way of expressing animosity.

Rush Tangos continued successfully right up into the late 1920's.

Chart I.
Smith Exhibits.

First Form - Smith Ex. 1.

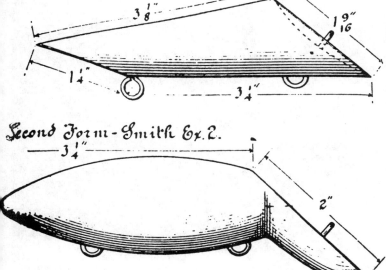

Second Form - Smith Ex. 2.

Third Form - Smith Ex. 3.

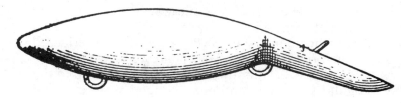

Fourth Form - Smith Ex. 5.

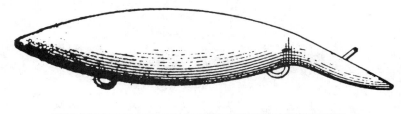

Chart II.
Yakeley Exhibits.

Yakeley Ex. 1-A.

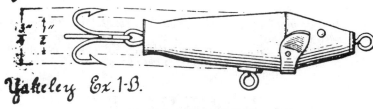

Yakeley Ex. 1-B.

Yakeley Ex. 1-C.

green

yellow

Yakeley Ex. 3.

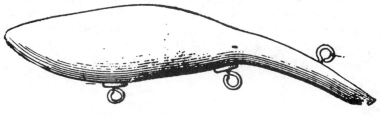

This illustration is a combination of two of the most important exhibits in the Smith vs Yakely/Rush lawsuit. The four side views of the lures in Chart I represent Smith's design transition from beginning to end. Chart II is meant to illustrate Yakely's. When you see them side by side it becomes quite obvious who had the legitimate claim. It's a wonder it ever got to court.

Rush's Tango (cont'd.)

Earliest Tangos had a unique line tie. It was a brass screw eye that was actually a machine screw eye that went all the way through the lip, secured on the bottom of the lip with a nut. This is reflected in the original patent. Hook hardware was the simple screw eye. Later the line tie was simplified to the regular screw eye and hook hangers were cup and screw eye type.

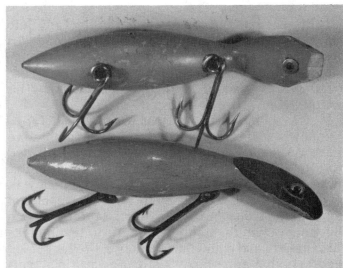

A pair of 5" Rush Tango Swimming Minnows. These have the line tie secured through the lip by the use of a machine threaded screw eye and a disk shaped nut at the underside. The hook hardware is a cup and screw eye arrangement, but the screw eyes are twisted in a way peculiar to Rush lures. The lip on the upper lure was modified by a fisherman. Collector value range: $5 to $10.

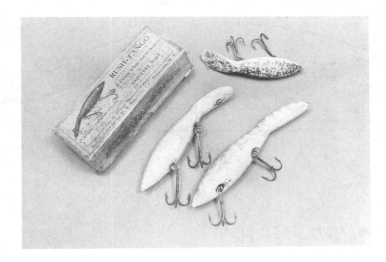

1916 or later Rush Tango box. Top Rush Tango shows the typical early Rush mottled paint pattern. Middle lure shows the brass nut securing the line tie on the bottom of the lip. Lower lure shows recessed screw eyes without cup hardware.
Collector value range: $5 to $10.

RUSH TANGO MINNOW

A 1916 listing in an Abbey and Imbrie catalog calls this lure "Rush's Swimming Minnow." It was offered there, in two sizes (4", 5") and three colors; white body with red head; white body, green and yellow mottled back; and yellow body with red head. Later, other colors were added. It had two belly trebles. Smaller and larger sizes were added to the line under different names. They will be discussed individually. Collector value range: $5 to $10.

NAME	BODY LENGTH	LURE WEIGHT
Minnow	4"	?
	5"	1 oz.

COLOR OR FINISH: *Luminous; White with red head; White, yellow, and green mottled back; Yellow with red head; Yellow, red and green mottled back; Red with white head; Solid white; White, red and green mottled back.*

A close-up view of the machine threaded screw eye and nut described in the previous photo. If you pick up one of these don't be tempted to unscrew it. With age they tend to freeze up or corrode. You might damage or break it if you try.

These two Rush Tangos have the green and yellow mottle back finish. Note the subtle body shape differences. This is often the case with Rush lures. It may be that he just didn't control the body shape too stringently. The upper plug measures 5-1/16" and the lower, 5-3/16". Both have cup and regular screw eye hook hangers. Collector value range: $5 to $10.

The upper lure here has the typical early Rush Tango twisted screw eye hook hangers. The lower lure is almost identical in body shape, however, it sports yellow glass eyes and smaller than usual cup and regular screw eye hook hardware. Both measure 4-1/8".

A close-up view of the belly of the previous lure showing the twisted screw eye described.

These two Swimming Minnows represent the two earlier style hook hangers. The upper lure (3-15/16") has the first style, the simple washer and regular screw eye. The lower (4-1/8") has the cup and twisted screw eye described previously.

TANGO JUNIOR SWIMMING MINNOW or RUSH TANGO JUNIOR

Rush Tango box and standard Rush Tango Collector value range: $5 to $10.

A 1924 listing in a William Mills catalog states the size of the "Tango Junior Swimming Minnow" is 3¾" and ½ oz. A later advertisement in an undated catalog says there are two available, 4½", ¾ oz. or 4", but the name was "Rush Tango Junior." This may be a change in design or two different plugs. To help in determining which is which, the number, size and color finish listing below is separated into the two names. Both had two belly trebles. Collector value range: $5 to $10.

NAME	BODY LENGTH	LURE WEIGHT
TANGO JUNIOR SWIMMING MINNOW	3¾"	½ oz.

COLOR OR FINISH: *Luminous white; White with red head; White, yellow and green mottled back; Yellow, red and green mottled back; Yellow with red head.*

NAME	BODY LENGTH	LURE WEIGHT
RUSH TANGO JUNIOR	4¼"	¾ oz.
	4"	5/8 oz.

COLOR OR FINISH: *White with red head; Red with yellow head; Red with white head; White, green and yellow mottled back.*

MUSKY TANGO MINNOW and FIELD SPECIAL MUSKY TANGO

This was the same basic body design as the other "Tangos" but was stronger and larger. Collector value range: $5 to $10.

NAME	BODY LENGTH	LURE WEIGHT
MUSKY TANGO FIELD SPECIAL	5½"	?
MUSKY TANGO	8"	?

COLOR OR FINISH: *White with red head; White with yellow & green mottled back; Red with white head.*

MIDGET TANGO

The lure on the far right in the photo here is the Midget Tango. It measures 1-13/16" and has the simple screw eye hook hanger. Collector value range: $5 to $10.

The remaining lures in the photo reading from left to right are: a #500 3-1/8" with the Victory Finish and cup/screw eye hardware. Collector value range: $5 to $10.; #400 (3-1/8") with a recessed (no cup) hook hanger. Collector value range: $5 to $10; and the last is a 2-3/8" unknown Rush Tango with the cup and twisted screw hook hardware. It has a very different, flattened squared off head plane that is not visible in the photo. Collector value range: $5 to $10.

NAME	BODY LENGTH	LURE WEIGHT
MIDGET	2¼"	?
	2½"	?

S.O.S. TANGO

Same as above but slightly larger sizes, 3" and 3-1/8".

TIGER TANGO

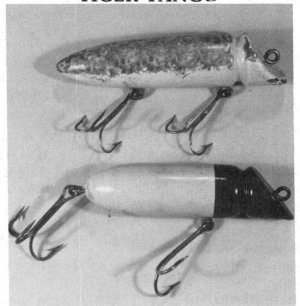

In the last edition the lower lure was erroneously identified as the Tiger Tango. It is now known that the upper lure here is the Tiger Tango. The unknown measures 3-3/8" and is a Rush product. It could be a prototype. The Tiger Tango measures 3-7/8". Collector value range: $20 to $40.

Two versions of the Deluxe Rush Tango. Both have metal head plate. Upper lure has no eyes and lower has glass eyes. Collector value range: $20 to $40.

SCHOONIE'S SCOOTER
John Ray Schoonmaker
Kalamazoo, Michigan

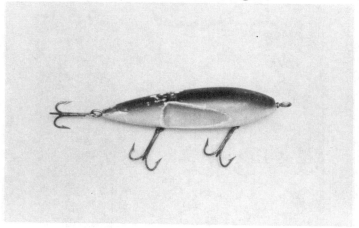

This lure was made in two sizes: 3½", 5/8 oz. and 4½", 1 oz. It was a floater at rest, but on retrieve it rode just below the surface weaving from side to side. Patented in 1916 by Schoonmaker. I found it consistently advertised to about 1920 when it disappeared from periodicals. The photo above is a side view consequently doesn't show that the groove on the other side is located further up toward the nose. The Junior size had only one belly treble. They were available in a rainbow finish (photo) and white with a red head. Collector value range: $10 to $20.

358

SCHROEDER'S WASHINGTON WONDER PLUG

Fred H. Schroeder   Tacoma, WA

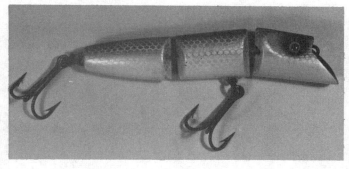

This high quality double joint lure measures 5-3/16" in length. The patent (see accompanying illustration) was granted to Schroeder on February 9, 1937. It has yellow glass eyes and the heavy duty hardware illustrated in the patent drawing. The example in the photograph here has a shiner scale finish. Another example I know of is gold with red flecks. There are four other finishes reported to have been available: silver with green flecks, white with red gill marks, an Allen Stripey finish and a white with red eyes and tail, the latter reportedly available only with two single hooks. It is known that in addition to this lure Schroeder also made a single joint version and a regular unjointed version. Collector value range: $10 to $20.

F. H. SCHROEDER

SALMON LURE

Filed May 16, 1934

Feb. 9, 1937.   **2,069,972**

THE SHAKESPEARE LURES

William Shakespeare
Kalamazoo, Michigan

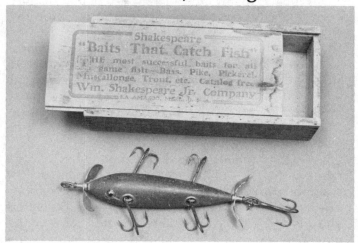

Many of the early plugs were sold in a slide-top wooden box such as pictured here. To find one of these with the lure in it or not is a fine catch. They are scarce indeed.

It is generally accepted that Shakespeare started his tackle business around 1900. Although William Shakespeare, Jr. had received a patent for a reel in 1896, the first lure he patented was for the wooden model of the Revolution. The patent was applied for in July of 1900 and granted about 6 months later (February 5, 1901). It was granted jointly to Shakespeare and William Locher, both of Kalamazoo. Interestingly, one of the witnesses signing was an Andrew J. Shakespeare, Jr. Who was Mr. Locher? Presumably he, or both of them, owned the Kalamazoo Shutter Company listed as their address

(cont'd next page)

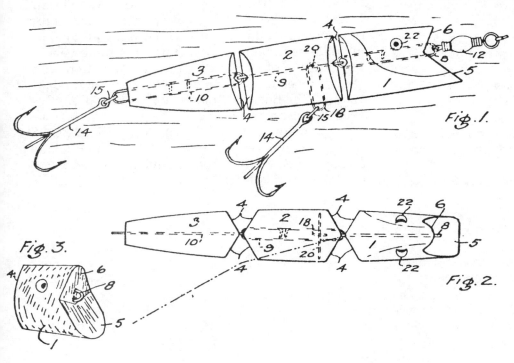

Fig. 1.

Fig. 3.

Fig. 2.

Shakespeare (cont'd.)

in the patent text. Another name important in the early development of the company was Fred D. Rhodes, also of Kalamazoo. He and his uncle, Jay Rhodes, were making lures around the same time as Shakespeare. In any case there was a patent dispute between Enterprise Manufacturing Company (Pflueger) and Shakespeare regarding a hook fastener. Shakespeare had acquired all rights to Jay Rhodes' lures by then and won the lawsuit. By 1904-05 Shakespeare had also struck some kind of agreement with Fred Rhodes. Whatever the relationship, most or all Rhodes products ended up in Shakespeare's line and the name frequently used in lure nomenclature (see Rhodes).

By 1910 the Shakespeare company had a large range of baits available. A 1910 catalog advertises a number of wooden minnows among these various offerings. As the years passed they added, deleted and modified their own baits. As did many of the other early companies, the Shakespeare company frequently included some of their competitors' lures in their catalogs. It is thought that some of their own lures were actually made for them by other companies.

By 1952 William Shakespeare had died (1950) and the company was sold to Creek Chub Bait Company.

Hints for Identifying Shakespeare Lures

While the following are observations and conclusions derived from catalog and advertisement studies, they should be regarded as general guidelines, not absolute facts to be taken without question. Shakespeare, like most other larger companies, did not always adhere to their policies regarding construction.

1. Rhodes wooden minnows are round bodied.
2. Earliest glass eyes had white irises and very small black pupils.
3. Pressed eyes came along about 1933.
4. The earliest painted eyes are about 1936.
5. The "Ball-head" tail hook hanger was patented in 1931 and appears on various lures through the 1930's (see patent illustration on page 88).
6. See-through gem clip hook hangers were pre-1910. The hooks were attached to a through-body wire.
7. Earliest cups used on Shakespeare lures were brass.
8. The see-through plate hangers came along about 1910 replacing the wired see-through hangers.
9. Cork-bodied Revolutions are probably early Fred Rhodes-made and pre-Shakespeare production.
10. The photograph of three 5T wooden minnows here shows the evolution of the Shakespeare style propeller spinners.

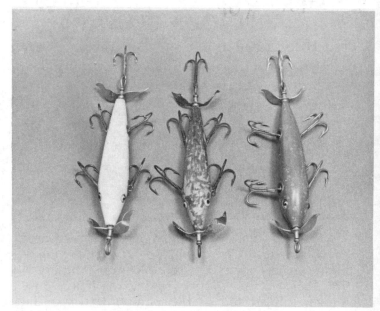

The white body lure has the first style propeller spinners sometimes called the "Long Horn" style that was used from the beginning until about 1910. The lure in the center has the two-hump propeller used in the 1910's and the last shows the smooth edge (no hump) propeller used thereafter. They also used a floppy bow tie type propeller on some of their less expensive lure lines.

11. See the Shakespeare Wooden Minnows on page 363 for more detailed dating and identification guidelines.

THE SHAKESPEARE "REVOLUTION" BAIT and THE SHAKESPEARE-WORDEN "BUCKTAIL SPINNER"

The first patent (applied for July 6, 1900, granted February 5, 1901) was for a wood body Revolution. It was advertised in 1901, but apparently was quite brief in availability for it and the Bucktail Spinner in hollow aluminum were offered the same year. A 1901 edition of Rawlings Sporting Goods Company catalog offered "an aluminum 3½" Revolution Bait" (actually the Bucktail Spinner in the illustration). The 1902 Shakespeare catalog offered both in aluminum only (no mention of wood). The Revolution was offered in three sizes, 3", 4" and 6", and the Bucktail Spinner in 4" only. The aluminum version was patented April 9, 1901.

Shakespeare (cont'd.)

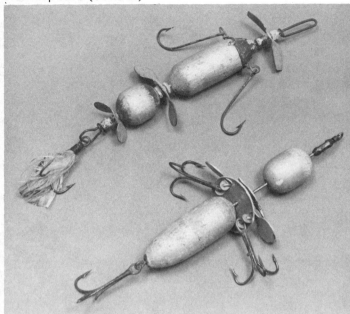

The lower lure is the Wooden Revolution. It matches the 1901 ad illustration and the patent drawing for the wood Revolution (first set of spinner blades broken off in photograph). The upper lure is thought to be the first Bucktail Spinner. All future aluminum models omit the small round second body section.

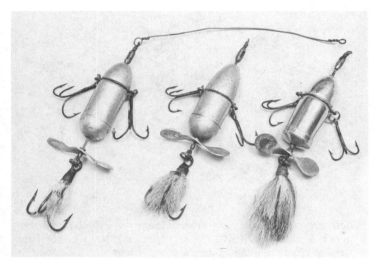

The Bucktail Spinner on the left (with wire leader) is a perfect match for the one illustrated in the 1902 catalog. Compare the shorter, rounder nose on it to the other two. This is the oldest version. The more pointed nose version was new in late 1901. A January, 1902 issue of the Sporting Goods Dealer illustrates this exact lure in an article. The nose, however, reverted to the shorter, rounder configuration and stayed that way. The last lure is a later, c1907 version with a cup closure at the end (called Acorn type by collectors). All these are marked as patent pending.

By 1907 the Revolution and Bucktail Spinner were offered in the original aluminum but also in three colors: green body with gold spots, white body with red head, yellow body with red head. Both had Acorn style body sections. Oddly, the illustration for the Revolutions shows the small second section reversed from the normal round part toward the nose of the lure. This shows up in subsequent catalogs only occasionally. Few examples have shown up. Both also have acquired the first generation plain, pointed blade propeller spinners. The last catalog in which this was listed as available was in the 1921 edition. Collector value range: $40 to $80.

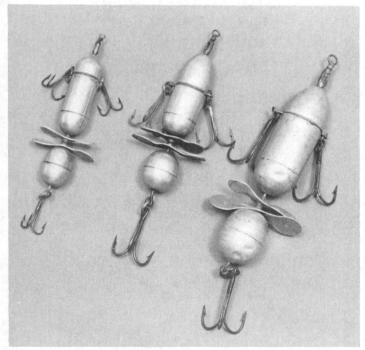

These three Revolutions match the illustration in the 1902 catalog. Note the rounded blade propellers (called Mickey Mouse props by collectors). Blades are stamped "patent pending".

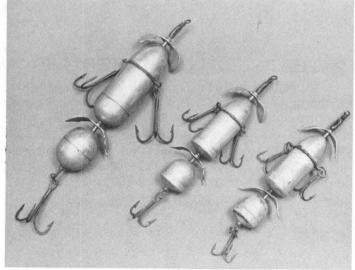

Left is a round end body style Revolution with two-hump propellers. Center also has two-hump propellers. It is Acorn body style. The last sports the latest pointed propellers (no-hump).

361

Shakespeare (cont'd.)

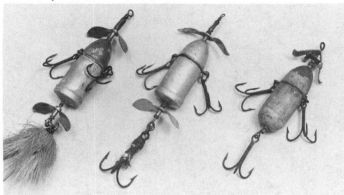

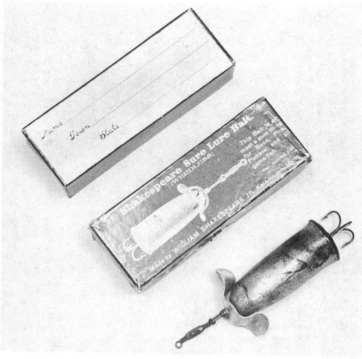

Left lure is a red headed Bucktail Spinner with two-hump propellers (Acorn body style). Center is the same but with the later smooth edge (no-hump) pointed props. Right lure is oddball. It is the original style body with the elaborate P & S Ball bearing Company style propeller spinner used on the Joe Pepper 20th Century Wonder. May have been modified by a fisherman.

This is an oddball Revolution. Note that the ball is at the leading end of the lure. Someone may have monkeyed around with it, but it appears to have come this way. It is painted yellow with gold dots and is 4½" long.

Sure Lure Weedless.

THE SHAKESPEARE "EVOLUTION BAIT"

THE "SURE LURE" WEEDLESS

Appearing in the 1902 catalog this bait was made with a pure rubber tube surrounding the hook. This supposedly gave it its weedless character. The rubber tube was at first of a solid aluminum color but later (c1910) gold spots were added. Available in one size only. Not found in post-1924 catalogs, this lure has a collector value of about $100 to $200.

The fourth and last bait to appear in Shakespeare's 1902 catalog is the "Evolution Bait". The body is in the shape of a minnow and made of soft rubber. It has propellers on both ends and has three treble hooks. It was available in three sizes.

The "Evolution" appears in a 1934 catalog and is essentially unchanged except that by the time it

Shakespeare (cont'd.)

was available only in the 2-5/8" body length. The earlier ones were also available in 2-1/8" and 4" lengths. It apparently was not available after 1936. The earliest models have "PAT. PENDING" stamped on the propeller. This bait is valued at $20 to $60.

SHAKESPEARE WOODEN MINNOWS

Sometime in 1905 Shakespeare acquired the rights to Fred D. Rhodes' patent for his wooden minnow. Prior to that they had been experimenting with various hook hangers. The following photo illustrates one of these experiments.

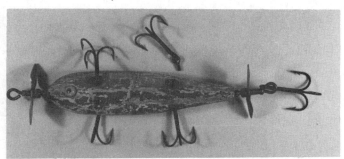

It isn't obvious in the photo but the hook that has been removed is attached to a device that is made by clipping a cotter key and giving it machine threads. It is screwed in or out of a bullet shaped, rimless brass cup inbedded in the lure body so that some of the rim extends beyond the body. Collector value range for this lure: $100 to $200.

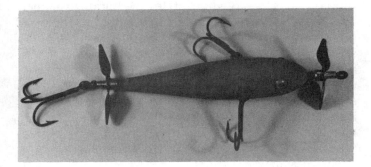

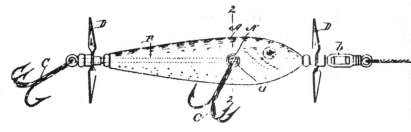

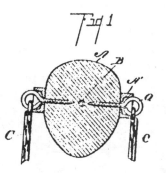

It appears that Shakespeare finally worked one out to his satisfaction for he applied for and was granted a patent for it. That patent and the lure bearing the hardware is shown above and left. It probably never went into production, however, for the Rhodes patent he acquired has much superior hook hanger hardware. Most Shakespeare Wooden Minnows utilize it. Collector value range for the patent model in the photo at left: $100 to $200.

The following examples of the Wooden Minnows date back to at least 1906 and probably represent some of the highest quality lures ever offered in the line.

These lures date back to at least 1907. It is the highest quality ever offered in their line. They were available in 5T (two on each side and one on tail) and 3T (both belly and side mounts) at the time. They later added a 2T (single belly and one trailing). These were glass eyed and had the gem-clip see-thru hook hangers with brass cup hardware and Longhorn style one-hump (or one notch) propeller spinners. This information from the catalog illustrations. It is known that earlier versions had the wired, see-through hook hangers. All of the earliest have a high forehead profile at the head of the body. Later this was not evident, being rounded off. All have shaped bodies.

Shakespeare (cont'd.)

The first sizes offered were 3″, 3½″ and 4½″ bodies for each of the three hook styles. By 1910 they had added 1¾″, 2½″, and 5¼″ body sizes.

The following chart will help you with number of hooks and props.

SERIES NO.	BODY LENGTH	PROPS	TREBLE HOOKS
00 (Floater)	1¾″	1 at nose	1T (tail)
03 (Sinker)	1¾″	2	3T (2 opp. side, 1 tail)
23 (Sinker)	2½″	2	3T (2 opp. side, 1 tail)
31 (Floater)	3″	2	2T (1 belly, 1 tail)
33 (Sinker)	3″	2	3T (2 opp. side, 1 tail)
43 (Sinker)	3½″	2	3T (2 opp. side, 1 tail)
44 (Floater and Sinker)	3½″	2	5T (4 opp. side, 1 tail)
53 (Sinker)	4½″	2	3T (2 opp. side, 1 tail)
64 (Floater and Sinker)	5¼″	2	5T (4 opp. side, 1 tail)

Any found with the see-thru plate hook hanger hardware will be from the 1910's. See photos for more dating guidelines. The 3T lure on the left in the

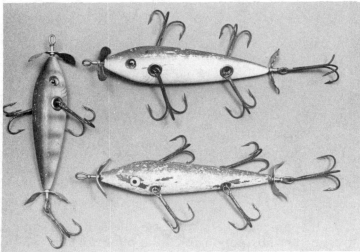

photograph here has the Rhodes 1904 patent gem clip type hook hanger and the second style, two-hump propeller. The upper right lure has clear glass eyes and the same type propeller and hook hangers. Body is more rounded. The bottom right lure is one of the oldest of the Wooden Minnows. It has the high forehead body profile, opaque yellow iris glass eyes, Longhorn style (one hump) propeller, and wired see-thru hook hangers.

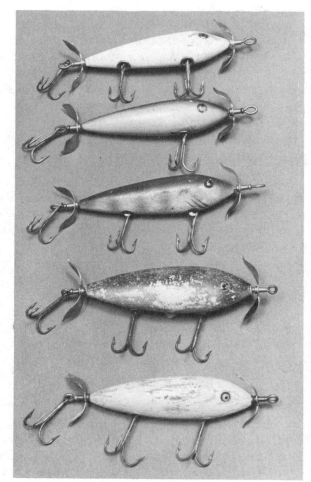

This photograph illustrates, among other things, the body style changes from earliest on. The white 3T is the earliest body style with the high forehead profile. It has the Longhorn style (one-hump) propeller and glass eyes. The second from the top has the two-hump propeller. The third lure clearly shows the plate style hook hanger and the later smooth edge, pointed propeller. The fourth lure shows a fatter body and the same propellers and the last shows the late style propeller with Shakespeare stamping on the blades. Refer to the photo of three Wooden Minnows on page 360 for a very clear illustration of the first three types of propeller spinners found on Shakespeare Wooden Minnows.

Shakespeare (cont'd.)

Colors found throughout the years are in the following list.

COLORS ON THE FIRST THREE SIZES

1907
Green back, white belly
Red back, white belly
Green back, yellow belly
Red back, yellow belly
Green back, aluminum belly
Red back, aluminum belly
Solid white
Solid red
Solid yellow
Yellow Perch, shaded

ADDED BY 1910
Fancy sienna back, yellow belly
Fancy green back, white belly
Solid bronze green
Solid aluminum

ADDED BY 1917
Metallized or Metal Plated
Solid Copper
Solid Nickel
Solid Gold

ADDED BY 1920
White body, green and red spots
Frog colors
Rainbow
Cracked gold

By 1923 they were utilizing many of their scale finishes on the Wooden Minnows. Collector value range: $10 to $40.

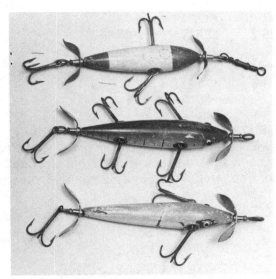

Upper lure in this photo is a #33 Rhodes Torpedo, white body with red head and tail. The Torpedo was also available in a white body with red head only in 1910. The other two are #33 and #44 Rhodes Minnows.

"RHODES" WOODEN MINNOWS

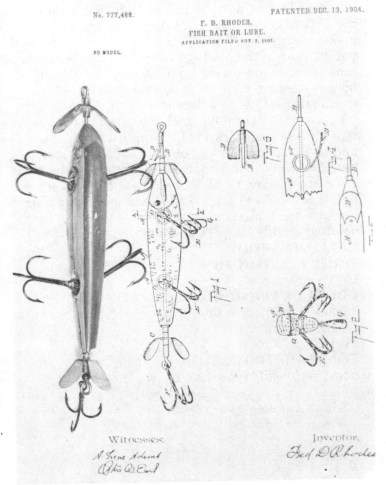

No. 777,488.   PATENTED DEC. 13, 1904.

F. D. RHODES.
FISH BAIT OR LURE.
APPLICATION FILED NOV. 2, 1903.

NO MODEL.

Witnesses: Inventor,

Regarding the Rhodes minnows a 1910 catalog states: "The 'Rhodes' Wooden Minnows are made of exactly the same high grade materials and with the same first class finish as the 'Shakespeare' Minnows." "They are identical in construction throughout except the Rhodes baits have **round** instead of **shaped** bodies."

Apparently Shakespeare was able to manufacture the Rhodes baits less expensively by utilizing a simpler round lure body. The catalog prices for a standard, shaped body Shakespeare 3" Fancy Back Minnow was 55¢ and that for a 3" round body Shakespeare "Rhodes Minnow was 42¢. Not a big difference by today's standards but if we place a price of say $3.00 on the Shakespeare and set up a ratio we find that the Rhodes minnow would cost about $2.30. That represents a 23% savings or 70¢.

The earliest (c1907) Rhodes baits used a See-Through type hook fastener and the 1910 catalogs depicts this type in the lure illustration. However, the text states that the" ...hook link shown in the illustration has now been discarded for a newer one, the same as depicted in the representations of the various 'Shakespeare' Minnows."* Those seen in the 1907 catalog are the early wired see-through type.The Rhodes patent that Shakespeare acquired was for, among other things, a gem-clip type hook fastener. it must have been used on the Shakespeare Rhodes Wooden Minnows until then. It appears that Shakespeare began to equip the second line Rhodes lures with the bar type fastener in 1910.

Basically there seem to be only three models of the Rhodes Wooden Minnow offered. All versions had side mounted trebles and one trailing. Each had two propellers, nose and tail and all were available with or without a bucktail " . . . in place of the tail hook." One can only assume that the bucktail also had a treble hook. The plugs are found with two side

Shakespeare (cont'd.)

CATALOG SERIES #	BODY LENGTH
*33F (Torpedo)	3″
33R	3″ (3T)
43R	3¾″ (3T)
44R	3¾″ (5T)

COLOR OR FINISH: *Green back, white belly; *Red back, white belly; Brown back, white belly, *Solid red; *Solid yellow; *Solid white; Green back, white belly, striped; Red back, white belly, striped; Brown back, white belly, striped.

*Torpedos were available in the asterisked colors above plus Solid Aluminum in 1920.

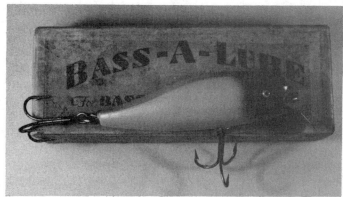

The body of this one is squared-off where the others are more rounded. The wood box is scarce. The plug measures 3¼″ without the lip, has yellow glass eyes and cup and screw eye belly hook hanger. This may be an early prototype.

THE BASS-A-LURE

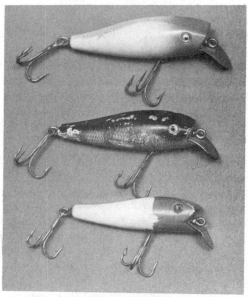

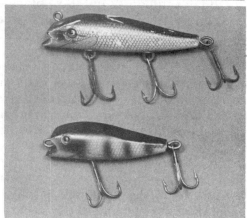

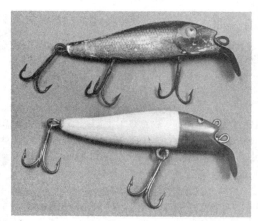

This lure came available in 1923 and is one of the first plugs to utilize a fairly large metal lip to make a normally floating lure dive on retrieve. As you can see in the photographs it was made at one time without the diving lip (first model, 1923). The lip was standard equipment by 1925. The Bass-A-Lure is probably a later development of the Hydroplane see page 315). According to all the catalogs the large size was made with two belly mounted treble hooks and one trailing, but as you can see in the photos here there were some made with only one belly treble and a trailing treble hook. There are also some lipless versions of both sizes to be found. These were not cataloged. The Bass-A-Lure had disappeared from catalogs by 1949. Collector value range: $5 to $10.

CATALOG SERIES #	BODY LENGTH
591	2¾″

COLOR OR FINISH: Black body, white head; Green "Fancy Back", scale finish; Green back, yellow belly, scale finish.

*591½	2¾″

COLOR OR FINISH: Rainbow, scale finish; White body, red head; Yellow perch, scale finish.

* The 591½ is the BASS-A-LURE JUNIOR. It is one inch shorter normally, has no blade lip, and has a trailing treble and only one belly mounted treble (2T).

366

SHAKESPEARE BASS-KAZOO

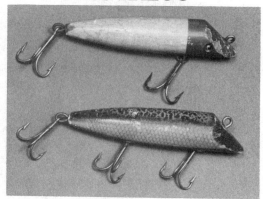

The 1924 catalog shows the Bass-Kazoo as being available in four colors and finish combination and no eyes. This was reduced to two colors about 1935-36 which is the last year it was observed in catalogs in this form. The plug had two belly mounted treble hooks and one trailing treble (3T) and a head sloped to make it dive. The collector value range: $5 to $10.

CATALOG SERIES #	BODY LENGTH
590	3-7/8"

COLOR OR FINISH: *Green "Fancy Back", scale finish; *Rainbow, scale finish; White body, red head; Yellow perch, scale finish.

*These two finishes had been eliminated by c1936.

SHAKESPEARE "BUDDY"

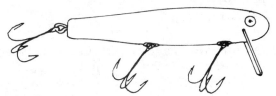

This wooden plug is unique in that it was advertised as having an "invisible lip". Upon close examination of the illustrations, it is apparent that the lip blade is made of clear plastic. This is the only occurance of the clear plastic lip wooden lure in the Shakespeare portion of the author's catalog collection. The "Buddy" had two belly mounted treble hooks and one trailing treble. The lure is included in a 1934 and a 1937 catalog but not from 1949 on. Collector value range: $20 to $40.

CATALOG SERIES #	BODY LENGTH	LURE WEIGHT
6568	4¼"	3/5 oz.

COLOR OR FINISH: White body, red head, silver flitters; Spotted; Green perch, scale finish; Natural pickerel, scale finish; Silver flitter; Green mullet, scale finish.

THE DARTING SHRIMP

This lure first appeared sometime around 1928-29 but was not fully patented until February 3, 1931. Looking sort of like a shrimp, it was jointed so that it would swim like one on retrieve. It had one belly mounted treble hook and one trailing treble. Does not appear in catalogs from late 1930's on. Collector value range: $10 to $30.

CATALOG SERIES #	BODY LENGTH	LURE WEIGHT
135	1¼"	7/10 oz.

COLOR OR FINISH: *Natural frog; *White body shaded red head, gold flitter; Copper sides, dark back, silver belly, and a red flash at throat and tail (photo on next page).

*Earliest color combinations offered.

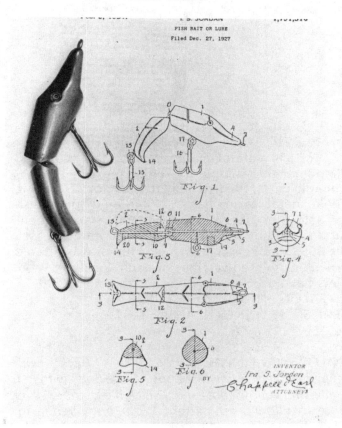

Darting Shrimp

Shakespeare (cont'd.)

THE EGYPTIAN WOBBLERS

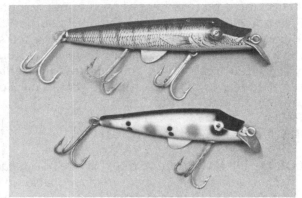

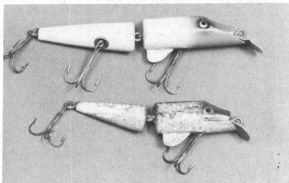

A 1934 catalog indicates that this plug had already been available for some time. The lure has a metal ventral fin, two belly treble hooks, a trailing treble, metal lip and has a gold colored hook finish for saltwater use. It is the same in subsequent catalogs and by the late 1940's and continuing into the 1950's an Egyptian Wobbler Junior was offered as well as jointed versions of each. Egyptian Wobblers have a collector value of from $5 to $10.

CATALOG SERIES #	BODY LENGTH	LURE WEIGHT
*6636	4-7/8"	1 oz.
6635	3-5/8"	½ oz.

COLOR OR FINISH: Green "Fancy Back" with tangerine, green and white body; White body with red, black, and yellow spots and a black back stripe; Silver flitters; Yellow perch pattern; White body, red head, silver flitters; Natural pickerel.

Jointed Egyptian Wobblers

CATALOG SERIES #	BODY LENGTH	LURE WEIGHT
6677	5½"	9/10 oz.
6676	4¾"	½ oz.

COLOR OR FINISH: Black back, scale finish and vertical stripes; White body with red, black, and yellow spots; Silver flitters; White body, red head.
*Sometimes known as the "STRIPED BASS WOBBLER".

THE "OO" SIZE FANCY BACK and METAL PLATE MINNOWS

This small plug is almost exactly the same design as the "Punkin-Seed" minnow (page 377) except made smaller. It was available in one body design and size only in the 1910 catalog, but several paint finishes were offered. The "Metal Plated" finish plugs were made by electroplating the body with copper, nickel, or gold, giving it a bright highly polished look. This finish was used on several other lures as well. The "Fancy Back" minnow was a crackle-like finish. This finish was also used on other lures.

These plugs had a propeller on the nose and only one treble hook (1T) trailing.* Feathers were bound to the hook. The photo shows one example with a bucktail. It was apparently added later by an angler. Collector value range: $5 to $10.

CATALOG SERIES #	BODY LENGTH
00's	1¾"

COLOR OR FINISH: "Fancy Back" in sienna, yellow belly; "Metal Plated" in copper, nickel & gold.

*The 3T plug in the photo is a #03 available in the 1910 catalog in fancy sienna back with yellow belly.

This same lure is listed in a post 1934 catalog (probably between 1934-37) as "The Midget", available in "one finish only". The illustration shows a Fancy Back finish with natural scale sides. The feathers are multicolored and the lure body is 1-7/8" long. It is valued at between $3 and $6.

RHODES "MECHANICAL SWIMMMING FROG" #3GWF

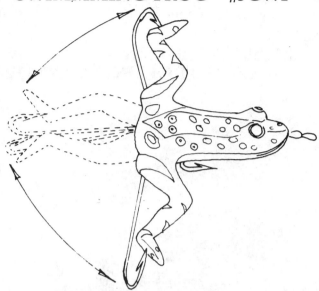

This ingenious invention, offered in the 1910 catalog, was a rubber body frog that had flexible legs which kicked back each time the fishing line was tugged. Each leg had single weedless hooks and the belly had a removable double hook in order to render it weedless. The body length is 2¼" and with legs extended, the overall length is about 4". The #3GWF does not appear in catalogs after the early 1920's. The collector can place a value range of about $30 to $60.

THE "PIN HEAD" BAIT

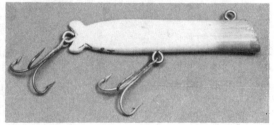

Appears in a 1934 catalog in one size, one weight. Heavily weighted in the head it wS made for salt water pier fishing. It has a belly treble hook and a trailing treble. The line tie is on top of the head (Screw eye type). It was in continued production until early 1950's. Collector value range: $4 to $8.

CATALOG SERIES #	BODY LENGTH	LURE WEIGHT
6566	3-3/8"	95/100 oz.

COLOR OR FINISH: *White body, red head; White body, red head, silver flitters; *Yellow body, red head.*
*Not one of the first two colors to be offered.

RHODES TORPEDO #6540

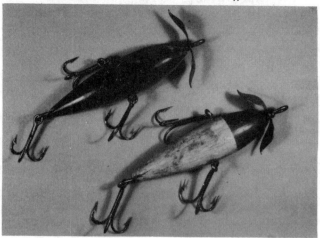

This 1934 catalog listing states that this" ...two spinner underwater lure with side hooks" ..."was first put on the market by Shakespeare Company over 25 years ago..." The collector should be aware of the possibility of this newer "Torpedo" being mistaken for the older one. Look at the hardware, size and body style closely in the illustrations of both if you find a "Torpedo" before deciding which you have. The propellers on each plug in the photo here have the Shakespeare name. Collector value range: $10 to $20.

CATALOG SERIES #	BODY LENGTH	LURE WEIGHT
6540	3"	5/8 oz.

COLOR OR FINISH: *Green back, white sides, silver flitters; Spotted green frog; White body, red head.*

"KAZOO" WOODEN MINNOW

Upper lure is an early Kazoo Wooden Minnow with simple screw-eye hook fastener (note off-set) and glass eyes. Lower lure is a later 3T model with tack and brass washer for eyes.

The "Kazoo" minnows were very inexpensively made second line lures for Shakespeare. They appear in 1910 catalogs as available in several versions: floating or submerged; different hook numbers and positions, two sizes, and several color designs. The body hooks (all treble) were attached by staples or a simple screw eye and now cup or cup hardware. All had a bow type tube propeller at the tail and nose and a trailing treble hook. Although the "Kazoo"

Shakespeare (cont'd.)

Wooden Minnow does not appear in catalogs from the early 1920's on, the name "Kazoo" is frequently used in connection with other Shakespeare lures. Collector value range: $10 to $20.

CATALOG SERIES #	BODY LENGTH
31 GWK	3"

Floating Style, 1 belly treble, 1 tail treble (2T), green back, white belly.

31 RWK   3"
Floating Style, 1 belly treble, 1 tail treble (2T), red back, white belly.

33 GWK   3"
Submerged style, 2 side trebles, 1 tail treble (3T), green back, white belly.

33 RWF   3"
Submerged style, 2 side trebles, 1 tail treble (3T), green back, white belly.

42 GWK   3¾"
Floating style, 2 side trebles, 1 tail treble (3T), red back, white belly.

42 RWK   3¾"
Floating style, 2 belly trebles, 1 tail treble (3T), red back, white belly.

43 GWK   3¾"
Submerged style, 2 side trebles, 1 tail treble (3T), green back, white belly.

43 RWK   3¾"
Submerged style, 2 side trebles, 1 tail treble (3T), red back, white belly.

44 GWK   3¾"
Submerged style, 4 side trebles, 1 tail treble (5T), green back, white belly.

44 RWK   3¾"
Submerged style, 4 side trebles, 1 tail treble (5T), red back, white belly.

KAZOO CHUB MINNOW

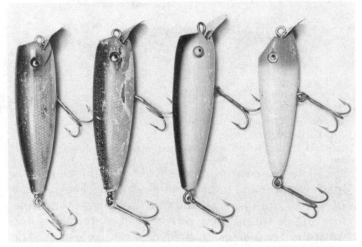

This lure was fist found listed in a 1923 catalog. It wasn't listed in any subsequent catalogs. All four of these have glass eyes. The third one in the photo has pink glass eyes. The body of each measures 3-3/8", except for the shorter uncataloged one. It may have been so similar to others in this line such as the Bass-A-Lure that it was dropped from production. There seems to be a large number of very similar size and action plugs in their line. Collector value range: $20 to $30.

MUSKIE TROLLING MINNOW or KAZOO TROLLING MINNOW

Called a "new type of lure" in the 1924 catalog this plug had a reed body built around a treble hook. The three points of the hook protruded from the body. It had a single hook at the tail covered by a bucktail and moose hair tail, and fluted spoon forward of the body. The lure was available in three sizes, the smallest being the "Bass" size and had no trailing hook. No actual sizes or weights were quoted. By 1929 the "bass" size had disappeared from catalogs and by the late 1930's the lure disappeared from the catalogs altogether. Collector value range: $10 to $20.

THE KAZOO WOBBLER

Called a "veteran bait" in the 1934 catalog, one would think it a later development of the Bass Kazoo or Pikie Kazoo. However both continue to be offered

Shakespeare Kazoo Wobbler (cont'd.)
in subsequent catalogs so its original availability is presently hazy. The plug has a metal lip, belly mounted fin, one belly mount treble hook and a trailing treble attached by regular eye or the Shakespeare "Ball Head Hook Retainer" used in the 1930's. Collector value range: $5 to $10.

CATALOG SERIES #	BODY LENGTH	LURE WEIGHT
6637	4"	4/5 oz.

COLOR OR FINISH: *Black back, tan and gold sides with vertical stripes; Black back, green & gold sides; Green back, golden yellow sides, white belly; Green back, salmon pink and silver sides; Green back, white sides and silver flitters; White body, red head.*

KAZOO WOBBLE TAIL #980

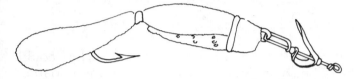

This lure was apparently short-lived for it appears only once in the catalog collection, a 1924. It has a reed body with a highly colored scale finish, silk wound with a crude rubber flapper tail, one single tail hook, and a single blade propeller at the nose. Collector value range: $10 to $15.

KAZOO FLAPPER WING #984

This lure is in the same catagory as the previous Kazoo Wobble Tail. It was first observed in the 1924 catalog and one other later one, a 1926. The 1924 catalog lists it as being available in the three color patterns but the 1926 listing says nothing about the available colors. The flapper wing also had a reed body with scale finish. It had two rubber wings, a single blade nose propeller and a long trailing bucktail hiding a single hook. As in the "Wobble Tail", there was no size or weight listed. Collector value range: $10 to $15.

THE PIKIE KAZOO

This lure, as depicted in a 1923 Shakespeare catalog, was available with two belly mounted treble hooks and a trailing treble. It is a long body pike lure with a metal lip which is "bendable" to vary the retrieve depth. Body length was 5-1/16" at first, but by 1924 it had a shortened to 4-3/4". It was last observed in this form in a catalog from between 1934 and 1937. The same color and finish combinations were available from first to last. The collector value range is $4 to $8.

CATALOG SERIES #	BODY LENGTH
637	5-1/16 & 4¾

COLOR OR FINISH: *Green "Fancy Back" with scale finish; Green back with scale finish; Rainbow with scale finish; White body, red head; Yellow perch with scale finish.*

BABY PIKIE KAZOO

This lure, a smaller version of the Pikie Kazoo appeared in the same catalog (c1935) that the larger one was last observed in. It actually has a slightly different design in that there is no metal lip, rather the nose is designed to impart the same action. It had only one belly treble and a trailing treble (2T). The catalog number assigned to it was #637½ and it was available in exactly the same finishes as the #637 above. Note eye location differences. Eyes on sides is oldest version. Collector value range: $5 to $10.

SHAKESPEARE "FAVORITE" FLOATING BAIT

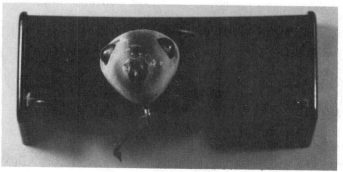

This is a nose view of the FAVORITE showing the unique triangular shape of the body.

(cont'd. next page)

Shakespeare (cont'd.)

I have found a small catalog calling this a new lure. Unfortunately it is not dated and all I have been able to do so far is pin it down to between 1910 and 1917 by using other catalog entries and catalog design style. It was offered in only one size. It has a double hook at the belly that is stabilized with a small pin. It is designed so that upon a fish striking the hook can pull of the pin and swing away from the lure body. This lure is very much like the Heddon Zaragossa and the Creek Chub Sarasota. It had disappeared from catalogs by the late 1920's. Collector value range: $30 to $60.

CATALOG SERIES #	BODY LENGTH
41F	3-5/8"

COLOR OR FINISH: *Solid red; Solid white; Solid yellow; Imitation frog color (later).*

SHAKESPEARE "ALBANY" FLOATING BAIT C1913 No. 64

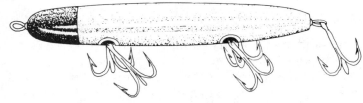

The earliest listing for this lure I was able to find was in a 1917 catalog. It was listed as available in a white body with blue head. It is known to exist with a red head also. It has plate hook hanger hardware and is 5½" long. Collector value range: $60 to $90.

THE FISHER BAIT

This floating plug was called a new lure in a 1940's catalog. It had a metal lip to make it dive on retrieve. Has a single belly mounted treble hook forward of a ventral fin and one trailing treble. There was a smaller version of this plug called the "JUNIOR FISHER BAIT." The plugs have a collector value range of $12 to $24.

CATALOG SERIES #	BODY LENGTH	LURE WEIGHT
6508	2-7/8"	½ oz.
6509	3¾"	3/5 oz.

COLOR OF FINISH: *Black and green, vertical stripes, scale finish; Green bronze back, silver sides, white belly, scale finish; White body, spotted red, green and black, narrow green back; white body, green head; White body, red head; Yellow perch scale finish.*

SHAKESPEARE FLOATING "SPINNER"

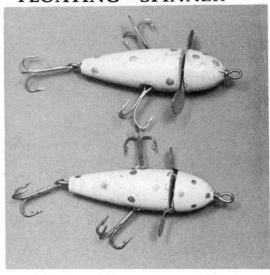

The 1910 catalog shows this wooden lure could be obtained in three color schemes. It was a floating bait designed so that the entire head of the bait rotated by means of an attached propeller. It sports three treble hooks (3T), one on each side and one trailing.

The side hook fasteners in the lures photographed are see-thru plate type. The original was available only in a 3-1/8" size and three color designs, but the early 1920's a 2-7/8" size was offered and a fourth color had been added. 1924 and subsequent catalogs do not offer the plug. Collector value range: $5 to $10.

CATALOG SERIES #	BODY LENGTH
3 S	2-7/8"
4 S	3-1/8"

COLOR OR FINISH: *White body, red head; *Solid yellow with gold dots; *Solid white with gold dots; Solid white and varigated dots.*

The original finishes offered. The fourth was not offered until around 1920-24.

FROG SKIN BAIT

Upper lure is the small Frog Skin Bait. The lower was not found cataloged anywhere.

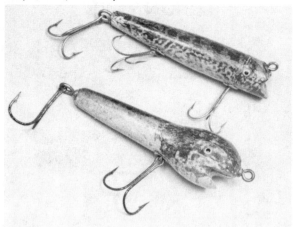

Upper lure is a frog skin Jerkin (see page 374). Lower is the larger (3¾") Frog Skin Bait.

New sometime in the early 1930's this was a wooden lure with actual frog skin stretched over the body. The fist listing I found for it was in a 1936 catalog. It said nothing about it being new, just offered matter-of-factly. It is thought by some that this lure was actually made for Shakespeare by Egar (see page 168). A point of interest is that Egar actually held the patent, applied for in 1936 and granted in September of 1937. They are practically identical. A general rule for differentiating the two is that the Shakespeare version has white iris glass eyes and Egars supposedly do not. Disappeared sometime in the late 1930's. Collector value range: $10 to $20.

CATALOG SERIES #	BODY LENGTH
6505	3¾"
6505-S	3"

COLOR OR FINISH: *All plugs had the natural frog skin stretched over the body.*

THE HYDROPLANE

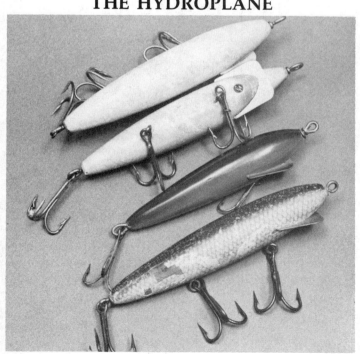

As shown in a 1920 catalog this bait was available in only one size but shortly thereafter it was offered in two sizes had two simple screw eye mounted belly treble hooks and one tail treble. However, one shown in the photo obviously was made with only one belly treble. This bait was gone from the catalogs by the mid 1920's and is probably the forerunner of the Bass-A-Lure (see page 366). Collector value range: $5 to $10.

CATALOG SERIES #	BODY LENGTH
709	4½"
709½	3"

COLOR OR FINISH: *Solid white; Solid red; Fancy green; Frog back; Spotted; Rainbow; Red and White; Yellow perch.*

INJUN JOE
LITTLE JOE

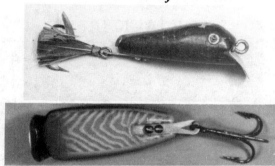

The photographs here are of the Little Joe. The Little Joe is a smaller version of the Injun Joe. The Little Joe was first found in a 1931 catalog with the Injun Joe first showing up in a 1934 edition. Neither of these were found in subsequent catalogs. Both have metal diving lips and one trailing treble with or without fasteners. The larger Injun Joe has an additional treble on the belly. Both have a unique scissor-type tail hook hanger (see photo). Collector value range: $5 to $10.

CATALOG SERIES #	BODY LENGTH	LURE WEIGHT
6530	2"	½ oz.
6593	2-1/8"	½ oz.

COLOR OR FINISH: *Rainbow with green back, Green back with green and red sides, White body with red head, Yellow perch, Black body with yellow stripe, Grey with tangerine striped belly, Tangerine body with black back and black and yellow spots, Black body with white head, Lavender body with black spots.*

(cont'd. next page)

JACKSMITH LURE

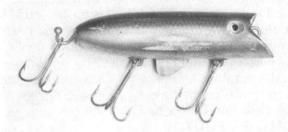

This is merely a heavy duty version of the "Jack Jr." It has two belly trebles instead of just the one. The 1934 catalog illustration shows the Shakespeare "Ball Post Hook Retainer", but by the mid 1940's it was the simple screw eye once again. It has a metal ventral fin and was made in the same color patterns as the "Jack Jr.", but the white body, red head color combination does not have silver flitters. Collector value range: $5 to $10.

THE JACK JR.

A small version of the previous Jacksmith Lure bait was first offered sometime around the later 1920's. It is a top water bait with one belly treble hook and a trailing treble. It was probably discontinued sometime in the 1940's. Collector value range: $5 to $10.

CATALOG SERIES #	BODY LENGTH	LURE WEIGHT
6560	2¾''	½ oz.

COLOR OR FINISH: *White body, red heat, silver flitters; Rainbow with green back; Spotted; Green and silver, scale finish; Green "Fancy Back", scale finish; Green perch, scale finish; White body, red head; Black back, white belly, green and gold sides, scale finish; Black back, tan and gold sides, with vertical stripes, scale finish.

*Later versions do not have silver flitters.

JERKIN LURE

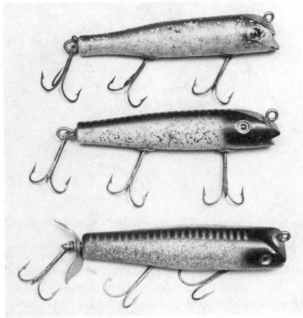

The 1934 catalog from the collection shows only one version of the "Jerkin Lure" available. By 1949 there was a second one offered that had a tail propeller. It was a surface popping plug and the 1934 illustration shows two belly trebles and a trailing treble attached by the Shakespeare "Ball Head Hook Retainer" (see photo, upper plug). Collector value range: $3 to $6.

CATALOG SERIES #	BODY LENGTH	LURE WEIGHT
6567	4''	3/5 oz.

COLOR OF FINISH: *Frog; Green and silver; scale finish; Natural pickerel, scale finish; Silver flitters; White body, red head; Green back, red & white sides, scale finish; Frog skin.*

KING FISH WOBBLER

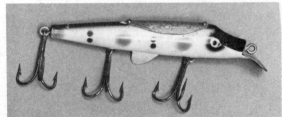

A 1934 catalog lists but does not illustrate this plug. It says it is the same body design as the "Egyptian Wobbler"(see page 368). It is listed and illustrated in later catalogs, but disappeared from them by the end of the 1940's. This is a most unusual plug in that is has a chrome plated back plate and a gold colored hook finish. It has a metal ventral fin, two belly mounted treble hooks, a trailing treble hook and a metal blade lip. The collector may place a value range of from $5 to $10 on them.

Shakespeare (cont'd.)

CATALOG SERIES #	BODY LENGTH	LURE WEIGHT
6535	4-7/8''	1¼ oz.

CATALOG SERIES #	BODY LENGTH	LURE WEIGHT
6601	1-7/8''	½ oz.

CATALOG SERIES #	BODY LENGTH	LURE WEIGHT
#6510	3¾''	5/8 oz.

LUMINOUS FLOATING NIGHT BAIT

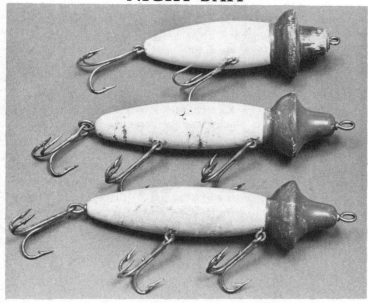

In a 1920 catalog this plug is advertised as being available in only one size. In a later one (1921-1923) it is offered in two sizes. By the 1924 catalog there is but one size again. In addition one of the two belly treble hooks has been eliminated. Judging from the catalog illustrations, there was apparently a slight design change as well.

All the plugs were coated with a white luminous paint and until the mid 1920's they had two belly mounted treble hooks and a trailing treble (3T). All those illustrated after had only one belly treble and the tail mounted treble (2T) as in the photograph here. In not a single instance were the actual sizes listed. The early models had a red head and white body, later ones were solid white. The Shakespeare catalog numbers were 680 for the larger one and 680½ for the smaller one. The Moonlight Bait Company also made one with the same size, shape, and hardware. Collectors could value their Shakespeare lure at between $5 and $10.

SHAKESPEARE MIDGET SPINNER

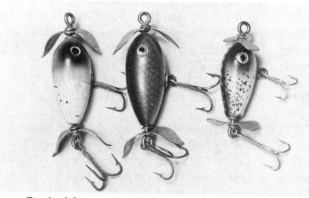

Probably a newer design of the old "Punkin Seed"(see page 377). This plug has a propeller at the nose and tail, a belly treble hook and a trailing treble. Appears in the 1934 catalog and still present in the early 1950's catalogs. This plug has a collector value range of $4 to $8, depending on age and condition.

CATALOG SERIES #	BODY	LURE WEIGHT
6601	1-7/8''	½ oz.

COLOR OR FINISH: *Shiner finish; Sienna fancy, back; Silver flitters; White body, red head; Pickerel finish; Green back, green & red sides.*

NU-CRIP MINNOW

This plug called new in the 1934 catalog, is shown in a minnow shape with a propeller spinner at the nose and tail. It has a trailing treble hook and two side-mounted trebles (3T). It does not appear in mid 1940's catalog. Collector value range: $5 to $10.

CATALOG SERIES #	BODY	LURE WEIGHT
#6510	3¾''	5/8 oz.

COLOR OR FINISH: *Silver flitter; Green frog; White body, red head; Green back, red sides, scale finish; Green back, golden yellow sides, scale finish; Green back, tan and gold sides, dark vertical stripes, white belly, scale finish.*

Shakespeare (cont'd.)

OREGON MIDGET

In the 1934 catalog this is described as a midget lure designed for use with a fly rod but some fishermen trolled and cast with it by adding a lead weight to the leader. Has one belly mounted double hook. Collector value range: $4 to $8.

CATALOG SERIES #	BODY LENGTH	LURE WEIGHT
6377	1 ¾"	?

COLOR OR FINISH: *White body, green head; Green perch, scale finish; Red, yellow and green spotted; Green back, red & green sides, scale finish; Yellow body, red head; White body, red head.*

THE PAD-LER

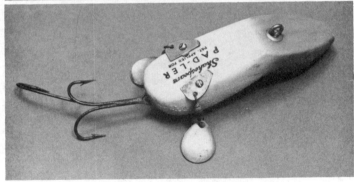

A Shakespeare catalog of 1936 calls this a new lure. It was made in the shape of a rodent, most particularly a mouse. The two small attached spoons in the illustration were meant to impart the swimming action of the mouse's rear legs. The plug had a trailing double hook. Found in three sizes, the collector value range is from: $5 to $10.

CATALOG SERIES #	BODY LENGTH	LURE WEIGHT
6678	3 ¼"	1 oz.
6679	3 ¾"	1 ½ oz.

COLOR OR FINISH: *Green spotted frog; Gray body, white belly; White body, red head.*

6680	2-7/8"	7/10 oz.

COLOR OR FINISH: *Gray body, white belly; White body, black wavy stripe on sides, White body, red head.*

"LITTLE PIRATE" MINNOW #23LP

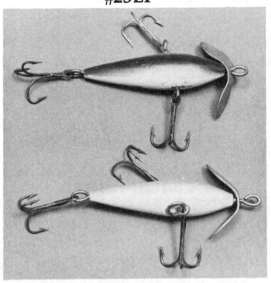

Little Pirate Minnows. Note the rather cheaply made propellers and simple screw eye hook hangers on upper Shakespeare model. The lower lure is a Pflueger model with the Neverfail hook hanger (Pflueger Peerless).

This inexpensive lure appears in two pre 1920's catalogs at 15¢ and 17¢ respectively. They do not appear in later catalogs. The Little Pirate was available in white belly with either a green or red back. They were all 2½" in length with one nose propeller spinner, two treble side hooks and one tail treble (3T). Collector value range: $3 to $4.

THE PLOPPER #6511 or #7-11

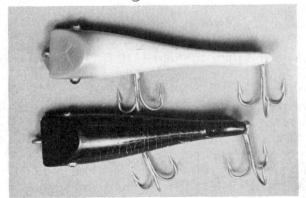

This lure is also known as the "Seven-eleven". It came along about 1926-27 and has been found with the 1930's Shakespeare "Ball Head Hook Retainer". Named for the sound it makes on retrieve it has one belly mounted treble hook and a trailing treble. Listed as available in only one size and color; 3/5 oz., white body with shaded red head. The photo shows another color and body shape. Collector value range: $5 to $10.

Shakespeare (cont'd.)
"POP-EYE"

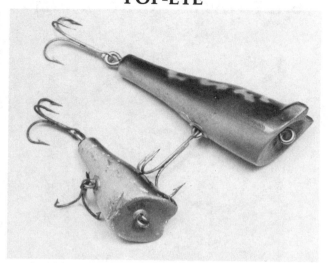

A 1949 catalog illustrates this as a top water plug. It is a cone shape with two bumps on the top of the larger and representing the "Pop Eyes". One belly treble and a trailing treble. Collector value range: $3 to $6.

CATALOG SERIES #	BODY LENGTH	LURE WEIGHT
6575	3½"	5/8 oz.

COLOR OR FINISH: *Green spotted frog; Green back, white belly and silver flitters.*

SHAKESPEARE "PUNKIN-SEED" MINNOW

Punkin-Seeds. The upper lure with cup hardware is a floater with glass eyes and the early two-hump prop. The middle lure is a painted eye floater with the late model marked floppy propeller spinner. Lower lure is an early sinker (no belly hook). Has the two-hump prop and glass eyes.

The 1910 catalog offers their lures in one size, six color styles and in a floating and underwater version. The plug probably didn't last much past 1920 for the author could not find it listed in that or subsequent catalogs with these catalog numbers or the exact design. It appears again as a #6601 in a 1937

catalog. There is use of the same numbers on substantially different plugs. The floating version had two treble hooks (2T), one trailing with bucktail and one belly treble attached with the cup and screw eye hardware (CUP). The underwater version was available with or without the belly treble. The collector may value these plugs at $40 to $60.

CATALOG SERIES #	BODY LENGTH
30P (sinker)	2-5/8"

COLOR OR FINISH: *Green back, aluminum color belly; Green back, white belly; Red back, aluminum color belly.*

31P (floater)	2-5/8"

COLOR OR FINISH: *Solid white with red on head; Solid white with green on head; Green back, white belly; Sienna Yellow "Fancy Back" with brown head.*

SHAKESPEARE'S RIVER PUP

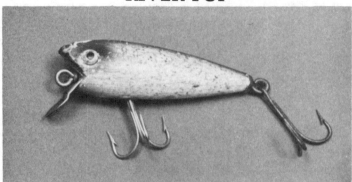

This smaller lure is weighted for deep running according to a 1934 catalog. It has a metal blade lip, one belly treble hook and one trailing treble (2T). The metal lip is notched on the early models and the later ones have no notch and the lip is longer and more squared off. See photo of Grumpy's following for the later model River Pup. Collector value range: $3 to $6.

CATALOG SERIES #	BODY LENGTH	LURE WEIGHT
6564	2-5/8"	½ oz.

COLOR OR FINISH: *Rainbow with green back; Pearl; Spotted; White body, red head, silver flitters; Green perch with red head, scale finish; *Yellow body; *Frog; *Silver Flitter.*

**These were not among the first five color patterns to be offered.*

"GRUMPY"

A 1941 catalog first illustrates this plug. It has a metal lip pointing very nearly straight down. A belly treble hook, and a trailing treble. Collector value range: $2 to $4.

CATALOG SERIES #	BODY LENGTH	LURE WEIGHT
6602	1¾"	4/10 oz.

COLOR OR FINISH: *Green spotted frog; Green perch; White body spotted red, green and black, narrow green back; Green back, white belly, silver flitter; White body, red head; Yellow perch.*

(cont'd.)

Shakespeare (cont'd.)

Photo shows a later model River Pup in center and two Grumpys.

"DOPEY"

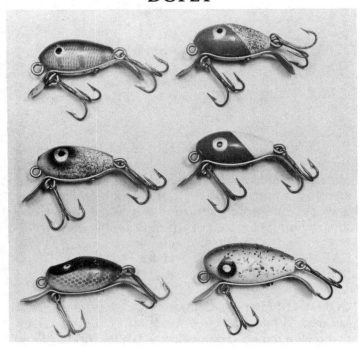

This is a very light, very small deep running plug. The "Dopey" had a metal piece beginning as a blade lip and running down the belly extending into another blade just under the trailing treble hook. There is a second treble hook attached just behind the front lip. First seen in a 1941 catalog. Collector value range: $2 to $4.

CATALOG SERIES #	BODY LENGTH	LURE WEIGHT
6603	1-5/16"	4/10 oz.

COLOR OR FINISH: *Black body, white ribs; Black body, white head; Green spotted frog; Green perch; Green back, white belly silver flitter; White body, red head; Solid yellow; Yellow perch.*

SHAKESPEARE SARDINIA SALT WATER MINNOW #721

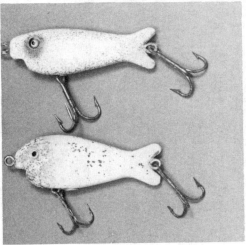

Upper lure is a glass eye #721 Sardinia Saltwater Minnow. The lower lure appears much like the following Saltwater Special #722, but has a notched mount and painted eyes. It could be, however, just a later model of the #721.

Although the first and last time this plug appears in the catalog collection is in 1924 and 1925, there can be no doubt that it was around longer than two years. It was made in the shape of a minnow complete with tail and cut-out mouth. It had one belly mounted treble hook and one trailing treble (2T). Collector value range: $20 to $40.

CATALOG SERIES #	BODY LENGTH
721	3"

COLOR OR FINISH: *Solid white; Solid white with gold speckles.*

SHAKESPEARE SALTWATER SPECIAL MINNOW #722

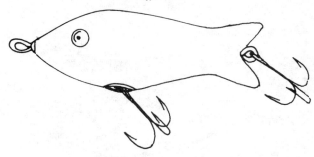

Essentially the same as the #721, the plug is only slightly different in body shape and has no mouth cut out. Available in same size and finishes. Collector value range: $20 to $40.

THE SEA WITCH
#133 & #6533

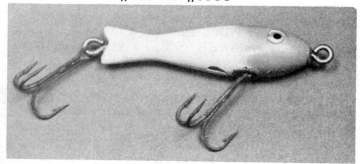

Sea Witches. The tail hook has been altered by an angler. It is not known if the unusual tail hook hanger is production or not.

As far as can be determined this is an earlier version of the #6531 "Sea Witch". The length of the #133 is more but otherwise it appears to be essentially the same plug. The catalog states that the #6533 is the same lure as the #133 Sea Witch the major difference being the addition of another line tie" ...in top of head". Thought to be of about 1928 vintage, the collector value range of these plugs is from $8 to $16.

CATALOG SERIES #	BODY LENGTH	LURE WEIGHT
133	4"	¾ oz.

COLOR OR FINISH: *White body, red head; White body, red head, gold flitters.*

6533	3/16"	½ oz.

COLOR OR FINISH: *White body, red head; White body, red head, gold flitters.*

BARNACLE BILL

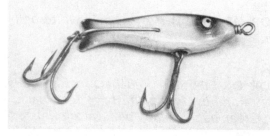

This very scarce saltwater lure is uniquely shaped. The photo here is a straight on side view. The drawing is a top view showing the curved shape of the lure. The wire you can see in the photo is both internal and external. It is continuous forming both the line tie and hook hangers. It appeared first in the 1931 catalog. Collector value range: $40 to $80.

CATALOG SERIES #	BODY LENGTH	LURE WEIGHT
6529	*3"	3/5 oz.

Actual measurement is 2-5/8".

COLOR OR FINISH: *White body, red head, gold flitters; White body, spotted red, yellow and black, gold flitters, black back; Mud puppy (silver flitters); Rainbow, blue, green, yellow, red and white; White body, eyes and tail shaded black.*

THE SEA WITCH #6531
THE SEA WITCH MIDGET #6534

The 1934 catalog describes these plugs as weighted and having "...special plated hooks". They each had a belly treble and a trailing treble. Their differences only in size, weight and color pattern availability, the body design being identical. Collector value range: $3 to $6.

CATALOG SERIES #	BODY LENGTH	LURE WEIGHT
6531	3¾"	1 oz.
6534	2¾"	½ oz.

COLOR OR FINISH: *Solid white; Solid white, red head; Solid white, red head, silver flitters; Solid white, red head, gold flitters; Spotted pattern; Pearl lustre finish.*

SHAKESPEARE "SHINER" MINNOW

This crackle back SHINER is a bit beat up but still serves as a good example for identifying any you may find. It measures 3-1/16" long, has white glass eyes, one internal belly weight and twisted thru-body wire and see-thru side hook hanger hardware.

This lure was offered in two sizes in the 1910 and subsequent catalogs, with or without a "fancy bucktail" on the trailing treble hook. It had two side treble hooks attached by the wire type "See Through" hook hanger. Both sizes had three treble hooks (3T) and a propeller on the nose. Collector value range: $10 to $20.

CATALOG SERIES #	BODY LENGTH
23 S	2½"
43 S	3¾"

COLOR OR FINISH: *Black back, white belly only.*

SHAKESPEARE "SLIM JIM MINNOW"

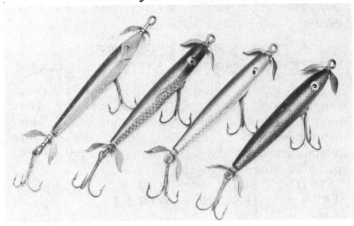

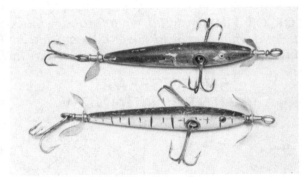

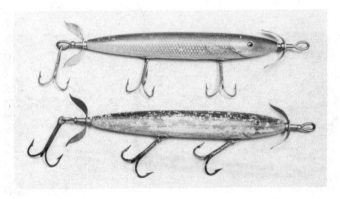

This plug is one of the earliest Shakespeares to have painted thin vertical stripes along the body sides. The three photographs are arranged in order from oldest, reading left to right in the one of four lures and top to bottom on the second and third photographs. They show changes in body style, hook hardware, eyes and propellers. The 1910 catalog offers it in two sizes. Smaller models have only one propeller spinner and larger models have two. Both have two side mounted treble hooks and one tail mounted treble hook. The side hooks utilize the "See Through" fastener on the earlier plugs. By 1920 only the larger size (3¾") seemed to be available. Although they continued to be a "Slim Jim" bait offered, the side hook #43 had disappeared from Shakespeare catalogs by 1924. The original offering listed the same five color variations for each size. The last listing offered eight. Examples of this plug are valued at $5 to $10.

CATALOG SERIES #	BODY LENGTH
33	3"
43	3¾"

COLOR OR FINISH: *Blue back, white belly, striped; Green back, white belly, striped; Red back, white belly, striped; Brown back, white belly, striped and spotted; Solid White; *Frog back, white belly, striped; *Solid red; *Solid yellow; *Solid aluminum color.*
These colors were not offered in catalogs prior to early 1920's.

SHAKESPEARE "SLIM JIM" MINNOW
(Underwater)

A 1924 catalog first lists this plug but a 1949 listing says they introduced the lure "...over 30 years ago". That dates the early ones around 1917-1918 and they are very likely the side hook #33½" and #43½". Similar to the earlier "Slim Jim" Minnow (see page 321), but the configuration and catalog numbers are different. This newer one is offered in two sizes, the larger having two belly mounted treble hooks and a trailing treble. The smaller being the same except only one belly treble. Both have nose and tail propellers. This plug continues in production until the 1950's with very little change. The bodies are weighted and finishes have varied considerably through the years. The collector value range is $5 to $15 depending upon age and condition.

CATALOG SERIES #	BODY LENGTH	PLUG WEIGHT
52 J or 6552	4½"	4/5 oz.

COLOR OR FINISH: *Blue back, white belly, scale finish.*

41 J or 6541	3¾"	3/5 oz.

COLOR OR FINISH: *Red back, white belly, scale finish; *Rainbow, scale finish; *Green back, yellow belly; Green back, yellow belly, scale finish; *Yellow perch, scale finish; Gold body, red head; White body, red head; Green back, silver sides, scale finish; Natural pickeral pattern; Green back, red and green striped sides; Dark crackle back, maroon & silver sides; Green back, golden yellow sides.*
Although these color patterns continue to be used through the years, they are the only finishes available in 1924 to around 1926-1932.

SHAKESPEARE SPECIAL

Two Shakespeare Specials. Frog finish and natural pickeral finish.

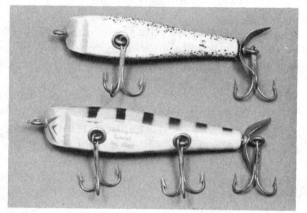

Belly view showing markings on Shakespeare Special.

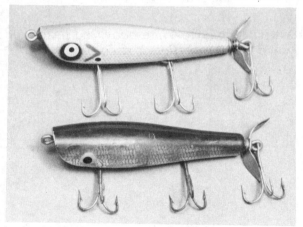

Lower plug is made by Florida Fishing Tackle Company. Upper plug is a Shakespeare product labeled Dalton Special.

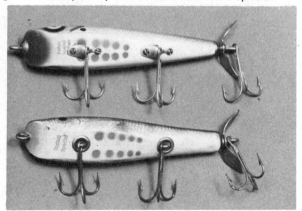

Belly view of the Shakespeare, (lower) and Florida Fishing Tackle Company (upper) Dalton Specials.

A surface lure with a tail mounted propeller. It has a notched mouth below a forward sloping nose, one belly mounted treble hook and a trailing treble. The collector may easily become confused if he were confronted with the four different plugs repesented by the photographs here. Three of them are unquestionably made by Shakespeare. Two, as you can see by the belly view photo, state Shakespeare Special right on the body. In the other belly view the one on the bottom is made by Shakespeare but the other is not. The one with the one piece surface hook hanger was made by the Florida Fishing Tackle Company (Barracuda Brand) in St. Petersburg, Florida. Both can be found with either "Tampa" or "St. Pete". Collector value range: $3 to $6.

CATALOG SERIES #	BODY LENGTH	LURE WEIGHT
6546	3″	½ oz.
6547	4″	5/8 oz.

COLOR OR FINISH: *Frog finish, white belly; Frog finish, yellow belly; Natural pickerel with vertical stripes; Solid yellow, black spots; Green back, white belly, silver flitters; *Yellow body, green stripes.
Available only on the larger size, #6547.

STRIKE-IT #6666

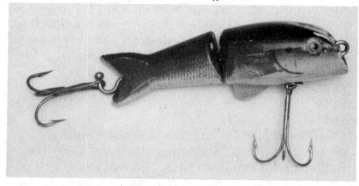

New around 1930 the Strike-It is similar to the Tantalizer. Note in photograph the Strike-It has no metal diving lip. There were only three colors available in the 1930 catalog. They are: Herring; Light grey back and sides, red at throat; White body, shaded red head. Missing from catalogs after 1931. Collector value range: $5 to $10.

CATALOG SERIES #	BODY LENGTH	LURE WEIGHT
6666	4″	4/5 oz.

COLOR OR FINISH: *(in addition to the above colors): Black body (white pickerel scale); Bluish green body, spotted red and yellow, black back; Mud puppy (light grey); White body, black head; White body, spotted red black and yellow, black back.*

381

THE MERMAID
and
THE LITTLE MERMAID

Mermaid #583, 3-5/8"

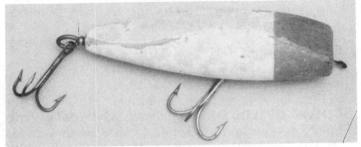

Little Mermaid #582, 3¼"

New for Shakespeare sometime in the early 1920's, it actually dates back to at least 1917. The McCormic Mermaid was patented by John Thomas McCormic of Kalamazoo, Michigan in 1917 (see page 252). The 1923 catalog was the only one I could find the Mermaids in. Appears never to have been given eyes of any type. Collector value range: $5 to $10.

CATALOG SERIES #	BODY LENGTH	LURE WEIGHT
582	3¼"	
583	3-5/8"	

COLOR OR FINISH: *Rainbow with scale finish; Yellow perch, scale finish; Fancy green, scale finish; Frog back with scale finish; Green back, yellow belly with scale finish; White body, red head; Black body, white head.*

THE SURE-LURE MINNOW

This familiar name was used for one of the first Shakespeare lures (see page 362). This newer lure is made of molded rubber in the shape of a minnow. It is remarkably similar to the "Evolution Minnow" originally marketed around 1902. It appears in the 1931 catalog but is gone from catalogs soon after. The collector value range is from $10 to $20.

CATALOG SERIES #	BODY LENGTH	LURE WEIGHT
6504	2-5/8"	½ oz.

COLOR OR FINISH: *Shiner pattern; Yellow perch pattern.*

"SURFACE WONDER"
#42 WW

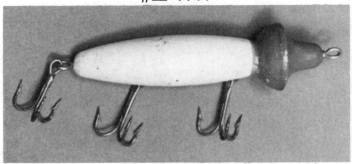

This plug was initially available in only one color design, a white body with a red head. An undated catalog (pre 1924) shows the "Surface Wonder" in a yellow body with red head and an "Imitation Frog Color" also.

A c1936 catalog lists the same lure as #42F, 3¾" body length, as available in one finish only; white body with a red head. It is called "The Floater". Collector value range: $10 to $20.

This plug is substantially similar to the "Luminous Floating Night Bait, #680", but is not luminous. It had two belly mounted treble hooks and one trailing treble (3T). Collector value range: $5 to $10.

CATALOG SERIES #	BODY LENGTH
42 WW	4"
42 YW	4"
42 FW	4"

COLOR OR FINISH: *White body, red head; Yellow body, red head; Imitation frog color.*

382

Shakespeare (cont'd.)

SHAKESPEARE SWIMMING MOUSE

This lure appears in a 1924 catalog and in various versions continues all the way into the fifties. it has always been around 3¼" long with the exception of a 2¾" "Junior Mouse" which appeared sometime in the early 1930's and a 2½" "Baby Mouse" which is first observed by the author in a 1949 catalog. All have had two belly mounted treble hooks as in the photograph here. The lure is frequently found missing the tail. Has been found with only one treble hook (1T) (post 1934). Collector value range: $3 to $6.

CATALOG SERIES #	BODY LENGTH	PLUG WEIGHT
578	3¼"	

COLOR OR FINISH: *Solid black, white head; Solid white, red head; Yellow, white belly, black back & head; Mouse gray, white belly; Solid black.*

6570	2¾"	5/8 oz.

COLOR OR FINISH: *Gray body, white belly, black back; Gray body, white belly; Tiger stripe; Solid white; White body, black head; White body, red head. All luminous.*

6577	2½"	½ oz.

COLOR OR FINISH: *Light gray; Imitation frog colors; Solid black; Black body, white head; Gray; Tiger stripe; White body, red head; Yellow body, red head.*

6578	3"	8/10 oz.

COLOR OR FINISH: *Black, shaded white belly.*

6580	2¾"	5/8 oz.

COLOR OR FINISH: *White, shaded red head; Mouse gray, white belly; Yellow, white belly, black shaded back and head; Tiger stripe, black over yellow; Yellow body, red head; Black body, yellow back stripe; Black body, white head.*

TANTALIZER

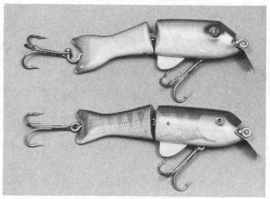

This is one of Shakespeare's first jointed baits. It appeared sometime around 1927-1929 as did the "Darting Shrimp" (see page 308). It is also one of the earliest of Shakespeare's use of the metal ventral fin. The plug has one belly mounted treble hook and one trailing treble (2T). Available with glass or painted eyes, in one size and weight, and only in two color patterns initially. In a 1934 catalog the trailing hook fastener has been changed to the "Ball Head Hook Retainer" from the original simple screw eye (see photograph). By 1937 this fastener had disappeared and again the screw eye came into use. The 1937 catalog also shows a slightly smaller "JR. TANTALIZER" and both had gained a second belly treble (3T). Collector value range: $10 to $20.

CATALOG SERIES #	BODY LENGTH	LURE WEIGHT
638 or 6638	4"	9/10 oz.

COLOR OR FINISH: **White body, shaded red head; *Natural pickerel.*

*The color patterns first available.

383   (cont'd.)

Shakespeare Tantalizer (cont'd.)

CATALOG SERIES #	BODY WEIGHT	LURE
639 or 6639	4″	¾ oz.

COLOR OR FINISH: *Yellow perch, scale finish; Shad finish; Black back with tan and gold vertical side stripes; Green back, silver & pink sides.*

THE TARPALUNGE

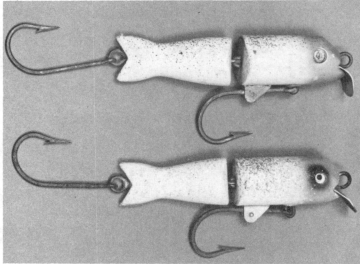

First observed in a 1930 catalog this is another jointed plug. It had a sloped head, ventral fin, a belly mounted single point hook and one trailing. It was absent from catalogs by the late 1930's to early 1940's. Collector value range: $20 to $30.

CATALOG SERIES #	BODY LENGTH	LURE WEIGHT
6640	5″$	2¾″

COLOR OR FINISH: *Shiner finish; Mullet finish; Red and white with silver flitters.*

WAUKAZOO SURFACE SPINNER

Note that each of the WAUKAZOO SURFACE SPINNERS have the patented Shakespeare ball-head hook hanger. Note also the different propeller spinners you may encounter. The one on the left plug has "Shakespeare Honorbilt" stamped into the blades.

The lure with no propeller spinner is a mystery. Never cataloged this way, the lure shows absolutely no wear at the nose. If it ever had a prop it would have to show some wear if it was used.

The earliest reference to this lure found so far was in an advertisement in the June, 1929 issue of Field and Stream. There is reason to believe it dates as early as 1924. It has a pear shaped body, ventral fin, one nose mounted propeller, a belly mounted treble hook and trailing treble. "Shakespeare No. 1" appears stamped on the propeller. It apparently wasn't too popular for it wasn't found in catalogs subsequent to 1931. Collector value range: $10 to $20.

CATALOG SERIES #	BODY LENGTH	LURE WEIGHT
6555	2-5/8″	¾ oz.

COLOR OR FINISH: *White body, shaded red head; Natural frog finish; Gray body, white belly with a flash or red at the throat.*

SHAKESPEARE "WEEDLESS FROG" #4 WF

As advertised in the 1910 catalog this was a lure cast in soft rubber in the shape and marking of a frog. There were rubber guards protecting the single trailing treble hook (1T). It was 3¼″ long and had a propeller on the nose. It apparently wasn't available long as subsequent catalogs offered weedless frogs made by others, and they do not list the #4 WF. Collector value range: $50 to $100.

SHAKESPEARE "WHIRLWIND SPINNER #65W"

The lure on the left has bow tie type propeller spinners. This is the earliest use prop.

This interesting plug apparently went out of production early on. By 1920 it was absent from the catalogs. It was listed in the 1910 catalog in one size only, 4" length overall, the body measuring 1¼". The colors offered were solid red, white, or yellow. All had a "Fancy feather bucktail" on the tail treble hook. The two side treble hooks were attached to the body with the see through fastener (3T). There were two propellers, tail and nose. These plugs range from $20 to $30 in collector value.

BABY POPPER

This little critter made its debut sometime in the early 1940's and had a short run as it had come and gone from catalogs in just a couple of years. Colors available unknown except for the two in the photograph here. Collector value range: $3 to $6.

WIGGLE-DIVER

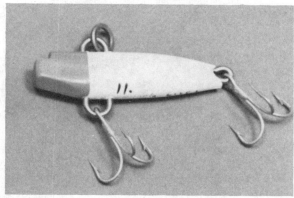

Tenite Wiggle Diver. Measures 2¼" body length.

The later lure (1940's), the Wiggle-Diver, was made of molded plastic (Tenite). Earlier ones have wooden bodies. Available in a 1940's catalog in three different sizes, each had one belly mounted treble hook and a trailing treble. Collector value range: $2 to $4.

CATALOG SERIES #	BODY LENGTH	LURE WEIGHT
6357	2¼"	½ oz.

COLOR OR FINISH: *Green bronze back, silver sides, white belly, scale finish.*

6538	3½"	1 oz.

COLOR OR FINISH: *Silver flitter, narrow green back, white belly.*

6539	4-5/8"	1¼ oz.

COLOR OR FINISH: *White body, red head; Yellow body, black head.*

SHAKESPEARE JIM DANDY LURES

It is not known exactly when, but sometime around 1930 Shakespeare either bought or somehow obtained the rights to the lure designs of the Wise Sportsman Supply of Chicago and incorporated them into the line. Specific information regarding the lures is sketchy due to incomplete catalog listings. What is known so far follows.

JIM DANDY SPOON BILL WOBBLER

This glass eyed Dandy shows up first in a 1931 catalog and is never again listed in any I was able to study through the the 1950's. The Jim Dandy line was an inexpensive selection of lures. Note the 1931 patent ball head tail hook hanger on the upper lure. The smaller size was not listed in the 1931 catalog entry. Collector value range: $5 to $10.

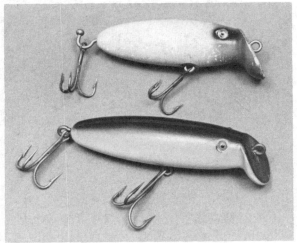

CATALOG SERIES #	BODY LENGTH	LURE WEIGHT
6400	3-¾ "	¾ oz.

COLOR OR FINISH: *Green back with red sides and white belly; Grey back shading down to white belly; Red body with black head and black over yellow spots; White body with red head; Yellow body with red over black spots and black back.*

JIM DANDY UNDERWATER

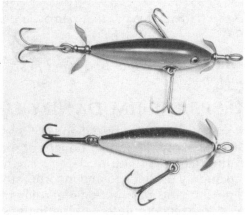

The upper glass eye 3T lure is the Jim Dandy Underwater. The other is unidentified but is most likely called the Jim Dandy Surface. The Jim Dandy Baits was an inexpensive line of Shakespeare lures. I only found one reference to the line (in a 1931 catalog). Collector value range: $5 to $10.

CATALOG SERIES #	BODY LENGTH	LURE WEIGHT
6406	3-¾ "	¾ oz.

COLOR OR FINISH: *Red body, black head; Rainbow; White body, red head; Greenish yellow sides, perch stripes with pink lower stripe, white belly and dark back.*

JIM DANDY NUMBER 6503

A 1931 catalog entry is the only place this lure was found. Part of a Shakespeare line meant to be inexpensive, this lure was un-named but looks something like a fat, unshaped Bass-A-Lure without the metal diving lip. They have pressed, painted eyes but might be found with glass eyes as some of the

other Jim Dandy Baits. No size or weight was listed. Colors listed were: Red body with black head, White body with red head, Green scale with silver sides and green back, Yellow perch scale finish, Black body with red head. Collector value range: $5 to $10.

JIM DANDY FLOATERS

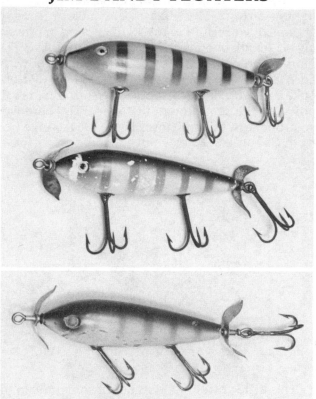

These are thought to be Jim Dandy floating lures because of their pressed, painted and zinc tack painted eyes. Also, the colors match one of those listed with the Jim Dandy Underwater Minnow above. They sport the late smooth edge, pointed Shakespeare propellers. The upper lure in the photograph has these propellers, marked Shakespeare. Collector value range: $5 to $10.

Shakespeare (cont'd.)

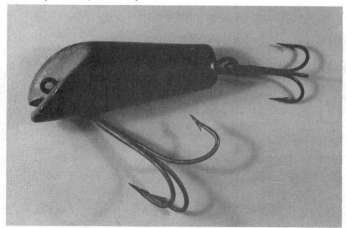

This is the original Schillinger patent JIM DANDY produced by Wise Sportsman Supply now owned by Shakespeare. It measures 2½" and has simple screw eye and washer hook hanger hardware. Collector value range: $5 to $10.

Two unidentified Jim Dandy lures. They each have the screw eye and washer hook hardware. The upper white body, red head lure has white iris glass eys and is 4¼" long. The lower measures 4-5/16" and has yellow glass eyes. Collector value range: $5 to $10.

Each of these are 4-1/8" long and has cup and screw eye hook hardware. The upper lure has white iris glass eyes while the lower sports embossed painted eyes. Note that the latter has a scale finish. Collector value range: $5 to $10.

SHAKESPEARE UNKNOWNS

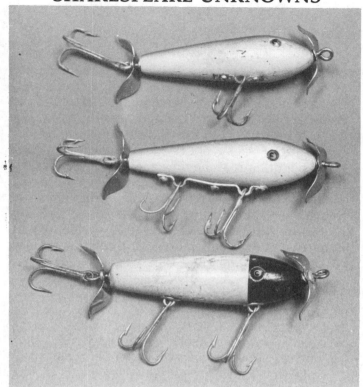

The three lures are wood belly with glass eyes and Shakespeare propeller spinners. There are two types of props and each have "Shakespeare Honorbuilt" stamped on the blades.

This strange looking plug is very well made and sports a marked Shakespeare propeller spinner.

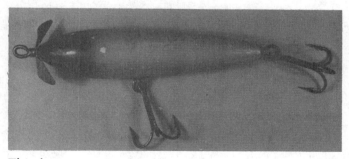

This lure was not found in any catalogs, but it has Shakespeare paint and hardware as well as the same unique triangular body shape as the Shakespeare FAVORITE. It measures 4-1/8" and utilizes screw eye and washer hook hanger hardware.

SILVER CREEK NOVELTY WORKS

Dowagiac, Michigan

Silver Creek Novelty Works started doing business sometime in the 1910's and continued until 1923 when the Moonlight Bait Company acquired them. This resulted in that company changing its name to the Moonlight Bait and Novelty Works. Be sure to turn to the Moonlight section for further information. The Silver Creek Company was making a number of lures at the time and many were carried on in the Moonlight line. There were, I'm sure, many more made by Silver Creek that Moonlight didn't continue to make, but just what they were is not presently known. Those I have been able to identify as originally made by Silver Creek and continued in the Moonlight line are listed following:

WIGGLER 3½"
  Colors and other size information unknown.
POLLY-WOG 4"
POLLY-WOG JUNIOR 3¼"
  Both were made in Solid yellow, Moss back, Yellow perch, White with red stripes, Yellow with black spots, and white with black stripes.
BASS-EAT-US 3"
BABE-EAT-US 2½"
TROUT-EAT-US 1¾"
  Each was available in Yellow perch, Rainbow, Moss back, White body with red head, Yellow body with red head, White body with green head and Yellow body with black head.
BUG-EAT-US 1½"
  Made in Moss back, White with red head, Yellow with red head, and White with a blue head.
PIKAROON MINNOW 5¼"
BABY PIKAROON 4¼"
  Colors available were Yellow, Moss back, White with red back, Yellow with black stripes, Solid white and Yellow perch.

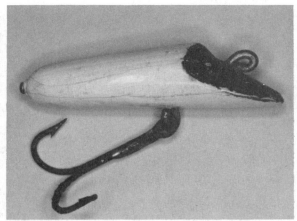

Silver Creek Novelty Works WIGGLER, 1¾". Collector value range: $100 to $200.

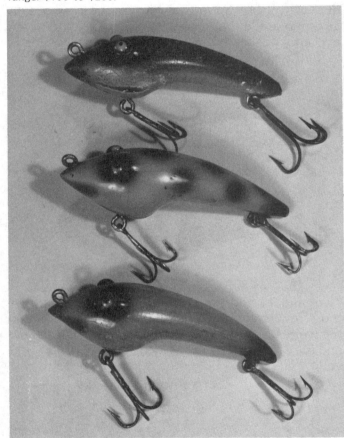

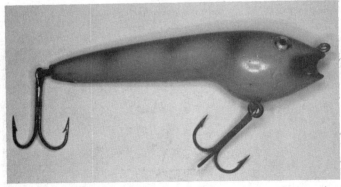

Silver Creek Novelty Works POLLYWOG, 3¾". The notched mouth version shown here is very rare and found only on Silver Creek models. Collector value range: $200 to $400.

As you have seen by a previous photo some Silver Creek Novelty Works Polly-Wogs came with a notched mouth (c1921). The top lure here is a Silver Creek Polly-Wog without the notch. It measures 3-1/8" and has white glass eyes said to be found on Silver Creek lures, but not on Moonlight. The next two are Moonlight Polly-Wogs. Note the fatter bodies. Silver Creek Polly-Wog Collector value range: $20 to $40.

Silver Creek (cont'd.)

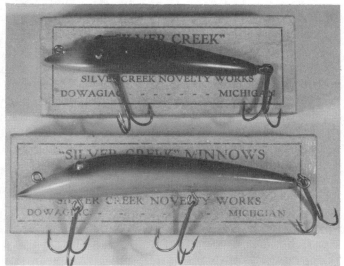

These two are the #1010 Baby Pikaroon (top) and the #903 Pikaroon. Each has a screw eye line tie and hook hangers and glass eyes. Collector value range: $20 to $40.

The 3" Bass-Eat-Us and the two 2-3/8" Babe-Eat-Us's are all Silver Creek made lures. Note the notches at the line tie areas. This is found only on the Eat-us type lures made by Silver Creek. Collector value range: $5 to $10.

A brochure from the Silver Creek Novelty Works showing four of their smaller lures. Note the notch at the line ties. This is a characteristic not found on the Moonlight versions of these produced after they acquired Silver Creek company in 1923.

This Polly-Wog measures 4-1/8", has yellow glass eyes and screw eye hook hangers and line tie. Collector value range: $30 to $40.

SOUTH BEND BAIT COMPANY

South Bend, Indiana

Sometime at the beginning of the 1900's F. G. Worden started a small factory to manufacture fishing tackle in South Bend, Indiana. At first the company specialized in the production of bucktail baits and over the next twenty years it evolved into the South Bend Bait Company. One of the early catalogs offered various bucktail spinners, flys and spoons, etc., but there were also eight or so wooden casting and trolling plugs. These early plugs usually employed one or more propellers and until around 1914 they were characterized by notched blades. Over the next few years several lures were added to the line and about the mid 1930's a new stronger hook-link hardware was introduced on the "Oreno" series plugs. it was an aluminum plate cemented and riveted inside the wood body. The metal eyes for attaching the hooks were the only parts to protrude from the body.

In 1938 the company introduced a series of "Obite" lures patterned after the "Oreno" plugs. The baits were molded of Tenite and employed a removable stainless steel wire running inside the length of the lure body instead of the aluminum plate mentioned above. This "Obite" series was meant to be less expensive line of plugs.

In the remaining years to the present changing technology and fishing habits and knowledge have dictated changes, additions and deletions, in their lures. The company continues successfuly today under the ownership of the Lazy Ike Corporation.

The listing of lures in this section is primarily of South Bend wooden lures from inception to the early 1950's. Although some early plastics are listed, most are not yet popularly collected. The metal products are far too complicated and not within the purview of this book, therefore they are not covered. A much more detailed study of the metal and all the wooden lures was undertaken and published by Jim Bourdon, **South Bend, Their Artificial Baits and Reels,** copyright 1985. This is highly recommended for the serious collector of South Bend. Refer to page 14 for source. It was prepared primarily for members of the National Fishing Lure Collectors Club, so Mr. Bourdon may not have it available for general distribution.

The lure listing does not contain photographs of all the lures with the same basic body design of the Bass-Oreno. I have grouped them all together following the Bass-Oreno #973. The last Bass-Oreno style lure is the Fish-Oreno on page 398. With this exception, the entries are arranged more or less chronologically according to when each was new to the line, ending with the series of "inexpensive" lures called "Best O Luck."

OBSERVATIONS AND CONCLUSIONS REGARDING IDENTIFICATION AND DATING OF SOUTH BEND LURES

1. Colors. The earliest South Bend catalog (1912) in the author's possession illustrates eight wooden plugs as available in some or all of the eighteen standard colors offered at that time. The body was of red cedar, the eyes were made of glass and counter sunk. Some were available in different hook configurations. The standard colors available at that time are listed below.

South Bend Standard Colors
As Listed in the 1912 Catalog

Solid white	Green cracked back, white belly
Solid red	Red back, white belly
Solid aluminum	Red back, yellow belly
Red head and tail, white body	Red cracked back, yellow belly
Red head and tail, aluminum body	Red cracked back, white belly
Red head and tail, white body	Sienna cracked back, yellow belly
Green back, white belly	Slate back, white belly
Green back, yellow belly	Rainbow
Green cracked back, yellow belly	Yellow perch

Around 1921-24 South Bend came out with a set of colors collectors refer to as the HEX colors. The new patterns were introduced ostensibly to imitate the Heddon hexagonal body design without resorting to the expense or possible litigation resulting from actually making the hexagonal body. The colors are quite similar and create the illusion, somewhat of the hexagonal body. They are listed as follows:

White body with green and red spots
Yellow body with green and red spots
Red body with black spots

There are shaded stripes oriented longitudinally on the body, helping to create the illusion. See photograph of Combination Minnow on page 331 for an example.

Other than the above, colors and finishes are not a reliable tool for identification and dating.

Eyes

a. Earliest South Bend lures had no eyes.

b. Glass eyes came along sometime prior to 1921, probably 1913-14.

c. The tack eye came along sometime around 1935-38. This period saw both glass eyes and tack eyes. Painted eyes (no tack) showed up on some of the very small lures such as the Ketch-Oreno in 1935.

d. Pressed eyes came along sometime in the late 1940's.

Propeller Spinners

a. Notched propellers almost identical to the early Shakespeare notched propellers are the first to be used on South Bend wooden lures.

b. The smooth blade, no notch propeller shows up around 1913-14. These are not marked with the South Bend name.

c. Sometime around 1919-20 they began stamping the propellers with "South Bend".

South Bend (cont'd.)

4. **Hardware**
   a. The first cup hardware was made of brass but soon it was nickel. The 1930's Best O Luck series have painted cup flanges (lure painted after cup installation). Most older South Bend lures have screw hook and cup hardware. Only the very earliest will be found with screw hooks.
   b. The only unique hook is called the Snap-Eye Detachable Single Hook (SD). First observed in a 1916 advertisement in Forest and Stream and then listed in catalogs until 1925. The following dated lists of lures show when they were available.

1916 Ad
Bass-Oreno
Surf-Oreno
Woodpeckers

1921 Catalog
Underwater Minnows
Panetella
Surface Minnows
Panetella Wobbler
Woodpeckers
Combination Minnows
Minbucks
Surf-Orenos
Babe-Oreno
Bass-Oreno
Musk-Oreno

1922 Catalog
Underwater Minnows
Panetella
Woodpeckers
Surf-Orenos
Babe-Oreno
Bass-Oreno
Musk-Oreno

The 1925 catalog stated they were available on all wooden lures. This may not be of much help, more a matter of interest. Because they were detachable, a fisherman could change them around with great ease. If you find a lure with the SD hook mint, in its original box, it will be helpful.

MIDGET MINNOW
#901

This is a very small version of the #902-#906 Underwater Minnows. It first appears in the author's earliest catalog (1912), but may have come along a bit before. They were gone by 1940. The plug is 2½" long weighing ½ ounce. The same colors as the #902-906 were available on this plug. It was available

with a treble hook mounted on each side, trailing treble and a nose mounted propeller spinner. Collector value range: $5 to $10.

UNDERWATER MINNOWS
Nos. 902, 903, 904, 905, 906
(c1912-1939)

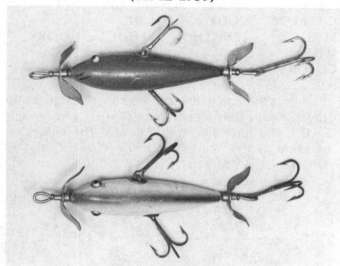

No. 902 and 903

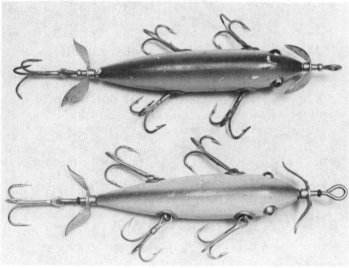

The upper lure has no name on big propeller (NNBP) and old style paint pattern with three hand painted gill marks (not visible in photo). Lower plug has name pressed on big propeller (NOBP).

The 1921 catalog illustrates several types of Underwater Minnows as available. The #903 and #904 both have three treble hooks, two propellers, and weight and length are the same. The only difference appears to be type of finish applied. Collector value range: $5 to $10

CATALOG SERIES #	BODY LENGTH	LURE WEIGHT	HOOKS
#904	3"	¾ oz.	3T

COLOR OR FINISH: *Rainbow; Yellow perch; Green cracked back with white belly; Red cracked back with yellow belly; Sienna cracked back with yellow belly; White body with dark shade back; Solid white; White body with red head; White body with red head and tail; Solid aluminum color; Solid red with black nose; Scale finish; Scale finish with red blend; Gold finish with red head.*

South Bend Underwater Minnows (cont'd.)

#904	3"	¾ oz.	3T

COLOR OR FINISH: *White body, red and green spots; Yellow body, red and green spots; Red body, black spots; Frog.*

The #902 Underwater Minnow is essentially the same as the others but has only two trebles and they are weedless hooks. Collector value range:

CATALOG SERIES #	BODY LENGTH	LURE WEIGHT	HOOKS
#902	3"	¾ oz.	.2T

COLOR OR FINISH: *Rainbow; White body, dark shaded back; Green cracked back, white belly.*

The #905 and **#906 are the same design as the others except they weigh more (1¼ oz.), are longer (3-5/8"), and have five treble hooks. The colors are the same as** #903 and #904 respectively. Collector value range: $5 to $10.

This is a #905 UNDERWATER MINNOW. It is identical to one illustrated in a 1918 South Bend catalog. It measures 3½", has yellow glass eyes and cup/screw eye hook hangers. Note the c1918 notched propeller spinners. Collector value range: $50 to $100.

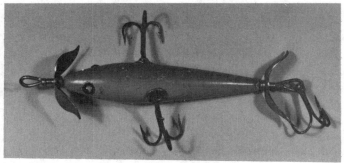

It is not known for certain that this lure is a South Bend product. It may not be apparent in the photo, but in handling this and the one above it becomes obvious that if South Bend didn't paint it then some other company did a remarkable job of copying their style. It's the same length and the eyes are yellow glass, but placed so that they are very cock-eyed. The cup and screw hook hardware is bigger and stronger than normal. Collector value range: $10 to $20.

THE PANATELLA MINNOW
(c1912-42)

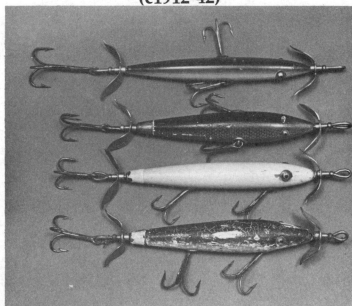

These plugs are arranged top to bottom, oldest to newest. Top lure has glass eyes, no tail cap and painted gill marks (not visible in photo) and no name on propellers. Second lure has tail cap, glass eyes and name pressed into props. Third lure has tail cap, large glass eyes and the propellers are different (may have been changed by an angler). Bottom lure is the strong saltwater version.

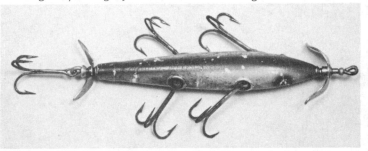

A five treble Panatella Minnow with a "Barracuda Brand" propeller on the tail. May have been changed by a fisherman.

This plug was newly introduced in 1912* in the 3T model and was removed sometime around the 1940's. It first weighed about 9/10 ounce and body length was 4¼". The last ones available weighted a bit more (1-1/8 ounce), but the length remained the same. Earliest versions had either three or five treble hooks (one trailing and the others side or belly mounted. Later catalogs made detachable single hooks an option. Collector value range: Early $10 to $15. Late $5 to $10.

CATALOG SERIES #	BODY LENGTH	LURE WEIGHT	HOOKS
#913	4¼"	9/10 oz.	3T
#915	4¼"	9/10 oz.	5T

COLOR OR FINISH: ***Green cracked back, white belly; **Rainbow; Yellow perch; White body, dark shaded back; Red body, dark shaded back; White body, red head and tail; Scale finish; Red head, aluminum color body; Frog; **Scale finish with red blend; Gold finish with red head; **Red head, white body.*
***These were the only four finishes available by 1940.**
**The 5T model is thought to be new in 1916.*

SURFACE MINNOW

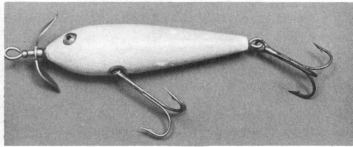

This particular plug shows up first in a 1912 catalog, the earliest South Bend catalog in the collection available. There were three versions first available there; The 920 W and 920 F, 921 RH, and 922 L. All have two trebles and one nose mounted propeller (notched until about 1914). The same numbers were used later for different plugs. A 1939 catalog lists #920 as a "Wounded Minnow", #921 as a "Panetella Wobbler", and #922 as a "Darting Bait". All are completely different plugs. Collector value range for the "Surface Minnows" is $5 to $10.

CATALOG SERIES #	BODY LENGTH	LURE WEIGHT
920	3½"	¾ oz.
921	3½"	¾ oz.
922	3½"	¾ oz.

COLOR OR FINISH: *Solid white or frog finish; White body with red head; Luminous.*

WEEDLESS SURFACE MINNOW

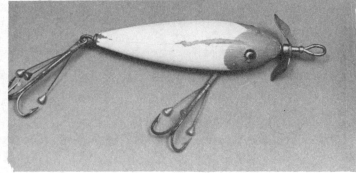

This is the same as 920 & 921 above except that it was offered with weedless hooks. Available only in white body with red head or frog finish. Collector Value Range: $5 to $10.

THE WOODPECKER

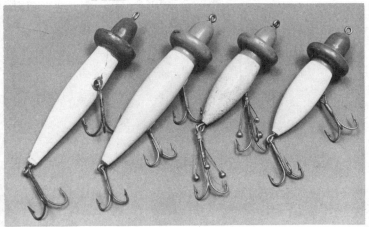

First found in a 1912 catalog as available in one design only; the body was white with head red. It had a distinct collar around the head (see far left in photo). By 1921 it was available with a frog finish and weedless hooks if desired. A "midget" size was also made available about in the 1914 catalog. By the mid 1910's it was being offered with a luminous surface paint. It had disappeared from South Bend catalogs by the late 1930's. The large two treble hook model in the photo is rare. The collector value range: $4 to $8.

CATALOG SERIES #	BODY LENGTH	LURE WEIGHT	HOOKS
923	4½"	1 oz.	3T

COLOR OR FINISH: *Red head with white body; Frog finish; All white.*

924	4½"	1 oz.	3T

COLOR OR FINISH: *Luminous.*

925(Midget)	3"	¾ oz.	2T

COLOR OR FINISH: *Red head with white body; All white.*

926(Midget)	3"	¾ oz.	2T

COLOR OR FINISH: *Luminous.*

COMBINATION MINNOWS

These baits appear in the 1912 catalog in two types (number of treble hooks). One has a single trailing treble and the other has the trailing treble and two more trebles, one mounted on each side. Both are in catalogs from the mid 1920's on. Collector value range: $10 to $15.

CATALOG SERIES #	BODY LENGTH	LURE WEIGHT	HOOKS
#931	2-5/8"	½ oz.	1T

COLOR OR FINISH: *White body, red and green spots, natural bucktail; Yellow body, red and green spots, natural bucktail; Red body, black spots, natural bucktail; Rainbow, natural bucktail; Green cracked back, white belly, natural bucktail; Yellow perch, natural bucktail; White body, dark shaded back, natural bucktail; Red body, dark shaded back, natural bucktail; White body, red head, natural bucktail; Luminous with white bucktail.*

#932	2-5/8"	½ oz.	1T

COLOR OR FINISH: *White body, red and green spots, white bucktail; yellow body, red and green spots, white bucktail; Red body, black spots, white bucktail.*

#933	2-5/8"	½ oz.	3T

South Bend (cont'd)

COLOR OR FINISH: *White body, red and green spots, natural bucktail; Yellow body, red and green spots, natural bucktail; Red body, black spots, natural bucktail.*

#934   2-5/8"   1 oz.   3T

COLOR OR FINISH: *White body, red and green spots, natural bucktail; Yellow body, red and green spots, natural bucktail; Red body, black spots, natural bucktail.*

THE MIN-BUCK
#943, #944, #945, #946, and #955

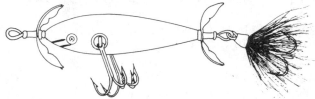

The 1912 catalog first offered the Min-Buck in "All Standard Colors". Two versions were available in the listing. The #943 with three trebles and the #945 with five trebles. The belly trebles were opposite side mounted. Both had trailing bucktail trebles. The illustration shows the early notched propeller. It is reproduced in the drawing above.

About 1914 two more, the #944 and the #946, were offered. These sport the smooth edge (no-notch) propeller spinners and new colors were added. They are the so-called "Hex" colors (see page 328). They were 3" long in 3T and 3-5/8" in 5T. The #955 was a Musky size Min-Buck, 5T at 5-1/4". No Min-Bucks were listed in catalogs from 1921 on. Collector value range: $5 to $10.

MUSKIE CASTING MINNOW
#953

This rare plug seems to have been offered for a very short time (c1914). Weighing in at 1¼ ounce, this fighter is 3-5/8 inches long. This lure is essentially the same body style as the #943 Min-Buck illustrated above, but it is bigger and heavier. It has the same hook configuration as well but is not supplied with a bucktail on the trailing treble. Collector value range: $5 to $10.

MUSKIE TROLLING MINNOW
#956

This is the same lure as the #955 Min-Buck (5T) but does not have a bucktail on the treble. 5¼ inch, 2¼ ounces. It has five trebles and was available in the 1912 catalog in all the standard colors listed on page 328. It was around until about 1922. Collector value range: $5 to $10.

SURF-ORENO
#963

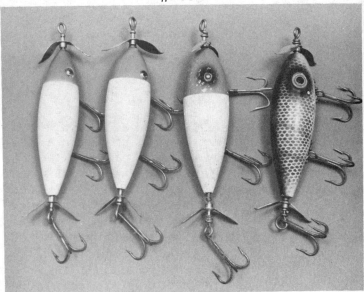

First appearing around 1916 this plug continued to be available throughout the years but the color design options dwindled from thirteen choices (1921) to only six by 1953. It sports two propellers and the later versions were available with ony three trebles. Early versions were available with either two or three. Body length is 3¾" and weight is one ounce. The earliest #963 Surf-Orenos had more elongated (TSB) bodies almost pointed at both ends and the later models were more rounded at the head. The original paint designs were: *red head with white body; *frog design; rainbow; solid red, black nose; green cracked back with white belly; white body with green and red spotted decorations, blue head with white body, *luminous; *scale finish; red head and aluminum color; *scale finish with red blend; and gold finish with red head. Collector value range: $3 to $6.

The only colors available by 1953. There was an additional finish, yellow body with red painted gills available then.

MIDGET SURF-ORENO

This plug appears around 1916 and is a smaller version of the #963 Surf-Oreno. It is 2¾" long and weights approximately ½ ounce. The same general comments made about the #963 apply to this #962 Midget Surf-Oreno. Collector value range: $3 to $10.

Midget Surf-Oreno

FLY ROD
SURF-ORENO
#961

This is a tiny 1½ inch version of the above Surf-Oreno. It was around from the late 1920's until the early 1940's. Weight was cataloged as "1 pound per dozen". You figure it out. Colors listed in 1927 were: Red head, white body; Rainbow; Imitation frog; White body with red and green decorations; Green scale finish; Scale finish with red blend. Collector value range: $2 to $3.

MUSKIE SURF-ORENO
#964

Appearing first around 1925 this is a beefy version of the Surf-Oreno. It has nose and tail mounted propellers, two belly mounted treble hooks and a trailing treble. Had disappeared by the mid 1930's. Collector value range: $3 to $10.

CATALOG SERIES #	BODY LENGTH	LURE WEIGHT
#964*	3¾"	1-1/18 oz.
#964	5½"	1-1/18 oz.

COLOR OR FINISH: **Red head, white body; **Rainbow; **Scale finish with green blend; Frog; Scale finish with red blend; yellow perch scale finish.

*This size appeared for a few years in the late 1930's.
**The first three finishes available.

BASS-ORENO
#973

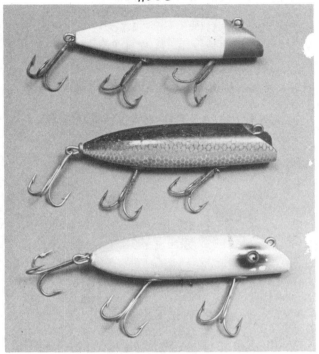

The most famous lure in the South Bend line. This lure first appeared in 1915 as part of their offerings, but it was probably available (in a slightly different design) before that. South Bend didn't invent the lure but rather bought the patent rights (J.S. Olds, December 19, 1915). Mr. Olds had been making and selling his lure before 1915. So if you see any weird looking plugs (the patent lure had an oval body) that seem much like the Bass-Oreno, it might be one of his. In any case the Bass-Oreno is still around today. It has undergone many changes through the years, but the design remains pretty much the same as the 1915 model. They have gone through eyes from no eyes to glass eyes (until 1920's) to tack eyes (c1935) to pressed eyes (c1951) and last to painted eyes in the 1960's. A major change in construction was introduced in 1934. Called the Better Bass-Oreno, the body was sawn out longitudinally, making a slot from the belly in. A die-cut aluminum plate was inserted, glued and riveted in. The result was that only the three hook hangers and line tie (integral with the plate) protruded from the body. This lasted only until 1942. The standard cup rig continued to be available throughout this period also.

It was available in a large variety of finishes by 1921. They are: red head, white body; yellow body, red and green spots; solid red, black nose; white body, red and green spots; rainbow; frog; red head, aluminum color body; luminous; scale; white body, blue head; scale with red blend; red head, gold color body; and solid black. The famous Bass-Oreno has survived throughout the years and has been expanded to include many sizes and finishes for just about any type of fishing. Collector value range for the earliest Bass-Orenos is $2 to $10.

South Bend (cont'd.)

CATALOG SERIES #	BODY LENGTH	LURE WEIGHT	HOOKS
#973	3½"	5/8 oz.	3T
#473*	3¾"	¾ oz.	3T
#73**	3¾"	¾ oz.	3T

*From 1934-35 this was the size listed in the catalogs.

**This is the number for the Better Bass-Oreno.

SALTWATER BASS-ORENO
#977

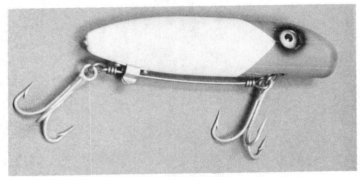

The lure in this photograph is a 1950's Saltwater Bass-Oreno called the King Basser. The older models do not have this wire and clip rigged hardware.

This is the same lure as the regular Bass-Oreno except that it is built with much stronger hardware. It has only one belly treble and a trailing treble hook. It was made from about 1924 through 1942; however, it was constructed exclusively with the aluminum plate hardware (discussed with the regluar Bass-Oreno) from 1934 on. Collector value range: $2 to $5.

CATALOG SERIES #	BODY LENGTH	LURE WEIGHT	HOOKS
#977	3½"	¾ oz.	2T

COLOR OR FINISH: *Red head, white body; Red arrow head, white body; *Rainbow; *Scale finish with green blend; *Scale finish with red blend; Red head, aluminum color body; Minnow scale finish; Iridescent pearl; Dace scale finish; Yellow perch scale finish; Pike scale finish; Yellow body, red & brown decorations; Luminous.

*These were the first four finishes available. The others had been added by 1939.

BASS-ORENO
WINDOW DISPLAY

One of these babies would be a prize addition to a South Bend plug collection. It was introduced for $4.00 in the late 1920's. Made of papier-mache it was two and one-half feet long and weighed about 10 pounds. Collector value range: $10 to $15.

BABE - ORENO' #972

1916 is thought to be the birth date for this baby. It is continuously available into the 1950's. At birth it was 2-¾ inches long, weighing ½ ounce. It was available in at least 14 finishes by 1927. It is the same shape body as the Bass-Oreno and has one belly treble and a trailing treble. It was also available in the Better Babe-Oreno aluminum plate construction (discussed with Bass-Oreno) from 1934 through 1942.

The oldest ones had no eyes and a shallower cupped head than the later versions and the paint line on the head was a straight vertical line. Size and weight has remained fairly constant through the years. Around 1926 eyes were added and a 1932 catalog illustrates it as available with detachable single hooks. By 1932-34 the paint design had changed to reflect an "arrow" design instead of the straight vertical paint line at the head. The accompanying photo illustrates eye type and paint design changes from oldest to the last glass eye model. Collector value range: $2 to $10.

CATALOG SERIES #	BODY LENGTH	LURE WEIGHT	HOOKS
#972	2¾"	½ oz.	2T

COLOR OR FINISH: *Red head, white body; Yellow body, red and green spots; Red body, black nose; White body, red and green spots; Rainbow; Frog; Red head, aluminum color body; Scale finish; Scale finish with red blend; Gold finish with red head; White body, blue head; Luminous.

MUSK-ORENO

This is a large version of the Bass-Oreno new about 1916. First found in a 1921 catalog supplement, it was offered with a "...5 inch piano wire leader having a snap arrangement, permitting easy removal if preferred." By 1930 this leader option was not mentioned. The earliest models have no eyes, but by 1925-26 eyes were present and sometime in 1934-35 the improved aluminum plate, hook-link was added.

South Bend (cont'd.)

The plug had two belly mounted trebles and one trailing. It was removed from the line sometime in the early 1940's. Collector value range: $5 to $6.

CATALOG SERIES #	BODY LENGTH	LURE WEIGHT	HOOKS
#976	4½"	1-1/8 oz.	3T

COLOR OR FINISH: *Red head, white body; Yellow body, red and green spots; White body, red and green spots; Red body, black nose; Rainbow; Frog; Red head, aluminum color body; Scale finish; Scale finish with red blend; Gold finish with red head; Blue head, white body; Luminous.*

TROLL-ORENO
#978

Called the "newest and latest number of the 'Oreno' baits" in the 1921 catalog. It was made of light cedar, had two belly treble hooks and one trailing treble. The same general comments concerning changes over the years that are made about the Bass-Oreno and Babe-Oreno apply here as well. Collector value range: $5 to $10.

CATALOG SERIES #	BODY LENGTH	LURE WEIGHT	HOOKS
#978	6½"	2 oz.	3T

COLOR OR FINISH: *Green back, white belly; Frog; Scale finish with red blend; Gold finish, red head; Red head, white body; Yellow body with red and green spots; White body with red and green spots; Solid red with black nose; Rainbow; Red head with aluminum color body; White body, blue head.*

TROUT-ORENO
#971

The Trout-Oreno came along in 1920 and stayed in the line into the 1950's. It is the same shape as the Bass-Oreno, is 1¾ inches long and has one belly mounted double hook. Collector value range: $2 to $3.

FLY-ORENO
#970

This little bit of a wooden lure was new about 1921 and continues to be available into the 1950's. It is one inch long with one belly mounted double hook. Collector value range: $2 to $3.

WIZ-ORENO
#967

This is an unusual plug that utilized the Babe-Oreno body. There was a belly mounted long shank single point hook with a special "swirling" propeller mounted on the hook shank and a gray hackle covering the point. There was a tail mounted pork rind attachment also. New in 1925, this lure had disappeared from catalogs by 1930. Collector value range: $5 to $10.

CATALOG SERIES #	BODY LENGTH	LURE WEIGHT
#967	2¾"	unk.

COLOR OR FINISH: *Red head, white body; Yellow perch scale finish; Rainbow; Scale finish with green blend; Red body, black nose; Red head, aluminum color body; Copper finish.*

TARP-ORENO
#979

Long about 1921-22 this large plug appeared. It is the same body design as the other "Oreno" type baits. In 1922 this plug was fitted with a belly mounted double hook and a trailing double, but by 1925 and from then on the hooks were single point. Collector value range: $5 to $10.

CATALOG SERIES #	BODY LENGTH	LURE WEIGHT
#979	8"	5 oz.

COLOR OR FINISH: *Mullet scale finish; Red head, white body; Red head, aluminum color body; Scale finish with green blend; Scale finish with red blend; Rainbow; Iridescent pearl; Minnow scale finish.*

KING-ORENO
#986

This is the same design as the Tarp-Oreno but smaller (6½" body length) and has only one single hook (belly mount). It first appears in the early 1920's and has disappeared from the line in the 1940's. Collector value range: $15 to $10.

CATALOG SERIES #	BODY LENGTH	LURE WEIGHT
#986	6½"	2 oz.

COLOR OR FINISH: *Yellow perch scale finish; Red head, white body; *Red arrowhead, white body; Red head, aluminum color body; *Scale finish with green blend; Scale finish with red blend; Rainbow; *Minnow scale finish.*

These are the only three finishes available by the time it was discontinued.

COAST-ORENO
#985

This bait is 4½" in body length and weighs 1½ oz. All comments made about the "King-Oreno" #986 apply to this plug as well.

MIDGE-ORENO
#968

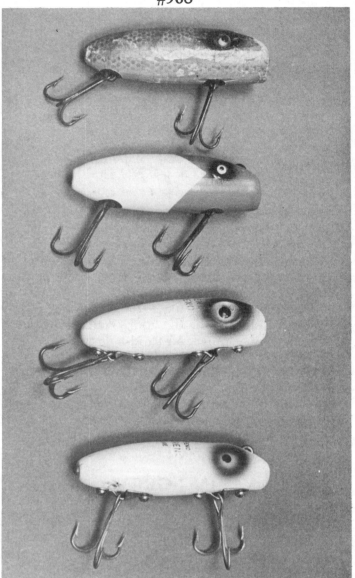

KETCH-ORENO

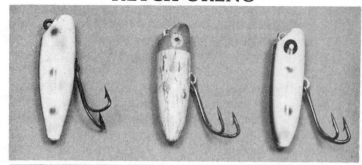

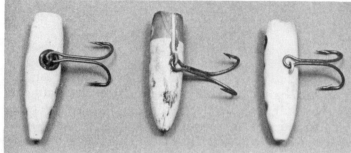

This small plug was first observed by the author in a 1932 catalog. It had one belly mounted double hook and was gone by 1940. Collector value range: $2 to $3.

CATALOG SERIES #	BODY LENGTH	LURE WEIGHT
#909	1½"	1 oz. minus

COLOR OR FINISH: *Red arrowhead, white body; Red arrowhead, yellow body; Scale finish with red blend; Scale finish, green; Pike scale finish; Frog.*

FISH-ORENO

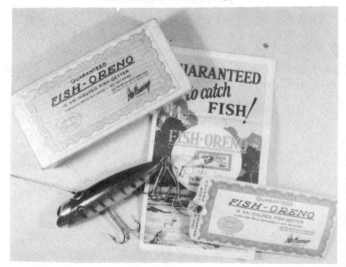

This interesting plug appeared in South Bend catalogs about 1927. The catalog states "The Fish-Oreno is the first lure ever produced that is **guaranteed** by the manufacturer to catch fish." "It is covered by an insurance policy attached to the bait, that is backed by the resources of the South Bend Bait Co." "Can be sold to any angler with positive guarantee of 'money back' if not satisfied after one year's use."

This plug was first found in the catalog collection in a 1932 issue and continued to be included from that point on. It had one belly treble and one treble mounted just under the tail end of the plug body. Collector value range: $2 to $4.

CATALOG SERIES #	BODY LENGTH	LURE WEIGHT
#968	2¼"	3/8 oz.

COLOR OR FINISH: **Red head, white body; Red arrowhead, white body; **Red arrowhead, yellow body; **Black arrowhead, white body; *Yellow perch, scale finish; **Green scale finish; **Pike; Silver speckled, white body, green back stripe; Rainbow; Copper scale finish; White head, black body; Minnow scale finish, silver, black, and red: Dace scale finish.*

Available for only a short time after 1932.
**These were the only colors available in 1932. Others added later.*

South Bend (cont'd.)

The plug is similar to the Bass-Oreno but has a polished metal head, a twisted wire lead permanently attached to a screw eye at the top of the head. One belly mounted treble hook and a trailing treble. The guarantee tag and promotion of the guarantee had disappeared by 1939, but the bait was produced on into the early 1950's. Collector value range: $3 to $6.

CATALOG SERIES #	BODY LENGTH	LURE WEIGHT
#953	3½''	5/8 oz.

COLOR OF FINISH: *White body, red head; Pike finish; Scale finish; Yellow body, green and red spots; Copper scale finish; Silver body; Frog; Rainbow; Pike scale finish; Silver speckled white body, green stripe; Minnow scale finish, silver, black and red; Yellow perch scale finish.*

VACUUM BAIT

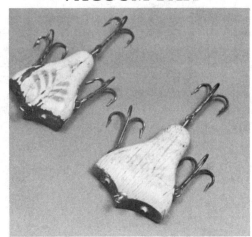

Belly view of two South Bend Vacuum Baits with glass eyes.

Belly view of three South Bend Vacuum Baits. Left had glass eyes. Center, no eyes. Right, smaller size with no eyes and Howe's swivel hook hangers.

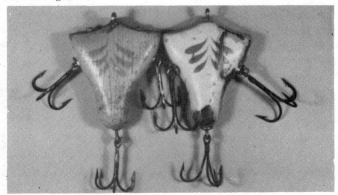

Belly view. Left is a South Bend Vacuum Bait with glass eyes. Right is Howe's Vacuum Bait.

This lure first occurs in a 1922 South Bend catalog but it is known to have been patented in 1909 by Howe (see page 270). Apparently South Bend obtained the rights to the patent. As you can see by the accompanying photographs, the earliest South Bend versions used the original Howe swivel hook hanger hardware. What probably happened is that upon purchasing the rights to manufacture the lure, South Bend also acquired some of Howe's inventory. As this was exhausted, South Bend began using their own hardware. Hence the mixture of hardware and possible bodies. At first South Bend only offered the larger size but soon after a second, smaller size was added. Some of the earliest South Bend Vacuum Baits had glass eyes. The lure remained in catalogs until continued in the 1940's. Collector value range: $15 to $30.

CATALOG SERIES #	BODY LENGTH	LURE WEIGHT
#1	2-3/8''	¾ oz.
#21	2''	½ oz.

COLOR OR FINISH: *White body, red stripes; Yellow spotted with red and green; Rainbow; Dragon fly; Frog, Red spotted with yellow & black.*

PIKE-ORENOS

Left to right: #957, #975, #956, #974. Shows major design changes discussed in the text.

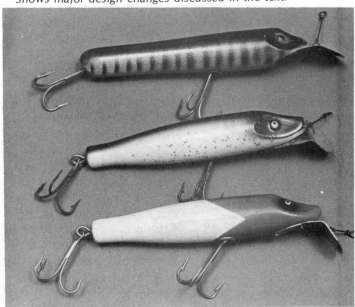

Shows three of the lip types. Top has long narrow lip with name on it. Middle has a hammered metal lip. Bottom has steep lip with no name. Shows body design changes.

South Bend (cont'd.)

The first of the Pike-Orenos show up around 1922. They were nothing like the familiar two curved eye scoop model at first. It came out in two models, the regular at 4¼″ inches and the Midget at 3 inches. The first body style was the same as the Bass-Oreno. They fitted a metal plate into the nose scoop that extended down creating a lip (see No's. 974 and 975 in upper photo at left). They had no eyes. The next model had the curved eye scoops resulting in a fish-like face and nose. The body was slightly tapered but remained chunky. They continued to refine the body to the more familiar shape (c1932). Two more sizes were added that year, the Baby Pike-Oreno (3¼″) and the Big Pike-Oreno (5-3/8″).

All three were the same design. It had changed to a more pointed nose with eye depression scooped out of each side of the nose. The metal lip no longer covered the nose but was mounted beneath the nose and bent downward to impart the deep diving action. It had a one inch wire leader permanently fastened to the plate. One of the treble hooks had been removed and the belly position of the two remaining trebles changed.

By 1935 an even smaller one, the Midget Pike-Oreno (2½″) was offered, and the newer arrow paint design was utilized on the three smallest versions. A third treble hook reappeared on the two largest sizes about 1935 also. Collector value range for old $3 to $6 and for newer $1 to $4.

CATALOG SERIES #	BODY LENGTH	LURE WEIGHT	HOOKS
*974	3″		2 SD
*975	4¼″		3T
955(Midget)	2½″	½ oz.	2T
956(Baby)	3¼″	5/8 oz.	2T
957(Reg.)	4½″	¾ oz.	3T, 2T
958(Big)	5-3/8′	1½ oz.	3T, 2T

COLOR OR FINISH: *Red head, white body; Red arrowhead, white body; Iridescent pearl; Green scale finish; yellow perch scale finish; Pike scale finish; Rainbow; **Silver speckled white body, green stripe; Scale finish with red blend; Red head, aluminum color body; Frog; Red with black nose; White body, green and red spots.*

*This was the first style Pike-Oreno.
**This finish was not used with the "Big Pike-Oreno".

JOINTED PIKE-ORENO
#960

The jointed version of the Pike-Oreno shows up first around the mid 1930's. It had undergone a design change by the 1950's and the number had changed to #2956. The old plug had a scoop taken out of the top of the head and was almost twice as long as the newer one. The newer version had two scoops in the head, one on either side making it more or less a pointed nose, old had two belly trebles and a trailer, new had the trailer but only one belly treble. Collector value range: $3 to $6.

CATALOG SERIES #	BODY LENGTH	LURE WEIGHT
#960	7″	2-1/8 oz.

COLOR OR FINISH: *Red arrowhead, white body; Scale finish, silver, black and red; Green scale finish; Red head, aluminum color body.*

WHIRL-ORENO
#935

New around the late 1920's this surface lure had feathers mounted on a trailing treble hook. The body was 3½″ long, overall, 3″ wide, and weighed in at 5/8 oz. It was available in three finishes; red head, white body; frog finish; butterfly. The plug was available up to the early 1940's. Collector value range: $15 to $30.

GULF-ORENO
and MIDGET GULF-ORENO

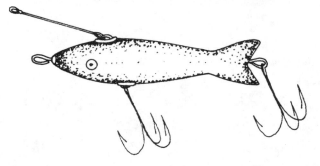

New around 1927 this plug was minnow shaped. It has a belly mounted treble, a trailing treble, and a removable wire leader attached to the top, aft portion of the head. Had disappeared from catalogs by the early 1930's. Collector value range: $15 to $30.

CATALOG SERIES #	BODY LENGTH	LURE WEIGHT
#983 (reg.)	3½″	
#982 (Midget)	2¾″	½ oz.

COLOR OR FINISH: *White body, red around eyes, red gills; White body, gold speckled, red head; White body, silver speckled, black around eyes.*

MINNOW
#999

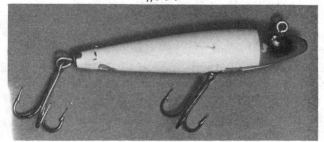

This slender plug was first found in a 1930 catalog. It has a line tie eye on top of the nose, a belly treble and a trailing treble hook. Note the small metal fin protruding from beneath the head. Collector value range: $5 to $10.

CATALOG SERIES #	BODY LENGTH	LURE WEIGHT
#999	4" overall	5/8 oz.

COLOR OR FINISH: *Red head, white body; Green cracked back; Scale finish; Red head, black nose; Yellow perch; Muskie finish.*

PLUNK-ORENO
#929

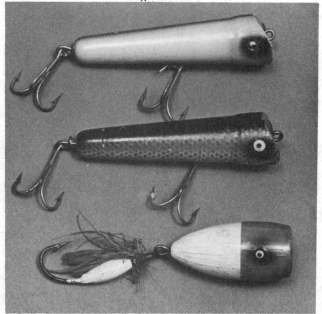

This plug shows up around the late 1920's and stayed in catalogs until 1932. It disappeared for several years to reappear as an entirely different design plug around 1939. (See photograph). The early plug was a long tapered body with a scoop head, one belly mounted treble hook, a trailing treble, and glass eyes. It was 3¾" long and weighted 5/8 ounce. It came in three color finishes; red head, white body; green scale finish; and yellow perch scale finish. The new design was a short wood body with a tail mounted weighted single hook covered with fancy feathers. It weighed 5/8 ounce and was 4" long overall, body less than 2". It was available in: red head, white body; black body; yellow perch; rainbow; and frog. Collector value range: $5 to $10.

TEASE-ORENO
#940

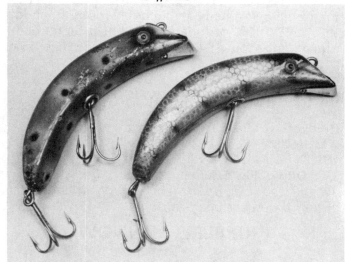

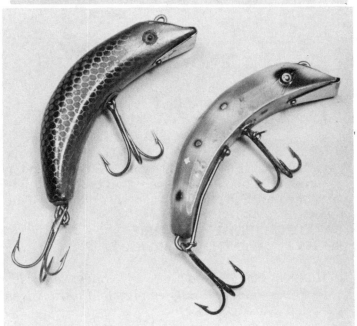

Midget Tease-Oreno. 2½" version of the Tease-Oreno. Collector value range: $3 to $6.

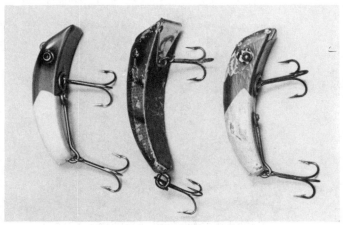

3¼" #939 Baby Tease-Oreno

(cont'd. next page)

401

South Bend (cont'd.)

This plug was introduced sometime prior to 1930. It has a chrome plated metal head plate, a trailing treble and a belly treble hook, looks much like the "LAZY IKE" of today. The Midget didn't come along until about 1940. Collector value range: $5 to $10.

CATALOG SERIES #	BODY LENGTH	LURE WEIGHT	HOOKS
#936 (Midget)	2-7/8"	½ oz.	2T
#939 (Baby)	3-¼"	½ oz	2T
#940	4-1/8"	5/8 oz.	2T

COLOR OR FINISH: *Red head, white body; Rainbow; Frog; Green scale finish; Yellow perch; Minnow scale finish; Iridescent pearl finish.*

CRIPPLED MINNOW

This plug first appears in a 1930 catalog but was gone by 1935. It had a belly mounted treble* and a trailing treble hook. There were two propeller spinners, one nose and one tail mounted. Collector value range: $2 to $4.

CATALOG SERIES #	BODY LENGTH	LURE WEIGHT
#965	3¼"	5/8 oz.

COLOR OR FINISH: *Red head, white body; Red head, black nose; Luminous; Green scale finish; Silver speckled; Muskie scale.*

Technically it is side mounted but the lure floats on its side therefore it is called belly mount.

PLUG-ORENO
#959

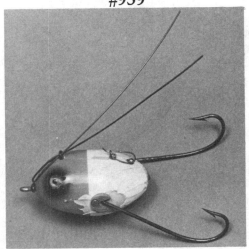

This is a weedless surface plug that was new in the 1930 catalog. Has two belly mounted single

hooks, a pork rind attachment on top of the body, and two wire weed guards. It was made into the 1940's. Collector value range: $2 to $4.

CATALOG SERIES #	BODY LENGTH	LURE WEIGHT
#959	2"	5/8 oz.

COLOR OR FINISH: *Red head, white body; Frog; Yellow body, red and green decorations.*

MOUSE-ORENO
#949

New in the early thirties this 2¾", 5/8 ounce mouse shaped plug had a flexible tail, a metal lip with wire leader attached and one belly mount treble hook. The original finishes available were: Gray mouse back with white belly; solid black; and white body with red blended eyes and gray stripes down the back. In 1934 a new finish was added. It was a fuzzy gray mouse-like skin finish. It replaced the first finish described above. The plug was available throughout the years after. There was a smaller fly rod version (#948) made as well. Collector value range (#949): $5 to $10.

MIN-ORENO

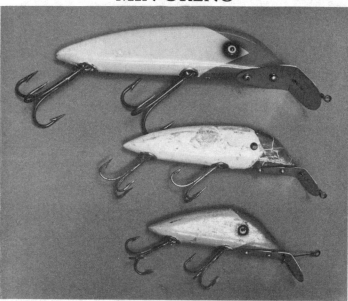

Three sizes of the Min-Oreno. Center lure has been repaired.

A new lure for 1932 the Min-Oreno was three years in designing according to the catalog. It is a departure from the usual shapes in the South Bend line. The plug was made in three different sizes each

South Bend (cont'd.)

available in six different finishes. It had an under tail mounted treble, belly treble, painted eyes and a metal diving lip under the nose. It was made throughout the 1930's. Collector value range: $5 to $10.

CATALOG SERIES #	BODY LENGTH	LURE WEIGHT
#926	3"	3½ oz.
#927	4"	4½ oz.
#928	5-5/8"	6 oz.

COLOR OR FINISH: *Red arrowhead, white body; Red arrowhead, yellow body; Yellow perch, scale finish; Pike, scale finish; Green scale finish; Scale finish with red blend.*

LUNGE-ORENO

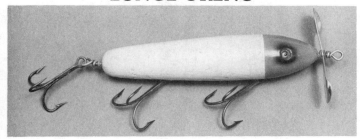

This large plug was new around 1930. The first version of it had two belly mount trebles and a trailing treble. There were two extra-large aluminum propellers, one at tail and nose. By 1932 the tail propeller had been eliminated for some reason. It remained this way all the way into the 1940's. The axis for the propeller was heavy wire passing all the way through the length of the body with the line tie incorporated at the front and the trailing treble at the back making a direct connection. Collector value range: $5 to $15.

CATALOG SERIES #	BODY LENGTH	LURE WEIGHT
#966	6"	2½ oz.
#965	3¾"	1-1/8 oz.

COLOR OR FINISH: *Red head, white body; Pike scale finihs; Yellow body, red and brown decorations; Scale finish with red blend.*

SLIM-ORENO
#912

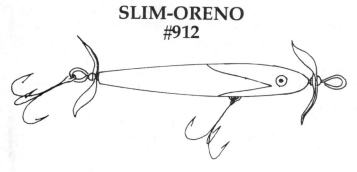

This was a new plug for 1932 that is very similar in design to the Panetella. It continues to be offered through the 1930's. The plug has nose and tail propellers a belly treble and trailing treble hook and painted eyes. Collector value range: $2 to $4.

CATALOG SERIES #	BODY LENGTH	LURE WEIGHT
#912	3¾"	½ oz.

COLOR OR FINISH: *Red arrowhead, white body; Green cracked back, white belly; Rainbow; Yellow perch, scale finish; Scale finish with red blend; Green scale finish.*

TRUCK-ORENO
#936

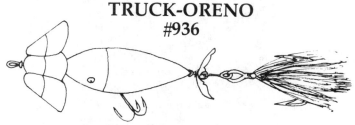

A new plug for 1938 and produced until sometime in the 1940's. This lure had an unusual head shaped so that it would turn like a propeller on retrieve. The body had one belly treble, a small trailing spinner forward of a trailing feathered treble hook. Collector value range: $40 to $60.

CATALOG SERIES #	BODY LENGTH	LURE WEIGHT
#936	9" overall	5 oz.

COLOR OR FINISH: *Red head, white body, red & white feathers; Frog, red & white feathers; Yellow with black stripe, black & red dots, red and white feathers.*

ENTICE-ORENO
#991

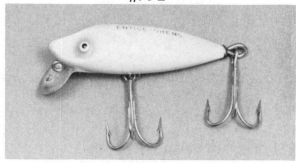

A new plug for 1938, it continued in production into the early 1940's. In 1939 apparently the Fish-Obite #1991 (Tenite body) was introduced to replace the Entice-Oreno #991 although the latter was still available at that time. The Entice-Oreno had one belly mount treble and a trailing treble hook. It has a metal lip and line tie under the nose. Collector value range: $2 to $4.

CATALOG SERIES #	BODY LENGTH	LURE WEIGHT
#991	2-5/8"	½ oz.

COLOR OR FINISH: *Red arrowhead, white body; White arrowhead, black body; Black arrowhead, white body; Silver speckle, white body, green back stripe; Yellow perch scale; Dace scale; Pike scale; White body, red and green decorations; Pearl finish; Rainbow, blue back; Minnow scale finish; Red body, black shaded eyes.*

TEX-ORENO
Sinker-#995
Floater-#996

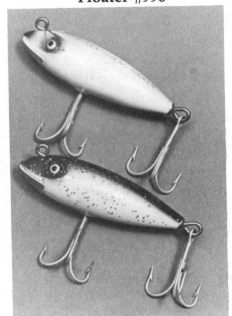

Appearing in the late 1930's this plug was available with or without a weighted head. It had one belly treble and a trailing treble hook. Originally developed for trout fishing in the Houston-Corpus Christi Gulf waters. Collector value range: $2 to $4.

CATALOG SERIES #	BODY LENGTH	LURE WEIGHT
#995 (Sinker)	2¾''	5/8 oz.
#966 (Floater)	2¾''	½ oz.

COLOR OR FINISH: *Red arrowhead, white body; White arrowhead, yellow body; Rainbow, blue back; Pearl finish; Silver speckled; Minnow scale finish; Dace scale.*

TWO-ORENO
and BABY TWO-ORENO

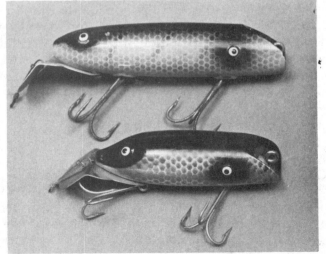

New in the mid to late 1930's this unique plug came in two sizes. Each had two belly trebles, four eyes (2 each end), two line ties and a metal lip. The line could be tied to either end. It had been eliminated from the line by the 1940's. Collector value range: $2 to $4.

CATALOG SERIES #	BODY LENGTH	LURE WEIGHT
#975	3¾''	¾ oz.
#974	3''	½ oz.

COLOR OR FINISH: *Red arrowhead, white body; Rainbow with blue back; Frog; Yellow perch scale; Pearl; Green scale finish.*

TWO-OBITE
and BASS-OBITE

These are the same plugs as the Two-Oreno and Bass-Oreno except that they are made of "Tenite". This came about 1938 and the "Tenite" material was used more and more for these and other plugs as the years passed by. Collector value range: Two-Obite $1 to $2; Bass-Obite $1 to $2.

DARTING BAIT

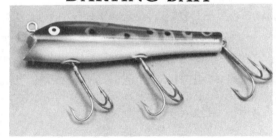

This is part of a series of low cost plugs marketed by South Bend in the 1930's and 1940's. It has a "V" shaped mouth notch, two belly trebles and one trailing treble hook. Collector value range: $2 to $3.

CATALOG SERIES #	BODY LENGTH	LURE WEIGHT
#922	4''	½ oz.

COLOR OR FINISH: *Splotch frog finish; Red head, white body; Silver speckled white body, green back stripe; Pike scale; Yellow perch scale finish; White head, black body.*

STANDARD PIKE LURE #930
BABY PIKE LURE #907
JOINTED STANDARD PIKE LURE #931
JOINTED BABY PIKE LURE #908

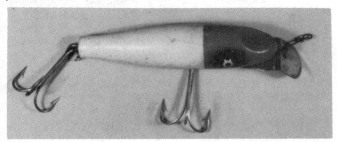

These four plugs are part of the low cost series called "Best-O-Luck" lures marketed by South Bend in the 1930's and 1940's. All have a trailing treble, one belly mount treble, a slope nose, and metal lip with wire leader attached. Collector value range: $3 to $6.

CATALOG SERIES #	BODY LENGTH	LURE WEIGHT
#907	3¼"	½ oz.
#908	3½"	½ oz.
#930	4-3/8"	5/8 oz.
#931	4½"	5/8 oz.

COLOR OR FINISH: *Red head, white body; Pike finish; Pike scale finish; Green striped; Silver speckled body, green back stripe; Yellow perch, scale finish; Rainbow; Green scale finish.*

STANDARD WOBBLER #943 and BABY WOBBLER #942

These plugs are part of the South Bend low cost series called Best-O-Luck and marketed through the 1930's and 1940's. They are the same design, the Baby Wobbler having one trailing treble and one belly treble hook and the larger having a second belly treble. Collector value range: $2 to $4.

CATALOG SERIES #	BODY LENGTH	LURE WEIGHT
#942	2¾"	½ oz.
#943	3¾"	5/8 oz.

COLOR OR FINISH: *Red head, white body; Green striped; Pike finish; Green scale finish; Pike scale finish; Yellow perch scale finish.*

WEIGHTED WOBBLER #941

This lure is part of the "Best-O-Luck" series of low cost plugs marketed by South Bend in the 1930's and 1940's. It has a metal lip belly mounted treble, and trailing treble hook. Collector value range: $1 to $2.

CATALOG SERIES #	BODY LENGTH	LURE WEIGHT
#941	2-5/8"	½ oz.

COLOR OR FINISH: *Red head, white body; Green striped; Iridescent pearl finish; White silver speckled, green back stripe; Rainbow, blue back; Red dace scale finish; Pike scale finish; Yellow perch scale finish.*

BABY WOUNDED MINNOW #914

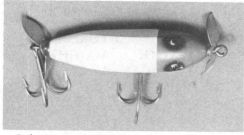

Baby Wounded Minnow. Note flat sides.

This plug is part of a low cost line lures marketed by South Bend in the 1930's and 1940's called the "Best-O-Luck" series. It had a nose and tail propeller, a trailing treble hook, and a belly mounted treble hook. Collector value range: $1 to $2.

CATALOG SERIES #	BODY LENGTH	LURE WEIGHT
#914	2¾"	½ oz.

COLOR OR FINISH: *Red head, with body; Silver speckled body, red and brown stripes; Pike finish; Yellow perch, scale finish.*

SURFACE LURE #916

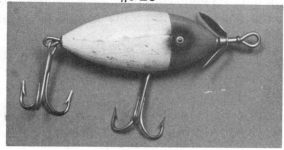

South Bend (cont'd.)

This is one of South Bends low cost line of lures marketed in the 1930's and 1940's. The lure was called "Best-O-Luck". This was an elongated egg shape plug with a propeller at the nose, a belly treble and trailing treble hook. Collector value range: $1 to $2.

CATALOG SERIES #	BODY LENGTH	LURE WEIGHT
#916	2¾"	5/8 oz.

COLOR OR FINISH: Red head, white body; Frog finish.

SURFACE LURE
#950

One of the "Best-O-Luck" bait series. This was a low cost line of lures marketed by South Bend in the 1930's and 1940's. This plug had a front propeller, belly treble, and a trailing treble hook. Collector value range: $1 to $2.

CATALOG SERIES #	BODY LENGTH	LURE WEIGHT
#950	3¼"	½ oz.

COLOR OR FINISH: Red head, white body; Green back blending to white belly; Silver body, red throat; Yellow body, red back stripe.

WEIGHTED
UNDERWATER LURE
#91 and #918

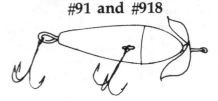

Part of the South Bend low cost lure series called "Best-O-Luck" and marketed through the 1930's and 1940's. The #910 had one nose propeller spinner, one trailing treble hook and two side-mounted trebles, one on each side of the body. The #918 is the same except has one belly treble in place of the two side-mounted ones. Collector value range: $2 to $4. #918 $4 to $8.

CATALOG SERIES #	BODY LENGTH	LURE WEIGHT
#910	3"	5/8 oz.

COLOR OR FINISH: Red head, white body; Green back, white belly; Yellow body, red back stripe; Silver body, red throat.

#918	3"	5/8 oz.

COLOR OR FINISH: Red head, white body; Rainbow with blue back; Pike finish.

WOUNDED MINNOW
#920

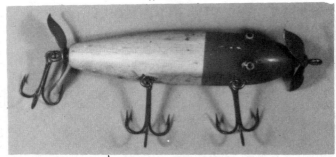

One of the "Best-O-Luck" series. This was a low cost line of lures marketed by South Bend in the 1930's and 1940's. It had a nose and tail propeller, two belly mounted trebles, and a trailing treble hook. Collector value range: $1 to $2.

CATALOG SERIES #	BODY LENGTH	LURE WEIGHT
#920	3-5/8"	¾ oz.

COLOR OR FINISH: Red head, white body; Silver speckled body, red & brown stripes; Pike finish; Yellow perch, scale finish.

PANATELLA WOBBLER
#921

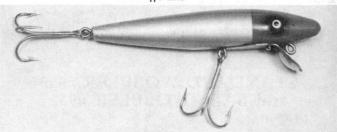

This plug is part of the low cost South Bend series of lures called Best-O-Luck marketed in the 1930's and 1940's. It has a metal lip belly mounted treble, and trailing treble hook. Collector value range: $4 to $8.

CATALOG SERIES #	BODY LENGTH	LURE WEIGHT
#921	4"	5/8 oz.

COLOR OR FINISH: Red head, white body; Red head, aluminum color body; Green striped.

SOUTH COAST MINNOW

H.C. Royer   **Los Angeles, CA**

The South Coast Minnow was first offered in advertising around 1910-11 with one of the ads commenting on their "...remarkable reception ... the last three years." A search turned up no patent, but the ads identified the inventor and source as a Dr. H.C. Royer of Terminal Island, Los Angeles, California. The ads disappeared after a couple of years. About then, roughly 1913, the Heddon company began offering a very similar lure in their catalogs. They were continually offered, undergoing small modifications, until they disappeared from the line

South Coast Minnow (cont'd.)

about 1927. The physical similarity of the Royer lure and the name leads to reasonable speculation that Heddon somehow obtained the rights to the South Coast Minnow around 1912-13, and renamed it the Coast Minnow. Collector value range: $15 to $30.

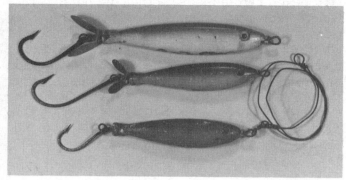

South Coast Minnows by H.C. Royer. The top lure is 4" long, has four internal belly weights. The lower two measure 3-1/8" and have three internal belly weights. Note the shaped tail on all three. Each also has the thru-body twisted wire hook hanger/line tie and yellow glass eyes. The propeller spinner on the middle lure is painted red. The prop on the lower lure may have been removed by a fisherman.

SPIKE-TAIL MOTION BAIT
Schmelzer's   **Kansas City**

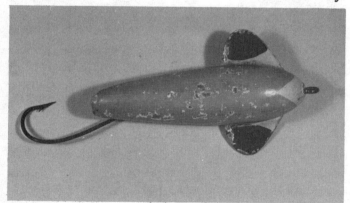

The Smelzer name above is not the manufacturer but is rather, a sporting goods store in Kansas City. They also printed catalogs. The manufacturer of the lure is unknown. The only reference I was able to find was in a 1915 edition of Schmelzer's catalog. Among other things it stated that the lure was "A new minnow..." and came in a red body, white fin or a white body, red fin finish. The one depicted in the accompanying photo has a yellow body with a white head and red and white fins, but could be a fisherman's repaint. It measures 3-5/8" long, has no eyes, and sports cup and screw hook hardware. The catalog entry also states that the single hook is detachable and reversible. Collector value range: $40 to $80.

SPINNING BARNEY
McCagg   **Mt. Kisco, NY**

When Jim Donaly of Jim Donaly Baits died in the mid-1930's, his family attempted to operate the company for a while, but apparently had difficulty without him. They began selling the rights to some of his patents to others. The most famous of these is a 1928 patent that eventually became the Heddon CRAZY CRAWLER. Apparently, at some point after his death the family sold the rights to manufacture their REDFIN FLOATER to a McCagg (no first name found) in Mt. Kisco, New York. An early 1950's advertisement states that it was available in five models in "...tantalizing finishes in red and white, perch, black, rainbow, frog and mouse." So far collectors have turned up three sizes: 1-5/8", 2-1/4" and 2-3/4". Collector value range: $5 to $10.

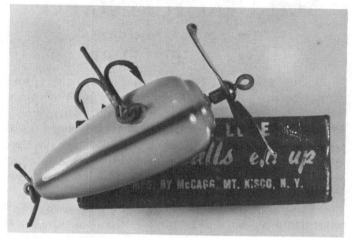

This big Spinning Barney measures 2¾". It has cup and screw eye belly hook hardware and a protective tail insert. New in the original box.

SPORTSMAN'S LURE COMPANY
Corpus Christi, Texas

There is little or nothing presently known about this company. The similarity of the one lure found to those of the PICO Company is San Antonio, Texas is striking. It is possible that the Sportsmans Company was somehow connected with Pico or merely copied the Pico Perch (see page 350). The lure illustrated here is called the "Talking Perch". It is plastic, two inches long and has a BB rattler inside. Age unknown. Collector value range: $4 to $8.

Sportsman Lure Co. (cont'd.)

Sportsman's Lure Talking Perch

SPRINGFIELD NOVELTY MANUFACTURING CO.
Springfield, Missouri
THE "REEL" LURE

The Springfield Novelty Manufacturing Company was founded in 1932 by Stanley F. Myers and Adolph A. Kunz. They began operation in Myers' garage. With the help of Kunz's son and Myers' two sons they produced an astounding 8000 lures in the first four months of operation. Even more amazing is that they worked only part-time, both hanging onto their regular jobs.

The photo accompanying shows seven different paint patterns on "REEL" lures. The other three are all what they called the "½ CHARMER." If you are familiar with the Charmer Minnow Company lures you may be struck by the similarity. Although it isn't likely that they would intentionally infringe on Charmer's patent, there is more to the story than coincidence. When Myers and Kunz first met, Kunz was an independent machinist in Springfield. However, prior to that he worked for the Charmer Minnow Company, also of Springfield, and was bound to have been influenced by his association with them. In any case Charmer apparently objected and Springfield Novelty suspended production. It is thought that only 40 or 50 were ever made so to find one would be a real event.

Early in production Springfield Novelty used the rear sections of raw Charmer Minnow bodies (apparently Kunz had a bunch left over from his time at Charmer) for part of their lure, but they soon began turning their own on a lathe. This may account for the fact that the earliest "Reel" lure bodies are 1/8" slimmer than those produced later. The lure body was 2" in length. They also started to make a musky size at 2¾", but for some unknown reason failed to place them into full-scale production and made only about a dozen examples. These, obviously, are very rare critters.

The lures made by Springfield Novelty were a very high quality product. They used select cedar, brass bushings, German silver hardware and imported hooks. Much work went into the fashioning and painting. They used multiple coats of enamel paint, each coat baked before the next. They did not advertise widely depending rather, on word-of-mouth. They were marketed only in northwestern Missouri, east Oklahoma and east Texas so to find one outside that area would be unusual. There isn't sufficient trade data to establish a realistic collector value for either the MUSKY REEL LURE or the ½ CHARMER, but the Collector value range for the 2" REEL Lure is $10 to $20.

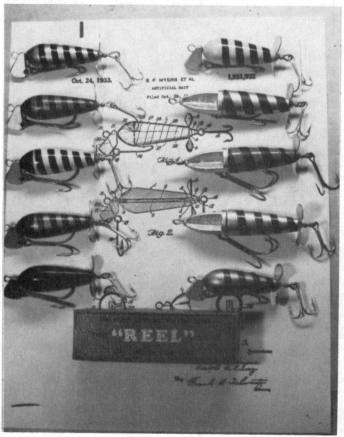

Left row shows five REEL lures and right row shows two REEL lures and three ½ CHARMERS. The box in the photo is the most common. It is red cardboard. The first was yellow and the second, white. Both had a picture of the lure on top.

(cont'd. next page)

Oct. 24, 1933.   S. F. MYERS ET AL   1,931,932
ARTIFICIAL BAIT
Filed Oct. 29, 1932

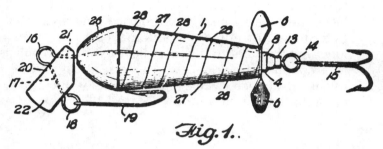

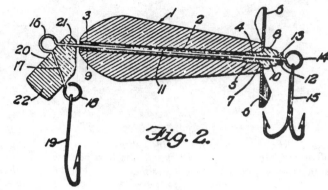

Fig.1..   *Fig.2.*

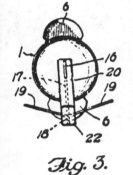   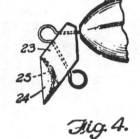   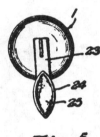

Fig.3.   *Fig.4.*   *Fig.5.*

Inventors
Stanley F. Myers
Adolph A. King
By Frank H. Schwartz
Attorney

The advertisement here gives you all the available colors for the REEL lure. Some are changed. The earliest Nos. 50 and 54 had red heads and the earliest No. 62 had a black head so there are 31 possible paint patterns to be found.

409

Springfield (cont'd)

Four 2" REEL LURES. Left to right: Yellow body with red stripe, Silver with green, Yellow with green, and Red body with yellow stripe. The propeller spinner is attached to the lure body so that the whole body rotates around the wire armature on retrieve.

Two REEL LURES on a red box. The one on the right is missing its hooks. Note the hook guard on the lure at right. It looks as if it is meant to prevent the hook from getting in the way of the spinner.

selling his wares. I know of at least five different lures he offered: the Crippled Mouse and the Musky Duck in the photographs here, the Crippled Wiggler, S.S.S. Minnow (Stewart's Shiny Shiner), and the Pad Popper. No good catalog or advertising illustrations of the latter three were found in the course of my research. Bud Stewart is retired and still makes a few of his lures, but they are strictly for collectors and sold only at a couple of regional swap meets in his area of Michigan. Collector value range for Musky Duck: $80 to $160; for Crippled Mouse: $6 to $12.

Stewart Musky Duck. 5" long.

STEWART TACKLE CO.
Flint, Michigan

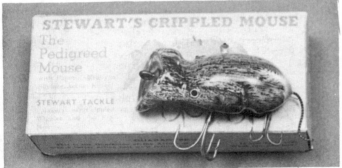

Stewart Crippled Mouse. 2-5/8" long.

As far as can be determined this company, also known as Bud Stewart Tackle, was in business in the 1940's and 1950's. He manufactured at least four lures: The Crippled Mouse, Crippled Wiggler, S.S.S. Minnow (Stewart's Shiny Shiner), and Pad Popper. No good illustrations were found excepting the photo here of the Crippled Mouse. Collector value range: $6 to $12.

Bud Stewart began manufacturing lures sometime in the 1930's and as far as can be determined, continued into the 1950's turning to plastics. He is known to have traveled the tackle show circuit

STRIKE-MASTER LURES
Strike-Master Tackle Company
Versailles, Ohio
and
Sure-Catch Bait Company
Versailles, Ohio

AUTHOR'S NOTE: This company has been a long time in getting sorted out. I have tried to for ten years now, with little success. What follows here is an article prepared by Jim Bourdon of Croton-on-Hudson, New York. Jim is a man of extraordinary talent. He is an avid collector, but beyond that he approaches his collecting as a scholar, an artist and a writer. His careful research and preparation of the garnered material into eminently usable form for his fellow collectors is well known to members of the National Fishing Lure Collectors' Association. What follows here was written by Jim Bourdon and finally resolves the confusion that has bedeviled so many of us for so long.

TWO STRIKE-MASTER HELLGRAMITES on a box with Sure-Catch Bait Company on it.

STRIKE-MASTER box with the name Strike-Master Tackle Company on it. The lures are the MOUSE (on box), BASS KING (left) and two HELLGRAMITES.

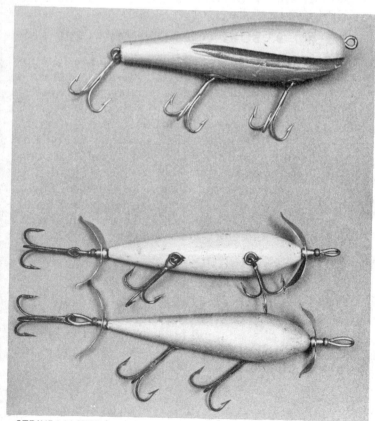

STRIKE-MASTER lures. Upper is THE ROLLING DIVER. Lower two are SURFACE KILLERS.

During the late 1920's in Union City, Indiana, A.T. Death was producing lures under the name Sure Catch Bait. In 1928, he travelled to Versailles, Ohio to raise capital in order to open a lure manufacturing facility. Mr. Death succeeded in raising $10,000 from soon to be partners Dr. John E. Gillette (Secretary), Dr. W.C. Guttermuth (President), August H. Grilliot (Vice President and owner of the Buckeye Overall factory) and Frank Ash (local banker) – an additional partner may have existed, possibly Charles Huber who was on the company's Board in 1929. The October 11, 1928 issue of *The Versailles Policy* proclaimed that a bait factory was coming to town and scheduled to start operations on November 1, 1928, with equipment transferred from Union City. This new factory was located at the corner of Water and Center Streets.

The start up was less than smooth, but by January 10, 1929, the local paper was reporting that the plant, "was now busy making baits to fill orders for several thousand lures," although operations had been delayed both in the transferring of old equipment and delivery of new equipment. This optimistic assessment evidently proved to be mostly hype. By October, A.T. Death was replaced as General Manager by C.O. Ellison whose forte was Sales Promotion. In 1930, the company's name was changed to the Strike-Master Tackle Co. Ellison's expertise proved temporarily positive as orders increased, and the company's work force was raised to 15-20 employees. This success was short-lived and the company finally shut down probably in 1931 when A.T. Death returned to Union City.

Although Strike-Master lures were produced for a very short period, numerous variations of the same lure appear from time to time. A partial explanation would be that A.T. Death produced many of these designs in Union City before and possibly after the Versailles facility's operation. Particular nuances to watch out for include:

Eye Styles

Some plugs can be found without eyes or with glass-eyes – either standard or all black. The no-eye variations of a particular lure were generally the latest version.

Lip Styles

Those lures employing metal wobbling lips may have a cup-like depression stamped into them or be simply drilled for line-tie attachment. The simple lips appear to be earlier.

Head Styles

Certain baits with slanted wooden heads (i.e.: Helgramite Crab) may sometimes appear with rounded (bullnose) heads. These bullnose plugs generally seem to be of later vintage than the slant-headed.

(cont'd. next page)

Rubber Legs

Strike-Master often utilized rubber legs or collars on its products. Variations have been noted as produced without these rubber appendages (later version).

Many examples of the company's product line are illustrated. The accompanying text when required will reference the Sure-Catch (pre-1930) name and/or model plus the later Strike-Master nomenclature separated by a slash mark. When available the color pattern number will be listed (parenthetically if Sure-Catch era).

It has only been in recent years that information has begun to surface regarding this company. With mounting interest by the Indiana collector community, many additional details should come to light in the next few years.

MR. DEATH

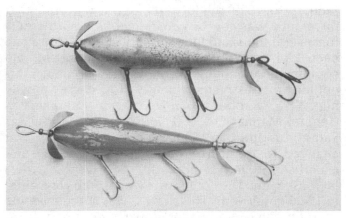

Although not found in any catalog or brochure, these 3¾" no-eyed lures have long been attributed to A.T. Death, dating to his early Indiana days. They utilize screw-eye hook-hangers around which are surface-mounted round wire bands. The top bait in silver (aluminum) and bottom in yellow are the only colors that have been noted. Collector value range: $20 to $40.

SURFACE KILLER No. 45/45XX

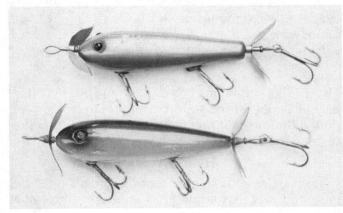

These 3¾" top water baits were a mainstay product of Mr. Death from his Union City days. The No. 4550 (top) has black glass-eyes. Note the prop style on the No. 4549 (bottom). During the Sure-Catch

period, this lure was also offered in a two-hook (model No. 35) rendition. The No. 45 was listed as available in White with Red Head (No. 46), all Silver with Red Head (No. 51) were added, and all Yellow, deleted. The No. 35 series was offered in Scaled and Striped, All Silver (No. 50) and White with Red Head (No. 46). Collector value range: $15 to $25.

NIGHT HAWK No. 36XX

The top lure illustrated in the photo above is No. 6352 is 3¼" in length and has no eye detail. Note the notched mouth. During the Sure-Catch period, the company offered a similarly shaped model No. 63; however, the brochure shows glass-eyes but does not illustrate the notched mouth. The No. 63XX was offered in colors No. 52 (White with Black Spots) and No. 46 (White with Red Head). Collector value range: $10 to $20.

No. 33 SURFACE MINNOW-TYPE

Center (above photo) Sure-Catch produced two groups of surface minnow-type lures. This style has a tapered rear half and was described as "slightly underwater." The No. 45/45XX series was full bodied and referred to as "surface." The illustrated No. 33 (Perch) measures 3½". A larger size was known as the No. 47 and a smaller the No. 55. The No. 33 colors include Natural Perch Scale and White with Red Head. The No. 47 was offered in similar colors plus All Silver and All Yellow (see Mr. Death). The No. 55 was listed in White with Red Head, All Silver and White with Blue Back. Collector value range: $10 to $20.

Injured Surface Killer
Uncataloged

Bottom (above photo.) This 3-5/8" lure is a modified No. 45XX SURFACE KILLER which has been shaved on one side and hooks mounted in injured minnow fashion. The included example is in Perch finish. Collector value range: $10 to $20.

(cont'd. next page)

HELGRAMITE No. 91XX Series
Photo below

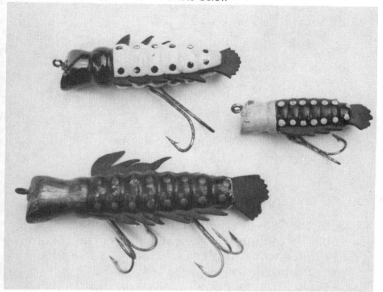

No. 31
Photo below

One of the company's most famous baits which was only offered during the Strike-Master era is the HELGRAMITE. Illustrated are three available sizes: Large No. 9153 (3¾") Black with Gold Head, Medium No. 9146 (measures 2-3/8" although catalog states 3") White with Red Head and Fly Rod No. 9147 (2") Black with White Head. This lure was also available in color No. 48 (Orange with Black Head) and has been found in the bullnose variation. Collector value range: $15 to $30.

Only described as "slightly underwater," the No. 31 is a handsome wood-tailed lure with bulging (a Sure-Catch characteristic) glass-eyes. This 3¼" lure is reflected in the catalog as having a single forward propeller only, although the above examples reflect additional variations. Note the prop style and typical Sure-Catch scale pattern. Available in the "Scaled" color-pattern only. Collector value range: $20 to $40.

CRAB No. 71/77XX Series
Photo below

The Sure-Catch catalog reflects this lure with bead-eyes, a metal lip, two trebles and available in one size only. The Strike-Master brochure reflects a no-eye slant-head model with a single double-hook and available in two sizes: Large (3¼" and Fly Rod (2-1/8"). The accompanying examples date to the Strike-Master period. The large bait measures 3¼" and has black bead eyes. The smaller bait (2¾") has a "bullnose" and no eyes. The only available color is No. 23 Natural Crab (Dark Green). Collector value range: $15 to $30.

BUG No. 19
Photo above

(Top) This 3 inch wooden plug was offered during the Sure-Catch period only. Depicted in the brochure and above with black glass-eyes, it may have been produced with regular glass-eyes as well. It was available in one size and three color-patterns: White with Red Head (No. 46). Black with Gold Head (No. 53) and All Silver (No. 50). Collector value range: $15 to $25.

MOUSE No. 65/65XX
Photo above

(Bottom) This 2½" lure with bead eyes and rubber ears is missing its rubber tail. Note similarity to Creek Chule's LUCKY MOUSE which was introduced in 1930. The MOUSE was available in three colors during the Strike-Master era: No. 27 (Natural Mouse), No. 46 (White with Red Head) and No. 47 (Black with White Head). Collector value range: $15 to $25.

FROG 67/67XX SERIES

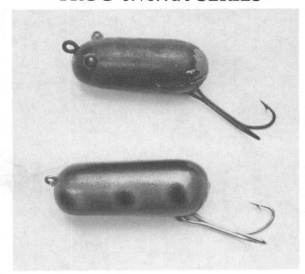

The top example (2¼") is missing its rubber legs but depicts the earlier glass-eyed version. The lower (2-3/8") is the later no-eyed, no-legged rendition. This lure was offered in one size and color (No. 25 Green with Black Spots) only. Collector value range: $10 to $20.

ROLLING DIVER No. 43/43XX

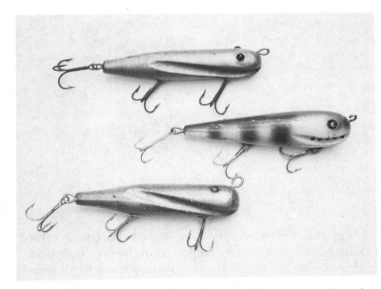

The accompanying photo depicts three examples of this bait. The Perch (4-1/8") colored lure (center) has a short flute, standard glass-eyes and red spots (a Strike-Master trademark) in the flute. The other two are All Silver and measure 4 inches. The upper plug (No. 4362) utilizes black glass-eyes while the lower has standard eyes. The ROLLING DIVER was offered in one size only and in colors: No. 46 (White with Red Head), No. 15 (Silver Flecked Natural Perch), No. 49 (Rainbow), No. 50 All Silver, No. 51 (Silver with Red Head) and the un-cataloged No. 62 (above, White with Green Back, Striped). Collector value range: $10 to $20.

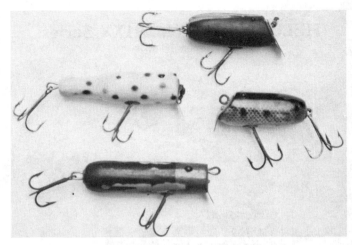

UNDERWATER LURES

During the Sure-Catch era the company marketed a number of nameless underwater plugs. The accompanying photo depicts the No. 23 and 53 series. Collector value range: $10 to $20.

No. 23 (center left, above photo). This lure measures 2-7/8", has black glass-eyes and employs a lip which is stamped with a cup-like depression, very similar to those found later on Paw Paw lips. The barrel-swivel on the line-tie is typical of this manufacturer. Collector value range: $10 to $20.

No. 23 (bottom, above photo). Except for its black glass-eyes, and a slightly different lip shape, this 3 inch lure is a dead ringer for a plug found in a Sure Catch Bait, Union City, Indiana box. Note the rounded tail-end compared to the tapered tail on the above version. This model was offered in three colors: Red with Silver head, Black with Gold head (No. 53) and White with Black spots (No. 52). Collector value range: $10 to $20.

No. 53 (center right, above photo). This 2-1/8" bait with black glass-eyes is identical to the Sure-Catch brochure illustration. The top bait is similar except that it utilizes a barrel-swivel on the line tie. These lures were cataloged as available in White with Red Head (No. 46) and Yellow with Black Spots and White with Red Spots. Other colors include All Black and Black Scale with Red Spots as in photograph. Collector value range: $10 to $20.

DEATH'S PRIDE No. 29/29XX

414

This lure provides an excellent example for comparison between Sure-Catch era (note the eye placement, next to line-tie), eye usage (standard glass-eye) and line-tie (no washer). The No. 2953 (bottom) is also 3½" but note its rear mounted black glass-eye and washered line-tie. The No. 29 was offered in White with Red Head (No. 46), Black with Gold Head (No. 53) and All Silver (No. 50). In addition to these colors, the No. 29XX could be had in No. 15 (Silver Flecked, Natural Perch), No. 47 (Black with White Head) and No. 51 (Silver with Red Head). Collector value range: $15 to $30.

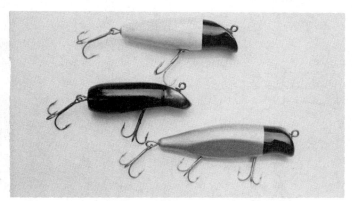

BASS KING No. 85XX
Photo above

(Top) This 3½" lure is one of four similarly shaped Strike-Master products. It can be most readily confused with the 3½" 89XX WITCH (not illustrated). The later has a more tapered rear and a grooved head. The BASS KING was offered in color patterns No. 46 (White with Red Head), No. 47 (Black with White Head), No. 48 (Orange with Black Head), No. 49 (Rainbow) and No. 53 (Black with Gold Head). The No. 89XX was available in the same colors plus No. 62 (White with Green Back, Striped). Collector value range: $10 to $20.

MUSKIE MINNOW No. 75XX
Photo above

(Bottom) The largest of these near surface swimmers, the MUSKIE MINNOW, was available rigged for either bass or musky (different hooks). The illustrated No. 7551 measured 3-7/8" and appears bass-rigged. It was offered in the same colors as the BASS KING plus No. 51 (Silver with Red Head). Collector value range: $15 to $25.

WATER WALTZER No. 19XX
Photo above

(Center) The fattest version of this group, the three inch WATER WALTZER was available in colors: No. 46 (White with Red Head), No. 47 (Black with White Head), No. 48 (Orange with Black head), No. 51 (Silver with Red Head) and No. 54 (All Black). Collector value range: $10 to $20.

SURFACE SPRAYING GLIDER 8746

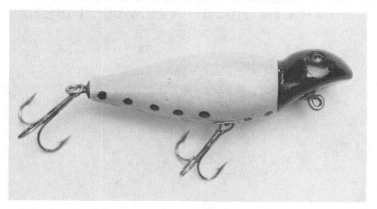

Most noteable due to its similarity to the Creek Club Jigger (introduced in 1933), this 3-5/8" lure has standard glass-eyes and bears characteristic Strike-Master spots on the belly. Available color patterns include: No. 46 (White with Red Head), No. 47 (Black with White Head), No. 48 (Orange with Black Head), No. 51 (Silver with Red Head) and No. 53 (Black with Gold Head). Collector value range: $15 to $30.

SURFACE TEASER No. 21/21XX

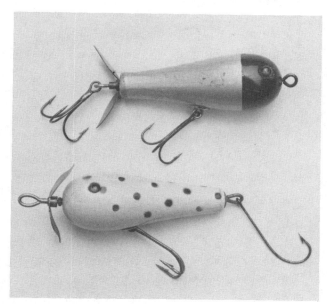

Offered in both the Sure-Catch and Strike-Master eras as a front-prop plug, it was obviously available in other configurations. Generally measuring 2¾" (top example No. 2151 is 2-7/8") this lure has been noted in the no-eye variation. The No. 21 was offered in: White with Red Head, No. 46; White with Black Spots, No. 52; All Silver, No. 50 and All Black, No. 54. The No. 21XX series dropped color pattern No. 50 and added No. 47 (Black with White Head) and No. 62 (White with Green Stripes). The upper illustrated example No. 2151 shows this bait as also available in Silver with Red Head. Collector value range: $10 to $15.

1905 SMITH MINNOW
Charles H. Smith   Lagrange, Indiana

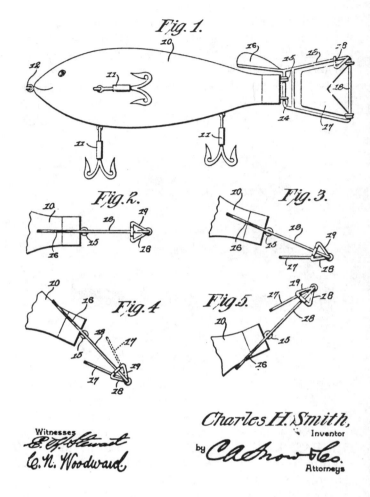

No. 781,794.

C. H. SMITH.
ARTIFICIAL BAIT.
APPLICATION FILED JULY 27, 1904.

PATENTED FEB. 7, 1905.

This rare little beauty sports glass eyes and a fairly complicated wagging tail fin. Smith was granted a patent for this lure February 7, 1905. The accompanying patent drawing shows the tail fin assembly clearly, but Smith apparently devised at least two variations. The two I have seen have tail fins that are slightly different so don't let that throw you if you are lucky enough to come across one. Collector value range: $200 to $300.

416

SPIRAL-LURE

Calumet Tackle Co.   Detroit, MI
Spiral Tackle Co.   Detroit, MI

The first name and address was revealed upon removal of a paper label on the box in the photo here. The lure is fluted, has no eyes and rotates around a heavy wire armature on retrieve. The line tie and both hook hangers are integral with the wire armature. The plug measures 3″ in length is is thought to date around the 1930's. Photo courtesy Clarence Zahn. Collector value range: $10 to $20.

SURKATCH BAITS

**Shurkatch Fishing Tackle Co., Inc.
Richfield Springs, New York**

All I was able to find regarding this lure is from the box in the photo. Scoop nose, eye depressions and cup and screw eye hardware. A well made lure. There are undoubtedly more from this company to be found. Collector value range: $3 to $6.

ECLIPSE MINNOW
William Stuart & Co.   Canton, Ohio

The ECLIPSE is a wooden lure that was in production as early as 1905. It has been found with yellow glass eyes and unusual white glass eyes with black pupils. It was made in two sizes, 5T at 3½″ and 3T at 2¾″. It sports fore and aft propeller spinners and a unique style of raised aluminum cup hook

Stewart Eclipse (cont'd.)

hanger hardware. It is thought to be the forerunner of an early Shakespeare plug. Perhaps they bought Stuart's rights. Collector value range: $100 to $200.

Stump Dodger (cont'd.)

STUMP DODGER
Albert Winnie Traverse City, Michigan

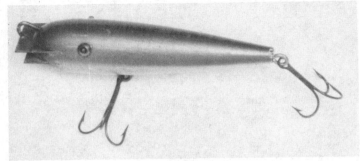

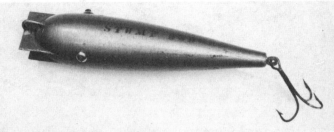

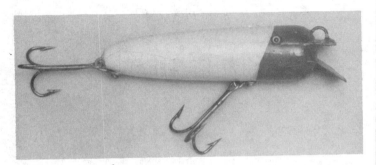

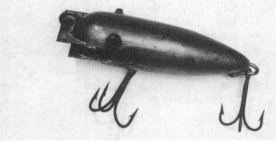

Stump Dodgers are unique early lures. Winnie patented it in 1914. The 1914 patent looks much like those pictured here with the exception of the line ties. It had two simple screw eye line ties, on top of the nose and beneath the nose. In 1916 he improved the patent with the line tie style shown in the photographs here. The only two references I found in catalogs were in a 1916 Abbey and Imbrie and in a mixed company section of a 1921 Shakespeare catalog. Both were 3½" long and colors (combined from both catalogs) were: Metallic finish (1916); Rainbow (1916); Green back, white belly ("slightly smaller"). They are found with no eyes but the greatest majority sport unpainted brass washer/tack eyes. Note different eye locations in the photographs. Almost all are found with the name stenciled on the side or back. Note different body styles and hook hanger hardware in the photographs. They are found with staple, screw eye and an L-rig type hook hangers the latter being modified to have a hump in it. Collector value range: $10 to $20.

SWAN LAKE WIGGLER
J. W. Reynolds Decoy Factory
Chicago, Illinois

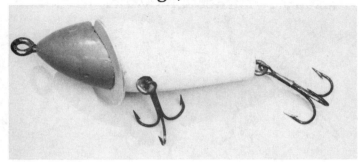

The one advertisement (1915) I was able to find said this lure was available " ...in any color desired," that it was patented, and the hooks were detachable and reversible. The ad illustration shows a lure with double hooks. The metal flange is made of aluminum. Ad text indicated that they made other lures but did not specify. Collector value range: $10 to $20.

SLIM SWEENEY'S TWINMINNOW
Twinminnow Bait Company
Fresno, California

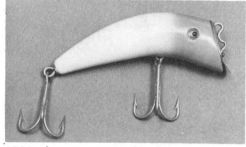

A c1939 glass eye, wooden lure. It was a surface or subsurface running lure depending upon which of the line ties used. 3-3/8" long, it was made in four finishes: Red head, white body; Green perch scale; Yellow perch scale; Black back with gold sides and white belly. Collector value range: $4 to $8.

TOLEDO WEEDLESS
Toledo Bait Company   **Toledo, OH**

An old but undated advertisement states that this lure was "...famous..." and that it was patented May 12, 1925 so that approximates its vintage. It is a wood body lure with slot and spring loaded single hook. The hook point is concealed in the body to come out as the fish bites down. Collector value range: $50 to $100.

THOREN MINNOW CHASER
Manufacturer & Location Unknown

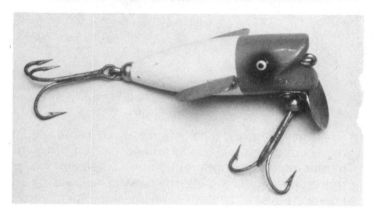

The accompanying photo of the single lure was in the UNKNOWN section in the last edition. It measures 2¾" long and has tack painted eyes. A collector spotted it and sent along the other photo here. Unfortunately it was an instant photo type and didn't reproduce too well, but it helps. The collector speculated that the one in the unknown section might be part of the MINNOW CHASER. I examined both very carefully. The Minnow Chaser (2 bodies on a wire) has a hole and fixture for attaching the following plug to the wire and the other exhibits no such hardware. The only conclusion that we can come to is that they made both a single lure and the double lure they called the Minnow Chaser. The lure box nor the lure box flyer had a name or address printed on it. It did say they were available in three finishes, Red head with white body, Red head with yellow body and Pike scale finish. Collector value range: $5 to $10.

419

L.J. TOOLEY TACKLE
Detroit, Michigan

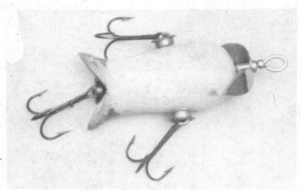

TOOLEY'S SPINNERED BUNTY. Also has the unusual surface mounted cup hardware.

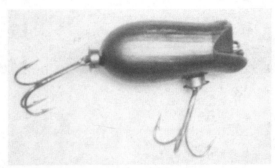

TOOLEY'S SURFACE BUNTY DARTER c1917. Note the unusual surface mounted cup and screw eye hook mounts.

I have learned a little more about Tooley since the second edition. It was known by two different names depending apparently upon when and where the company was doing business. They were also knonw as the L.J. Tooley Company at another Detroit address. Whatever the name or address, the company was owned by Lloyd J. Tooley of Kalamazoo and Detroit. Tooley was a champion bait caster in 1904, 1905 and 1906 setting a world record in 1905 with the then newly developed shorter Shakespeare bait casting rod called the "Kazoo" rod. The record was 199⅔ feet, a prodigious distance even today over eighty years later!

The company manufactured silk lines and fishing rods as well as a few lures. The only reference to lures other than the two here was to a "Tooley Minnow Tandem." The other two lures are the Surface Bunty Darter and the Spinnered Bunty. The TOOLEY'S SURFACE BUNTY DARTER is 2" to 2-1/8" long and was available in three finishes: Red head, white body; Red head, gold body; White head red body.

The second lure attributed to Tooley is 2½" long with a nose mounted propeller spinner. We do not know its actual name so for now call it TOOLEY'S SPINNERED BUNTY. Collector value range: Surface Bunty Darter - $20 to $40; Spinnered Bunty - $30 to $60.

TURNER CASTING BAIT
TURNER NIGHT CASTER
Zachary T. Turner Coldwater, Michigan

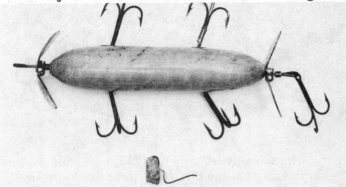

TURNER CASTING BAIT. Top view with belly weight removed.

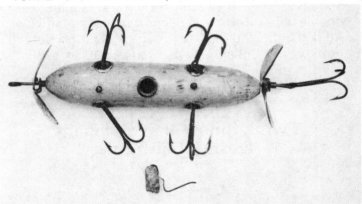

Belly view showing hook pins and hole for removable belly weight.

This 4-1/8" (actual measure) wooden plug dates from around 1904-10. A unique feature is the removable lead belly weight. The weight was cast with a spring wire so that it would have the weight firmly in the hole, but by squeezing the spring against the weight it could be removed. This feature made the plug a floater or sinker at will. Be very careful if you find one. The spring gets rusty and might break if you try to pull it out. The hook hardware was cup and see-thru gem-clip type hook hangers held fast by pins inserted from the belly. Colors were: frog back, orange and black, brown and white, mauve, dark back and orange belly, gold, aluminum, yellow white, orange, yellowish lemon and the Night Caster was luminous white. Collector value range: $90 to $180

TORPEDO RAY
North American Tackle Company
Royal Oak, Michigan

March 16, 1948. J. I. BELL 2,437,803
FISH LURE
Filed Dec. 1, 1943

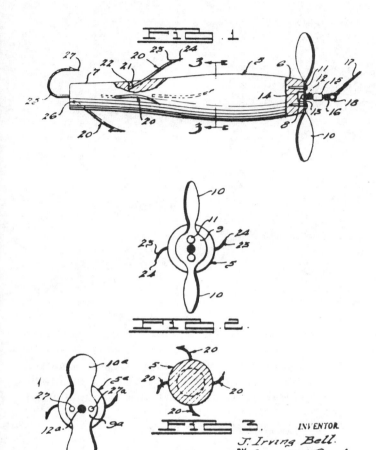

I had no example of this lure available to photograph but have included the original patent drawing for you here. The patent was filed in 1943 and granted over four years later on March 16, 1948. The grantee was John Irving Bell of Royal Oak, Michigan. Collector value range: $3 to $7.

In the last edition I had only the patent for this lure and no example to photograph. As you can see we know have a couple of good examples, but still precious little information regarding the North American Tackle Company. Both lures in the photo measure 3-5/8". The upper one is in a black and silver scale finish and the other is yellow with black and red spots and a red head. The yellow may have been white and has turned yellow over the years. Note that the prop in the patent is not the same as the production model. Those on the lures are really swinging blades. The band in one of the two blades seems intentional.

TRENTON MANUFACTURING COMPANY
Covington, Kentucky

This company was in business during the 1940's. As far as can be determined presently, collectors have uncovered five wooden plugs and two or three propeller type lures so far, that the company manufactured. The plugs are: Surface Doodler, Gurglehead, Tail Spin, Spin Diver, and the Mad Mouse. Only four are illustrated or discussed here.

(cont'd. next page)

Trenton (cont'd.)

GURGLEHEAD
or
SURFACE DOODLER

This is a 2-7/8" plug with a metal spoon shaped, round wing attached to each side, three trebles and the name stenciled on the back. Catalog illustrations of the Gurglehead are extremely similar to the Surface Doodler, but show only two trebles and indicated that the plug is larger. Collector value range: $3 to $6.

TRENTON GURGLEHEAD

A 3¼", 5/8 ounce wooden plug with a large metal spoon-like wing attached to either side of the body. It had a belly treble and trailing treble hook. Color options unknown. Collector value range: $3 to $6.

MAD MOUSE

The only reference found to this plug says it is 2¾" long. The lure in the photo here is no doubt a Mad Mouse, but it actually measures only 2" in body length. There may be two sizes to be found or the measurement in the reference included the metal diving lip. Collector value range: $3 to $6.

TRENTON TAIL SPIN

This wooden lure is 4-5/8" long and weighs 5/8 ounce. It had nose and tail propellers, a belly treble, and trailing treble hook. Colors are presently unknown. Collector value range: $3 to $6.

THE SPEED SHAD c1940
True Temper Products*
Geneva, Ohio

This lure also came in a smaller size called the "Speed Shad Junior", each had a wooden body and a metal diving lip under the nose. Both had a belly treble and trailing treble hook. Collector value range: $2 to $4.

NAME	BODY LENGTH	LURE WEIGHT
Speed Shad	2-3/8"	5/8 oz.
Speed Shad	2"	½ oz.

COLOR OR FINISH: *Natural shad; Chub; Pearl; Perch; Red and white; Black and white.*

CRIPPLED SHAD C1910
True Temper Products*
Geneva, Ohio

The originals were wooden floating plugs and plastic with a curved metal lip (shown in photo). It had one belly mounted treble* and a trailing treble

*See Al Foss page 198

(cont'd. next page)

422

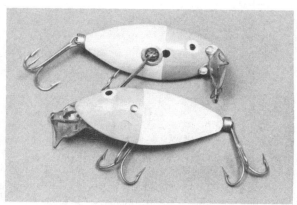

hook. The later models were made of plastic. It weights 5/8 ounce and the lure body length is 2¾" Collector value range: $1 to $2.
COLOR OR FINISH: *Natural shad; Chub; Pearl; Perch; Red and white; Black and white.*
Technically it is a side mount but the lure floats on its side therefore it is called belly mount.

TWEEDLER
Bear Creek Bait Company
Keleva, Michigan

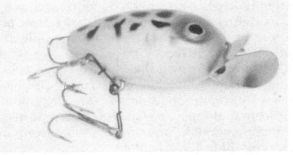

A late 1940's lure, the TWEEDLER was first made of wood and later of plastic. It was available in six unlisted finishes. The company was in business from the 1940's to around the 1970's. They made two other lures, the COHO KING and the SUCKER MINNOW Both had metal diving lips. It is reported that they made fewer than 1000 of each of their lures. Collector value range: $2 to $4.

UNDER-TAKER

Glen L. Evans, Inc.   **Caldwell, Idaho**

A collector from Montana identified this lure from the UNKNOWN section in the last edition. He sent a photo of several lures in which an example of this lure appeared. His is new in the box. It has a red face, green body with yellow spray spots and bulging painted (tack?) eyes. The box yielded what information we now have. On the box was printed "CRAFTSMAN Fishing Tackle. A product of Glen L. Evans, Inc., Caldwell, Idaho." There was also much printed information on how to fish the plug. The one in the photo here measures 3-7/8" and the one from the box measured 3-3/8". Presently nothing else is known about the lure or the company. Collector value range: $5 to $10.

VAUGHN'S LURE
Vaughn's Tackle Company
Cheboygan, Michigan

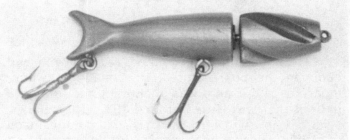

This lure appeared in the unknown section of the first edition of this book. It has since been identified. It has a green body and fully rotating head with three flutes. The flutes are painted red, yellow and white respectively. The body is 3½". Dates and other information still unknown. Collector value range: $5 to $10.

Listed as unknown in the first edition of this book this 3-5/8" lure was identified for the second edition. Little more has been learned for this edition. This mint-in-the-box lure is yellow bodied with red and green flutes.

THE VEE-BUG

Martz Tackle   **Detroit, Michigan**

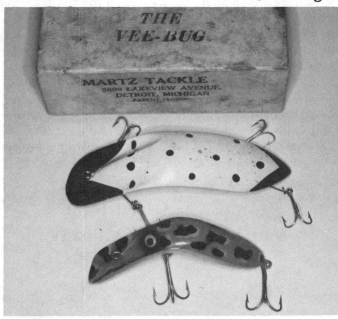

The upper lure in the photo is red and white and came in the box pictured. It is made of wood, measures 4¾" and was manufactured under a patrent that was issued around 1937. The smaller, 3-5/8" version with a frog finish is a later model made of plastic. The wooden model is difficult to find and has a Collector value range of $5 to $10. Plastic ones are more common and have a value range that is probably less.

VERMILION MEADOW MOUSE
(Other Vermilion Lures)
Frank Knill   **Vermilion, Ohio**

The slim body version of the VERMILION MEADOW MOUSE. Collector value range: $5 to $10.

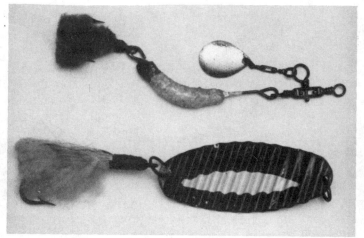

Upper lure is the VERMILION PEARL FLASHER. Lower lure is the VERMILION WOBBLER. Collector value range: $5 to $10.

Earliest reference found was to a patent application filed by Frank Knill in 1922 for a lure unrelated to the MEADOW MOUSE. The earliest advertisement found was in a September issue of SPORTING GOODS JOURNAL for VERMILION SPINNERS. Knill had a small operation, employing only a few part-time workers. The lures were assembled in his garage, the metal pieces being made by metal shops in Vermilion. He may have been a small operation, but he was serious, filing at least three patent applications, 1922, 1924 and 1926.

As far as is known the MEADOW MOUSE was the only wooden plug he made. The rest of his products were spoons and spinners. Advertisements by Knill seem to disappear after 1933. It is reported that a company named Patterson Manufacturing made some Vermilion lures in 1949.

There are two models of the MEADOW MOUSE to be found. The oldest is a fat body and the later version has a slimmer body. Both have eyes that are faceted like a rhine stone, cup and screw eye hardware and leather tail as in the photo. They are 3½" long.

WADHAM NATURE BAITS
Percy Wadham   **Address Unknown**

(cont'd. next page)

These lures are remarkable reproductions of minnows in beautiful colors. They were fashioned of celluloid. As you can see in the accompanying photo they were highly detailed. Readily identifiable, they were made in six sizes ranging from 1¼" to 3½" and available in five patterns. I found them listed in a 1925 vintage sporting goods catalog, but nowhere did I find them independently advertised. This is why there is no address or city location listed. The original box had no address, but did have a patent number printed on it. The number "21411/09" doesn't fit the normal patent numbering system. I believe it is a design patent, not a lure patent. Collector value range: $10 to $20.

WEEZEL BAIT COMPANY
Cincinnati, Ohio

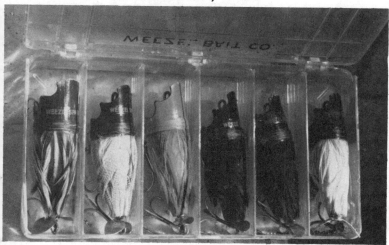

The best date I can come up with for this company is mid-1930's to the late 1940's. They manufactured at least ten basic lure designs most of which were feathered metal spoon, spinner or jig types. The most sought after lures from this company are the WEEZEL SPARROW pictured here and the BOPPER which is essentially the same lure without the feathers. They are both wood bodied ½ ounce lure manufactured under a patent number that date about 1948. Photo courtesy Dennis Hyder. Collector value range: $4 to $8.

WELLER'S
CLASSIC MINNOW c1925
Erwin Weller Company,
Sioux City, Iowa

The company was born of Erwin Weller's idea for a natural swimming action wooden minnow while fishing. He devised a three-piece articulated minnow. Thus was born the Weller Classic Minnow. About 1920-21 he and his wife started turning out the lure in their home. He made them and she painted them. By 1924 the company had grown considerably, now making three sizes of the Classic Minnow. Over the

years they added a fourth Classic, a Mouse lure and a couple more, unjointed wooden plugs. 1942 was the last year Weller made wooden lures, although they continued in operation and are in fact still in business. After 1942 the tackle they offered was all metal.

WELLER'S CLASSIC MINNOW

The Classic Minnow was, as we have seen, the first lure offered by the company (1920-21). It had a three-piece jointed body (the joints were hinges), glass eyes, two belly trebles and a combination, one-piece metal lip/line tie (see photograph on page 352) and was 4¾" long, not including the flexible rubberized fiber tail. The latter had a tendency to rot away, hence are difficult to find intact.

Sometime around 1924 Weller included two more sizes of the jointed Classic. Both were smaller, 4" and 3¼". They exhibit all the characteristics of the 4¾" lure, except they have only two-piece bodies.

A very typical Weller characteristic of jointed lures is the red-painted area of articulation to simulate injury. In fact, some of their advertisements said "HORRORS"! It Has Two Bloody Tooth Marks On Each Side."

Sometime around 1932 the rubber tail had disappeared from all sizes. That year saw the introduction of a fourth size, The new Classic, 3¼". This one departed form the original Classic style in two ways. The one piece lip/line tie had changed to a screw eye line tie and a more standard screw-on Metal diving lip. The hooks had changed from two belly trebles to one belly treble and one trailing treble. It still had glass eyes and hinged articulation. Finishes of the various Classics found listed so far are: chub, white body with red head, white body with blue head, brown pike, green pike, perch and Red Devil. Hints for dating:

1. 1920-21 to 1933 lures will have the flexible tail or the slot where it was once located.
2. 1934 to 1942 Wellers will have small pins or brads in tail and nose to fill up the holes made by the lathe. No tail fin.

Collector value range for Weller's Classic Minnows: $8 to $12.

WELLER'S MOUSE

Weller's Mouse. This one has black bead eyes measures 1-13/16" and has one internalized belly weight. White in color.

The Mouse was introduced in 1928 and continued in production until 1942. This is a mouse body shaped, 1¾″ glass eyed plug with a double hook hidden in the fancy tail feathers. They were available with a single hook by "Special Order", so presumably the single hook model would be the hardest to find. Weight was 3/8 ounce and colors available were: gray, red and white, solid black, or solid white with pink eyes. Collector value range: $10 to $20.

WELLER OZARK MINNOW

This is an unjointed model of the fourth Classic, The New Classic. It is 2½″ long and shares the same characteristics, but it has been reported with tack-painted eyes. It came along about 1934, I believe. Finishes available were: brown pike, green pike, perch, chub, white with red head, blue with white head, yellow with white head. Collector value range: $5 to $10.

WELLER SIMPLEX WIGGLER

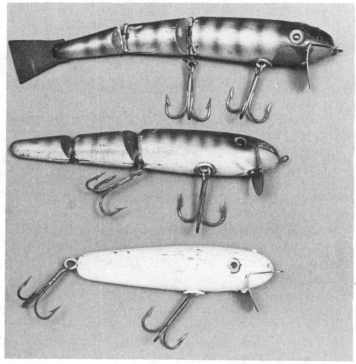

The two upper lures are Weller Classic Minnows. The bottom lure is the Simplex Wiggler.

This lure was introduced sometime prior to 1933 when the metal diving lip style changed and continued in production, so presumably it may be found with both styles. The only one I have seen (see photograph) has the old style. It is 3¼″ long with glass eyes (latest models have pressed eyes), a belly treble and trailing treble hook. Finishes available were the same as the Classic Minnow. The one in the photo is solid white. It could be a repaint. Collector value range: $5 to $10.

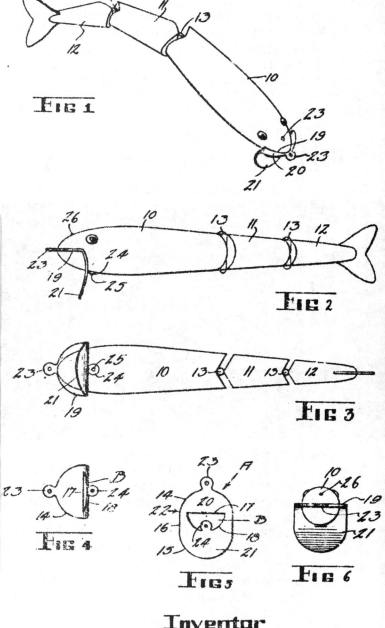

Nov. 16 , 1926   E. E. WELLER   1,607,107
FISH LURE MOUTHPIECE
Filed Feb. 11. 1926

Patent illustration for Weller's Classic Minnow. Granted November 16, 1926. The patent actually claims only the mouthpiece.

1929 WIGGLER
or POLLYWOG WIGGLER
Anthony J. Sobecki   **South Bend, IN**

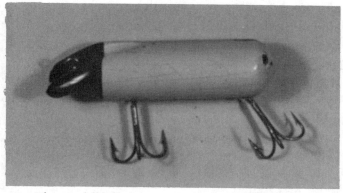

This oddball lure was patented in 1929. It measures 3-5/8" long and the hooks utilize the cup and screw eye hardware. This example has a white body with red head. Little else is known about Sobecki or his lures. Collector value range: $10 to $20.

April 1, 1930.   A. J. SOBECKI   1,752,706

FISH LURE

Filed Aug. 16, 1928

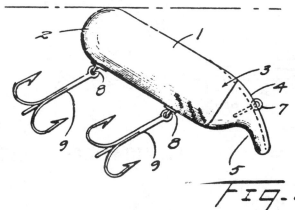

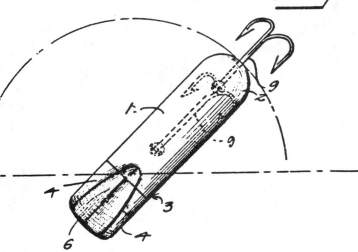

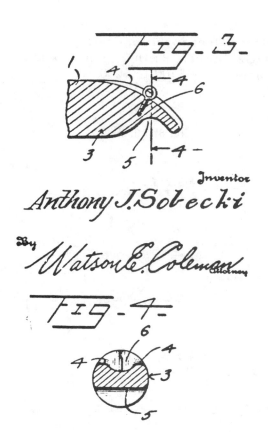

CHARLES M. WILCOX
New Paris, Ohio
WILCOX WIGGLER

This WILCOX WIGGLER measures 3-7/16" in length, has yellow iris glass eyes and See-thru side hook hangers.

Although not found advertised or cataloged anywhere, this very rare lure was patented and available to fishermen. The patent was granted November 5, 1907 to three people: Charles M. Wilcox of New Paris, Ohio, inventor; James E. Kirkpatrick of Anderson, Indiana, and Charles P. Kirkpatrick of New Paris, Ohio. There was one 1916 advertisement found for a "Wilcox Wiggler Red Head Floater" placed by E. C. Campbell of Eaton, Ohio. The lure in the ad is not the same as this jointed wiggler but it may be related. The lure in the ad does have the same single blade tail spinner.

The Wilcox Wiggler in the photo matches the accompanying patent drawing. It is a very strongly constructed with single joint articulation, yellow glass eyes and one surface-flush internal belly weight. The name "Wiggler" is arbitrarily assigned to this lure because the patent application text says it is designed to wiggle. The actual name is not yet known. Collector value range: $100 to $200.

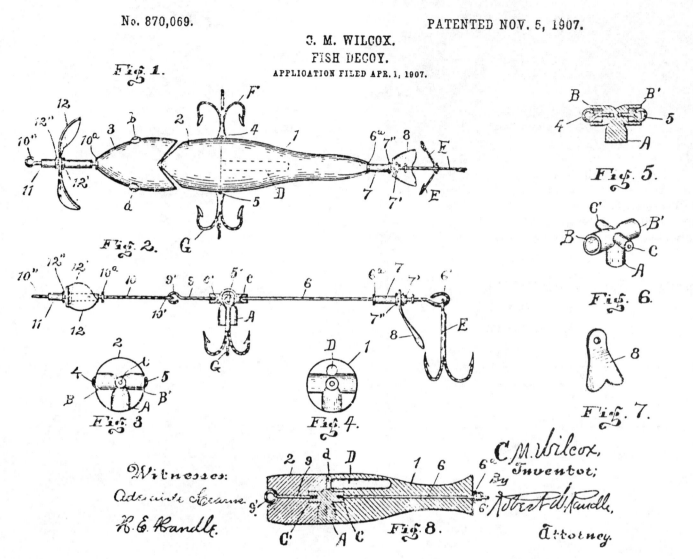

No. 870,069.

PATENTED NOV. 5, 1907.

J. M. WILCOX.
FISH DECOY.
APPLICATION FILED APR. 1, 1907.

Fig. 1.

Fig. 2.

Fig. 3.

Fig. 4.

Fig. 5.

Fig. 6.

Fig. 7.

Fig. 8.

Witnesses:

Inventor;

Attorney.

WILCOX RED HEADED FLOATER

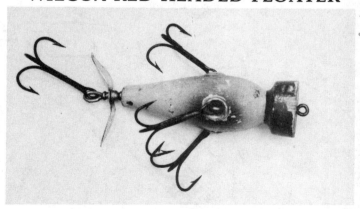

This very rare lure measures 2-7/8″ long. It has raised cup and screw eye hook hanger hardware, three trebles around the body and one trailing with a propeller spinner. Collector value range: $50 to $100.

428

CLINTON WILT MANUFACTURING COMPANY

Springfield, Missouri

Clinton Wilt "Little Wonder Bait" #70, 2-1/8". Patent applied for in 1911, granted September 16, 1913.

Clinton Wilt "Champion Bait" #50, 3¼"

There have only been two lures positively identified as products of this company so far. Both are thought to have been made in the following fifteen different color patterns: white, orange, or gold body with red stripes; white, orange, gold, or red body with green stripes; green body with orange stripes. Note the three bladed propeller spinners aft. Collector value range: $40 to $80.

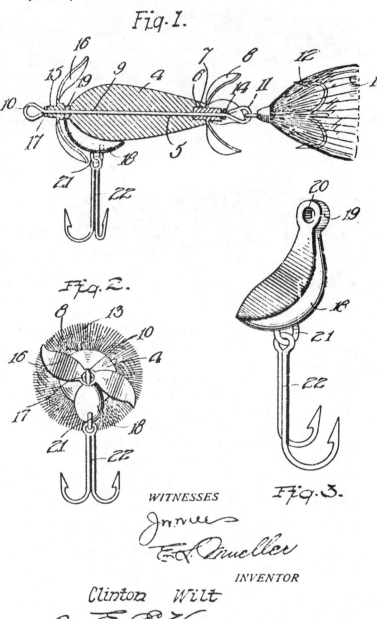

Patent illustration of the Clinton Wilt Champion Bait. Granted Sept. 16, 1913.

WINCHESTER BAIT and MANUFACTURING CO.
Muncie, Indiana

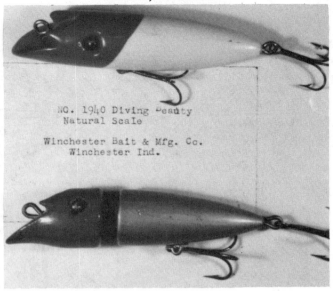

O.L. Williams   Muncie, IN

The two plugs depicted in the photo are examples of only a handful to have been found so far. There are unjointed versions as well as the jointed ones shown here. The ones here measure 4-1/8" long and have glass eyes as do all found so far. They are high quality in construction and paint finish. Five years ago I received a very nice letter from a lady saying that she was one of two daughters of a Mr. O.L. Williams and that they were pleased that their father's lure were included as collectible in this book. She went on to say that Mr. Williams was still alive and living in Elkhart, Indiana and about to celebrate his 97th birthday. To make a long story short I wrote her a letter asking for more information and never heard from her again. To my great chagrin, when I went to my files to get the address and try again, the letter was not there or anywhere else I looked. Recently, I literally went through all my research files page by page and I turned up the long lost letter finally. Williams' daughter said she thought that he made thirteen different styles of lures and that he made them for only about four years quitting about l935. That's all we know folks. Perhaps if we keep digging we'll turn something else up. If you find one of the little beauties the collector value range is $50 to $100.

WINCHESTER REPEATING ARMS COMPANY
New Haven, Connecticut

The famous Winchester company was in the fishing tackle business for a short time in the 1920's. Among other things they made flies, spinner baits and plugs. It is the plugs we will cover here. They are limited and catalogs are incomplete. The author would appreciate any additional information the collector may have. Because they marketed plugs for such a short time, almost any would be quite a find and a rare addition to your collection. Most have the famous Winchester Trademark on them. Some had propellers and these are distinctly different from others, especially the aft propeller. The only list of color or finishes available seems to apply to all the plugs that were marketed. Only time will tell if this following list of eight colors is correct.

COLOR OR FINISH: *White body, red head, green back stripes; Green and gold back, yellow belly; Green with silver sides; Gold scale finish; Silver scale finish; Solid red; Rainbow; Crackle back.*

(cont'd. next page)

WINCHESTER MULTI-WOBBLER

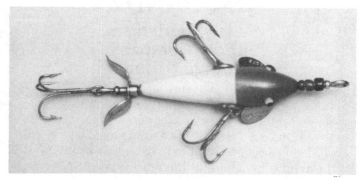

These lures had glass eyes and the distinctive Winchester nose and aft mount propeller shapes. The colors are listed on page 355. They each had a trailing treble and opposite side mounted trebles (2 or 4). Collector value range: $50 to $75.

This was a tear drop shape 3½" wooden plug with two adjustable metal nose mounted side planes. It had two belly mounted double hooks. Collector value range: $40 to $60.

WINCHESTER THREE TREBLE HOOK MINNOW
WINCHESTER FIVE TREBLE HOOK MINNOW

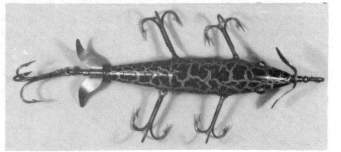

THE WINNER WOODEN MINNOW

Sears, Roebuck and Co.   Chicago, Illinois

This lure presents something of a contradiction. The upper lure in the photo came in the wooden box and a slight remnant of the word "WINNER" remains on its side. Both of these are thought to be WINNERS. The problem arises when you read the entry for the lure in the 1908 Sears catalog. Complete with detailed illustration the entry reads in part "...New Winner Wood Minnow... as you will note in the illustration above, has the new patented link and detachable hooks." Further reading leads one to believe that this is the "see-thru, Gem clip" hook hanger often used by Shakespeare prior to 1910. That in itself is fine, for many companies produced lures for Sears to market. The problem is that the two lures in the photo here have thru-body, twisted wire hook hangers. Perhaps they are earlier models and the "new" in the catalog refers to the lure with the new hook hanger. Those in the photo have opaque yellow glass eyes, tube type propeller spinners and are 3" long. Collector value range: $40 to $80.

JIM DANDY
Wise Sportsman Supply Company, Chicago, Illinois

The Jim Dandy was new around 1915. Henry H. Schillinger, Paw Paw, Michigan, invented the lure, assigning rights to Wise Sportsman's Supply. The two in the photo are the bass size and the musky size, 2¼" and 3½" respectively. It isn't too clear in the photo but the lip is notched in the middle, resulting in two "wings". The sloped head is scooped out to create a concave head. The hook rings are distinctive, having metal guards to prevent the hooks from damaging the body. See Figure I and Figure II of patent drawing for this feature. The Jim Dandys were available in solid white, white with red head or green spotted (frog finish). Collector value range: $5 to $10.

H. H. SCHILLINGER.
FISH BAIT OR LURE.
APPLICATION FILED MAY 12, 1915.

1,226,701.

Patented May 22, 1917.

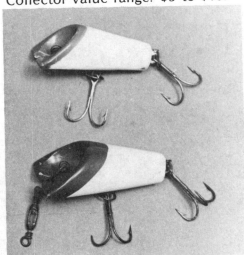

This little 2" mouse lure is said to be a product of Leo Wise of Wise Sportsmans Supply Company. It has large black bead eyes and is handsomely painted in very fine detail. The single trailing treble is attached by the use of a simple screw eye. Collector value range: $10 to $20.

WOOD'S LURES
Wood Manufacturing Company
Conway, Arkansas

The earliest I have been able to trace this company back to is 1937-40. They were listed in a McClean Sporting Goods catalog of that approximate vintage.

The majority of Wood's plugs are found made of plastic, but have been found made of wood, notably the Poppa-Doodle. There may be others.

The following list of colors were available on almost all their lures. The first ten on the list were the original finishes available. The last two were added at some later date.

COLOR OR FINISH: *Pearl; Smokey Joe; Chub; Red head; Shad; Perch; Yellow; Shiner; Black; Frog; Silver flash; Grass pike.*

DEEP-R-DOODLE

This lure was made in three sizes. Each had a metal diving plane, a belly and a trailing treble hook. Collector value range: $2 to $4.

CATALOG SERIES#	BODY LENGTH	LURE WEIGHT
300	1-3/8"	1/6 oz.
800	2¼"	½ oz.
1000	3"	5/8 oz.

COLOR OR FINISH: *all colors listed above.*

DIPSY DOODLE

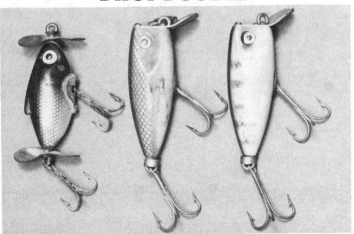

There are two body styles for this lure the "old" (flat nose) and the new, a slightly rounded pointed nose and dorsal fin molded in. As far as can be determined the old style came in only a 1¾" size: #1400 (¼ oz.), #1500 (3/8 oz.), and #1800 (½ oz.). *All three had an adjustable metal belly plate and a round spoon type diving lip blade. They had a belly treble and trailing treble hook. Found in all twelve finishes. Collector value range: $2 to $4.

There was an older model of the #1800 with two propeller spinners and no metal lip.

DOODLER

A surface lure available in two sizes; #1600 (½ oz., 2T) and #1700 (5/8 oz. 4", 3T). There was a tail mounted propeller on each size. Available in all twelve finishes. Collector value range: $2 to $4.

SPOT TAIL MINNOW

This lure was made in five styles. Each had a metal nose lip, a belly treble and a tail treble. One is jointed and one has a tail propeller. They were available in all twelve colors with a spot on the tail. Collector value range: $2 to $4.

CATALOG SERIES #	BODY LENGTH	LURE WEIGHT
700	2¼"	½ oz.
1100	2¾"	½ oz.
1300	3"	½ oz.
Jointed 2000	unknown	

(cont'd.)

433

Wood's Lures (cont'd.)

2000 S   unknown   3/8 oz.
Propeller
Spinner   unknown
COLOR OR FINISH: *Available in all twelve colors. #2000 also available in solid white.*

WOODS DOODLER
(Series 600)

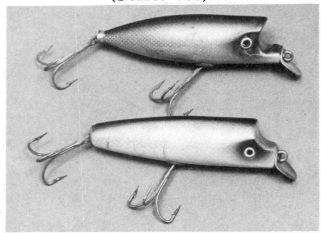

This is a different body style from the #1600 and #1700 Doodler. It had a metal diving lip and no propeller. It was made in two sizes: 3¼", 2T and 4", 3T. Collector value range: $2 to $4.

POPPA-DOODLE

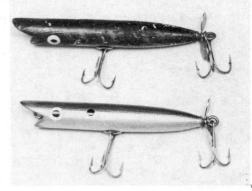

This is a surface plug with a long slender 3-5/8" body weighing ¼ ounce. It had a belly treble, a trailing treble, and a tail mounted propeller. It was made in seven unknown colors plug solid white. These two are made of wood. It also was made in a larger (4") size and a smaller ¼ oz. size. Neither of the latter had the propeller spinner. Collector value range: $2 to $4.

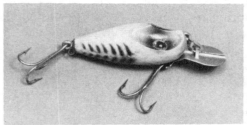

Unknown Woods Lure. 2' body length. Possibly a Di-Dipper.

WORDEN
South Bend, Indiana

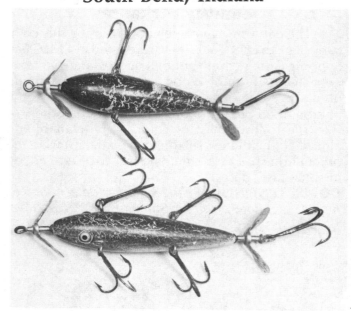

Upper lure is a #173 WORDEN WOODEN MINNOW. It is a 3" long, no eyes. Lower lure is a 5T model wooden minnow with eyes. It has "Ketchum 03" stamped on the prop.

Mr. F. G. Worden of South Bend began manufacturing a particular lure in the 1900's. This most famous lure being known as the Bucktail Worden. Because of the widespread interest in his lure, he began making others and during the twenty year growth of his company it became the South Bend Bait Company of today. There have been at least four wooden Worden lures found. They can be tentatively identified by the shape of the propeller. So far they have all been the shape shown in the photo accompanying the text here. The propellers almost always have the patent date of Dec. 29, 1903 stamped on the blade. The upper lure shown in this photo is a #173 Wooden Minnow, 3" long. This and other Worden lures are rare. All fall into the Collector value range of $60 to $120.

"Ketch-Em" Wooden Minnow.

New Patent Spinner

Good sized Hooks—Fish won't tear loose.

Color Red and White   No. KM4.

This is an original box for the Worden Ketchum Wooden Minnow.

434

WRIGHT AND McGILL COMPANY

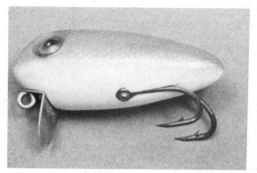

This Wright and McGill plug is 2½" long and called "Big Hawk" Collector value range: $5 to $10.

This well known firm has been doing business continuously since 1925. Their "Eagle Claw" products are widely used and respected by the number of artifical lures they have made is quite limited. They are heavily into fishing reels, rods, and hooks and presently produce no lures. The author has a few miscellaneous ads and sporting goods catalogs from which to draw information as well as the 1930, 1951 and 1956 Wright and McGill Company catalogs. These represent the majority of the plugs marketed by the company

BASS-O-GRAM

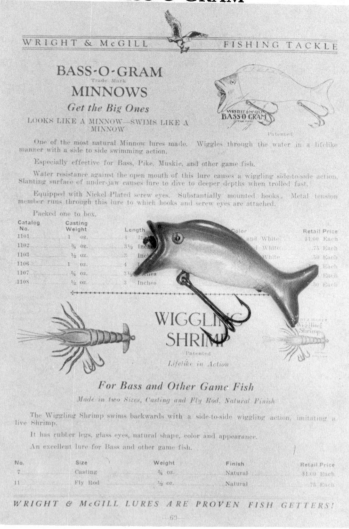

This is a minnow like lure with a large open mouth and two belly treble hooks. It appeared in the 1930 catalog as available in three sizes and two finishes. Collector value range: $20 to $40.

CATALOG SERIES #	BODY LENGTH	LURE WEIGHT
1101	4"	1 oz.
COLOR OR FINISH: *Red and white.*		
1102	3½"	¾ oz.
COLOR OR FINISH: *Red and white.*		
1103	3"	½ oz.
COLOR OR FINISH: *Red and white.*		
1106	4"	1 oz.
COLOR OR FINISH: *Natural.*		
1107	3½"	¾ oz.
COLOR OR FINISH: *Natural.*		
1108	3"	½ oz.
COLOR OR FINISH: *Natural.*		

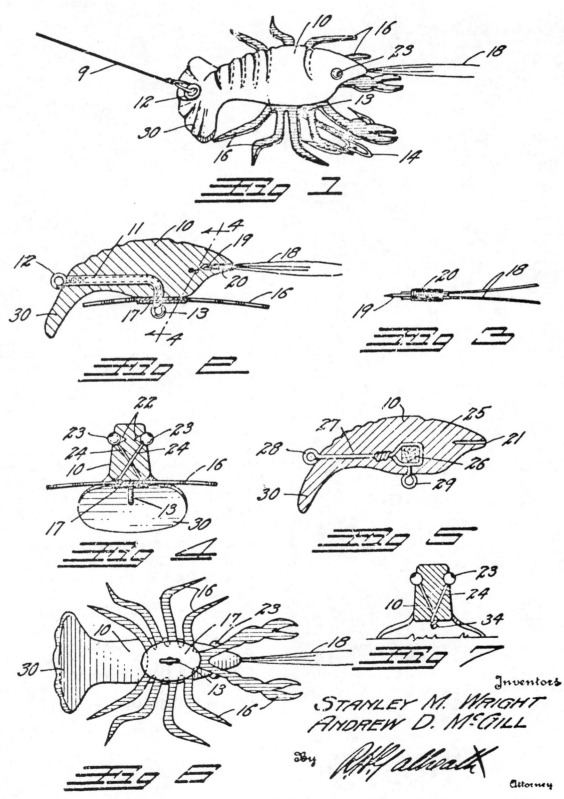

July 7, 1931.   S. M. WRIGHT ET AL   1,813,722

FISH LURE AND PROCESS OF MAKING THE SAME

Filed Dec. 14, 1928

Inventors
STANLEY M. WRIGHT
ANDREW D. McGILL

By

Attorney

Illustration accompanying the patent application for the "Flapper Crab". Granted July 7, 1931 to Stanley M. Wright and Andrew D. McGill of Denver, Colorado.

BUG-A-BOO

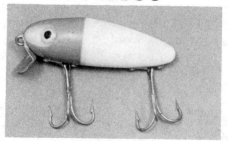

The Bug-A-Boo was a 2-3/8", 1 oz. plastic body lure with two belly trebles and a metal lip. It had scooped out (concave) eye sockets and the line tie was at the nose above the diving lip. Collector value range: $3 to $6.

CATALOG SERIES #	BODY LENGTH	LURE WEIGHT
303	2-3/8"	½ oz.
467 (600)	1¾"	3/8 oz.

COLOR OR FINISH: *Red and white; Pike scale; Perch scale; Silver scale; Gold scale; Chub scale; Yellow with silver scale; Black and white; Frog; Rainbow; Pearl; Pearl with red stripe.*

BASSKIL

This is almost exactly the same plug as the Bug-A-Boo but longer (3"). Colors unknown. Collector value range: $3 to $6.

RUSTLER

This early Wright and McGill plug was made of wood. It weighed 3/8 ounce, length unknown. It had two belly mounted treble hooks and a vertically concave face sloped to make it submerge on retrieve. Colors unknown. Collector value range: $3 to $6.

CRAWFISH

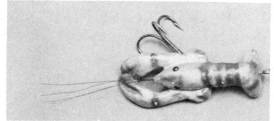

This lure was found in the 1930 catalog as available in only size (2¾", ½ ounce). It was a reverse running plug with rubber legs and bristle antennae at the nose of the crawfish body. It had one belly treble. Collector value range: $5 to $10.

THE FLAPPER CRAB

Pictured here is a side/under and top view of the Flapper Crab. One of the rubber pincers is missing from the nose area and two or three of the rubber legs are also missing. Found in the 1930 catalog this lure was made in two sizes, one color. They had glass eyes, one treble and were reverse running. Small fly rod size: ½ ounce. Large, casting size: 1 ounce, 2½" Collector value range: $5 to $6. (See page 360.)

HIJACKER

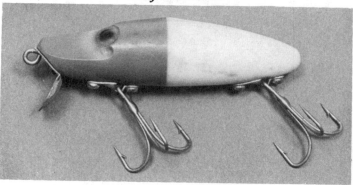

This is a plastic body plug weighing 5/8 ounce and 3½ inches long and has scooped out eye sockets extended to the nose making it more or less pointed. There is a metal lip and two belly treble hooks. It came in the same colors as the Bug-A-Boo. Collector value range: $3 to $6.

MIRACLE MINNOW
MIRACLE MINNOW MIDGET
JOINTED MIRACLE MINNOW

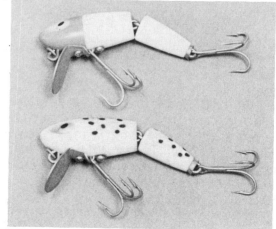

Wright & McGill (cont'd.)

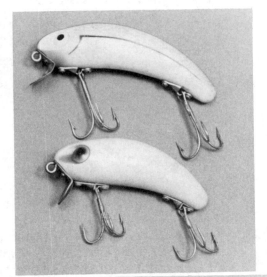

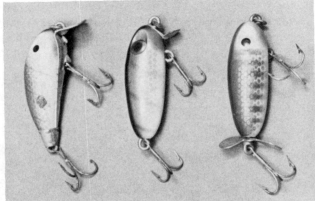

There are at least six different "Miracle Minnow" styles the collector may encounter. One was jointed but all five had the same body design, one belly treble and one trailing treble. The principal differences were in size and type or finish on the hardware. Collector value range: $3 to $6.

CATALOG SERIES #	BODY LENGTH	LURE WEIGHT
305	3"	½ oz.
472 Jointed	2½"	3/8 oz.
601 Plain	1¾"	1/8 oz.
470-W Silver bright fittings	1¾"	3/8 oz.
466-W Weighted	1¾"	¼ oz.
471-W Gold plated fittings	1¾"	3/8 oz.

COLOR OR FINISH: *Red and white; Pike scale; Perch scale; Silver scale; Gold scale; Chub scale; *Brown scale; Yellow, silver scale; Frog; Pearl; White with red stripe; White with black dot; White with black rib; *Black with white rib; White with black dot; Yellow with black dot; **Metallic finishes.*

*Available only on the jointed versions.
**Not available on the lures with "silver bright" or "gold plated" fittings.

POP-A-LURE

This is the same 3/8 ounce body as that of the "Rustler." The difference is that the body is turned over so that the face would make the lure a top water popper on proper retrieve. Colors unknown. Collector value range: $3 to $6.

DIXIE DANDY

Left: #470 Series Miracle Minnow with metal belly plate. Center: #600 Dixie Dandy. Right: Bug-A-Boo.

This is a surface spinning plug with a belly treble, trailing treble hook and a tail mounted propeller spinner. Size and colors unknown. Collector value range: $3 to $6.

SWIMMING MOUSE

This 1930 catalog listing looks to be one of the most life-like mouse lures ever marketed. It was made in three sizes (¼, ½, and 1 ounce). It had one belly treble hook and lead eyes. Collector value range: $5 to $10.

WIGGLING SHRIMP

The 1930 catalogs states this life-like lure was available in two sizes (¾ oz. and ½ oz.) It had rubber legs, glass eyes and one treble hook. Collector value range: $5 to $10.

YPSILANTI MINNOW BAIT COMPANY
circa 1909

Hillsdale, Michigan

There is little known about this company other than its time of operation and that isn't at all certain. Somewhere around 1904 to 1910 is the best estimate for now. They may have been some how connected to the Shakespeare company in that company's early days. Shakespeare, like many other companies, may have had other companies to make some of their lures before they were in a position to manufacture their entire line. That the Yspilanti company did so for Shakespeare is only a theory, but the following photos illustrate a reasonable progression that lends some credence to the theory.

This photo is not part of the progression discussed above, but is a photo of an earlier more crude lure that is said to be a 1904-05 Ypsilanti Minnow. It is the badly worn lure in the photo. Its color is green with a white belly and has a thick black line and a thin red line for gill marks. It measures 3-1/16″, has tube type propeller spinners and an unusual nose cap. The nose cap is more easily seen on the lower, unknown lure placed here because of its similarity to the Ypsilanti lure. The belly hook hangers are offset and are screw eyes with soldered disks to present the hook better and keep it from contacting the lure body upon retrieve. Collector value range: $40 to $80.

The other two, Ypsilanti Minnows of later vintage, c1909 are much more polished and professional in contruction. They have painted eyes with gold iris's and black pupils, tube-type propeller spinners that are more refined than those above, and the same screw eye hook hangers with preventers. The lower lure is 3-1/8″ and the belly hook hangers are offset. The other lure sports the same hook hangers, but they are installed in line.

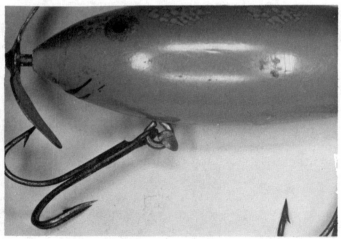

A close-up view of the disk or washer soldered onto the screw eye. This holds the lure out away from the body and makes a better hook presentation.

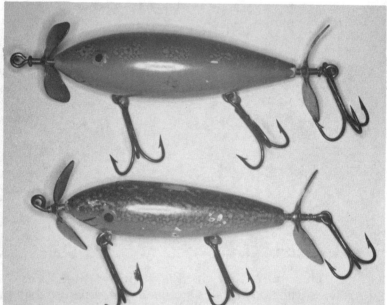

439

Ypsilanti (cont'd.)

The two unknown lures pictured here each sport the same painted gold iris and black pupil eyes and hook hangers as the above. The paint job is also somewhat similar. Collector value range: $40 to $80.

These two also share all the same characteristics, but they both have Shakespeare style propeller spinners. Note also the Shakespeare style painted gill marks on the lower lure. They measure 3" and 3-5/8" respectively. Collector value range: $20 to $40.

These two unknown lures have the same mottled paint pattern on their backs as do the preceding lures. They also have early Shakespeare propeller spinners and painted gill marks. The hook hardware is deep cup and screw eye type and they have glass eyes. Collector value range: $40 to $80.

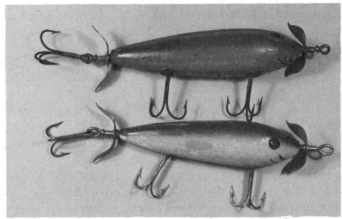

Last in the progression are these two. The upper is an unknown 3-7/8" lure. The one at bottom is a known Shakespeare measuring 3-5/8". Collector value range for both: $20 to $40.

To some collectors the progression theory illustrated here is a bit far fetched, but most advanced collectors know that almost anything is possible and don't scoff. It's sort of the classic "I may not agree with you, but will defend to the death that you're right to say it" attitude. In the early days of lure and company development almost nothing was sacred. They copied ideas, bought (and probably even a few stole) lures and ideas from each other. Companies merged, folded, prospered, scraped along, and competed and cooperated. Many patented their designs consequently patent infringements were rampant and lawsuits numerous.

ZINK SCREWTAIL

Zink Artificial Bait Company
Dixon, Illinois

This peculiar looking dude measures 2-2½". The body rotates around a wire armature that makes up the line tie and tail hook hanger. The metal device at the head is adjustable rendering it a surface or diving plug. The eyes are painted and located in a depression. It is a 1940's era lure. The only advertisement found stated that is was available in four colors but did not list them. The one in the photo here has a pearl white body and a red head. Collector value range: $5 to $10.

UNKNOWN LURES

In the first edition there were a number of these unknowns that are now known, thanks to collectors who either recognized them or did a little detective work. A little over one-half of them were identified and they have been placed appropriately in this book with what was learned about them.

Following here is a new and more extensive challenge. Hopefully we can get them identified. There are some left from the first edition. They have remained unknown for six years now. Where there is anything known or suspected, it will be noted. If you can help, by all means drop the author a line. Your contribution will be shared with other collectors in subsequent editions.

White with red head, 3¾" long. Painted eyes. Belly hooks are mounted on a wire bridle extending the hooks out to either side.

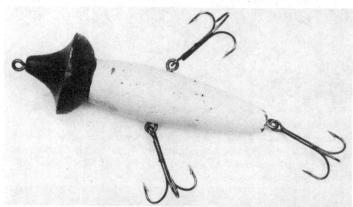

This woodpecker type lure is 4½" long with brass screw eye hook hangers. It is extremely nose heavy, but a dunking in the sink showed me it floats beautifully.

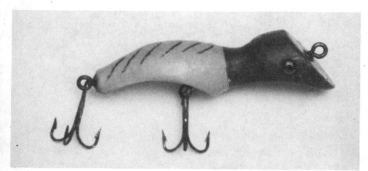

Yellow body with red spots and black stripe down the back, 3¾" long. Painted eyes. Hook hardware is screw eye with staples mounted forward as hook restrainers. Stenciled on the belly is XXUR-TEES. The X's represent two letters that are illegible. Probably SHUR-TEES.

A very unusual wooden lure carved in the shape of a propeller 2½" across. PAT PEND is stamped into the wood. Note glass bead at aft end. There is a tube forced through the center so that the propeller will spin easily around the armature.

White with red head, 3½" long. Has tack eyes and screw eye and washer hook hangers.

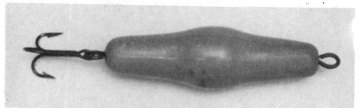

Solid yellow, 3-1/8" long. Has internallized belly weight.

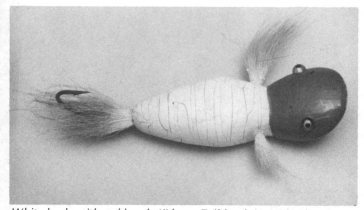

White body with red head, 4" long. Tail hook is rigid. Glass bug eyes.

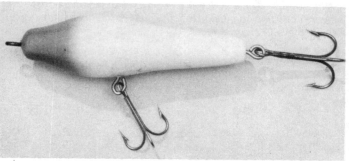

White body with red head, 3½" long.

441

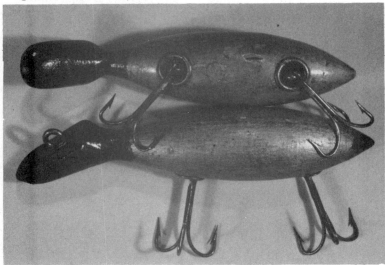

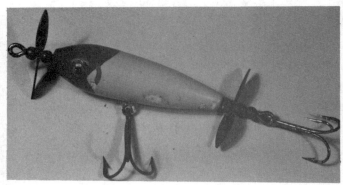

This unknown white body, red headed lure measures 2-3/4" and has brass floppy propeller spinners. The red and black bearing beads are wooden. Eyes are made by the placement of a plastic washer, brass washer and black bead in that order.

These two lures are attributed to a company in Southaven, Michigan whose name is presently unknown. They measure 4-3/8" and 4-3/4" respectively, have cup and screw eye hook hardware and one internal belly weight each. They are bright gold in color with red heads.

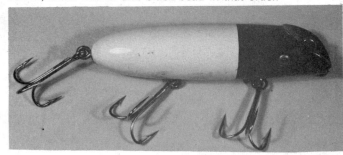

This lure appears to be a South Bend product due to its hook hangers, eyes and paint job, but the metal face plate/diving lip is decidedly not. There is a narrow strip of silver scale finish along the belly of this white body, red head lure. It measures 4".

Body has yellowed with age but was originally white. Other markings are red. Deep brass cup with no bottom and screw eye hook hardware and brass propeller spinners. Line tie and tail hook hanger is not thru-body.

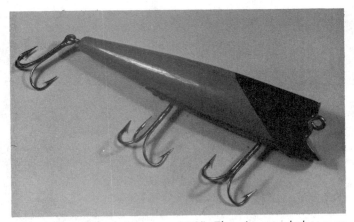

This plug has a black and white frog finish and is 2" long. The eyes are wooden pegs. One has been removed in the photo.

White body/red head. Measures 4-3/8". There is a metal plate over a wire belly hook hanger. Note the metal protective plate shaped to fit the odd shaped face.

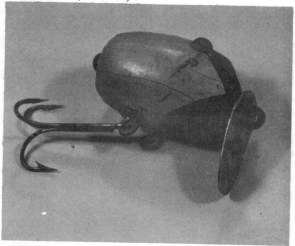

This peculiar little chunk measures 1-5/8" and has two line ties on the unusual style head plate. It is a topwater or diver depending upon which line tie is used. It has a washer and screw eye hook hanger and large brass tack eyes. The same tack is found at the tail.

This egg shaped plug has a frog finish and measures 2" long. The nose mounted dive plane is triangular in shape and made of brass. Note the spike eye at the top. This is probably a remnant of a bead eye.

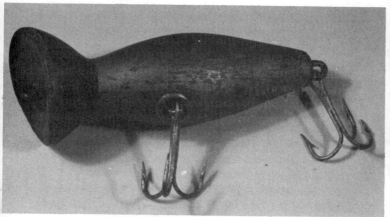

Measures 3". Note the carved-in grooves. Cup and screw eye hardware. The eyes were carved and were installed before painting.

This unknown lure has a gold body with black head and measures 3-1/8". It has brass cup and screw eye belly hook hardware and a tail hook insert.

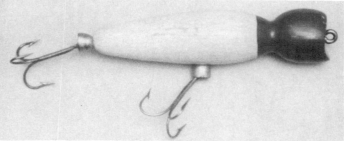

This red head, white body lure has the same hook limiter hanger patented by O. L. Strausborger in 1932. Could be a Strausborger but nothing else is known. Patent drawing illustrated on page 92.

This 4-1/8" lure has large deep cup screw eye hook hardware. Note the head/face shape. White body with red head.

Unknown Lures (cont'd.)

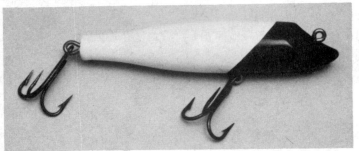

White body with black head, 4¼" long. No eyes. Nose and body similar to Creek Chub Pikies.

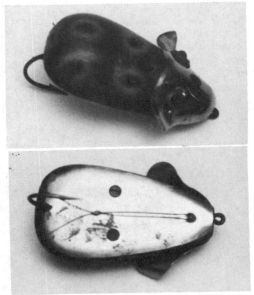

Head and belly covered with metal. The head plate has big, bright red glass eyes set in it. Green with frog spots. Rigid mounted single hook with wire and guard. 2½" long.

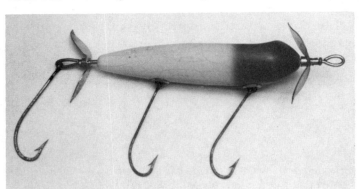

White with red head, 3¾" long. Cup and screw eye hardware. No eyes.

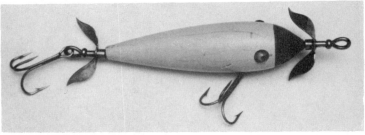

White body with red head, 3½" long. Glass eyes. Cup and screw eye hook hanger and unmarked propeller spinners.

May have been solid white. The head appears to have been painted red by a fisherman. Has painted eyes (gold with black pupil) and is 4" long. Screw eye only, hook hanger.

White with red head, 3" long. Note the double ring eye treble hooks. Unmarked floppy propeller forward spinner. Has opaque yellow glass eyes.

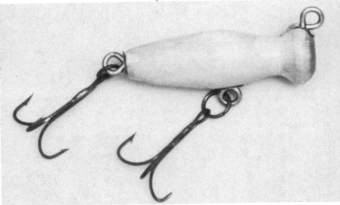

Solid white, 2½" long. Note small metal plate on top of head under line tie. Screw eye and washer hook hangers. O-ring hook fasteners.

Yellow body with black tail and red, white and green stripes at the head. Metal (brass?) fins at head to make the lure rotate. The body rotates around a one-piece brass wire that incorporates the hook hanger method. 4" long.

Solid black body, 4¼" long. Woodpecker type lure with all brass hardware. Screw eye and cone shaped inverted cup on surface (not counter sunk as regular cup hardware).

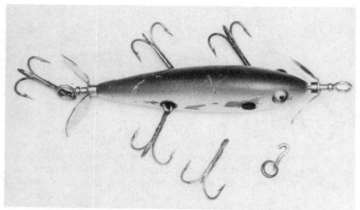

This is suspected to be a Shakespeare product. Has typical Shakespeare paint job, body style and propellers (unmarked). Note the flanged sleeve use instead of standard cup. Glass eyes.

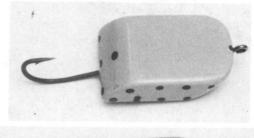

Top and belly view. Yellow with black spots. Has brad inserted through the side for the single hook to swing on. Triangular lead weight on belly.

Frog style lure with huge bulbous eyes and one rigid single hook.

White body, red head with painted eyes. Weedless.

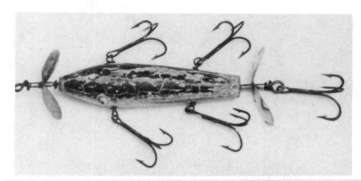

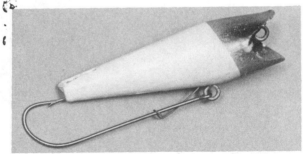

White body with red head and no eyes. Weedless.

Top and belly views of a lure with reversed gill stripes typical of Joe Pepper lures. Has yellow glass eyes, through-body twisted wire hook hangers and line tie/trailing hook hanger. Yellow glass eyes and tube-type bow tie propellers.

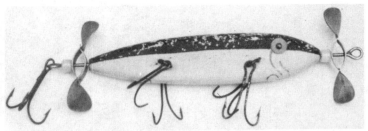

Note the very unique two piece soldered reinforced propellers and flattened end white bearing beads. The hook hangers are staple type. This could be a homemade lure.

This green back lure has a brass bow tie type non-floppy propeller spinner. Yellow glass eyes and two very small internal belly weights. The knob on the end is wrapping that used to hold a bucktail like the South Bend Combination Minnows.

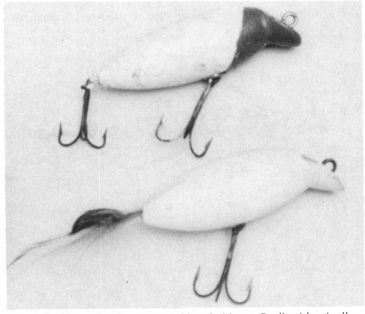

Solid white and white body red headed lures. Bodies identically shaped. Simple screw eye hardware.

Upper lure is natural unvarnished wood. The lower is similar in shape and is crudely repainted black. Simple screw eye hardware.

Unusual shaped blades on tube-type propellers spinners. Through-body twisted wire hook hangers and line tie/trailing hook com-·bination. Painted eyes.

ADDENDUM

The following group of photographs and related information was provided by a prominent collector, Clyde Harbin. Even though it arrived too late to be integrated into the main body of text and photos, the publishers felt it of sufficient import to be included here as an addendum.

The "DAWAGIAC KILLER" no. 400 (box end marked Yellow). The lure has 3 inserted belly weights (Killers come with 2 and/or one belly weight(s)). The front prop is unmarked. The screw hooks and cups are brass as well as the line tie and tail hook hanger. The propeller is nickled. Look close and see the under label is "THE DAWAGIAC CASTING BAIT". The "KILLERS" offered on in the 1905 and 1906 catalogs. The cardboard box bottom was marked: "Protect and Perpetuate the Black Bass" by killing the big ones with a "Dowagiac" Bait and returning to the water all under one pound. The patent date refers only to the first patent of the "SLOPE NOSE BAIT", the lure on the under label. Collector value range with box: $80 to $160.

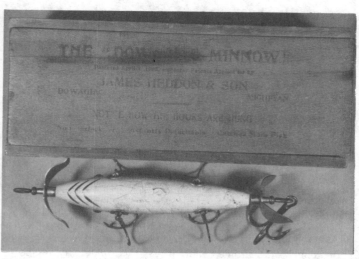

Same box and lure as in previous photo. The No. 150 has the light GREEN FANCY BACK, unmarked nickel props, line tie, rear screw eye, screw hook hangers, and cups of brass. The glass eyes have YELLOW IRIS, three hand painted gill marks, and three internal belly weights. The Heddon 3 belly weight lures are thought to be the first style, as well as the light green fancy back (notice very faint white cracks). The Wood Box marked James Heddon and "SONS" came about in 1908. Collector value range with box: $100 to $200.

The sliding-top wood box is marked on both ends: "HEDDON'S DOWAGIAC MINNOW...fancy Back, No. 150" and is marked "DOWAGIAC" Minnow No. 150. It is listed as rainbow, fancy back, plain white, aluminum, or red yellow or copper. The 1905 book has a letter dated August 6, 1904 stating that a No. 150 was left out of a shipment. Collector value range with box: $100 to $200.

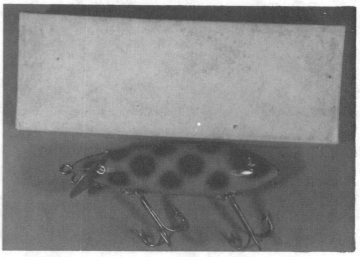

Plain white cardboard box marked only 1805 on each end. This is the Spotted Heddon Crab Wiggler (stamped on "U" collar back and Heddon's Dowagiac on collar front). Notice the two different line ties and "L" hook hangers. Also found was a second plain carboard box with 1705 marked on both ends. The No. 1800 size offered 1915-1929. Inch Worm (first in catalogue) and single screw eye or this double line tie should be before 1920. Catalogs often used the same picture many years running. Collector value range with box: $20 to $40.

Here's a puzzle...both ends of the cardboard box are faintly stamped "No. 7500's." This is the number for the "VAMPIRE" Minnow with white body with red and green spots. Yet, in the 1918 Von Lengerke & Antoine catalog the No. is 2000's...White Spotted. Also, one end is marked WIGGLE KING, swimming bait. The lure has nickel cups, a screw eye tail hanger and belly screw hook hangers. Both sides of the box marked: "Heddon's Dowagiac Minnows, Dowagiac, Michigan." Could be introductory box. Collector value range with box: $40 to $80.

This cardboard box is marked 7009K...Goldfish, Scale in 1920 Heddon Catalog. However in the VL&A 1920 catalog it is marked "NEW" and with line tie hump down; both books showing the pork rind attachment on the rear hook. Again, an introductory box. Collector value range with box: $40 to $80.

Introductory cardboard box. No number marked on end. The 1918 VL&A catalog shows the No. 6000 "HEART (or apple) SHAPED" lip with the lip engraved or stamped - Heddon Dowagiac parallel to high hump (very first style) line tie. This box, the 1918 VL&A and 1920 Heddon catalog pictures show this style line tie. Collector value range with box: $60 to $120.

This 5 3/4" cardboard box is marked on both ends: "Heddon's Genuine "Dowagiac Crab Wiggler No. 1802" and patent date April 1, 1902. The word "Genuine" first used in the 1914 Catalog. However, this lure has the third style of line tie. This number was listed only as Red Head until 1924 when it was listed as White Body with Red Head and Tail. In 1925 No. 1802 it was just White with Red Head (same for 1926). In 1927 and 1928 it was back to White with Red Head and Tail. This box style should date before 1912 Crab Wiggler introduced in 1915. This marked Crab Wiggler box was in Catalog No. 14 in 1916. Collector value range with box: $40 to $80.

This blue border "00" cardboard box has both ends marked HEDDON'S "Genuine Dowagiac" MINNOW, no number. Both sides are marked, "All Genuine Dowagiac Minnows have 'Heddon's Dowagiac' stamped on the spinners". Collector value range with box: $40 to $80.

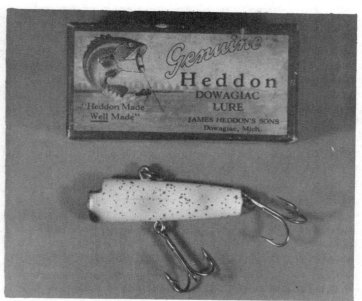

This cardboard box is 3 1/8". One end is marked: "Heddon Dowagiac 79p1 Drewco." One side reads: "In 22 years of Field & Stream's Fishing contest..." Collector value range with box: $40 to $80.

This 5 3/4" cardboard box is marked on both ends: "Genuine Heddon Dowagiac Minnow No. 3509BB." On one side it reads: "If Heddon didn't make it, it isn't a Dowagiac. Look for the Heddon Trade Mark." On the other side it reads: "James Heddon's Sons, Dowagiac, Michigan. HEDDON Fishing Tackle. Heddon Made-Well and if not made by Heddon it is not a Genuine Dowagiac". The Luny Frog has two-piece toilet seat hardware (second style hook hanger). Collector value range with box: $75 to $125.

This 4 1/2" cardboard box pictures a leaping fish with a River-Runt in its mouth and has the odd shaped regular Heddon logo (red on black) that first appeared on the cover of the 1949 Heddon Catalog. However, the fish was pictured only on the 1940, 1941 and 1942/1943 catalog covers. This was a 3 1/2" length, glass eye wood lure with screw eye hangers and line tie made only for Japan. Notice the 6400-Zaragossa, Jr. pamphlet. Collector value range with box: $100 to $200.

K & K Animated Minnow. Cardboard box with both ends marked "Pat, June 25, 1907 No. 857 & 883". Collector value range with and without box: $50 to $140.

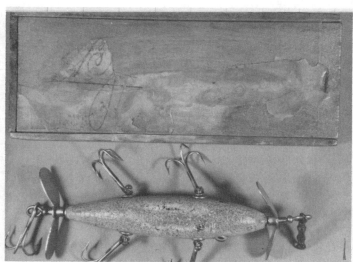

Pontiac 5 treble wood-body Minnow with the Delux hook hangers. This sliding-top wood box is stamped on both ends: "R. M. 5" Collector value range with box: $200 to $400.

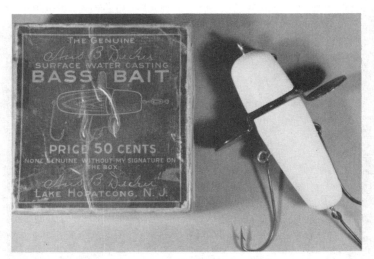

Decker cardboard box. One side is stamped. Lure is white with red wings. Collector value range with box: $40 to $80.

The Manitou Minnow with its cardboard box. No side or end information. Collector value range with box: $200 to $400.

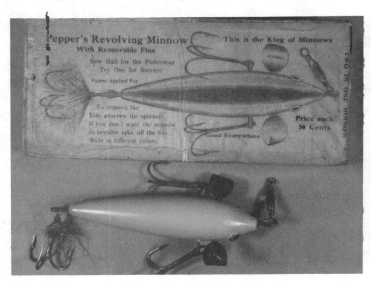

Wooden box with a sliding closure. Pepper's Revolving Minnow. Collector value range with box: $200 to $300.

FLOOD'S Florida Shinner. 6½", tack eye, cardboard box with instruction pamphlet, circa 1928. Collector value range with box & pamphlet: $200 to $400.

The Biff Bait cardboard box is marked on both ends: "BIFF BAIT GODEVIL BIFF. Surface Weedless No. 881, Red and White." On one long side is: "USED FOR CASTING and TROLLING" and on the other side: "TRY OUR WHOOPEE BIFF PLUG, Weedless." Collector value range with box: $20 to $40.

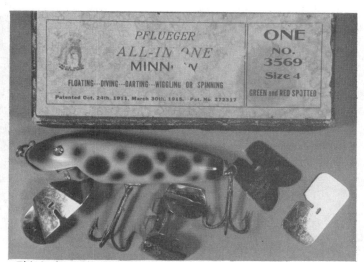

This is the earliest cardboard Pflueger box. All maroon except for the label. Collector value range with box: $200 to $400.

Baby Pikaroon No. 1010. Horned Ace No. 1000 Series made by Silver Creek Novelty Works, Dowagiac, Michigan with White Iris Glass Eyes and straight nose. The Paw-Paw made Pikaroons have a turned up nose. Collector value range with box: $40 to $80.

Yellow cardboard box. Lure has name stenciled on belly. Collector value range with box: $80 to $160.

This sliding top wood box is photographed on its side. Collector value range with box: $100 to $200.

Shakespeare's cardboard box and lure. One end marked: SHAKESPEARE Sure Lure Bait (Weedless), No. SL...1-12 dozen. Collector value range with box: $200 to $400.

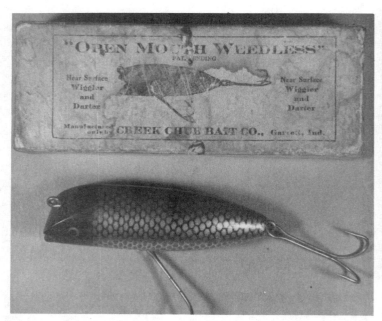

Open Mouth Shinner cardboard box by Creek Chub Bait Co. Garrett, Indiana. One end marked: "Open Mouth Weedless." Collector value range with box: $40 to $80.

This cardboard box is marked on one end: Creek Chub Wiggler, No. 101, Natural Perch Scale finish. Collector value range with box: $40 to $80.

AL&W Lure cardboard box - marked on both ends: AL&W Lure No.-One side marked: AL&W Nature Lures catch more fish. Collector value range with box: $100 to $150.

Can barely make out Shakespeare stamped under"FOR PIKE." Both sides marked Bass-A-Lure. One end marked: BO 2. Collector value range with box: $40 to $80.

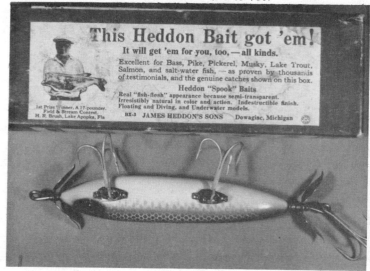

This 7 3/16" Heddon box is marked on one end: Heddon-Dowagiac 179P. Both sides feature many pictures of fish. This 170 SOS has thru body lengthwise one heavy duty metal wire. Collector value range with box: $20 to $40.

452

James Heddon's Sons bought Outing out in 1927 and offered inventory for sale from Dowagiac, Michigan. Collector value range with box: $20 to $40.

Sliding wood top box. "Winner" is stenciled on one side (worn off here). In 1908 Sears Catalog this lure and box (described and pictured) as No. 6K9006. Collector value range with box: $80 to $160.

This is James Heddon & Sons Artistic Minnow, No. 50 Series. The cardboard box is 4 3/16" with maroon border. The first Artistic minnows had three concealed belly weights. Collector value range with box: $40 to $80. Good box: $80 to $100.

This cardboard box hand-marked as No. 5 White. However, pictured is the smaller Red and White Leeper's Bass Bait. Collector value range with box: $40 to $80.

This sliding top wood box is thought to be c.1905/1906. The hook hanger is wire thru body with a small see thru hole. The front larger propeller is marked Pflueger, no mark on rear smaller propeller. Has yellow iris glass eyes. Collector value range with box. $80 to $100.

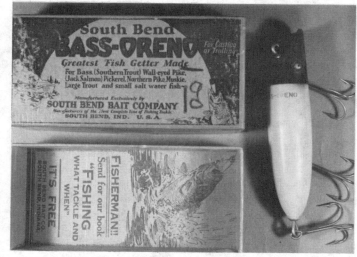

This South Bend Bass-Oreno cardboard box was in stock in 1933 at a Wilson Dam, Alabama bait store. In addition to a pamphlet the inside of the box is pictured. One box end is marked: Genuine SOUTH BEND BASS-ORENO, the Wobbling Motion Bait...973 with RH stenciled in. The other end marked: Patented December 19, 1916 Trade Mark registered. Both sides showing trade mark logo. Collector value range with box: $10 to $20.

LANE'S AUTOMATIC MINNOW patented July 29, 1913 by Charles W. Lane, Madrid, New York. The tail propeller operates the pectoral fins in a natural manner when pulled through the water in a swimming manner. The double hooks release and swing free on striking the fish, saving the all metal bait. Collector value range: $300 to $400.

This South Bend cardboard box has one end marked: "South Bend Minnow No. 913, Color GCBW." Collector value range with box: $20 to $40.

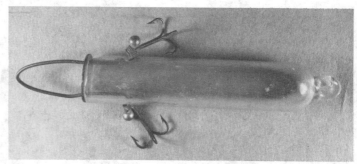

Trout size of the Detroit Glass Minnow-Tube Co. The rarest of this lure. 2 ¾ " in length, circa1914. Collector value range: $75 to $150.

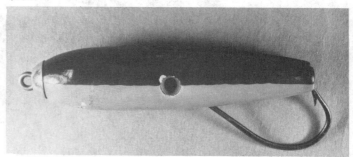

This sliding top wood box is not marked on end or sides. The lure is No. 44SR with 1917 plate hook hangers, two hump propellers (second style) and glass eyes with three hand painted gill marks (yellow) between the two front hooks. This may not be the lure for this box. No catalog information when wood boxes were offered by Shakespeare. Collector value range with box: $50 to $100.

TOLEDO WEEDLESS No. 2. Patented May 12, 1925 by Toledo Bait Company, Toledo, Ohio. It was offered in five different color designs. Collector value range: $40 to $80.

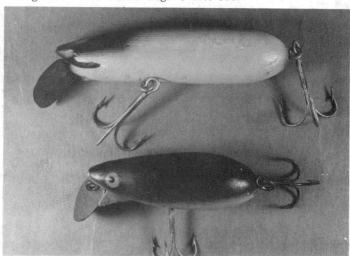

This Chippewa cardboard box is marked on one end: Chippewa Floater. However, the lure pictured is a sinker. Someone changed lures. Collector value range with box: $50 to $100.

KIMMICH HAIRLESS MICE...both lips marked patented January 22, 1929. The large one is 3 1/4" and the small one 2 1/4". Manufactured in Ellwood City, Pennsylvania. In the second edition of this book, page 277, upper right side the HAIRY KIMMICH MOUSE is misidentified as the Paw-paw mouse. Collector value range: $20 to $30.

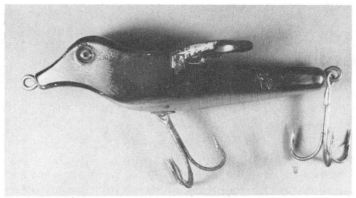

KINNEY'S BIRD LURE patented September 20, 1927 by Herbert A. Kinney and made by Old Hickory Rod & Tackle Co., Tampa, Florida. Assembled and painted by the James Heddon's Sons of Dowagiac, Michigan. This is the Red Wing Black Bird finish with cup hardware and "L" rigging. Collector value range: $400 to $500. range: $400 to $500.

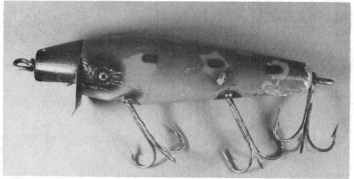

CLAY'S RED HEAD LURE by T. H. Clay, Clay's Bait Company, Thomasville, Georgia. This is one of the early ones with a spring loaded line tie (the unsnagger feature), reversible metal lip (unmarked), glass eyes and the plate hook hardware, circa 1935/1940. Collector value range: $80 to $160.

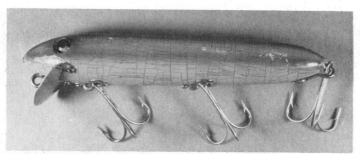

HEDDON·ROUND NOSE VAMP...marked lip of Heddon Dowagiac, glass eye, "L" rigged belly hooks and the tail hook hanger of the "short loop" Stolley patent issued August 1, 1922. This style round nose about 1922-1925...no catalog information. Collector value range: $15 to $30.

HEDDON ICE SPOOK, so stenciled on belly lead weight. No catalog information available. However, a pamphlet may surface...circa 1930's. Collector value range: $90 to $180.

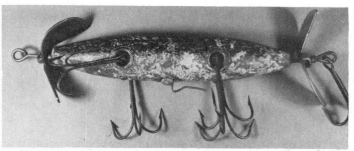

TURNER CASTING BAIT, Zachery T. Turner, Coldwater, Michigan, circa1904-1910. 4" in length, no eye detail, see-thru body hook rigging. Front propeller is brass and the rear one nickel plated. It has the removable belly weight (recently hand-made to complete the lure). Collector value range: $90 to $180.

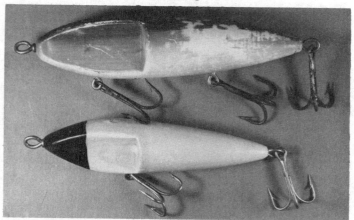

SCHOONIE'S SCOOTERS. John Ray Schoomaker, Kalamazoo, Michigan. Top lure is 4½" and bottom lure is 3½" (appears to be repainted), circa1916. Collector value range: $10 to $20.

THE SNAKERABAIT, THE FROGGERBAIT and THE BIG MOUTH MINS by Robert L. Clewell, Canton, Ohio, circa 1926. Collector value ranges: $80 to $160, $30 to $50, and $30 to $50.

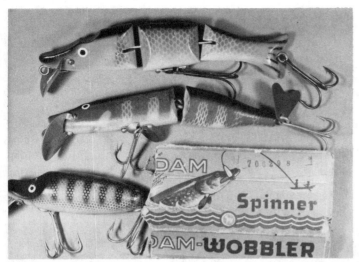

DER SPORTFISHER KATALOG Nr. 26 (1962) of "MIT DAM GERAT UND ULTRA DAMYL"... German fishing lure catalog. The surface hook hangers appear to be the Heddon style, as well as the scale paint finishes and metal lips. The lower left Wobbler lure came in a damaged box. Collector value range: $10 to $20.

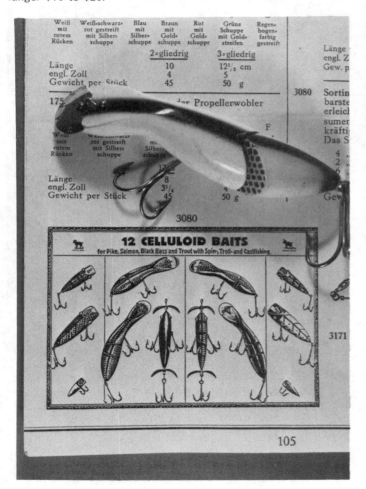

The Heddon made CELLULOID Gamefisher. Note the fitted joint. The lip is marked "VAMPIR". Plastic body. Collector value range: $30 to $40.

Thought to be a F.C. Woods or a J.C. Holzwarth lure. The finish, the hook hangers, body style or configuration, hardware and the rear tube/bow tie propeller all are Woods or Holzworth, either with holes in propeller or not. The front propeller styles could be a fisherman change or a company transitional propeller. collector value range: $50 to $80.

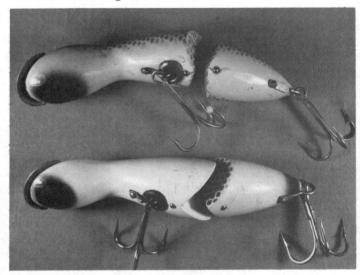

Top lure came from the Dowagiac, Michigan factory from a former salesman (featured on pages no. 254, 255). The bottom lure has the belly hanger similar to an early style Creek Chub one, yet the tail hanger is Heddon (Stolley patent). The German lure has the standard Heddon "L" belly hanger and the tail as featured above (Stolley style). Notice the different style joints. Collector value range, top: $40 to $80, bottom: $30 to $40.

A rare one-word "STANLEY" propeller installed on a Heddon No. 1600 body (front metal fins removed). Collector value range: $100 to $200.

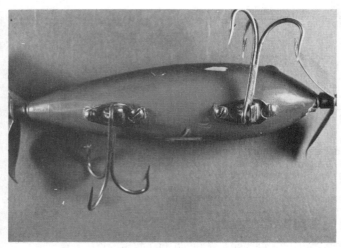

The "small" (2-7/8") RADIUM MINNOW by Pontiac Manufacturing Co., Pontiac, Michigan, c1908. This is the standard style of side, brass screw hook hangers rather than the Delux style as pictured on page 351. Collector value range: $40 to $80.

This is a 3½" Heddon No. 140 Flipper with unmarked thin metal Heddon propellers and the 1935 (Bear patent) style two piece rectangular (or flap) belly hangers. This lure, however, was originally marked Heddon 210 Surface before being rebuilt into the Flipper. A closer look reveals the overpaint letters. By removing the metal collar of a beater-body 210 and installing a front and rear tube propeller this makes a great bass fishing lure and a successful top water lure. Collector value range: $20 to $60.

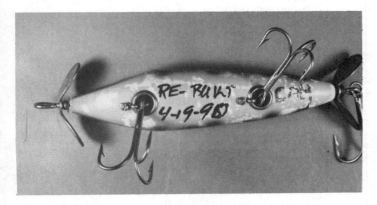

A rebuilt (so marked) STANLEY FAT FLIPPER as the prototype found in the HEDDON/PRADCO, Ft. Smith, Arkansas collection in May 1988. There is a regular round end Heddon/Stanley propeller on the tail hook hanger. This No. 1600 did not have a metal tail hook insert. Collector value range: $100 to $200.

457

Holz=Zelluloid=Spinner „Wobler"

(Siehe Farbtafel)

„Die größte Sensation auf dem Gebiete der Spinnangelei mit künstlichem Köderfisch."

Der Vorteil bei diesen künstlichen Fischen aus Holz liegt darin, daß sie die Bewegung eines lebenden Fisches täuschend imitieren und durch hervorragend leuchtende Farben den Raubfisch besonders stark anlocken.

Der besondere Vorzug ist aber der, daß diese Holzwobler infolge ihres geringen Gewichtes schwimmen. Besonders Anfängern passiert es bei der Wurffischerei, daß die Schnur verheddert und hierdurch die alten Metallköder auf den Boden sinken. Die Folge davon ist oftmals der vollständige Verlust des Gerätes durch Verhängen. Anders beim Holzwobler; dieser schwimmt an der Oberfläche und fängt erst an zu tauchen und sich zu bewegen, wenn die Rolle in Bewegung gesetzt wird.

Nachdem ich festgestellt hatte, daß die Zelluloidspinner außerordentlich fängisch sind, habe ich keinen Augenblick gezögert und mich sofort mit der Herstellung befaßt. Ich stieß hierbei auf große Schwierigkeiten, denn die Lacke sind außerordentlich schwierig herstellbar, da sie besonders hart, elastisch und widerstandsfähig gegen Wassereinflüsse sein müssen. Nach vielen Monaten gelang es mir, dann endlich brauchbare Lacke zu erhalten.

Als einziger und größter Fabrikant dieses Artikels in Europa habe ich große Verkaufserfolge aufzuweisen und bin ich sicher, auch Beifall bei der Kundschaft zu finden, die den Artikel bisher noch nicht gekannt und geführt hat.

Wie die Farbentafel zeigt, stelle ich diese Wobler in den effektvollsten Farbenzusammensetzungen her. Eine besondere Brillanz haben die geschuppten Fische, aber auch die weißrot-leuchtende A-Farbe hat sich als äußerst fängisch erwiesen.

Die Wobler sind alle mit extra starken und vernickelten Drillingen montiert und werden im vierfarbig bedruckten Einzelkarton geliefert.

3035 „Vampir"-Serie, der bewegliche Gliederfisch, täuschende Imitation eines lebenden Fisches

Farben

A	B	C	D	E	F	G
Weiß mit rotem Rücken	Weiß-schwarz rot gestreift mit Silber-schuppe	Blau mit Silber-schuppe	Braun mit Gold-schuppe	Rot mit Gold-schuppe	Grüne Schuppe mit Gold-streifen	Regen-bogen-farbig gestreift

	2=gliedrig	3=gliedrig
Länge	10	12¹/₂ cm
engl. Zoll	4	5
Gewicht per Stück	45	50 g

1756/1486 „Monarch"-Serie, der Propellerwobler

Farben

A	B	C	D	E	F
Weiß mit rotem Rücken	Weiß-schwarz rot gestreift mit Silber-schuppe	Blau mit Silber-schuppe	Braun mit Gold-schuppe	Grün mit Gold-schuppe	Bunt gefleckt

	1756	1486
Länge	8	10 cm
engl. Zoll	3¹/₄	4
Gewicht per Stück	45	50 g

3030 „Oreno"-Serie, Taumel-Köder, der kranke Fisch

Farben	A	B	C	D	F
	Siehe wie 1756/1486				

	Forelle	Hecht		
Länge	30	55	75	95 mm
engl. Zoll	1¹/₄	2¹/₄	3	3³/₄
Gew. p. Dtz.	60	180	360	600 g

3080 Sortimentskarten 12 verschiedener, gangbarster Typen von Woblern aller Größen. erleichtert den Verkauf gegenüber dem Konsumenten und dient im Schaufenster als zugkräftigste Reklame

Das Sortiment besteht aus:

4	„Vampir"-Woblern: 2 und 3gliedrig
2	„Monarch"-Woblern: 80 mm
6	„Oreno"-Woblern: 30, 55, 75 mm
12	

Gewicht: 300 g

3080

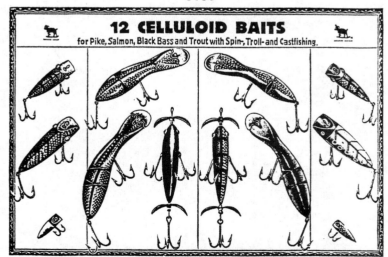

3171

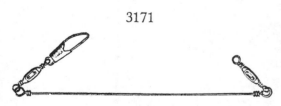

3171 Sicherheitskarabiner, mit 2 Wirbeln und Kettenvorschlag aus Neusilber, speziell für die Wobler angefertigt.

Länge 20 cm = 8 engl. Zoll

Gewicht per Dutzend 60 g

A German lure distributor's 1926 catalog page featuring the 12 "CELLULOID BAITS", notably the Heddon No. 5500 and 5400 Gamefisher lures.

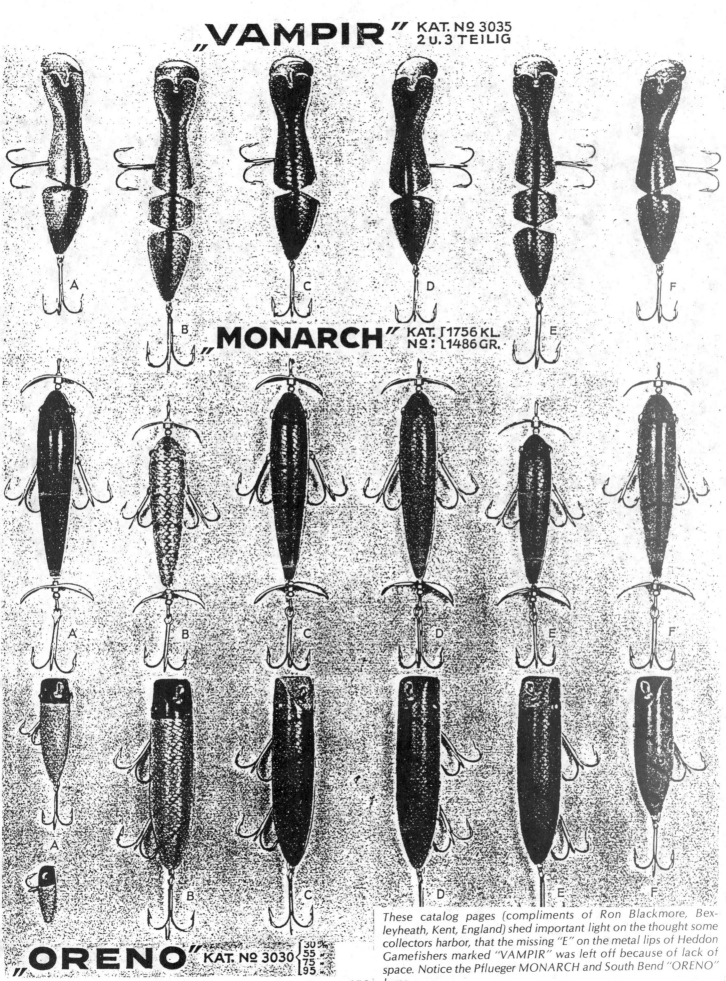

„VAMPIR" KAT. No 3035
2 u. 3 TEILIG

A B C D E F

„MONARCH" KAT. No: {1756 KL. 1486 GR.}

A B C D E F

„ORENO" KAT. No 3030 {30% 55 " 75 " 95 "}

A B C D E F

These catalog pages (compliments of Ron Blackmore, Bexleyheath, Kent, England) shed important light on the thought some collectors harbor, that the missing "E" on the metal lips of Heddon Gamefishers marked "VAMPIR" was left off because of lack of space. Notice the Pflueger MONARCH and South Bend "ORENO" lures.

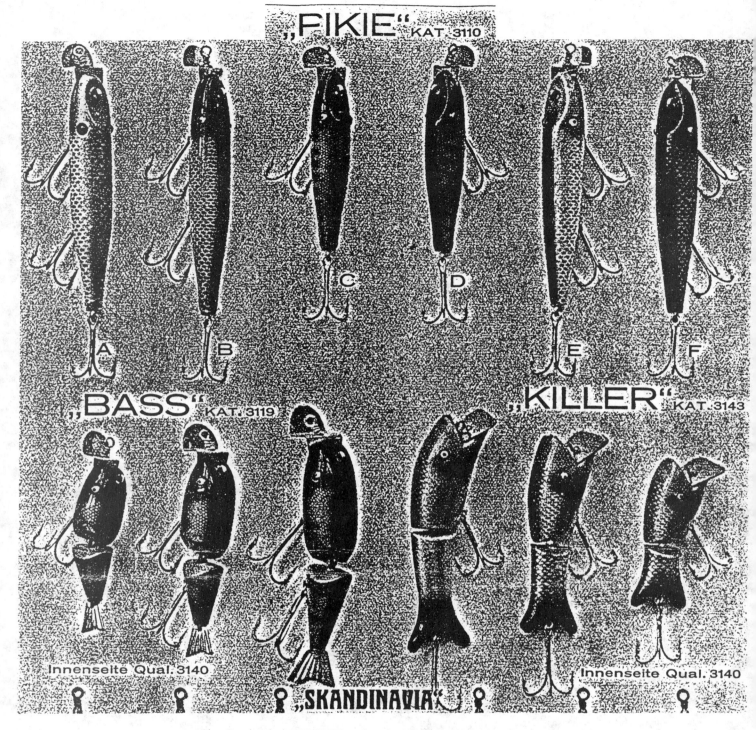

The Creek Chub "PICKIE" style as well as the Wiggle Fish style "BASS" and the Shakespeare style "KILLER" lures. The "WOBBLER" could be the lower right lure picture.

KINNEY'S BIRD LURES
FOR GAME FISH
Anglers, This Bird Don't "Sing"—It's a "Thriller"

This "BIRD" a fishing lure
Patented by Herbert A. Kinney Sept. 20-1927 73503
HEDDON FINISH"

THE WORLD'S FIRST BIRD LURE
For All Game Fish

ANGLERS know that a fluttering bird or fledgling on the water, is "desert" for all game fish. They strike it savagely. Our BIRD LURES positively imitate a fluttering bird on the water, when retrieved slowly, in short, "choppy" jerks, and if MR. BASS is around, "you got him." He don't "strike it," he "KILLS IT." **(No mistake about this.)**

Our BIRDS are each one finished and decorated in true AMERICAN BIRD colors, by one of the best artists in the Country.

PRICE $1.00 EACH, Postpaid
[STATE COLOR]

THE BEST DOLLAR'S WORTH YOU EVER GOT

This lure is the most expensive one made to sell at $1.00, but, anticipating an enormous sale—you get quality —we get ours in quantity.

Kinney's Famous BIRD LURES are proven BIG FISH GETTERS, and will give you Anglers "thrills" aplenty.

"THRILLS THAT LAST"

Just slip us a Dollar Bill, and get yours. State color of BIRD wanted, and pass this along to your fishing Buddy, (a sportsman's favor.) He will thank you.

ADDRESS
Old Hickory Rod & Tackle Company
Route No. 1, Box 137 A   Tampa, Florida

A box pamphlet of the KINNEY'S BIRD LURES see previous picture on p. 455 for data. Collector value range: $10 to $20.

INDEX

This key should prove very helpful in your research and indentification efforts. While using the index you will frequently find more than one page reference listed with the subject you have looked up. In this case, if there is a bold face page reference, this is the main entry for the subject. The other pages listed are where the same subject is mentioned or discussed in relation to another company, lure etc.